Clojure Programming

Chas Emerick, Brian Carper, and Christophe Grand

O'REILLY®

Beijing · Cambridge · Farnham · Köln · Sebastopol · Tokyo

Clojure Programming

by Chas Emerick, Brian Carper, and Christophe Grand

Published by O'Reilly Media, Inc., 1005 Gravenstein Highway North, Sebastopol, CA 95472.

O'Reilly books may be purchased for educational, business, or sales promotional use. Online editions are also available for most titles (*http://my.safaribooksonline.com*). For more information, contact our corporate/institutional sales department: (800) 998-9938 or *corporate@oreilly.com*.

Editors: Mike Loukides and Julie Steele	**Indexer:** Fred Brown
Production Editor: Teresa Elsey	**Cover Designer:** Karen Montgomery
Copyeditor: Nancy Reinhardt	**Interior Designer:** David Futato
Proofreader: Linley Dolby	**Illustrator:** Robert Romano

April 2012:   First Edition.

Revision History for the First Edition:
   2012-03-28   First release
   2014-05-14   Second release
See *http://oreilly.com/catalog/errata.csp?isbn=9781449394707* for release details.

ISBN: 978-1-449-39470-7

[LSI]

1399902411

Table of Contents

Preface xi

1. **Down the Rabbit Hole** 1
   Why Clojure?   1
   Obtaining Clojure   3
   The Clojure REPL   3
   No, Parentheses Actually Won't Make You Go Blind   6
   Expressions, Operators, Syntax, and Precedence   7
   Homoiconicity   9
   The Reader   12
      Scalar Literals   13
      Comments   18
      Whitespace and Commas   19
      Collection Literals   19
      Miscellaneous Reader Sugar   20
   Namespaces   20
   Symbol Evaluation   23
   Special Forms   23
      Suppressing Evaluation: quote   24
      Code Blocks: do   25
      Defining Vars: def   26
      Local Bindings: let   27
      Destructuring (let, Part 2)   28
      Creating Functions: fn   36
      Conditionals: if   42
      Looping: loop and recur   43
      Referring to Vars: var   44
      Java Interop: . and new   44
      Exception Handling: try and throw   45
      Specialized Mutation: set!   45
      Primitive Locking: monitor-enter and monitor-exit   45
   Putting It All Together   46

eval   46
This Is Just the Beginning   48

Part I.   Functional Programming and Concurrency

2. **Functional Programming** **51**
What Does Functional Programming Mean?   52
On the Importance of Values   52
About Values   53
Comparing Values to Mutable Objects   54
A Critical Choice   58
First-Class and Higher-Order Functions   59
Applying Ourselves Partially   65
Composition of Function(ality)   68
Writing Higher-Order Functions   71
Building a Primitive Logging System with Composable Higher-Order
Functions   72
Pure Functions   76
Why Are Pure Functions Interesting?   78
Functional Programming in the Real World   81

3. **Collections and Data Structures** **83**
Abstractions over Implementations   84
Collection   87
Sequences   89
Associative   99
Indexed   103
Stack   104
Set   105
Sorted   106
Concise Collection Access   111
Idiomatic Usage   112
Collections and Keys and Higher-Order Functions   113
Data Structure Types   114
Lists   114
Vectors   115
Sets   117
Maps   117
Immutability and Persistence   122
Persistence and Structural Sharing   123
Transients   130
Metadata   135

Putting Clojure's Collections to Work   136
  Identifiers and Cycles   137
  Thinking Different: From Imperative to Functional   138
  Navigation, Update, and Zippers   151
In Summary   157

4. Concurrency and Parallelism **159**
Shifting Computation Through Time and Space   160
  Delays   160
  Futures   162
  Promises   163
Parallelism on the Cheap   166
State and Identity   168
Clojure Reference Types   170
Classifying Concurrent Operations   172
Atoms   174
Notifications and Constraints   176
  Watches   176
  Validators   178
Refs   180
  Software Transactional Memory   180
  The Mechanics of Ref Change   181
  The Sharp Corners of Software Transactional Memory   191
Vars   198
  Defining Vars   198
  Dynamic Scope   201
  Vars Are Not Variables   206
  Forward Declarations   208
Agents   209
  Dealing with Errors in Agent Actions   212
  I/O, Transactions, and Nested Sends   214
Using Java's Concurrency Primitives   224
  Locking   225
Final Thoughts   226

Part II.   Building Abstractions

5. Macros **229**
What Is a Macro?   229
  What Macros Are Not   231
  What Can Macros Do that Functions Cannot?   232
  Macros Versus Ruby eval   234

Writing Your First Macro   235
Debugging Macros   237
    Macroexpansion   237
Syntax   239
    quote Versus syntax-quote   240
    unquote and unquote-splicing   241
When to Use Macros   243
Hygiene   244
    Gensyms to the Rescue   246
    Letting the User Pick Names   248
    Double Evaluation   249
Common Macro Idioms and Patterns   250
The Implicit Arguments: &env and &form   251
    &env   252
    &form   254
    Testing Contextual Macros   258
In Detail: -> and ->>   259
Final Thoughts   262

6. **Datatypes and Protocols** **263**
Protocols   264
Extending to Existing Types   266
Defining Your Own Types   270
    Records   272
    Types   277
Implementing Protocols   280
    Inline Implementation   281
    Reusing Implementations   285
Protocol Introspection   289
Protocol Dispatch Edge Cases   290
Participating in Clojure's Collection Abstractions   292
Final Thoughts   299

7. **Multimethods** **301**
Multimethods Basics   301
Toward Hierarchies   304
Hierarchies   306
    Independent Hierarchies   308
Making It Really Multiple!   311
A Few More Things   313
    Multiple Inheritance   313
    Introspecting Multimethods   314
    type Versus class; or, the Revenge of the Map   314

The Range of Dispatch Functions Is Unlimited   316
Final Thoughts   317

Part III. Tools, Platform, and Projects

8. Organizing and Building Clojure Projects **321**
Project Geography   321
    Defining and Using Namespaces   322
    Location, Location, Location   332
    The Functional Organization of Clojure Codebases   334
Build   336
    Ahead-of-Time Compilation   337
    Dependency Management   339
    The Maven Dependency Management Model   339
    Build Tools and Configuration Patterns   344
Final Thoughts   353

9. Java and JVM Interoperability **355**
The JVM Is Clojure's Foundation   356
Using Java Classes, Methods, and Fields   357
Handy Interop Utilities   360
Exceptions and Error Handling   362
    Escaping Checked Exceptions   364
    with-open, finally's Lament   364
Type Hinting for Performance   366
Arrays   370
Defining Classes and Implementing Interfaces   371
    Instances of Anonymous Classes: proxy   372
    Defining Named Classes   374
    Annotations   381
Using Clojure from Java   385
    Using deftype and defrecord Classes   388
    Implementing Protocol Interfaces   390
Collaborating Partners   392

10. REPL-Oriented Programming **393**
Interactive Development   393
    The Persistent, Evolving Environment   397
Tooling   398
    The Bare REPL   399
    Eclipse   403
    Emacs   405

Debugging, Monitoring, and Patching Production in the REPL   411
    Special Considerations for "Deployed" REPLs   414
Limitations to Redefining Constructs   415
In Summary   417

Part IV. Practicums

11. Numerics and Mathematics 421
Clojure Numerics   421
    Clojure Prefers 64-bit (or Larger) Representations   422
    Clojure Has a Mixed Numerics Model   422
    Rationals   424
    The Rules of Numeric Contagion   425
Clojure Mathematics   427
    Bounded Versus Arbitrary Precision   428
    Unchecked Ops   430
    Scale and Rounding Modes for Arbitrary-Precision Decimals Ops   432
Equality and Equivalence   433
    Object Identity (identical?)   433
    Reference Equality (=)   434
    Numeric Equivalence (==)   435
Optimizing Numeric Performance   436
    Declare Functions to Take and Return Primitives   438
    Use Primitive Arrays Judiciously   442
Visualizing the Mandelbrot Set in Clojure   449

12. Design Patterns 457
Dependency Injection   459
Strategy Pattern   462
Chain of Responsibility   463
Aspect-Oriented Programming   466
Final Thoughts   470

13. Testing 471
Immutable Values and Pure Functions   471
    Mocking   472
clojure.test   473
    Defining Tests   474
    Test "Suites"   477
    Fixtures   479
Growing an HTML DSL   481
Relying upon Assertions   486

      Preconditions and Postconditions   487

14. Using Relational Databases **491**
    clojure.java.jdbc   491
      with-query-results Explained   494
      Transactions   496
      Connection Pooling   496
    Korma   498
      Prelude   498
      Queries   499
      Why Bother with a DSL?   500
    Hibernate   503
      Setup   503
      Persisting Data   506
      Running Queries   506
      Removing Boilerplate   507
    Final Thoughts   509

15. Using Nonrelational Databases **511**
    Getting Set Up with CouchDB and Clutch   512
    Basic CRUD Operations   512
    Views   514
      A Simple (JavaScript) View   514
      Views in Clojure   516
    _changes: Abusing CouchDB as a Message Queue   520
    À la Carte Message Queues   522
    Final Thoughts   525

16. Clojure and the Web **527**
    The "Clojure Stack"   527
    The Foundation: Ring   529
      Requests and Responses   529
      Adapters   531
      Handlers   532
      Middleware   534
    Routing Requests with Compojure   535
    Templating   545
      Enlive: Selector-Based HTML Transformation   546
    Final Thoughts   554

17. Deploying Clojure Web Applications **557**
    Java and Clojure Web Architecture   557
      Web Application Packaging   560

Running Web Apps Locally   565
Web Application Deployment   566
    Deploying Clojure Apps to Amazon's Elastic Beanstalk   567
Going Beyond Simple Web Application Deployment   570

Part V. Miscellanea

18. Choosing Clojure Type Definition Forms Wisely 573

19. Introducing Clojure into Your Workplace 577
Just the Facts...   577
Emphasize Productivity   579
Emphasize Community   580
Be Prudent   582

20. What's Next? 583
(dissoc Clojure 'JVM)   583
    ClojureCLR   583
    ClojureScript   584
4Clojure   584
Overtone   585
core.logic   585
Pallet   586
Avout   587
Clojure on Heroku   587

Index 589

Preface

Clojure is a dynamically and strongly typed programming language hosted on the Java Virtual Machine (JVM), now in its fifth year. It has seen enthusiastic adoption by programmers from a variety of backgrounds, working in essentially all problem domains. Clojure offers a compelling mix of features and characteristics applicable to solving modern programming challenges:

- Functional programming foundations, including a suite of persistent data structures with performance characteristics approaching typical mutable data structures
- A mature, efficient runtime environment, as provided by the host JVM
- JVM/Java interoperability capabilities suited for a wide variety of architectural and operational requirements
- A set of mechanisms providing reliable concurrency and parallelism semantics
- A Lisp pedigree, thereby providing remarkably flexible and powerful metaprogramming facilities

Clojure offers a compelling practical alternative to many who strain against the limitations of typical programming languages and environments. We aim to demonstrate this by showing Clojure seamlessly interoperating with existing technologies, libraries, and services that many working programmers already use on a day-to-day basis. Throughout, we'll provide a solid grounding in Clojure fundamentals, starting from places of common expertise and familiarity rather than from (often foreign) computer science first principles.

Who Is This Book For?

We wrote this book with a couple of audiences in mind. Hopefully, you consider yourself a part of one of them.

Clojure matches and often exceeds your current favorite language's expressivity, concision, and flexibility while allowing you to effortlessly leverage the performance, libraries, community, and operational stability of the JVM. This makes it a natural next step for Java developers (and even JVM developers using interpreted or otherwise not particularly fast non-Java languages), who simply will not accept a performance hit or who do not want to give up their JVM platform investment. Clojure is also a natural step for Ruby and Python developers who refuse to compromise on language expressivity, but wish they had a more reliable, efficient execution platform and a larger selection of quality libraries.

Engaged Java Developers

There are millions of Java developers in the world, but some fewer number are working in demanding environments solving nontrivial, often domain-specific problems. If this describes you, you're probably always on the hunt for better tools, techniques, and practices that will boost your productivity and value to your team, organization, and community. In addition, you're probably at least somewhat frustrated with the constraints of Java compared to other languages, but you continue to find the JVM ecosystem compelling: its process maturity, massive third-party library selection, vendor support, and large skilled workforce is hard to walk away from, no matter how shiny and appealing alternative languages are.

You'll find Clojure to be a welcome relief. It runs on the JVM with excellent performance characteristics, interoperates with all of your existing libraries, tools, and applications, and is *simpler* than Java, yet is demonstrably more expressive and less verbose.

Ruby, Python, and Other Developers

Ruby and Python are not new languages by any means, but they have garnered significant (dare we say, "mainstream"?) traction over recent years. It's not hard to see why: both are expressive, dynamic languages that, along with their thriving communities, encourage maximal developer productivity in many domains.

Clojure is a natural next step for you. As a Ruby or Python programmer, you're probably unwilling to compromise on their strengths, but you may wish for a more capable execution platform, better runtime performance, and a larger selection of libraries. The fact that Clojure is efficiently hosted on the JVM fulfills those desires—and it matches or exceeds the degrees of language sophistication and developer productivity that you've come to expect.

 We will frequently compare and contrast Clojure with Java, Ruby, and Python to help you translate your existing expertise to Clojure. In such comparisons, we will always refer to the canonical implementations of these other languages:

- Ruby MRI (also called CRuby)
- CPython
- Java 6/7

How to Read This Book

In formulating our approach to this book, we wanted to provide a fair bit of concrete detail and practical examples that you could relate to, but stay clear of what we thought were generally unsuccessful approaches for doing so. In particular, we've been frustrated in the past by books that attempted to thread the implementation of a single program or application through their pages. Such approaches seem to result in a disjointed narrative, as well as the dominance of a tortured "practical" example that may or may not apply or appeal to readers.

With that in mind, we split the book in two, starting with foundational, instructional narrative that occupies roughly two-thirds of the book, followed in Part IV by a number of discrete, practical examples from real-world domains. This clear segmentation of content with decidedly distinct objectives may qualify this book as a "duplex book." (This term may have been coined by Martin Fowler in *http://martinfowler.com/bliki/ DuplexBook.html*.) In any case, we can conceive of two obvious approaches to reading it.

Start with Practical Applications of Clojure

Often the best way to learn is to dig straight into the nitty-gritty of how a language is used in the real world. If that sounds appealing, the hope is that you will find that at least a couple of the practicums resonate with what you do on a day-to-day basis, so that you can readily draw parallels between how you solve certain categories of problems in your current language(s) and how they may be solved using Clojure. You're going to bump into a lot of potentially foreign concepts and language constructs in those chapters—when you do, use that context within the domain in question as your entry point for understanding those concepts using the relevant instructional material in the first part of the book.

Start from the Ground Up with Clojure's Foundational Concepts

Sometimes the only way to truly understand something is to learn it inside-out, starting with the fundamentals. If you prefer that approach, then you will likely find that digesting this book starting from the first page of Chapter 1 will be best. We have attempted to provide a comprehensive treatment of all of Clojure's foundational principles and constructs in a narrative that progresses such that it will be *very* rare for you to need to look ahead in the book to understand concepts in earlier sections. As you begin to get a handle on Clojure's fundamentals, feel free to jump ahead into the practicums you find most interesting and relevant to your work.

Who's "We"?

We are three software developers who have each taken different paths in coming to use and appreciate Clojure. In writing this book, we have attempted to distill all that we've learned about why and how you should use Clojure so that you can be successful in your use of it as well.

Chas Emerick

Chas has been a consistent presence in the Clojure community since early 2008. He has made contributions to the core language, been involved in dozens of Clojure open source projects, and frequently writes and speaks about Clojure and software development generally.

Chas maintains the Clojure Atlas (*http://clojureatlas.com*), an interactive visualization of and learning aid for the Clojure language and its standard libraries.

The founder of Snowtide (*http://snowtide.com*), a small software company in Western Massachusetts, Chas's primary domain is unstructured data extraction, with a particular specialty around PDF documents. He writes about Clojure, software development, entrepreneurship, and other passions at *http://cemerick.com*.

Brian Carper

Brian is a Ruby programmer turned Clojure devotee. He's been programming Clojure since 2008, using it at home and at work for everything from web development to data analysis to GUI apps.

Brian is the author of Gaka (*https://github.com/briancarper/gaka*), a Clojure-to-CSS compiler, and Oyako (*https://github.com/briancarper/oyako*), an Object-Relational Mapping library. He writes about Clojure and other topics at *http://briancarper.net*.

Christophe Grand

Christophe was a long-time enthusiast of functional programming lost in Java-land when he encountered Clojure in early 2008, and it was love at first sight! He authored Enlive (*http://github.com/cgrand/enlive*), an HTML/XML transformation, extraction, and templating library; Parsley (*http://github.com/cgrand/parsley*), an incremental parser generator; and Moustache (*http://github.com/cgrand/moustache*), a routing and middleware application DSL for Ring.

As an independent consultant, he develops, coaches, and offers training in Clojure. He also writes about Clojure at *http://clj-me.cgrand.net*.

Acknowledgments

Like any sizable piece of work, this book would not exist without the tireless efforts of dozens, probably hundreds of people.

First, Rich Hickey, the creator of Clojure. In just a few short years, he has designed, implemented, and shepherded a new programming language into the world that, for so many, has been not just another tool, but a reinvigoration of our love of programming. Beyond that, he's personally taught us a great deal—certainly about programming, but also about patience, humility, and perspective. Thanks, Rich.

Dave Fayram and Mike Loukides were essential in helping to formulate the initial concept and approach of the book. Of course, you likely wouldn't be reading this book right now if it weren't for Julie Steele, our editor, and all of the fine people at O'Reilly who took care of the logistics and minutiae that go along with publishing.

The quality of this book would be far less than it is were it not for the efforts of our technical reviewers, including Sam Aaron, Antoni Batchelli, Tom Faulhaber, Chris Granger, Anthony Grimes, Phil Hagelberg, Tom Hicks, Alex Miller, William Morgan, Laurent Petit, and Dean Wampler. We'd also like to thank all of those who provided feedback and comments on the early releases and Rough Cuts of the book, both on the O'Reilly forums and via email, Twitter, and so on.

Michael Fogus and Chris Houser have inspired us in many ways large and small. One of the smaller ways was the style and presentation of the REPL interactions in their Clojure book, *The Joy of Clojure*, which we shamelessly copied and iterated.

If we've neglected to mention anyone, please accept our implicit thanks and our apologies; at the end of this endeavor, we are quite lucky to be upright and coherent at all!

And Last, but Certainly Far from Least

The Clojure community has been my home away from home for a number of years. The hospitality and positive, helpful energy I see anywhere Clojure programmers congregate continues to be an inspiration and example to me. In particular, many of the regular denizens of #clojure on Freenode IRC—in addition to becoming good friends—have guided me toward learning things I never would have otherwise.

To my coauthors, Christophe and Brian: working with you has been a great honor for me. There is absolutely no way that I would have been able to complete this work without you.

To my parents, Charley and Darleen: my compulsive curiosity about how things work, my love of language and rhetoric, and my interest in business—all of these can be traced back over the years to your consistent influence. Without it, I am certain I would not have found my unique path, started a software company, or written this book, each done against all odds.

Finally, to my wife, Krissy: the sacrifices you've made to enable me to chase my ambitions are legion. It is likely that I'll never be able to thank you sufficiently. So, I'll just say: I love you.

—*Chas Emerick, February 2012*

To everyone in the community who helped create Clojure: thank you for your tireless hard work, for making my professional and personal coding life so much more enjoyable, and for opening my eyes to what's possible.

To my coauthors, Christophe and Chas: I've never worked with a smarter group of people. It's been an honor and a privilege.

To my wife Nicole: sorry I kept you awake all night with my typing.

—*Brian Carper, February 2012*

To Rich Hickey for creating Clojure and fostering such a friendly community.

To this community for having brought me to higher standards.

To my coauthors, Brian and Chas: it has been a great honor to work with you.

A mon professeur Daniel Goffinet, et à ses exercices improbables, qui a radicalement changé mon approche de la programmation et de l'informatique—sur ces sujets je lui suis plus redevable qu'à nul autre.

(To Pr. Daniel Goffinet, and his meta mind twisters, who radically altered the way I think about programming and computing—on those subjects there is no one I'm more indebted to.)

A mes parents pour votre amour bien sûr mais aussi pour tout le temps à s'inquiéter que je passais trop de temps sur l'Amstrad.

(To my parents: for your love obviously and for buying me that 8-bit computer you worried I was spending too much time on.)

A ma compagne Emilie, et mon fils Gaël, merci d'être là et de m'avoir supporté pendant l'écriture de ce livre.

(To my wife Emilie and to my son Gaël: thank you for being there and having supported me throughout the writing of this book.)

—*Christophe Grand, February 2012*

Conventions Used in This Book

The following typographical conventions are used in this book:

Italic
> Indicates new terms, URLs, email addresses, filenames, and file extensions.

Constant width

> Used for program listings, as well as within paragraphs to refer to program elements such as variable or function names, databases, data types, environment variables, statements, and keywords.

; listing lines prefixed with a semicolon

> Used to indicate content *printed* (i.e., to standard out/err) by code evaluated in the REPL.

;= listing lines prefixed with a semicolon + equal sign

> Used to indicate the *result/return value* of a REPL evaluation.

Constant width bold

> Shows commands or other text that should be typed literally by the user.

Constant width italic

> Shows text that should be replaced with user-supplied values or by values determined by context.

 This icon signifies a tip, suggestion, or general note.

 This icon indicates a warning or caution.

Using Code Examples

This book is here to help you get your job done. In general, you may use the code in this book in your programs and documentation. You do not need to contact us for permission unless you're reproducing a significant portion of the code. For example, writing a program that uses several chunks of code from this book does not require permission. Selling or distributing a CD-ROM of examples from O'Reilly books does require permission. Answering a question by citing this book and quoting example code does not require permission. Incorporating a significant amount of example code from this book into your product's documentation does require permission.

We appreciate, but do not require, attribution. An attribution usually includes the title, author, publisher, and ISBN. For example: "*Clojure Programming* by Chas Emerick, Brian Carper, and Christophe Grand (O'Reilly). Copyright 2012 Chas Emerick, Brian Carper, and Christophe Grand, 978-1-449-39470-7."

If you feel your use of code examples falls outside fair use or the permission given above, feel free to contact us at *permissions@oreilly.com*.

Safari® Books Online

Safari Books Online is an on-demand digital library that lets you easily search over 7,500 technology and creative reference books and videos to find the answers you need quickly.

With a subscription, you can read any page and watch any video from our library online. Read books on your cell phone and mobile devices. Access new titles before they are available for print, and get exclusive access to manuscripts in development and post feedback for the authors. Copy and paste code samples, organize your favorites, download chapters, bookmark key sections, create notes, print out pages, and benefit from tons of other time-saving features.

O'Reilly Media has uploaded this book to the Safari Books Online service. To have full digital access to this book and others on similar topics from O'Reilly and other publishers, sign up for free at *http://my.safaribooksonline.com*.

How to Contact Us

Please address comments and questions concerning this book to the publisher:

O'Reilly Media, Inc.
1005 Gravenstein Highway North
Sebastopol, CA 95472
800-998-9938 (in the United States or Canada)
707-829-0515 (international or local)
707-829-0104 (fax)

We have a web page for this book, where we list errata, examples, and any additional information. You can access this page at:

http://shop.oreilly.com/product/0636920013754.do

To comment or ask technical questions about this book, send email to:

bookquestions@oreilly.com

For more information about our books, courses, conferences, and news, see our website at *http://www.oreilly.com*.

Find us on Facebook: *http://facebook.com/oreilly*

Follow us on Twitter: *http://twitter.com/oreillymedia*

Watch us on YouTube: *http://www.youtube.com/oreillymedia*

## CHAPTER 1

Down the Rabbit Hole

If you're reading this book, you are presumably open to learning new programming languages. On the other hand, we assume that you expect reciprocity for the time and effort you'll expend to learn a new language, some tangible benefits that can make you more productive, your team more effective, and your organization more flexible.

We believe that you will find this virtuous cycle in effect as you learn, apply, and leverage Clojure. As we are fond of saying, *Clojure demands that you raise your game, and pays you back for doing so.*

As software developers, we often build up a complex and sometimes very personal relationship with our tools and languages. Deciding which raw materials to use is sometimes dominated by pragmatic and legacy concerns. However, all other things being equal, programmers prefer using whatever maximally enhances their productivity and hopefully enables us to fulfill our potential to build useful, elegant systems. As the old saying goes, we want whatever makes the easy stuff easy, and the hard stuff possible.

Why Clojure?

Clojure is a programming language that lives up to that standard. Forged of a unique blend of the best features of a number of different programming languages—including various Lisp implementations, Ruby, Python, Java, Haskell, and others—Clojure provides a set of capabilities suited to address many of the most frustrating problems programmers struggle with today and those we can see barreling toward us over the horizon. And, far from requiring a sea-change to a new or unfamiliar architecture and runtime (typical of many otherwise promising languages over the years), Clojure is hosted on the Java Virtual Machine, a fact that puts to bed many of the most pressing pragmatic and legacy concerns raised when a new language is considered.

To whet your appetite, let's enumerate some of Clojure's marquee features and characteristics:

Clojure is hosted on the JVM
> Clojure code can use any Java library, Clojure libraries can in turn be used from Java, and Clojure applications can be packaged just like any Java application and deployed anywhere other Java applications can be deployed: to web application servers; to desktops with Swing, SWT, or command-line interfaces; and so on. This also means that Clojure's runtime is Java's runtime, one of the most efficient and operationally reliable in the world.

Clojure is a Lisp
> Unlike Java, Python, Ruby, C++, and other members of the Algol family of programming languages, Clojure is part of the Lisp family. However, forget everything you know (or might have heard rumored) about Lisps: Clojure retains the best of Lisp heritage, but is unburdened by the shortcomings and sometimes anachronistic aspects of many other Lisp implementations. Also, being a Lisp, Clojure has *macros*, an approach to metaprogramming and syntactic extension that has been the benchmark against which other such systems have been measured for decades.

Clojure is a functional programming language
> Clojure encourages the use of first-class and higher-order functions with values and comes with its own set of efficient immutable data structures. The focus on a strong flavor of functional programming encourages the elimination of common bugs and faults due to the use of unconstrained mutable state and enables Clojure's solutions for concurrency and parallelization.

Clojure offers innovative solutions to the challenges inherent in concurrency and parallelization
> The realities of multicore, multi-CPU, and distributed computing demand that we use languages and libraries that have been designed with these contexts in mind. Clojure's *reference types* enforce a clean separation of *state* and *identity*, providing defined concurrency semantics that are to manual locking and threading strategies what garbage collection is to manual memory management.

Clojure is a dynamic programming language
> Clojure is dynamically and strongly typed (and therefore similar to Python and Ruby), yet function calls are compiled down to (fast!) Java method invocations. Clojure is also dynamic in the sense that it deeply supports updating and loading new code at runtime, either locally or remotely. This is particularly useful for enabling interactive development and debugging or even instrumenting and patching remote applications without downtime.

Of course, we don't expect you to understand all of that, but we do hope the gestalt sounds compelling. If so, press on. By the end of this chapter, you'll be able to write simple programs in Clojure, and be well on your way to understanding and leveraging it to help realize your potential.

Obtaining Clojure

You'll need two things to work with the code in this chapter and otherwise explore Clojure on your own:

1. The Java runtime. You can download the Oracle JVM for free for Windows and Linux (*http://java.com/en/download/*); it is bundled with or automatically installed by all versions of Mac OS X. Clojure requires Java v1.5 or higher; the latest releases of v1.6 or v1.7 are preferable.

2. Clojure itself, available from clojure.org (*http://clojure.org/downloads*). *All of the code in this book requires v1.3.0 or higher, and has been tested against v1.4.0 as well.*[1] Within the zip file you download, you'll find a file named something like *clojure-1.4.0.jar*; this is all you'll need to get started.

There are a number of different Clojure plug-ins for popular development environments like Eclipse and Emacs; see "Tooling" on page 398 for an overview of Clojure tooling. While Clojure's command-line REPL is sufficient for your first few steps in understanding Clojure, we encourage you to use your favorite text editor or IDE if it has quality Clojure support, or to pick up one that does.

If you don't yet want to commit to a particular editor or IDE for Clojure development, you should at least use Leiningen, the most popular project management tool for Clojure. It will download Clojure for you, give you a better REPL than Clojure's default, and you'll likely be using it on a daily basis for your own projects in short order anyway. See "Leiningen" on page 347 for an introduction to it.

If you want to avoid downloading anything right now, you can run many of the samples in this book in the online, in-browser Clojure implementation available at *http://tryclj.com*.

The Clojure REPL

Many languages have REPLs, often also referred to as interpreters: Ruby has `irb`; Python has its command-line interpreter; Groovy has its console; even Java has something akin to a REPL in BeanShell. The "REPL" acronym is derived from a simple description of what it does:

1. Read: code is read as text from some input (often `stdin`, but this varies if you're using a REPL in an IDE or other nonconsole environment).
2. Eval: the code is evaluated, yielding some value.

---

1. Given Clojure's history with regard to backwards compatibility, the code and concepts in this book should remain applicable to future versions of Clojure as well.

3. Print: the value is printed to some output device (often `stdout`, sometimes preceded by other output if the code in question happened to print content itself).

4. Loop: control returns to the *read* step.

Clojure has a REPL too, but it differs from many other languages' REPLs in that it is not an interpreter or otherwise using a limited or lightweight subset of Clojure: all code entered into a Clojure REPL is *compiled* to JVM bytecode as part of its evaluation, with the same result as when code is loaded from a Clojure source file. In these two scenarios, compilation is performed entirely at runtime, and requires no separate "compile" step.[2] In fact, Clojure is *never* interpreted. This has a couple of implications:

1. Operations performed in the REPL run at "full speed"; that is to say, there is no runtime penalty or difference in semantics associated with running code in the REPL versus running the same code as part of a "proper" application.

2. *Once you understand how Clojure's REPL works (in particular, its read and eval phases), you'll understand how Clojure itself works at the most fundamental level.*

With this second point in mind, let's dig into the Clojure REPL and see if we can find bedrock.

 The optimal workflow for programming in Clojure makes much more use of the REPL than is typical in other languages to make the development process as interactive as possible. Taking advantage of this is a significant source of the enhanced productivity—and really, fun!—that Clojure enables. We talk about this extensively in Chapter 10.

Example 1-1. Starting a Clojure REPL on the command line

```
% java -cp clojure-1.4.0.jar clojure.main
Clojure 1.4.0
user=>
```

This incantation starts a new JVM process, with a *classpath* that includes the *clojure.jar* file in the current directory, running the `clojure.main` class as its main entry point.[3] See "A classpath primer" on page 331 if you don't yet know what the classpath is; for now, you can just think of the classpath as the JVM's analogue to Python's `PYTHONPATH`, Ruby's `$:`, and your shell's `PATH`, the set of files and directories from which the JVM will load classes and resources.

When you see the `user=>` prompt, the REPL is ready for you to enter some Clojure code. The portion of the Clojure REPL prompt preceding `=>` is the name of the *current*

---

2. If necessary, you can ahead-of-time compile Clojure to Java class files. See "Ahead-of-Time Compilation" on page 337 for details.

3. Alternatively, you can use `java -jar clojure.jar`, but the `-cp` flag and the `clojure.main` entry point are both important to know about; we talk about both in Chapter 8.

---

namespace. Namespaces are like modules or packages; we discuss them extensively later in this chapter in "Namespaces" on page 20. Clojure REPL sessions always start in the default user namespace.

Let's look at some real code, a function that calculates the average of some numbers in Java, Ruby, and Python:

Example 1-2. Averaging numbers in Java, Ruby, and Python

```
public static double average (double[] numbers) {
  double sum = 0;
  for (int i = 0; i < numbers.length; i++) {
    sum += numbers[i];
  }
  return sum / numbers.length;
}

def average (numbers)
  numbers.inject(:+) / numbers.length
end

def average (numbers):
    return sum(numbers) / len(numbers)
```

Here is the Clojure equivalent:

```
(defn average                          ❶
  [numbers]                            ❷
  (/ (apply + numbers) (count numbers))) ❸
```

❶ defn defines a new function named average in the current namespace.

❷ The average function takes one argument, referred to within its body as numbers. Note that there is no type declaration; this function will work equally well when provided with any collection or array of numbers of any type.

❸ The body of the average function, which sums the provided numbers with (apply + numbers),[4] divides that sum by the number of numbers provided—obtained with (count numbers)—and returns the result of that division operation.

We can enter that defn expression at the REPL, and then call our function with a vector of numbers, which yields the expected result:

```
user=> (defn average
          [numbers]
          (/ (apply + numbers) (count numbers)))
#'user/average
user=> (average [60 80 100 400])
160
```

---

4. Note that + here is not a special language operator, as in most other languages. It is a regular function, no different in type than the one we're defining. apply is also a function, which applies a function it is provided with to a collection of arguments (numbers here); so, (apply + [a b c]) will yield the same value as (+ a b c).

No, Parentheses Actually Won't Make You Go Blind

Many programmers who don't already use a Lisp or secretly harbor fond memories of their last usage of Lisp from university blanch at the sight of Lisp syntax. Typical reasons offered for this reaction include:

1. The particular usage of parentheses to delimit scope, rather than the more familiar braces {...} or do ... end blocks

2. The use of prefix notation indicating the operation being performed; e.g., (+ 1 2) rather than the familiar infix 1 + 2

These objections are born first out of simple unfamiliarity. The braces that Java (and C and C++ and C# and PHP and…) uses for delimiting scope seem perfectly fine— why bother with what appears to be an ill-conceived animal? Similarly, we've all known and used infix notation for mathematics since early childhood—why work to use an unusual notation when what we've been using seems to have been so reliable? We are creatures of habit, and outside of building an understanding of why any particular difference may be significant, we understandably prefer the familiar and reliable.

In both cases, the answer is that Clojure did not import its syntactic foundations from other Lisp implementations on a whim; their adoption carries powerful benefits that are worth a minor shift in perspective:

- Prefixed operations used uniformly simplify the language's syntax significantly and eliminate potential ambiguity from nontrivial expressions.
- The use of parentheses (as a textual representation of lists) is an outgrowth of Clojure being a *homoiconic* language. We'll see what this means in "Homoiconicity" on page 9, but the ramifications of it are manifold: homoiconicity enables the development and use of metaprogramming and domain-specific language constructs simply unavailable in any programming language that is not homoiconic.

After getting through an initial period of unfamiliarity, you will very likely find that Clojure's syntax reduces the cognitive load necessary to read and write code. Quick: is << (bit-shift left) in Java executed before or after & (bitwise and) in order of operations? Every time a programmer has to pause and think about this (or look it up in a manual), every time a programmer has to go back and add grouping parentheses "just in case," a mental page fault has occurred. And, every time a programmer forgets to think about this, a potential error has entered his code. Imagine a language with no order of operations to worry about at all; Clojure is that language.

You might be saying, "But there are so many parentheses!" Actually, there aren't.

In places where it makes sense, Clojure has borrowed a lot of syntax from other languages—like Ruby—for its data literals. Where other Lisps you might have seen use parenthesized lists *everywhere*, Clojure provides a rich set of literals for data and collections like vectors, maps, sets, and lists, as well as things like records (roughly, Clojure's corollary to structs).

If you count and compare the number of delimiting characters and tokens of all kinds ((), [], {}, Ruby's || and end, and so on) in Clojure, Java, Ruby, and Python codebases of similar sizes, you will find that the Clojure code won't have appreciably more than the others—and will often have many fewer thanks to its concision.

Expressions, Operators, Syntax, and Precedence

All Clojure code is made up of expressions, each of which evaluates to a single value. This is in contrast to many languages that rely upon valueless statements—such as if, for, and continue—to control program flow imperatively. Clojure's corollaries to these statements are all expressions that evaluate to a value.

You've already seen a few examples of expressions in Clojure:

- 60
- [60 80 100 400]
- (average [60 80 100 400])
- (+ 1 2)

These expressions all evaluate to a single value. The rules for that evaluation are extraordinarily simple compared to other languages:

1. Lists (denoted by parentheses) are calls, where the first value in the list is the operator and the rest of the values are parameters. The first element in a list is often referred to as being in *function position* (as that's where one provides the function or symbol naming the function to be called). Call expressions evaluate to the value returned by the call.

2. Symbols (such as **average** or **+**) evaluate to the named value in the current scope—which can be a function, a named local like **numbers** in our **average** function, a Java class, a macro, or a special form. We'll learn about macros and special forms in a little bit; for now, just think of them as functions.

3. All other expressions evaluate to the literal values they describe.

Lists in Lisps are often called *s-expressions* or *sexprs*—short for *symbolic expressions* due to the significance of symbols in identifying the values to be used in calls denoted by such lists. Generally, valid s-expressions that can be successfully evaluated are often referred to as *forms*: e.g., (if condition then else) is an if form, [60 80 100 400] is a vector form. Not all s-expressions are forms: (1 2 3) is a valid s-expression—a list of three integers—but evaluating it will produce an error because the first value in the list is an integer, which is not callable.

The second and third points are roughly equivalent to most other languages (although Clojure's literals are more expressive, as we'll see shortly). However, an examination of how calls work in other languages quickly reveals the complexity of their syntax.

Table 1-1. Comparison of call syntax between Clojure, Java, Python, and Ruby

Clojure expression	Java equivalent	Python equivalent	Ruby equivalent
(not k)	!k	not k	not k or ! k
(inc a)	a++,++a,a += 1,a + 1[a]	a += 1,a + 1	a += 1
(/ (+ x y) 2)	(x + y) / 2	(x + y) / 2	(x + y) / 2
(instance? java.util.List al)	al instanceof java.util.List	isinstance(al, list)	al.is_a? Array
(if (not a) (inc b) (dec b))[b]	!a ? b + 1 : b - 1	b + 1 if not a else b - 1	!a ? b + 1 : b - 1
(Math/pow 2 10)[c]	Math.pow(2, 10)	pow(2, 10)	2 ** 10
(.someMethod some Obj "foo" (.otherMe thod otherObj 0))	someObj.someMe thod("foo", other Obj.otherMethod(0))	someObj.someMe thod("foo", other Obj.otherMethod(0))	someObj.someMe thod("foo", other Obj.otherMethod(0))

[a] In-place increment and decrement operations have no direct corollary in Clojure, because unfettered mutability isn't available. See Chapter 2, particularly "On the Importance of Values" on page 52 for a complete discussion of why this is a good thing.

[b] Remember, even forms that influence control flow in Clojure evaluate to values just like any other expression, including if and when. Here, the value of the if expression will be either (inc b) or (dec b), depending on the value of (not a).

[c] Here's your first taste of what it looks like to call Java libraries from Clojure. For details, see Chapter 9.

Notice that call syntax is all over the map (we're picking on Java here the most, but Python and Ruby aren't so different):

- Infix operators are available (e.g., `a + 1`, `al instanceof List`), but any nontrivial code ends up having to use often-significant numbers of parentheses to override default precedence rules and make evaluation order explicit.
- Unary operators are seemingly arbitrary in regard to whether they use prefix (e.g., `!k` and `++a`) or postfix position (e.g., `a++`).
- Static method calls have prefix position, such as `Math.pow(2, 10)`, but…
- Instance method calls use an unusual variety of infix positions, where the target of the method (which will be assigned to `this` within the body of the method being called) is specified first, with the formal parameters to the method coming after the method name.[5]

In contrast, Clojure call expressions follow one simple rule: the first value in a list is the operator, the remainder are parameters to that operator. There are no call expressions that use infix or postfix position, and there are no difficult-to-remember precedence rules. This simplification helps make Clojure's syntax very easy to learn and internalize, and helps make Clojure code very easy to read.

Homoiconicity

Clojure code is composed of literal representations of its own data structures and atomic values; this characteristic is formally called *homoiconicity*, or more casually, *code-as-data*.[6] This is a significant simplification compared to most other languages, which also happens to enable metaprogramming facilities to a much greater degree than languages that are not homoiconic. To understand why, we'll need to talk some about languages in general and how their code relates to their internal representations.

Recall that a REPL's first stage is to *read* code provided to it by you. Every language has to provide a way to transform that textual representation of code into something that can be compiled and/or evaluated. Most languages do this by parsing that text into an *abstract syntax tree* (AST). This sounds more complicated than it is: an AST is simply a data structure that represents formally what is manifested concretely in text. For example, Figure 1-1 shows some examples of textual language and possible transformations to their corresponding syntax trees.[7]

---

5. Python uses the same sort of infix position for its instance methods, but varies from Algol-family brethren by requiring that methods explicitly name their first parameter, usually `self`.

6. Clojure is by no means the only homoiconic language, nor is homoiconicity a new concept. Other homoiconic languages include all other Lisps, all sorts of machine language (and therefore arguably Assembly language as well), Postscript, XSLT and XQuery, Prolog, R, Factor, Io, and more.

7. The natural language parse tree was mostly lifted from *http://en.wikipedia.org/wiki/Parse_tree*.

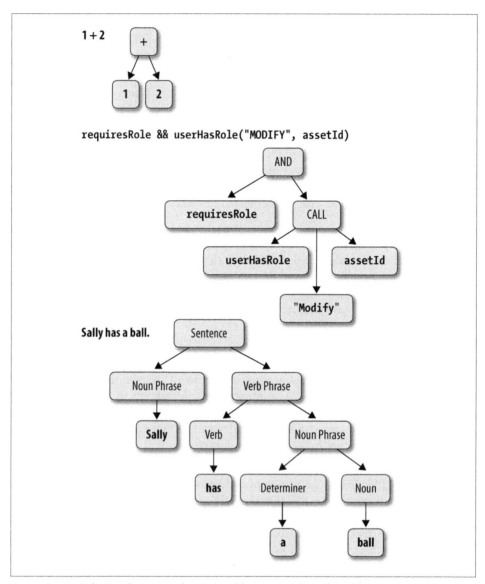

Figure 1-1. Sample transformations from textual language to formal models

These transformations from a textual manifestation of language to an AST are at the heart of how languages are defined, how expressive they are, and how well-suited they are to the purpose of relating to the world within which they are designed to be used. Much of the appeal of domain-specific languages springs from exactly this point: if you have a language that is purpose-built for a given field of use, those that have expertise in that field will find it far easier to define and express what they wish in that language compared to a general-purpose language.

The downside of this approach is that most languages do not provide any way to control their ASTs; the correspondence between their textual syntax and their ASTs is defined solely by the language implementers. This prompts clever programmers to conjure up clever workarounds in order to maximize the expressivity and utility of the textual syntax that they have to work with:

- Code generation
- Textual macros and preprocessors (used to legendary effect by C and C++ programmers for decades now)
- Compiler plug-ins (as in Scala, Project Lombok for Java, Groovy's AST transformations, and Template Haskell)

That's a lot of incidental complexity—complexity introduced solely because language designers often view textual syntax as primary, leaving formal models of it to be implementation-specific (when they're exposed at all).

Clojure (like all Lisps) takes a different path: rather than defining a syntax that will be transformed into an AST, Clojure programs are written using Clojure data structures that represent that AST directly. Consider the `requiresRole...` example from Figure 1-1, and see how a Clojure transliteration of the example *is* an AST for it (recalling the call semantics of function position in Clojure lists).

`(and requiresRole (userHasRole "MODIFY" assetId))`

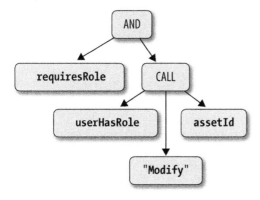

The fact that *Clojure programs are represented as data* means that Clojure programs can be used to write and transform other Clojure programs, trivially so. This is the basis for macros—Clojure's metaprogramming facility—a far different beast than the gloriously painful hack that are C-style macros and other textual preprocessors, and the ultimate escape hatch when expressivity or domain-specific notation is paramount. We explore Clojure macros in Chapter 5.

In practical terms, the direct correspondence between code and data means that the Clojure code you write in the REPL or in a text source file isn't text at all: you are programming using Clojure data structure literals. Recall the simple `averaging` function from Example 1-2:

```
(defn average
  [numbers]
  (/ (apply + numbers) (count numbers)))
```

This isn't just a bunch of text that is somehow transformed into a function definition through the operation of a black box; this is a list data structure that contains four values: the symbol `defn`, the symbol `average`, a vector data structure containing the symbol `numbers`, and another list that comprises the function's body. Evaluating that list data structure is what defines the function.

The Reader

Although Clojure's compilation and evaluation machinery operates exclusively on Clojure data structures, the practice of programming has not yet progressed beyond storing code as plain text. Thus, a way is needed to produce those data structures from textual code. This task falls to the Clojure *reader*.

The operation of the reader is completely defined by a single function, `read`, which reads text content from a character stream[8] and returns the next data structure encoded in the stream's content. This is what the Clojure REPL uses to read text input; each complete data structure read from that input source is then passed on to be evaluated by the Clojure runtime.

More convenient for exploration's sake is `read-string`, a function that does the same thing as `read` but uses a string argument as its content source:

```
(read-string "42")
;= 42
(read-string "(+ 1 2)")
;= (+ 1 2)
```

The operation of the reader is fundamentally one of deserialization. Clojure data structures and other literals have a particular textual representation, which the reader deserializes to the corresponding values and data structures.

You may have noticed that values printed by the Clojure REPL have the same textual representation they do when entered into the REPL: numbers and other atomic literals are printed as you'd expect, lists are delimited by parentheses, vectors by square brackets, and so on. This is because there are duals to the reader's `read` and `read-string` functions: `pr` and `pr-str`, which prints to `*out*`[9] and returns as a string the `readable` textual representation of Clojure values, respectively. Thus, Clojure data structures and

---

8. Technically, `read` requires a `java.io.PushbackReader` as an implementation detail.

9. `*out*` defaults to `stdout`, but can be redirected easily. See "Building a Primitive Logging System with Composable Higher-Order Functions" on page 72 for an example.

---

values are trivially serialized and deserialized in a way that is both human- and reader-readable:

```
(pr-str [1 2 3])
;= "[1 2 3]"
(read-string "[1 2 3]")
;= [1 2 3]
```

 It is common for Clojure applications to use the reader as a general-purpose serialization mechanism where you might otherwise choose XML or java.io.Serializable serialization or pickling or marshaling, especially in cases where human-readable serializations are desirable.

Scalar Literals

Scalar literals are reader syntax for noncollection values. Many of these are bread-and-butter types that you already know intimately from Java or very similar analogues in Ruby, Python, and other languages; others are specific to Clojure and carry new semantics.

Strings

Clojure strings are Java Strings (that is, instances of java.lang.String), and are represented in exactly the same way, delimited by double quotes:

```
"hello there"
;= "hello there"
```

Clojure's strings are naturally multiline-capable, without any special syntax (as in, for example, Python):

```
"multiline strings
are very handy"
;= "multiline strings\nare very handy"
```

Booleans

The tokens true and false are used to denote literal Boolean values in Clojure, just as in Java, Ruby, and Python (modulo the latter's capitalization).

nil

nil in Clojure corresponds to null in Java, nil in Ruby, and None in Python. nil is also logically false in Clojure conditionals, as it is in Ruby and Python.

Characters

Character literals are denoted by a backslash:

```
(class \c)
;= java.lang.Character
```

Both Unicode and octal representations of characters may be used with corresponding prefixes:

```
\u00ff
;= \ÿ
\o41
;= \!
```

Additionally, there are a number of special named character literals for cases where the character in question is commonly used but prints as whitespace:

- \space
- \newline
- \formfeed
- \return
- \backspace
- \tab

Keywords

Keywords evaluate to themselves, and are often used as accessors for the values they name in Clojure collections and types, such as hash maps and records:

```
(def person {:name "Sandra Cruz"
             :city "Portland, ME"})
;= #'user/person
(:city person)
;= "Portland, ME"
```

Here we create a hashmap with two slots, :name and :city, and then look up the value of :city in that map. This works because keywords are functions that look themselves up in collections passed to them.

Syntactically, keywords are always prefixed with a colon, and can otherwise consist of any nonwhitespace character. A slash character (/) denotes a *namespaced keyword*, while a keyword prefixed with two colons (::) is expanded by the reader to a name-spaced keyword in the current namespace—or another namespace if the keyword started by a namespace alias, ::alias/kw for example. These have similar usage and motivation as namespaced entities in XML; that is, being able to use the same name for values with different semantics or roles:[10]

```
(def pizza {:name "Ramunto's"
            :location "Claremont, NH"
            ::location "43.3734,-72.3365"})
;= #'user/pizza
pizza
;= {:name "Ramunto's", :location "Claremont, NH", :user/location "43.3734,-72.3365"}
```

---

10. Namespaced keywords are also used prominently with multimethods and isa? hierarchies, discussed in depth in Chapter 7.

```
(:user/location pizza)
;= "43.3734,-72.3365"
```

This allows different modules in the same application and disparate groups within the same organization to safely lay claim to particular names, without complex domain modeling or conventions like underscored prefixes for conflicting names.

Keywords are one type of "named" values, so called because they have an intrinsic name that is accessible using the name function and an optional namespace accessible using namespace:

```
(name :user/location)
;= "location"
(namespace :user/location)
;= "user"
(namespace :location)
;= nil
```

The other named type of value is the symbol.

Symbols

Like keywords, symbols are identifiers, but they evaluate to values in the Clojure runtime they name. These values include those held by vars (which are named storage locations used to hold functions and other values), Java classes, local references, and so on. Thinking back to our original example in Example 1-2:

```
(average [60 80 100 400])
;= 160
```

average here is a symbol, referring to the function held in the var named average.

Symbols must begin with a non-numeric character, and can contain *, +, !, -, _, and ? in addition to any alphanumeric characters. Symbols that contain a slash (/) denote a *namespaced symbol* and will evaluate to the named value in the specified namespace. The evaluation of symbols to the entity they name depends upon their context and the namespaces available within that context. We talk about the semantics of namespaces and symbol evaluation extensively in "Namespaces" on page 20.

Numbers

Clojure provides a plethora of numeric literals (see Table 1-2). Many of them are pedestrian, but others are rare to find in a general-purpose programming language and can simplify the implementation of certain algorithms—especially in cases where the algorithms are defined in terms of particular numeric representations (octal, binary, rational numbers, and scientific notation).

While the Java runtime defines a particular range of numeric primitives, and Clojure supports interoperability with those primitives, Clojure has a bias toward longs and doubles at the expense of other widths, including bytes, shorts, ints, and floats. This means that these smaller primitives will be produced as needed from literals or runtime values for interop operations (such as calling Java methods), but pure-Clojure operations will default to using the wider numeric representations.

For the vast majority of programming domains, you don't need to worry about this. If you are doing work where mathematical precision and other related topics is important, please refer to Chapter 11 for a comprehensive discussion of Clojure's treatment of operations on primitives and other math topics.

Table 1-2. Clojure numeric literals

Literal syntax	Numeric type
42, 0xff, 2r111, 040	long (64-bit signed integer)
3.14, 6.0221415e23	double (64-bit IEEE floating point decimal)
42N	clojure.lang.BigInt (arbitrary-precision integer[a])
0.01M	java.math.BigDecimal (arbitrary-precision signed floating point decimal)
22/7	clojure.lang.Ratio

[a] clojure.lang.BigInt is automatically coerced to java.math.BigInteger when needed. Again, please see Chapter 11 for the in-depth details of Clojure's treatment of numerics.

Any numeric literal can be negated by prefixing it with a dash (-).

Let's take a quick look at the more interesting numeric literals:

Hexadecimal notation
Just as in most languages, Clojure supports typical hexadecimal notation for integer values; 0xff is 255, 0xd055 is 53333, and so on.

Octal notation
Literals starting with a zero are interpreted as octal numbers. For example, the octal 040 is 32 in the usual base-10 notation.

Flexible numeral bases
You can specify the base of an integer in a prefix BrN, where N is the digits that represent the desired number, and B is the base or radix by which N should be interpreted. So we can use a prefix of 2r for binary integers (2r111 is 7), 16r for hexadecimal (16rff is 255), and so on. This is supported up to base 36.[11]

11. The implementation limit of java.math.BigInteger's radix support. Note that even though BigInteger is used for parsing these literals, the concrete type of the number as emitted by the reader is consistent with other Clojure integer literals: either a long or a big integer if the number specified requires arbitrary precision to represent.

Arbitrary-precision numbers

Any numeric literal (except for rational numbers) can be specified as arbitrary-precision by suffixing it appropriately; decimals with an M, integers with an N. Please see "Bounded Versus Arbitrary Precision" on page 428 for a full exploration of why and when this is relevant.

Rational numbers

Clojure directly supports rational numbers, also called *ratios*, as literals in the reader as well as throughout its numeric operators. Rational number literals must always be two integers separated by a slash (/).

For a full discussion of rational numbers in Clojure and how they interact with the rest of Clojure's numerical model, please see "Rationals" on page 424.

Regular expressions

The Clojure reader treats strings prefixed with a hash character as regular expression (regex) literals:

```
(class #"(p|h)ail")
;= java.util.regex.Pattern
```

This is exactly equivalent to Ruby's /.../ regex syntax, with a minor difference of pattern delimiters. In fact, Ruby and Clojure are *very* similar in their handling of regular expressions:

```
# Ruby
>> "foo bar".match(/(...) (...)/).to_a
["foo bar", "foo", "bar"]

;; Clojure
(re-seq #"(...) (...)" "foo bar")
;= (["foo bar" "foo" "bar"])
```

Clojure's regex syntax does not require escaping of backslashes as required in Java:

```
(re-seq #"(\d+)-(\d+)" "1-3")     ;; would be "(\\d+)-(\\d+)" in Java
;= (["1-3" "1" "3"])
```

The instances of `java.util.regex.Pattern` that Clojure regex literals yield are entirely equivalent to those you might create within Java, and therefore use the generally excellent `java.util.regex` regular expression implementation.[12] Thus, you can use those `Pattern` instances directly via Clojure's Java interop if you like, though you will likely find Clojure's related utility functions (such as `re-seq`, `re-find`, `re-matches`, and others in the `clojure.string` namespace) simpler and more pleasant to use.

---

12. See the `java.util.regex.Pattern` javadoc for a full specification of what forms the Java regular expression implementation supports: *http://docs.oracle.com/javase/7/docs/api/java/util/regex/Pattern.html*.

Comments

There are two comment types that are defined by the reader:

- Single-line comments are indicated by prefixing the comment with a semicolon (;); all content following a semicolon is ignored entirely. These are equivalent to // in Java and JavaScript, and # in Ruby and Python.
- *Form-level* are available using the #_ reader macro. This cues the reader to elide the next Clojure *form* following the macro:

```
(read-string "(+ 1 2 #_(* 2 2) 8)")
;= (+ 1 2 8)
```

What would have been a list with four numbers—(+ 1 2 4 8)—yields a list of only three numbers because the entire multiplication form was ignored due to the #_ prefix.

Because Clojure code is defined using data structure literals, this comment form can be far more useful in certain cases than purely textual comments that affect lines or character offsets (such as the /* */ multiline comments in Java and JavaScript). For example, consider the time-tested debugging technique of printing to stdout:

```
(defn some-function
  [...arguments...]
  ...code...
  (if ...debug-conditional...
    (println ...debug-info...)
    (println ...more-debug-info...))
  ...code...)
```

Making those println forms functionally disappear is as easy as prefixing the if form with the #_ reader macro and reloading the function definition; whether the form spans one or a hundred lines is irrelevant.

There is only one other way to comment code in Clojure, the comment macro:

```
(when true
  (comment (println "hello")))
;= nil
```

comment forms can contain any amount of ignored code, but they are not elided from the reader's output in the way that #_ impacts the forms following it. Thus, comment forms always evaluate to nil. This often is not a problem; but, sometimes it can be inconvenient. Consider a reformulation of our first #_ example:

```
(+ 1 2 (comment (* 2 2)) 8)
;= #<NullPointerException java.lang.NullPointerException>
```

That fails because comment returns nil, which is not a valid argument to +.

Whitespace and Commas

You may have noticed that there have been no commas between forms, parameters to function calls, elements in data structure literals, and so on:

```
(defn silly-adder
  [x y]
  (+ x y))
```

This is because whitespace is sufficient to separate values and forms provided to the reader. In addition, *commas are considered whitespace by the reader*. For example, this is functionally equivalent to the snippet above:

```
(defn silly-adder
  [x, y]
  (+, x, y))
```

And to be slightly pedantic about it:

```
(= [1 2 3] [1, 2, 3])
;= true
```

Whether you use commas or not is entirely a question of personal style and preference. That said, they are generally used only when doing so enhances the *human* readability of the code in question. This is most common in cases where pairs of values are listed, but more than one pair appears per line:[13]

```
(create-user {:name new-username, :email email})
```

Collection Literals

The reader provides syntax for the most commonplace Clojure data structures:

```
'(a b :name 12.5)        ;; list

['a 'b :name 12.5]       ;; vector

{:name "Chas" :age 31}   ;; map

#{1 2 3}                  ;; set
```

Since lists are used to denote calls in Clojure, you need to quote (') the list literal in order to prevent the evaluation of the list as a call.

The specifics of these data structures are explored in detail in Chapter 3.

---

13. Questions of style are notoriously difficult to answer in absolutes, but it would be very rare to see more than two or three pairs of values on the same line of text in any map literal, set of keyword arguments, and so on. Further, some forms that expect pairs of values (such as bindings in `let`) are essentially *always* delimited by linebreaks rather than being situated on the same line.

Miscellaneous Reader Sugar

The reader provides for some additional syntax in certain cases to improve concision or regularity with other aspects of Clojure:

- Evaluation can be suppressed by prefixing a form with a quote character (`'`); see "Suppressing Evaluation: quote" on page 24.

- Anonymous function literals can be defined very concisely using the #() notation; see "Function literals" on page 40.

- While symbols evaluate to the values held by vars, vars themselves can be referred to by prefixing a symbol with #'; see "Referring to Vars: var" on page 44.

- Instances of reference types can be dereferenced (yielding the value contained within the reference object) by prefixing @ to a symbol naming the instance; see "Clojure Reference Types" on page 170.

- The reader provides three bits of special syntax for macros: `` ` ``, `~`, and `~@`. Macros are explored in Chapter 5.

- While there are technically only two Java interop forms, the reader provides some sugar for interop that expands into those two special forms; see "Java Interop: . and new" on page 44.

- All of Clojure's data structures and reference types support *metadata*—small bits of information that can be associated with a value or reference that do not affect things like equality comparisons. While your applications can use metadata for many purposes, metadata is used in Clojure itself where you might otherwise use keywords in other languages (e.g., to indicate that a function is namespace-private, or to indicate the type of a value or return type of a function). The reader allows you to attach metadata to literal values being read using the ^ notation; see "Metadata" on page 135.

Namespaces

At this point, we should understand much of how the nontrivial parts of the Clojure REPL (and therefore Clojure itself) work:

- Read: the Clojure reader reads the textual representation of code, producing the data structures (e.g., lists, vectors, and so on) and atomic values (e.g., symbols, numbers, strings, etc.) indicated in that code.

- Evaluate: many of the values emitted by the reader evaluate to themselves (including most data structures and scalars like strings and keywords). We explored earlier in "Expressions, Operators, Syntax, and Precedence" on page 7 how lists evaluate to calls to the operator in *function position*.

The only thing left to understand about evaluation now is how symbols are evaluated. So far, we've used them to both name and refer to functions, locals, and so on. Outside of identifying locals, the semantics of symbol evaluation are tied up with namespaces, Clojure's fundamental unit of code modularity.

All Clojure code is defined and evaluated within a namespace. Namespaces are roughly analogous to modules in Ruby or Python, or packages in Java.[14] Fundamentally, they are dynamic mappings between *symbols* and either *vars* or imported Java classes.

One of Clojure's *reference types*,[15] vars are mutable storage locations that can hold any value. Within the namespace where they are defined, vars are associated with a symbol that other code can use to look up the var, and therefore the value it holds.

Vars are defined in Clojure using the def special form, which only ever acts within the current namespace.[16] Let's define a var now in the user namespace, named x; the name of the var is the symbol that it is keyed under within the current namespace:

```
(def x 1)
;= #'user/x
```

We can access the var's value using that symbol:

```
x
;= 1
```

The symbol x here is *unqualified*, so is resolved within the current namespace. We can also redefine vars; this is critical for supporting interactive development at the REPL:

```
(def x "hello")
;= #'user/x
x
;= "hello"
```

Vars are not variables

Vars should only ever be defined in an interactive context—such as a REPL—or within a Clojure source file as a way of defining named functions, other constant values, and the like. In particular, top-level vars (that is, globally accessible vars mapped within namespaces, as defined by def and its variants) should only ever be defined by top-level expressions, never in the bodies of functions in the normal course of operation of a Clojure program.

See "Vars Are Not Variables" on page 206 for further elaboration.

---

14. In fact, namespaces correspond precisely with Java packages when types defined in Clojure are compiled down to Java classes. For example, a Person type defined in the Clojure namespace app.entities will produce a Java class named app.entities.Person. See more about defining types and records in Clojure in Chapter 6.

15. See "Clojure Reference Types" on page 170 for a full discussion of Clojure's reference types, all of which contribute different capabilities to its concurrency toolbox.

16. Remember that the Clojure REPL session always starts in the default user namespace.

Symbols may also be namespace-qualified, in which case they are resolved within the specified namespace instead of the current one:

```
*ns*                        ❶
;= #<Namespace user>
(ns foo)
;= nil
*ns*
;= #<Namespace foo>
user/x
;= "hello"
x
;= #<CompilerException java.lang.RuntimeException:
;=   Unable to resolve symbol: x in this context, compiling:(NO_SOURCE_PATH:0)>
```

❶ The current namespace is always bound to *ns*.

Here we created a new namespace using the ns macro (which has the side effect of switching us to that new namespace in our REPL), and then referred to the value of x in the user namespace by using the namespace-qualified symbol user/x. Since we only just created this new namespace foo, it doesn't have a mapping for the x symbol, so attempting to resolve it fails.

 You need to know how to create, define, organize, and manipulate namespaces in order to use Clojure effectively. There is a whole suite of functions for this; please refer to "Defining and Using Namespaces" on page 322 for our guidelines in their use.

We mentioned earlier that namespaces also map between symbols and imported Java classes. All classes in the java.lang package are imported by default into each Clojure namespace, and so can be referred to without package qualification; to refer to unimported classes, a package-qualified symbol must be used. Any symbol that names a class evaluates to that class:

```
String
;= java.lang.String
Integer
;= java.lang.Integer
java.util.List
;= java.util.List
java.net.Socket
;= java.net.Socket
```

In addition, namespaces by default alias all of the vars defined in the primary namespace of Clojure's standard library, clojure.core. For example, there is a filter function defined in clojure.core, which we can access without namespace-qualifying our reference to it:

```
filter
;= #<core$filter clojure.core$filter@7444f787>
```

These are just the barest basics of how Clojure namespaces work; learn more about them and how they should be used to help you structure your projects in "Defining and Using Namespaces" on page 322.

Symbol Evaluation

With a basic understanding of namespaces under our belt, we can turn again to the example `average` function from Example 1-2 and have a more concrete idea of how it is evaluated:

```
(defn average
  [numbers]
  (/ (apply + numbers) (count numbers)))
```

As we learned in "Homoiconicity" on page 9, this is just a canonical textual representation of a Clojure data structure that itself contains other data. Within the body of this function, there are many symbols, each of which refers to either a var in scope in the current namespace or a local value:

- `/`, `apply`, `+`, and `count` all evaluate to functions held in vars defined and so named in the `clojure.core` namespace
- `numbers` either defines the sole argument to the function (when provided in the argument vector `[numbers]`),[17] or is used to refer to that argument's value in the body of the function (when used in the `(apply + numbers)` and `(count numbers)` expressions).

With this information, and recalling the semantics of lists as calls with the operator in function position, you should have a nearly complete understanding of how calls to this function are evaluated:

```
(average [60 80 100 400])
;= 160
```

The symbol `average` refers here to the value of `#'average`, the var in the current namespace that holds the function we defined. That function is called with a vector of numbers, which is locally bound as `numbers` within the body of the `average` function. The result of the operations in that body produce a value—160—which is then returned to the caller: in this case, the REPL, which prints it to `stdout`.

Special Forms

Ignoring Java interoperability for a moment, symbols in function position can evaluate to only two things:

---

17. We'll get into all the details of how to define functions and therefore their arguments in "Creating Functions: fn" on page 36.

1. The value of a named var or local, as we've already seen.
2. A Clojure *special form*.[18]

Special forms are Clojure's primitive building blocks of computation, on top of which all the rest of Clojure is built. This foundation shares a lineage with the earliest Lisps, which also defined a limited set of primitives that define the fundamental operations of the runtime, and are taken as sufficient to describe any possible computation.[19] Further, special forms have their own syntax (e.g., many do not take arguments per se) and evaluation semantics.

As you've seen, things that are often described as primitive operations or statements in most languages—including control forms like when and operators like addition and negation—are not primitives in Clojure. Rather, everything that isn't a special form is implemented in Clojure itself by bootstrapping from that limited set of primitive operations.[20] The practical effect of this is that, if Clojure doesn't provide a language construct that you want or need, you can likely build it yourself.[21]

Though all of Clojure is built on top of its special forms, you need to understand what each one does—as you'll use many of them constantly. Let's now discuss each one in turn.

Suppressing Evaluation: quote

quote suppresses evaluation of a Clojure expression. The most obvious impact of this relates to symbols, which, if they name a var, evaluate to that var's value. With quote, evaluation is suppressed, so symbols evaluate to themselves (just like strings, numbers, and so on):

```
(quote x)
;= x
(symbol? (quote x))
;= true
```

There is reader syntax for quote; prefixing any form with a quote character (') will expand into a usage of quote:

---

18. Special forms are always given precedence when resolving symbols in function position. For example, you can have a var or local named def, but you will not be able to refer to the value of that var or local in function position—though you can refer to that value anywhere else.

19. Paul Graham's *The Roots of Lisp* (*http://www.paulgraham.com/rootsoflisp.html*) is a brief yet approachable precis of the fundamental operations of computation, as originally discovered and enumerated by John McCarthy. Though that characterization of computation was made more than 50 years ago, you can see it thriving in Clojure today.

20. If you were to open the *core.clj* file from Clojure's source repository, you will see this bootstrapping in action: everything from when and or to defn and = is defined in Clojure itself. Indeed, if you were so motivated, you could implement Clojure (or another language of your choosing) from scratch, on your own, on top of Clojure's special forms.

21. This sort of syntactic extension generally requires *macros*, which are treated in detail in Chapter 5.

```
'x
;= x
```

Any Clojure form can be quoted, including data structures. Doing so returns the data structure in question, with evaluation recursively suppressed for all of its elements:

```
'(+ x x)
;= (+ x x)
(list? '(+ x x))
;= true
```

While lists are usually evaluated as calls, quoting a list suppresses that evaluation, yielding the list itself; in this case, a list of three symbols: '+, 'x, and 'x. Note that this is exactly what we get if we "manually" construct the list without using a list literal:

```
(list '+ 'x 'x)
;= (+ x x)
```

 You can usually have a peek at what the reader produces by quoting a form. Let's go meta for a moment and try it first on quote itself:

```
''x
;= (quote x)
```

It's informative to use this trick on other reader sugars:

```
'@x
;= (clojure.core/deref x)
'#(+ % %)
;= (fn* [p1__3162792#] (+ p1__3162792# p1__3162792#))
'`(a b ~c)
;= (seq (concat (list (quote user/a))
;=               (list (quote user/b))
;=               (list c)))                    ❶
```

❶ clojure.core namespace-prefixes elided for legibility.

Code Blocks: do

do evaluates all of the expressions provided to it in order and yields the last expression's value as its value. For example:

```
(do
  (println "hi")
  (apply * [4 5 6]))
; hi
;= 120
```

The values of all but the last expression are discarded, although their side effects do occur (such as printing to standard out as we're doing here, or manipulations of a stateful object available in the current scope).

Note that many other forms (including fn, let, loop, and try—and any derivative of these, such as defn) wrap their bodies in an implicit do expression, so that multiple inner expressions can be evaluated. For example, let expressions—like this one that defines two locals—provide an implicit do context to their bodies:

```
(let [a (inc (rand-int 6))
      b (inc (rand-int 6))]
  (println (format "You rolled a %s and a %s" a b))
  (+ a b))
```

This allows any number of expressions to be evaluated within the context of the let form, with only the final one determining its ultimate result. If let didn't wrap its body with a do form, you would have to add it explicitly:[22]

```
(let [a (inc (rand-int 6))
      b (inc (rand-int 6))]
  (do
    (println (format "You rolled a %s and a %s" a b))
    (+ a b)))
```

Defining Vars: def

We've already seen def in action;[23] it defines (or redefines) a var (with an optional value) within the current namespace:

```
(def p "foo")
;= #'user/p
p
;= "foo"
```

Many other forms implicitly create or redefine vars, and therefore use def internally. It is customary for such forms to be prefixed with "def," such as defn, defn-, defprotocol, defonce, defmacro, and so on.

> Although forms that create or redefine vars have names that start with "def," unfortunately not all forms that start with "def" create or redefine vars. Examples of the latter include deftype, defrecord, and defmethod.

---

22. The other alternative would be for let (and all other forms that utilize do) to (re?) implement its own semantics of "do several things and return the value of the last expression": hardly a reasonable thing to do.

23. See "Namespaces" on page 20 for a discussion of the typical usage of vars as stable references to values in namespaces; see "Vars" on page 198 for more a more comprehensive treatment of them, including esoteric usages related to dynamic scope and thread-local references.

Local Bindings: let

let allows you to define named references that are lexically scoped to the extent of the let expression. Said another way, let defines locals. For example, this rudimentary static method in Java:

```
public static double hypot (double x, double y) {
    final double x2 = x * x;
    final double y2 = y * y;
    return Math.sqrt(x2 + y2);
}
```

is equivalent to this Clojure function:

```
(defn hypot
  [x y]
  (let [x2 (* x x)
        y2 (* y y)]
    (Math/sqrt (+ x2 y2))))
```

The x2 and y2 locals in the respective function/method bodies serve the same purpose: to establish a named, scoped reference to an intermediate value.

There are many terms used to talk about named references established by let in Clojure parlance:

- *locals*
- *local bindings*
- particular values are said to be *let-bound*

Bindings and *bound* used in connection with let are entirely distinct from the binding macro, which controls scoped thread-local variables; see "Dynamic Scope" on page 201 for more about the latter.

Note that let is implicitly used anywhere locals are required. In particular, fn (and therefore all other function-creation and function-definition forms like defn) uses let to bind function parameters as locals within the scope of the function being defined. For example, x and y in the hypot function above are let-bound by defn. So, the vector that defines the set of bindings for a let scope obeys the same semantics whether it is used to define function parameters or an auxiliary local binding scope.

Occasionally, you will want evaluate an expression in the binding vector provided to let, but have no need to refer to its result within the context of the let's body. In these cases, it is customary to use an underscore as the bound name for such values, so that readers of the code will know that results of such expressions are going unused intentionally.

This is only ever relevant when the expression in question is side-effecting; a common example would be printing some intermediate value:

```
(let [location (get-lat-long)
      _ (println "Current location:" location)
      location (find-city-name location)]
  …display city name for current location in UI…)
```

Here we're retrieving our current latitude and longitude using a hypothetical API, and we'd like to print that out before converting the location data to a human-recognizable city name. We might want to rebind the same name a couple of times in the course of the let's binding vector, paving over those intermediate values. To print out that intermediate value, we add it to the binding vector prior to rebinding its name, but we indicate that we are intentionally ignoring the return value of that expression by naming it _.

let has two particular semantic wrinkles that are very different from locals you may be used to in other languages:

1. All locals are *immutable*. You can *override* a local binding within a nested let form or a later binding of the same name within the same binding vector, but there is no way to bash out a bound name and change its value within the scope of a single let form. This eliminates a source of common errors and bugs without sacrificing capability:
   - The loop and recur special forms provide for looping cases where values need to change on each cycle of a loop; see "Looping: loop and recur" on page 43.
   - If you really need a "mutable" local binding, Clojure provides a raft of reference types that enforce specific mutation semantics; see "Clojure Reference Types" on page 170.
2. let's binding vector is interpreted at compile time to provide optional *destructuring* of common collection types. Destructuring can aid substantially in eliminating certain types of verbose (and frankly, dull) code often associated with working with collections provided as arguments to functions.

Destructuring (let, Part 2)

A lot of Clojure programming involves working with various implementations of data structure abstractions, *sequential* and *map* collections being two of those key abstractions. Many Clojure functions accept and return seqs and maps generally—rather than specific implementations—and most Clojure libraries and applications are built up relying upon these abstractions instead of particular concrete structures, classes, and so on. This allows functions and libraries to be trivially composed around the data being handled with a minimum of integration, "glue code," and other incidental complexity.

One challenge when working with abstract collections is being able to concisely access multiple values in those collections. For example, here's a collection, a Clojure vector:

```
(def v [42 "foo" 99.2 [5 12]])
;= #'user/v
```

Consider a couple of approaches for accessing the values in our sample vector:

```
(first v)      ❶
;= 42
(second v)
;= "foo"
(last v)
;= [5 12]
(nth v 2)      ❷
;= 99.2
(v 2)          ❸
;= 99.2
(.get v 2)     ❹
;= 99.2
```

❶ Clojure provides convenience functions for accessing the `first`, `second`, and `last` values from a sequential collection.

❷ The `nth` function allows you pluck any value from a sequential collection using an index into that collection.

❸ Vectors are functions of their indices.

❹ All of Clojure's sequential collections implement the `java.util.List` interface, so you can use that interface's `.get` method to access their contents.

All of these are perfectly fine ways to access a single "top-level" value in a vector, but things start getting more complex if we need to access multiple values to perform some operation:

```
(+ (first v) (v 2))
;= 141.2
```

Or if we need to access values in nested collections:

```
(+ (first v) (first (last v)))
;= 47
```

Clojure destructuring provides a concise syntax for declaratively pulling apart collections and binding values contained therein as named locals within a `let` form. And, because destructuring is a facility provided by let, it can be used in any expression that implicitly uses let (like fn, defn, loop, and so on).

There are two flavors of destructuring: one that operates over sequential collections, and another that works with maps.

Sequential destructuring

Sequential destructuring works with any sequential collection, including:

- Clojure lists, vectors, and seqs
- Any collection that implements java.util.List (like ArrayLists and LinkedLists)
- Java arrays
- Strings, which are destructured into their characters

Here's a basic example, where we are destructuring the same value v discussed above:

Example 1-3. Basic sequential destructuring

```
(def v [42 "foo" 99.2 [5 12]])
;= #'user/v
(let [[x y z] v]
  (+ x z))
;= 141.2
```

In its simplest form, the vector provided to let contains pairs of names and values, but here we're providing a vector of symbols—[x y z]—instead of a scalar symbol name. What this does is cause the value v to be destructured sequentially, with the first value bound to x within the body of the let form, the second value bound to y, and the third value bound to z. We can then use those destructured locals like any other locals. This is equivalent to:

```
(let [x (nth v 0)
      y (nth v 1)
      z (nth v 2)]
  (+ x z))
;= 141.2
```

Python has something similar to Clojure's sequential destructuring, called *unpacking*. The equivalent to the preceding code snippet in Python would be something like:

```
>>> v = [42, "foo", 99.2, [5, 12]]
>>> x, y, z, a = v
>>> x + z
141.19999999999999
```

The same goes for Ruby:

```
>> x, y, z, a = [42, "foo", 99.2, [5, 12]]
[42, "foo", 99.2, [5, 12]]
```

```
>> x + z
141.2
```

Clojure, Python, and Ruby all seem pretty similar on their face; but, as you'll see as we go along, Clojure goes quite a long ways beyond what Python and Ruby offer.

Destructuring forms are intended to mirror the structure of the collection that is being bound.[24] So, we can line up our destructuring form with the collection being destructured and get a very accurate notion of which values are going to be bound to which names:[25]

```
[x  y    z]
[42 "foo" 99.2 [5 12]]
```

Destructuring forms can be composed as well, so we can dig into the nested vector in v with ease:[26]

```
(let [[x _ _ [y z]] v]
  (+ x y z))
;= 59
```

If we visually line up our destructuring form and the source vector again, the work being done by that form should again be very clear:

```
[x  _    _  [y z ]]
[42 "foo" 99.2 [5 12]]
```

 If our nested vector had a vector inside of it, we could destructure it as well. The destructuring mechanism has no limit to how far it can descend into a deeply nested data structure, but there are limits to good taste. If you're using destructuring to pull values out of a collection four or more levels down, chances are your destructuring form will be difficult to interpret for the next person to see that code—even if that next person is you!

There are two additional features of sequential destructuring forms you should know about:

Gathering extra-positional sequential values

You can use & to gather values that lay beyond the positions you've named in your destructuring form into a sequence; this is similar to the mechanism underlying varargs in Java methods and is the basis of **rest** arguments in Clojure functions:

24. Thus the term: destructuring is undoing (*de-*) the creation of the data *structure*.

25. Values in the source collection that have no corresponding bound name are simply not bound within the context of the 1et form; you do not need to fully match the structure of the source collection, but sequential destructuring forms do need to be "anchored" at the beginning of the source.

26. Again, note the use of underscores (_) in this destructuring form to indicate an ignored binding, similar to the idiom discussed in the note earlier in this chapter.

```
(let [[x & rest] v]
  rest)
;= ("foo" 99.2 [5 12])
```

This is particularly useful when processing items from a sequence, either via recursive function calls or in conjunction with a loop form. Notice that the value of rest here is a sequence, and *not* a vector, even though we provided a vector to the destructuring form.

Retaining the destructured value

You can establish a local binding for the original collection being destructured by specifying the name it should have via the :as option within the destructuring form:

```
(let [[x _ z :as original-vector] v]
  (conj original-vector (+ x z)))
;= [42 "foo" 99.2 [5 12] 141.2]
```

Here, original-vector is bound to the unchanged value of v. This comes in handy when you are destructuring a collection that is the result of a function call, but you need to retain a reference to that unaltered result in addition to having the benefit of destructuring it. Without this feature, doing so would require something like this:

```
(let [some-collection (some-function ...)
      [x y z [a b]] some-collection]
  ...do something with some-collection and its values...)
```

Map destructuring

Map destructuring is conceptually identical to sequential destructuring—we aim to mirror the structure of the collection being bound. It works with:

- Clojure hash-maps, array-maps, and records[27]
- Any collection that implements java.util.Map
- Any value that is supported by the get function can be map-destructured, using indices as keys:
  — Clojure vectors
  — Strings
  — Arrays

Let's start with a Clojure map and a basic destructuring of it:

```
(def m {:a 5 :b 6
        :c [7 8 9]
        :d {:e 10 :f 11}
        "foo" 88
        42 false})
;= #'user/m
```

27. See "Records" on page 272 to learn more about records.

```
(let [{a :a b :b} m]
  (+ a b))
;= 11
```

Here we're binding the value for :a in the map to a, and the value for :b in the map to b. Going back to our visual alignment of the destructuring form with the (in this case, partial) collection being destructured, we can again see the structural correspondence:

```
{a  :a b  :b}
{:a 5  :b 6}
```

Note that there is no requirement that the keys used for map lookups in destructuring be keywords; any type of value may be used for lookup:

```
(let [{f "foo"} m]
  (+ f 12))
;= 100
(let [{v 42} m]
  (if v 1 0))
;= 0
```

Indices into vectors, strings, and arrays can be used as keys in a map destructuring form.[28] One place where this can be helpful is if you are representing matrices by using vectors, but only need a couple of values from one. Using map destructuring to pull out two or three values from a 3×3 matrix can be much easier than using a potentially nine-element sequential destructuring form:

```
(let [{x 3 y 8} [12 0 0 -18 44 6 0 0 1]]
  (+ x y))
;= -17
```

Just as sequential destructuring forms could be composed, so can the map variety:

```
(let [{{e :e} :d} m]
  (* 2 e))
;= 20
```

The outer map destructuring—{{e :e} :d}—is acting upon the top-level source collection m to pull out the value mapped to :d. The inner map destructuring—{e :e}— is acting on the value mapped to :d to pull out its value for :e.

The *coup de grâce* is the composition of both map and sequential destructuring, however they are needed to effectively extract the values you need from the collections at hand:

```
(let [{[x _ y] :c} m]
  (+ x y))
;= 16
(def map-in-vector ["James" {:birthday (java.util.Date. 73 1 6)}])
;= #'user/map-in-vector
(let [[name {bd :birthday}] map-in-vector]
```

28. This is due to the polymorphic behavior of get, which looks up values in a collection given a key into that collection; in the case of these indexable sequential values, get uses indices as keys. For more about get, see "Associative" on page 99.

```
    (str name " was born on " bd))
;= "James was born on Thu Feb 06 00:00:00 EST 1973"
```

Map destructuring also has some additional features.

Retaining the destructured value.   Just like sequential destructuring, adding an :as pair to the destructuring form to hold a reference to the source collection, which you can use like any other let-bound value:

```
(let [{r1 :x r2 :y :as randoms}
       (zipmap [:x :y :z] (repeatedly (partial rand-int 10)))]
  (assoc randoms :sum (+ r1 r2)))
;= {:sum 17, :z 3, :y 8, :x 9}
```

Default values.   You can use an :or pair to provide a defaults map; if a key specified in the destructuring form is not available in the source collection, then the defaults map will be consulted:

```
(let [{k :unknown x :a
       :or {k 50}} m]
  (+ k x))
;= 55
```

This allows you to avoid either merging the source map into a defaults map ahead of its destructuring, or manually setting defaults on destructured bindings that have nil values in the source collection, which would get *very* tiresome beyond one or two bindings with desired default values:

```
(let [{k :unknown x :a} m
       k (or k 50)]
  (+ k x))
;= 55
```

Furthermore, and unlike the code in the above example, :or knows the difference between no value and a false (nil or false) value:

```
(let [{opt1 :option} {:option false}
       opt1 (or opt1 true)
       {opt2 :option :or {opt2 true}} {:option false}]
  {:opt1 opt1 :opt2 opt2})
;= {:opt1 true, :opt2 false}
```

Binding values to their keys' names.   There are often stable names for various values in maps, and it's often desirable to bind those values by using the same names in the scope of the let form as they are mapped to in the source map. However, doing this using "vanilla" map destructuring can get very repetitive:

```
(def chas {:name "Chas" :age 31 :location "Massachusetts"})
;= #'user/chas
(let [{name :name age :age location :location} chas]
  (format "%s is %s years old and lives in %s." name age location))
;= "Chas is 31 years old and lives in Massachusetts."
```

Having to type the content of each key twice is decidedly contrary to the spirit of destructuring's concision. In such cases, you can use the :keys, :strs, and :syms options

---

to specify keyword, string, and symbol keys (respectively) into the source map and the names the corresponding values should be bound to in the `let` form without repetition. Our sample map uses keywords for keys, so we'll use `:keys` for it:

```
(let [{:keys [name age location]} chas]
  (format "%s is %s years old and lives in %s." name age location))
;= "Chas is 31 years old and lives in Massachusetts."
```

...and switch to using `:strs` or `:syms` when we know that the source collection is using strings or symbols for keys:

```
(def brian {"name" "Brian" "age" 31 "location" "British Columbia"})
;= #'user/brian
(let [{:strs [name age location]} brian]
  (format "%s is %s years old and lives in %s." name age location))
;= "Brian is 31 years old and lives in British Columbia."

(def christophe {'name "Christophe" 'age 33 'location "Rhône-Alpes"})
;= #'user/christophe
(let [{:syms [name age location]} christophe]
  (format "%s is %s years old and lives in %s." name age location))
;= "Christophe is 31 years old and lives in Rhône-Alpes."
```

You will likely find yourself using `:keys` more than `:strs` or `:syms`; keyword keys are by far the most common key type in Clojure maps and keyword arguments, and are the general-purpose accessor by dint of their usage in conjunction with records.

Destructuring rest sequences as map key/value pairs.   We've already seen how extra-positional values in sequential destructuring forms can be gathered into a "rest" seq, and map and sequential destructuring can be composed as needed to drill into any given data structure. Here's a simple case of a vector that contains some positional values, followed by a set of key/value pairs:

```
(def user-info ["robert8990" 2011 :name "Bob" :city "Boston"])
;= #'user/user-info
```

Data like this isn't uncommon, and handling it is rarely elegant. The "manual" approach in Clojure is tolerable as these things go:

```
(let [[username account-year & extra-info] user-info      ❶
      {:keys [name city]} (apply hash-map extra-info)]    ❷
  (format "%s is in %s" name city))
;= "Bob is in Boston"
```

❶ We can destructure the original vector into its positional elements, gathering the remainder into a rest seq.

❷ That rest seq, consisting of alternating keys and values, can be used as the basis for creating a new hashmap, which we can then destructure as we wish.

However, "tolerable" isn't a very high bar given the prevalence of sequences of key/value pairs in programming. A better alternative is a special variety of the compositional behavior offered by `let`'s destructuring forms: map destructuring of rest seqs. If a rest seq has an even number of values—semantically, key/value pairs—then it can be destructured as a map of those key/value pairs instead of sequentially:

```
(let [[username account-year & {:keys [name city]}] user-info]
  (format "%s is in %s" name city))
;= "Bob is in Boston"
```

That is a far cleaner notation for doing exactly the same work as us manually building a `hash-map` out of the rest seq and destructuring that map, and is the basis of Clojure functions' optional keyword arguments described in "Keyword arguments" (page 39).

Creating Functions: fn

Functions are first-class values in Clojure; creating them falls to the `fn` special form, which also folds in the semantics of `let` and `do`.

Here is a simple function that adds 10 to the number provided as an argument:

```
(fn [x]      ❶
  (+ 10 x))  ❷
```

❶ fn accepts a `let`-style binding vector that defines the names and numbers of arguments accepted by the function; the same optional destructuring forms discussed in "Destructuring (let, Part 2)" on page 28 can be applied to each argument here.

❷ The forms following the binding vector constitute the *body* of the function. This body is placed in an implicit `do` form, so each function's body may contain any number of forms; as with `do`, the last form in the body supplies the result of the function call that is returned to the caller.

The arguments to a function are matched to each name or destructuring form based on their positions in the calling form. So in this call:

```
((fn [x] (+ 10 x)) 8)
;= 18
```

8 is the sole argument to the function, and it is bound to the name x within the body of the function. This makes the function call the equivalent of this `let` form:

```
(let [x 8]
  (+ 10 x))
```

You can define functions that accept multiple arguments:

```
((fn [x y z] (+ x y z))
 3 4 12)
;= 19
```

In this case, the function call is the equivalent of this `let` form:

```
(let [x 3
      y 4
      z 12]
  (+ x y z))
```

Functions with *multiple arities* can be created as well; here, we'll put the function in a var so we can call it multiple times by only referring to the var's name:

```
(def strange-adder (fn adder-self-reference
                      ([x] (adder-self-reference x 1))
                      ([x y] (+ x y))))
;= #'user/strange-adder
(strange-adder 10)
;= 11
(strange-adder 10 50)
;= 60
```

When defining a function with multiple arities, each arity's binding vector and implementation body must be enclosed within a pair of parentheses. Function calls dispatch based on argument count; the proper arity is selected based on the number of arguments that we provide in our call.

In this last example, notice the optional name that we've given to the function, adder-self-reference. This optional first argument to fn can be used within the function's bodies to refer to itself—in this case, so that the single-argument arity can call the two-argument arity with a default second argument without referring to or requiring any containing var.

Mutually recursive functions with letfn

Named fns (like the above adder-self-reference) allow you to easily create self-recursive functions. What is more tricky is to create *mutually* recursive functions.

For such rare cases, there is the letfn special form, which allows you to define several named functions at once, and all these functions will know each other. Consider these naive reimplementations of odd? and even?:

```
(letfn [(odd? [n]
           (if (zero? n)
             false
             (even? (dec n))))
        (even? [n]
           (or (zero? n)
               (odd? (dec n))))]  ❶
  (odd? 11))
;= true
```

❶ The vector consists of several regular fn bodies, only the fn symbol is missing.

defn builds on fn. We've already seen defn used before, and the example above should look familiar; defn is a macro that encapsulates the functionality of def and fn so that you can concisely define functions that are named and registered in the current namespace with a given name. For example, these two definitions are equivalent:

```
(def strange-adder (fn strange-adder
                      ([x] (strange-adder x 1))
                      ([x y] (+ x y))))

(defn strange-adder
  ([x] (strange-adder x 1))
  ([x y] (+ x y)))
```

and single-arity functions can be defined, with the additional parentheses eliminated as well; these two definitions are also equivalent:

```
(def redundant-adder (fn redundant-adder
                       [x y z]
                       (+ x y z)))

(defn redundant-adder
  [x y z]
  (+ x y z))
```

We'll largely use defn forms to illustrate fn forms for the rest of this section, simply because calling functions bound to named vars is easier to read than continually defining the functions to be called inline.

Destructuring function arguments

defn supports the destructuring of function arguments thanks to it reusing let for binding function arguments for the scope of a function's body. You should refer to the prior comprehensive discussion of destructuring to remind yourself of the full range of options available; here, we'll discuss just a couple of destructuring idioms that are particularly common in conjunction with functions.

Variadic functions.   Functions can optionally gather all additional arguments used in calls to it into a seq; this uses the same mechanism as sequential destructuring does when gathering additional values into a seq. Such functions are called *variadic*, with the gathered arguments usually called *rest arguments* or *varargs*. Here's a function that accepts one named positional argument, but gathers all additional arguments into a remainder seq:

```
(defn concat-rest
  [x & rest]
  (apply str (butlast rest)))
;= #'user/concat-rest
(concat-rest 0 1 2 3 4)
;= "123"
```

The seq formed for the rest arguments can be destructured just like any other sequence; here we're destructuring rest arguments to make a function behave as if it had an explicitly defined zero-arg arity:

```
(defn make-user
  [& [user-id]]
  {:user-id (or user-id
                (str (java.util.UUID/randomUUID)))})
```

```
;= #'user/make-user
(make-user)
;= {:user-id "ef165515-6d6f-49d6-bd32-25eeb024d0b4"}
(make-user "Bobby")
;= {:user-id "Bobby"}
```

Keyword arguments.   It is often the case that you would like to define a function
that can accept many arguments, some of which might be optional and some of which
might have defaults. Further, you would often like to avoid forcing a particular argument ordering upon callers.[29]

fn (and therefore defn) provides support for such use cases through *keyword arguments*, which is an idiom built on top of the map destructuring of rest sequences that
let provides. Keyword arguments are pairs of keywords and values appended to any
strictly positional arguments in a function call, and if the function was defined to accept
keyword arguments, those keyword/value pairs will be gathered into a map and destructured by the function's map destructuring form that is placed in the same position
as the rest arguments seq:

```
(defn make-user
  [username & {:keys [email join-date]          ❶
               :or {join-date (java.util.Date.)}}]   ❷
  {:username username
   :join-date join-date
   :email email
   ;; 2.592e9 -> one month in ms
   :exp-date (java.util.Date. (long (+ 2.592e9 (.getTime join-date))))})
;= #'user/make-user
(make-user "Bobby")                               ❸
;= {:username "Bobby", :join-date #<Date Mon Jan 09 16:56:16 EST 2012>,
;=  :email nil, :exp-date #<Date Wed Feb 08 16:56:16 EST 2012>}
(make-user "Bobby"                                ❹
  :join-date (java.util.Date. 111 0 1)
  :email "bobby@example.com")
;= {:username "Bobby", :join-date #<Date Sun Jan 01 00:00:00 EST 2011>,
;=  :email "bobby@example.com", :exp-date #<Date Tue Jan 31 00:00:00 EST 2011>}
```

❶ The make-user function strictly requires only one argument, a username. The rest of
the arguments are assumed to be keyword/value pairs, gathered into a map, and
then destructured using the map destructuring form following &.

❷ In the map destructuring form, we define a default of "now" for the join-date value.

❸ Calling make-user with a single argument returns the user map, populated with de-
faulted join- and expiration-date values and a nil email value since none was provided in the keyword arguments.

❹ Additional arguments provided to make-user are interpreted by the keyword destructuring map, without consideration of their order.

---

29. Python is a language that supports this usage pervasively, where every argument may be named and
    provided in any order in a function call, and argument defaults can be provided when a function is defined.

Because keyword arguments are built using let's map destructuring, there's nothing stopping you from destructuring the rest argument map using types of key values besides keywords (such as strings or numbers or even collections). For example:

```
(defn foo
  [& {k ["m" 9]}]
  (inc k))
;= #'user/foo
(foo ["m" 9] 19)
;= 20
```

["m" 9] is being treated here as the name of a "keyword" argument.

That said, we've never actually seen non-keyword key types used in named function arguments. Keywords are overwhelmingly the most common argument key type used, thus the use of *keyword arguments* to describe the idiom.

Pre- and postconditions.   fn provides support for pre- and postconditions for performing assertions with function arguments and return values. They are valuable features when testing and for generally enforcing function invariants; we discuss them in "Preconditions and Postconditions" on page 487.

Function literals

We mentioned function literals briefly in "Miscellaneous Reader Sugar" on page 20. Equivalent to blocks in Ruby and lambdas in Python, Clojure function literals' role is straightforward: when you need to define an anonymous function—especially a very simple function—they provide the most concise syntax for doing so.

For example, these anonymous function expressions are equivalent:

```
(fn [x y] (Math/pow x y))
```

```
#(Math/pow %1 %2)
```

The latter is simply some reader sugar that is expanded into the former; we can clearly see this by checking the result of reading the textual code:[30]

```
(read-string "#(Math/pow %1 %2)")
;= (fn* [p1__285# p2__286#] (Math/pow p1__285# p2__286#))
```

The differences between the fn form and the shorter function literal are:

No implicit do form.   "Regular" fn forms (and all of their derivatives) wrap their function bodies in an implicit do form, as we discussed in "Creating Functions: fn" on page 36. This allows you to do things like:

---

30. Since the name of the arguments to the function is irrelevant, the function literal generates a unique symbol for each argument to refer to them; in this case, p1__285# and p2__286#.

```
(fn [x y]
  (println (str x \^ y))
  (Math/pow x y))
```

The equivalent function literal requires an explicit do form:

```
#(do (println (str %1 \^ %2))
     (Math/pow %1 %2))
```

Arity and arguments specified using unnamed positional symbols. The fn examples above use the named symbols x and y to specify both the arity of the function being defined, as well as the names of the arguments passed to the function at runtime. In contrast, the literal uses unnamed positional % symbols, where %1 is the first argument, %2 is the second argument, and so on. In addition, the highest positional symbol defines the arity of the function, so if we wanted to define a function that accepted four arguments, we need only to refer to %4 within the function literal's body.

There are two additional wrinkles to defining arguments in function literals:

1. Function literals that accept a single argument are so common that you can refer to the first argument to the function by just using %. So, #(Math/pow % %2) is equivalent to #(Math/pow %1 %2). You should prefer the shorter notation in general.

2. You can define a variadic function[31] and refer to that function's rest arguments using the %& symbol. These functions are therefore equivalent:

```
(fn [x & rest]
  (- x (apply + rest)))
```

```
#(- % (apply + %&))
```

Function literals cannot be nested. So, while this is perfectly legal:

```
(fn [x]
  (fn [y]
    (+ x y)))
```

This is not:

```
#(#(+ % %))
;= #<IllegalStateException java.lang.IllegalStateException:
;=    Nested #()s are not allowed>
```

Aside from the fact that the bodies of function literals are intended to be terse, simple expressions, making the prospect of nested function literals a readability and comprehension nightmare, there's simply no way to disambiguate which function's first argument % is referring to.

---

31. See "Variadic functions" (page 38).

Conditionals: if

if is Clojure's sole primitive conditional operator. Its syntax is simple: if the value of the first expression in an if form is *logically* true, then the result of the if form is the value of the second expression. Otherwise, the result of the if form is the value of the third expression, if provided. The second and third expressions are only evaluated as necessary.

Clojure conditionals determine logical truth to be anything other than nil or false:

```
(if "hi" \t)
;= \t
(if 42 \t)
;= \t
(if nil "unevaluated" \f)
;= \f
(if false "unevaluated" \f)
;= \f
(if (not true) \t)
;= nil
```

Note that if a conditional expression is logically false, and no else expression is provided, the result of an if expression is nil.[32]

Many refinements are built on top of if, including:

- when, best used when nil should be returned (or no action should be taken) if a condition is false.
- cond—similar to the else if construction in Java and Ruby, and elif in Python—allows you to concisely provide multiple conditions to check, along with multiple then expressions if a given conditional is true.
- if-let and when-let, which are compositions of let with if and when, respectively: if the value of the test expression is logically true, it is bound to a local for the extent of the then expression.

Clojure provides true? and false? predicates, but these are unrelated to if conditionals. For example:

```
(true? "string")
;= false
(if "string" \t \f)
;= \t
```

true? and false? check for the Boolean values true and false, not the logical truth condition used by if, which is equivalent to (and (not (nil? x)) (not (false? x))) for any value x.

---

32. when is far more appropriate for such scenarios.

Looping: loop and recur

Clojure provides a number of useful imperative looping constructs, including `doseq` and `dotimes`, all of which are built upon `recur`. `recur` transfers control to the local-most *loop head* without consuming stack space, which is defined either by `loop` or a function. Let's take a look at a very simple countdown loop:

```
(loop [x 5]        ❶
  (if (neg? x)
    x              ❷
    (recur (dec x))))) ❸
;= -1
```

❶ `loop` establishes bindings via an implicit `let` form, so it takes a vector of binding names and initial values.

❷ If the final expression within a `loop` form consists of a value, that is taken as the value of the form itself. Here, when x is negative, the `loop` form returns the value of x.

❸ A `recur` form will transfer control to the local-most loop head, in this case the `loop` form, resetting the local bindings to the values provided as arguments to `recur`. In this case, control jumps to the beginning of the `loop` form, with x bound to the value `(dec x)`.

Loop heads are also established by functions, in which case `recur` rebinds the function's parameters using the values provided as arguments to `recur`:

```
(defn countdown
  [x]
  (if (zero? x)
    :blastoff!
    (do (println x)
        (recur (dec x)))))
;= #'user/countdown
(countdown 5)
; 5
; 4
; 3
; 2
; 1
;= :blastoff!
```

Appropriate use of recur.   `recur` is a very low-level looping and recursion operation that is usually not necessary:

- When they can do the job, use the higher-level looping and iteration forms found in Clojure's core library, `doseq` and `dotimes`.
- When "iterating" over a collection or sequence, functional operations like `map`, `reduce`, `for`, and so on are almost always preferable.

Because `recur` does not consume stack space (thereby avoiding stack overflow errors), `recur` *is* critical when implementing certain recursive algorithms. In addition, because it allows you to work with numerics without the overhead of boxed representations, `recur` is very useful in the implementation of many mathematical and data-oriented operations. See "Visualizing the Mandelbrot Set in Clojure" on page 449 for a live example of `recur` within such circumstances.

Finally, there are scenarios where the accumulation or consumption of a collection or set of collections is complicated enough that orchestrating things with a series of purely functional operations using `map`, `reduce`, and so on is either difficult or inefficient. In these cases, the use of `recur` (and sometimes `loop` in order to set up intermediate loop heads) can provide an important escape hatch.

Referring to Vars: var

Symbols that name a var evaluate to that var's value:

```
(def x 5)
;= #'user/x
x
;= 5
```

However, there are occasions when you'd like to have a reference to the var itself, rather than the value it holds. The `var` special form does this:

```
(var x)
;= #'user/x
```

You've seen a number of times now how vars are printed in the REPL: `#'`, followed by a symbol. This is reader syntax that expands to a call to `var`:

```
#'x
;= #'user/x
```

You'll learn a lot more about vars in "Vars" on page 198.

Java Interop: . and new

All Java interoperability—instantiation, static and instance method invocation, and field access—flows through the `new` and `.` special forms. That said, the Clojure reader provides some syntactic sugar on top of these primitive interop forms that makes Java interop more concise in general and more syntactically consistent with Clojure's notion of function position for method calls and instantiation. Thus, it's rare to see `.` and `new` used directly, but you will nevertheless come across them out in the wild at some point:

Table 1-3. Sugared Java interop forms and their fully expanded equivalents

Operation	Java code	Sugared interop form	Equivalent special form usage
Object instantiation	`new java.util.Array List(100)`	`(java.util.ArrayList. 100)`	`(new java.util.Array List 100)`
Static method invocation	`Math.pow(2, 10)`	`(Math/pow 2 10)`	`(. Math pow 2 10)`
Instance method invocation	`"hello".sub string(1, 3)`	`(.substring "hello" 1 3)`	`(. "hello" substring 1 3)`
Static field access	`Integer.MAX_VALUE`	`Integer/MAX_VALUE`	`(. Integer MAX_VALUE)`
Instance field access	`someObject.some Field`	`(.someField some- object)`	`(. some-object some- field)`

The sugared syntax shown in Table 1-3 is idiomatic and should be preferred in every case over direct usage of the . and new special forms. Java interop is discussed in depth in Chapter 9.

Exception Handling: try and throw

These special forms allow you to participate in and use the exception-handling and -throwing mechanisms in Java from Clojure. They are explained in "Exceptions and Error Handling" on page 362.

Specialized Mutation: set!

While Clojure emphasizes the use of immutable data structures and values, there are contexts where you need to effect an in-place mutation of state. The most common settings for this involve the use of setter and other stateful methods on Java objects you are using in an interop setting; for the remaining cases, Clojure provides set!, which can be used to:

- Set the thread-local value of vars that have a non-root binding, discussed in "Dynamic Scope" on page 201
- Set the value of a Java field, demonstrated in "Accessing object fields" (page 359)
- Set the value of mutable fields defined by deftype; see "Types" on page 277 for details of that usage

Primitive Locking: monitor-enter and monitor-exit

These are lock primitives that allow Clojure to synchronize on the monitor associated with every Java object. You should never need to use these special forms, as there's a macro, locking, that ensures proper acquisition and release of an object's monitor. See "Locking" on page 225 for details.

Putting It All Together

We've continued to pick at the running example from Example 1-2 throughout our first explorations of Clojure:

```
(defn average
    [numbers]
    (/ (apply + numbers) (count numbers)))
```

We learned how this expression is simply a canonical representation of Clojure data structures in "Homoiconicity" on page 9. In the beginning, in "Expressions, Operators, Syntax, and Precedence" on page 7, we established that lists are evaluated as calls, with the value in function position as the operator. After exploring namespaces, we saw in "Symbol Evaluation" on page 23 how the symbols in that data structure are evaluated at runtime in the course of a call. Now, after we've learned about special forms—in particular, def and fn—we have the final pieces in hand to comprehensively understand what happens when you evaluate this expression (whether at the REPL or as part of loading a Clojure source file from disk in a production application).

defn is simply a shorthand for:

```
(def average (fn average
                 [numbers]
                 (/ (apply + numbers) (count numbers))))
```

So, fn creates the average function (recall from "Creating Functions: fn" on page 36 that the first argument to fn here, average, is a self-reference, so the function can be called recursively if necessary without looking up the value of the corresponding var again), and def registers it as the value of the average var in the current namespace.

eval

All of the evaluation semantics we've been discussing are encapsulated within eval, a function that evaluates a single argument form. We can see very clearly that, for example, scalars and other literals evaluate to the values they describe:

```
(eval :foo)
;= :foo
(eval [1 2 3])
;= [1 2 3]
(eval "text")
;= "text"
```

...and a list will evaluate to the return value of the call it describes:

```
(eval '(average [60 80 100 400]))
;= 160
```

While `eval`'s semantics underly all of Clojure, it is itself very rarely used within Clojure programs. It provides the ultimate in flexibility—allowing you to evaluate any data that represents a valid Clojure expression—that you simply don't need most of the time. In general, if you're using `eval` in application code, it's likely that you're working with far more rope than you need, and might end up hanging yourself in the process.

Most problems where `eval` is applicable are better solved through judicious application of macros, which we explore in Chapter 5.

Knowing everything we do now, we can *reimplement* the Clojure REPL quite easily. Remember that `read` (or `read-string`) is used to produce Clojure values from their textual representations:

```
(eval (read-string "(average [60 80 100 400])"))
;= 160
```

...and we can construct a control loop using a `recur` within a function (a `loop` form would work as well). Just a sprinkling of I/O-related functions for printing results and the REPL prompt, and we have a functioning REPL:

Example 1-4. A naive reimplementation of Clojure's REPL

```
(defn embedded-repl
  "A naive Clojure REPL implementation.  Enter `:quit`
  to exit."
  []
  (print (str (ns-name *ns*) ">>> "))
  (flush)
  (let [expr (read)
        value (eval expr)]
    (when (not= :quit value)
      (println value)
      (recur))))

(embedded-repl)
; user>>> (defn average2
;           [numbers]
;           (/ (apply + numbers) (count numbers)))
; #'user/average2
; user>>> (average2 [3 7 5])
; 5
; user>>> :quit
;= nil
```

This REPL implementation is ill-behaved in a variety of ways—for example, any thrown error leaks out of the loop in `embedded-repl`—but it's a start.[33]

---

33. Clojure's actual REPL is also implemented in Clojure, in the `clojure.main` namespace, and is waiting for you if you are interested in seeing how the REPL you'll use every day is built.

This Is Just the Beginning

What we've explored here is the bedrock of Clojure: the fundamental operations of computation (special forms), the interchangeability of code and data, and the tip of the iceberg that is interactive development. On top of this foundation, and in conjunction with the facilities of its JVM host, Clojure provides immutable data structures; concurrency primitives with defined, tractable semantics; macros; and much, much more.

We'll help you understand much of it throughout the rest of the book, and hopefully tie Clojure into your day-to-day life as a programmer with the practicums in Part IV.

There are some key resources you'll may want to keep close at hand along the way:

- The core API documentation, available at *http://clojure.github.com/clojure*
- The main Clojure mailing list, available at *http://groups.google.com/group/clojure*, and the #clojure IRC channel on Freenode,[34] both friendly places to get quality help with Clojure, no matter your skill or experience level
- The companion site for this book, *http://clojurebook.com*, which will be maintained over time with additional resources to help you along in learning and using Clojure effectively

Are you ready to take the next step?

---

34. You can use *http://webchat.freenode.net/?channels=#clojure* if you aren't on IRC regularly enough to maintain a desktop client.

## PART I

Functional Programming and Concurrency

## CHAPTER 2

Functional Programming

Functional programming (FP) is one of those amorphous concepts in software development that means different things to different people. Despite the many shades of gray that exist in the FP spectrum, it's easy to assert that Clojure is a functional programming language, and that that character is the root of many of its most attractive facilities and advantages.

In this chapter, we will:

1. Give you a reasonable introduction to what functional programming is
2. Explain why you should care about it
3. Discuss the details of Clojure's implementation that make it a desirable functional programming language

Along the way, we hope to make the case that FP—and Clojure's flavor of FP in particular—far from being an academic exercise, can improve your practice of software design and development just as structural- and object-oriented programming concepts have over the years.

If you're already familiar with functional programming (whether via Ruby, or JavaScript, or even more opinionated functional languages like Scala, F#, or Haskell, et al.), much of what follows will appear to be old hat, but it's worth internalizing so that you can understand Clojure's cut at FP.

If you are completely new to FP or initially skeptical of it, we'd urge you in particular to hang on for the ride, it'll be worth your time and effort.[1] Recall again from Chapter 1 the adage *Clojure demands that you raise your game, and pays you back for doing so*; just as you may have had to grow to learn object-oriented programming, or Java generics, or Ruby, you'll have to reach a little to be able to understand and make the most of FP—and therefore Clojure. But in return, you'll have not just a "new way of

---

1. After you've internalized what we provide here, you may find the Wikipedia entry for functional programming to be a surprisingly good springboard for diving deeper into a variety of related topics: *http://en.wikipedia.org/wiki/Functional_programming*.

thinking," but a set of tools and practices highly applicable to day-to-day programming challenges.[2]

What Does Functional Programming Mean?

Functional programming is an umbrella term that encompasses a number of language-level primitives and capabilities of which different languages provide different treatments. In Clojure, functional programming means:

- A preference for working with immutable *values*; this includes:
  - — The use of immutable data structures that satisfy simple abstractions, rather than mutable bags of state
  - — The treatment of functions as values themselves, enabling *higher-order functions*
- A preference for declarative processing of data over imperative control structures and iteration
- The natural incremental composition of functions, higher-order functions, and immutable data structures in order to solve complex problems by working with higher-level (or, *right-level*) abstractions

These are all part of the foundation for many of the more advanced features of Clojure that you may have heard of—in particular, Clojure's fantastic support for concurrency, parallelism, and more generally, providing defined semantics for the management of identities and changing state, which we'll cover separately in Chapter 4.

On the Importance of Values

The notion of *program state* is a broad one with a long history, but in general, it refers to all of the scalars and aggregate data structures that you use to represent entities within your application, along with all of the connections that your application maintains with the external world (such as open files, sockets, and so on). Much of the character of a programming language is determined by its posture toward handling state: what it provides, what it prevents, and what it encourages.

Most programming languages, either through idiom or explicit design, encourage the use of *mutable* state, whether within the guise of objects or not. Functional programming languages tend to encourage the use of *immutable* objects—referred to as *values*—to represent program state. Clojure is no different in this respect.

---

2. Note that it *is* possible to use functional programming principles even in languages—like Java—that do little to encourage (and sometimes actively *discourage*) FP styles. This is made much easier if you have some quality persistent data structures and implementations of FP fundamentals like those provided by the Google Guava (*https://code.google.com/p/guava-libraries/*) or Functional Java (*http://functionaljava .org*) libraries.

"But wait," you might say, "talking about eliminating mutability doesn't make any sense—my programs need to *do things in the world*, so changing state is inevitable." You would certainly be right in that all useful programs need to interact with the outside world, to take input and deliver output...

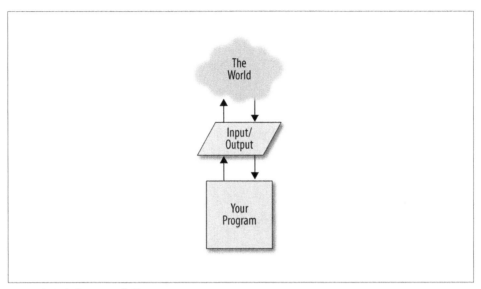

Figure 2-1. A diagram of all programs ever

...but this does not preclude the use of immutable values. On the contrary, the more you can make your program rely upon operations over values, the easier it will be to reason about the program's behavior compared with what is possible given mutable state. We'll come to see how this is true throughout this chapter.

The shift from mutable state and objects to immutable values can be jarring for many, but it may be encouraging to know that you are already using immutable values every day as a programmer, and that they are probably the most reliable, easy-to-reason-about elements within your applications.

About Values

What are values, exactly, and how do they and their immutable nature compare to mutable objects? Here are a few examples of values:

```
true  false  5  14.2  \T  "hello"  nil
```

These standard JVM Booleans, numbers, characters, and strings—which Clojure conveniently reuses—are all immutable, are all values, and you use and rely upon them (or, values analogous to them in other languages) every day.

A key characteristic of values are the semantics they ensure with regard to equality and comparison, at a single point in time as well as over time. For example, these expressions will *always* be true:

```
(= 5 5)
```

```
(= 5 (+ 2 3))
```

```
(= "boot" (str "bo" "ot"))
```

```
(= nil nil)
```

```
(let [a 5]
  (do-something-with-a-number a)
  (= a 5))
```

The equivalent expressions in Java, Python, and Ruby are *always* true, too,[4] and this fact helps us reason about operations in our programs that involve such values. To understand why, it would be helpful to see what would happen if one of these so familiar types were to lose its value semantics.

Comparing Values to Mutable Objects

Choosing between mutable objects and immutable values is a momentous decision that carries significant consequences, even for the most trivial of examples; yet, this decision is often made out of habit or familiarity or based on what's close at hand, rather than by considering the consequences of the respective options. Because the state held by mutable objects can change, and potentially be changed without your knowledge, using them when an immutable alternative is available can only be described as dangerous.

That may sound like hyperbole, especially if your current practice of using mutable objects on a daily basis seems to be working out for you. However, let's take a moment to consider the effect of making mutable something that nearly every programmer takes for granted to be an immutable value, the reliable integer:

Example 2-1. Implementation of a mutable integer in Java

```java
public class StatefulInteger extends Number {
    private int state;

    public StatefulInteger (int initialState) {
        this.state = initialState;
    }

    public void setInt (int newState) {
        this.state = newState;
    }
```

---

4. Aside from the (= nil nil) example; many languages provide limited support for checks involving nil or null, and bad things generally happen when you pass an object's equals method a null pointer. nil is just another value in Clojure.

```
public int intValue () {
    return state;
}

public int hashCode () {
    return state;
}

public boolean equals (Object obj) {
    return obj instanceof StatefulInteger &&
        state == ((StatefulInteger)obj).state;
}

// remaining xxxValue() methods from java.lang.Number...
}
```

This class is fundamentally identical to java.lang.Integer, aside from the absence of a variety of static utility methods. The one big change is that its sole field is mutable (i.e., it is not declared final), and it provides a setter for that field, setInt(int). Let's see what working with a mutable number looks like:[5]

```
(def five (StatefulInteger. 5))      ❶
;= #'user/five
(def six (StatefulInteger. 6))
;= #'user/six
(.intValue five)                     ❷
;= 5
(= five six)                         ❸
;= false
(.setInt five 6)                     ❹
;= nil
(= five six)                         ❺
;= true
```

❶ We create a couple instances of StatefulInteger, one containing the value 5, the other, 6.

❷ We can verify that, yes, five contains the value "5"...

❸ ...and 5 does not equal 6.

❹ We change the state of five to 6, and...

❺ five is now equal to 6.

You should find this deeply troubling. Our common conception is that numbers really *are* values, in far more than a technical sense—honest-to-goodness universal Platonic forms. 5 should always be 5, and certainly shouldn't be subject to the sadistic whims of a programmer somewhere.

---

5. We'll be working with this Java class from Clojure, which provides a rich set of Java and JVM interoperability features. See Chapter 9 for details.

A final example, illustrating the consequences of mutable objects in connection with any function or method invocation:

```
(defn print-number          ❶
  [n]
  (println (.intValue n))
  (.setInt n 42))
;= #'user/print-number
(print-number six)          ❷
; 6
;= nil
(= five six)                ❸
;= false
(= six (StatefulInteger. 42))
;= true
```

❶ A simple print-number function, which ostensibly should just print the value of the given number to stdout. Unbeknownst to us, it additionally modifies StatefulInteger arguments.[6]

❷ We call the print-number function with our StatefulInteger instance of six. By the time this function returns, that object has been changed as well.

❸ Now, while the prior example showed that six was equal to five, that is no longer true either.

In the general case, the function called with mutable arguments above does not have to be malicious code, nor does it need to be implemented by an incompetent developer; the mutation of arguments provided to methods and functions is common, and chances are you've encountered (and likely produced!) bugs that were due to an object being modified by a method to which it was passed as an argument. The same holds true for mutable objects held in global pools of state. Neither of these conditions are suitably guarded against with documentation (which is read even more rarely than it is written!), and indeed, such pitfalls of mutability are the *raison d'être* for the notion of deep object copying and copy constructors.

If numbers in your programming language worked this way, you might just quit your job tomorrow morning and take up carpentry. Unfortunately, nearly all other objects *do* work this way.

In Ruby, even strings, often faithfully immutable in other languages, are mutable. This can be the source of all sorts of trouble:

```
>> s = "hello"
=> "hello"
>> s << "*"
=> "hello*"
>> s == "hello"
=> false
```

---

6. We could just as easily implement this as a Java method; presenting the same functionality here as a Clojure function is merely convenient.

Ruby collections like hashes and sets work around this by "freezing" strings when they are added to a collection. However, any classes or structs you write that contain strings must take similar precautions to prevent potentially serious bugs—the same class of errors that can occur when you attempt to use mutable objects as keys in a hash:

```
>> h = {[1, 2] => 3}          ❶
=> {[1, 2]=>3}
>> h[[1,2]]                    ❷
=> 3
>> h.keys[0] << 3             ❸
=> [1, 2, 3]
>> h[[1,2]]                    ❹
=> nil
```

❶ A hash(map) is created, mapping an array to a number...

❷ ...which, as expected, provides that number when we look up the value corresponding to the array.

❸ If any keys in a hash ever changed...

❹ ...then lookups that had succeeded before will fail.[7]

Problems like this exist in any language where mutable objects are available, but their effects are most pernicious in languages where immutable values are rarely used: many programmers learn the hard way to avoid sharp edges, so even if a particular programming task is most efficiently modeled with, say, a map that has collections for keys, past lessons preclude the simplest solution in favor of other approaches that are generally more complicated and baroque. Create a new class that contains and guards the map with a restricted set of operations? Use unsophisticated immutable collections that provide some sane semantics, but that require full copies to produce changed versions? Ouch.

In contrast, you can use collections in Clojure's maps (or as entries in its sets or vectors or records) safely, without any concern for the values of those keys or thread safety when in concurrent contexts, all because Clojure data structures are immutable *and* efficient:

```
(def h {[1 2] 3})             ❶
;= #'user/h
(h [1 2])
;= 3
(conj (first (keys h)) 3)     ❷
;= [1 2 3]
(h [1 2])                     ❸
;= 3
h                             ❹
;= {[1 2] 3}
```

7. Yes, we could use the hash's **rehash** method, which would "solve" the problem. That's fine if you're happy to rehash maps prior to any lookup, and potentially hold a lock for the map for the duration of the rehashing and any lookup or update operation in a map shared by multiple threads.

❶ A Clojure map is created, mapping a vector key to a number value, which has the lookup behavior we would expect.

❷ We can "add" a value to the vector key, which returns the "updated" vector. However...

❸ ...this has no impact at all upon the original map, vector, or any lookups that have succeeded in the past. This is because...

❹ ...the vector key was not modified, and indeed, *could never be modified*; when we added a value to it, a completely new vector reference was returned.

This is absolutely just the tip of the iceberg. Understanding and utilizing Clojure's data abstractions and data structure implementations is fundamental to wielding the language effectively. While we'll use Clojure's data structures casually for various examples in this chapter, we'll spend all of the next chapter exploring them in detail.

A Critical Choice

In summary, the use of unfettered object state means that:[8]

- Mutable objects cannot be safely passed to methods.
- Mutable objects cannot be reliably used as keys in maps, entries in sets, and so on, because their equality and lookup semantics change over time.
- Mutable objects cannot be reliably cached.
- Mutable objects cannot be reliably used in a multithreaded environment because of the requirement for proper synchronization of action among different threads.

Entire classes of bugs made possible solely by the use of mutable objects simply cannot occur if you were to use immutable values in their place. The consequences of mutability are actually well-established and have been understood for some time,[9] and apply to any language that does not provide easy alternatives to mutability. These issues are so common that a range of fairly pathological coping mechanisms have developed in the object-oriented world to deal with the problem of unfettered mutability of state, including:

- Copy constructors and deep copy methods in order to ensure reliable access to an object in a particular state.[10]

---

8. Brian Goetz discusses these pitfalls in detail at *http://www.ibm.com/developerworks/java/library/j-jtp02183.html*.

9. For example, Joshua Bloch, one of the key architects of the Java standard libraries, recommends that you should "minimize mutability" (*http://www.artima.com/intv/bloch11.html*), and said in his 2001 book *Effective Java* that "classes should be immutable unless there's a very good reason to make them mutable."

10. Even going so far in certain settings as to use serialization as a reliable deep copy mechanism when an object model doesn't provide a reliable copy constructor or duplication method.

- A host of patterns for tracking and managing change over time, including "Observer," "Reactor," and so on.[11]

- A plethora of utilities for erecting relatively flimsy immutable facades in front of mutable data structures, such as those provided by `java.util.Collections`. Such facades almost uniformly simply delegate to the underlying mutable collection; thus, if the underlying collection is changed, the "immutable" view of that collection does, too.

- Reams of documentation and bad advice[12] given over the course of years on how to sanely manage concurrent access and modification of shared mutable state via manual lock management; the result being, deadlocks and race conditions are some of the most common sources of quality issues industry-wide.

In the end, much of the challenge of programming is in identifying and holding tight to every *invariant* you can find, those things in your algorithms, applications, or business rules that do not change. The more invariants you can identify, the more you can focus on the local effects of a particular piece of code, and the more risk you can drive out of whatever system you are building. Immutable values establish a whole new beachhead of invariants; using them, you can know with absolute certainty that calling a function with a collection won't result in changes to that collection, that multiple threads can touch a value without risking its consistency or imposing a complexity tax in the form of complicated lock strategies, and that time-dependent changes will not result in timing-dependent behavior.[13] These things are guaranteed when working with values like numbers; there are few reasons to not demand the same from your aggregates, such as Clojure's immutable collections and records.

First-Class and Higher-Order Functions

Despite the great variability about what "functional programming" means in different languages, one requirement is consistent: functions must themselves be values, so that they may be treated like any other data, accepted as arguments and returned as results by other functions.

Functions as data permits a means of abstraction that a language without first-class functions lacks. As a simple example, imagine writing a function that simply calls some other function twice. Rather than call a specific function, our `call_twice` function should be generic enough to call *any* function on *any* argument.

---

11. In Chapter 12, we provide examples of how Clojure's facilities make many familiar object-oriented patterns unnecessary or invisible.

12. Perhaps you recall the confusion and uncertainty that existed around *double-checked locking* some years ago—eventually resolved, but with much complexity and the help of a new JVM memory model: *http://www.cs.umd.edu/~pugh/java/memoryModel/DoubleCheckedLocking.html*.

13. A.k.a. Heisenbugs, *https://en.wikipedia.org/wiki/Heisenbug*.

This is trivial in a language with first-class functions. In Ruby[14] and Python:

```
# Ruby
def call_twice(x, &f)
  f.call(x)
  f.call(x)
end

call_twice(123) {|x| puts x}

# Python
def call_twice(f, x):
  f(x)
  f(x)

call_twice(print, 123)
```

The Clojure code is just as simple:

```
(defn call-twice [f x]
  (f x)
  (f x))

(call-twice println 123)
; 123
; 123
```

By contrast, it would be difficult to write even this trivial function in Java. Ironically, the majority language on the JVM does not provide for functions as first class values. In Java, code may only exist within methods, which must be associated with a class, and methods can't be referenced as objects short of resorting to Java's reflection API.

Classes defined only to contain static utility methods—like `java.lang.Math`—end up functioning as impoverished namespaces created to compensate for the lack of first-class functions. Other useful methods—like many of the string-manipulation operations defined by `java.lang.String`—are *not* static methods, and so must be invoked in conjunction with a specific instance.

```
Math.max(a, b);

someString.toLowerCase();
```

This may seem reasonable; what could be simpler than grouping related utility methods in a dedicated class, or tying operations for a particular type to instances of that type?

Really, doing neither of those things is simpler and more powerful in so many ways.

For example, what do you need to do in Java to determine the largest number in an array, or perhaps transform a list of strings into a list containing their lowercase counterparts?

---

14. Ruby's *blocks*, the objects created via `lambda`, and `Proc.new`, and even class methods via `SomeClass.method(:foo)` are all slightly different variants of first-class functions. On the other hand, Clojure's functions fill all of those roles.

Example 2-2. Some static utility methods in Java

```java
public static int maxOf (int[] numbers) {
    int max = Integer.MIN_VALUE;
    for (int i : numbers) {
        max = Math.max(i, max);
    }
    return max;
}

public static void toLowerCase (List<String> strings) {
    for (ListIterator<String> iter = strings.listIterator(); iter.hasNext(); ) {
        iter.set(iter.next().toLowerCase()); ❶
    }
}
```

❶ A tangent: this is modifying the **strings** **List** in place...we sure hope no one else was holding a reference to it without expecting this mutation to occur.

In contrast, all functions in Clojure are first-class values. They exist of their own right, can be called directly (without any intervening classes/quasi-namespaces), and can be provided as arguments in function calls and returned as results from functions. They are data, just as much as data structures, numbers, and strings are.

Clojure defines a **max** function and a **lower-case** function (the latter in the **clo jure.string** namespace), which correspond to **Math.max** and **String.toLowerCase** as shown above.[15] Of course, they can be used directly:

```clojure
(max 5 6)
;= 6
(require 'clojure.string)
;= nil
(clojure.string/lower-case "Clojure")
;= "clojure"
```

But that isn't intended to impress. What is different is that, because Clojure functions are values themselves, they can be used with *higher-order functions*, sometimes referred to as "HOFs"; these are any functions that take other functions as arguments or return a function as a result.

Clojure comes with far too many higher-order functions for us to discuss comprehensively, so we'll talk about some key ones as we go along—including map, **reduce**, **par tial**, **comp**, **complement**, **repeatedly**, and others. Let's look at map first; it is perhaps the most frequently used HOF in Clojure codebases.[16]

---

15. These Clojure functions actually just delegate to the corresponding Java methods.

16. This is likely due to the great utility of the sequence abstraction, described in "Sequences" on page 89.

map.   map accepts a single function argument, followed by one or more collections, and returns a sequence of the results of applying that function to successive members of the provided collections. More formally, any usage of map of the form (map *f* [a b c]) is equivalent to [(*f* a) (*f* b) (*f* c)], usage of the form (map *f* [a b c] [x y z]) is equivalent to [(*f* a x) (*f* b y) (*f* c z)], and so on.

A few examples will make map's semantics obvious:

```
(map clojure.string/lower-case ["Java" "Imperative" "Weeping"      ❶
                                "Clojure" "Learning" "Peace"])
;= ("java" "imperative" "weeping" "clojure" "learning" "peace")
(map * [1 2 3 4] [5 6 7 8])                                         ❷
;= (5 12 21 32)
```

❶ Just about the simplest usage of map: given lower-case and a collection of strings, map will return a sequence of those strings lowercased.

❷ Given * and *n* collections of numbers, map will return a sequence of the products of the corresponding numbers from each collection.

The first example above is the Clojure corollary to the toLowerCase static utility method in Example 2-2. The contrast between the two approaches is striking, even for such a trivial example:

- The toLowerCase static method mutated its argument in place, whereas map, like all other well-behaved functions in Clojure, returns immutable values.

- If we were to make toLowerCase return a new collection containing the transformed strings, we would need to explicitly consider and define the allocation and type of a return collection. map always returns a sequence.[17]

- In Java, we are constantly concerned with the imperative flow of control, from manually iterating over an input collection to which methods are called to how they are ordered. Python's list comprehensions and Ruby's each idiom improve on Java in this regard. Clojure goes even further though, encouraging the separation of operations from the specifics of their application. For example, there's nothing in the general contract of "mapping" over a sequence or set of sequences that requires that a given function must be applied to the provided collections in order, or even all on one thread.[18]

Where map is the fundamental higher-order function for transforming the contents of any sequential collection, we often need to coalesce a collection into a single value that might not be sequential. For such cases, reduce awaits.

---

17. The sequences returned by map are *lazy*, as are most other sequence-producing functions in Clojure. We discuss lazy sequences fully in "Lazy seqs" on page 93; for now, you can ignore this detail.

18. This is incredibly useful, and makes possible things like pmap, which you can use to easily parallelize the application of a *pure* function across collection(s). See "Pure Functions" on page 76 for a discussion of them, and "Parallelism on the Cheap" on page 166 for details on pmap and related parallelization facilities.

reduce.   Flexibly producing any value from the application of a function to a collection is called a *reduction* in many circles. Clojure implements this concept via a higher-order function called reduce.[19] The simplest possible example of reduce provides us with a Clojure analogue to the maxOf static method from Example 2-2:

```
(reduce max [0 -3 10 48])
;= 48
```

Given a function and a collection to operate over, reduce applies the function to each of the items of the collection, accumulating and returning a single result value. The key to reduce is understanding how it manages the application of the function to the collection's items. If you were to invoke the same operations yourself manually, they'd look like this:

```
(max 0 -3)
;= 0
(max 0 10)
;= 10
(max 10 48)
;= 48
```

or, in a single expression:[20]

```
(max (max (max 0 -3) 10) 48)
;= 48
```

On the first "iteration" of reduce's operation, it applies the provided function to the first two items in the collection, obtaining a result. After that, reduce applies the function to the previous result (e.g., 0 above) and the next item in the collection (e.g., 10 above, since it had only consumed 0 and -3 so far) to obtain its next result, and so on. You can also optionally provide an initial value to "seed" the reduction:

```
(reduce + 50 [1 2 3 4])
;= 60
```

Here, reduce is doing nothing different, except that the first time it invokes the provided function, it uses the initial value as the first argument to the function, with the second argument being the first item from the collection. Being able to provide an initial value to seed the reduction is a key capability, as this allows us to easily reduce a collection of values into a result of any type. For example, we can reduce a collection of numbers into a map, with numbers for keys, and their squares for values:

```
(reduce
  (fn [m v]              ❶
    (assoc m v (* v v)))
  {}                     ❷
```

---

19. And somewhat confusingly named inject in Ruby.

20. Clojure provides plenty of options for making sure that code like this should never be seen in the wild. For example, max is variadic already, so (max 0 -3 10 48) is far preferable compared to the pointlessly nested parentheses shown here purely for illustrative purposes.

```
   [1 2 3 4])
 ;= {4 16, 3 9, 2 4, 1 1}
```

❶ We provide a function to reduce as in our other examples, but in this case, one that we define inline. It takes two arguments, a map (always the result of the prior step of the reduction, or the initial value we provide), and the next item in the collection we're reducing over. The function we supply here is simply assoc'ing[21] into the map the next item from the collection and that item's square; assoc returns a new map that contains that entry, which will be used as the first argument to our function for the next step in the reduction.

❷ We provide our initial value to "seed" the reduce here, just before our collection to be reduced over. {} is a Clojure literal for an empty map.

When to Use Anonymous Functions or Function Literals

The previous example is written using an anonymous function created with the fn form. Providing anonymous functions like this in conjunction with usage of map, reduce, and other higher-order functions is incredibly common. However, you should also ensure that you're familiar with Clojure's function literals; as we saw in "Function literals" on page 40, they do away with the fn symbol and an explicit argument vector, thus eliminating a fair bit of verbosity when the function being defined is particularly simple.

For example, here's the previous reduce example rewritten using a function literal instead of the longer fn form:

```
(reduce
  #(assoc % %2 (* %2 %2))
  {}
  [1 2 3 4])
 ;= {4 16, 3 9, 2 4, 1 1}
```

Whether you use the longer form of anonymous function or a function literal is largely a matter of personal taste. The latter are certainly more concise, and make sense for very short functions, whereas the former allows you to be more explicit and informative about arguments and their purpose. In either case, Clojure code in the wild often uses both forms, so you need to be able to read them equally well.

Many of the same comparisons can be made between our use of reduce with max and the maxOf static method we defined in Java in Example 2-2 as we made between the use of map with lower-case and the toLowerCase static method: the separation of operations from their modes of application, the avoidance of explicitly defining imperative control flow, and so on. However, perhaps the most significant point of contrast is that, *no one would define functions analogous to the maxOf and toLowerCase static methods in Clojure*; it is far more sensible to define core operations like max and lower-case, and

---

21. That is, *associate*, the equivalent of java.util.Map.put(Object, Object) in Java or hash_map[key] = value in Python and Ruby. We cover maps, assoc, and all of the rest of Clojure's rich collections in Chapter 3.

then apply them to your data in place as needed by using whatever higher-order function is most appropriate.

Applying Ourselves Partially

Function application is the invocation of a function with a sequence of arguments, in contrast to function calls indicated by syntactic convention. For example, in Ruby and Python (Examples 2-3 and 2-4), a function can be applied to an array or list of arguments by prepending the argument reference with an asterisk:

Example 2-3. Function (method) application in Ruby

```
>> interval = [-10, 10]
=> [-10, 10]
>> Range.new(*interval)
=> -10..10

>> h = {}
=> {}
>> pair = ['a', 5]
=> ["a", 5]
>> h.store(*pair)
=> 5
>> h
=> {"a"=>5}
```

This capability is absolutely fundamental if a language is to be able to support various functional programming idioms—especially when the function you need to invoke is unknown (perhaps provided to you in a particular context as an argument), and arguments to that function are data of indefinite size, it would simply be impossible (or, prohibitively verbose and error-prone) to have to pluck arguments out of the data and align them as necessary to construct a "regular" function call.

Function application is available in Clojure via `apply`:

```
(apply hash-map [:a 5 :b 6])
;= {:a 5, :b 6}
```

As a convenience, `apply` allows you to prefix the argument sequence with any number of explicit arguments. In many cases where you have some discrete values as well as a sequence of arguments, this allows you to avoid having to create a new sequence that includes the former:

```
(def args [2 -2 10])
;= #'user/args
(apply * 0.5 3 args)
;= -60.0
```

Whereas function application is when a function is applied to its arguments held in a sequential collection—`apply` must be provided with *all* arguments to that function—*partial application* is where you can provide only *some* of the arguments to a function, yielding a new function that can be called with the remainder of the arguments to the original function later.

Example 2-4. Partial application in Python

```
>> from functools import partial
>> only_strings = partial(filter, lambda x: isinstance(x, basestring))
>> only_strings(['a', 5, 'b', 6])
['a', 'b']
```

What's happening here? `partial` accepts some function (`filter` above, but can be any f), and one or more arguments to that function (a string type predicate above, but can be any a, b, ...), and returns a new function g that retains those arguments as well as a reference to f:

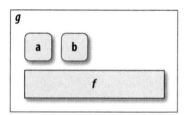

When g, the function returned from `partial`, is invoked, its return is the result of calling the original function f with the arguments provided to `partial` (a, b, ...) *plus* any arguments provided to g:

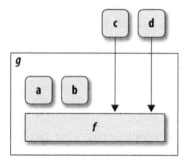

`partial` provides for partial application in Clojure:

```
(def only-strings (partial filter string?))
;= #'user/only-strings
(only-strings ["a" 5 "b" 6])
;= ("a" "b")
```

Partial application is commonly used in a number of contexts. For example, functions that require some configuration (maybe to connect to a database, maybe to indicate where a file should be written) often have that configuration as their first (or first couple) arguments. This allows you to easily use `partial` to create a derivative of such functions that have the necessary configuration "locked in," without necessarily worrying about what additional arguments the underlying function requires:

```
(def database-lookup (partial get-data "jdbc:mysql://..."))
```

This characteristic of `partial`—where it can be used to easily toss off a derivative of a function without concern for what the remainder of the function's arguments should be—can be very useful and is part of what makes `partial` attractive to use in conjunction with `comp`.[22]

Be aware that, compared to a regular function call with explicit arguments, higher-order functions like `apply` and `partial` do carry a performance penalty, albeit a small one and only on large arities: `comp` up to three arguments and `partial` up to four use specialized implementations, which create plain closures without requiring packing and unpacking arguments in a varargs sequence.

The performance penalty associated with larger arities of `apply` and `partial` is because such functions need to unpack sequence(s) of provided arguments in order to call the arity of the function that corresponds to the total number of arguments provided. This can never be as fast as "regular" Clojure function calls, which simply reuse the JVM's (*really* fast) method invocation machinery. On the bright side, because of that underlying efficient machinery, calling functions with `apply` and the functions returned by `partial` remain leaps and bounds faster in Clojure than, for example, direct, explicit method calls in Python or Ruby.

partial versus function literals.   You might have noticed that function literals technically provide a superset of what `partial` provides: they allow you to concisely create a function that calls another function with some subset of its arguments predefined.

```
(#(filter string? %) ["a" 5 "b" 6])
;= ("a" "b")
```

However, function literals do not limit you to defining only the initial arguments to the function:

```
(#(filter % ["a" 5 "b" 6]) string?)
;= ("a" "b")
(#(filter % ["a" 5 "b" 6]) number?)
;= (5 6)
```

---

22. We'll get to `comp` shortly, in "Composition of Function(ality)" on page 68.

The tradeoff is that function literals force you to fully specify all of the arguments to the functions it calls, whereas `partial` allows you to be ignorant of such details:

```
(#(map *) [1 2 3] [4 5 6] [7 8 9])                    ❶
;= #<ArityException clojure.lang.ArityException:
;=   Wrong number of args (3) passed to: user$eval812$fn>
(#(map * % %2 %3) [1 2 3] [4 5 6] [7 8 9])            ❷
;= (28 80 162)
(#(map * % %2 %3) [1 2 3] [4 5 6])                    ❸
;= #<ArityException clojure.lang.ArityException:
;=   Wrong number of args (2) passed to: user$eval843$fn>
(#(apply map * %&) [1 2 3] [4 5 6] [7 8 9])           ❹
;= (28 80 162)
(#(apply map * %&) [1 2 3])
;= (1 2 3)

((partial map *) [1 2 3] [4 5 6] [7 8 9])            ❺
;= (28 80 162)
```

❶ We can't avoid providing a full accounting of the arguments to `map`; the function literal ends up taking zero arguments, because functions defined by literals have a single arity based on the number of arguments they refer to.

❷ We can "solve" this for some inputs by enumerating additional arguments to `map`...

❸ ...but this will fail if the usage of our function literal does not align exactly with what we define.

❹ A solution for such cases is to use `apply`, along with the function literal syntax indicating the acceptance of rest args, `%&`.

❺ This is essentially duplicating what `partial` will do for you with ease, and without the syntactic penalties.

As you can see, there are cases where the use of `partial` will produce more easily readable code, and others where `partial` is a clearly preferable way to bind some initial subset of arguments to a function with unknown arities.

Composition of Function(ality)

Compositionality is an overloaded term; we use it to refer to the ability of various parts to be joined together to create a well-formed composite that is itself reusable.

Different programming models provide varying support for assembling constituent parts into larger wholes. Imperative, procedural code is generally not composable at all; calling a subroutine or method in the course of a procedure is little more than a difference in notation. Object orientation offers some basic facilities for composition, most notably the concept of an attribute where a composite establishes a "has-a" relationship between itself and another entity. Patterns like delegation and pluggable strategies are other ways you can coherently glom smaller pieces together.

Functional programming puts an even greater emphasis on compositionality, making it astonishingly easy to start with small pieces and loosely join them into purpose-built abstractions. We dig into Clojure's additional specific mechanisms for building abstractions at length in Part II, but the simplest abstraction of all is the function. Because they are generally divorced from data entirely—and, ideally, able to polymorphically work with whatever concrete types of data might be semantically suitable—functions can be used to assemble very powerful composites with a minimum of ceremony.

Function composition has a very distinct meaning in functional programming circles:[23] given any number of functions, it is the creation of a function that applies its arguments to one of the provided functions, using each successive result as the argument to the next provided function, usually in the reverse order that the functions were originally specified.

For example, say we frequently needed the negation of a sum of some given numbers, but as a string. That's simple enough to write:

```
(defn negated-sum-str
  [& numbers]
  (str (- (apply + numbers))))
;= #'user/negated-sum-str
(negated-sum-str 10 12 3.4)
;= "-25.4"
```

Function composition, implemented in Clojure via comp, can bring together operations like this more concisely, and usually with more clarity:

```
(def negated-sum-str (comp str - +))
;= #'user/negated-sum-str
(negated-sum-str 10 12 3.4)
;= "-25.4"
```

These two definitions of `negated-sum-str` are functionally equivalent; they differ only in their construction.

What's going on here? You can think of comp as defining a pipeline: it accepts any number of functions—str, -, and + above, but can be any ƒ, g, and h—and produces a new function (labeled k in the figure) that accepts the same arguments as h (since it is the first stage in the pipeline), and then calls g with the result given by h, calls ƒ with the result given by g, and so on.

---

23. Function composition even has special notation in some settings. For example, mathematical notation for composition of functions f and g is f ∘ g, while Haskell uses a period as the composition operator, f . g.

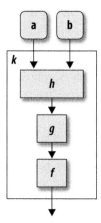

The final result is that given by the first function provided to comp.

The sole limitation of comp is that the result of each function in the composite *must* be a suitable argument for the function that precedes it syntactically. So, if we reverse the order of functions in the composition that produced the negated-sum-str function, we get an error:

```
((comp + - str) 5 10)
;= #<ClassCastException java.lang.ClassCastException:
;=    java.lang.String cannot be cast to java.lang.Number>
```

...because the result of the call (str 5 10) is a string, which cannot be negated by -.

Far from being relegated to toy examples, comp can be used to build up significant chains of functionality, either in a single composition, or as a result of composing functions that are themselves products of comp. For example, many identifiers—in Java, in XML and other markup, and so on—are often provided in CamelCase style. We may reasonably want to put data that uses such identifiers as keys into a Clojure map, but we would like to idiomatically continue to use lowercase, hyphen-delimited keywords to refer to those entries in Clojure.

A function to do this might reasonably use comp, and look like so:

```
(require '[clojure.string :as str])                    ❶

(def camel->keyword (comp keyword
                          str/join
                          (partial interpose \-)
                          (partial map str/lower-case)
                          #(str/split % #"(?<=[a-z])(?=[A-Z])"))) ❷
;= #'user/camel->keyword
(camel->keyword "CamelCase")
;= :camel-case
(camel->keyword "lowerCamelCase")
;= :lower-camel-case
```

❶ We use `require` here to ensure that the `clojure.string` namespace is loaded, and establish a `str` prefix for its vars in the current namespace.

❷ There's no need to use predefined functions with `comp`. This function literal uses a regular expression[24] to split provided strings between a lowercase character and an uppercase character to suit `CamelCase` identifiers.

> You can achieve much the same effect as `comp` in another way, using the `->` and `->>` macros.[25] Being macros, they do not operate over functions; rather, they rearrange the code you provide to "thread" a value or collection as either the first or last argument in each form. For example, this is functionally equivalent to the `camel->keyword` function we produce using `comp` above:
>
> ```
> (defn camel->keyword
>   [s]
>   (->> (str/split s #"(?<=[a-z])(?=[A-Z])")
>     (map str/lower-case)
>     (interpose \-)
>     str/join
>     keyword))
> ```
>
> Whether you use `comp` or threading macros for any given task is largely a matter of style.[26]

We can use `camel->keyword` as part of a further composition, defining a function that returns an idiomatic Clojure map given a sequence of key/value pairs that use Camel Case-style keys:

```
(def camel-pairs->map (comp (partial apply hash-map)
                            (partial map-indexed (fn [i x]
                                                   (if (odd? i)
                                                     x
                                                     (camel->keyword x))))))
;= #'user/camel-pairs->map
(camel-pairs->map ["CamelCase" 5 "lowerCamelCase" 3])
;= {:camel-case 5, :lower-camel-case 3}
```

Writing Higher-Order Functions

The notion of function composition as embodied by `comp` is just one possible way to compose functionality—a useful one to be sure, but just as it is broadly applicable, it

---

24. The reader supports convenient regular expression literals as we described in "Regular expressions" on page 17.

25. We discuss `->` and `->>` at length in "In Detail: -> and ->>" on page 259.

26. `comp` and `partial` enable *point-free style* (also known as *tacit programming*), the distinguishing feature of which is that functions are defined without explicitly naming or referring to arguments ("points").

is in some sense the lowest common denominator of compositionality. While Clojure provides a number of general-purpose higher-order functions, they are by no means reserved for general-purpose things.

More sophisticated and sometimes more utilitarian composites are only made possible by tailoring your own contracts between functions and higher-order functions. Once you are accustomed to treating functions as just another category of values, you'll find yourself writing function-producing and function-accepting functions quite naturally.

Let's look at some fairly trivial examples. First, a HOF that returns a function that adds a given number to its argument:

```
(defn adder
  [n]
  (fn [x] (+ n x)))
;= #'user/adder
((adder 5) 18)
;= 23
```

Less trivial might be a higher-order function that doubles the result of calling the provided function:

```
(defn doubler
  [f]
  (fn [& args]
    (* 2 (apply f args))))
;= #'user/doubler
(def double-+ (doubler +))
;= #'user/double-+
(double-+ 1 2 3)
;= 12
```

Let's build something more interesting, and along the way, see how some aspects of functional programming are actually very well-suited for solving problems related to state and IO in addition to those dealing with immutable data and algorithms.

Building a Primitive Logging System with Composable Higher-Order Functions

Logging is a common necessity of applications large and small, and the configuration of logging is often fairly cumbersome and complicated for a variety of reasons. We can skin this cat in a slightly different way using a couple of higher-order functions.[27] We'll end up having to use a couple of bits of Clojure that we've not discussed in detail yet, but you'll be able to follow along easily.

---

27. What we're going to build here should not be confused for any sort of replacement for the accepted general-purpose Clojure logging library, tools.logging from *https://github.com/clojure/tools.logging*.

We're all guilty of using `System.out.println` or `puts` or `print` for logging—it's brutish, yet effective in a pinch. To improve on this, let's start simply, with a simple HOF that returns a function that prints messages to any writer we provide to the HOF:

```
(defn print-logger
  [writer]                    ❶
  #(binding [*out* writer]    ❷
     (println %)))            ❸
```

❶ Our HOF accepts as a single argument any instance of `java.io.Writer`, the base of any type that provides for the writing of character data to some output device.

❷ `print-logger` returns a function that *binds* *out*[28] with the value of `writer`, the `Writer` we provided to the HOF.

❸ The body of our returned function writes its sole argument (the message we want to log) using `println`, which always writes to `*out*` (which we've replaced in this scope with our `writer`).

Let's see how it works:

```
(def *out*-logger (print-logger *out*))  ❶
;= #'user/*out*-logger
(*out*-logger "hello")                   ❷
; hello
;= nil
```

❶ We provide `*out*` to `print-logger`, so all messages sent to the returned function will be logged to `*out*`—or rather to the value of `*out*` at the moment when `*out*-logger` was defined.

❷ `print-logger` always returns a function that accepts a single argument, which we call here with a string.

Okay, all we did there was produce a more complicated `println` that dumps output to stdout. More interesting would be capturing logging output in an in-memory buffer. `java.io.StringWriter` does this for us; it is a `java.io.Writer` implementation that is backed not by an output device, but by a character buffer:

```
(def writer (java.io.StringWriter.))    ❶
;= #'user/writer
(def retained-logger (print-logger writer))
;= #'user/retained-logger
(retained-logger "hello")               ❷
;= nil
(str writer)                            ❸
;= "hello\n"
```

---

28. `*out*` is bound to a `Writer` that writes to stdout by default; by rebinding it, content written to `*out*` is redirected to the writer we specify. You can learn more about *binding* in "Dynamic Scope" on page 201.

❶ We create and retain a `StringWriter` separately, so we can poke at it after we use `print-logger` to produce a logging function targeting it.

❷ Calling our logging function doesn't write anything to `stdout`...

❸ ...because it's been `println`ed to our `StringWriter` instead.

This is slightly more interesting; but any logging approach worth its salt can log to files. The contract of `print-logger` allows us to get there pretty easily: given a `Writer`, it will return a function that writes provided messages to that `Writer`. So, as long as we can obtain a `Writer` that dumps output to a file of our choosing, we'll be good to go.

```
(require 'clojure.java.io)

(defn file-logger
  [file]                                              ❶
  #(with-open [f (clojure.java.io/writer file :append true)] ❷
     ((print-logger f) %)))                           ❸
```

❶ The `file-logger` HOF accepts a single `file` argument, to which log messages will be written. Because of the semantics of `clojure.java.io/writer`, this argument can be a string naming a file path or an instance of either `java.io.File`, `java.net.URL`, or `java.net.URI` that does the same.

❷ The function literal that `file-logger` returns creates a new `Writer` for the `file`, opens it for appending (so we don't clobber any messages written to it in the past), and names it `f` within the local scope.[29]

❸ Instead of repeating the binding of `*out*` and use of `println` here, we just call `print-logger` with our file's `Writer`, and call the function it returns straight off with the message to be logged. Remember that since functions are values, there's no need to define a top-level var in order to call one; the function returned by `print-logger` is created, called, and then discarded immediately.

Let's see how we're doing:

```
(def log->file (file-logger "messages.log"))
;= #'user/log->file
(log->file "hello")
;= nil

% more messages.log
hello
```

Fabulous: we can create a function that logs to a given file (`messages.log` in the current directory here), and messages logged via that function are written to that logfile as we'd expect. This is not so bad for 10 lines of code, and you could easily add to the set of `*-logger` HOFs; having ones that produced functions that logged to databases, message

---

29. The `with-open` form will ensure that `f` is closed at the end of its body; this is equivalent to the "try with resources" syntax in Java 7 and `with` in Python. See "with-open, finally's Lament" on page 364 for more on `with-open`.

queues, and other sinks would be straightforward enough, and they could all be swapped around however your needs dictate.

But, what if we needed to log to multiple destinations? That's not a detail that code using a logger function should have to care about. For this, we need a different kind of logging HOF, one that produces a function that doesn't do any logging itself, but that routes a message to multiple other loggers:

```
(defn multi-logger
  [& logger-fns]          ❶
  #(doseq [f logger-fns]  ❷
     (f %)))
```

❶ multi-logger accepts any number of other logging functions.

❷ The function it returns will imperatively loop over the sequence of logging functions,[30] calling each with the message to be logged.

Having this available makes it easy for us to define logging functions that dump messages to multiple sinks:

```
(def log (multi-logger          ❶
            (print-logger *out*)
            (file-logger "messages.log")))
;= #'user/log
(log "hello again")
; hello again
;= nil

% more messages.log
hello
hello again
```

❶ We create a new "top-level" logging function that, thanks to multi-logger, will direct messages to *out* as well as to our *messages.log* logfile.

Yes, now we can log to any number of destinations.

Let's look at one final enhancement to our miniature logging library. Because the data being passed around by all of the functions produced by our logging HOFs is uniform (just a string at the moment), there's nothing stopping us from defining other higher-order functions that can enhance and transform that data in various ways. Log messages almost always include a timestamp, so maybe a HOF that prepends timestamps to messages is a good start:

---

30. See "Sequences are not iterators" on page 91 for details on doseq and "iterating" over sequences in Clojure.

Example 2-5. Adding a piece of "logging middleware" to include a timestamp with each log message

```
(defn timestamped-logger
  [logger]
  #(logger (format "[%1$tY-%1$tm-%1$te %1$tH:%1$tM:%1$tS] %2$s" (java.util.Date.) %))) ❶

(def log-timestamped (timestamped-logger
                       (multi-logger
                         (print-logger *out*)
                         (file-logger "messages.log"))))

(log-timestamped "goodbye, now")
; [2011-11-30 08:54:00] goodbye, now
;= nil

% more messages.log
hello
hello again
[2011-11-30 08:54:00] goodbye, now
```

❶ The function returned by `timestamped-logger` simply prepends a timestamp to the string message passed to it and calls the logging function provided to the HOF with the enhanced message. `format` is a Clojure function that uses Java's `String.format` method to apply `sprintf`-style formatting to some number of objects.

We can imagine transforming logged messages in a variety of ways—adding the current namespace, implicit contextual information (e.g., which host the application is running on), maybe the source line number of a logging message,[31] and so on. More significantly, if you were to use something like this in nontrivial applications, the most pressing improvement would be to make logging messages richer and more flexible than strings, so that logging data itself was open and more easily enhanced. For example, if each logging event were a map of data,[32] then that map could be easily enhanced with all sorts of useful information without complicating the consumption or processing of logging data down the road. Such a structured approach would also make it very simple to compose in filtering of log events based on their "level" or importance.

Pure Functions

While the use of immutable values eliminates many classes of errors when working with data in our programs, there are many other sorts of errors that are rooted in how we write the functions that work with those values. Most of these errors are due to *side effects*, changes that functions make to their environment in addition to their response of a return value.

---

31. This one would require a macro in order to access the line number of a call to a logger function via :line metadata; see "Producing useful macro error messages" on page 254.

32. Of course, the logging of strings should remain possible; it would be trivial to ensure that logging "foo" would be always be implicitly converted into a structured log map like {:message "foo"}.

Thinking back to our diagram in Figure 2-1, side effects are any interaction that a function has with the outside world in either direction. Any function that works with random numbers[33] is a perfect example of a side-effecting function, as it:

1. Depends upon the state of the random number generator being used[34]
2. Necessarily modifies the state of that random number generator, so the next caller of the function will end up working with a different series of random numbers than it otherwise would have

 By definition, performing I/O of any kind or the modification of any shared mutable object are side effects.

Random numbers seem a bit prosaic, so perhaps these not-really-hypothetical functions are a bit more illustrative:[35]

```
(defn perform-bank-transfer!
  [from-account to-account amount]
  ...)

(defn authorize-medical-treatment!
  [patient-id treatment-id]
  ...)

(defn launch-missiles!
  [munition-type target-coordinates]
  ...)
```

Maybe more concretely, consider a naive implementation of a function that accepts Twitter usernames and returns the number of followers of the named user:

```
(require 'clojure.xml)

(defn twitter-followers
  [username]
  (->> (str "https://api.twitter.com/1/users/show.xml?screen_name=" username)
    clojure.xml/parse
    :content
    (filter (comp #{:followers_count} :tag))
    first
    :content
    first
    Integer/parseInt))
```

---

33. Generally provided by rand and rand-int in Clojure.

34. In Clojure's case, an instance of java.math.Random.

35. It is common for the names of functions that manipulate external state to be suffixed with an exclamation point, which serves as an immediate reminder for users (and readers!) that the operation being considered has side effects.

```
(twitter-followers "ClojureBook")
;= 106
(twitter-followers "ClojureBook")                    ❶
;= 107
```

❶ The results of calling `twitter-followers` with the same argument at different times *may* yield a different result.

It should be obvious that it's impossible to deterministically test a function that depends upon a random number generator. For all intents and purposes however, the same is true of any function that depends upon or produces external state, since it is often very difficult to enumerate (never mind comprehensively reason about) all the potential edge cases and failure conditions related to that state. This is what mocks are for in testing, to dummy up an external data source or sink so that it will reliably behave in ways we know ahead of time so as to provoke particular results from a function under test. Unfortunately, any mock you produce—really, any test of any kind you may produce—will never have the same range of behavior or exercise your code in the same ways that it will be abused in the real world.

In contrast with side-effecting functions, *pure functions* are those that do not depend upon external data sources, do not provoke side effects of any kind in their environment, and, when invoked with a particular set of arguments, will always respond with the same return value.[36] All arithmetic functions are pure—e.g., + does not depend upon its environment, produces no side effects, and always returns the same value for a given set of arguments—and the same goes for any other well-behaved operation over immutable values.

Why Are Pure Functions Interesting?

We've already hinted at a couple of practical implications of working with and writing pure functions. For a number of reasons, they can have a profound simplifying effect upon the practice and experience of writing software, especially in conjunction with the use of a capable set of immutable value types.

Pure functions are easier to reason about.   Recall our discussion in "Comparing Values to Mutable Objects" on page 54 about how immutable values allow you to identify whole new categories of invariants. Pure functions provide much the same aid, but with regard to *operations* and not just the state of data. If you know that some function f always returns γ when called with arguments α and β, and you know that calling f will never modify a database or write to a file or read from a socket, then you can call f in *any* context with those arguments and be confident about the results.

---

36. This final characteristic is called *idempotence*, a close cousin of function purity. For example, a function that always returns the same value for a given set of arguments but that does have side effects—say, writing to a logfile—is idempotent but not pure.

Pure functions are easier to test.   This follows naturally from prior points of discussion. If you know your functions have no side effects, and that their results are derived deterministically from their arguments, testing those functions becomes markedly easier. You can strictly define the domain of each function's inputs, and equally strictly define the range of each function's results. Since the results of pure functions are determined solely by their inputs, mocking becomes unnecessary. These characteristics allow you to—if you are so inclined—comprehensively test a pure function to a degree that is simply not possible with side-effecting functions.

You're probably doing this already by driving as much functionality as possible into unit-testable methods, which leaves the (far more difficult-to-test) highly stateful bits over for integration and functional testing. Thinking in terms of pure functions may help you to brighten the line between these two domains and further motivate you to maximize the time you spend in the more pleasant one of them.

Pure functions are cacheable and trivial to parallelize.   Expressions that involve only pure functions are said to be *referentially transparent*; meaning, such expressions are semantically indistinguishable from their results. For example, all these expressions are equivalent, because all the functions involved are pure:

```
(+ 1 2)  (- 10 7)  (count [-1 0 1])
```

Each of these expressions could be replaced by its result value of 3 without affecting the body of code within which it might be found.

In practical terms, this means that the results of pure functions may be freely cached, where the result of each call of a function is retained so that future calls of the function with the same arguments can immediately return the prior result instead of recalculating it. This technique, called *memoization*, is used to help solve a variety of problems where the costs of computing the result of some function call is too high to bear more than once per set of arguments. Clojure includes a simple implementation of this called `memoize`; calling it with a function will return another function that has been *memoized*:

```
(defn prime?                           ❶
  [n]
  (cond
    (== 1 n) false
    (== 2 n) true
    (even? n) false
    :else (->> (range 3 (inc (Math/sqrt n)) 2)
            (filter #(zero? (rem n %)))
            empty?)))

(time (prime? 1125899906842679))       ❷
; "Elapsed time: 2181.014 msecs"
;= true
(let [m-prime? (memoize prime?)]
  (time (m-prime? 1125899906842679))
  (time (m-prime? 1125899906842679)))
; "Elapsed time: 2085.029 msecs"       ❸
```

```
; "Elapsed time: 0.042 msecs"                    ❹
;= true
```

❶ First, the definition of a function that checks whether a given integer is prime (here a naive implementation of the naive prime-testing approach of trial division).

❷ For large primes, this test will take some time.

❸ After being memoized, that same function takes the same amount of time for the first call with a given set of arguments. However...

❹ ...subsequent calls with previously provided arguments return instantly, the corresponding result having been cached by the function returned by `memoize`.

Side-effecting functions, however, are not referentially transparent, and so are generally not safe to memoize. For example, what if we memoized `rand-int`?[37]

```
(repeatedly 10 (partial rand-int 10))
;= (3 0 2 9 8 8 5 7 3 5)
(repeatedly 10 (partial (memoize rand-int) 10))
;= (4 4 4 4 4 4 4 4 4 4)
```

Right, the expression that uses memoization isn't going to yield random numbers! Because memoization elides the invocation of the function in question, any side effects the underlying function might have caused or relied upon will not occur when a memoized result is returned.

In order to work its magic, `memoize` retains all arguments and return values from all calls to the function it produces, so none of that data will ever be garbage-collected. Thus, memoized functions that have highly variable domains or particularly memory-intensive arguments or return values are often the source of memory "leaks," especially when they are naively defined in a top-level var with `def` or similar.

The solution for such situations is to either:

1. Keep a tight leash on the scope of memoized functions. In particular, don't define them in top-level vars; rather, create memoized functions local to a high-level function call as necessary.

2. Use `core.memoize` (*https://github.com/clojure/core.memoize*), a library that provides a number of different memoization strategies, including ones that expire cached arguments and return values based on various criteria.

---

37. Note that the same effect will occur whether `rand-int` itself is memoized or the result of (`partial rand-int 10`) were to be memoized. Understanding why is left as an exercise for the reader. Hint: think about what argument(s) are being passed to the memoized function in each case.

Functional Programming in the Real World

At the beginning of our discussion of functional programming, we looked at a diagrammatic characterization of all programs (Figure 2-1) and we waved at any potential objections that, yes, dealing with potentially messy, unreliable external state is necessary in order to write software that does useful things. What we'd like to leave you with is a slightly adjusted perspective that indicates how you might enjoy the fruits of functional programming within your everyday programming practice without sacrificing any degree of practicality at all.

No matter what kind of software you build, you likely tend to try to isolate the bulk of what makes your creation unique from all the chaos that might surround it once you get it out in the world. We build models of our domain, construct abstractions for key operations, define core algorithms, try to avoid repeating ourselves, and winnow implementations down to fine-grained, easily testable units, all in an effort to find and define invariants, thereby circumscribing an area of sanity and control in stark contrast to the unforgiving wilds of "production."

Taking that existing effort and recasting it with a functional approach can yield huge benefits, as we've described throughout this chapter. Given such a solid foundation, you can tackle the task of coping with the wooly outside world more confidently than before, knowing that at least one side of the bridge between that world and the rest of your application is reliable. The result can be characterized with a slight yet critical adjustment to our original diagram.

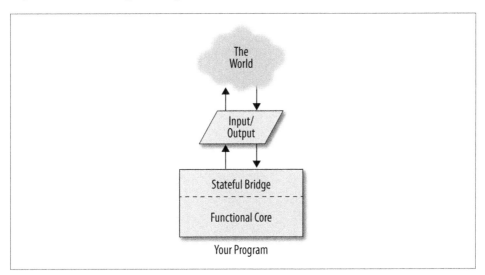

Figure 2-2. A diagram of all programs ever, functional programming style

So many of Clojure's most attractive facilities depend upon the use of immutable data structures, functions as first class, composable values, and the emphasis on minimizing side effects in general. As we've summarized in this chapter, the repercussions of this orientation are far-reaching, making code easier to reason about, test, and compose, while turning otherwise esoteric notions like parallelization and reliable concurrency semantics into low-hanging fruit. It is functional programming that provides the sort of raw materials you should want to build the core of your programs upon.

## CHAPTER 3

Collections and Data Structures

Maps, vectors, sets, and lists are the basic data structures provided by Clojure. As you've seen already, each of these has its own convenient literal notation:

```
'(a b :name 12.5)        ;; list

['a 'b :name 12.5]       ;; vector

{:name "Chas" :age 31}   ;; map

#{1 2 3}                  ;; set

{Math/PI "~3.14"
 [:composite "key"] 42
 nil "nothing"}          ;; another map

#{{:first-name "chas" :last-name "emerick"}
  {:first-name "brian" :last-name "carper"}
  {:first-name "christophe" :last-name "grand"}}  ;; a set of maps
```

These categories of data structures and their notations are likely familiar to you for the most part; particularly with regard to notation, Ruby and Python are quite similar. However, Clojure data structures have a couple of distinctive characteristics:

1. They are first and foremost used in terms of abstractions, not the details of concrete implementations.
2. They are *immutable* and *persistent*, both essential to Clojure's flavor of efficient functional programming.

Each data structure has its own characteristics and idiomatic patterns of usage that we'll explore progressively, but it is far more important to internalize the above points and what they imply about Clojure, its data structures, and how you can and should design your Clojure applications.

Abstractions over Implementations

> It is better to have 100 functions operate on one data structure than 10 functions on 10 data structures.[1]

> —Alan J. Perlis in the foreword to *Structure and Interpretation of Computer Programs*, *http://mitpress.mit.edu/sicp/toc/toc.html*

Clojure's stance is that it is even better to have those 100 functions to operate on one *abstraction*. In some ways, the primacy of Clojure's collection abstractions over particular implementations parallels the polymorphism of operations in Python and Ruby, and the use of interfaces in Java, but there are subtle (and not so subtle) ways in which Clojure's emphasis is more thorough and yields more powerful effects.

To set the stage, let's jump ahead and look at some operations on a vector:

```
(def v [1 2 3])
;= #'user/v
(conj v 4)
;= [1 2 3 4]
(conj v 4 5)
;= [1 2 3 4 5]
(seq v)
;= (1 2 3)
```

seq always yields a sequential view over a collection—called a *sequence*—and conj[2] adds new value(s) into the provided collection. This is pretty pedestrian so far; but, the same operations work on maps:

```
(def m {:a 5 :b 6})
;= #'user/m
(conj m [:c 7])
;= {:a 5, :c 7, :b 6}
(seq m)
;= ([:a 5] [:b 6])
```

...and sets:

```
(def s #{1 2 3})
;= #'user/s
(conj s 10)
;= #{1 2 3 10}
(conj s 3 4)
;= #{1 2 3 4}
(seq s)
;= (1 2 3)
```

...and lists:

```
(def lst '(1 2 3))
;= #'user/lst
```

---

1. More wonderful Perlisisms may be found at *http://www.cs.yale.edu/quotes.html*.

2. conj is derived from "conjoin," to bring together.

```
(conj lst 0)
;= (0 1 2 3)
(conj lst 0 -1)
;= (-1 0 1 2 3)
(seq lst)
;= (1 2 3)
```

Clearly, seq and conj are polymorphic over the type of collection they are operating upon. conj appends a value to a vector; or, prepends a value to a list; or, properly adds a key/value entry to a map with any preexisting keys having their values properly replaced; or, adds a value to a set, presuming that value is not already present. seq provides an intuitive sequential view over a vector or set or list, and brings maps into the fold by yielding a sequential view over a map's key/value pairs, represented as vector pairs.

It is the essence of Clojure to have small, approachable APIs, on top of which auxiliary functions are built. From a user standpoint, "core" functions and helper functions are indistinguishable, and nothing forces the developer to prematurely specialize new helper functions or to make a false choice between which interfaces and types to support for a given operation.

For example, into is built on top of seq and conj, which means that into automatically works on any values that support seq and conj:

```
(into v [4 5])
;= [1 2 3 4 5]
(into m [[:c 7] [:d 8]])
;= {:a 5, :c 7, :b 6, :d 8}
(into #{1 2} [2 3 4 5 3 3 2])
;= #{1 2 3 4 5}
(into [1] {:a 1 :b 2})          ❶
;= [1 [:a 1] [:b 2]]
```

❶ Because the seq of a map is a sequence of its key/value pairs, conjing those pairs into a vector retains the structure of those pairs.

In contrast, Java maps are not even collections within the java.util framework, and Python relies upon concrete data structures that each have their own set of siloed operations. Ruby fares a little better insofar as both lists and hashes provide an .each method to support imperative iteration, but they otherwise remain entirely distinct data structures with their own vocabularies. Meanwhile, Clojure encourages the use of unifying abstractions (sequences, protocols, collection interfaces, and so on), leaving you to have to explicitly go out of your way to depend upon the specific behavior of concrete types.

Abstraction Dilemmas

It is common in Java to have a small interface (a particular type of abstraction), but at the same time need to provide convenience functions. These are very often added to the interface (hence making it more difficult to implement) and implemented in an abstract base class, with only the core methods unimplemented. This leaves code reuse tied to inheritance. Since Java supports only single inheritance, when a user needs to develop a new class that implements two such interfaces, she has to choose which helper methods to reimplement because she can't reuse the existing implementations from two abstract classes.

Thus goes a primary dilemma of the main tools of abstraction in Java, leaving many developers caught between the devil and the deep blue sea—their own personal Scylla and Charybdis (*https://en.wikipedia.org/wiki/Scylla_and_Charybdis*)—left with a choice between maintaining multiple implementations (and minimal code reuse),or a poor API.

In Chapter 6, we'll look at some Clojure facilities you can use to design your own abstractions and types while adhering to its principle of ensuring that common abstractions remain primary.

Small and widely supported abstractions are one of the Clojure design principles that cannot be stressed enough. It is easy to see parallels with HTTP, which achieves robust interoperability and flexibility while defining just one small interface, which is usually less than half-implemented. Similarly, many Clojure data structures support many different abstractions partially, just as they implement only the *read-only* portions of the Java collection API's interfaces (doing more would open Clojure's collections to in-place mutation). An abstraction does not necessarily require full conformance by all of its participants in order to be useful.[3]

There are seven different primary abstractions in which Clojure's data structure implementations participate:

- Collection
- Sequence
- Associative
- Indexed
- Stack
- Set
- Sorted

In the following pages, we'll explore the semantics of the operations that define each abstraction's API. Along the way, you'll learn how to use Clojure's data structures in terms of those abstractions, and therefore, *any* data structure that participates in those abstractions.

---

3. A strategy used throughout software to good effect: witness all of the various "unsupported operation" errors and exception types in nearly all languages, used to indicate a corner of an abstraction that remains unimplemented.

Collection

All data structures in Clojure participate in the common *collection* abstraction. A collection is a value that you can use with the set of core collection functions:

- `conj` to add an item to a collection
- `seq` to get a sequence of a collection
- `count` to get the number of items in a collection
- `empty` to obtain an empty instance of the same type as a provided collection
- `=` to determine value equality of a collection compared to one or more other collections[4]

These functions are all polymorphic with regard to the concrete type of collection being operated upon. Said another way, each operation provides semantics consistent with the constraints of each data structure implementation.

We've already previewed `seq`, but we'll learn much more about it in "Sequences" on page 89, as it is the gateway to Clojure's other most pervasive abstraction, the sequence.

Similarly, we've seen `conj` applied to vectors where it appends items; to maps, it adds a key/value association; and to sets, where it ensures the membership of a given value. One guarantee of `conj` however, is that it will always add a given value to the subject collection *efficiently*. This leads to an initially surprising effect: due to their implementation—which we'll detail later in "Lists" on page 114—`conj` prepends items to lists:

```
(conj '(1 2 3) 4)
;= (4 1 2 3)
(into '(1 2 3) [:a :b :c])
;= (:c :b :a 1 2 3)
```

Doing anything else would require traversing the list, a costly operation if you are working with larger datasets. The broader point is that the specific action of `conj` is dependent upon the local characteristics of the subject collection.

empty.   `empty` likely represents an unfamiliar concept. In many circumstances, you must know what concrete type of data structure you're working with, and therefore you simply create the structure in question directly. `empty` allows you to break out of that pattern and generically work with collections of the same type as a given instance, such as one you have received as an argument to a function. For example, we can write a function that will swap pairs of values in a sequential collection:

```
(defn swap-pairs
  [sequential]
  (into (empty sequential)
        (interleave
```

---

4. Equality is a subtle subject that goes beyond the topic of collections; see "Equality and Equivalence" on page 433.

```
              (take-nth 2 (drop 1 sequential))
              (take-nth 2 sequential)))))

(swap-pairs (apply list (range 10)))
;= (8 9 6 7 4 5 2 3 0 1)
(swap-pairs (apply vector (range 10)))
;= [1 0 3 2 5 4 7 6 9 8]
```

Notice that `swap-pairs`' return type is the same as its argument: a list if we provide a list, and a vector if we provide a vector. This is thanks to the polymorphic behavior of `into` (bolstered by `conj` and `seq`), and the semantics of `empty` that allow us to obtain an empty data structure that we can guarantee will be of the same concrete type as what our caller provided.[5]

This doesn't only work with sequential types; consider a function that allows you to map a given function over every value in a map. What if the map you're provided is sorted...or not? No problem, just use `empty` to work with a fresh instance of the given concrete type—in this case, a map that preserves the sorting guarantees of some other provided map:

```
(defn map-map
  [f m]
  (into (empty m)
        (for [[k v] m]  ❶
          [k (f v)])))
```

❶ `for` is a list comprehension form, very similar in spirit to list comprehensions in Python; this one produces a lazy sequence of vector pairs [k (f v)], one for each key/value pair [k v] destructured from the entries in the map argument m.

```
(map-map inc (hash-map :z 5 :c 6 :a 0))
;= {:z 6, :a 1, :c 7}
(map-map inc (sorted-map :z 5 :c 6 :a 0))
;= {:a 1, :c 7, :z 6}
```

Unsorted in, unsorted out; or, sorted in, sorted out. The caller gets to determine the types of values they get in return, if you allow for it.

count. count does just what you'd expect: indicates the number of entries in a collection:

```
(count [1 2 3])
;= 3
(count {:a 1 :b 2 :c 3})
;= 3
(count #{1 2 3})
;= 3
(count '(1 2 3))
;= 3
```

---

5. Compare this to, for example, Java collections helper methods that can opt to accept generic types like `java.util.List`, but then must either specialize their return type or only guarantee that they also return something equally generic.

---

count guarantees efficient operation on all collections other than sequences (the lengths of which can be undefined, as we'll see next).

count helpfully works on Java types that aren't Clojure collections, like Strings,[6] maps, collections, and arrays.

Sequences

The *sequence* abstraction defines a way to obtain and traverse sequential views over some source of values: either another collection, or successive values that are the result of some computation. Sequences—often called "seqs"—involve a couple of operations in addition to the base provided by the collection abstraction:

- seq produces a sequence over its argument.
- first, rest, and next provide ways to consume sequences.
- lazy-seq produces a *lazy sequence* that is the result of evaluating an expression.

The set of types that are *seqable*—that is, those for which seq can produce a valid value—include:

- All Clojure collection types
- All Java collections (i.e., java.util.*)
- All Java maps
- All java.lang.CharSequences, including Strings
- Any type that implements java.lang.Iterable[7]
- Arrays
- nil (i.e., null as returned from Java methods)
- Anything that implements Clojure's clojure.lang.Seqable interface

Demonstrating all of these comprehensively would be excessive; a small subset will suffice:

```
(seq "Clojure")
;= (\C \l \o \j \u \r \e)
(seq {:a 5 :b 6})
;= ([:a 5] [:b 6])
(seq (java.util.ArrayList. (range 5)))
;= (0 1 2 3 4)
(seq (into-array ["Clojure" "Programming"]))
```

---

6. Really, any java.lang.CharSequence, including java.lang.StringBuilders, java.lang.StringBuffers, and java.nio.CharBuffers instances.

7. seq works on Iterable objects directly; iterator-seq and enumerator-seq are available for obtaining a seq of a java.lang.Iterator or java.lang.Enumerator, respectively. These functions are separate from seq because they are destructive: an Iterator or Enumerator can only be traversed *once*, which is required if you obtain and consume a seq over either of them. In contrast, seq is nondestructive with regard to Iterable objects because they can always provide a fresh Iterator for each seq call.

```
;= ("Clojure" "Programming")
(seq [])
;= nil
(seq nil)
;= nil
```

❶ The seq of nil or any empty collection is nil. This is convenient in many circumstances, including in places where you need a conditional that is equivalent to (not
(empty? some-collection)).

Note that many functions that work with sequences call seq on their argument(s) implicitly. For example, we don't have to wrap this String in a seq call just to use it with
map or set:

```
(map str "Clojure")
;= ("C" "l" "o" "j" "u" "r" "e")
(set "Programming")
;= #{\a \g \i \m \n \o \P \r}
```

> Your own functions will get this behavior for free if you are building
> them on top of others' sequence functions. If you use lazy-seq then it
> is your responsibility to call seq on your arguments to maintain this
> convenient characteristic of seq.

Traversing and processing sequences can be done in many ways, and the Clojure standard library contains many dozens of functions for manipulating and producing sequences in clojure.core. However, most fundamental are first, rest, and next:

```
(first "Clojure")
;= \C
(rest "Clojure")
;= (\l \o \j \u \r \e)
(next "Clojure")
;= (\l \o \j \u \r \e)
```

first and rest should strike you as quite obvious. The latter should seem familiar to
you if you recall how to define and work with variadic functions in Clojure, with their
"rest arguments"; it is rest that lies beneath such functions.[8]

The distinction between rest and next is not so clear though: their results are identical
for most values, as we see above. They only differ in their treatment of sequences containing zero or one value:

Example 3-1. rest versus next

```
(rest [1])
;= ()
(next [1])
;= nil
```

---

8. See "Variadic functions" (page 38).

```
(rest nil)
;= ()
(next nil)
;= nil
```

As you can see, `rest` will always return an empty sequence, whereas `next` will return `nil` if the resulting sequence is empty. In short, this will always be true for any value x:

```
(= (next x)
   (seq (rest x)))
```

The distinction is a small one, but makes it possible for sequences to be realized entirely lazily. We'll learn about lazy sequences and `lazy-seq` in a little bit.

 Sequences are colloquially referred to as "seqs" (perhaps a natural consequence of the key sequence-producing function being called seq), and we'll do so as well throughout the rest of the book.

Sequences are not iterators

When you see code like this:

```
(doseq [x (range 3)]
  (println x))
; 0
; 1
; 2
```

it might be reasonable to think that the `doseq` form here is pulling x values from some iterator that is walking over the sequential collection returned by `range`. While it's true that x is bound to successive values from the `seq` of (`range` 3), that seq is an immutable, persistent collection just like any other in Clojure:

```
(let [r (range 3)
      rst (rest r)]
  (prn (map str rst))
  (prn (map #(+ 100 %) r))
  (prn (conj r -1) (conj rst 42)))
; ("1" "2")
; (100 101 102)
; (-1 0 1 2) (42 1 2)
```

The "derivative" `rst` seq works just as its "parent" seq `r` does, and both can be operated upon separately by using the breadth of functions available for sequences and collections. In particular, we can map a function over a seq without affecting it or its source values, any of its "descendants" or its parents. None of these characteristics are shared by mutably stateful iterators and generators, which cannot be checkpointed, safely used as the basis for other iterators, and, once consumed, cannot be consumed again.

Sequences are not lists

At first sight, sequences look very much like lists: they are either empty or consist of a head value and a tail that is itself a sequence. In addition, lists are their own sequences.[9] However, they are quite different in some important ways:

- Obtaining the length of a seq carries a cost.
- The contents of sequences may be computed lazily and actually *realized* only when the values involved are accessed.
- The computation that is producing values for a lazy sequence can opt to produce an unlimited progression of those values, thus making it possible for sequences to be *infinite* and therefore uncountable.

In contrast, lists track their length, so getting the count of one is a cheap, constant-time operation. Seqs cannot provide the same guarantee, because they may be produced lazily and can potentially be infinite. Thus, the only way to obtain a count of a seq is to force a full traversal of it. You can see the effect of this when count is applied to a lazy sequence versus a fully realized list:

```
(let [s (range 1e6)]           ❶
  (time (count s)))
; "Elapsed time: 147.661 msecs"
;= 1000000
(let [s (apply list (range 1e6))]     ❷
  (time (count s)))
; "Elapsed time: 0.03 msecs"
;= 1000000
```

❶ range returns a lazy seq of numbers that are produced *only* when needed. counting a lazy seq is one way to ensure that it is fully realized, since all of the seq's values must be produced in order to count them. Here, we're including that realization within the scope of activity we're timing.

❷ Lists always track their size, so getting the count of one will always return immediately.

Creating seqs

You may have noticed that we've not explicitly created any seqs so far. Given that seqs are just sequential views over other collections, this makes sense; generally, a seq is produced by a collection, either explicitly via seq or via another function (like map) calling seq on its argument(s) implicitly. However, there are two ways to *create* a seq: cons and list*.[10]

---

9. This is an implementation detail, but currently (identical? some-list (seq some-list)) is always true.

10. If you have any experience with other Lisps, take note that Clojure's cons has little to nothing to do with the cons found elsewhere. Similarly, Clojure's lists are not composed of a series of cons cells.

cons accepts two arguments, a value to serve as the head of the new seq, and another collection, the seq of which will serve as its tail:

```
(cons 0 (range 1 5))
;= (0 1 2 3 4)
```

You can think of cons as *always* "prepending" to the tail collection's sequence regardless of the collection's concrete type, thus distinguishing itself from conj:

```
(cons :a [:b :c :d])
;= (:a :b :c :d)
```

list*[11] is just a helper for producing seqs with any number of head values, followed by a sequence. So, these two expressions are equivalent:

```
(cons 0 (cons 1 (cons 2 (cons 3 (range 4 10)))))
;= (0 1 2 3 4 5 6 7 8 9)
(list* 0 1 2 3 (range 4 10))
;= (0 1 2 3 4 5 6 7 8 9)
```

cons and list* functions are most commonly used when writing macros—where seqs and lists are equivalent, and you just need to prepend a value to a list or seq—and when assembling the next step of a lazy sequence, as we'll see next.

Lazy seqs

It is possible for the contents of a sequence to be evaluated *lazily*, where values are produced as the result of a computation performed on demand when a consumer attempts to access them. Each such value is always computed once and only once. The process of accessing a lazy sequence is called *realization*; when all values in a lazy sequence have been computed, it is said that the sequence has been *fully realized*.

You can create a lazy sequence with lazy-seq, a macro that accepts any expression that will evaluate to a seqable value. Here's a silly example:

```
(lazy-seq [1 2 3])
;= (1 2 3)
```

That's not very interesting, insofar as the lazy sequence here is "realizing" its values from a fully formed data structure to begin with. More interesting is a sequence that lazily produces a sequence of random integers:

Example 3-2. Implementing a lazy sequence

```
(defn random-ints
  "Returns a lazy seq of random integers in the range [0,limit)."
  [limit]
```

---

11. Confusingly, list* does *not* return a list—i.e., (list? (list* 0 (range 1 5))) will return false—unless only one value is provided. This will not cause any problems, unless you were to use the concrete type of a data structure to dictate program behavior by using, for example, list?. As always, it is better to code to abstractions instead of concrete types, so anywhere you might want to use list?, use seq? or sequential? instead.

```
(lazy-seq
  (cons (rand-int limit)      ❶
        (random-ints limit))))  ❷

(take 10 (random-ints 50))
;= (32 37 8 2 22 41 19 27 34 27)
```

❶ We return a lazy seq that is defined by a head of (rand-int limit)...

❷ ...and a tail that is itself a lazy sequence as produced by a recursive call to this same
random-ints function.

The result of this might not look very special, but the sequence of digits in the seq
returned from random-ints is produced lazily—it's only shown in its entirety here because printing a sequence forces its contents to be realized.[12] Let's prove this by modifying random-ints a bit to print something every time a value is realized:

```
(defn random-ints
  [limit]
  (lazy-seq
    (println "realizing random number")  ❶
    (cons (rand-int limit)
          (random-ints limit))))

(def rands (take 10 (random-ints 50)))    ❷
;= #'user/rands
(first rands)                             ❸
; realizing random number
;= 39
(nth rands 3)
; realizing random number
; realizing random number
; realizing random number
;= 44
(count rands)                             ❹
; realizing random number
; realizing random number
; realizing random number
; realizing random number
; realizing random number
; realizing random number
;= 10
(count rands)                             ❺
;= 10
```

❶ Each time lazy-seq is evaluated (which will occur every time a concrete value is
produced by looking at the head of the cons), we'll print a message.

12. That means that you should be cautious about evaluating references to infinite or otherwise very large
sequences without constraining their scope, such as via (take 100 infinite-seq) to limit the printed
subsequence to the first 100 values. Alternatively, you can set! *print-length* to some reasonable value
(maybe 100) to limit the number of entries shown from each printed collection.

❷ We define the lazy sequence so it's not printed, which would force its full evaluation. Notice that no message is printed; the sequence is entirely lazy, and has not yet produced any values.

❸ Asking the seq for its head value via `first` *forces* the production of that value based on whatever calculation or logic defined in the `lazy-seq` form. We get a random number and a corresponding printed message as expected.

❹ If we ask for values later in the lazy seq, it and all preceding values are necessarily realized; here, we see that `count` forces the entire sequence to be realized so it can determine its size.

❺ Asking for the count again (or, similarly, if we asked for the `nth` value in the seq) does not require recomputing each value: once realized, values in lazy seqs are retained.

When we first define the lazy seq in a var, its contents simply do not exist:

Once we attempt to access its first value, that value is realized and retained so that the computation that produced it does not have to be repeated:

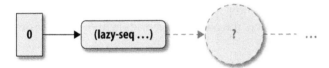

Its head is a concrete value, but its tail is defined entirely by a computation suspended in a function that `lazy-seq` creates from the expression it is provided that will not be invoked by our accessing its corresponding value. This points to a key advantage of `cons` and `list*`: these functions do *not* force the evaluation of the (potentially lazy) sequences they are provided as their final argument. This makes these functions a key helper in building up lazy seqs, where a common pattern is to return the result of a `cons` or `list*` call with one or more concrete seq values, followed by a `lazy-seq` that suspends the call or computation that will produce the rest of the lazy sequence.

`random-ints` is actually a very poor, overly complex implementation of functionality you can obtain just from composing a couple of standard-library Clojure functions together: `rand-int`, which `random-ints` already uses, and `repeatedly`, which produces a lazy seq that contains values obtained by invoking a given function for each value:

```
(repeatedly 10 (partial rand-int 50))
;= (47 19 26 14 18 37 44 13 41 38)
```

 It's worth reemphasizing that the expression provided to `lazy-seq` can do just about anything—you're not limited simply to numerical tricks like random numbers or operations on small bits of data. Any pure function implementing computation that is appropriate for a value in a sequence is fair game.

Note that the single-argument arity of `repeatedly` would return an infinite lazy sequence of random numbers. It is not uncommon to work with infinite lazy sequences in Clojure. There is a considerable body of functions both in Clojure's standard library and throughout Clojure's community libraries that deal in (potentially infinite) lazy sequences transparently. Handily, all of the core sequence-processing functions in the standard library—such as `map`, `for`, `filter`, `take`, and `drop`[13]—return lazy sequences, and can be layered as needed without affecting the laziness of underlying seqs. Given these facilities, it is very common to characterize many problems as processing sequences of values, from things as general as the lazy processing of data from queues and parallelized search[14] to the lazy consumption and transformation of data from various sources, as with `file-seq`, `line-seq`, and `xml-seq`.

There are cases where you will want to be very careful to minimize the degree to which you force the realization of a lazy sequence—for example, if each value required some I/O or a significant amount of computation to produce. This is where the difference between `next` and `rest` is critical. Remember from Example 3-1 that `next` always returns `nil` instead of an empty sequence? This is only possible because `next` checks for a nonempty tail seq; this check necessarily forces the potential realization of the head of that nonempty tail seq:

```
(def x (next (random-ints 50)))
; realizing random number
; realizing random number
```

In contrast, `rest` will "blindly" return the tail of a given sequence, thereby avoiding realizing its head and therefore maximizing laziness:

```
(def x (rest (random-ints 50)))
; realizing random number
```

---

13. ...and their derivatives, like `take-nth`, `take-while`, `drop-while`, `remove`, and so on.

14. Being able to filter gigabytes of data on multiple cores simply by using `pmap` in conjunction with a lazy seq while using just a couple of megabytes of memory inspires giddiness. See "Parallelism on the Cheap" on page 166 for more on `pmap`.

Sequential destructuring *always* uses `next`, and not `rest`. Thus, destructuring a lazy seq will always realize its tail's head value:

```
(let [[x & rest] (random-ints 50)])
; realizing random number
; realizing random number
;= nil
```

On the other hand, there are times when you need to force the complete realization of a lazy sequence. In such cases, you should use `doall` if you wish to retain the contents of the sequence,[15] or `dorun` if you want the contents disposed of as each value in the sequence is produced:

```
(dorun (take 5 (random-ints 50)))
; realizing random number
; realizing random number
; realizing random number
; realizing random number
; realizing random number
;= nil
```

Not retaining the contents of a lazy sequence might seem like a waste, but this can be a very useful if a lazy seq's computations are side-effecting, and you are only interested in ensuring that those side effects occur. For example, if you have a lazy sequence of files (via `file-seq`), and you need to perform the some set of operations on them, characterizing that as one or many functions `mapped` across that lazy sequence is very convenient. Then, `dorun` will actually apply those operations, but not wastefully retain any return values of the functions involved in the operations performed.

Usually, documentation for functions that operate over seqs is explicit about whether they produce lazy seqs or force their realization:

```
(doc iterate)
; -----------------------
; clojure.core/iterate
; ([f x])
;   Returns a lazy sequence of x, (f x), (f (f x)) etc.
;   f must be free of side-effects

(doc reverse)
; -----------------------
; clojure.core/reverse
; ([coll])
;   Returns a seq of the items in coll in reverse order. Not lazy.
```

Clearly, `iterate` is lazy, `reverse` is not. The admonition that the function provided to `iterate` "must be free of side effects" deserves some explanation, though.

---

15. As we saw before, `count` (and a few other functions) will do the same, but only as an implementation detail. It is *possible* (though very rare) for a lazy sequence to know its length, and therefore return it as the result of `count` without realizing its contents.

Code defining lazy sequences should minimize side effects. We already learned of many of the advantages of pure functions in "Pure Functions" on page 76, but those characteristics—and the pitfalls of side-effecting code—are accentuated in the context of lazy sequences. Because values in lazy seqs are realized when they are accessed and not when they are defined, it's very, very easy to lose track of when and where any side effects associated with the production of those values will happen, if they ever happen! For example, changing a logging level while a lazy seq is being consumed may cause log events to be suddenly passed through, even if the log level was set to squelch such messages when the lazy seq was defined.

To make things worse, the evaluation of some lazy sequences may be batched as a performance optimization,[16] thus making the realization of items run ahead of consumption by some amount, causing any side effects to occur in bursts as opposed to being coincident with the consumption of each value.

The moral of this story is that you should generally not rely upon the evaluation of sequences to control execution flow. Clojure's laziness does not serve the same purpose as in other languages where lazy evaluation is pervasive. In Clojure, laziness is restricted to sequences, with the rest of the language and its data structures being otherwise entirely "eagerly" evaluated. Lazy sequences allow Clojure to transparently process big datasets that don't fit in memory and to express algorithms in a more uniform, declarative, pipelined way; in this context, sequences can be considered *an ephemeral medium of computation*, not as collections.

You will often notice this pattern in Clojure code: given one or more data sources, you extract a sequence from it, process it, and turn it back into a more appropriate data structure. This pattern can be spotted in code as simple as this:

```
(apply str (remove (set "aeiouy")
                   "vowels are useless! or maybe not..."))
;= "vwls r slss! r mb nt..."
```

Here we have a data source, the `String` `"vowels are useless! or maybe not..."`, which is implicitly turned into a sequence of characters. All vowels are then removed from it before aggregating the resulting sequence back into a `String`.

Head retention

One fact often overlooked by newcomers to Clojure is that lazy sequences are persistent: an item is computed once, but is still retained by the sequence.[17] This means that, as long as you maintain a reference to a sequence, you'll prevent its items from being

---

16. Some data structures like vectors generate "chunked" sequences, and many sequence functions (e.g., `map`, `filter`) process those sequences one chunk (containing 32 values per chunk in the case of seqs obtained from vectors) at a time rather than one value at a time.

17. This is in sharp contrast with generators in Python and `Enumerator`s in Ruby, which can lazily produce potentially infinite series of values on demand, but which do not provide a consistent way to retain previously generated values if desired.

garbage-collected. This type of fault is called *head retention* (or, *holding onto head*) and can put pressure on the VM that will impact performance, potentially even causing an out of memory error if the realized portion of a sequence grows too large.

`split-with` is a function that, given a predicate and seq-able value, will return a vector of two lazy seqs; the prefix that satisfies the predicate and the suffix starting at the first item that does not satisfy the predicate:

```
(split-with neg? (range -5 5))
;= [(-5 -4 -3 -2 -1) (0 1 2 3 4)]
```

Consider a case using `split-with` where you know that the prefix is going to be very small, but the suffix will be very large. If you retain a reference to the prefix, all of the values in the sequence will be retained even if your processing of the suffix is lazy. If the sequence in question is very large, then this head retention will ensure that an out of memory error will occur:

```
(let [[t d] (split-with #(< % 12) (range 1e8))]
  [(count d) (count t)])
;= #<OutOfMemoryError java.lang.OutOfMemoryError: Java heap space>
```

Reversing the order of evaluation solves the problem:

```
(let [[t d] (split-with #(< % 12) (range 1e8))]
  [(count t) (count d)])
;= [12 99999988]
```

Since the last reference of `t` occurs before the processing of `d`, no reference to the head of the `range` sequence is kept, and no memory issues arise.

Insertion into a map or set, `=`, and `count` are also common causes of "head retention"[18] since they force complete realization of lazy sequences.

Associative

The *associative* abstraction is shared by data structures that link keys and values in some way. It is defined by four operations:

- `assoc`, which establishes new associations between keys and values within the given collection
- `dissoc`, which drops associations for given keys from the collection
- `get`, which looks up the value for a particular key in a collection
- `contains?`, which is a predicate that returns `true` only if the collection has a value associated with the given key

The canonical associative data structure is the map, which also happens to be the most versatile data structure provided by Clojure. You'll soon find maps to be your best friend.

---

18. Or rather, premature realization—but the end result of an out-of-memory condition is the same.

As we have already seen, maps are seen as collections of entries (key/value pairs) when used with the core collection functions of conj and seq, but the associative functions are a more natural fit.

```
(def m {:a 1, :b 2, :c 3})
;= #'user/m
(get m :b)
;= 2
(get m :d)
;= nil
(get m :d "not-found")
;= "not-found"
(assoc m :d 4)
;= {:a 1, :b 2, :c 3, :d 4}
(dissoc m :b)
;= {:a 1, :c 3}
```

Conveniently, you can also use assoc and dissoc to affect multiple entries in the given map:

```
(assoc m
  :x 4
  :y 5
  :z 6)
;= {:z 6, :y 5, :x 4, :a 1, :c 3, :b 2}
(dissoc m :a :c)
;= {:b 2}
```

Though they are used more frequently with maps, get and assoc are supported by vectors too. While it might be initially counterintuitive, maps and vectors are *both* associative collections, where vectors associate values with indices:

```
(def v [1 2 3])
;= #'user/v
(get v 1)                    ❶
;= 2
(get v 10)
;= nil
(get v 10 "not-found")
;= "not-found"
(assoc v
  1 4
  0 -12
  2 :p)                      ❷
;= [-12 4 :p]
```

❶ v "associates" the index 1 with the value 2.

❷ You can update the value at an index in a vector using assoc; again, following the intent of the associative abstraction, but having data structure-dependent effects. Note that this assoc call is structurally identical to the multiple-entry assoc in the previous listing that operated on a map.

Just as `conj` appends to vectors because that is where value may be added efficiently, you can also use `assoc` to append to vectors—with the caveat that you need to know what the new value's index *will be*:

```
(assoc v 3 10)
;= [1 2 3 10]
```

Finally, `get` works on sets, where if the "key" is present, it is returned:

```
(get #{1 2 3} 2)
;= 2
(get #{1 2 3} 4)
;= nil
(get #{1 2 3} 4 "not-found")
;= "not-found"
```

While sets by themselves have no key/value semantics, `get`'s return values when operating on a set imply that a set "associates" its values with themselves. This may seem strange, but it allows sets to satisfy the semantics of `get`, while remaining consistent with typical usage as a test in a conditional:

```
(when (get #{1 2 3} 2)
  (println "it contains `2`!"))
; it contains `2`!
```

Clojure maps and sets support the semantics of `get` quite directly, beyond being usable with `get` itself. See Collections are functions on page 111 for how lookups can be done concisely, without touching `get`.

contains?   `contains?` is a predicate that returns true for an associative collection only if the given key is present:

```
(contains? [1 2 3] 0)
;= true
(contains? {:a 5 :b 6} :b)
;= true
(contains? {:a 5 :b 6} 42)
;= false
(contains? #{1 2 3} 1)
;= true
```

It is a common mistake for Clojure programmers to initially believe that `contains?` always searches for the presence of a *value* in a collection, that is, that it would be appropriate to use to determine if the vector [0 1 2 3] contained a particular numeric value. This misconception can lead to some very confusing results:

```
(contains? [1 2 3] 3)
;= false
(contains? [1 2 3] 2)
;= true
```

```
(contains? [1 2 3] 0)
;= true
```

Of course, the results above are correct, since contains? is only checking to see if any mapping exists for the provided *key*—in this case, the indices 3, 2, and 0. To check for the existence of a particular *value* in a collection, it is typical to use some, described in "Collections and Keys and Higher-Order Functions" on page 113.

get and contains? are particularly versatile: they work effectively on vectors, maps, sets, Java maps, Strings, and Java arrays:

```
(get "Clojure" 3)
;= \j
(contains? (java.util.HashMap.) "not-there")
;= false
(get (into-array [1 2 3]) 0)
;= 1
```

Beware of nil values

get returns nil when there's no entry for a given key and when no default value is provided. However, nil is a perfectly valid value, and is obviously returned when it is associated with a given key:

```
(get {:ethel nil} :lucy)
;= nil
(get {:ethel nil} :ethel)
;= nil
```

How can we tell the difference between a key that is associated with nil and a key that is not present?

We could use contains?, but then we'd be doing two map lookups all the time: one so that contains? could determine that an entry exists for a given key, and then the same lookup again to actually get the value. We could get clever and use a special default value, assuming that a key was not found if a get call returns the default value. However, such schemes have serious drawbacks as well: it's often too easy for that special default value to leak into a map as a normal key, and using one ensures that the result of a get lookup won't play nicely with conditionals, since any special default value will always be logically true, even when the given key is absent.

The answer is to use find. find works very much like get except that, instead of returning the associated value, it returns the whole entry; or, nil when not found.

```
(find {:ethel nil} :lucy)
;= nil
(find {:ethel nil} :ethel)
;= [:ethel nil]
```

Additionally find works very well with destructuring and conditional forms like if-let (or when-let):

```
(if-let [e (find {:a 5 :b 6} :a)]
  (format "found %s => %s" (key e) (val e))
  "not found")
;= "found :a => 5"
(if-let [[k v] (find {:a 5 :b 6} :a)]
  (format "found %s => %s" k v)
  "not found")
;= "found :a => 5"
```

Of course, if you *only* want to check for the presence of a given key, just use `contains?`.

Beware of false too

When used with a conditional, false values in associative collections present nearly the same problems as `nil`, and the same measures must be taken to gracefully handle them.

Indexed

So far, we've talked about vectors while mostly avoiding talking about how to reach directly for the nth item in one, or changing the value at that position. There's a reason for that: *indices are the new pointers.*[19]

Honestly, indices—be they for strings or arrays or other sequential data—are rarely mandated by your algorithms.[20] In many cases, dealing with indices induces complexity: either through index arithmetic and bounds-checking or through unneeded indirections. Outside of special circumstances, we feel safe in saying that excessive indexed lookup or modification is a code smell.

That said, there is a time and place for such things, and this is where the *indexed* abstraction comes in. It consists of a single function, `nth`, which is a specialization of `get`. They differ on how they deal with out-of-bounds indices: `nth` throws an exception while `get` returns `nil`:

Example 3-3. Comparing nth and get on vectors

```
(nth [:a :b :c] 2)
;= :c
(get [:a :b :c] 2)
;= :c
(nth [:a :b :c] 3)
;= java.lang.IndexOutOfBoundsException
(get [:a :b :c] 3)
```

---

19. Alternatively, an `IndexOutOfBoundsException` is the new core dump.

20. Every generalization has its exceptions; if you are writing numerical libraries or implementing sublinear algorithms like the Boyer-Moore string search, you need indices. Sometimes you need to step back when considering a given algorithm for implementation in Clojure. Many textbooks and other guides use arrays and indices everywhere simply because they are a *lingua franca*, a kind of least common denominator between languages. That doesn't mean that the cleanest or most efficient implementation in Clojure won't use a different approach.

```
;= nil
(nth [:a :b :c] -1)
;= java.lang.IndexOutOfBoundsException
(get [:a :b :c] -1)
;= nil
```

Despite this difference, when you provide a default return value, their semantics are identical:

```
(nth [:a :b :c] -1 :not-found)
;= :not-found
(get [:a :b :c] -1 :not-found)
;= :not-found
```

nth and get convey different meaning. First, nth can only work with numerical indices and works on many things that can be numerically indexed: vectors, lists, sequences, Java arrays, Java lists, strings, and regular expression matchers. On the other hand, get is more general: it works on any kind of associative type, as we've already seen, and treats numerical indices as keys into the collection or value in question.

Another major difference between nth and get is that get is more resilient. We have already seen that get returns nil when an index (treated as a key) is not found, rather than throwing an exception. get goes even further: it returns nil when the subject of the lookup is not supported, while nth throws an exception.

```
(get 42 0)
;= nil
(nth 42 0)
;= java.lang.UnsupportedOperationException: nth not supported on this type: Long
```

 Clojure vectors support the semantics of nth quite directly, beyond being usable with nth itself. See "Collections are functions" (page 111) for how lookups can be done concisely, without touching nth.

Stack

Stacks are collections that classically support last-in, first-out (LIFO) semantics; that is, the most recent item added to a stack is the first one that can be pulled off of it. Clojure doesn't have a distinct stack data structure, but it does support a stack abstraction via three operations:

- conj, for pushing a value onto the stack (conveniently reusing the collection-generalized operation)
- pop, for obtaining the stack with its top value removed
- peek, for obtaining the value on the top of the stack

Both lists and vectors can be used as stacks (Examples 3-4 and 3-5), where the top of the stack is the end of each respective data structure where conj can efficiently operate.

Example 3-4. Using a list as a stack

```
(conj '() 1)
;= (1)
(conj '(2 1) 3)
;= (3 2 1)
(peek '(3 2 1))
;= 3
(pop '(3 2 1))
;= (2 1)
(pop '(1))
;= ()
```

Example 3-5. Using a vector as a stack

```
(conj [] 1)
;= [1]
(conj [1 2] 3)
;= [1 2 3]
(peek [1 2 3])
;= 3
(pop [1 2 3])
;= [1 2]
(pop [1])
;= []
```

popping an empty stack will result in an error.

Set

We've already seen how sets participate partially in the associative abstraction, where they are treated as a sort of degenerate map, associating keys with themselves:

```
(get #{1 2 3} 2)
;= 2
(get #{1 2 3} 4)
;= nil
(get #{1 2 3} 4 "not-found")
;= "not-found"
```

To be complete though, the *set* abstraction requires `disj`, which removes value(s) from the given set:

```
(disj #{1 2 3} 3 1)
;= #{2}
```

While the set abstraction itself is slight, reusing common collection and associative semantics for most of the fundamental operations on sets, we recommend that you become familiar with `clojure.set`. A namespace in Clojure's standard library, `clojure.set` provides a suite of functions implementing various higher-level operations and predicates over sets, including `subset?`, `superset?`, `union`, `intersection`, `project`, and more.

Sorted

Collections that participate in the *sorted* abstraction guarantee that their values will be maintained in a stable ordering that is optionally defined by a predicate or implementation of a special comparator interface. This allows you to efficiently obtain in-order and reverse-order seqs over all or a subrange of such collections' values. These operations are provided by:

- rseq, which returns a seq of a collection's values in reverse, with the guarantee that doing so will return in constant time
- subseq, which returns a seq of a collection's values that fall within a specified range of keys
- rsubseq, the same as subseq, but the seq is in reversed order

Only maps and sets are available in sorted variants. They do not have any literal notation; they may be created by sorted-map and sorted-set, or sorted-map-by and sorted-set-by if you provide your own predicate or comparator to define sort order.

Given a sorted collection, you can use any of the abstraction's functions to query it:

```
(def sm (sorted-map :z 5 :x 9 :y 0 :b 2 :a 3 :c 4))
;= #'user/sm
sm
;= {:a 3, :b 2, :c 4, :x 9, :y 0, :z 5}
(rseq sm)                                              ❶
;= ([:z 5] [:y 0] [:x 9] [:c 4] [:b 2] [:a 3])
(subseq sm <= :c)                                      ❷
;= ([:a 3] [:b 2] [:c 4])
(subseq sm > :b <= :y)                                 ❸
;= ([:c 4] [:x 9] [:y 0])
(rsubseq sm > :b <= :y)                                ❹
;= ([:y 0] [:x 9] [:c 4])
```

❶ rseq will return a seq over sm in reverse order in constant time.

❷ Here we are querying sm for all values that have keys that sort before or equal to :c.

❸ This query is looking for all values that have keys that sort after :b *and* before or equal to :y.

❹ rsubseq performs the same query as subseq, but returns results in reverse order.

Because sm is sorted, each of these operations have far better performance characteristics than their seq-only corollaries, which would need various linear-time operations (e.g., filter, take-while) to yield the same results. In particular, rseq is guaranteed to return in constant time, in contrast to reverse, which can be used to obtain a seq of any collection in reverse order, but which operates in linear time.[21]

---

21. We're fibbing a bit here: rseq is technically part of another minor abstraction—*reversible*—that establishes this guarantee. We're glossing over it because, aside from sorted collections, only vectors are also reversible (and so rseq may be used with vectors as well).

The compare function defines the default sort: ascending, supporting all Clojure scalars and sequential collections, sorting lexicographically at each level:[22]

```
(compare 2 2)
;= 0
(compare "ab" "abc")
;= -1
(compare ["a" "b" "c"] ["a" "b"])
;= 1
(compare ["a" 2] ["a" 2 0])
;= -1
```

In truth, compare supports more than strings, numbers, and sequential collections: it supports anything that implements java.lang.Comparable—which includes Booleans, keywords, symbols, and all Java and third-party classes implementing this interface. compare is a potent function but is only the default *comparator*.

Comparators and predicates to define ordering

A *comparator* is a two-argument function that returns a positive integer when the first argument is greater than the second one, a negative integer when the first is less than the second, and zero when both arguments are equal.

All Clojure functions implement java.util.Comparator and can therefore be used as comparators—although obviously, not all functions are intended to be used as such. Specifically, you don't have to do anything special to make a function implement that Comparator interface—any two-argument predicate will do.

Beyond not having to implement special interfaces to produce a comparator, this fact means that it is much easier to create composite orderings: a secondary sort is just a function composition away. Comparison functions can be passed directly to sorted collections' factory functions as well as sort and sort-by:[23]

```
(sort < (repeatedly 10 #(rand-int 100)))
;= (12 16 22 23 41 42 61 63 83 87)
(sort-by first > (map-indexed vector "Clojure"))
;= ([6 \e] [5 \r] [4 \u] [3 \j] [2 \o] [1 \l] [0 \C])
```

How Does Clojure Turn a Predicate into a Comparator?

It may seem confusing that predicates—like <, which return Boolean values—can be used as comparators, since their return values are defined as negative or positive integers, or zero if arguments are equal.

The algorithm used to turn a predicate into a comparator is quite simple: the predicate is called first with the two arguments in the order given to the comparator. If the predicate returns true, then -1 is returned. Otherwise, the predicate is called again but with

---

22. It follows that, for example, vectors of vectors of vectors can be reliably sorted.

23. Or any Java API that expects a java.util.Comparator.

the order of the two arguments reversed. If this time it returns true, then 1 is returned. Otherwise, given that no argument appears to be dominated by the other, the arguments are considered equal, and 0 is returned.

comparator will explicitly turn a two-argument predicate into a comparator function that uses this logic:

```
((comparator <) 1 4)
;= -1
((comparator <) 4 1)
;= 1
((comparator <) 4 4)
;= 0
```

although this is rarely used, since functions implicitly provide this conversion when used with the various Clojure functions that accept comparators, and two-argument functions already implement the java.util.Comparator interface.

So, while sorted-map and sorted-set create maps and sets where their keys are sorted according to the default compare, sorted-map-by and sorted-set-by will accept a comparator (again, any two-argument predicate function will do) to drive their sort order. The simplest comparator you can pass to a sorted collection (apart from compare itself) is probably (comp - compare), which negates the result of compare, and therefore the sort order of the collection:

```
(sorted-map-by compare :z 5 :x 9 :y 0 :b 2 :a 3 :c 4)
;= {:a 3, :b 2, :c 4, :x 9, :y 0, :z 5}
(sorted-map-by (comp - compare) :z 5 :x 9 :y 0 :b 2 :a 3 :c 4)
;= {:z 5, :y 0, :x 9, :c 4, :b 2, :a 3}
```

It must be noted that *sort order defines equality within a sorted map or set*; this can sometimes lead to rational but surprising results. For example, say we have a function that returns the order of magnitude of numbers:

```
(defn magnitude
  [x]
  (-> x Math/log10 Math/floor))
;= #'user/magnitude
(magnitude 100)
;= 2.0
(magnitude 100000)
;= 5.0
```

Straightforward enough, and we can create a comparison predicate that uses magnitude, which will return the difference in orders of magnitude between its first and second arguments:

```
(defn compare-magnitude
  [a b]
  (neg? (- (magnitude a) (magnitude b))))

((comparator compare-magnitude) 10 10000)
;= -1
((comparator compare-magnitude) 100 10)
```

```
;= 1
((comparator compare-magnitude) 10 75)
;= 0
```

Things get interesting when we use this as a comparator with a sorted collection:

```
(sorted-set-by compare-magnitude 10 1000 500)   ❶
;= #{10 500 1000}
(conj *1 600)                                    ❷
;= #{10 500 1000}
(disj *1 750)                                    ❸
;= #{10 1000}
(contains? *1 1239)                              ❹
;= true
```

❶ Each of 10, 1000, and 500 have different orders of magnitude, so they are all retained in the set as different elements according to the comparator.

❷ Adding 600 to that set is a no-op because 600 is the same order of magnitude as 500, and therefore is considered equal to 500 by the comparator.[24]

❸ Because 750 is also considered equal to 500 by the comparator, 500 is removed from the set even though 750 was provided as the argument to disj.

❹ Similarly, 1239 has the same order of magnitude as 1000, so contains? returns true because a key equal to its argument is found in the given set.

Sometimes this behavior is what you want, sometimes not. Keep in mind that you have complete control over the implementation of your comparators; while it is convenient to use (or reuse) predicates, you can opt to return negative or positive integers or zero at any time in order to enforce the equality semantics you desire. compare-magnitude can be rewritten to ensure that only equivalent numbers are considered equal, by delegating to compare when its arguments have the same order of magnitude:

```
(defn compare-magnitude
  [a b]
  (let [diff (- (magnitude a) (magnitude b))]
    (if (zero? diff)
      (compare a b)
      diff)))

(sorted-set-by compare-magnitude 10 1000 500)
;= #{10 500 1000}
(conj *1 600)
;= #{10 500 600 1000}
(disj *1 750)
;= #{10 500 600 1000}
```

---

24. *1 holds the value of the last expression evaluated in the REPL. See REPL-bound vars on page 399 for details.

Now our set's values remain sorted by their order of magnitude, but operations that rely upon numerical equality (like `conj` and `disj`) will behave as we might intuitively expect.

`subseq` and `rsubseq` continue to work as you'd expect to extract intervals (in natural or reverse order) from a sorted collection defined with a custom comparator:

```
(sorted-set-by compare-magnitude 10 1000 500 670 1239)
;= #{10 500 670 1000 1239}
(def ss *1)
;= #'user/ss
(subseq ss > 500)
;= (670 1000 1239)
(subseq ss > 500 <= 1000)
;= (670 1000)
(rsubseq ss > 500 <= 1000)
;= (1000 670)
```

 The interval specification required by these functions uses `<`, `<=`, `>`, and `>=` solely as hints with regard to the actual comparator in use in the sorted collection; the corresponding predicates are not used.

One amusing use of these functions is to implement linear interpolation:

```
(defn interpolate
  "Takes a collection of points (as [x y] tuples), returning a function
  which is a linear interpolation between those points."
  [points]
  (let [results (into (sorted-map) (map vec points))]   ❶
    (fn [x]
      (let [[xa ya] (first (rsubseq results <= x))       ❷
            [xb yb] (first (subseq results > x))]
        (if (and xa xb)                                  ❸
          (/ (+ (* ya (- xb x)) (* yb (- x xa)))         ❹
             (- xb xa))
          (or ya yb))))))
```

❶ `(map vec points)` ensures that each point is a vector and thus can be added as an entry to a map.

❷ Here and at the line below we find the two closest neighbors of x in the known points.

❸ When we are out of range either xa or xb is `nil` and we return `(or ya yb)`, which is the only value we know.

❹ The linear interpolation formula for the regular case.

Let's test it; say we have three known points, [0 0], [10 10], and [15 5]:

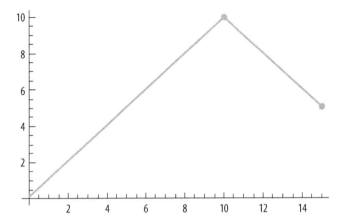

For known x coordinates, we can find the y that fits the data we have:

```
(def f (interpolate [[0 0] [10 10] [15 5]]))
;= #'user/f
(map f [2 10 12])
;= (2 10 8)
```

Perfect!

Concise Collection Access

Accessing values is easily the most common operation performed over collections, especially those that support the associative abstraction. That being the case, having to constantly type get or nth could get very tiring. Thankfully, Clojure collections and the most common types of keys used in associative collections *are also functions* with the semantics of get or nth (as appropriate for the concrete type of collection involved).

Collections are functions.   Very simply, Clojure collections are functions that look up the value associated with the key or index that is provided. So these:

```
(get [:a :b :c] 2)
;= :c
(get {:a 5 :b 6} :b)
;= 6
(get {:a 5 :b 6} :c 7)
;= 7
(get #{1 2 3} 3)
;= 3
```

are exactly equivalent to these more concise expressions:

```
([:a :b :c] 2)
;= :c
({:a 5 :b 6} :b)
;= 6
({:a 5 :b 6} :c 7)
```

```
;= 7
(#{1 2 3} 3)
;= 3
```

In each of these cases, the collection is in function position, so *it* is being called with the key or index to look up within itself. Maps accept an optional second argument just like `get`, the optional default value returned if the lookup fails. Both vectors and sets accept only a single value/index for the lookup; defaults are not supported. Indices provided for vector lookups must also be within the range of the vector, just as with `nth`:

```
([:a :b :c] -1)
;= #<IndexOutOfBoundsException java.lang.IndexOutOfBoundsException>
```

Collection keys are (often) functions.   Similarly, the most common types of keys—keywords and symbols—are also functions that look themselves up in the provided collection. Thus, these:

```
(get {:a 5 :b 6} :b)
;= 6
(get {:a 5 :b 6} :c 7)
;= 7
(get #{:a :b :c} :d)
;= nil
```

are exactly equivalent to these more concise expressions:

```
(:b {:a 5 :b 6})
;= 6
(:c {:a 5 :b 6} 7)
;= 7
(:d #{:a :b :c})
;= nil
```

Since the value in function position must be a function, numeric indices can't be used; therefore, vector lookups cannot be performed using this approach.

Idiomatic Usage

Great, so there are less verbose ways to access values in collections. That's clearly good, but without some additional guidance, it might not be so clear as to how and when to use each variation: when should the collection be used as the lookup function versus the keyword or symbol?

This is treading dangerously into the realm of taste; but, *in general*, we recommend using the keyword or symbol being looked up as the function. The most immediate advantage of this idiom is that null pointer exceptions are usually avoided, since keywords and symbols are most often literals when used as lookup functions. Consider:

```
(defn get-foo
  [map]
  (:foo map))
;= #'user/get-foo
(get-foo nil)
```

```
;= nil
(defn get-bar
  [map]
  (map :bar))
;= #'user/get-bar
(get-bar nil)
;= #<NullPointerException java.lang.NullPointerException>
```

Additionally, the form `(coll :foo)` assumes that `coll`, a collection, is also a function. That is true for most Clojure data structures, but is not true for (for example) lists, and is not necessarily true for other types that participate in Clojure's collection abstractions but that are not also functions. This makes `(:foo coll)` more desirable, insofar as you can be certain that the literal keyword `:foo` is always a function and is never `nil`, whereas the value referenced by `coll` may satisfy neither condition.

Of course, if a collection has keys other than keywords or symbols, then you must use the collection or `get` or `nth` as the lookup function.

Collections and Keys and Higher-Order Functions

Because keywords, symbols, and many collections are functions, using them as inputs to higher-order functions is both common and incredibly convenient. Say we want all the names of our customers; no need to define any functions, and no need to explicitly use `get`:

```
(map :name [{:age 21 :name "David"}
            {:gender :f :name "Suzanne"}
            {:name "Sara" :location "NYC"}])
;= ("David" "Suzanne" "Sara")
```

`some` searches for the first value in a sequence that returns a logically true value from a provided predicate; using it in conjunction with sets is a common pattern:

```
(some #{1 3 7} [0 2 4 5 6])
;= nil
(some #{1 3 7} [0 2 3 4 5 6])
;= 3
```

This makes `some` a very concise way to use the result of searching a collection in a conditional. A more generalized operation is `filter`, which returns a lazy sequence that retains only values that are true according to a given predicate. Again, we can just use a collection or a keyword or symbol when appropriate, potentially composed with other functions as necessary:

```
(filter :age [{:age 21 :name "David"}
              {:gender :f :name "Suzanne"}
              {:name "Sara" :location "NYC"}])
;= ({:age 21, :name "David"})

(filter (comp (partial <= 25) :age) [{:age 21 :name "David"}
                                     {:gender :f :name "Suzanne" :age 20}
```

```
                                    {:name "Sara" :location "NYC" :age 34}])
;= ({:age 34, :name "Sara", :location "NYC"})
```

`remove` is the complement to `filter`, quite literally: it is implemented by filtering the given collection with the `complement` of the given function, `(filter (complement f) collection)`.

Beware of the nil (again)

It is so simple to use sets to test whether some value belongs to a given collection that it is easy to forget that when the value in question is `nil` or `false`, results may not align with our expectations because both of them are logically false:

```
(remove #{5 7} (cons false (range 10)))
;= (false 0 1 2 3 4 6 8 9)
(remove #{5 7 false} (cons false (range 10)))
;= (false 0 1 2 3 4 6 8 9)
```

So, when you don't know for sure that you'll never have `nil` or `false` in the set you're using as a predicate, prefer `contains?` over `get` or a direct call:

```
(remove (partial contains? #{5 7 false}) (cons false (range 10)))
;= (0 1 2 3 4 6 8 9)
```

Data Structure Types

Clojure provides a number of concrete data structures, each of which satisfy various abstractions as appropriate. We've already been working with these concrete implementations quite a lot—indeed, as we'd hope, their behavior and semantics are defined for the most part by the abstractions (or parts of abstractions) they participate in.

Here, we'll rapidly move through some of the implementation details that separate each of the concrete data structure types, most of which have to do with their construction.

Lists

Lists are the simplest collection type in Clojure. Their primary and most typical purpose is to serve as a representation for calls in Clojure code, as we explained in "Expressions, Operators, Syntax, and Precedence" on page 7; as such, you'll use them far more as literals in your source files than you ever will at runtime in your programs.[25]

Clojure lists are singly linked, but are only efficiently accessed or "modified" at their head, using `conj` to push a new head value on, or `pop` or the sequence operator `rest` to obtain a reference to the sublist without the prior head value. Because they are linked

---

25. This is a departure from prior Lisps, where lists and cons cells play a central role. Clojure's use of richer composites—like maps, sets, vectors, and the list's abstract cousin, the sequence—markedly diminish the cases for which lists are themselves applicable.

lists, they do not support efficient random access; thus, nth on a list will run in linear time (as opposed to constant time when used with vectors, arrays, and so on), and get does not support lists at all because doing so would not align with get's objective of sublinear efficiency.

It is worth noting that lists are their own sequences; therefore, seq of a list will always return that list and not a separate sequential view over the list.

We've only really seen list literals before:

```
'(1 2 3)
;= (1 2 3)
```

If we didn't quote this list, it would be evaluated as a call of the value 1, which would fail.[26] The side effect of this is that expressions within the list literal are also not evaluated:

```
'(1 2 (+ 1 2))
;= (1 2 (+ 1 2))
```

Most people simply use a vector literal for such cases, within which member expressions will always be evaluated. However, there are some cases where you really do need a list, and no other data structure will do.[27] For those times, reach for list:

```
(list 1 2 (+ 1 2))
;= (1 2 3)
```

list accepts any number of values, where each value will become an element of the returned list.

Finally, you can use the list? predicate to test if a value is specifically a list.

Vectors

Vectors are a sequential data structure that supports efficient random access lookup and alteration that will match the expectations of programmers used to java.util.ArrayList, Python's lists, and Ruby's arrays. Vectors are also particularly versatile, participating in the associative, indexed, and stack abstractions as we've seen.

Aside from now-familiar vector literals, vectors can be created using vector and vec:

```
(vector 1 2 3)
;= [1 2 3]
(vec (range 5))
;= [0 1 2 3 4]
```

vector is the analog to list, whereas vec expects only a single sequential argument whose entire contents will be used to create the new vector. This is useful when you

---

26. Note that an *empty* list does not need to be quoted, since there is no first item that could be construed as a callable value. Thus, () is a valid empty list literal.

27. The most common such cases are when writing macros; see Chapter 5.

have some data in an array, list, sequence, or other seqable value, but further manipulation of that data needs to benefit from a vector's capabilities.

vector? is the predictable analog to list?, used for testing whether a value is a vector.

Vectors as tuples

Tuples are one of the most common use cases for vectors. Any time several values should be batched together with as little ceremony as possible—like when returning multiple values from a function—they can be put into a vector:

```
(defn euclidian-division    ❶
  [x y]
  [(quot x y) (rem x y)])

(euclidian-division 42 8)
;= [5 2]
```

❶ Just in case you're golfing for concision, (juxt quot rem) returns a function that is equivalent to this one.

This pairs nicely with Clojure's pervasive destructuring mechanism (see "Destructuring (let, Part 2)" on page 28), allowing us to easily unpack such return values into their constituents:

```
(let [[q r] (euclidian-division 53 7)]
  (str "53/7 = " q " * 7 + " r))
;= "53/7 = 7 * 7 + 4"
```

As tempting and easy as tuples are, you should not forget that they are an expeditive mean to an end: they are best kept hidden in your libraries' and modules' internals rather than exposed as part of a public API. The rationale behind this is twofold:

- Tuples are not self-documenting. You have to consistently recall the respective roles of each index.
- Tuples are inflexible. You have to provide values even in middle slots that aren't appropriate for a particular return value and you can't extend a tuple in ways other than appending to its tail.

Maps don't suffer from those two limitations; thus, for functions that are part of a public API and for nontrivial return values, maps are a better fit.

Of course, as with any rule, this one has exceptions. In places where the purpose of a tuple is obvious for the domain at hand—coordinates, oriented edges in graphs, and so on—using vectors as tuples is entirely appropriate:

```
(def point-3d [42 26 -7])

(def travel-legs [["LYS" "FRA"] ["FRA" "PHL"] ["PHL" "RDU"]])
```

In the latter case above, note that we have two different usages of vectors: the outer vector is just a better list, while the inner vectors are acting as tuples of airport trigrams, [from to].

Sets

There is little to say about sets as a concrete data structure implementation that we've not touched on already when discussing the associative and set abstractions. Like Clojure's other data structure types, sets have a literal notation we've seen already:

```
#{1 2 3}
;= #{1 2 3}
#{1 2 3 3}   ❶
;= #<IllegalArgumentException java.lang.IllegalArgumentException:
;=   Duplicate key: 3>
```

❶ Since sets by definition cannot contain duplicate values, literals including duplicate values will be rejected.

And the hash-set function is available to create unsorted sets from any number of arguments:

```
(hash-set :a :b :c :d)
;= #{:a :c :b :d}
```

Finally, you can create a set from the values in any collection by using the set function:

```
(set [1 6 1 8 3 7 7])
;= #{1 3 6 7 8}
```

This actually works with anything that is seqable, and allows for some very succinct idioms given that sets are functions themselves:

```
(apply str (remove (set "aeiouy") "vowels are useless"))
;= "vwls r slss"

(defn numeric? [s] (every? (set "0123456789") s))
;= #'user/numeric?
(numeric? "123")
;= true
(numeric? "42b")
;= false
```

Sorted set variants are also available, as we saw in "Sorted" on page 106.

Maps

Aside from the now-familiar map literal:

```
{:a 5 :b 6}
;= {:a 5, :b 6}
{:a 5 :a 5}                                    ❶
;= #<IllegalArgumentException java.lang.IllegalArgumentException:
;=   Duplicate key: :a>
```

❶ As with values in sets, keys in maps must be unique; literals that violate this requirement are rejected.

unsorted maps can be created using `hash-map`, which accepts any number of key/value pairs. This is most often used in conjunction with `apply` when you have a collection of key/value pairs that are not themselves grouped into vector tuples:

```
(hash-map :a 5 :b 6)
;= {:a 5, :b 6}
(apply hash-map [:a 5 :b 6])
;= {:a 5, :b 6}
```

Sorted map variants are also available, as we saw in "Sorted" on page 106.

keys and vals.   Though specific to maps, these functions are handy shortcuts that return a sequence of keys or values from a source map:

```
(keys m)
;= (:a :b :c)
(vals m)
;= (1 2 3)
```

They are fundamentally just shortcuts for using `seq` on a map to obtain its sequence of entries, and then obtaining the `key` or `val` from each entry:

```
(map key m)
;= (:a :c :b)
(map val m)
;= (1 3 2)
```

Maps as ad-hoc structs

Since map values can be of any type, they are frequently used as simple, flexible models, most often with keywords for keys to identify each field (also called *slots*).

```
(def playlist
  [{:title "Elephant", :artist "The White Stripes", :year 2003}
   {:title "Helioself", :artist "Papas Fritas", :year 1997}
   {:title "Stories from the City, Stories from the Sea",
    :artist "PJ Harvey", :year 2000}
   {:title "Buildings and Grounds", :artist "Papas Fritas", :year 2000}
   {:title "Zen Rodeo", :artist "Mardi Gras BB", :year 2002}])
```

It is very common for data modeling in Clojure to start with simple maps. Especially when you aren't sure of what slots your entities will consist of, maps allow you to get to work right away without having to predefine a rigid data model.

Once you are using maps (and other data structures that participate in Clojure's abstractions) for your model, all of their capabilities flow into any work you do with it. For example, assuming you're using keywords as keys, "querying" data aggregates becomes trivial:

```
(map :title playlist)
;= ("Elephant" "Helioself" "Stories from the City, Stories from the Sea"
;=  "Buildings and Grounds" "Zen Rodeo")
```

Similarly, things like associative destructuring, introduced in "Map destructuring" on page 32, can help simplify operations on individual map "structs," eliminating more verbose (:slot data) accesses:

```
(defn summarize [{:keys [title artist year]}]
  (str title " / " artist " / " year))
```

Clojure tries to save you from premature over-architecting by offering a clear upgrade path—if you need it—from prototyping using map-based "structs" to a more mature model. Thus, modeling with maps is not a dead end. Rather, as long as you program to Clojure's collection abstractions instead of any particular implementation (the latter being something you really need to go out of your way to do), you'll be able to cleanly swap out a map-based model for a specialized type—like one defined by defrecord, which always produces associative types.

We'll discuss defrecord in detail in "Defining Your Own Types" on page 270, and compare them with maps in "When to use maps or records" on page 277.

Other usages of maps

Maps are also often used as summaries, indexes, or translation tables; think here of database indexes and views.

For example, group-by is very useful to partition a collection according to a key function:

```
(group-by #(rem % 3) (range 10))
;= {0 [0 3 6 9], 1 [1 4 7], 2 [2 5 8]}
```

Here we see numbers grouped together under keys defined by the provided function. Following on with our playlist data, we can easily create an index on albums by artist:

```
(group-by :artist playlist)
;= {"Papas Fritas" [{:title "Helioself", :artist "Papas Fritas", :year 1997}
;=                  {:title "Buildings and Grounds", :artist "Papas Fritas"}]
;= ...}
```

Indexing on two "columns" is as easy as (group-by (juxt :col1 :col2) data).

Sometimes you just want to compute a summary of items for a given key rather than returning a vector of those items. You could use group-by and then process each value to summarize it:

```
(into {} (for [[k v] (group-by key-fn coll)]
            [k (summarize v)]))
```

...where key-fn and summarize are placeholders for your actual functions. However, this can become cumbersome if your collections are particularly large, as when dealing with large result sets from a database query. In this case, you have to resort to your own mix of group-by and reduce. reduce-by will help to compute all kinds of summaries on data, not unlike a SELECT ... GROUP BY ... query in SQL:

```
(defn reduce-by
  [key-fn f init coll]
```

```
(reduce (fn [summaries x]
          (let [k (key-fn x)]
            (assoc summaries k (f (summaries k init) x))))
  {} coll))
```

x, xs, and other not-so-cryptic names

Newcomers to Clojure often find the usage of very brief names like x
and xs confusing. The meaning of each letter is partly codified by the
Library Coding Standards style guide (*http://dev.clojure.org/display/de
sign/Library+Coding+Standards*). In essence, when you use the name
x, you are saying that your code is generic and oblivious to x's type, so
there's no point in calling it invoice. Likewise, a collection or sequence
of x values is often named xs, and so on. *The more generic your code is,
the less specific the names you use are going to be.*

Let's assume we have a list of purchase orders to ACME Corp, represented using plain
maps as "structs":

```
(def orders
  [{:product "Clock", :customer "Wile Coyote", :qty 6, :total 300}
   {:product "Dynamite", :customer "Wile Coyote", :qty 20, :total 5000}
   {:product "Shotgun", :customer "Elmer Fudd", :qty 2, :total 800}
   {:product "Shells", :customer "Elmer Fudd", :qty 4, :total 100}
   {:product "Hole", :customer "Wile Coyote", :qty 1, :total 1000}
   {:product "Anvil", :customer "Elmer Fudd", :qty 2, :total 300}
   {:product "Anvil", :customer "Wile Coyote", :qty 6, :total 900}])
```

With reduce-by, we can easily compute order totals by customer:

```
(reduce-by :customer #(+ %1 (:total %2)) 0 orders)
;= {"Elmer Fudd" 1200, "Wile Coyote" 7200}
```

Likewise, you can get the customers for each product:

```
(reduce-by :product #(conj %1 (:customer %2)) #{} orders)
;= {"Anvil" #{"Wile Coyote" "Elmer Fudd"},
;=  "Hole" #{"Wile Coyote"},
;=  "Shells" #{"Elmer Fudd"},
;=  "Shotgun" #{"Elmer Fudd"},
;=  "Dynamite" #{"Wile Coyote"},
;=  "Clock" #{"Wile Coyote"}}
```

What if you want a two-level breakup, say, all orders by customer, and then by product?
You simply need to return a vector of the two values as the key. There are several ways
to write such a function:

```
(fn [order]
  [(:customer order) (:product order)])

#(vector (:customer %) (:product %))

(fn [{:keys [customer product]}]
  [customer product])
```

```
(juxt :customer :product)
```

We'll prefer the most clear and succinct one:

```
(reduce-by (juxt :customer :product)
  #(+ %1 (:total %2)) 0 orders)
;= {["Wile Coyote" "Anvil"] 900,
;=  ["Elmer Fudd" "Anvil"] 300,
;=  ["Wile Coyote" "Hole"] 1000,
;=  ["Elmer Fudd" "Shells"] 100,
;=  ["Elmer Fudd" "Shotgun"] 800,
;=  ["Wile Coyote" "Dynamite"] 5000,
;=  ["Wile Coyote" "Clock"] 300}
```

Not quite what we were expecting—we don't have a map of maps. This problem boils down to reduce-by assuming that the map is shallow. You can either "fix" reduce-by by creating a version for nested maps, or you can massage your result map.

Making reduce-by work with nested maps is as easy as replacing calls to assoc and the implicit get (when the map is used as a function) with assoc-in and get-in:

```
(defn reduce-by-in
  [keys-fn f init coll]
  (reduce (fn [summaries x]
            (let [ks (keys-fn x)]
              (assoc-in summaries ks
                (f (get-in summaries ks init) x))))
    {} coll))
```

As expected, we now get a two-level breakup:

```
(reduce-by-in (juxt :customer :product)
  #(+ %1 (:total %2)) 0 orders)
;= {"Elmer Fudd" {"Anvil" 300,
;=                "Shells" 100,
;=                "Shotgun" 800},
;=  "Wile Coyote" {"Anvil" 900,
;=                 "Hole" 1000,
;=                 "Dynamite" 5000,
;=                 "Clock" 300}}
```

The second option is to transform our previous result data:

```
(def flat-breakup
  {["Wile Coyote" "Anvil"] 900,
   ["Elmer Fudd" "Anvil"] 300,
   ["Wile Coyote" "Hole"] 1000,
   ["Elmer Fudd" "Shells"] 100,
   ["Elmer Fudd" "Shotgun"] 800,
   ["Wile Coyote" "Dynamite"] 5000,
   ["Wile Coyote" "Clock"] 300})
```

...into the expected map of maps. To do so, we are also going to use `assoc-in`:

```
(reduce #(apply assoc-in %1 %2) {} flat-breakup)
;= {"Elmer Fudd" {"Shells" 100,
;=                "Anvil" 300,
;=                "Shotgun" 800},
;=  "Wile Coyote" {"Hole" 1000,
;=                 "Dynamite" 5000,
;=                 "Clock" 300,
;=                 "Anvil" 900}}
```

Each value in the seq provided by the `flat-breakup` map is a map entry like `[["Wile Coyote" "Anvil"] 900]`. Thus, when our reduction function uses `apply` with each of these map entries, the resulting call to `assoc-in`—e.g., `(assoc-in {} ["Wile Coyote" "Anvil"] 900)`—conveniently uses the data in each entry to define both the structure of the resulting map and its deepest values.

Immutability and Persistence

We've now gone through much of the nuts and bolts of Clojure's collections and surveyed many of their abstractions. What we haven't yet emphasized and explored are two characteristics that are shared by all of Clojure's data structures: they are *immutable*, and they are *persistent*.

We explored the notion of immutability in Chapter 2 and learned how the value semantics provided by working with immutable entities can be a great simplifying force. However, you might have some lingering concerns. For example, consider this operation over numbers:

```
(+ 1 2)
;= 3
```

3 here is a value entirely separate from the arguments to `+`. Certainly, the act of adding numbers doesn't modify one of the addends to make it *be* another number. This is in stark contrast to how most data structures work in languages that encourage unfettered mutation, like Python here:

```
>>> lst = []
>>> lst.append(0)
>>> lst
[0]
```

append really did modify `lst`. That has many implications, not necessary all pleasant, but you can be certain that such operations are *efficient*, almost regardless of the size of the collection in question. On the other hand, this looks like it might be problematic:

```
(def v (vec (range 1e6)))   ❶
;= #'user/v
(count v)
;= 1000000
(def v2 (conj v 1e6))       ❷
;= #'user/v2
(count v2)
;= 1000001
(count v)                   ❸
;= 1000000
```

❶ Start with a vector, containing the range of all integers from 0 through 1e6: a million elements, a reasonably sized collection.

❷ Using conj, append an integer to the vector, which now has 1,000,001 items in it.

❸ As we've said though, all of Clojure's data structures are immutable, so v is not changed.

v2 here is a whole separate data structure. You might say, "Surely that isn't efficient: it looks like conj (and maybe every other operation on Clojure data structures) creates a *full copy* of the collection it's *modifying*!"

Thankfully, that is not the case.

Persistence and Structural Sharing

Operations over Clojure's immutable data structures *are* efficient; often as fast as the equivalent operations in Java. This is because the data structures are *persistent*, an implementation technique where collections reuse internal structure to minimize the number of operations needed to represent altered versions of an instance of a collection while ensuring that all versions of a collection will maintain the same efficiency guarantees.

The semantics of "persistence"

Clearly, we're not talking about "persistence" as it applies to the serialization and storage of data, objects, and so on. The notion under consideration here is rooted in Okasaki's *Purely Functional Data Structures* (*http://www.amazon.com/dp/0521663504*), where he describes techniques that allow the performance guarantees of immutable data structures to *persist* in later versions of those collections produced by various operations.

Purely Functional Data Structures is a seminal work in functional programming, and the designs of Clojure and many other current functional programming languages owe a great deal to its foundational vision. Those interested in deepening their understanding of functional programming as it intersects with data structures should consider it required reading.

To achieve persistence without sacrificing performance, Clojure's data structures implement *structural sharing*. That is, they never perform deep copies to satisfy an operation; rather, only the portions of the data structure affected by a change are swapped out, while references are retained to those parts that are uninvolved.

Visualizing persistence: lists

The simplest example of this dynamic in play involves operations over lists. Consider this list:

```
(def a (list 1 2 3))
```

Recalling that Clojure lists are linked lists, we can visualize this like so:

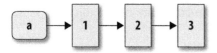

Let's conj a new value onto the list, remembering that conj always prepends to lists:

```
(def b (conj a 0))
;= #'user/b
b
;= (0 1 2 3)
```

We can visualize this operation:

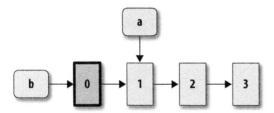

conj *does* create a new list with 0 as the first value, but it reuses the entirety of a to form the new list's tail. Clearly, this is an efficient operation:

- There is no copying of data.
- The original list a remains as-is and can be accessed and used as the basis of other lists as needed.
- The new list b shares the structure of a, with the addition of a single value.

As we said earlier, part of the contract of `conj` is that it operates in constant time: conjoining a value onto a collection of three elements should take the same amount of time as the same operation on a collection of a million elements, and that is certainly true in the case of lists. Thus, the characteristics of a *persist* on to a later version of it, the list b.

What about other operations? Clojure lists aren't random access (just like all other linked lists), so we know we can't use, for example, `nth` to obtain a value within a list in anything better than linear time. However, we can pop the head off of lists efficiently:

```
(def c (rest a))
;= #'user/c
c
;= (2 3)
```

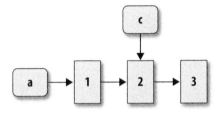

`rest` on a list is similarly a constant-time operation, thanks to the data structure ensuring that it shares structure however possible across versions. `rest`[28] will return that list's tail in the same time, regardless of the size of the list in question, and the result continues to maintain the same guarantees for future operations.

Visualizing persistence: maps (and vectors and sets)

So operations on a linked list can be made efficient. What about the data structures that carry the load of most of the work in Clojure programming? Maps, vectors, and sets all share the same fundamental implementation strategy,[29] even though their internal structure is considerably more involved than that of lists.

For the sake of our example, let's look at a map:

```
(def a {:a 5 :b 6 :c 7 :d 8})
```

28. We could have just as easily used `pop` here.

29. There are many subtle differences in their internals, but those do not prevent us from discussing their persistent semantics in general. Please keep in mind that the map data structure visualizations in this section are intended solely to highlight those semantics, not to accurately reflect implementation details.

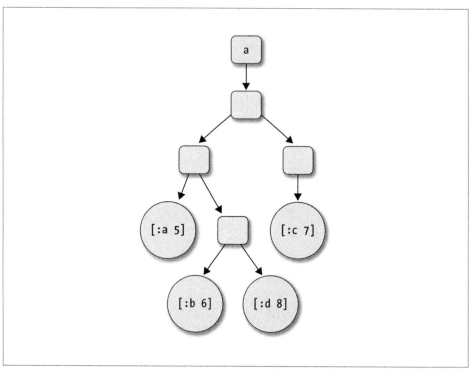

Figure 3-1. The internal structure of the map {:a 5 :b 6 :c 7 :d 8}

Like most maps, Clojure's is implemented as a tree structure, with values in the map stored in the tree's leaves.

Let's update our map:

```
(def b (assoc a :c 0))
;= #'user/b
b
;= {:a 5, :c 0, :b 6, :d 8}
```

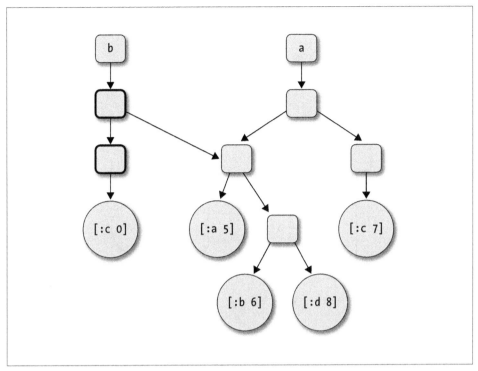

Figure 3-2. Effect of (assoc a :c 0)

More so than in the example where we added a value to a list using `conj`, you can see that the map produced by **assoc** shares a great deal of structure with the prior version of that map. The entire subtree that contains the entries for `:a`, `:b`, and `:d` is reused in its entirety without modification, and the only allocations required are for the leaf associated with the change and the internal nodes that lead back up to the new tree's root.

Removing an entry from the map has much the same result in terms of the structural sharing in play:

```
(def c (dissoc a :d))
;= #'user/c
c
;= {:a 5, :c 7, :b 6}
```

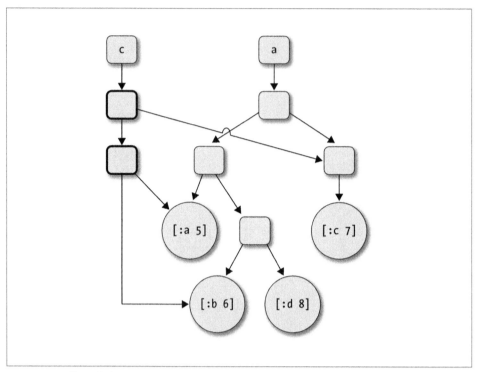

Figure 3-3. Effect of (dissoc a :d)

Again, much of the tree's structure is not impacted by the change, so the new tree shares most of its structure with its basis.

A Forest of Trees

To provide persistent semantics, nearly all of Clojure's data structures are implemented as trees, including hash maps and sets, sorted maps and sets, and vectors. The specific tree structure that is used varies significantly though: hash maps use a persistent variant of hash array mapped tries,[31] vectors use a further variant called an array mapped hash trie,[32] while sets are built on top of hash maps and sorted sets and sorted maps use a persistent variant of red-black trees so as to guarantee sort order efficiently.

In all of these cases, Clojure's tree implementations are such that operations you would expect to be fast (e.g., appending to a vector, adding to a set, establishing a new association in a map, and performing lookups across all collections) *are* fast. In "big-O"

---

31. See *http://blog.higher-order.net/2009/09/08/understanding-clojures-persistenthashmap-deftwice* for an overview of the hash array mapped trie implementation in Clojure's `PersistentHashMap` class.

32. See *http://blog.higher-order.net/2009/02/01/understanding-clojures-persistentvector-implementation* for an overview of the implementation in Clojure's `PersistentVector` class.

---

terms, these operations are either $O(\log_{32} n)$ (for unsorted collections) or $O(\log_2 n)$ (for sorted collections), where n is the number of values in the collection. The upshot? Operations over immutable data structures that are as fast or nearly as fast as the analogous operations performed over mutable collections, while ensuring all of the beneficial semantics we've talked about that only immutable values can provide.

Interestingly, many systems are emerging that utilize the same implementation strategy of using immutable, persistent trees. Aside from Clojure, other examples include Git and CouchDB. A high-level overview of the similarities involved can be found at *http: //eclipsesource.com/blogs/2009/12/13/persistent-trees-in-git-clojure-and-couchdb-data -structure-convergence*.

Tangible benefits

While this might have seemed like a diversion into the implementation details of Clojure's data structures (as appealing and interesting as that may be), there are some distinct tangible benefits that you enjoy *because of* the fact they are persistent and immutable. We already detailed in Chapter 2 how working with immutable values can be a powerful simplifying force, eliminating entire categories of bugs and unintended consequences that can crop up when unfettered mutable data structures are in play. There's more, though.

Enabling concurrency.   Clojure's reference types—explored in "Clojure Reference Types" on page 170—would not exist as they do if there were no useful, efficient, immutable values for them to hold. Insofar as those reference types define the semantics of change over time for a particular identified piece of data, it would be pointless to store mutable data structures in them. At any time, some other code could potentially be making changes to such mutable collections, thereby undermining the purpose of the reference types and again putting the onus on you to ensure correctness in your systems in the face of concurrent access and modification.

Free versioning.   One requirement in many systems is the need to keep and refer to multiple versions of some data. This can be challenging to implement and represent if your data structures are mutable. How do you make a copy of some data so future modifications can't affect it? How do you reasonably roll back to some prior state?

Immutable collections make answering these questions easy:

```
(def version1 {:name "Chas" :info {:age 31}})
;= #'user/version1
(def version2 (update-in version1 [:info :age] + 3))   ❶
;= #'user/version2
version1
;= {:info {:age 31}, :name "Chas"}
version2
;= {:info {:age 34}, :name "Chas"}
```

❶ update-in updates the value (identified by the vector argument) located in the (potentially nested) associative structure by applying the given function (+ here) to it and any additional arguments (3 here).

Each "update" to a Clojure collection leaves that collection in its original state, and provides the new version. Each can be used, modified, and stored however your application needs; but, you never have to strain yourself to do the housekeeping around the production of such useful versioned data, because that naturally falls out of the collections' implementation for free.

Transients

Transient collections are the dual to those that are persistent: while persistent collections make guarantees about the integrity of prior revisions of a value, transient collections do not. After modification, any reference to an old revision of a transient collection cannot be relied upon; it may be valid, it may be the new value, or it may be garbage.

This may seem like a foolish notion, but it is born of an adaptation of an age-old notion: *if a data structure is mutated, and no one sees it happen, does that mutation hurt anyone?*

In stark contrast to nearly everything else in Clojure, *transient collections are mutable*:

```
(def x (transient []))  ❶
;= #'user/x
(def y (conj! x 1))     ❷
;= #'user/y
(count y)               ❸
;= 1
(count x)               ❹
;= 1
```

❶ We create a transient vector using a persistent vector as a basis.

❷ A single value is added to the transient vector using conj!, the transient analog to conj...

❸ ...which unsurprisingly returns a new reference to a transient vector containing that one value. However...

❹ ...our old transient vector reflects that change as well![33]

So, given everything we've said so far, why would transients ever be a good idea? Clojure's persistent data structures possess a number of *very* attractive characteristics, and for what they deliver, they are *very* fast. However, there are some inescapable realities about them that cannot be ignored: chiefly, that the semantic guarantees of persistent

---

33. As we said at the start of this section, old revisions of transient collections *must not* be relied upon; we're simply illustrating here that transient collections are quite mutable and have semantics that run counter to persistent collections.

data structures require allocation on every update, something that does carry some overhead. However marginal that overhead might be, when you need to perform mass updates where, for example, hundreds or thousands of values are being conjed into a collection, the result in aggregate is subpar.

Transients are nothing more than an optimization for this scenario. In some cases, transients can reduce or eliminate the cumulative object allocation rate of an operation, thereby minimizing garbage collection time and improving overall collection construction times. In particular, they are an easy way to reduce object churn in a tight loop.[34]

What sort of circumstances are we talking about, exactly? Well, let's look at a core Clojure function we've seen before, into; it takes a collection, some seq of values, and conj's all of the latter into the former:

```
(into #{} (range 5))
;= #{0 1 2 3 4}
```

What would it take for us to reimplement this? As a first draft, not much:

```
(defn naive-into
  [coll source]
  (reduce conj coll source))

(= (into #{} (range 500))
   (naive-into #{} (range 500)))
;= true
```

Great, so we have our own implementation of into, and it will work with any persistent collection. However, let's look at the performance of our implementation versus Clojure's:

```
(time (do (into #{} (range 1e6))        ❶
          nil))
; "Elapsed time: 1756.696 msecs"
(time (do (naive-into #{} (range 1e6))
          nil))
; "Elapsed time: 3394.684 msecs"
```

❶ We don't want to print a set of a million numbers to the REPL, so we make sure to return nil from the do form.

Ouch, naive-into is 2× slower! The reason is that into uses a transient collection when it can,[35] that is, when the "destination" collection is a vector or unsorted map or set, the only types of collections for which transient variants exist to date.

---

34. When confronted with a performance problem, allocations are generally the first thing to profile in a Clojure program.

35. Other core Clojure functions use transients under the covers when they can as well, including frequencies and group-by.

We can do the same though:

```
(defn faster-into
  [coll source]
  (persistent! (reduce conj! (transient coll) source)))
```

Prior to entering the reduction, we turn the initial collection into a `transient`. At each step of the reduction, we use `conj!`—the transient analogue to `conj`—to add the next value from `source` to the transient collection. `reduce` returns the newly populated transient collection, which we make persistent again using `persistent!`. What is the upshot?

```
(time (do (faster-into #{} (range 1e6))
          nil))
; "Elapsed time: 1639.156 msecs"
```

Yes, performance parity with `into`. Let's take a step back for just a moment though: faster is almost always better, but are we losing all that we gained by using persistent, immutable collections? In short, no. It's true that we are working with a mutable collection throughout the course of `faster-into`'s reduction, but *that transient never escapes the scope of the function that uses it*! This means that `faster-into` has *exactly* the same semantics as `naive-into`—persistent collection in, persistent collection out. Thus, users get all the beneficial semantics of persistent collections and all the speed of unfettered mutation.

 Remember that only vectors and unsorted maps and sets have transient variants. Therefore, `faster-into` will fail if it is provided with, for example, a sorted set as the collection to populate.

There is unfortunately no standard predicate to indicate if a given collection's type has a transient variant. You need to check if a given collection is an instance of `clojure.lang.IEditableCollection`, the interface Clojure uses to indicate that a collection can produce a transient variant. A predicate to check for this might be `transient-capable?`:

```
(defn transient-capable?
  "Returns true if a transient can be obtained for the given collection.
   i.e. tests if `(transient coll)` will succeed."
  [coll]
  (instance? clojure.lang.IEditableCollection coll))
```

Now that we've seen the benefits of transients and understand the limited scope within which they should be used, let's look at the finer details of their mechanics.

True to its name, a persistent collection used as the basis of a transient is unaffected:

```
(def v [1 2])
;= #'user/v
(def tv (transient v))
;= #'user/tv
(conj v 3)
;= [1 2 3]
```

On the other hand, turning a transient collection into a persistent one by using `persis` `tent!` makes the source transient unusable:[36]

```
(persistent! tv)
;= [1 2]
(get tv 0)
;= #<IllegalAccessError java.lang.IllegalAccessError:
;=   Transient used after persistent! call>
```

Both `transient` and `persistent!` return in constant time.

Transient collections support many of the access functions of their persistent parents, but not all:

```
(nth (transient [1 2]) 1)
;= 2
(get (transient {:a 1 :b 2}) :a)
;= 1
((transient {:a 1 :b 2}) :a)        ❶
;= 1
((transient [1 2]) 1)
;= 2
(find (transient {:a 1 :b 2}) :a)
;= #<CompilerException java.lang.ClassCastException:
;=   clojure.lang.PersistentArrayMap$TransientArrayMap
;=   cannot be cast to java.util.Map (NO_SOURCE_FILE:0)>
```

❶ Transients are functions too!

A notable exception is that `seq` is not supported on transients, the rationale being that a sequence can outlive its source, and transients cannot be relied upon to satisfy the guarantees that seqs make as persistent collections themselves.

However, none of the persistent update functions may be used with transients. Transients have their own update functions that, other than being dedicated for use with transients, perform the same operations as their namesakes: `conj!`, `assoc!`, `dissoc!`, `disj!`, and `pop!`.

All transient functions end with an exclamation mark to denote their invalidating behavior with regard to the collection passed as their first argument. Once you use any of these functions on a transient collection, *that collection should never be touched again*—even for read-only purposes. Just as you must always use the result of `conj` and `assoc` and `disj`, et al., in order to benefit from their effect, you must always use the result of their transient analogues. That is, you cannot bash transient collections in-place, or bad things happen:

```
(let [tm (transient {})]
  (doseq [x (range 100)]
    (assoc! tm x 0))        ❶
  (persistent! tm))
;= {0 0, 1 0, 2 0, 3 0, 4 0, 5 0, 6 0, 7 0}
```

---

36. Thus the exclamation point to indicate that `persistent!` is a destructive operation.

❶ Even though we `assoc!` 100 entries into the transient map, nearly all of them are lost because we are not using the result of `assoc!`.

Transients are intended to be used just like their persistent counterparts, with the additional restriction that prior revisions of a transient must not be used again. The easiest and safest way to use transients is to write normal Clojure code, add the required `transient` and `persistent!` calls, and tack exclamation marks at the end of functions that return modified transients. You still have to be sure that the linear use of transients is respected (that is, once modified, a transient is never used again). As we saw with `faster-into` earlier, reductions are perhaps the easiest operations to transform to use transients.

Because transients are solely an optimization, they should be used with discretion and strictly locally, usually local to a single function (or perhaps, local to a cluster of related private functions within a single library). Part of this good practice is enforced: there is a concurrency safeguard built into transients ensuring that only the thread that creates a given transient can ever use or modify it. We'll talk about concurrency in general in Chapter 4, but suffice it to say that `future` here will cause the `get` call to run in a different thread than the one that establishes the local binding `t` and creates the transient map:

```
(let [t (transient {})]
  @(future (get t :a)))
;= #<IllegalAccessError java.lang.IllegalAccessError:
;=   Transient used by non-owner thread>
```

Transients may be an effective optimization but they don't come for free: you have to restructure your code to follow their restrictions and work around their limited support of Clojure core functions. As with any optimization technique, you should analyze whether this is the best optimization strategy for your code, and once implemented, whether it's effective.

Transients don't compose.   Transients don't compose well; `persistent!` will not traverse a hierarchy of nested transients you may have created, so calling `persistent!` on the top level reference will not apply to subcollections:

```
(persistent! (transient [(transient {})]))
;= [#<TransientArrayMap clojure.lang.PersistentArrayMap$TransientArrayMap@b57b39f>]
```

In any case, because transients are mutable, they do not have value semantics and cannot be treated as such:

```
(= (transient [1 2]) (transient [1 2]))
;= false
```

This should drive home the point that transients and their mutability should not be let out to mix with collections with polite semantics. They are strictly a local optimization that you should keep hidden, like the proverbial falling tree that no one has a chance to hear.

Metadata

Metadata is data about other data. Metadata has many other names and takes many forms in other languages:

- Type declarations and access modifiers (like `private`, `protected`, and so on) are metadata about the values, variables, and functions with which they are associated.
- Java annotations are metadata about classes, methods, method arguments, and so on.

While metadata in Clojure *is* used for these particular purposes,[37] it is a much more generalized facility that you can use in your applications and with your data.

Metadata can be attached to any Clojure data structure, sequence, record, symbol, or reference type, and always takes the form of a map. There is a convenient reader syntax for declaratively attaching metadata to a value literal:

```
(def a ^{:created (System/currentTimeMillis)}
        [1 2 3])
;= #'user/a
(meta a)
;= {:created 1322065198169}
```

As a convenience, metadata that contains only slots whose keys are keywords and whose value is Boolean `true` can be provided in a short form, and can be additively "stacked" onto the next value being read:

```
(meta ^:private [1 2 3])
;= {:private true}
(meta ^:private ^:dynamic [1 2 3])
;= {:dynamic true, :private true}
```

There are `with-meta` and `vary-meta` functions that will update metadata associated with a given value:

```
(def b (with-meta a (assoc (meta a)
                       :modified (System/currentTimeMillis))))
;= #'user/b
(meta b)
;= {:modified 1322065210115, :created 1322065198169}
(def b (vary-meta a assoc :modified (System/currentTimeMillis)))
;= #'user/b
(meta b)
;= {:modified 1322065229972, :created 1322065198169}
```

37. See "Type Hinting for Performance" on page 366 for how metadata is used to provide type information to Clojure's compiler, "Vars" on page 198 for how metadata attached to vars can set access policy and concurrency semantics, and "Annotations" on page 381 for how metadata is used to apply Java annotations to Clojure types.

While `with-meta` replaces a value's metadata, `vary-meta` updates the metadata map that is already in place based on the update function (`assoc` above) and additional arguments to that function.

Remember, though, that metadata is data *about* other data. In other words, changing a value's metadata does not impact things like how the value prints or its equality (or inequality) with other values:

```
(= a b)
;= true
a
;= [1 2 3]
b
;= [1 2 3]
(= ^{:a 5} 'any-value
   ^{:b 5} 'any-value)
;= true
```

Of course, values that have metadata attached are just as immutable as those that don't; so, operations that "modify" data structures return new data structures that retain the original metadata:

```
(meta (conj a 500))
;= {:created 1319481540825}
```

This is far more useful compared to the handling of application-level metadata in other languages, where such information must be carefully kept isolated from the "real" data in an application, lest it improperly affect equality comparisons or not get carried along into updated values and aggregates. We already saw that things like creation and modification times can be held in metadata; consider also the tracking of provenance of data loaded from different sources, such as an authoritative database and a cache. We can decorate values representing data from these sources with different metadata without impacting their equality, and then use the metadata to determine how to treat those values: for example, what to do with requests to update a value loaded from the database versus a value loaded from cache.

Putting Clojure's Collections to Work

Why are data structures so important? In *The Mythical Man-Month*, Frederick Brooks says:

> Show me your flowchart and conceal your tables, and I shall continue to be mystified. Show me your tables, and I won't usually need your flowchart; it'll be obvious.

Two decades later, Eric Raymond modernized it into:

> Show me your code and conceal your data structures, and I shall continue to be mystified. Show me your data structures, and I won't usually need your code; it'll be obvious.

The way you structure and model your data determines the shape of your code; hence, you cannot write good functional Clojure code if you persist with old habits, modeling everything out of arrays, dedicated objects, and the occasional map.

Modeling data well in Clojure puts the focus on values (and particularly composite values), natural identifiers, and sets and maps. The mindset to adopt is akin to the one for relational[38] modeling. However, what constitutes a value is highly context-dependent: thanks to composite values, a value can be hierarchical, so it's up to the developer to define the granularity at which relationships are maintained.

Identifiers and Cycles

Natural identifiers are opposed to synthetic or surrogate identifiers, where the latter are usually strings or an artificially generated number, akin to sequences or autoincrements in databases or object references themselves in most object-oriented languages. Thus, synthetic identifiers are by definition artifacts of incidental complexity.

Without those middlemen, there is no need to maintain a canonical mapping of *things* to their *IDs*: either the "things" are different and, as values, are enough to identify themselves, or they are not. As a bonus, eliminating synthetic identifiers means that different threads or even processes no longer need to communicate to assign unique identifiers to chunks of data, because you can derive natural identifiers from the data at hand.

The debate of the respective virtues of synthetic keys versus natural keys is not new, but is still very much alive when it comes to database schema design. The arguments for synthetic identifiers revolve around two preoccupations: that data is going to survive the process that created it (and the rules it embodies), and that data is hard to refactor. The implication is that synthetic identifiers are of little use for in-process or otherwise application-level computation.

A typical example of unnecessary synthetic identifiers is the distinct states generated by parsers or regular expression engines. This generally involves mechanically numbering each parser or lexer state, while in Clojure you can construct complex valued states that fully describe themselves in a semantically significant way. Computing transitions from a state can then be done with a simple function, taking only the actual state as argument. In contrast to typical practice, there's no need to pass a separate mapping of states-as-numbers to data defining those states; *just the data is enough*.

You can still number states later on for efficiency reasons, but the two important lessons are that:

1. You are not required to.

---

38. The `clojure.set` namespace is an implementation of the relational algebra's operators.

2. You can perform the numbering or renaming in a separate step, cleanly separating concerns and complexities. This means that you can readily maintain multiple sets of synthetic identifiers if necessary, as is often required when working with data owned or affected by multiple interacting systems.

The only taboo in this picture is cycles: the only reasonable way to introduce them is through identifiers and indirection. Similarly, no cycles also means no back-references.

Cycles, values, and identities. Let's suppose we have an immutable tree node (e.g., a DOM node) that has `:parent-node` and `:children` slots. What happens to these slots when you "update" (create a new version of) this node? If you don't change the values under `:parent-node` and `:children`, then a roundtrip through these properties will get you back...to the old, unmodified value of the node, not the new one! Quite a problematic situation, one that must force you to modify the parent and child nodes to point to the updated node.

However, to be correct, this update must be propagated to all the nodes of the tree. One way out might be to use reference types, which we discuss in detail in "State and Identity" on page 168, for those properties. But this results in your tree no longer being an immutable value, and nodes will need to grow special logic to keep all those mutable references coherent. Welcome back to spaghetti mutations and incidental complexity!

Most of the time, cycles (a.k.a. back-references) are built into data structures for navigational purposes. Such cases are covered by paths or *zippers*, which we explore in "Navigation, Update, and Zippers" on page 151. The rest of the time, you'll have to add an indirection layer to introduce cycles.

This indirection layer can be plain reference types or IDs (used to look up into an index, usually a map). It may feel cumbersome at times, but breaking cycles in such a fashion forces you to ask important questions about which pieces of data are pure values and which deserve their own identifiers—and what those identifiers are for.[39] Those questions and their answers will save you time later when you share your data outside of your application, by sending it to the network, to the disk, to a database, or expose it as a service of some kind.

Thinking Different: From Imperative to Functional

We have already argued against numeric indices and promoted the use of sequences instead. However, despite being a nice abstraction, sequences are still linear and by themselves won't help you to think differently about problems and how to effectively solve them with Clojure data structures. You need to fully embrace programming with values, and use them to their fullest in order to get the most out of Clojure.

---

39. This questioning about identifying the identities of a system and their boundaries is closely related to the concerns of *domain-driven design*, explored in *Domain-Driven Design: Tackling Complexity in the Heart of Software* (Addison-Wesley Professional) by Eric Evans.

Revisiting a classic: Conway's Game of Life

Conway's Game of Life (*https://en.wikipedia.org/wiki/Conway%27s_Game_of_Life*) is the sort of algorithm that seems to beg for arrays. We will implement its rules here; first, in a traditional manner—the board will be a vector of vectors with each item being either :on or nil—and later in a more Clojure-idiomatic fashion, without the complexity (and restrictions) of indices.

```
(defn empty-board
  "Creates a rectangular empty board of the specified width
   and height."
  [w h]
  (vec (repeat w (vec (repeat h nil)))))
```

Now that we can create an empty board, we need to add some living cells to it:

```
(defn populate
  "Turns :on each of the cells specified as [y, x] coordinates."
  [board living-cells]
  (reduce (fn [board coordinates]
            (assoc-in board coordinates :on))
          board
          living-cells))

(def glider (populate (empty-board 6 6) #{[2 0] [2 1] [2 2] [1 2] [0 1]}))

(pprint glider)
; [[nil :on nil nil nil nil]
;  [nil nil :on nil nil nil]
;  [:on :on :on nil nil nil]
;  [nil nil nil nil nil nil]
;  [nil nil nil nil nil nil]
;  [nil nil nil nil nil nil]]
```

Now for the real meat of it: an indexed-step function, which takes a board's state, returning its successor according to the game's rules:

Example 3-6. Implementation and helpers for indexed-step

```
(defn neighbours
  [[x y]]
  (for [dx [-1 0 1] dy [-1 0 1] :when (not= 0 dx dy)]
    [(+ dx x) (+ dy y)]))

(defn count-neighbours
  [board loc]
  (count (filter #(get-in board %) (neighbours loc))))   ❶

(defn indexed-step
  "Yields the next state of the board, using indices to determine neighbors,
   liveness, etc."
  [board]
  (let [w (count board)
        h (count (first board))]
    (loop [new-board board x 0 y 0]
```

```
(cond
  (>= x w) new-board
  (>= y h) (recur new-board (inc x) 0)
  :else
    (let [new-liveness
            (case (count-neighbours board [x y])
              2 (get-in board [x y])
              3 :on
              nil)]
        (recur (assoc-in new-board [x y] new-liveness) x (inc y)))))))))
```

❶ Note that, because `count-neighbours` uses `get-in`—built on top of `get`, which as we have seen, returns `nil` for unknown indices—it will not throw any index-related errors.

Let's see how well this works:

```
(-> (iterate indexed-step glider) (nth 8) pprint)
; [[nil nil nil nil nil nil]
;  [nil nil nil nil nil nil]
;  [nil nil nil :on nil nil]
;  [nil nil nil nil :on nil]
;  [nil nil :on :on :on nil]
;  [nil nil nil nil nil nil]]
```

We now have a functioning implementation of Conway's Game of Life, with a nice glider there!

Let's see how you can rework this solution to avoid indices. The first step is to get rid of manual iteration. Each loop is replaced by a `reduce` over a range:

```
(defn indexed-step2
  [board]
  (let [w (count board)
        h (count (first board))]
    (reduce
      (fn [new-board x]
        (reduce
          (fn [new-board y]
            (let [new-liveness
                    (case (count-neighbours board [x y])
                      2 (get-in board [x y])
                      3 :on
                      nil)]
                (assoc-in new-board [x y] new-liveness)))
          new-board (range h)))
      board (range w))))
```

Nested reductions can always be collapsed to make code less noisy:

```
(defn indexed-step3
  [board]
  (let [w (count board)
        h (count (first board))]
    (reduce
      (fn [new-board [x y]]
```

```
(let [new-liveness
        (case (count-neighbours board [x y])
          2 (get-in board [x y])
          3 :on
          nil)]
      (assoc-in new-board [x y] new-liveness)))
    board (for [x (range h) y (range w)] [x y])))))
```

Now we have a loop-less version that nevertheless still uses indices.

It has been said and repeated that sequences replace indices, but our count-neighbours and neighbours functions depend heavily on indices to compute and access the neighbourhood of a cell. How can we express the concept of neighbourhood with sequences and without relying upon indices?

If we were working in only one dimension, it would be easy; just use partition:

```
(partition 3 1 (range 5))
;= ((0 1 2) (1 2 3) (2 3 4))
```

The result of partition here can be seen as a sequence of the items 1, 2, and 3 along with their neighbours. The only problem is that this code only create "windows" around items which have enough neighbours: entries for 0 and 4 and their neighbours are missing! We can fix this by padding the original collection:

```
(partition 3 1 (concat [nil] (range 5) [nil]))
;= ((nil 0 1) (0 1 2) (1 2 3) (2 3 4) (3 4 nil))
```

Let's factor this into a window function:

```
(defn window
  "Returns a lazy sequence of 3-item windows centered around each item of coll."
  [coll]
  (partition 3 1 (concat [nil] coll [nil])))
```

Now, how can we make the transition to two dimensions? Well, the trick is that when we apply this window function to a collection of n rows, we get n triples of 3 rows and each triple of 3 rows (of length m) can be transformed in a sequence of m triples; formally speaking this is a *transposition*. Applying window again to such a sequence yields a sequence of triples of triples, we can readily create 3 by 3 windows around each item.

Let's look at the code:

```
(defn cell-block
  "Creates a sequences of 3x3 windows from a triple of 3 sequences."
  [[left mid right]]
  (window (map vector
              (or left (repeat nil)) mid (or right (repeat nil)))))
```

The two or forms are there to replace the nil padding generated by window with repeating sequences of nil, because map stops as soon as one of its argument is empty.[40] We can simplify this code by allowing window to take an optional pad argument:

```
(defn window
  "Returns a lazy sequence of 3-item windows centered
  around each item of coll, padded as necessary with
  pad or nil."
  ([coll] (window nil coll))
  ([pad coll]
    (partition 3 1 (concat [pad] coll [pad])))))

(defn cell-block
  "Creates a sequences of 3x3 windows from a triple of 3 sequences."
  [[left mid right]]
  (window (map vector left mid right)))
```

We need to compute the liveness of the cell at the center of a block; that should probably be factored out as well, this time using destructuring to concisely separate a cell block into its constituent parts:

```
(defn liveness
  "Returns the liveness (nil or :on) of the center cell for
  the next step."
  [block]
  (let [[[_ [_ center _] _] block]
    (case (- (count (filter #{:on} (apply concat block)))
             (if (= :on center) 1 0))
      2 center
      3 :on
      nil)))
```

So, at last, we can reexpress the indexed-step function, now depending strictly upon index-free helper functions:

```
(defn- step-row
  "Yields the next state of the center row."
  [rows-triple]
  (vec (map liveness (cell-block rows-triple))))

(defn index-free-step
  "Yields the next state of the board."
  [board]
  (vec (map step-row (window (repeat nil) board))))
```

Even though index-free-step depends upon strictly index-free helper functions, it is equivalent to indexed-step:

```
(= (nth (iterate indexed-step glider) 8)
   (nth (iterate index-free-step glider) 8))
;= true
```

---

40. In other words, the result of a map is as long as the shortest of its arguments; so if one of the arguments is nil or empty, map will return an empty sequence.

Each step along the way may be simple, but the path from an "imperative" solution to a "sequential" one may be mind-bending the first couple of times you travel it.

Getting to the next level.   The problem with what we've done so far is that it stays close to the spirit of the original *implementation*. However, there's a way to find a far more elegant approach. For this to happen, we have to take a deep breath, step back, and really examine the rules for the Game of Life.

At each step in time, the following transitions occur:

- Any live cell with fewer than two live neighbours dies, as if caused by under-population.
- Any live cell with two or three live neighbours lives on to the next generation.
- Any live cell with more than three live neighbours dies, as if by overcrowding.
- Any dead cell with exactly three live neighbours becomes a live cell, as if by reproduction.

This expression of the rules does not mention rows, columns, or indices. It only talks about cells and neighbours; to be more precise, it talks about living cells, neighbours, and dead cells that are in the vicinity of living cells. Hence, the two main concepts are living cells and neighborhood: dead cells are neighbour cells that are not alive, so they can be derived from *neighbourhood* and *living cells*.

If we stick to these two concepts, *the only state of the world is the set of living cells*. To generate each successive state, we simply have to first compute all living cells' neighbours and then count how many times a given "neighbour cell" occurs (it occurs as many times as it has living neighbours).

If we try to translate this to Clojure, we end with:

Example 3-7. An elegant implementation of Conway's Game of Life

```
(defn step
 "Yields the next state of the world"
 [cells]
 (set (for [[loc n] (frequencies (mapcat neighbours cells))
            :when (or (= n 3) (and (= n 2) (cells loc)))]
        loc)))
```

And that's all! Only our original `neighbours` helper function is needed; no indexed, vector-of-vectors board, no limit to the size of the board for that matter, and the representation of the world is sparse—only the coordinates of living cells are represented explicitly.[41]

Let's try this new `step` on a glider pattern; the state of the world isn't a board anymore—just a set of the locations of living cells—but we can reuse the `populate` function to produce a delimited board that is easily visualized:

---

41. This is on par with array processing languages such as APL or J, despite the implementation being fundamentally different.

```
(->> (iterate step #{[2 0] [2 1] [2 2] [1 2] [0 1]}) ❶
  (drop 8)
  first
  (populate (empty-board 6 6))
  pprint)
; [[nil nil nil nil nil nil]
;  [nil nil nil nil nil nil]
;  [nil nil nil :on nil nil]
;  [nil nil nil nil :on nil]
;  [nil nil :on :on :on nil]
;  [nil nil nil nil nil nil]]
```

❶ Starting with the same glider pattern as before, we can see it drift by one unit every four steps as expected.

An interesting point is that the step in Example 3-7 uses the neighbours previously defined for the imperative indexed-step in Example 3-6. However, in the context of this solution, neighbours is *not* dealing with numerical indices into a concrete data structure anymore, but with coordinates: the [x y] pairs are opaque identifiers with regard to step while in the original imperative indexed-step, those pairs where built from indices by indexed-step itself.

Therefore, neighbours is now the sole part of this algorithm that cares about the content of the cell identifiers. As such, it defines the topology of the grid. By tweaking neigh bours, this code can be made to support finite grids, torus grids, hexgrids, N-dimensional grids, and so on, all without changing step. By letting go of our imperative mindset, we are left a much better separation of concerns and a clear solution that is very close to the expression of the problem that happens to be more generic.

We can easily make something really generic out of this step: a higher-order function, stepper, which acts as a factory for step functions.

```
(defn stepper
  "Returns a step function for Life-like cell automata.
   neighbours takes a location and return a sequential collection
   of locations. survive? and birth? are predicates on the number
   of living neighbours."
  [neighbours birth? survive?]
  (fn [cells]
    (set (for [[loc n] (frequencies (mapcat neighbours cells))
               :when (if (cells loc) (survive? n) (birth? n))]
           loc))))
```

Our step implementation is equivalent to the function returned by (stepper neighbours #{3} #{2 3}). This stepper HOF can accommodate different liveness rules and topologies as previously mentioned (hexagonal, 3D, finite, infinite, spherical, torus, mobius, and so on). For example, the Life-like automaton H.B2/S34 (with a hexagonal grid, birth for 2, survive when 3 or 4) is simply implemented as:

```
(defn hex-neighbours
  [[x y]]
  (for [dx [-1 0 1] dy (if (zero? dx) [-2 2] [-1 1])]
    [(+ dx x) (+ dy y)]))
```

```
(def hex-step (stepper hex-neighbours #{2} #{3 4}))

;= ; this configuration is an oscillator of period 4
(hex-step #{[0 0] [1 1] [1 3] [0 4]})
;= #{[1 -1] [2 2] [1 5]}
(hex-step *1)
;= #{[1 1] [2 4] [1 3] [2 0]}
(hex-step *1)
;= #{[1 -1] [0 2] [1 5]}
(hex-step *1)
;= #{[0 0] [1 1] [1 3] [0 4]}
```

So the four-line long stepper function is effectively a generic factory for all Life-like cell automata. This was possible not by getting rid of indices (since our sequence-based implementation wasn't generic) but by profoundly changing the data structures to use sets, natural identifiers, and maps (the frequency map). It is because of this focus on sets and natural identifiers that this solution can be said to be "relational."

There *is* a difference between step and indexed-step besides the generic use of data structures instead of concrete indices: the latter acts on a (finite) rectangular grid, while the former acts on an (infinite) planar grid. However, we can easily recreate index-step with stepper as well, assuming w and h are globally or locally bound to the width and height of the desired finite grid:

```
(stepper #(filter (fn [[i j]] (and (< -1 i w) (< -1 j h)))
          (neighbours %)) #{3} #{2 3})
```

Maze generation

Let's study another example: Wilson's maze generation algorithm.[42]

Wilson's algorithm is a carving algorithm; it takes a fully walled "maze" and carves an actual maze out of it by removing some walls. Its principle is:

1. Randomly pick a location and mark it as *visited*.
2. Randomly pick a location that isn't *visited* yet—if there's none, return the maze.
3. Perform a random walk starting from the newly picked location until you stumble on a location that is *visited*—if you pass through a location more than once during the random walk, always remember the direction you take to leave it.
4. Mark all the locations of the random walk as *visited*, and remove walls according to the last known "exit direction."
5. Repeat from 2.

---

42. For those interested in maze generators, there is a great illustrated blog post series by Jamis Buck at *http: //weblog.jamisbuck.org/2011/2/7/maze-generation-algorithm-recap*.

Generally, maze algorithms use a matrix to represent the maze, and each item of this matrix is a bitset indicating which walls are still up. The astute reader may twitch at the idea that in such a setup, as the state of a wall is stored twice: once in each location on each side of it.

Wilson's algorithm further requires you to remember the exit direction for each location, a source of further complexity when you try to cram everything into the bitset or "location state." These are some reasons why Wilson's algorithm is regarded as complex to implement; however, equipped with Clojure and "relational" modeling, we can minimize and eliminate much of that complexity with the help of sets, maps, and natural identifiers!

If we study the outline of this algorithm, we spot several entities: locations, the *visited* state, the maze itself, random walks, and exit directions. Let's see how to best represent them in Clojure.

At this point it should come to no surprise that a location should simply be represented by a vector of its coordinates, [x y].

If a location is reduced to its coordinates, how do you store that additional visited state? The answer is easy: this state is stored outside of locations because it does not belong in them; a location is just a (natural) identifier. Hence a *visited set* of locations is maintained.

The maze itself is made of walls, and a wall is between two locations, so a wall should be a pair of locations; [[0 0] [1 0]] would then denote the wall between the locations [0 0] and [1 0]. The problem is that [[1 0] [0 0]] represents the same wall. Since we are indifferent to the order of the locations in the pair, we should store them in a collection that is not ordered...like a set. #{[0 0] [1 0]} is thus a unique natural identifier for a single wall. A maze is a bunch of walls, and so naturally can be represented as a set of walls![43]

The representation of the walk is an easy one: a walk is just a sequence of locations. Here, *sequence* is used in its broadest sense: any sequential type fits the bill, including seqs, but vectors or lists would do as well.

Last, exit directions: an exit direction is from the exited location to the newly entered location, thus a direction is a pair of locations [from to]—unlike walls, the order of locations matters, so vectors are used.

Now that we have defined our data structures, we can jump to the code:

```
(defn maze
  "Returns a random maze carved out of walls; walls is a set of
   2-item sets #{a b} where a and b are locations.
   The returned maze is a set of the remaining walls."
  [walls]
```

---

43. A maze is then a set of two-item sets of locations. Don't let data structure vertigo makes your head spin: don't look into the depth of the nesting, think about only one level at a time.

```
(let [paths (reduce (fn [index [a b]]
                      (merge-with into index {a [b] b [a]}))
                  {} (map seq walls))
      start-loc (rand-nth (keys paths))]
  (loop [walls walls
         unvisited (disj (set (keys paths)) start-loc)]
    (if-let [loc (when-let [s (seq unvisited)] (rand-nth s))]
      (let [walk (iterate (comp rand-nth paths) loc)
            steps (zipmap (take-while unvisited walk) (next walk))]
        (recur (reduce disj walls (map set steps))
          (reduce disj unvisited (keys steps))))
      walls))))
```

❶ paths is an index (map) from locations to adjacent locations (as vectors, see ❻).

❷ (map seq walls) turns walls into sequences so that they can be destructured by [a b].[44]

❸ By construction, (keys path) contains all the locations, so rand-nth returns a random starting location for the walk.

❹ Instead of maintaining the *visited set*, we are using its complement, the *unvisited set*, because writing the code with *visited set* was a bit more complex; see ❺ and ❼.

❺ This call to seq serves two purposes: ensuring the set is not empty and providing a sequential view so rand-nth may be used. If *visited* locations had been used instead of *unvisited*, (seq unvisited) would need to be replaced by (seq (remove visited (keys paths))).

❻ (iterate (comp rand-nth paths) loc) generates an infinite random walk: it takes a location, applies paths on it to get the vector of adjacent locations and rand-nth to pick one. If paths had returned sets instead of a sequential type (like a vector), then (comp rand-nth seq paths) would have been necessary instead.

❼ (take-while unvisited walk) is the part of the random walk until (but not including) a visited location. (take-while unvisited walk) would be (take-while (complement visited) walk) if the code had been written with visited.

❽ (next walk) is infinite, but (take-while unvisited walk) is not, so zipmap only looks at the *n* first items of (next walk) (where *n* is (count (take-while unvisited walk))). The *n* first items of (next walk) is thus the random walk without the start location and including the first *visited* location. Since the two sequences are shifted by one, each key-value pair is going to be a *direction*. Creating a map out of these pairs will only retain the most recent direction for a given key, and therefore the last exit direction. *Entries of the resulting map are the last exit directions* for each location of the random walk.

❾ (map set steps) turn the directions (entries) into walls (sets) that we remove from the maze.

---

44. [& [a b]] is able to directly destructure sets but feels hacky.

To test this nice implementation, we need two utility functions: grid, which creates a fully walled maze, and draw, which renders the maze (in this case, to a Swing JFrame):

```
(defn grid
  [w h]
  (set (concat
         (for [i (range (dec w)) j (range h)] #{[i j] [(inc i) j]})
         (for [i (range w) j (range (dec h))] #{[i j] [i (inc j)]}))))

(defn draw
  [w h maze]
  (doto (javax.swing.JFrame. "Maze")
    (.setContentPane
      (doto (proxy [javax.swing.JPanel] []
              (paintComponent [^java.awt.Graphics g]
                (let [g (doto ^java.awt.Graphics2D (.create g)
                          (.scale 10 10)
                          (.translate 1.5 1.5)
                          (.setStroke (java.awt.BasicStroke. 0.4)))]
                  (.drawRect g -1 -1 w h)
                  (doseq [[[xa ya] [xb yb]] (map sort maze)]
                    (let [[xc yc] (if (= xa xb)
                                    [(dec xa) ya]
                                    [xa (dec ya)])]
                      (.drawLine g xa ya xc yc))))))
        (.setPreferredSize (java.awt.Dimension.
                             (* 10 (inc w)) (* 10 (inc h))))))
    .pack
    (.setVisible true)))

(draw 40 40 (maze (grid 40 40)))
```

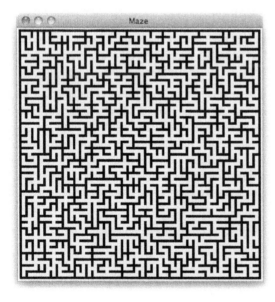

The True Wilson's Algorithm

Actually, we fibbed: `maze` is not exactly an implementation of Wilson's algorithm.

In our code, when the random walk reaches a location already in the graph (maze), we add a whole tree constituted by all the locations visited during the random walk instead of just the branch of this tree going from the starting point to the end location. Obviously, our algorithm is faster since it adds more locations to the maze at once. However, the selling point of Wilson's algorithm is that each maze has the same probability to be generated.

Empirical measures (looking at the maze distribution over samples generated by both Wilson's and our algorithms) hint that this property still holds in our variant, but we haven't proved it formally and we haven't computed its time complexity. This is left as an exercise to the reader.[45]

The interesting story behind this patent lie is that we literally stumbled on this algorithm: it was just easier to write in Clojure, it was begging to be written.

A true implementation of the Wilson's algorithm is not very different, it's only two extra lines:

```
(defn wmaze
  "The original Wilson's algorithm."
  [walls]
  (let [paths (reduce (fn [index [a b]]
                        (merge-with into index {a [b] b [a]}))
                {} (map seq walls))
        start-loc (rand-nth (keys paths))]
    (loop [walls walls unvisited (disj (set (keys paths)) start-loc)]
      (if-let [loc (when-let [s (seq unvisited)] (rand-nth s))]
        (let [walk (iterate (comp rand-nth paths) loc)
              steps (zipmap (take-while unvisited walk) (next walk))
              walk (take-while identity (iterate steps loc)) ❶
              steps (zipmap walk (next walk))]              ❷
          (recur (reduce disj walls (map set steps))
            (reduce disj unvisited (keys steps))))
        walls))))
```

❶ Retraces only one "branch" of the random walk, by starting over at `loc`.

❷ Turns this path into a map of [`from-loc to-loc`] entries.

Formally speaking, Wilson's algorithm generates random spanning trees of graphs. In the original paper,[46] the pseudocode, despite being imperative, uses sets and maps—but relies on synthetic identifiers (nodes are numbered). This implementation is still succinct and clear but has been forgotten by most programmers of maze generators.

---

45. We are interested in the answers though!

46. *Generating Random Spanning Trees More Quickly than the Cover Time* by David Bruce Wilson *http://citeseer.ist.psu.edu/viewdoc/summary?doi=10.1.1.47.8598.*

As a bonus, you may have noticed that, like step previously, maze is oblivious to what constitutes a location.[47] Consequently, maze works for any topology: hexagonal, N-dimensional, and so on. As an example of this genericity here is the grid generation and the rendering code for hexagonal mazes:

```
(defn hex-grid
  [w h]
  (let [vertices (set (for [y (range h) x (range (if (odd? y) 1 0) (* 2 w) 2)]
                        [x y]))
        deltas [[2 0] [1 1] [-1 1]]]
    (set (for [v vertices d deltas f [+ -]
               :let [w (vertices (map f v d))]
               :when w] #{v w}))))

(defn- hex-outer-walls
  [w h]
  (let [vertices (set (for [y (range h) x (range (if (odd? y) 1 0) (* 2 w) 2)]
                        [x y]))
        deltas [[2 0] [1 1] [-1 1]]]
    (set (for [v vertices d deltas f [+ -]
               :let [w (map f v d)]
               :when (not (vertices w))] #{v (vec w)}))))

(defn hex-draw
  [w h maze]
  (doto (javax.swing.JFrame. "Maze")
    (.setContentPane
      (doto (proxy [javax.swing.JPanel] []
              (paintComponent [^java.awt.Graphics g]
                (let [maze (into maze (hex-outer-walls w h))
                      g (doto ^java.awt.Graphics2D (.create g)
                          (.scale 10 10)
                          (.translate 1.5 1.5)
                          (.setStroke (java.awt.BasicStroke. 0.4
                                        java.awt.BasicStroke/CAP_ROUND
                                        java.awt.BasicStroke/JOIN_MITER)))
                      draw-line (fn [[[xa ya] [xb yb]]]
                                  (.draw g
                                    (java.awt.geom.Line2D$Double.
                                      xa (* 2 ya) xb (* 2 yb))))]
                  (doseq [[[xa ya] [xb yb]] (map sort maze)]
                    (draw-line
                      (cond
                        (= ya yb) [[(inc xa) (+ ya 0.4)] [(inc xa) (- ya 0.4)]]
                        (< ya yb) [[(inc xa) (+ ya 0.4)] [xa (+ ya 0.6)]]
                        :else [[(inc xa) (- ya 0.4)] [xa (- ya 0.6)]]))))))
        (.setPreferredSize (java.awt.Dimension.
                             (* 20 (inc w)) (* 20 (+ 0.5 h))))))
    .pack
    (.setVisible true)))

(hex-draw 40 40 (maze (hex-grid 40 40)))
```

47. As long as it's not a nil or a false.

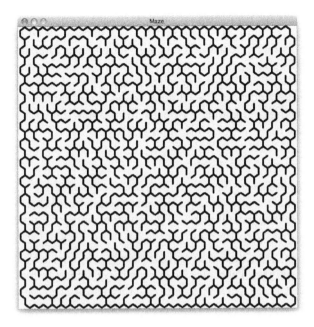

Porting maze to Java, Python, or Ruby is doable, but the result would be brittle since it would rely on mutable objects as values;[48] on such a limited example it may be fine, but on a large project it is difficult to marshal enough discipline to enforce. Alternatively, you can program defensively, and perform deep copies of input data—although this would incur inefficiencies at the module's boundaries. Those languages are *viscous* toward this solution while Clojure is *viscous* toward imperative solutions, insofar as its defaults and foundational capabilities enable implementations like these relative to other languages.

Generally, when you find the code you are writing painful or awkward, you are most certainly fighting the language, working against its grain. Chances are that in such cases you'll be able to find a more pleasant solution by rethinking your data structures. As Brooks's quote said, code follows from data modeling, so pleasant Clojure code flows from good data representation, which so often implies natural composite identifiers, sets, and maps.

Navigation, Update, and Zippers

Since immutability precludes back references, you cannot rely on them to navigate trees. A typical functional solution to this problem is *zippers*, an implementation of which can be found in the clojure.zip namespace.

---

48. This could be mitigated with extensive use of freeze in Ruby or unmodifiable wrappers as found in Java.

A zipper is not unlike Ariadne's thread, which helped Theseus to find his way out of the Labyrinth after having killed the Minotaur:[49] essentially, it is a stack of all nodes and node children we traverse. It is therefore a kind of cursor, both a navigation and an editing mechanism. You can move a zipper, examine the current node and position and update the tree at its current position, and then run back through your traversal path to obtain a reconstituted tree. And, just like Clojure's collections, zippers are persistent and immutable, so moving or updating a zipper returns a new zipper and does not modify the original or the tree it is operating upon.

Manipulating zippers

`clojure.zip` provides a generic `zipper` factory function and three more specialized ones: `seq-zip` for nested sequences, `vector-zip` for nested vectors, and `xml-zip` for XML data represented as per `clojure.xml`. We'll see later how to define a custom zipper; for now, our examples will use zippers created by `vector-zip`.

The basic functions to move a zipper are up (toward the root), down (toward the leaves), and left and right to move along siblings. There are also prev and next, which perform depth-first traversals, and leftmost and rightmost to move to the first or last sibling (but will not move the zipper if it is already at one extreme).

To examine the current position/node, `clojure.zip`'s functions include node, branch?, children, lefts, rights, and root, which respectively return: the current node, whether the current node is a branch,[50] the child nodes (for branches), and all of the left and right siblings of the current nodes. root is key when modifying a tree with zippers, since it is the only way to get an updated tree changed to cumulatively reflect all of the modifications made by the zipper since its creation.

```
(require '[clojure.zip :as z])

(def v [[1 2 [3 4]] [5 6]])
;= #'user/v
(-> v z/vector-zip z/node)
;= [[1 2 [3 4]] [5 6]]
(-> v z/vector-zip z/down z/node)
;= [1 2 [3 4]]
(-> v z/vector-zip z/down z/right z/node)
;= [5 6]
```

You can remove the current node, replace it with another, insert a child node at the front, or append it to the rear. More generally, you can edit a node. edit uses the uniform update model: in addition to the zipper, it takes a function f and extra arguments; the current node is then replaced by the result of applying f to itself and the extra arguments.

---

49. See *https://en.wikipedia.org/wiki/Ariadne* for the mythology.

50. A branch is a node that *may* have children: a branch can have no children.

You can also create a new node based on the current position of a zipper with make-node. However, this node won't be added to the final tree; for this to happen, you have to use one the above functions.

```
(-> v z/vector-zip z/down z/right (z/replace 56) z/node)
;= 56
(-> v z/vector-zip z/down z/right (z/replace 56) z/root)        ❶
;= [[1 2 [3 4]] 56]
(-> v z/vector-zip z/down z/right z/remove z/node)              ❷
;= 4
(-> v z/vector-zip z/down z/right z/remove z/root)
;= [[1 2 [3 4]]]
(-> v z/vector-zip z/down z/down z/right (z/edit * 42) z/root) ❸
;= [[1 84 [3 4]] [5 6]]
```

❶ z/vector-zip and z/root together act like boundaries of a "transaction."

❷ z/remove moves the zipper to the previous location in a depth-first walk.

❸ The 2 node is multiplied by 42.

That's nearly[51] all that is to know about the zipper API. We can now study how we can create custom zippers, and see how it can help us in our mazes.

Custom zippers

Zippers are in general created using the zipper function, which accepts three functions, followed by the root node of the structure to which the zipper will be applied:

- A predicate that returns true if a node *can* have children.
- A function that, given a branch node, returns a seq of its children.
- A function that returns a new branch node, given an existing node and a seq of children.

Let's try to implement a zipper for a custom data schema: vectors representing HTML elements. The first item is the tag name, the second may be the attributes map, and the remaining ones are children, including text nodes as strings. Hence [:h1 "zipper"] and [:a {:href "http://clojure.org/"} "Clojure"] are both valid nodes. This schema is just irregular enough to make its zipper implementation interesting:

```
(defn html-zip [root]
  (z/zipper
    vector?
    (fn [[tagname & xs]]
      (if (map? (first xs)) (next xs) xs))
    (fn [[tagname & xs] children]
      (into (if (map? (first xs)) [tagname (first xs)] [tagname])
        children))
    root))
```

51. We didn't mention end? to test when the end of a depth-first walk is reached.

On top of generic zipper functions, we can create helper domain-specific functions such as `wrap`:

```
(defn wrap
  "Wraps the current node in the specified tag and attributes."
  ([loc tag]
    (z/edit loc #(vector tag %)))
  ([loc tag attrs]
    (z/edit loc #(vector tag attrs %))))

(def h [:body [:h1 "Clojure"]
              [:p "What a wonderful language!"]])
;= #'user/h
(-> h html-zip z/down z/right z/down (wrap :b) z/root)
;= [:body [:h1 "Clojure"] [:p [:b "What a wonderful language!"]]]
```

Creating custom zippers for nested data structures is not difficult. However, we can also create read-only[52] zippers on hierarchical data stored in a nonhierarchical manner—for example, like the mazes we created in "Maze generation" on page 145. In such cases, the key is that the arguments to `zipper` are closures over the data structure, and nodes are the natural identifiers into that data structure.

Ariadne's zipper

Speaking of mazes and epic adventures, what about literally using a zipper as Ariadne's thread and helping Theseus use it to keep track of his traversal of the labyrinth?

To set the stage, we need a labyrinth:

```
(def labyrinth (maze (grid 10 10)))
```

But this labyrinth is full of walls while we are only interested in passages—or missing walls:

```
(def labyrinth (let [g (grid 10 10)] (reduce disj g (maze g))))
```

Let's add the characters:

```
(def theseus (rand-nth (distinct (apply concat labyrinth))))
(def minotaur (rand-nth (distinct (apply concat labyrinth))))
```

`[(rand-int 10) (rand-int 10)]` would have been effective but at the cost of introducing coupling between the `labyrinth` definition and the characters' locations.

At first glance, it may seem that a location is enough to identify the position of Theseus while he's searching for the minotaur. However, that's not enough: we have to remember where we came from so we can distinguish between the passages leading to new unvisited rooms and the one Theseus just came out from. We need a direction, which is best represented as a pair of locations.

So, our Ariadne's zipper is going to have directions as nodes:

---

52. Read-write is possible but more complex.

```
(defn ariadne-zip
  [labyrinth loc]
  (let [paths (reduce (fn [index [a b]]
                        (merge-with into index {a [b] b [a]}))
                  {} (map seq labyrinth))
        children (fn [[from to]]
                   (seq (for [loc (paths to)                    ❶
                              :when (not= loc from)]
                          [to loc])))]
    (z/zipper (constantly true)                                 ❷
      children
      nil                                                       ❸
      [nil loc])))                                              ❹
```

❶ zipper documentation requires the children function passed as argument to return a *seq* and not any sequential type, so seq should be called on its return value.

❷ We use (constantly true) as our branch predicate, since all locations potentially lead to other ones.

❸ nil is provided as the node factory function, since this zipper is purely navigational: it can't perform updates.

❹ [nil loc] is the initial direction, the root of Theseus's exploration.

Now we just have to perform a depth-first walk of the maze to find the path to the Minotaur:

```
(->> theseus
     (ariadne-zip labyrinth)
     (iterate z/next)
     (filter #(= minotaur (second (z/node %))))
     first z/path
     (map second))
([3 9] [4 9] [4 8] [4 7] [4 6] [5 7] [5 6] [5 5] [5 4]
 [5 8] [6 8] [6 7] [6 6] [6 5] [7 6] [8 6] [9 6] [9 5]
 [9 4] [9 3] [9 2] [9 1] [9 0] [8 2] [8 1] [8 0] [7 0]
 [6 0] [7 1] [7 2] [6 2] [6 1] [5 1] [4 1] [4 0] [5 0]
 [3 0] [4 2] [5 2] [3 2] [3 3] [4 3] [4 4] [4 5] [3 5])
```

After the minotaur is slaughtered, Theseus can thus find his way back to his starting point!

We can visualize the whole story; the first step is modifying draw to accommodate an extra argument: the actual path from Theseus to the Minotaur.

```
(defn draw
  [w h maze path]
  (doto (javax.swing.JFrame. "Maze")
    (.setContentPane
      (doto (proxy [javax.swing.JPanel] []
              (paintComponent [^java.awt.Graphics g]
                (let [g (doto ^java.awt.Graphics2D (.create g)
                          (.scale 10 10)
                          (.translate 1.5 1.5)
                          (.setStroke (java.awt.BasicStroke. 0.4)))]
```

```
            (.drawRect g -1 -1 w h)
            (doseq [[[xa ya] [xb yb]] (map sort maze)]
              (let [[xc yc] (if (= xa xb)
                             [(dec xa) ya]
                             [xa (dec ya)])]
                (.drawLine g xa ya xc yc)))
            (.translate g -0.5 -0.5)
            (.setColor g java.awt.Color/RED)
            (doseq [[[xa ya] [xb yb]] path]  ❶
              (.drawLine g xa ya xb yb)))))
        (.setPreferredSize (java.awt.Dimension.
                            (* 10 (inc w)) (* 10 (inc h)))))))
    .pack
    (.setVisible true)))
```

❶ The path is expected to be a collection of location pairs, so it differs from the path previously computed where only the locations were returned thanks to the (map second) step.

Now we can tell the whole mythical story, narrated and visualized in Clojure:

```
(let [w 40, h 40
      grid (grid w h)
      walls (maze grid)
      labyrinth (reduce disj grid walls)
      places (distinct (apply concat labyrinth))
      theseus (rand-nth places)
      minotaur (rand-nth places)
      path (->> theseus
             (ariadne-zip labyrinth)
             (iterate z/next)
             (filter #(= minotaur (first (z/node %))))
             first z/path rest)]  ❶
  (draw w h walls path))
```

❶ A rest replaces the (map second) because the first pair of locations is irregular from initializing ariadne-zip with [nil theseus].

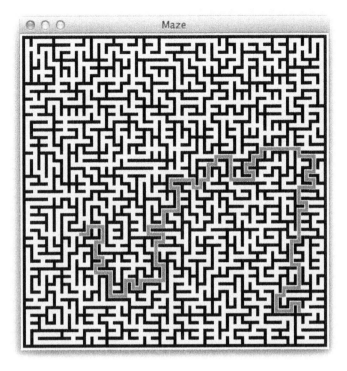

In Summary

Clojure's collection abstractions and data structure implementations sit at the very heart of the language and dictate its capabilities, character, and worldview more than nearly anything else. Understanding their semantics, mechanics, and idiomatic usage allows you to wring the most out of functional programming within Clojure on a daily basis, and enables you to better understand all the other parts of Clojure that depend upon them.

## CHAPTER 4

Concurrency and Parallelism

Writing multithreaded programs is one of the most difficult tasks many programmers will face. They are difficult to reason about, and often exhibit nondeterministic behavior: a typical program that utilizes concurrency facilities will sometimes yield different results given the same inputs, a result of ill-defined execution order that can additionally produce race conditions and deadlocks. Some of these conditions are hard to detect, and none of them are easy to debug.

Most languages give us paltry few resources to cope with the cognitive burden of concurrency. Threads and locks, in all their forms, are often the only real tools at our disposal, and we are often victims of how difficult they are to use properly and efficiently. In which order should locks be acquired and released? Does a reader have to acquire a lock to read a value another thread might be writing to? How can multithreaded programs that rely upon locks be comprehensively tested? Complexity spirals out of control in a hurry; meanwhile, you are left debugging a race condition that only occurs in production or a deadlock that happens on *this* machine, but not *that* one.

Considering how low-level they are, the continued reliance upon threads, locks, and pale derivatives as the sole "user-facing" solution to the varied complexities of concurrency is a remarkable contrast to the never-ending stampede of activity seen over the years in developing more effective and less error-prone abstractions. Clojure's response to this has many facets:

1. As we discussed in Chapter 2, minimize the amount of mutable state in your programs, with the help of immutable values and collections with reliable semantics and efficient operations.

2. When you do need to manage changing state over time and in conjunction with concurrent threads of execution, isolate that state and constrain the ways in which that state can be changed. This is the basis of Clojure's *reference types*, which we'll discuss shortly.

3. When you absolutely have no other choice—and are willing to shrug off the benefits of the semantic guarantees of Clojure's reference types—make it

straightforward to drop back to bare locks, threads, and the high-quality concurrency APIs provided by Java.

Clojure provides no silver bullet that makes concurrent programming instantly trivial, but it does provide some novel and now battle-tested tools to makes it far more tractable and reliable.

Shifting Computation Through Time and Space

Clojure provides a number of entities—delays, futures, and promises—that encapsulate discrete use cases for controlling when and how computations are performed. While only futures are solely concerned with concurrency, they are all often used to help implement specific concurrent semantics and mechanics.

Delays

A *delay* is a construct that suspends some body of code, evaluating it only upon demand, when it is dereferenced:

```
(def d (delay (println "Running...")
              :done!))
;= #'user/d
(deref d)
; Running...
;= :done!
```

 The deref abstraction is defined by Clojure's clojure.lang.IDeref interface; any type that implements it acts as a container for a value. It may be dereferenced, either via deref, or the corresponding reader syntax, @.[1] Many Clojure entities are dereferenceable, including delays, futures, promises, and all reference types, atoms, refs, agents, and vars. We talk about them all in this chapter.

You can certainly accomplish the same sort of thing just by using functions:

```
(def a-fn (fn []
            (println "Running...")
            :done!))
;= #'user/a-fn
(a-fn)
; Running...
;= :done!
```

However, delays provide a couple of compelling advantages.

---

1. @foo is nearly always preferred to (deref foo), except when using deref with higher-order functions (to, for example, dereference all of the delays in a sequence) or using deref's timeout feature, available only with promises and futures.

Delays only evaluate their body of code *once*, caching the return value. Thus, subsequent accesses using `deref` will return instantly, and not reevaluate that code:[2]

```
@d
;= :done!
```

A corollary to this is that multiple threads can safely attempt to dereference a delay for the first time; all of them will block until the delay's code is evaluated (only once!), and a value is available.

When you may want to provide a value that contains some expensive-to-produce or optional data, you can use delays as useful (if crude) optimization mechanisms, where the end "user" of the value can opt into the costs associated with that data.

Example 4-1. Offering opt-in computation with a delay

```
(defn get-document
  [id]
  ; ... do some work to retrieve the identified document's metadata ...
  {:url "http://www.mozilla.org/about/manifesto.en.html"
   :title "The Mozilla Manifesto"
   :mime "text/html"
   :content (delay (slurp "http://www.mozilla.org/about/manifesto.en.html"))})  ❶
;= #'user/get-document
(def d (get-document "some-id"))
;= #'user/d
d
;= {:url "http://www.mozilla.org/about/manifesto.en.html",
;=  :title "The Mozilla Manifesto",
;=  :mime "text/html",
;=  :content #<Delay@2efb541d: :pending>}                                        ❷
```

❶ We can use `delay` to cheaply suspend some potentially costly code or optional data.

❷ That `delay`'s code will remain unevaluated until we (or our code's caller) opt to dereference its value.

Some parts of our program may be perfectly satisfied with the metadata associated with a document and not require its content at all, and so can avoid the costs associated with retrieving that content. On the other hand, other parts of our application may absolutely require the content, and still others might make use of it *if it is already available*. This latter use case is made possible with `realized?`, which polls a delay to see if its value has been materialized yet:

```
(realized? (:content d))
;= false
@(:content d)
;= "<!DOCTYPE html><html>..."
(realized? (:content d))
;= true
```

---

2. And, therefore, not cause any potential side effects associated with the code provided to create the delay.

Note that `realized?` may also be used with futures, promises, and lazy sequences.

`realized?` allows you to immediately use data provided by a delay that has already been dereferenced, but perhaps opt out of forcing the evaluation of a delay if you know that doing so will be too expensive an operation than you're willing to allow at that point in time and can do without its eventual value.

Futures

Before getting to more sophisticated topics like reference types, Clojure programmers often start off asking, "How do I start a new thread and run some code in it?" Now, you can use the JVM's native threads if you *have* to (see "Using Java's Concurrency Primitives" on page 224), but Clojure provides a kinder, gentler option in futures.

A Clojure *future* evaluates a body of code in another thread:[3]

```
(def long-calculation (future (apply + (range 1e8))))
;= #'user/long-calculation
```

`future` returns immediately, allowing the current thread of execution (such as your REPL) to carry on. The result of evaluation will be retained by the future, which you can obtain by dereferencing it:

```
@long-calculation
;= 4999999950000000
```

Just like a delay, dereferencing a future will block if the code it is evaluating has not completed yet; thus, this expression will block the REPL for five seconds before returning:

```
@(future (Thread/sleep 5000) :done!)
;= :done!
```

Also like delays, futures retain the value their body of code evaluated to, so subsequent accesses via `deref` will return that value immediately.

Unlike delays, you can provide a timeout and a "timeout value" when dereferencing a future, the latter being what `deref` will return if the specified timeout is reached:[4]

```
(deref (future (Thread/sleep 5000) :done!)
       1000
       :impatient!)
;= :impatient!
```

---

3. `future-call` is also available if you happen to have a zero-argument function you'd like to have called in another thread.

4. This option is not available when using the @ reader sugar.

Futures are often used as a device to simplify the usage of APIs that perform some concurrent aspect to their operation. For example, say we knew that all users of the `get-document` function from Example 4-1 would need the `:content` value. Our first impulse might be to synchronously retrieve the document's `:content` within the scope of the `get-document` call, but this would make every caller wait until that content is retrieved fully, even if the caller doesn't need the content immediately. Instead, we can use a future for the value of `:content`; this starts the retrieval of the content in another thread right away, allowing the caller to get back to work without blocking on that I/O. When the `:content` value is later dereferenced for use, it is likely to block for less time (if any), since the content retrieval had already been in motion.

```
(defn get-document
  [id]
  ; ... do some work to retrieve the identified document's metadata ...
  {:url "http://www.mozilla.org/about/manifesto.en.html"
   :title "The Mozilla Manifesto"
   :mime "text/html"
   :content (future (slurp "http://www.mozilla.org/about/manifesto.en.html"))}) ❶
```

❶ The only change from Example 4-1 is replacing `delay` with `future`.

This requires no change on the part of clients (since they continue to be interested only in dereferencing the value of `:content`), but if callers are likely to always require that data, this small change can prove to be a significant improvement in throughput.

Futures carry a couple of advantages compared to starting up a native thread to run some code:

1. Clojure futures are evaluated within a thread pool that is shared with potentially blocking agent actions (which we discuss in "Agents" on page 209). This pooling of resources can make futures more efficient than creating native threads as needed.

2. Using `future` is much more concise than setting up and starting a native thread.

3. Clojure futures (the value returned by `future`) are instances of `java.util.concurrent.Future`, which can make it easier to interoperate with Java APIs that expect them.

Promises

Promises share many of the mechanics of delays and futures: a promise may be dereferenced with an optional timeout, dereferencing a promise will block until it has a value to provide, and a promise will only ever have one value. However, promises are distinct from delays and futures insofar as they are not created with any code or function that will eventually define its value:

```
(def p (promise))
;= #'user/p
```

promise is initially a barren container; at some later point in time, the promise may be fulfilled by having a value `delivered` to it:

```
(realized? p)
;= false
(deliver p 42)
;= #<core$promise$reify__1707@3f0ba812: 42>
(realized? p)
;= true
@p
;= 42
```

Thus, a promise is similar to a one-time, single-value pipe: data is inserted at one end via `deliver` and retrieved at the other end by `deref`. Such things are sometimes called *dataflow variables* and are the building blocks of *declarative concurrency*. This is a strategy where relationships between concurrent processes are explicitly defined such that derivative results are calculated on demand as soon as their inputs are available, leading to deterministic behavior. A simple example would involve three promises:

```
(def a (promise))
(def b (promise))
(def c (promise))
```

We can specify how these promises are related by creating a future that uses (yet to be delivered) values from some of the promises in order to calculate the value to be delivered to another:

```
(future
  (deliver c (+ @a @b))
  (println "Delivery complete!"))
```

In this case, the value of c will not be delivered until both a and b are available (i.e., `realized?`); until that time, the future that will `deliver` the value to c will block on dereferencing a and b. Note that attempting to dereference c (without a timeout) with the promises in this state will block your REPL thread indefinitely.

In most cases of dataflow programming, other threads will be at work doing whatever computation that will eventually result in the delivery of values to a and b. We can short-circuit the process by delivering values from the REPL;[5] as soon as both a and b have values, the future will unblock on dereferencing them and will be able to deliver the final value to c:

```
(deliver a 15)
;= #<core$promise$reify__5727@56278e83: 15>
(deliver b 16)
; Delivery complete!
;= #<core$promise$reify__5727@47ef7de4: 16>
@c
;= 31
```

---

5. Which, technically, *is* in another thread!

Promises don't detect cyclic dependencies

This means that (deliver p @p), where p is a promise, will block indefinitely.

However, such blocked promises are not locked down, and the situation can be resolved:

```
(def a (promise))
(def b (promise))
(future (deliver a @b))   ❶
(future (deliver b @a))

(realized? a)             ❷
;= false
(realized? b)
;= false

(deliver a 42)            ❸
;= #<core$promise$reify__5727@6156f1b0: 42>
@a
;= 42
@b
;= 42
```

❶ Futures are used there to not block the REPL.

❷ a and b are not delivered yet.

❸ Delivering a allows the blocked deliveries to resume—obviously (deliver a @b) is going to fail (to return nil) but (deliver b @a) proceeds happily.

An immediately practical application of promises is in easily making callback-based APIs synchronous. Say you have a function that takes another function as a callback:

```
(defn call-service
  [arg1 arg2 callback-fn]
  ; ...perform service call, eventually invoking callback-fn with results...
  (future (callback-fn (+ arg1 arg2) (- arg1 arg2))))
```

Using this function's results in a synchronous body of code requires providing a callback, and then using any number of different (relatively unpleasant) techniques to wait for the callback to be invoked with the results. Alternatively, you can write a simple wrapper on top of the asynchronous, callback-based API that uses a promise's blocking behavior on **deref** to enforce the synchronous semantics for you. Assuming for the moment that all of the asynchronous functions you're interested in take the callback as their last argument, this can be implemented as a general-purpose higher-order function:

```
(defn sync-fn
  [async-fn]
  (fn [& args]
    (let [result (promise)]
      (apply async-fn (conj (vec args) #(deliver result %&)))
      @result)))
```

```
((sync-fn call-service) 8 7)
;= (15 1)
```

Parallelism on the Cheap

We'll be examining all of Clojure's flexible concurrency facilities in a bit, one of which—agents—can be used to orchestrate very efficient parallelization of workloads. However, sometimes you may find yourself wanting to parallelize some operation with as little ceremony as possible.

Parallelism Versus Concurrency

Lest our discussion of concurrency and parallelism lead you to think they are the same thing, let's disentangle the two notions.

Concurrency is the coordination of multiple, usually interleaved threads of execution that are accessing or modifying some shared state.

Parallelism involves state as well, but usually in the inverse. Being an optimization technique used to efficiently utilize all of the available resources (usually computational, but sometimes other resources, like bandwidth) to improve the performance of an operation, approaches to parallelization generally aim to maximize the window of exclusive access to state (or, often, chunks of state) so as to minimize coordination overhead. Rather than involving interleaved threads of execution, the multiple evaluations of a parallelized operation run simultaneously—sometimes on different CPU cores, other times on different physical machines entirely.

The flexibility of Clojure's seq abstraction[6] makes implementing many routines in terms of processing sequences very easy. For example, say we had a function that uses a regular expression to find and return phone numbers found within other strings:

```
(defn phone-numbers
  [string]
  (re-seq #"(\d{3})[\.-]?(\d{3})[\.-]?(\d{4})" string))
;= #'user/phone-numbers
(phone-numbers " Sunil: 617.555.2937, Betty: 508.555.2218")
;= (["617.555.2937" "617" "555" "2937"] ["508.555.2218" "508" "555" "2218"])
```

Simple enough, and applying it to any seq of strings is easy, fast, and effective. These seqs could be loaded from disk using slurp and file-seq, or be coming in as messages from a message queue, or be the results obtained by retrieving large chunks of text from a database. To keep things simple, we can dummy up a seq of 100 strings, each about 1MB in size, suffixed with some phone numbers:

```
(def files (repeat 100
                   (apply str
```

---

6. Which we discussed in "Sequences" on page 89.

```
(concat (repeat 1000000 \space)
        "Sunil: 617.555.2937, Betty: 508.555.2218"))))
```

Let's see how fast we can get all of the phone numbers from all of these "files":

```
(time (dorun (map phone-numbers files)))  ❶
; "Elapsed time: 2460.848 msecs"
```

❶ We're using dorun here to fully realize the lazy seq produced by map and simultaneously release the results of that realization since we don't want to have all of the
found phone numbers printed to the REPL.

This is parallelizable though, and trivially so. There is a cousin of map—pmap – that will
parallelize the application of a function across a sequence of values, returning a lazy
seq of results just like map:

```
(time (dorun (pmap phone-numbers files)))  ❶
; "Elapsed time: 1277.973 msecs"
```

Run on a dual-core machine, this roughly doubles the throughput compared to the use
of map in the prior example; for this particular task and dataset, roughly a 4x improvement could be expected on a four-core machine, and so on. Not bad for a single-char-
acter change to a function name! While this might look magical, it's not; pmap is simply
using a number of futures—calibrated to suit the number of CPU cores available—to
spread the computation involved in evaluating phone-numbers for each file across each
of those cores.

This works for many operations, but you still must use pmap judiciously. There *is* a
degree of overhead associated with parallelizing operations like this. If the operation
being parallelized does not have a significant enough runtime, that overhead will dom-
inate the real work being performed; this can make a naive application of pmap *slower*
than the equivalent use of map:

```
(def files (repeat 100000
                   (apply str
                     (concat (repeat 1000 \space)
                             "Sunil: 617.555.2937, Betty: 508.555.2218"))))

(time (dorun (map phone-numbers files)))
; "Elapsed time: 2649.807 msecs"
(time (dorun (pmap phone-numbers files)))
; "Elapsed time: 2772.794 msecs"
```

The only change we've made here is to the data: each string is now around 1K in size
instead of 1MB in size. Even though the total amount of work is the same (there are
more "files"), the parallelization overhead outstrips the gains we get from putting each
evaluation of phone-numbers onto a different future/core. Because of this overhead, it is
very common to see speedups of something less than Nx (where N is the number of
CPU cores available) when using pmap. The lesson is clear: use pmap when the operation
you're performing is parallelizable in the first place, and is significant enough for each
value in the seq that its workload will eclipse the process coordination inherent in its

parallelization. Trying to force `pmap` into service where it's not warranted can be disastrous.

There is often a workaround for such scenarios, however. You can often efficiently parallelize a relatively trivial operation by *chunking* your dataset so that each unit of parallelized work is larger. In the above example, the unit of work is just 1K of text; however, we can take steps to ensure that the unit of work is larger, so that each value processed by `pmap` is a seq of 250 1K strings, thus boosting the work done per future dispatch and cutting down on the parallelization overhead:

```
(time (->> files
           (partition-all 250)
           (pmap (fn [chunk] (doall (map phone-numbers chunk))))  ❶
           (apply concat)
           dorun))
; "Elapsed time: 1465.138 msecs"
```

❶ `map` will return a lazy seq, so we use `doall` to force the realization of that lazy seq within the scope of the function provided to `pmap`. Otherwise, `phone-numbers` would never be called at all in parallel, leaving the work of applying it to each string to whatever process might have consumed the lazy seq later.

By changing the chunk size of our workload, we've regained the benefits of parallelization even though our per-operation computation complexity dropped substantially when applied to many more smaller strings.

Two other parallelism constructs are built on top of `pmap`: `pcalls` and `pvalues`. The former evaluates any number of no-arg functions provided as arguments, returning a lazy sequence of their return values; the latter is a macro that does the same, but for any number of expressions.

State and Identity

In Clojure, there is a clear distinction between *state* and *identity*. These concepts are almost universally conflated; we can see that conflation in its full glory here:

```
class Person {
    public String name;
    public int age;
    public boolean wearsGlasses;

    public Person (String name, int age, boolean wearsGlasses) {
        this.name = name;
        this.age = age;
        this.wearsGlasses = wearsGlasses;
    }
}

Person sarah = new Person("Sarah", 25, false);
```

Nothing particularly odd, right? Just a Java class[7] with some fields, of which we can create instances. Actually, the problems here are legion.

We have established a reference to a `Person`, meant to represent "`Sarah`", who is apparently 25 years old. Over time, Sarah has existed in many different states: Sarah as a child, as a teenager, as an adult. At each point in time—say, last Tuesday at 11:07 a.m.—Sarah has precisely *one* state, and each state in time is inviolate. It makes absolutely no sense to talk about changing one of Sarah's states. Her characteristics last Tuesday don't change on Wednesday; her state may change from one point in time to another, but that doesn't modify what she was previously.

Unfortunately, this `Person` class and low-level references (really, just pointers) provided by most languages are ill-suited to representing even this trivial—we might say fundamental—concept. If Sarah is to turn 26 years old, our only option is to clobber the particular state we have available:[8]

```
sarah.age++;
```

Even worse, what happens when a particular change in Sarah's state has to modify multiple attributes?

```
sarah.age++;
sarah.wearsGlasses = true;
```

At any point in time between the execution of these two lines of code, Sarah's age has been incremented, but she does not yet wear glasses. For some period of time (technically, an indeterminate period of time given the way modern processor architectures and language runtimes operate), Sarah may exist in an inconsistent state that is factually and perhaps semantically impossible, depending on our object model. This is the stuff that race conditions are made of, and a key motivator of deadlock-prone locking strategies.

Note that we can even change this `sarah` object to represent a completely different person:

```
sarah.name = "John";
```

This is troublesome. The `sarah` object does not represent a single state of Sarah, nor even the concept of Sarah as an identity. Rather, it's an unholy amalgam of the two. More generally, we cannot make any reliable statements about prior states of a `Person` reference, particular instances of `Person` are liable to change at any time (of particular concern in programs with concurrent threads of execution), and not only is it easy to put instances into inconsistent states, *it is the default.*

---

7. Note that this discussion is by no means limited to Java. Many—really, nearly all—other languages conflate state and identity, including Ruby, Python, C#, Perl, PHP, and so on.

8. Don't get hung up on the lack of accessors and such; whether you work with fields or getters and setters has no impact on the semantics involved.

The Clojure approach.   What we really want to be able to say is that Sarah has an *identity* that represents her; not her at any particular point in time, but her as a logical entity throughout time. Further, we want to be able to say that that identity can have a particular *state* at any point in time, but that each state transition does not change history; thinking back to "On the Importance of Values" on page 52 and the contrast between mutable objects and immutable values, this characterization of state would seem to carry many practical benefits as well as being semantically more sound. After all, in addition to wanting to ensure that a state of some identity is never internally inconsistent (something guaranteed by using immutable values), we may very well want to be able to easily and safely refer to Sarah as she was last Tuesday or last year.

Unlike most objects, Clojure data structures are immutable. This makes them ideal for representing state:

```
(def sarah {:name "Sarah" :age 25 :wears-glasses? false})
;= #'user/sarah
```

The map we store in the `sarah` var is one state of Sarah at some point in time. Because the map is immutable, we can be sure that any code that holds a reference to that map will be able to safely use it for all time regardless of what changes are made to other versions of it or to the state held by the var. The var itself is one of Clojure's *reference types*, essentially a container with defined concurrency and change semantics that can hold any value, and be used as a stable identity. So, we can say that Sarah is represented by the `sarah` var, the state of which may change over time according to the var's semantics.

This is just a glimpse of how Clojure treats identity and state and how they relate over time as distinct concepts worthy of our attention.[9] The rest of this chapter will be devoted to exploring the mechanics of that treatment. In large part, this will consist of exploring Clojure's four reference types, each of which implement different yet well-defined semantics for changing state over time. Along with Clojure's emphasis on immutable values, these reference types and their semantics make it possible to design concurrent programs that take maximum advantage of the increasingly capable hardware we have available to us, while eliminating entire categories of bugs and failure conditions that would otherwise go with the territory of dealing with bare threads and locks.

Clojure Reference Types

Identities are represented in Clojure using four reference types: `vars`, `refs`, `agents`, and `atoms`. All of these are very different in certain ways, but let's first talk about what they have in common.

---

9. Rich Hickey gave a talk in 2009 on the ideas of identity, state, and time and how they informed the design of Clojure. We highly recommend you watch the video of that talk: *http://www.infoq.com/presentations/ Are-We-There-Yet-Rich-Hickey*.

At their most fundamental level, references are just boxes that hold a value, where that value can be changed by certain functions (different for each reference type):

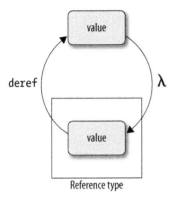

Reference type

All references always contain *some* value (even if that value is `nil`); accessing one is always done using `deref` or `@`:

```
@(atom 12)
;= 12
@(agent {:c 42})
;= {:c 42}
(map deref [(agent {:c 42}) (atom 12) (ref "http://clojure.org") (var +)])
;= ({:c 42} 12 "http://clojure.org" #<core$_PLUS_ clojure.core$_PLUS_@65297549>)
```

Dereferencing will return a *snapshot* of the state of a reference when `deref` was invoked. This doesn't mean there's copying of any sort when you obtain a snapshot, simply that the returned state—assuming you're using immutable values for reference state, like Clojure's collections—is inviolate, but that the reference's state at later points in time may be different.

One critical guarantee of `deref` within the context of Clojure's reference types is that `deref` *will never block*, regardless of the change semantics of the reference type being dereferenced or the operations being applied to it in other threads of execution. Similarly, dereferencing a reference type will never interfere with other operations. This is in contrast with delays, promises, and futures—which can block on `deref` if their value is not yet realized—and most concurrency primitives in other languages, where readers are often blocked by writers and vice versa.

"Setting" the value of a reference type is a more nuanced affair. Each reference type has its own semantics for managing change, and each type has its own family of functions for applying changes according to those semantics. Talking about those semantics and their corresponding functions will form the bulk of the rest of our discussion.

In addition to all being dereferenceable, all reference types:

- May be decorated with metadata (see "Metadata" on page 135). Rather than using `with-meta` or `vary-meta`, metadata on reference types may only be changed with `alter-meta!`, which modifies a reference's metadata in-place.[10]
- Can notify functions you specify when the their state changes; these functions are called *watches*, which we discuss in "Watches" on page 176.
- Can enforce constraints on the state they hold, potentially aborting change operations, using *validator* functions (see "Validators" on page 178).

Classifying Concurrent Operations

In thinking about Clojure's reference types, we'll repeatedly stumble across a couple of key concepts that can be used to characterize concurrent operations. Taken together, they can help us think clearly about how each type is best used.

Coordination.   A *coordinated* operation is one where multiple actors must cooperate (or, at a minimum, be properly sequestered so as to not interfere with each other) in order to yield correct results. A classic example is any banking transaction: a process that aims to transfer monies from one account to another must ensure that the credited account not reflect an increased balance prior to the debited account reflecting a decreased balance, and that the transaction fail entirely if the latter has insufficient funds. Along the way, many other processes may provoke similar transactions involving the same accounts. Absent methods to coordinate the changes, some accounts could reflect incorrect balances for some periods, and transactions that should have failed (or should have succeeded) would succeed (or fail) improperly.

In contrast, an *uncoordinated* operation is one where multiple actors cannot impact each other negatively because their contexts are separated. For example, two different threads of execution can safely write to two different files on disk with no possibility of interfering with each other.

Synchronization.   *Synchronous* operations are those where the caller's thread of execution waits or blocks or sleeps until it may have exclusive access to a given context, whereas *asynchronous* operations are those that can be started or scheduled without blocking the initiating thread of execution.

Just these two concepts (or, four, if you count their duals) are sufficient to fully characterize many (if not most) concurrent operations you might encounter. Given that, it makes sense that Clojure's reference types were designed to implement the semantics necessary to address permutations of these concepts, and that they can be conveniently classified according to the types of operations for which each is suited:[11]

---

10. `atom`, `ref`, and `agent` all accept an optional `:meta` keyword argument, allowing you to provide an initial metadata map when creating those references.

11. Vars do not fit into this particular classification; their primary mode of change is thread-local, and thus are orthogonal to notions of coordination or synchronization.

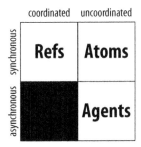

	coordinated	uncoordinated
synchronous	**Refs**	**Atoms**
asynchronous		**Agents**

When choosing which reference type(s) to use for a given problem, keep this classification in mind; if you can characterize a particular problem using it, then the most appropriate reference type will be obvious.

You'll notice that none of Clojure's reference types are slated as implementing coordinated and asynchronous semantics. This combination of characteristics is more common in distributed systems, such as eventually consistent databases where changes are only guaranteed to be merged into a unified model over time. In contrast, Clojure is fundamentally interested in addressing in-process concurrency and parallelism.

A Demonstration Utility

In order to demonstrate concurrency understandably, we'll be using a couple of helpers in this chapter's examples. `futures` is a macro that produces code that creates n futures for each expression provided to the macro to be evaluated:

```
(defmacro futures
  [n & exprs]
  (vec (for [_ (range n)
             expr exprs]
         `(future ~expr))))
```

This gives us an easy way to evaluate expressions on different threads. However, `futures` forms will themselves evaluate to a vector of the created futures. This could be handy in other contexts, but we'll always want to wait for all of the futures to complete, so we can be sure our expressions have all finished evaluating. So, another helper, `wait-futures`, will provide the same capabilities as `futures`, but will always return `nil` and will block our REPL until the futures are all realized:

```
(defmacro wait-futures
  [& args]
  `(doseq [f# (futures ~@args)]
     @f#))
```

We've not talked much about macros yet, so it's okay if you don't quite understand how these helpers work; don't worry, we'll discuss macros in detail in Chapter 5.

Atoms

Atoms are the most basic reference type; they are identities that implement synchronous, uncoordinated, atomic *compare-and-set* modification. Thus, operations that modify the state of atoms block until the modification is complete, and each modification is isolated—on their own, there is no way to orchestrate the modification of two atoms.

Atoms are created using `atom`. `swap!` is the most common modification operation used with them, which sets the value of an atom to the result of applying some function to the atom's value and any additional arguments provided to `swap!`:

```
(def sarah (atom {:name "Sarah" :age 25 :wears-glasses? false}))
;= #'user/sarah
(swap! sarah update-in [:age] + 3)                              ❶
;= {:age 28, :wears-glasses? false, :name "Sarah"}              ❷
```

❶ Here, when `swap!` returns, the value held by the `sarah` atom will have been set to the result of `(update-in @sarah [:age] + 3)`.

❷ `swap!` always returns the new value that was swapped into the atom.

Atoms are the minimum we need to do right by Sarah: every modification of an atom occurs atomically, so it's safe to apply any function or composition of functions to an atom's value. You can be sure that no other threads of execution will ever see an atom's contents in an inconsistent or partially applied state:

```
(swap! sarah (comp #(update-in % [:age] inc)
                   #(assoc % :wears-glasses? true)))
;= {:age 29, :wears-glasses? true, :name "Sarah"}
```

One thing you must keep in mind when using `swap!` is that, because atoms use compare-and-set semantics, if the atom's value changes before your `update` function returns (as a result of action by another thread of execution), `swap!` will retry, calling your update function again with the atom's newer value. `swap!` will continue to retry the compare-and-set until it succeeds:

```
(def xs (atom #{1 2 3}))
;= #'user/xs
(wait-futures 1 (swap! xs (fn [v]
                            (Thread/sleep 250)
                            (println "trying 4")
                            (conj v 4)))
                (swap! xs (fn [v]
                            (Thread/sleep 500)
                            (println "trying 5")
                            (conj v 5))))
;= nil
; trying 4
; trying 5      ❶
; trying 5
@xs
;= #{1 2 3 4 5}
```

---

❶ The thread of execution that aimed to conj 5 into the set held in xs ended up retrying the application of the function passed to swap!; while it was sleeping, the other thread was able to modify the atom (conjing 4 into the set), so the compare-and-set failed the first time.

We can visualize the retry semantics of swap! like so:

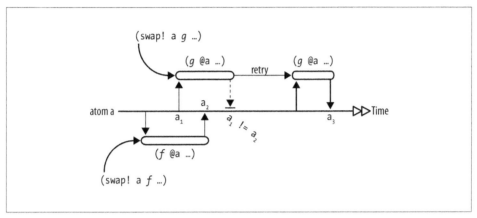

Figure 4-1. Interaction of conflicting swap! operations on a shared atom

If the value of atom a changes between the time when function g is invoked and the time when it returns a new value for a (a_1 and a_2, respectively), swap! will discard that new value and reevaluate the call with the latest available state of a. This will continue until the return value of g can be set on a as the immediate successor of the state of a with which it was invoked.

There is no way to constrain swap!'s retry semantics; given this, the function you provide to swap! *must* be pure, or things will surely go awry in hard-to-predict ways.

Being a synchronous reference type, functions that change atom values do not return until they have completed:

```
(def x (atom 2000))
;= #'user/x
(swap! x #(Thread/sleep %))    ❶
;= nil
```

❶ This expression takes at least two seconds to return.

A "bare" compare-and-set! operation is also provided for use with atoms, if you already think you know what the value of the atom being modified is; it returns true only if the atom's value was changed:

```
(compare-and-set! xs :wrong "new value")
;= false
(compare-and-set! xs @xs "new value")
;= true
```

```
@xs
;= "new value"
```

 `compare-and-set!` does *not* use value semantics; it requires that the value in the atom be identical[12] to the expected value provided to it as its second argument:

```
(def xs (atom #{1 2}))
;= #'user/xs
(compare-and-set! xs #{1 2} "new value")
;= false
```

Finally, there is a "nuclear option": if you want to set the state of an atom without regard for what it contains currently, there is `reset!`:

```
(reset! xs :y)
;= :y
@xs
;= :y
```

Now that we know about atoms, this is a good time to look at two facilities that all reference types support, since some later examples will use them.

Notifications and Constraints

We already learned about one common operation in "Clojure Reference Types" on page 170—dereferencing—which allows us to obtain the current value of a reference regardless of its particular type. There are certain other common things you'll sometimes want to do with every type of reference that involve being able to monitor or validate state changes as they happen. All of Clojure's reference types provide hooks for these, in the form of *watches* and *validators*.

Watches

Watches are functions that are called whenever the state of a reference has changed. If you are familiar with the "observer" design pattern, you will recognize the applicable use cases immediately, although watches are decidedly more general: a watch can be registered with any reference type, and all watches are functions—there are no special interfaces that must be implemented, and the notification machinery is provided for you.

All reference types start off with no watches, but they can be registered and removed at any time. A watch function must take four arguments: a key, the reference that's changed (an atom, ref, agent, or var), the old state of the reference, and its new state:

```
(defn echo-watch                              ❶
  [key identity old new]
```

12. As defined by `identical?`; see "Object Identity (identical?)" on page 433.

```
  (println key old "=>" new))
;= #'user/echo-watch
(def sarah (atom {:name "Sarah" :age 25}))
;= #'user/sarah
(add-watch sarah :echo echo-watch)
;= #<Atom@418bbf55: {:name "Sarah", :age 25}>
(swap! sarah update-in [:age] inc)
; :echo {:name Sarah, :age 25} => {:name Sarah, :age 26}
;= {:name "Sarah", :age 26}
(add-watch sarah :echo2 echo-watch)                          ❷
;= #<Atom@418bbf55: {:name "Sarah", :age 26}>
(swap! sarah update-in [:age] inc)                           ❸
; :echo {:name Sarah, :age 26} => {:name Sarah, :age 27}
; :echo2 {:name Sarah, :age 26} => {:name Sarah, :age 27}
;= {:name "Sarah", :age 27}
```

❶ Our watch function prints to stdout every time the atom's state may have changed.

❷ If we add the same watch function under a new key...

❸ It'll now be called twice for each state change.

 Watch functions are called synchronously on the same thread that effected the reference's state change in question. This means that, by the time your watch function has been called, the reference it is attached to could have been updated *again* from another thread of execution. Thus, you should rely only on the "old" and "new" values passed to the watch function, rather than dereferencing the host ref, agent, atom, or var.

The key you provide to **add-watch** can be used to remove the watch later on:

```
(remove-watch sarah :echo2)
;= #<Atom@418bbf55: {:name "Sarah", :age 27}>
(swap! sarah update-in [:age] inc)
; :echo {:name Sarah, :age 27} => {:name Sarah, :age 28}
;= {:name "Sarah", :age 28}
```

Note that watches on a reference type are called whenever the reference's state has been modified, but this does not guarantee that the state is *different*:

```
(reset! sarah @sarah)
; :echo {:name Sarah, :age 28} => {:name Sarah, :age 28}
;= {:name "Sarah", :age 28}
```

Thus, it's common for watch functions to check if the old and new states of the watched reference are equal before proceeding.

Generally speaking, watches are a great mechanism for triggering the propagation of local changes to other references or systems as appropriate. For example, they make it dead easy to keep a running log of a reference's history:

```
(def history (atom ()))

(defn log->list
  [dest-atom key source old new]
```

```
      (when (not= old new)
        (swap! dest-atom conj new)))

   (def sarah (atom {:name "Sarah", :age 25}))
   ;= #'user/sarah
   (add-watch sarah :record (partial log->list history))  ❶
   ;= #<Atom@5143f787: {:age 25, :name "Sarah"}>
   (swap! sarah update-in [:age] inc)
   ;= {:age 26, :name "Sarah"}
   (swap! sarah update-in [:age] inc)
   ;= {:age 27, :name "Sarah"}
   (swap! sarah identity)                                  ❷
   ;= {:age 27, :name "Sarah"}
   (swap! sarah assoc :wears-glasses? true)
   ;= {:age 27, :wears-glasses? true, :name "Sarah"}
   (swap! sarah update-in [:age] inc)
   ;= {:age 28, :wears-glasses? true, :name "Sarah"}
   (pprint @history)
   ;= ;= nil
   ;= ; ({:age 28, :wears-glasses? true, :name "Sarah"}
   ;= ;   {:age 27, :wears-glasses? true, :name "Sarah"}
   ;= ;   {:age 27, :name "Sarah"}
   ;= ;   {:age 26, :name "Sarah"})
```

❶ We use partial here to bind in the atom to which the watch function will always log history.

❷ Since identity always returns its sole argument unchanged, this swap! will result in a state change in the reference, but the old and new states will be equal. log->list only adds an entry if the new state is different, so this "repeated" state will not appear in the history.

Depending on how clever you get in your use of watches, you can also make the behavior of the watch function vary depending upon the key it's registered under. A simple example would be a watch function that logged changes, not to an in-memory sink but to a database identified by its registered key:

```
(defn log->db
  [db-id identity old new]
  (when (not= old new)
    (let [db-connection (get-connection db-id)]
      ...)))

(add-watch sarah "jdbc:postgresql://hostname/some_database" log->db)
```

We'll combine watches with refs and agents to great effect in "Persisting reference states with an agent-based write-behind log" on page 215.

Validators

Validators enable you to constrain a reference's state however you like. A validator is a function of a single argument that is invoked just before any *proposed* new state is installed into a reference. If the validator returns logically false or throws an exception, then the state change is aborted with an exception.

A proposed change is the result of any change function you attempt to apply to a reference. For example, the map of sarah that has had its :age slot incremented, but before swap! installs that updated state into the reference. It is at this point that a validator function—if any has been set on the affected reference—has a chance to veto it.

```
(def n (atom 1 :validator pos?))
;= #'user/n
(swap! n + 500)
;= 501
(swap! n - 1000)
;= #<IllegalStateException java.lang.IllegalStateException: Invalid reference state>
```

Because validator functions take a single argument, you can readily use any applicable predicate you might have available already, like pos?.

While all reference types may have a validator associated with them, atoms, refs, and agents may be *created* with them by providing the validator function as a :validator option to atom, ref, or agent. To add a validator to a var, or to change the validator associated with an atom, ref, or agent, you can use the set-validator! function:

```
(def sarah (atom {:name "Sarah" :age 25}))
;= #'user/sarah
(set-validator! sarah :age)
;= nil
(swap! sarah dissoc :age)
;= #<IllegalStateException java.lang.IllegalStateException: Invalid reference state>
```

You can make the message included in the thrown exception more helpful by ensuring that the validator you use throws its own exception, instead of simply returning false or nil upon a validation failure:[13]

```
(set-validator! sarah #(or (:age %)           ❶
                      (throw (IllegalStateException. "People must have `:age`s!"))))
;= nil
(swap! sarah dissoc :age)
;= #<IllegalStateException java.lang.IllegalStateException: People must have `:age`s!>
```

❶ Remember that validators must return a logically true value, or the state change will be vetoed. In this case, if we implemented the validator using, for example, #(when-not (:age %) (throw ...)), the validator would return nil when the state *did* have an :age slot, thus causing an unintentional validation failure.

While validators are very useful in general, they hold a special status with regard to refs, as we'll learn about next and in particular in "Enforcing local consistency by using validators" on page 189.

---

13. Alternatively, you can use a library like Slingshot to throw *values*, instead of encoding useful information in a paltry string: *https://github.com/scgilardi/slingshot*.

Refs

Refs are Clojure's coordinated reference type. Using them, you can ensure that multiple identities can participate in overlapping, concurrently applied operations with:

- No possibility of the involved refs ever being in an observable inconsistent state
- No possibility of race conditions among the involved refs
- No manual use of locks, monitors, or other low-level synchronization primitives
- No possibility of deadlocks

This is made possible by Clojure's implementation of *software transactional memory*, which is used to manage all change applied to state held by refs.

Software Transactional Memory

In general terms, software transactional memory (STM) is any method of coordinating multiple concurrent modifications to a shared set of storage locations. Doing this in nearly any other language means you have to take on the management of locks yourself, accepting all that comes along with them. STM offers an alternative.

Just as garbage collection has largely displaced the need for manual memory management—eliminating a wide range of subtle and not-so-subtle bugs associated with it in the process—so has STM often been characterized as providing the same kind of systematic simplification of another error-prone programming practice, manual lock management. In both instances, using a proven, automated solution to address what is otherwise an error-prone manual activity both frees you from having to develop expertise in low-level details unrelated to your domain, and often produces end results with more desirable runtime characteristics than those attainable by experts in those low-level details.[14]

Clojure's STM is implemented using techniques that have been relied upon by database management systems for decades.[15] As the name implies, each change to a set of refs has transactional semantics that you are sure to be familiar with from your usage of databases; each STM transaction ensures that changes to refs are made:

1. *Atomically*, so that all the changes associated with a transaction are applied, or none are.
2. *Consistently*, so that a transaction will fail if the changes to affected refs do not satisfy their respective constraints.

---

14. Modern garbage collection implementations can enable programs to outperform alternatives written using manual memory management in many contexts; and, each time a new garbage collector implementation or optimization is added to the JVM, every program everywhere benefits from it without any involvement from individual programmers. The same dynamic has played out with Clojure's STM.

15. In particular, *multiversion concurrency control* (often abbreviated *MVCC*): *https://en.wikipedia.org/wiki/ Multiversion_concurrency_control*.

3. In *isolation*, so that an in-process transaction does not affect the states of involved refs as observed from within other transactions or other threads of execution in general.

Clojure's STM therefore satisfies the A, C, and I properties of ACID (*https://en.wikipedia.org/wiki/ACID*), as you may understand it from the database world. The "D" property, durability, is not something that the STM is concerned with since it is purely an in-memory implementation.[16]

The Mechanics of Ref Change

With that background out of the way, let's see what refs can do for us. Earlier in "Classifying Concurrent Operations" on page 172, we talked about banking transactions being an example of an operation that requires coordination among multiple identities and threads of execution. While this is true, banking is perhaps an overwrought example when it comes to demonstrating transactional semantics. It might be more enlightening (and entertaining!) to explore refs and Clojure's STM as an ideal foundation for implementing a multiplayer game engine.

While some problems are rightfully described as "embarrassingly parallel" because of their potential to be parallelized given suitable facilities, we can say that multiplayer games are embarrassingly concurrent: the datasets involved are often massive, and it's possible to have hundreds or thousands of independent players each provoking changes that must be applied in a coordinated, consistent fashion so as to ensure the game's rules are reliably enforced.

Our "game"[17] will be in the fantasy/role-playing genre, the sort that contains classes like wizards and rangers and bards. Given that, we'll represent each player's character as a ref holding a map, which will contain all of the data relevant to the player's character's class and abilities. Regardless of their class, all characters will have a minimal set of attributes:

- `:name`, the character's name within the game.
- `:health`, a number indicating the character's physical well-being. When `:health` drops to 0, that character will be dead.
- `:items`, the set of equipment that a character is carrying.

Of course, specific character classes will have their own attributes. `character` is a function that implements all this, with default values for `:items` and `:health`:

---

16. We present a way to address durability of ref state with the help of agents in "Persisting reference states with an agent-based write-behind log" on page 215.

17. We're not game designers, and what we build here is obviously a contrivance, but there's no reason the mechanisms we demonstrate here could not be utilized and extended to implement a thoroughly capable game engine.

```
(defn character
  [name & {:as opts}]
  (ref (merge {:name name :items #{} :health 500}
              opts)))
```

With this available, we can now define some actual characters that different players could control:[18]

```
(def smaug (character "Smaug" :health 500 :strength 400 :items (set (range 50)))) ❶
(def bilbo (character "Bilbo" :health 100 :strength 100))
(def gandalf (character "Gandalf" :health 75 :mana 750))
```

❶ We've created smaug with a set of items; here, just integers, which might correspond to item IDs within a static map or external database.

In a game like this, if Bilbo and Gandalf were to defeat Smaug in a battle, they would be able to "loot" Smaug of the items he's carrying. Without getting into gameplay details, all this means is that we want to take some item from Smaug and transfer it to another character. This transfer needs to occur so that the item being transferred is only in one place at a time from the perspective of any outside observers.

Enter Clojure's STM and transactions. dosync establishes the scope of a transaction.[19] *All modifications of refs must occur within a transaction*, the processing of which happens synchronously. That is, the thread that initiates a transaction will "block" on that transaction completing before proceeding in its execution.

Similar to atoms' swap!, if two transactions attempt to make a conflicting change to one or more shared refs, one of them will retry. Whether two concurrently applied transactions are in conflict depends entirely upon which functions are used to modify refs shared between those transactions. There are three such functions—alter, commute, and ref-set—each of which has different semantics when it comes to producing (or avoiding) conflict.

With all that said, how do we implement looting of items among characters in our game? The loot function transfers one value from (:items @from) to (:items @to) transactionally, assuming each is a set,[20] and returns the new state of from:

Example 4-2. loot

```
(defn loot
  [from to]
  (dosync
    (when-let [item (first (:items @from))]          ❶
```

---

18. In a real game engine, you would almost surely not use vars to hold characters; rather, it would make sense to use a single map containing all online players' characters, itself held within a ref. As players were to go on- and offline, their characters would be assoced and dissoced from that map.

19. Note that nested transaction scopes—either due to lexically nested dosync forms, or the joining of scopes in, for example, different functions thanks to the flow of execution—are joined into a single logical transaction that commits or retries as a unit when control flows out of the *outermost* dosync.

20. Recall from "Set" on page 105 that disj returns a set that does not contain a given value.

```
(alter to update-in [:items] conj item)
(alter from update-in [:items] disj item))))
```

❶ If (:items @from) is empty, first will return nil, the body of when-let will remain unevaluated, the transaction will be a no-op, and loot itself will return nil.

Again, assuming Smaug is dead, we can cause Bilbo and Gandalf to loot his items:

```
(wait-futures 1
              (while (loot smaug bilbo))
              (while (loot smaug gandalf)))
;= nil
@smaug
;= {:name "Smaug", :items #{}, :health 500}
@bilbo
;= {:name "Bilbo", :items #{0 44 36 13 ... 16}, :health 500}
@gandalf
;= {:name "Gandalf", :items #{32 4 26 ... 15}, :health 500}
```

Right, so Gandalf and Bilbo have now taken all of Smaug's items. The important point to notice is that the bilbo and gandalf characters divvied up Smaug's loot from different futures (therefore, threads), and that all the looting occurred atomically: no items are unaccounted for, no item references were duplicated, and at no point was an item owned by multiple characters.

Example 4-3. Verifying the consistency of loot

```
(map (comp count :items deref) [bilbo gandalf])    ❶
;= (21 29)
(filter (:items @bilbo) (:items @gandalf))          ❷
;= ()
```

❶ If these counts were to add up to anything other than 50 (the original number of items held by Smaug), or...

❷ ...if Gandalf ended up with any items that Bilbo also held, then the effect of our loot transactions would have been cumulatively inconsistent.

This was accomplished without the manual management of locks, and this process will scale to accommodate transactions involving far more refs and far more interleaving transactions applied by far more separate threads of execution.

Understanding alter

loot uses alter, which is similar to swap! insofar as it takes a ref, a function f, and additional arguments to that function. When alter returns, the *in-transaction value* of the ref in question will have been changed to the return of a call to f, with the ref's value as the first argument, followed by all of the additional arguments to alter.

The notion of an in-transaction value is an important one. All the functions that modify the state of a ref actually operate on a speculative timeline for the ref's state, which starts for each ref when it is first *modified*. All later ref access and modification works on this separate timeline, which only exists and can only be accessed from within the transaction. When control flow is to exit a transaction, the STM attempts to commit it. In the optimistic case, this will result in the in-transaction, speculative states of each affected ref being installed as the refs' new shared, non-transaction state, fully visible to the rest of the world. However, depending upon the semantics of the operation(s) used to establish those in-transaction values, any change made to the refs' state outside of the transaction *may* conflict with the transaction's modifications, resulting in the transaction being restarted from scratch.

Throughout this process, any thread of execution that is solely *reading* (i.e., derefer-encing) refs involved in a transaction can do so without being blocked or waiting in any circumstance. Further, until a given transaction commits successfully, its changes will not affect the state of refs seen by readers outside of that transaction, including readers operating within the scope of entirely different transactions.

The unique semantic of `alter` is that, when the transaction is to be committed, the value of the ref outside of the transaction must be the same as it was prior to the first in-transaction application of `alter`. Otherwise, the transaction is restarted from the beginning with the new observed values of the refs involved.

This dynamic can be visualized as the interaction between two transactions, t_1 and t_2, which both affect some shared ref a using `alter`:

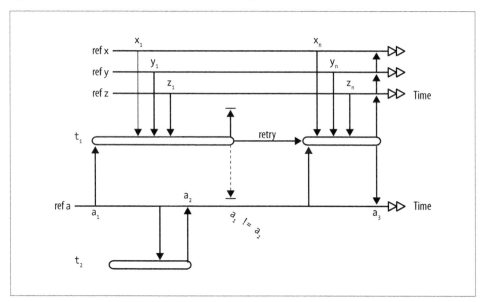

Figure 4-2. Interaction of transactions using alter, with conflict on a shared ref

Even though t_1 starts before t_2, its attempt to commit changes to a fails because t_2 has already modified it in the interim: the current state of a (a_2) is different than the state of a (a_1) when it was first modified within t_1. This conflict aborts the commit of any and all in-transaction modifications to refs affected by t_1 (e.g., x, y, z, ...). t_1 then restarts, using up-to-date values for all of the refs it touches.

Depicted and described this way, you can think of Clojure's STM as a process that optimistically attempts to reorder concurrent change operations so they are applied serially. Unsurprisingly, the same semantics are found in the database world as well, often called *serializable snapshot isolation* (*https://en.wikipedia.org/wiki/Serializability*).

A transaction's effects will not be committed to the refs involved if *any* conflicts exist at commit time. That is, just a single contested ref change is enough to cause a transaction to retry, even if 100 other ref changes could be committed cleanly.

Minimizing transaction conflict with commute

Because it makes no assumptions about the reorderability of the modifications made to affected refs, `alter` is the safest mechanism for effecting ref change. However, there *are* situations where the modifications being made to refs can be reordered safely; in such contexts, `commute` can be used in place of `alter`, potentially minimizing conflicts and transaction retries and therefore maximizing total throughput.

As its name hints, `commute` has to do with *commutative* functions (*https://en.wikipedia.org/wiki/Commutative_property*)—those whose arguments may be reordered without impacting results, such as +, *, `clojure.set/union`...—but it doesn't mandate that the functions passed to it be commutative. What really matters is that the function applications performed using `commute` are reorderable without violating program semantics. It follows that in such cases, it is the final result of all commutable function applications that matters, and not any intermediate results.

For example, although division is not commutative, it may be often used with `commute` when you are not concerned with intermediate results:

```
(= (/ (/ 120 3) 4) (/ (/ 120 4) 3))
;= true
```

Thus, `commute` can be used when the functional composition is commutative for the functions involved:

```
(= ((comp #(/ % 3) #(/ % 4)) 120) ((comp #(/ % 4) #(/ % 3)) 120))
;= true
```

Generally, `commute` should only be used to apply changes to ref states where reordering of that application is acceptable.

`commute` differs from `alter` in two ways. First, the value returned by `alter` on a ref will be the committed value of this ref; in other words, the in-transaction value is the eventual committed value. On the other hand, the in-transaction value produced by `commute` is not guaranteed to be the eventual committed value, because the `commute`d function will be applied again at commit time with the latest value for the `commute`d ref.

Second, a change made to a ref by using commute will *never* cause a conflict, and therefore never cause a transaction to retry. This obviously has potentially significant performance and throughput implications: transaction retries are fundamentally rework and time that a thread is "blocked" waiting for a transaction to complete successfully instead of moving on to its next task.

We can demonstrate this very directly. Given some ref x:

```
(def x (ref 0))
;= #'user/x
```

We'll beat on it with 10,000 transactions that do some small amount of work (just obtaining the sum of some integers), and then alter x's value:

```
(time (wait-futures 5
                    (dotimes [_ 1000]
                      (dosync (alter x + (apply + (range 1000)))))
                    (dotimes [_ 1000]
                      (dosync (alter x - (apply + (range 1000)))))))
; "Elapsed time: 1466.621 msecs"
```

At least some of the time taken to process these transactions was spent in retries, thus forcing the resumming of the integer sequence. However, the operations used with alter here (addition and subtraction) can safely be used with commute:

```
(time (wait-futures 5
                    (dotimes [_ 1000]
                      (dosync (commute x + (apply + (range 1000)))))
                    (dotimes [_ 1000]
                      (dosync (commute x - (apply + (range 1000)))))))
; "Elapsed time: 818.41 msecs"
```

Even though it applies the change function to the ref's value twice—once to set the in-transaction value (so x would have an updated value if we were to refer to it again later in the transaction), and once again at commit-time to make the "real" change to the (potentially modified) value of x—our cumulative runtime is cut nearly in half because commute will never retry.

commute is not magic though: it needs to be used judiciously, or it can produce invalid results. Let's see what happens if we carelessly use commute instead of alter in the loot function from Example 4-2:

Example 4-4. A flawed-loot function that uses commute

```
(defn flawed-loot
  [from to]
  (dosync
    (when-let [item (first (:items @from))]
      (commute to update-in [:items] conj item)
      (commute from update-in [:items] disj item))))
```

Let's reset our characters and see what our new looting function does:

```
(def smaug (character "Smaug" :health 500 :strength 400 :items (set (range 50))))
(def bilbo (character "Bilbo" :health 100 :strength 100))
(def gandalf (character "Gandalf" :health 75 :mana 750))

(wait-futures 1
              (while (flawed-loot smaug bilbo))
              (while (flawed-loot smaug gandalf)))
;= nil
(map (comp count :items deref) [bilbo gandalf])
;= (5 48)
(filter (:items @bilbo) (:items @gandalf))
;= (18 32 1)
```

Using the same checks from Example 4-3, we can see that flawed-loot has produced some problems: Bilbo has 5 items while Gandalf has 48 (with 18, 32, and 1 being the three duplicated items), a situation that should never happen since Smaug started with 50.

What went wrong? In three instances, the same value was pulled from Smaug's set of :items and conjed into both Bilbo's and Gandalf's :items. This is prevented in the known-good implementation of loot because using alter properly guarantees that the in-transaction and committed values will be identical.

In this peculiar case, we *can* safely use commute to add the looted item to the recipient's set (since the order in which items are added to the set is of no importance); it is the removal of the looted item from its source that requires the use of alter:

Example 4-5. A fixed-loot function that uses both commute and alter

```
(defn fixed-loot
  [from to]
  (dosync
    (when-let [item (first (:items @from))]
      (commute to update-in [:items] conj item)
      (alter from update-in [:items] disj item))))

(def smaug (character "Smaug" :health 500 :strength 400 :items (set (range 50))))
(def bilbo (character "Bilbo" :health 100 :strength 100))
(def gandalf (character "Gandalf" :health 75 :mana 750))

(wait-futures 1
              (while (fixed-loot smaug bilbo))
              (while (fixed-loot smaug gandalf)))
;= nil
(map (comp count :items deref) [bilbo gandalf])
;= (24 26)
(filter (:items @bilbo) (:items @gandalf))
;= ()
```

On the other hand, commute is perfect for other functions in our game. For example, attack and heal functions are just going to be incrementing and decrementing various character attributes, so such changes can be made safely using commute:

```
(defn attack
  [aggressor target]
  (dosync
    (let [damage (* (rand 0.1) (:strength @aggressor))]
      (commute target update-in [:health] #(max 0 (- % damage))))))
```

```
(defn heal
  [healer target]
  (dosync
    (let [aid (* (rand 0.1) (:mana @healer))]
      (when (pos? aid)
        (commute healer update-in [:mana] - (max 5 (/ aid 5)))
        (commute target update-in [:health] + aid)))))
```

With a couple of additional functions, we can simulate a player taking some action within our game:

Example 4-6. Player-simulation functions

```
(def alive? (comp pos? :health))
```

```
(defn play
  [character action other]
  (while (and (alive? @character)
              (alive? @other)
              (action character other))
    (Thread/sleep (rand-int 50))))     ❶
```

❶ Surely no one can spam a particular action more than 20 times a second!

Now we can have duels:

```
(wait-futures 1
              (play bilbo attack smaug)
              (play smaug attack bilbo))
;= nil
(map (comp :health deref) [smaug bilbo])     ❶
;= (488.80755445030337 -12.0394908759935)
```

❶ All by his lonesome, Bilbo understandably cannot hold his own against Smaug.

...or, "epic" battles:

Example 4-7. A battle between three characters

```
(dosync                                  ❶
  (alter smaug assoc :health 500)
  (alter bilbo assoc :health 100))
```

```
(wait-futures 1
              (play bilbo attack smaug)
              (play smaug attack bilbo)
```

```
                (play gandalf heal bilbo))
;= nil
(map (comp #(select-keys % [:name :health :mana]) deref) [smaug bilbo gandalf]) ❷
;= ({:health 0, :name "Smaug"}
;=  {:health 853.6622368542827, :name "Bilbo"}
;=  {:mana -2.575955687302212, :health 75, :name "Gandalf"})
```

❶ Just resetting our characters back to full health.

❷ Bilbo can ably take down Smaug as long as Gandalf is healing him throughout the course of the fight.

Clobbering ref state with ref-set

`ref-set` will set the in-transaction state of a ref to the given value:

```
(dosync (ref-set bilbo {:name "Bilbo"}))
;= {:name "Bilbo"}
```

Just like `alter`, `ref-set` will provoke a retry of the surrounding transaction if the affected ref's state changes prior to commit-time. Said differently, `ref-set` is semantically equivalent to using `alter` with a function that returns a constant value:

```
(dosync (alter bilbo (constantly {:name "Bilbo"})))
; {:name "Bilbo"}
```

Since this change is made without reference to the current value of the ref, it is quite easy to change a ref's value in a way that is consistent with regard to the STM's transactional guarantees, but that violates application-level contracts. Thus, `ref-set` is generally used only to reinitialize refs' state to starting values.

Enforcing local consistency by using validators

If you'll notice, Bilbo has a *very* high `:health` value at the end of Example 4-7. Indeed, there is no limit to how high a character's `:health` can go, as a results of heals or other restorative actions.

These sorts of games generally do not allow a character's health to exceed a particular level. However, from both a technical and management perspective—especially given a large team or codebase—it may be too onerous to guarantee that every function that might increase a character's health would not produce a health "overage." Such functions may, as part of their own semantics, attempt to avoid such an illegal condition, but we must be able to protect the integrity of our model separately. Maintaining local consistency like this—the C in "ACID"—in the face of concurrent changes is the job of validators.

We talked about validators already in "Validators" on page 178. Their use and semantics with refs is entirely the same as with other reference types, but their interaction with the STM is particularly convenient: if a validator function signals an invalid state, the exception that is thrown (just like any other exception thrown within a transaction) causes the current transaction itself to fail.

With this in mind, we should refactor our game's implementation details a bit. First, `character` should be changed so that:

1. A common set of validators is added to every character.
2. Additional validators can be provided for each character, so as to enforce constraints related to a character's class, level, or other status in the game:

```
(defn- enforce-max-health                                            ❶
  [name health]
  (fn [character-data]
    (or (<= (:health character-data) health)
      (throw (IllegalStateException. (str name " is already at max health!"))))))

(defn character
  [name & {:as opts}]
  (let [cdata (merge {:name name :items #{} :health 500}
                     opts)
        cdata (assoc cdata :max-health (:health cdata))        ❷
        validators (list* (enforce-max-health name (:health cdata)) ❸
                          (:validator cdata))]
    (ref (dissoc cdata :validator)
      :validator #(every? (fn [v] (v %)) validators))))        ❹
```

❶ enforce-max-health returns a function that accepts a character's *potential* new state, throwing an exception if the new :health attribute is above the character's original health level.

❷ We record the character's initial :health as their :max-health, which will come in handy later.

❸ In addition to always ensuring that a character's maximum health is never exceeded, it is easy to allow individual characters to be created with their own additional set of validator functions...

❹ ...which can be easily rolled into the validation of their containing refs.

Now, no character can ever be healed past his original health level:

```
(def bilbo (character "Bilbo" :health 100 :strength 100))
;= #'user/bilbo
(heal gandalf bilbo)
;= #<IllegalStateException java.lang.IllegalStateException: Bilbo is already at max
    health!>
```

One limitation of validators is that they are strictly *local*; that is, their charter does not extend past ensuring that the next state held by a reference satisfies the constraints they check:

```
(dosync (alter bilbo assoc-in [:health] 95))
;= {:max-health 100, :strength 100, :name "Bilbo", :items #{}, :health 95, :xp 0}
(heal gandalf bilbo)
;= #<IllegalStateException java.lang.IllegalStateException: Bilbo is already at max
    health!>
```

Here, Bilbo's :health is set just short of his :max-health, so he really should be heal-able. However, the implementation of heal does not yet take :max-health into account, and there is no way for the relevant validator to "tweak" Bilbo's new state to suit its constraints—in this case, to make his :health the lesser of his :max-health or the sum of his current :health and Gandalf's heal amount. If validators *were* allowed to make changes like this, then it would be difficult to avoid introducing inconsistency into the refs modified within a transaction. Validators exist solely to maintain invariants within your model.

A tweak to heal is warranted to ensure that "partial" heals are possible, up to a char-acter's maximum health:

```
(defn heal
  [healer target]
  (dosync
    (let [aid (min (* (rand 0.1) (:mana @healer))
                   (- (:max-health @target) (:health @target)))]
      (when (pos? aid)
        (commute healer update-in [:mana] - (max 5 (/ aid 5)))
        (alter target update-in [:health] + aid)))))
```

Now heal will improve a character's health *up to* his maximum health, returning nil when the character's health is already at that level:

```
(dosync (alter bilbo assoc-in [:health] 95))
;= {:max-health 100, :strength 100, :name "Bilbo", :items #{}, :health 95}
(heal gandalf bilbo)
;= {:max-health 100, :strength 100, :name "Bilbo", :items #{}, :health 100}
(heal gandalf bilbo)
;= nil
```

Note that our modification to target now potentially depends upon its prior state, so we use alter instead of commute. This isn't strictly required: perhaps you would be happy enough to have the validator catch errant heals, which would happen only if some other concurrently applied transaction also increased the health of the target character. This points to a potential downside to how we've modeled our characters, as all-encompassing bags of state (maps in this case) held by a single ref: if concurrent transactions modify unrelated parts of that state using alter, a transaction will retry unnecessarily.[21]

The Sharp Corners of Software Transactional Memory

As we said at the beginning of this chapter, Clojure does not offer any silver bullet to solve the problem of concurrency. Its STM implementation may sometimes seem

---

21. Determining ideal *ref granularity* for your particular model is an optimization step that you'll have to figure through benchmarking, experimentation, and some degree of forethought. Always start with the simplest approach—all-encompassing values are just fine most of the time—only reaching for a more complicated solution when necessary. See *http://clj-me.cgrand.net/2011/10/06/a-world-in-a-ref/* for one such potential direction.

magical—and, compared to the typical alternatives involving manual lock management, it sorta is—but even the STM has its own sharp corners and rough edges of which you should be aware.

Side-effecting functions strictly verboten

The only operations that should ever be performed within the scope of a transaction are things that are safe to retry, which rules out many forms of I/O. For example, if you attempt to write to a file or database inside a **dosync** block, you will quite possibly end up writing the same data to the file or database multiple times.

Clojure can't detect that you're attempting to perform an unsafe operation inside a transaction; it will happily and silently retry those operations, perhaps with disastrous results. For this reason, Clojure provides an **io!** macro, which will throw an error if it is ever evaluated within a transaction. Thus, if you have a function that may be used within a transaction, you can wrap the side-effecting portion of its body in an **io!** form to help guard against accidentally calling unsafe code:

```
(defn unsafe
  []
  (io! (println "writing to database...")))
;= #'user/unsafe
(dosync (unsafe))
;= #<IllegalStateException java.lang.IllegalStateException: I/O in transaction>
```

 As a corollary, operations on atoms should generally be considered side-effecting, insofar as **swap!**, et al., do not participate in the STM's transactional semantics. Thus, if a transaction is retried three times, and it contains a **swap!** call, **swap!** will be invoked three times and the affected atom will be modified three times...rarely what you want, unless you're using an atom to count transaction retries.

Note also that the values held by refs *must* be immutable.[22] Clojure isn't going to stop you from putting mutable objects into a ref, but things like retries and the usual foibles associated with mutability will likely result in undesirable effects:

```
(def x (ref (java.util.ArrayList.)))
;= #'user/x
(wait-futures 2 (dosync (dotimes [v 5]
                          (Thread/sleep (rand-int 50))    ❶
                          (alter x #(doto % (.add v))))))
;= nil
@x
;= #<ArrayList [0, 0, 1, 0, 2, 3, 4, 0, 1, 2, 3, 4]>    ❷
```

---

22. Or, at the very least, effectively mutable due to your usage of them. For example, it is possible to use a mutable Java list as the state of a ref with proper transactional semantics if you strictly copy-on-write when producing modified lists, but this is both bad form and almost always unnecessary.

---

❶ The randomized `sleep` call ensures that the two transactions will overlap; at least one of them will retry, leading to…

❷ …hopelessly flawed results.

Minimize the scope of each transaction

Remember from the discussion around Figure 4-2 that the STM's job is to ensure that all of the work encapsulated as transactions be applied to affected refs in a serial fashion, reordering that work and those ref state changes if necessary. This implies that, the shorter each transaction is, the easier it will be for the STM to schedule that transaction, thus leading to faster application and higher total throughput.

What happens if you have out-sized transactions, or transactions with a mix of scopes and scales? In general, the largest transactions will be delayed (along with whatever else the thread waiting on that transaction would otherwise be doing). Consider a bunch of transactions, all affecting some ref a:

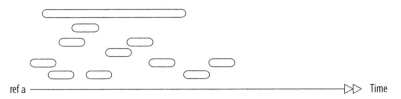

ref a ————————————————————————————————▷▷ Time

Assuming each of them is `altering` a, the execution of those transactions will be retried until they can be applied serially. The longest-running transaction will end up being retried repeatedly, with the likely result that it will be delayed until a long enough slot opens up in the contended ref's timeline for it to fit:

ref a ————————————————————————————————▷▷ Time

 Remember that `commute` (discussed in "Minimizing transaction conflict with commute" on page 185) does not provoke change conflicts and retries. Therefore, if you can use it safely with the change functions applicable to your state's domain, you will effectively sidestep any potential hazards associated with long-running transactions.

Doing a lot of time-consuming computation can result in a long-running transaction, but so can retries prompted by contention over other refs. For example, the long-running transaction depicted above may be performing some complex computation, which may need to be restarted repeatedly due to contention over another ref. Thus, you should aim to minimize the scope of transactions in general as much as possible both in terms of the computational runtime involved and in the number of affected refs.

Live lock. You might wonder: what happens if, particularly in times of heavy load, a large transaction *never* gets a chance to commit due to ref contention? This is called *live lock*, the STM equivalent to a deadlock, where the thread(s) driving the transactions involved are blocked indefinitely attempting to commit their respective transactions. Without suitable fallbacks, and we'd be no better off than if we were manually managing locks and causing our own deadlocks!

Thankfully, Clojure's STM does have a couple of fallbacks. The first is called *barging*, where an older transaction is allowed to proceed in certain circumstances, forcing newer transactions to retry. When barging fails to push through the older transaction in a reasonable amount of time, the STM will simply cause the offending transaction to fail:

```
(def x (ref 0))
;= #'user/x
(dosync
  @(future (dosync (ref-set x 0)))
  (ref-set x 1))
;= #<RuntimeException java.lang.RuntimeException:
;=    Transaction failed after reaching retry limit>
@x
;= 0
```

The transaction running in the REPL thread above always starts a new future, itself running a transaction that modifies the state of the contended ref. Dereferencing that future ensures that the REPL thread's transaction waits until the future's transaction has completed, thus ensuring a retry—and therefore the spawning of a new future, and so on.

Clojure's STM will permit a transaction to retry only so many times before throwing an exception. An error thrown with a stack trace you can examine is infinitely better than an actual deadlock (or live lock), where the only solution is to forcibly kill the application's process with little to no information about the problem's locale.

Readers may retry

In the case of reference types, `deref` is guaranteed to never block. However, *inside a transaction* dereferencing a ref may trigger a transaction retry!

This is because, if a new value is committed by another transaction since the beginning of the current transaction, the value of the ref *as of the start of the transaction* cannot be provided.[23] Helpfully, the STM notices this problem and maintains a bounded history of the states of refs involved in a transaction, where the size of the history is incremented by each retry. This increases the chance that—at some point—the transaction won't have to retry anymore because, while the ref is concurrently updated, the desired value is still present in the history.

---

23. See "Write skew" on page 196 for more subtleties on the value returned by `deref` inside a transaction.

History length can be queried (and tuned) with ref-history-count, ref-max-history, and ref-min-history. Minimum and maximum history sizes can also be specified when a ref is created by using the named arguments :min-history and :max-history:

```
(ref-max-history (ref "abc" :min-history 3 :max-history 30))
;= 30
```

This allows you to potentially tune a ref to suit expected workloads.

Retries on deref generally occur in the context of read-only transactions, which attempt to snapshot a lot of very active refs. We can visualize this behavior with a single ref and a slow reading transaction:

```
(def a (ref 0))
(future (dotimes [_ 500] (dosync (Thread/sleep 200) (alter a inc))))
;= #<core$future_call$reify__5684@10957096: :pending>
@(future (dosync (Thread/sleep 1000) @a))
;= 28                          ❶
(ref-history-count a)
;= 5
```

❶ The read value being 28 means that the reader transaction has been able to complete before all the writers have been run.

So, the a ref has grown its history to accommodate the needs of the slow reading transaction. What happens if the writes occur even faster?

```
(def a (ref 0))
(future (dotimes [_ 500] (dosync (Thread/sleep 20) (alter a inc))))
;= #<core$future_call$reify__5684@10957096: :pending>
@(future (dosync (Thread/sleep 1000) @a))
;= 500
(ref-history-count a)
;= 10
```

This time the history has been maxed out and the reader transaction has only been executed after all the writers. This means that the writers blocked the reader in the second transaction. If we relax the max history, the problem should be fixed:

```
(def a (ref 0 :max-history 100))
(future (dotimes [_ 500] (dosync (Thread/sleep 20) (alter a inc))))
;= #<core$future_call$reify__5684@10957096: :pending>
@(future (dosync (Thread/sleep 1000) @a))
;= 500
(ref-history-count a)
;= 10
```

It didn't work because by the time there's enough history, the writers are done. So, the key is to set the minimum history to a good value:

```
(def a (ref 0 :min-history 50 :max-history 100)) ❶
(future (dotimes [_ 500] (dosync (Thread/sleep 20) (alter a inc))))
@(future (dosync (Thread/sleep 1000) @a))
;= 33
```

❶ We choose 50 because the reader transaction is 50 times slower than the writer one.

This time the reader transaction completes quickly and successfully with no retry!

Write skew

Clojure's STM provides for the transactional consistency of ref state, but so far we've only seen that to be the case for refs that are modified by the transactions involved. If a ref isn't modified by a transaction, but the consistency of that transaction's changes depend upon the state of a ref that is read but not modified, there is no way for the STM to know about this through calls to `alter`, `commute`, and `set-ref`. If the read ref's state happens to change mid-transaction, that transaction's effects on other refs may end up being inconsistent with the read ref; this state of affairs is called *write skew*.

Such a circumstance is rare; generally, refs involved in a transaction are all being modified in some way. However, when that's not the case, `ensure` may be used to prevent write skew: it is a way to dereference a ref such that that read will conflict with any modifications prompted by other transactions, causing retries as necessary.

An example of this within the game's context might be the current amount of daylight. It's safe to say that attacks made with the benefit of mid-day sun will be more successful than those made at night, so a modification to `attack` to take into consideration the current amount of daylight would make sense:

```
(def daylight (ref 1))

(defn attack
  [aggressor target]
  (dosync
    (let [damage (* (rand 0.1) (:strength @aggressor) @daylight)]
      (commute target update-in [:health] #(max 0 (- % damage))))))
```

However, if the state of `daylight` is changed between the time it is read within a transaction and when that transaction commits its changes, those changes may be inconsistent. For example, a separate game process may shift `daylight` to reflect a sunset-appropriate amount of light (e.g., (dosync (ref-set daylight 0.3))). If `attack` is running while that change is being made, and uses the old value of `daylight`, more damage will be attributed to an attack action than is appropriate.

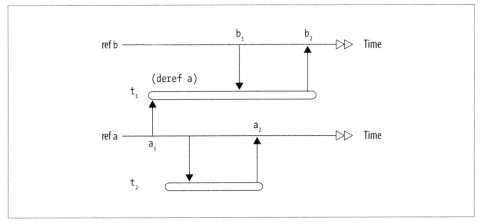

Figure 4-3. Write skew, where state b_2 depends upon state read from a at some prior time

Formally, if the state b_2 that a transaction t_1 writes to ref b depends upon the state of ref a at a_1, and t_1 never writes to a, and another transaction t_2 modifies a to hold some state a_2 prior to t_1 committing, then the world will be inconsistent: b_2 corresponds with a past state a_1, not the current state a_2. This is write skew.

Simply changing `attack` to `(ensure daylight)` instead of dereferencing via `@daylight` will avoid this by guaranteeing that `daylight` will not change before the reading transaction commits successfully.

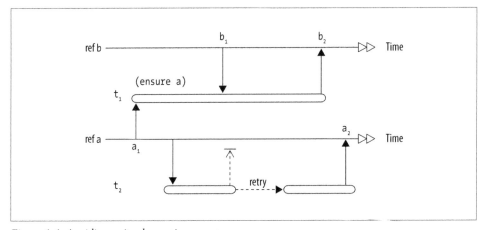

Figure 4-4. Avoiding write skew using ensure

When a transaction t_1 reads a ref a using `ensure` instead of `deref`, any changes to that ref's state by any other transaction t_2 prior to t_1 completing will retry until t_1 has successfully committed. This will avoid write skew: the change to b will always be consistent with the latest state of a, even though t_1 never changes the state of a.

In terms of avoiding write skew, (ensure a) is semantically equivalent to (alter a identity) or (ref-set a @a)—both effectively *dummy writes*—which end up requiring that the read value persist until commit time. Compared to dummy writes, ensure will generally minimize the total number of transaction retries involving read-only refs.

Vars

You've already used and worked with vars a great deal. Vars differ from Clojure's other reference types in that their state changes are not managed in time; rather, they provide a namespace-global identity that can optionally be rebound to have a different value on a *per-thread* basis. We'll explain this at length starting in "Dynamic Scope" on page 201, but first let's understand some of their fundamentals, since vars are used throughout Clojure, whether concurrency is a concern or not.

Evaluating a symbol in Clojure normally results in looking for a var with that name in the current namespace and dereferencing that var to obtain its value. But we can also obtain references to vars directly and manually dereference them:

```
map
;= #<core$map clojure.core$map@501d5ebc>
#'map                                    ❶
;= #'clojure.core/map
@#'map
;= #<core$map clojure.core$map@501d5ebc>
```

❶ Recall from "Referring to Vars: var" on page 44 that #'map is just reader sugar for (var map).

Defining Vars

Vars make up one of the fundamental building blocks of Clojure. As we mentioned in "Defining Vars: def" on page 26, top level functions and values are all stored in vars, which are defined within the current namespace using the def special form or one of its derivatives.

Beyond simply installing a var into the namespace with the given name, def copies the metadata[24] found on the symbol provided to name the new (or to-be-updated) var to the var itself. Particular metadata found on this symbol can modify the behavior and semantics of vars, which we'll enumerate here.

Private vars

Private vars are a basic way to delineate parts of a library or API that are implementation-dependent or otherwise not intended to be accessed by external users. A private var:

---

24. See "Metadata" on page 135 for a primer on metadata in Clojure.

1. Can only be referred to using its fully qualified name when in another namespace.
2. Its value can only be accessed by manually dereferencing the var.

A var is made private if the symbol that names it has a `:private` slot in its metadata map with a `true` value. This is a private var, holding some useful constant value our code might need:

```
(def ^:private everything 42)
```

Recall from "Metadata" on page 135 that this notation is equivalent to:

```
(def ^{:private true} everything 42)
```

We can see that `everything` is available outside of its originating namespace only with some effort:

```
(def ^:private everything 42)
;= #'user/everything
(ns other-namespace)
;= nil
(refer 'user)
;= nil
everything
;= #<CompilerException java.lang.RuntimeException:
;=    Unable to resolve symbol: everything in this context, compiling:(NO_SOURCE_PATH:0)>
@#'user/everything
;= 42
```

You can declare a private function by using the `defn-` form, which is entirely identical to the familiar `defn` form, except that it adds in the `^:private` metadata for you.

Docstrings

Clojure allows you to add documentation to top-level vars via *docstrings*, which are usually string literals that immediately follow the symbol that names the var:

```
(def a
  "A sample value."
  5)
;= #'user/a
(defn b
  "A simple calculation using `a`."
  [c]
  (+ a c))
;= #'user/b
(doc a)
; -------------------------
; user/a
;   A sample value.
(doc b)
; -------------------------
; user/b
; ([c])
;   A simple calculation using `a`.
```

As you can see, docstrings are just more metadata on the var in question; `def` is doing a little bit of work behind the scenes to pick up the optional docstring and add it to the var's metadata as necessary:

```
(meta #'a)
;= {:ns #<Namespace user>, :name a, :doc "A sample value.",
;=  :line 1, :file "NO_SOURCE_PATH"}
```

This means that, if you want, you can add documentation to a var by specifying the `:doc` metadata explicitly, either when the var is defined, or even afterward by altering the var's metadata:

```
(def ^{:doc "A sample value."} a 5)
;= #'user/a
(doc a)
; -------------------------
; user/a
;   A sample value.
(alter-meta! #'a assoc :doc "A dummy value.")
;= {:ns #<Namespace user>, :name a, :doc "A dummy value.",
;=  :line 1, :file "NO_SOURCE_PATH"}
(doc a)
; -------------------------
; user/a
;   A dummy value.
```

This is a rare requirement, but can be very handy when writing var-defining macros.

Constants

It is common to need to define constant values, and using top level `def` forms to do so is typical. You can add `^:const` metadata to a var's name symbol in order to declare it as a constant to the compiler:

```
(def ^:const everything 42)
```

While a nice piece of documentation on its own, `^:const` does have a functional impact: any references to a constant var aren't resolved at runtime (as per usual); rather, the value held by the var is retained permanently by the code referring to the var when it is compiled. This provides a slight performance improvement for such references in hot sections of code, but more important, ensures that your constant actually *remains* constant, even if someone stomps on a var's value.

This certainly isn't what we'd like to have happen:

```
(def max-value 255)
;= #'user/max-value
(defn valid-value?
  [v]
  (<= v max-value))
;= #'user/valid-value?
(valid-value? 218)
;= true
(valid-value? 299)
```

```
;= false
(def max-value 500)     ❶
;= #'user/max-value
(valid-value? 299)
;= true
```

❶ `max-value` is redefined, after which point `valid-value?` implements different semantics due to its reliance on our "constant."

We can prevent such mishaps using `^:const`:

```
(def ^:const max-value 255)
;= #'user/max-value
(defn valid-value?
  [v]
  (<= v max-value))
;= #'user/valid-value?
(def max-value 500)
;= #'user/max-value
(valid-value? 299)
;= false
```

Because `max-value` is declared `^:const`, its value is captured by the `valid-value?` function at compile-time. Any later modifications to `max-value` will have no effect upon the
semantics of `valid-value?` until it is itself redefined.

Dynamic Scope

For the most part, Clojure is lexically scoped: that is, names have values as defined by
the forms that circumscribe their usage and the namespace within which they are evaluated. To demonstrate:

```
(let [a 1
      b 2]
  (println (+ a b))      ❶
  (let [b 3
        + -]
    (println (+ a b))))) ❷
;= 3
;= -2
```

❶ a and b are names of locals established by `let`; `+` and `println` are names of vars
containing functions defined in the `clojure.core` namespace, which are available
within our current namespace.

❷ The local b has been bound with a different value, as has `+`; since these definitions
are more lexically local than the outer local binding of b and the original var named
`+`, they shadow those original values when evaluated within this context.

The exception to this rule is *dynamic scope*, a feature provided by vars. Vars have a *root
binding*; this is the value bound to a var when it is defined using `def` or some derivative,
and the one to which references to that var will evaluate in general. However, if you

define a var to be *dynamic* (using ^:dynamic metadata),[25] then the root binding can be overridden and shadowed on a per-thread basis using the binding form.

```
(def ^:dynamic *max-value* 255)
;= #'user/*max-value*
(defn valid-value?
  [v]
  (<= v *max-value*))
;= #'user/valid-value?
(binding [*max-value* 500]
  (valid-value? 299))
;= true
```

 Dynamic vars intended to be rebound with binding should be surrounded with asterisks — like *this*—also known as "earmuffs." This is merely a naming convention, but is helpful to alert a reader of some code that dynamic scope is possible.

Here we are able to change the value of *max-value* outside of the lexical scope of its usage within valid-value? by using binding. This is only a thread-local change though; we can see that *max-value* retains its original value in other threads:[26]

```
(binding [*max-value* 500]
  (println (valid-value? 299))
  (doto (Thread. #(println "in other thread:" (valid-value? 299)))
    .start
    .join))
;= true
;= in other thread: false
```

Dynamic scope is used widely by libraries and in Clojure itself[27] to provide or alter the default configuration of an API without explicitly threading context through each function call. You can see very practical examples in both Chapters 15 and 14, where dynamic scope is used to provide database configuration information to a library.

---

25. Attempting to use binding on a var that is not :dynamic will result in an exception being thrown.

26. Please excuse the momentary slew of Java interop; it is necessary to use a native thread in order to demonstrate this characteristics of dynamic vars. See "Using Java's Concurrency Primitives" on page 224 and Chapter 9 for explanations of what's going on here.

27. Examples include *warn-on-reflection* as detailed in "Type Hinting for Performance" on page 366 and "Type errors and warnings" on page 440. *out*, *in*, and *err*, and indirect usages of binding, like with-precision are discussed in "Scale and Rounding Modes for Arbitrary-Precision Decimals Ops" on page 432.

Visualizing dynamic scope.   To illustrate, consider a var: it has a root value, and for each thread, it *may* have any number of thread-local bindings, which stack up as nested dynamic scopes come into effect via `binding`.

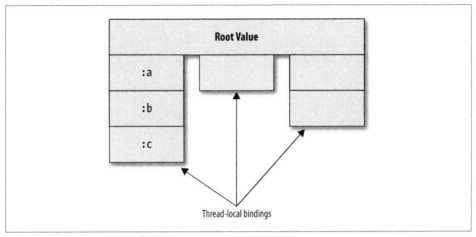

Figure 4-5. A var holding a single root value, and many thread-local stacks of thread-local bindings

Only the heads of these stacks may be accessed (shown bolded above). Once a binding is established, the prior binding is shadowed for the duration of the dynamic scope put into place by `binding`. So within the innermost dynamic scope here, `*var*` (and therefore, `(get-*var*)`) will never evaluate to `:root`, `:a`, or `:b`:

```
(def ^:dynamic *var* :root)
;= #'user/*var*
(defn get-*var* [] *var*)
;= #'user/get-*var*
(binding [*var* :a]
  (binding [*var* :b]
    (binding [*var* :c]
      (get-*var*))))
;= :c
```

Each level of dynamic scope pushes a new "frame" onto the stack for the var being bound:

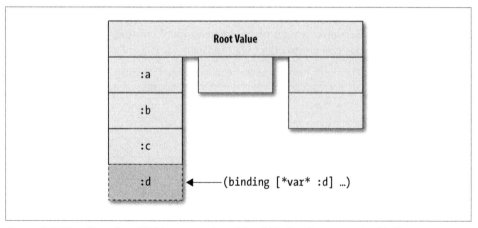

Figure 4-6. The effect of establishing a new thread-local binding for a var using binding

```
(binding [*var* :a]
  (binding [*var* :b]
    (binding [*var* :c]
      (binding [*var* :d]
        (get-*var*)))))
;= :d
```

We've seen how dynamic scope can be used to control the behavior of functions at a distance, essentially allowing callers to provide an implicit argument to functions potentially many levels down in a call tree. The final piece of the puzzle is that dynamic scope can also work in reverse, to allow functions to provide multiple side-channel return values to callers potentially many levels *up* in a call tree.

For example, while Clojure provides some incredibly convenient IO functions to simply retrieve the content of a URL (e.g., slurp and others in the clojure.java.io namespace), such methods provide no easy way to retrieve the corresponding HTTP response code when you require it (a necessary thing sometimes, especially when using various HTTP APIs). One option would be to *always* return the response code in addition to the URL's content in a vector of [response-code url-content]:

```
(defn http-get
  [url-string]
  (let [conn (-> url-string java.net.URL. .openConnection)
        response-code (.getResponseCode conn)]
    (if (== 404 response-code)
      [response-code]
      [response-code (-> conn .getInputStream slurp)])))

(http-get "http://google.com/bad-url")
;= [404]
(http-get "http://google.com/")
;= [200 "<!doctype html><html><head>..."]
```

That's not horrible, but as users of http-get, this approach forces us to deal with the response code for every call in every context, even if we aren't interested in it.

As an alternative, we could use dynamic scope to establish a binding that http-get can set *only when we're interested in the HTTP response code*:

```
(def ^:dynamic *response-code* nil)                                ❶

(defn http-get
  [url-string]
  (let [conn (-> url-string java.net.URL. .openConnection)
        response-code (.getResponseCode conn)]
    (when (thread-bound? #'*response-code*)                         ❷
      (set! *response-code* response-code))                         ❸
    (when (not= 404 response-code) (-> conn .getInputStream slurp))))) ❹

(http-get "http://google.com")
;= "<!doctype html><html><head>..."
*response-code*
;= nil
(binding [*response-code* nil]
  (let [content (http-get "http://google.com/bad-url")]
    (println "Response code was:" *response-code*)
    ; ... do something with `content` if it is not nil ...
    ))
;= Response code was: 404
;= nil
```

❶ We define a new var, *response-code*; users of http-get opt into accessing the response code it obtains by binding this var.

❷ We use thread-bound? to check if the caller of http-get has established a thread-local binding on *response-code*. If not, we do nothing with it.

❸ set! is used to *change* the value of the current thread-local binding on *response-code* so that the caller can access that value as desired.

❹ Now that http-get can use the optional dynamic scope around *response-code* to communicate auxiliary information to its callers, it can simply return the string content loaded from the URL instead of the compound vector of [response-code url-content] (assuming the URL is not 404).

Again, to illustrate:

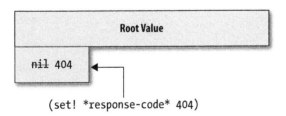

Because set! acts on a var's binding by replacing the current thread-local value, a caller within the dynamic scope established by binding—whether a direct one or one 50 frames up the call stack—can access that new value without it having been threaded back through the return values of all the intervening function calls. This works for any number of vars, any number of bindings, and any number or type of set!-ed values, including functions. Such flexibility enables simple API extensions like auxiliary returns as we've demonstrated here, up to more elaborate and powerful things like non-local return mechanisms.

Dynamic scope propagates through Clojure-native concurrency forms. The thread-local nature of dynamic scope is useful—it allows a particular execution context to remain isolated from others—but without mitigation, it would cause undue difficulty when using Clojure facilities that by necessity move computation from one thread to another. Thankfully, Clojure does propagate dynamic var bindings across threads—called *binding conveyance*—when using agents (via send and send-off), futures, as well as pmap and its variants:

```
(binding [*max-value* 500]
  (println (valid-value? 299))
  @(future (valid-value? 299)))
; true
;= true
```

Even though valid-value? is invoked on a separate thread than the one that originally set up the dynamic scope via binding, future propagates that scope across to the other thread for the duration of its operation.

Note that, while pmap does support binding conveyance, the same does *not* hold true for lazy seqs in general:

```
(binding [*max-value* 500]
  (map valid-value? [299]))
;= (false)
```

The workaround here is to ensure that you push the dynamic scope required for each step in the lazy seq into the code that will actually be evaluated when values in the seq are to be realized:

```
(map #(binding [*max-value* 500]
        (valid-value? %))
     [299])
;= (true)
```

Vars Are Not Variables

Vars should *not* be confused with variables in other languages. Coming from a language like Ruby, where code usually looks like this:

```
def foo
  x = 123
  y = 456
```

```
  x = x + y
end
```

It's incredibly tempting for new Clojure users to try to write code like this:

```
(defn never-do-this []
  (def x 123)
  (def y 456)
  (def x (+ x y)
  x))
```

This is very poor form in Clojure. But, what's the worst that could happen?

```
(def x 80)
;= #'user/x
(defn never-do-this []
  (def x 123)
  (def y 456)
  (def x (+ x y))
  x)
;= #'user/never-do-this
(never-do-this)
;= 579
x                               ❶
;= 579
```

❶ "Waitaminute, I declared x to be 80 at the start!"

def always defines *top level* vars—it is *not* an assignment operation affecting some local scope. x and y in this example are globally accessible throughout your namespace, and will clobber any other x and y vars already in your namespace.

With the exception of dynamic scope, vars are fundamentally intended to hold constant values from the time they are defined until the termination of your application, REPL, etc. Use one of Clojure's other reference types for identities that provide useful and proper semantics for changing state in place, if that is what you are looking for. Define a var to hold one of those, and use the appropriate function (swap!, alter, send, send-off, et al.) to modify the state of those identities.

Changing a var's Root Binding.   Despite our various warnings against using vars as variables as understood in other languages, there is value in mutating their root bindings occasionally and with great care. To change a var's root binding as a function of its current value, there's alter-var-root:

```
(def x 0)
;= #'user/x
(alter-var-root #'x inc)
;= 1
```

When the var in question contains a function, this provides a superset of the functionality found in most aspect-oriented programming frameworks. Concrete examples in that vein are provided in "Aspect-Oriented Programming" on page 466 and "Building mixed-source projects" on page 351.

You can also temporarily change the root binding of a bunch of vars with with-redefs, which will restore the vars' root bindings upon exiting its scope; this can be very useful in testing, for mocking out functions or values that depend upon environment-specific context. See "Mocking" on page 472 for an example.

Forward Declarations

You can opt not to provide a value for a var; in this case, the var is considered "unbound," and dereferencing it will return a placeholder object:

```
(def j)
;= #'user/j
j
;= #<Unbound Unbound: #'user/j>
```

This is useful for when you need to refer to a var that you haven't defined a value for yet. This can happen when implementing certain types of algorithms that benefit from alternating recursion—or, you may simply want to have the implementation of a function to come after where it is used as a matter of style or in an attempt to call attention to primary or public API points. Clojure compiles and evaluates forms in the order presented in your source files, so any vars you refer to must at least be declared prior to those references. Assuming such vars' values are only required at runtime (e.g., if they are placeholders for functions), then you can redefine those vars later with their actual values. This called a *forward declaration*.

In such cases, the declare macro is somewhat more idiomatic. Using it instead of def alone makes explicit your intention to define an unbound var (rather than leaving open the possibility that you simply forgot to provide a value), and it allows you to define many unbound vars in a single expression:

```
(declare complex-helper-fn other-helper-fn)          ❶

(defn public-api-function
  [arg1 arg2]
  ...
  (other-helper-fn arg1 arg2 (complex-helper-fn arg1 arg2)))   ❷

(defn- complex-helper-fn                             ❸
  [arg1 arg2]
  ...)

(defn- other-helper-fn
  [arg1 arg2 arg3]
  ...)
```

❶ We declare our helper functions' vars before they are referred to.

❷ Now we can put our primary/public API near the top of our source file and refer to our helper functions freely.

❸ We properly define our helper functions later on in the source file.

Agents

Agents are an uncoordinated, asynchronous reference type. This means that changes to an agent's state are independent of changes to other agents' states, and that all such changes are made away from the thread of execution that schedules them. Agents further possess two characteristics that uniquely separate them from atoms and refs:

1. I/O and other side-effecting functions may be safely used in conjunction with agents.
2. Agents are STM-aware, so that they may be safely used in the context of retrying transactions.

Agent state may be altered via two functions, send and send-off. They follow the same pattern as other reference state change functions, accepting another function that will determine the agent's new state that accepts as arguments the agent's current state along with optional additional arguments to pass to the function.

Taken together, each function + optional set of arguments passed to send or send-off is called an agent *action*, and each agent maintains a queue of actions. Both send and send-off return immediately after queueing the specified action, each of which are evaluated serially, in the order in which they are "sent," on one of many threads dedicated to the evaluation of agent actions. The result of each evaluation is installed as the agent's new state.

The sole difference between send and send-off is the type of action that may be provided to each. Actions queued using send are evaluated within a fixed-size thread pool that is configured to not exceed the parallelizability of the current hardware.[28] *Thus, send must never be used for actions that might perform I/O or other blocking operations*, lest the blocking action prevent other nonblocking, CPU-bound actions from fully utilizing that resource.

In contrast, actions queued using send-off are evaluated within an unbounded thread pool (incidentally, the same one used by futures), which allows any number of potentially blocking, non-CPU-bound actions to be evaluated concurrently.

Knowing all this, we can get a picture of how agents work in general:

---

28. For example, a two-core CPU will have a send thread pool configured to contain a maximum of four threads, a four-core CPU will have a pool of eight threads, etc.

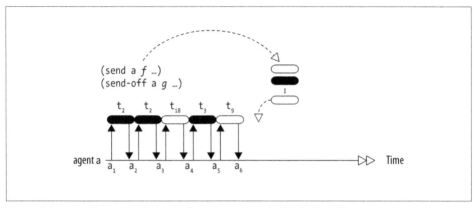

Figure 4-7. Queueing and evaluation of agent actions resulting in state changes

Actions are queued for an agent using either send or send-off (represented in Figure 4-7 as different-colored units of work). The agent applies its state to those actions in order, performing that evaluation on a thread from the pool associated with the function used to queue the action. So, if the black actions are CPU-bound, then threads t_2 and t_3 are from the dedicated, fixed-size send thread pool, and t_9 and t_{18} are from the unbounded send-off thread pool. The return value of each action becomes the agent's new state.

Agents Do Not Correspond to Threads

There is no connection between the number of agents created by a program and the number of live threads created to service those agents. Rather, the number of live threads related to agents is determined largely by the number of *concurrently processed* actions dispatched using send-off: because those are the only actions that can utilize an unbounded thread pool, they are the only actions that can prompt the creation of a new system thread. Remember that agent actions are serialized, so in order to force the creation of 100 threads (for example), you would need to have a minimum of 100 agents, each concurrently evaluating a send-off action.

This implies two things:

1. You can create as many agents as memory allows.[29]
2. The number of concurrent actions dispatched using send is essentially unlimited, but the number of threads dedicated to processing such actions is capped, so again, memory is the only bottleneck.

---

29. Many thousands of agents may be created without strain with a default heap configuration; millions may be created by tweaking the JVM's heap settings.

While the semantics of agents may be subtle, using them is extraordinarily easy:

```
(def a (agent 500))                              ❶
;= #'user/a
(send a range 1000)                              ❷
;= #<Agent@53d2f8be: 500>
@a
;= (500 501 502 503 504 ... 999)
```

❶ An agent is created with an initial value of 500.

❷ We send an action to the agent, consisting of the range function and an additional
argument 1000; in another thread, the agent's value will be set to the result of (range
@a 1000).

Both send and send-off return the agent involved. When sending actions in the
REPL, it is possible that you'll see the result of the sent action's evaluation immediately
in the printing of the agent; depending on the complexity of the action and how quickly
it can be scheduled to be evaluated, it may be complete by the time the REPL has a
chance to print the agent returned from send or send-off:

```
(def a (agent 0))
;= #'user/a
(send a inc)
;= #<Agent@65f7bb1f: 1>
```

On the other hand, you may find yourself needing the result of a pending action's
evaluation, and polling the agent for the result would be daft. You can block on an
agent(s) completing evaluation of all actions sent from your current thread using
await:[30]

```
(def a (agent 5000))
(def b (agent 10000))

(send-off a #(Thread/sleep %))
;= #<Agent@da7d7b5: 5000>
(send-off b #(Thread/sleep %))
;= #<Agent@c0cd75b: 10000>
@a                                               ❶
;= 5000
(await a b)                                       ❷
;= nil
@a                                               ❸
;= nil
```

❶ The function sent to a will take five seconds to complete, so its value has not been
updated yet.

---

30. It is an implementation detail—and so may change in the future—but you can call (.getQueueCount some-
agent) in order to check the current size of an some-agent's action queue.

❷ We can use `await` to block until all of the actions sent to the passed agents from this thread have completed. This particular call will block for up to 10 seconds, since that is how long the function sent to b will take to evaluate.

❸ After `await` has returned, the sent actions will have been evaluated, and the agent(s) values will have been updated. Note that another action could have modified a's value before you dereference it!

`await-for` does the same but allows you to provide a timeout.

Dealing with Errors in Agent Actions

Because agent actions are run asynchronously, an exception thrown in the course of their evaluation cannot be dealt with in the same thread of execution that dispatches the offending action. By default, encountering an error will cause an agent to fail silently: you'll still be able to dereference its last state, but further actions will fail to queue up:

```
(def a (agent nil))
;= #'user/a
(send a (fn [_] (throw (Exception. "something is wrong"))))
;= #<Agent@3cf71b00: nil>
a
;= #<Agent@3cf71b00 FAILED: nil>
(send a identity)                                            ❶
;= #<Exception java.lang.Exception: something is wrong>
```

❶ Attempting to send an action to a failed agent will return the exception that caused the failure. If you explicitly want to check for an error, you should use `agent-error`, which will return the exception or `nil` if the provided agent isn't in a failed state.

A failed agent can be salvaged with `restart-agent`, which will reset the agent's state to the provided value and enable it to receive actions again. An optional flag to `restart-agent`, `:clear-actions`, will clear any pending actions on the agent. Otherwise those pending actions will be attempted immediately.

```
(restart-agent a 42)
;= 42
(send a inc)                                                 ❶
;= #<Agent@5f2308c9: 43>
(reduce send a (for [x (range 3)]                            ❷
                 (fn [_] (throw (Exception. (str "error #" x))))))
;= #<Agent@5f2308c9: 43>
(agent-error a)
;= #<Exception java.lang.Exception: error #0>
(restart-agent a 42)
;= 42
(agent-error a)                                              ❸
;= #<Exception java.lang.Exception: error #1>
(restart-agent a 42 :clear-actions true)                    ❹
;= 42
```

```
(agent-error a)
;= nil
```

❶ Restarting an agent will reset its failed status and allow it to receive actions again.

❷ However, if an agent's queue contains other actions that will cause further errors...

❸ ...then `restart-agent` would need to be called once per erroring action.

❹ Adding the `:clear-actions` option to a `restart-agent` call will clear the agent's queue prior to resetting its failed status, ensuring that any doomed actions in the queue will not immediately fail the agent.

This default error-handling mode—where agents drop into a failed status and need to be resuscitated again—is most useful when you can rely upon manual intervention, usually via a REPL.[31] More flexible and potentially hands-off error handling can be had by changing the defaults for each agent as appropriate.

Agent error handlers and modes

The default behavior where an error causes an agent to enter a failed status is one of two failure modes supported by agents. `agent` accepts an `:error-mode` option of `:fail` (the default) or `:continue`;[32] an agent with a failure mode of `:continue` will simply ignore an error thrown by the evaluation of an agent action, carrying on with processing any actions in its queue and receiving new actions without difficulty:

```
(def a (agent nil :error-mode :continue))
;= #'user/a
(send a (fn [_] (throw (Exception. "something is wrong"))))
;= #<Agent@44a5b703: nil>
(send a identity)
;= #<Agent@44a5b703: nil>
```

This makes `restart-agent` unnecessary, but dropping errors on the floor by default and without any possible intervention is generally not a good idea. Thus, the `:continue` error mode is almost always paired with an error handler, a function of two arguments (the agent, and the precipitating error) that is called any time an agent action throws an exception; an error handler can be specified for an agent by using the `:error-handler` option:[33]

```
(def a (agent nil
              :error-mode :continue
              :error-handler (fn [the-agent exception]
                               (.println System/out (.getMessage exception)))))
;= #'user/a
(send a (fn [_] (throw (Exception. "something is wrong"))))
```

---

31. That is, via a REPL connected to your environment, wherever it may be; see "Debugging, Monitoring, and Patching Production in the REPL" on page 411.

32. You can change an agent's error mode with `set-error-mode!`.

33. You can change an agent's error handler with `set-error-handler!`.

```
;= #<Agent@bb07c59: nil>
; something is wrong
(send a identity)
:= #<Agent@bb07c59: nil>
```

Of course, far more sophisticated things can be done within an `:error-handler` function beyond simply dumping information about the exception to the console: some data in the application may be changed to avoid the error, an action or other operation might be retried, or the agent's `:error-mode` can be switched back to `:fail` if you know that shutting down the agent is the only safe course of action:

```
(set-error-handler! a (fn [the-agent exception]
                        (when (= "FATAL" (.getMessage exception))
                          (set-error-mode! the-agent :fail))))
;= nil
(send a (fn [_] (throw (Exception. "FATAL"))))
;= #<Agent@6fe546fd: nil>
(send a identity)
;= #<Exception java.lang.Exception: FATAL>
```

I/O, Transactions, and Nested Sends

Unlike refs and atoms, it is perfectly safe to use agents to coordinate I/O and perform other blocking operations. This makes them a vital piece of any complete application that use refs and Clojure's STM to maintain program state over time. Further, thanks to their semantics, agents are often an ideal construct for simplifying asynchronous processing involving I/O even if refs are not involved at all.

Because agents serialize all actions sent to them, they provide a natural synchronization point for necessarily side-effecting operations. You can set up an agent to hold as its state a handle to some context—an `OutputStream` to a file or network socket, a connection to a database, a pipe to a message queue, etc.—and you can be sure that actions sent to that agent will each have exclusive access to that context for the duration of their evaluation. This makes it easy to integrate the Clojure sphere—including refs and atoms—which generally aims to minimize side effects with the rest of the world that demands them.

You might wonder how agents could possibly be used from within STM transactions. Sending an agent action is a side-effecting operation, and so would seem to be just as susceptible to unintended effects due to transaction restarts as other side-effecting operations like applying change operations to atoms or writing to a file. Thankfully, this is not the case.

Agents are integrated into Clojure's STM implementation such that actions dispatched using `send` and `send-off` from within the scope of a transaction will be held in reserve until that transaction is successfully committed. This means that, even if a transaction retries 100 times, a sent action is only dispatched once, and that all of the actions sent during the course of a transaction's runtime will be queued at once after the transaction commits. Similarly, calls to `send` and `send-off` made within the scope of evaluation of an agent action—called a *nested send*—are also held until the action has completed. In both cases, sent actions held pending the completion of an action evaluation or STM transaction may be discarded entirely if a validator aborts the state change associated with either.

To illustrate these semantics and see what they enable, let's take a look at a couple of examples that use agents to simplify the coordination of I/O operations in conjunction with refs and the STM, and as part of a parallelized I/O-heavy workload.

Persisting reference states with an agent-based write-behind log

The game we developed in "The Mechanics of Ref Change" on page 181 using refs to maintain character state in the face of relentlessly concurrent player activity proved the capabilities of Clojure's STM in such an environment. However, any game like this, especially those providing multiplayer capabilities, will track and store player activity and the impact it has on their characters. Of course, we wouldn't want to stuff any kind of logging, persistence, or other I/O into the core game engine: any persistence we want to perform may itself end up being inconsistent because of transaction restarts.

The simplest way to address this is to use watchers and agents to implement a write-behind log for characters in the game. First, let's set up the agents that will hold our output sinks; for this example, we'll assume that all such agents will contain `java.io.Writer`s, the Java interface that defines the API of character output streams:

```
(require '[clojure.java.io :as io])

(def console (agent *out*))
(def character-log (agent (io/writer "character-states.log" :append true)))
```

One of these agents contains `*out*` (itself an instance of `Writer`), the other a `Writer` that drains to a *character-states.log* file in the current directory. These `Writer` instances will have content written to them by an agent action, `write`:

```
(defn write
  [^java.io.Writer w & content]
  (doseq [x (interpose " " content)]
    (.write w (str x)))
  (doto w
    (.write "\n")
    .flush))
```

`write` takes as its first argument a `Writer` (the state of one of the agents it will be queued for), and any number of other values to write to it. It writes each value separated by a space, then a newline, and then flushes the `Writer` so outputted content will actually hit the disk or console rather than get caught up in any buffers that might be in use by the `Writer`.

Finally, we need a function that will add a watcher to any reference type, which we'll use to connect our character refs with the agents that hold the `Writer` instances:

```
(defn log-reference
  [reference & writer-agents]
  (add-watch reference :log
             (fn [_ reference old new]
               (doseq [writer-agent writer-agents]
                 (send-off writer-agent write new)))))
```

Every time the reference's state changes, its new state will be sent along with our
write function to each of the agents provided to log-reference. All we need to do now
is add the watcher for each of the characters for which we want to log state changes,
and fire up a battle:

```
(def smaug (character "Smaug" :health 500 :strength 400))
(def bilbo (character "Bilbo" :health 100 :strength 100))
(def gandalf (character "Gandalf" :health 75 :mana 1000))

(log-reference bilbo console character-log)
(log-reference smaug console character-log)

(wait-futures 1
              (play bilbo attack smaug)
              (play smaug attack bilbo)
              (play gandalf heal bilbo))

; {:max-health 500, :strength 400, :name "Smaug", :items #{}, :health 490.052618}
; {:max-health 100, :strength 100, :name "Bilbo", :items #{}, :health 61.5012391}
; {:max-health 100, :strength 100, :name "Bilbo", :items #{}, :health 100.0}          ❶
; {:max-health 100, :strength 100, :name "Bilbo", :items #{}, :health 67.3425151}
; {:max-health 100, :strength 100, :name "Bilbo", :items #{}, :health 100.0}
; {:max-health 500, :strength 400, :name "Smaug", :items #{}, :health 480.990141}
; ...
```

❶ You can see the healing effects of Gandalf made concrete each time
  Bilbo's :health goes up in the log.

You'll find this same content in the *character-states.log* file as well. Fundamentally,
we're logging states to the console and a file because they're the most accessible sinks;
this approach will work just as well if you were to stream updates to a database, message
queue, and so on.

Using a watcher like this gives us the opportunity to make each state change to our
characters' refs durable (e.g., by writing them to disk or to a database) without modifying the functions used to implement those changes.

In order to track and persist in-transaction information—like the amount of each attack
and heal, who did what to whom, and so on—we just need to dispatch a write action
to our writer agents within the body of any function that makes a change we might
want to persist:

```
(defn attack
  [aggressor target]
  (dosync
    (let [damage (* (rand 0.1) (:strength @aggressor) (ensure daylight))]
      (send-off console write
```

```
        (:name @aggressor) "hits" (:name @target) "for" damage)
      (commute target update-in [:health] #(max 0 (- % damage))))))

(defn heal
  [healer target]
  (dosync
    (let [aid (min (* (rand 0.1) (:mana @healer))
                   (- (:max-health @target) (:health @target)))]
      (when (pos? aid)
        (send-off console write
          (:name @healer) "heals" (:name @target) "for" aid)
        (commute healer update-in [:mana] - (max 5 (/ aid 5)))
        (alter target update-in [:health] + aid)))))

(dosync
  (alter smaug assoc :health 500)
  (alter bilbo assoc :health 100))
; {:max-health 100, :strength 100, :name "Bilbo", :items #{}, :health 100}
; {:max-health 500, :strength 400, :name "Smaug", :items #{}, :health 500}

(wait-futures 1
              (play bilbo attack smaug)
              (play smaug attack bilbo)
              (play gandalf heal bilbo))
; {:max-health 500, :strength 400, :name "Smaug", :items #{}, :health 497.414581}
; Bilbo hits Smaug for 2.585418463393845
; {:max-health 100, :strength 100, :name "Bilbo", :items #{}, :health 66.6262521}
; Smaug hits Bilbo for 33.373747881474934
; {:max-health 500, :strength 400, :name "Smaug", :items #{}, :health 494.667477}
; Bilbo hits Smaug for 2.747103668676348
; {:max-health 100, :strength 100, :name "Bilbo", :items #{}, :health 100.0}
; Gandalf heals Bilbo for 33.37374788147494
; ...
```

The end result of composing these small pieces together with our character refs is a fire-and-forget persistence mechanism that is safe to use in conjunction with the retries that are inevitable when using atoms and transactions over refs. We wrote to the console and a logfile to keep the example simple, but you can just as easily write ref state updates to a database. In any case, this demonstrates how, just as with the general usage of atoms and refs, even things like sharing I/O resources within a concurrent environment can be done without touching a single low-level lock and taking on the risks inherent in their management.

Using agents to parallelize workloads

It may initially seem unnecessary or inconvenient to have to segregate agent actions into two sorts. However, without the separation between blocking and nonblocking actions, agents would lose their ability to efficiently utilize the resources needed to service the different kinds of workloads—CPU, disk I/O, network throughput, and so on.

For example, say our application was dedicated to processing messages pulled from a queue; reading messages from the queue would likely be a blocking operation due to waiting on the network if the queue was not in-process, and depending on the semantics of the queue, waiting for work to be available. However, processing each message is likely to be CPU-bound.

This sounds a lot like a web crawler. Agents make building one that is efficient and flexible quite easy. The one we'll build here will be extraordinarily basic,[34] but it will demonstrate how agents can be used to orchestrate and parallelize potentially very complicated workloads.

First, we need some basic functions for working with the content of web pages we crawl. links-from takes a base URL and that URL's HTML content, returning a seq of the links found within that content; words-from takes some HTML content and extracts its text, returning a seq of the words found therein, converted to lowercase:

```
(require '[net.cgrand.enlive-html :as enlive])
(use '[clojure.string :only (lower-case)])
(import '(java.net URL MalformedURLException))

(defn- links-from
  [base-url html]
  (remove nil? (for [link (enlive/select html [:a])]
                 (when-let [href (-> link :attrs :href)]
                   (try
                     (URL. base-url href)
                     ; ignore bad URLs
                     (catch MalformedURLException e))))))

(defn- words-from
  [html]
  (let [chunks (-> html
                   (enlive/at [:script] nil)
                   (enlive/select [:body enlive/text-node]))]
    (->> chunks
         (mapcat (partial re-seq #"\w+"))
         (remove (partial re-matches #"\d+"))
         (map lower-case))))
```

This code uses Enlive, a web templating and scraping library that we discuss in detail in "Enlive: Selector-Based HTML Transformation" on page 546, but its details aren't key to our main focus, the use of agents to soak up all of the resources we have to maximize crawling throughput.

There will be three pools of state associated with our web crawler:

1. One of Java's thread-safe queues will hold URLs that are yet to be crawled, which we'll call url-queue. Then, for each page we retrieve, we will...

---

34. And not very well-behaved, especially insofar as it doesn't throttle connections, a key point of politeness when crawling web content. Our apologies to the BBC for (ab)using them as an example crawl root!

---

2. Find all of the links in the page so as to crawl them later; these will all be added to a set held within an atom called `crawled-urls`, and URLs we haven't visited yet will be queued up in `url-queue`. Finally...

3. We'll extract all of the text of each page, which will be used to maintain a count of cumulative word frequencies observed throughout the crawl. This count will be stored in a map of words to their respective counts, held in an atom called `word-freqs`:

```
(import '(java.util.concurrent BlockingQueue LinkedBlockingQueue))
(def url-queue (LinkedBlockingQueue.))
(def crawled-urls (atom #{}))
(def word-freqs (atom {}))
```

We'll set up a bunch of agents in order to fully utilize all the resources we have available,[35] but we need to think through what state they'll hold and what actions will be used to transition those states. In many cases, it is useful to think about agent state and the actions applied to it as forming a finite state machine; we've already walked through the workflow of our crawler, but we should formalize it.

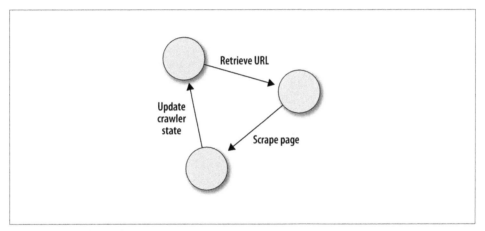

Figure 4-8. A web crawler's primary state transitions

The state of an agent at each point in this process should be obvious: prior to retrieving a URL, an agent will need a URL to retrieve (or some source of such URLs); prior to scraping, an agent will need a page's content to scrape; and, prior to updating the cumulative crawler state, it will need the results of scraping. Since we don't have very many potential states, we can simplify things for ourselves by allowing each action implementing these transitions to indicate the *next* action (transition) that should be applied to an agent.

---

35. Another shortcoming of our basic web crawler: at nearly any scale, a useful web crawler would use a message queue and suitable database instead of maintaining all state in memory. This thankfully does not affect the semantics of our example, which could be adapted to use such things with relative ease.

To see what this looks like, let's define our set of agents; their initial state, corresponding with the initial state preceding the "Retrieve URL" transition in Figure 4-8, is a map containing the queue from which the next URL may be retrieved, and the next transition itself, a function we'll call get-url:

```
(declare get-url)

(def agents (set (repeatedly 25 #(agent {::t #'get-url :queue url-queue})))) ❶
```

❶ Our agents' state will always have a ::t slot,[36] mapped to the next function that implements the next transition.[37]

The three transitions shown in Figure 4-8 are implemented by three agent actions: get-url, process, and handle-results.

get-url will wait on a queue (remember, each of our agents has url-queue as its initial value) for URLs to crawl. It will leave the state of the agent set to a map containing the URL it pulls off the queue and its content:

```
(use '[clojure.java.io :only (as-url)])
(declare run process handle-results)           ❶

(defn ^::blocking get-url
  [{:keys [^BlockingQueue queue] :as state}]
  (let [url (as-url (.take queue))]
    (try
      (if (@crawled-urls url)                   ❷
        state
        {:url url
         :content (slurp url)
         ::t #'process})
      (catch Exception e
        ;; skip any URL we failed to load
        state)
      (finally (run *agent*)))))
```

❶ We'll show run and explain what it's doing in a little bit.

❷ If we've already crawled the URL pulled off the queue (or if we encounter an error while loading the URL's content), we leave the agent's state untouched. This implementation detail in our finite state machine adds a cycle to it where get-url will sometimes be invoked on a single agent multiple times before it transitions states.

---

36. We use a namespaced keyword to avoid any potential naming clashes with other parts of state that might be added to the agents, if this crawler implementation were to ever be extended outside of its own namespace.

37. Depending on the range of states that are to be held by your agents, sending a multimethod or protocol function to them can be an elegant, efficient option to discriminate between a number of different potential agent state transitions. We talk about multimethods and protocols in Chapter 7 and "Protocols" on page 264, respectively.

process will parse a URL's content, using the links-from and words-from functions to obtain the URL's content's links and build a map containing the frequencies of each word found in the content. It will leave the state of the agent set to a map containing these values as well as the originating URL:

```
(defn process
  [{:keys [url content]}]
  (try
    (let [html (enlive/html-resource (java.io.StringReader. content))]
      {::t #'handle-results
       :url url
       :links (links-from url html)
       :words (reduce (fn [m word]
                        (update-in m [word] (fnil inc 0)))      ❶
                      {}
                      (words-from html))})
    (finally (run *agent*))))
```

❶ The :words map associates found words with their count within the retrieved page, which we produce by reducing a map through the seq of those words. fnil is a HOF that returns a function that uses some default value(s) (here, 0) in place of any nil arguments when calling the function provided to fnil; this keeps us from having to explicitly check if the value in the words map is nil, and returning 1 if so.

handle-results will update our three key pieces of state: adding the just-crawled URL to crawled-urls, pushing each of the newfound links onto url-queue, and merging the URL's content's word frequency map with our cumulative word-freqs map. handle-results returns a state map containing url-queue and the get-url transition, thus leaving the agent in its original state.

```
(defn ^::blocking handle-results
  [{:keys [url links words]}]
  (try
    (swap! crawled-urls conj url)
    (doseq [url links]
      (.put url-queue url))
    (swap! word-freqs (partial merge-with +) words)

    {::t #'get-url :queue url-queue}
    (finally (run *agent*))))
```

You may have noticed that each of the functions we'll use as agent actions has a try form with a finally clause that contains a sole call to run with *agent* as its sole argument.[38] We didn't define *agent* anywhere; usually unbound, it is a var provided by Clojure that, within the scope of the evaluation of an agent action, is bound to the *current agent*. So, (run *agent*) in each of these actions is calling run with a single argument, the agent that is evaluating the action.

---

38. We've repeated this pattern in three functions at this point; any more, and it would be a no-brainer to write a macro that would eliminate that boilerplate.

This is a common idiom used with agents that allow them to run continuously. In our web crawler's case, run is a function that queues up the next transition function to be applied to an agent based on that agent's ::t state. If each action already knows which transition function should be applied next, why add a level of indirection in calling run? Two reasons:

1. While it is reasonable to expect each function used as an agent action to know what the next transition should be given the new agent state it is returning, there's no way for it to know whether that next transition is a blocking action or not. This is something that is best left up to the transitions themselves (and their informed authors); thus, run will use the presence (or, absence) of ::blocking metadata on each transition to determine whether to use send or send-off to dispatch transition functions.[39]

2. run can check to see if the agent has been marked as being paused—a condition indicated simply by the presence of a logically true ::paused value in the agent's metadata.

Example 4-8. run, the web crawler's "main loop"

```
(defn paused? [agent] (::paused (meta agent)))

(defn run
  ([] (doseq [a agents] (run a)))
  ([a]
   (when (agents a)
     (send a (fn [{transition ::t :as state}]
               (when-not (paused? *agent*)
                 (let [dispatch-fn (if (-> transition meta ::blocking)
                                     send-off
                                     send)]
                   (dispatch-fn *agent* transition)))
               state)))))
```

run doubles as a way to start all of our (unpaused) agents when called with no arguments.

The pausing capability is particularly important, as we wouldn't want to have the crawler run without interruption. With the use of metadata to indicate that run should not dispatch the next transition for an agent's state, pause and restart give us a way to pause or restart the agents' operation just from changing their metadata:

```
(defn pause
  ([] (doseq [a agents] (pause a)))
  ([a] (alter-meta! a assoc ::paused true)))

(defn restart
```

---

39. This metadata access explains in part why we're using the functions' vars to denote transitions instead of the functions themselves. Beyond that, using vars helps make it easier to modify the behavior of the web crawler; see "Limitations to Redefining Constructs" on page 415 for why.

```
([] (doseq [a agents] (restart a)))
([a]
  (alter-meta! a dissoc ::paused)
  (run a)))
```

Now we can crawl some web pages! We'll want to run the crawler repeatedly from a fresh state, so it will be handy to have a testing function that will reset the crawler state. `test-crawler` does this, as well as adding a starting URL to `url-queue`, and letting the agents run for just 60 seconds so we can make some informal throughput comparisons:

```
(defn test-crawler
  "Resets all state associated with the crawler, adds the given URL to the
   url-queue, and runs the crawler for 60 seconds, returning a vector
   containing the number of URLs crawled, and the number of URLs
   accumulated through crawling that have yet to be visited."
  [agent-count starting-url]
  (def agents (set (repeatedly agent-count
                      #(agent {::t #'get-url :queue url-queue}))))  ❶
  (.clear url-queue)
  (swap! crawled-urls empty)
  (swap! word-freqs empty)
  (.add url-queue starting-url)
  (run)
  (Thread/sleep 60000)
  (pause)
  [(count @crawled-urls) (count url-queue)])
```

❶ We warned you against redefining vars within the body of a function in "Vars Are Not Variables" on page 206, but this may be one of the few contexts where doing so is okay: a function that is never called outside of the REPL, used solely for experimentation and testing.

To establish a baseline, let's first try it with a single agent, using the BBC's news page as a crawl root:

```
(test-crawler 1 "http://www.bbc.co.uk/news/")
;= [86 14598]
```

Eighty-six pages crawled in a minute. Surely we can do better; let's use 25 agents, which will parallelize both the blocking retrieval workload as well as the CPU-bound scraping and text processing workload:

```
(test-crawler 25 "http://www.bbc.co.uk/news/")
;= [670 81775]
```

Not bad, 670 pages crawled in 60 seconds, a very solid order of magnitude gained simply by tweaking the number of agents being applied to the problem.[40]

Let's check on the word frequencies being calculated. We can get a selection of the most and least common terms with their frequencies quite easily:

---

40. Of course, your specific results will vary greatly depending upon the CPU power you have available and the speed and latency of your Internet connection; however, the relative improvement from 1 to 25 agents should be similar.

```
(->> (sort-by val @word-freqs)
  reverse
  (take 10))
;= (["the" 23083] ["to" 14308] ["of" 11243] ["bbc" 10969] ["in" 9473]
;=  ["a" 9214] ["and" 8595] ["for" 5203] ["is" 4844] ["on" 4364])
(->> (sort-by val @word-freqs)
  (take 10))
;= (["relieved" 1] ["karim" 1] ["gnome" 1] ["brummell" 1] ["mccredie" 1]
;=  ["ensinar" 1] ["estrictas" 1] ["arap" 1] ["forcibly" 1] ["kitchin" 1])
```

Looks like we have a fully functioning crawler that does some marginally interesting work. It's surely not optimal—as we've said, it's quite basic, and would need a variety of subtle enhancements in order to be used at scale, but the foundation is clearly there.

Now, remember what we were saying earlier in this section, that the division of agent actions into those that may block (due to I/O or other wait conditions) and those that won't (i.e., CPU-bound processing) enables the maximal utilization of all of the resources at our disposal. We can test this; for example, by marking process as a blocking operation, we will ensure that it is always sent to agents using send-off, and thus handled using the unbounded thread pool:

```
(alter-meta! #'process assoc ::blocking true)
;= {:arglists ([{:keys [url content]}]), :ns #<Namespace user>,
;=  :name process, :user/blocking true}
```

The practical effect of this is that all of the HTML parsing, searching for links, and text processing associated with the word frequency calculations will happen without limit.

```
(test-crawler 25 "http://www.bbc.co.uk/news/")
;= [573 80576]
```

This actually has a negative impact on throughput—approaching 15 percent overall—as now there can be up to 25 active (and hungry) agents contending for CPU cores, which can cumulatively slow our CPU-bound workload.

Using Java's Concurrency Primitives

Now that we've done a deep dive into Clojure's extensive concurrency and state-management features, it's worth pointing out that Java's native threads, primitive lock mechanisms, and its own very useful concurrency libraries—especially the java.util.concurrent.* packages—are quite usable in Clojure. In particular, the latter are used extensively in the implementation of Clojure's own concurrency primitives, but Clojure does not wrap or subsume them, so you should learn about them and use them as appropriate in your applications.

We've not yet explored all the mechanics of Clojure's Java interoperability—we'll get to that in Chapter 9—but the examples we show here should be basic enough for you to understand before you dig into that.

Java defines a couple of key interfaces—`java.lang.Runnable` and `java.util.concurrent.Callable`—which are implemented by Clojure functions that take no parameters. This means you can pass no-arg Clojure functions to any Java API that requires an object that implements one of these interfaces, including native `Thread`s:

```
(.start (Thread. #(println "Running...")))
;= Running...
;= nil
```

The `java.util.concurrent.*` packages offer a number of concurrency facilities that are used in the implementation of Clojure's own features, many of which you should take advantage when appropriate. We already demonstrated the operation of one type of thread-safe queue implementation in "Using agents to parallelize work-loads" on page 217, `LinkedBlockingQueue`; there are many others like it but with subtle yet important differences in semantics and performance. Then there are thread pools, thread-safe concurrent data structures (a better fallback than the vanilla, e.g., `java.util.HashMap` if your Clojure program needs to share a mutable-in-place data structure with some Java code), and special-purpose objects like `CountDownLatch`, which allow you block a thread (or future, or agent action dispatched with `send-off`) until some number of other events have occurred.

If you would like to know how to use these facilities effectively and develop a thorough understanding of concurrency at the lower levels of the JVM, we recommend *Java Concurrency in Practice* by Goetz, et al.

Locking

Even given all of the (safer) concurrency primitives provided by Clojure, you may still occasionally need a primitive lock, often when working with mutable Java entities such as arrays. Of course, once you make this decision, you're on your own: you are no longer benefiting from the defined semantics that those primitives guarantee. In any case, you can use the `locking` macro to obtain and hold a lock on a given object for the duration of execution within the body of the `locking` form.

So, this Clojure code:

```
(defn add
  [some-list value]
  (locking some-list
    (.add some-list value)))
```

is equivalent to this code in Java, Ruby, and Python, respectively:

```
// Java
public static void add (java.util.List someList, Object value) {
    synchronized (someList) {
        someList.add(value);
    }
}
```

```
# Ruby
require 'thread'
m = Mutex.new

def add (list, value)
    m.synchronize do
        list << value
    end
end


# Python
import threading
lock = threading.Lock()
def add (list, value):
    lock.acquire()
    list.append(value)
    lock.release()
```

Final Thoughts

Concurrent programming is hard, and many popular programming languages are set up in such a way to make it harder. By having a clear separation of identity and state, promoting immutability, and offering built-in constructs for safe multithreaded programming, Clojure goes a long way to making concurrent programming easier and more accessible.

## PART II

Building Abstractions

## CHAPTER 5

Macros

Historically, Lisps have been described as "programmable programming languages." This description fits Clojure, and a large part of the reason for that is macros. Macros allow a programmer to extend the Clojure language in ways that are difficult or impossible in most other languages.

A programming language is a means for building abstractions. Instead of doing tedious manual work, a programmer can write code once and treat that code as a reusable unit. Code can be executed repeatedly in a loop; or, code can be grouped as a unit and given a name as a function; or, using conditionals, the same code can do different things in different circumstances.

It should be clear that some languages offer more powerful means of abstraction than others. Imagine for a moment a programming language without loops. Such a language might be usable, but unrolling all loops by hand would be incredibly tedious. Similarly, a language without functions might be able to do anything any other Turing-complete language can do, but code would have to be repeated over and over.

In short, when a language lacks proper means of abstraction, the result is boilerplate and repetition, both signs of fundamental weaknesses in that language. Macros are powerful because they give you a way to define entirely new levels of abstraction within the language itself. Macros are the ultimate tool for eliminating boilerplate and growing a programming language up to meet your needs.

What Is a Macro?

Macros allow you to control the Clojure compiler. Within their scope, they can be used to effect subtle syntactic tweaks or to upend the language's rules of physics. Where Java might be "C++ without guns, knives, and clubs,"[1] and languages like Ruby and Python might provide a reasonable yet well-defined arsenal, Clojure's macros allow you to

---

1. This quotation is often attributed to James Gosling, the original architect of Java.

build any weapon you want and have it feel like it came with the language as a built-in armament.

The key to understanding macros is to keep clear in your mind the distinction between *runtime* and *compile time*.

As you learned in "The Reader" on page 12, Clojure source code is read by the Clojure reader, which produces Clojure data structures from textual Clojure code—the very same Clojure data structures you have access to in your own code. For example, from the string "(foo [bar] :baz 123)", the reader yields a list containing a symbol, a vector containing a symbol, a keyword, and an integer. This property, where a language's code is represented using its own data structures, is called *homoiconicity*, and is critical in enabling macros.[2]

Normally these data structures are then *evaluated*. Each type of data has particular rules that govern its evaluation:

- Many literals evaluate to themselves (e.g., integers, strings, keywords, vectors).
- Symbols resolve to a value in a var from some namespace.
- Lists denote calls, either to functions, special forms, or macros.

It is between the *read* and *evaluation* steps where compilation happens and macros occupy a privileged status compared to functions. Whereas function calls in source code carry through to the compiled representation of that code where arguments are evaluated and passed to the function as parameters yielding some result at runtime, *macros are called by the compiler* with their unevaluated data structures as arguments and must return a Clojure data structure that can itself be evaluated. For example, if foo is a function, then

```
(foo a b)
```

compiles down to a runtime invocation of the foo function with the two values named by a and b, whereas if bar is a macro, then

```
(bar a b)
```

bar is called by the Clojure compiler with two arguments, the *symbols* a and b—*not* the values they name.[3] bar can choose to evaluate those symbols in the same way as they normally are, or it can implement its own semantics, and it can do all this using all of Clojure's facilities and all of the data and functions defined thus far: macros are not limited to a subset of the language. In any case, bar must return to the compiler a Clojure data structure that will be used in its place. This is recursive, as a macro can return a

---

2. We talked about homoiconicity at some length in "Homoiconicity" on page 9.

3. The Clojure compiler knows to treat macro calls differently than calls of functions or special forms because of the implementation detail that macros are themselves functions with a bit of metadata hanging off of them identifying them as such. You can see this by inspecting the metadata of a macro's var, such as (meta #'or).

Clojure data structure that includes other macro calls as well; this continues for each expression until it is no longer a macro call.

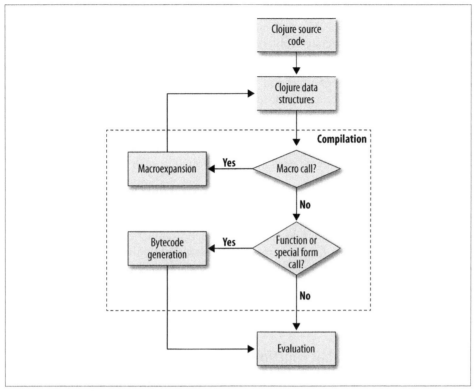

Figure 5-1. The Clojure compilation model

Macros being a tool of abstraction, each macro call generally produces code with a larger footprint than the macro call itself. Thus, this process of replacing macro calls with the code they produce is called *macroexpansion*. As we first said in "The Clojure REPL" on page 3, all Clojure code is always compiled, even at the REPL, and macroexpansion is a critical and inseparable part of compilation.

 The compilation process ensures that any macro calls are replaced wholesale with their expansions long before a program's runtime; thus, *macros are only ever evaluated at compile time*.

What Macros Are Not

Writing code that manipulates code is not a unique feature of Clojure, or Lisps in general. However, not all code-manipulating systems are created equal.

For example, C has a preprocessor, which does textual substitution of source code with other source code at compile time. Such textual macro systems are fundamentally less capable than Lisp-style macros, due to their reliance upon string processing rather than working with code as structured data. Some of the same weaknesses are evident in textual code evaluation mechanisms such as Ruby's eval, which we contrast with Clojure macros in "Macros Versus Ruby eval" on page 234.

Similarly, facilities providing *code generation* are not equivalent to macros. These generally take a high-level representation, say, a formal grammar or a description of an object model, and produce a body of code that implements it. While these systems are often useful, they often suffer from a discrete compilation step (whereas macros are folded into the same compilation process as all other Clojure code), siloed data models (whereas macros just use regular Clojure data structures), and noncomposability (whereas macros can readily be used in conjunction with each other).

Finally, there are a number of languages that provide compiler APIs, allowing you to modify code written in that language. Examples here include Java's annotation processors, Groovy's AST builders, Template Haskell, and Scala's compiler plug-ins. These are very powerful systems that do allow you to build syntactic abstractions and optimizations similar to what Clojure's macros support. While there are many potential points of contrast, the most striking is that these systems are by definition exposing an internal API and language data model that is generally far removed from its originating source code. Clojure being homoiconic makes the interface and model of macros as simple as working with Clojure data structures.

What Can Macros Do that Functions Cannot?

It may be difficult to understand at first the power or utility of macros. A simple example should make it clear.

Java was first released in 1996. Eight years later, in Java 5, enhanced for loops were added to the language, a useful addition long in the making. This lets you replace fairly verbose code like this:

```
for (int i = 0; i < collection.size(); i++) {
    SomeType var = (SomeType)collection.get(i);
    ...
}
```

with a more concise alternative:

```
for (SomeType var : collection) {
    ...
}
```

These kinds of changes to a language are important. The enhanced for loop in Java reduces complexity and eliminates possibilities for error: using enhanced for, it's impossible to exceed an array bounds, or accidentally iterate i starting from 1 instead of 0.

As programmers, we can look at a particular usage of the enhanced `for` syntax and mechanically transform the code into an equivalent loop using the old `for` syntax. The name of the loop variable and the collection to iterate over are the only important things here. The rest—tracking indices, bounds-checking, etc.—is just boilerplate.

So why didn't anyone add enhanced `for` to Java sooner? The problem is that Java lacks the expressive power to let you write code to do so. Enhanced `for` can't be a normal method call, and methods are the only tool at your disposal in Java. Methods can't set up bindings for local variables outside the scope of the method itself. Methods can't conditionally execute their arguments—their arguments are always evaluated, and the resulting values are passed to the method. It would be possible to create something that behaved similar to enhanced `for` in Java, but it certainly wouldn't look or feel anything like what shipped with Java 5.

Adding enhanced `for` to Java requires a change at the compiler level, and the average user does not have the knowledge or ability to make that change. So what did Java developers do for those first eight years without this helpful language feature? They lived without it.

In contrast, *any* Clojure programmer, in matter of minutes and in a few lines of unprivileged Clojure code, can write a macro to add an imperative looping construct to Clojure that is similar to Java 5's enhanced `for`:[4]

```
(defmacro foreach [[sym coll] & body]
  `(loop [coll# ~coll]
     (when-let [[~sym & xs#] (seq coll#)]
       ~@body
       (recur xs#))))
;= #'user/foreach
(foreach [x [1 2 3]]
  (println x))
; 1
; 2
; 3
```

Functions are excellent tools of abstraction, but there are certain things they simply cannot do because they are only called at runtime and have no access to the compiler; in this case, there is no way to lift an unevaluated body of code (our `println` call) into a looping construct by relying upon functions alone. In short, macros allow a Clojure programmer to add new language constructs to the language.

Built-ins versus macros.   Compared to most languages, Clojure's set of built-in operators—called *special forms*—is very small. Recall that the complete list (see "Special Forms" on page 23) contained only 16 items.

There are a lot of things missing from that list that we might expect to find there. Where are iteration constructs like `while`, `for`, and `doseq`? Defining constructs like `defn`,

---

4. This `foreach` macro is purely illustrative; Clojure already provides a superset of functionality offered by Java's enhanced imperative looping in `doseq`, in addition to `for`, its functional counterpart.

defmacro, defrecord? Conditionals like when, cond, and condp? All of these are fundamental to our everyday experience as Clojure programmers.

Perhaps surprisingly, those are all macros. If they didn't exist, you could write them
yourself in plain Clojure, without coordinating with or convincing the language's
authors. This is in stark contrast to many languages, where the thought of writing your
own loop or conditional construct is pure fantasy. Of course, this generalizes to very
application- and domain-specific requirements, where a syntactic tweak can make all
the difference in making the language itself more suitable for your particular needs.
Thus, macros blur the line between what is "built in" to the language and what is user-
defined; because the latter have the same status as the former, the distinction loses
much of its meaning.

Macros Versus Ruby eval

At a glance, macros may seem similar to eval in Ruby.[5] eval in Ruby is a built-in function that executes code at runtime. Ruby also has class_eval and instance_eval, which
similarly execute code at runtime, in different contexts.

In Ruby, we could write this:

```
x = 123
code = "puts VAR"
code.sub!(/VAR/, 'x')
eval code
```

And this would print 123. We've created code as a string, manipulated that code, and
executed it.

One important distinction between macros and eval is that eval executes at *runtime*.
This means, for example, that errors that would normally be caught at compile time
are impossible to catch in evaled code. Consider:

```
code = <<END
  def foo
    puts "foo!       # oops, forgot a closing quote
  end
END

if(rand(2) == 0)
  eval code
end
```

Half the time, this code will compile and run without error, because our code string is
never evaled. The other half of the time, we'll get an error at runtime.

By contrast, Clojure macros are compiled at compile time. A similar error would be
caught in Clojure immediately; because macros are just more Clojure code, so

---

5. Or Python, or JavaScript, or PHP, or Perl, or really any other language the allows you to evaluate a string
   containing code.

attempting to use improper syntax will fail in the reader. For example, this code will never even get to the point of being compiled, never mind used:

```
(defmacro foo []
  `(if (= 0 (rand-int 2))
     (println "foo!)))    ;; oops, forgot a closing quote
;= #<Exception java.lang.Exception: EOF while reading string>
```

Another difference between macros and Ruby's eval is apparent as soon as we try to manipulate our code. With Ruby eval, our code is a String. This String is structureless; to manipulate it, we are limited to the tools that work with Strings: regular expressions, concatenation, and substringing.

In contrast, Clojure macros don't operate over structureless strings. Since Clojure is homoiconic, they deal directly with Clojure data structures like lists, vectors, symbols, and so on.

Manipulation of source code in Strings is fragile and error-prone. And errors are not caught until the code is evaled, making the process dangerous. Thus, it's common to hear strong caveats in the Ruby world against ever using eval at all, and rightly so.

So, this monstrosity would be considered very poor form in Ruby:

```
>> def print_sym(x)
>>   code = "p(" + x + ".to_sym)"
>> end
nil
>> eval print_sym "\"foo\""
:foo
nil
```

while this Clojure equivalent is just fine:

```
(defmacro print-keyword [x]
  `(println (keyword ~x)))
;= #'user/print-keyword
(print-keyword "foo")
;  :foo
;= nil
```

Writing Your First Macro

Let's write a silly macro that does something that a function could never do. Suppose in a quest to annoy our coworkers, we want to write all of the symbols in our code in reverse. Our goal is to write this:

```
(reverse-it (nltnirp "foo"))
```

and have Clojure end up evaluating this:

```
(println "foo")
```

It should be apparent that this would be impossible to do in a language like Java without altering the Java parser or compiler. But in Clojure, thanks to macros, we can do it easily.

Our `reverse-it` macro receives source code as its arguments in the form of Clojure data structures. All we have to do is locate all of the symbols, fetch the symbols' `String` "names," reverse those strings and return new symbols in their place.

`clojure.walk` provides a handy function `postwalk`, which lets us recursively walk a series of nested lists and do something to certain elements. This fits our requirements nicely:

Example 5-1. reverse-it, a symbol-reversing macro

```
(require '(clojure [string :as str]
                   [walk :as walk]))

(defmacro reverse-it
  [form]                                          ❶
  (walk/postwalk #(if (symbol? %)                 ❷
                    (symbol (str/reverse (name %)))) ❸
                  %)
                 form))
```

❶ Our macro takes a single argument, named `form` here.

❷ It uses the `postwalk` function to recursively apply the given anonymous function to every element in `form`.

❸ That anonymous function replaces all symbols in `form` with symbols that have a reversed name, but leaves the rest of the elements in `form` untouched.

And now we can write absurdities[6] like this:

```
(reverse-it
  (qesod [gra (egnar 5)]
    (nltnirp (cni gra))))
; 1
; 2
; 3
; 4
; 5
;= nil
```

because after expanding the macro, Clojure sees normal, familiar code:

```
(macroexpand-1 '(reverse-it
                  (qesod [gra (egnar 5)]
                    (nltnirp (cni gra)))))
;= (doseq [arg (range 5)]
;=   (println (inc arg)))
```

---

6. While `reverse-it` provides a striking demonstration of one type of possible syntactic transformation made possible by macros, actually using something like it would surely be considered evil.

We're using the `macroexpand-1` function here to see what code our macro call is providing to the Clojure compiler. The `macroexpand` family of functions are key tools used in testing and debugging macros, which we'll discuss next.

Debugging Macros

Macros can be notoriously difficult to debug. Clojure helpfully catches a variety of compile-time errors, but care must be taken to use the power that macros offer without being snared by their traps.

Consider what happens when referring to a var that isn't yet defined. In a function, this will trigger a compile-time error:

```
(defn oops [arg] (frobnicate arg))
;= #<CompilerException java.lang.Exception:
;=   Unable to resolve symbol: frobnicate in this context (NO_SOURCE_FILE:1)>
```

Sadly, we can define a similar macro without any warning:

```
(defmacro oops [arg] `(frobnicate ~arg))
;= #'user/oops
```

Trying to use this macro will produce an error when it is *used*:

```
(oops 123)
;= #<CompilerException java.lang.IllegalStateException:
;=   Var user/frobnicate is unbound. (NO_SOURCE_FILE:0)>
```

What happened? Remember that macros execute at *compile time*. At compile time, Clojure doesn't (and can't) know if the symbol `frobnicate` will refer to a var that has a defined value at runtime or not. The macro sees and returns only lists, symbols, and other data structures. Whether those symbols are valid when the code produced by the macro is executed is not for the macro to decide. This can make debugging macros tricky, but we have a couple of tools at our disposal.

Macroexpansion

The most fundamental tool in debugging macros is `macroexpand-1`. This function takes a data structure (in debugging contexts, often a quoted macro form) and taps into the Clojure compiler to return the code—which, remember, is just a data structure—that will be executed in its place if it were to be evaluated. Here we can see that the `oops` macro invoked with an integer will return a list with two elements, the namespaced `frobnicate` symbol (referring to a nonexistent var) and the integer argument:

```
(macroexpand-1 '(oops 123))
;= (user/frobnicate 123)
```

`macroexpand-1` only expands the macro once. Remember that macroexpansion can happen many times if a macro returns code that itself contains macro calls; if your macro produces another macro call, and you want to continue expanding until the top level form is no longer a macro, use `macroexpand` instead.

Because so many core facilities in Clojure are themselves macros, `macroexpand-1` is often quite helpful in avoiding a verbose and unclear macro expansion. Going back to the `reverse-it` macro that we defined in Example 5-1, we can readily see the difference between `macroexpand-1` and `macroexpand`:

```
(macroexpand-1 '(reverse-it
                  (qesod [gra (egnar 5)]
                    (nltnirp (cni gra)))))
;= (doseq [arg (range 5)]
;=   (println (inc arg)))

(pprint (macroexpand '(reverse-it
                        (qesod [gra (egnar 5)]
                          (nltnirp (cni gra))))))
; (loop*
;   [seq_1647
;    (clojure.core/seq (range 5))
;    chunk_1648
;    nil
;    count_1649
;    (clojure.core/int 0)
;    i_1650
;    (clojure.core/int 0)]
;   (if
;    (clojure.core/< i_1650 count_1649)
;    (clojure.core/let
;     [arg (.nth chunk_1648 i_1650)]
;     (do (println (inc arg)))
;     (recur
;      seq_1647
;      chunk_1648
;      count_1649
;      (clojure.core/unchecked-inc i_1650)))
;    (clojure.core/when-let
;     [seq_1647 (clojure.core/seq seq_1647)]
;     (if
;      (clojure.core/chunked-seq? seq_1647)
;      (clojure.core/let
;       [c__3798__auto__ (clojure.core/chunk-first seq_1647)]
;       (recur
;        (clojure.core/chunk-rest seq_1647)
;        c__3798__auto__
;        (clojure.core/int (clojure.core/count c__3798__auto__))
;        (clojure.core/int 0)))
;      (clojure.core/let
;       [arg (clojure.core/first seq_1647)]
;       (do (println (inc arg)))
;       (recur
;        (clojure.core/next seq_1647)
;        nil
;        (clojure.core/int 0)
;        (clojure.core/int 0)))))))
```

`reverse-it` returns a `doseq` form, itself a macro that is based upon the `loop` special form, whose full macroexpansion is lengthy. In most cases, you will find that you only need to see the "top level" expansion of a macro, making `macroexpand-1` far preferable.

Completely expanding macros. Neither `macroexpand` nor `macroexpand-1` expand nested forms. For example, here we attempt to macroexpand a `cond` form, which emits an `if` call, with the "else" branch itself consisting of a `cond` form that will remain unexpanded:

```
(macroexpand '(cond a b c d))
;= (if a b (clojure.core/cond c d))
```

Being able to obtain the complete expansion of a macro can be very helpful. In many cases, the `clojure.walk/macroexpand-all` function fills that need:

```
(require '[clojure.walk :as w])

(w/macroexpand-all '(cond a b c d))
;= (if a b (if c d nil))
```

`macroexpand-all` is useful, but it is fundamentally a simple hack that only partially emulates the full macroexpansion performed by the compiler. For example, it does not handle special forms precisely right:

```
(w/macroexpand-all ''(when x a))
;= (quote (if x (do a)))
```

That expression should expand into `(quote (when x a))`—macroexpansion shouldn't progress past the `quote` special form. Similarly, `macroexpand-all` does not support the implicit `&env` and `&form` arguments, which we discuss in full in "The Implicit Arguments: &env and &form" on page 251, along with an improved `macroexpand` variant that can support those implicit arguments.

Syntax

Since macros return Clojure data structures, we will often want to return lists to represent further calls, either of functions, special forms, or other macros. Therefore, we need tools to build these lists. It's perfectly acceptable to use the simplest tool in our toolbox, the `list` function:

```
(defmacro hello
  [name]
  (list 'println name))

(macroexpand '(hello "Brian"))
;= (println "Brian")
```

However, for more complex macros that return something more than a simple flat list, this quickly becomes unwieldy. This is how the source code for the standard macro `while` would look, written in this manner:

```
(defmacro while
  [test & body]
  (list 'loop []
    (concat (list 'when test) body
      '((recur))))))
```

The gist of this macro is lost in all the calls to `list` and `concat`.

Therefore, Clojure offers some syntactic sugar for working with lists and interpolating named values into them. Using this sugar, the `while` macro[7] is much more readable:

```
(defmacro while
  [test & body]
  `(loop []
    (when ~test
      ~@body
      (recur))))
```

This macro uses three tools: syntax-quote,[8] unquote, and `splicing-unquote`. This syntax is not intrinsic to macros. You can use it in functions or other code as well, but because macros deal so heavily with lists, macros are the place you'll use these the most.[9]

quote Versus syntax-quote

You should be familiar with the `quote` special form already, which returns its arguments unevaluated. As a shortcut, we can write `(quote (a b))` as `'(a b)`, both of which evaluate to a list with two elements, the symbols `a` and `b`.

Clojure contains another form of quoting. *Syntax-quoting* looks similar to quoting, except it uses a backtick (`` ` ``) instead.

There are two differences between `quote` and `syntax-quote`. First, the latter fully qualifies unqualified symbols with the current namespace:

```
(def foo 123)
;= #'user/foo
[foo (quote foo) 'foo `foo]
;= [123 foo foo user/foo]
```

The syntax-quoted `` `foo `` (the last "foo" in the vector) results in the namespaced symbol `user/foo` because it was evaluated in the `user` namespace. In another namespace, `` `foo `` will be read as a symbol qualified to that other namespace.

```
(in-ns 'bar)
```

---

7. Shown here exactly as it is implemented in Clojure's standard library.

8. Similar facilities are called "backquote" or "quasi-quote" in other Lisps. The term "syntax-quote" was coined by Rich Hickey to distinguish it from those alternatives.

9. For example, we use `syntax-quote` and `unquote` outside of the scope of a macro in "In Detail: -> and ->>" on page 259.

```
`foo
;= bar/foo
```

However, if the symbol is namespace-aliased or is known to refer to a var from another namespace, syntax-quote qualifies it with the corresponding namespace.

```
(ns baz (:require [user :as u]))

`map
;= clojure.core/map
`u/foo
;= user/foo
`foo
;= baz/foo
```

This default qualification of symbols is critical for ensuring that a macro does not produce code that inadvertently refers to or redefines an already-named value within the context where it is used. This is called macro *hygiene*, and is discussed in "Hygiene" on page 244.

The second difference between quoting and syntax-quoting is that syntax-quoting allows *unquoting*: some elements of the list can be selectively *unquoted*, causing them to be evaluated within the scope of the syntax-quoted form.

unquote and unquote-splicing

When building a skeleton of source code in a macro, it's common to create lists where some elements need to be evaluated and some should not. One way of doing this—painful if it were your only option—is to use `list` and individually syntax-quote each element in the list that needs to be quoted, leaving the others unquoted.

```
(list `map `println [foo])
;= (clojure.core/map clojure.core/println [123])
```

A shorter and more readable option is to syntax-quote the entire list, and then *unquote* only those elements you would like to have evaluated in-place. This is done via ~.

```
`(map println [~foo])
;= (clojure.core/map clojure.core/println [123])

`(map println ~[foo])
;= (clojure.core/map clojure.core/println [123])
```

Note that compared to the explicit `list` version, the syntax-quoted form looks identical to how we'd write the form unquoted, with additional ` and ~ added.

Note also the second example: unquoting a list or vector unquotes the entire form. This can be used to evaluate function calls inside syntax-quoted forms:

```
`(println ~(keyword (str foo)))
;= (clojure.core/println :123)
```

Another common case is starting with a list of forms and unpacking the *contents* of another list into the first. Again, the most straightforward version using `list` and `concat` is pretty awkward:

```
(let [defs '((def x 123)
             (def y 456))]
  (concat (list 'do) defs))
;= (do (def x 123) (def y 456))
```

The `unquote-splicing` operator `~@` is a better option, and does the concatenation for you.

```
(let [defs '((def x 123)
             (def y 456))]
  `(do ~@defs))
;= (do (def x 123) (def y 456))
```

Here the elements within the list `defs` are spliced into the surrounding `syntax-quoted` list. This is a very common idiom in writing macros. For example, a macro that accepts multiple forms as a "code body" will often look like this:

```
(defmacro foo
  [& body]
  `(do-something ~@body))

(macroexpand-1 '(foo (doseq [x (range 5)]
                       (println x))
                     :done))
;= (user/do-something
;=   (doseq [x (range 5)]
;=     (println x))
;=   :done)
```

The rest argument `body` holds a sequential collection of the parameters to the macro, and then `~@body` in the macro unpacks that list into the surrounding context.

`syntax-quote` combined with `unquote` and `unquote-splicing` allow you to treat Clojure data structures—and therefore Clojure code that you may return from macros—as templates: you can form a skeleton of a form with `syntax-quote`, and then selectively fill in key parameterized parts of that skeleton with values and evaluated expressions thanks to the `unquote` syntaxes.

> `syntax-quote`, `unquote`, and `unquote-splicing` aren't magic: they are functions in Clojure's standard library that are swapped in by the reader in place of their various syntaxes, `` ` ``, `~`, and `~@`. You can take a look at what is going under the hood by quoting a `syntax-quoted` expression to suppress *its* evaluation:
>
> ```
> '`(map println ~[foo])
> ;= (clojure.core/seq
> ;=   (clojure.core/concat
> ;=     (clojure.core/list (quote clojure.core/map))
> ;=     (clojure.core/list (quote clojure.core/println))
> ;=     (clojure.core/list [foo])))
> ```

When to Use Macros

Macros are clearly a powerful tool, but with that power inevitably comes responsibility—and a list of caveats.

Macros operate at compile time. This means they are not first-class citizens of a running Clojure program like functions are. A macro has no access to runtime information, such as the current runtime values of a var. A macro sees only unevaluated data structures read from source code.

Consider a simple function that returns a greeting. It's possible to write this as either a function or a macro:

```
(defn fn-hello [x]
  (str "Hello, " x "!"))

(defmacro macro-hello [x]
  `(str "Hello, " ~x "!"))
```

These appear to behave similarly in some usages:

```
(fn-hello "Brian")
;= "Hello, Brian!"
(macro-hello "Brian")
;= "Hello, Brian!"
```

But they behave very differently in different contexts:

```
(map fn-hello ["Brian" "Not Brian"])
;= ("Hello, Brian!" "Hello, Not Brian!")
(map macro-hello ["Brian" "Not Brian"])
;= #<CompilerException java.lang.RuntimeException:
;=   Can't take value of a macro: #'user/macro-hello, compiling:(NO_SOURCE_PATH:1)>
```

This latter usage of `macro-hello` breaks because we are attempting to apply the macro's value at runtime. They functionally don't exist at runtime,[10] they can't be composed or passed as values, and therefore it makes no sense to `map` a macro across a collection of values as we attempted to do above.

To use macros in such contexts, we would need to wrap their usage in an enclosing `fn` or anonymous function literal. This brings the macro's application back to compile time, when the enclosing function is compiled. This will generally lead to some awkward situations where passing a function value would be far simpler and idiomatic:

```
(map #(macro-hello %) ["Brian" "Not Brian"])
;= ("Hello, Brian!" "Hello, Not Brian!")
```

An alternative to awkward wrapping in `fn` or #(...) would be to try to maintain clean-looking code by introducing another macro that would be a wrapper for `map`. This is a

---

10. This isn't entirely true, as we show in "Testing and debugging &env usage" (page 253)...but as you'll see there, using macros at runtime is messy, an unsupported implementation detail, and generally not worth the trouble.

rabbit-hole though, as macros encourage more macros: the more macros you write, the more macros you need to solve the issue of their being unavailable at runtime, and therefore not suitable for use in many functional programming idioms that call for passing higher-order functions around.

There are two lessons here, one minor and one more substantial. First, a macro is convenient or powerful in one context (compilation), but can make life difficult in another (runtime); consider splitting the core functionality out of your macro's implementation and keeping it in its own function. The macro can simply delegate to it at compile time, but if you need to leverage its capabilities in a setting that benefits from a simple function, that route is readily available to you.

Second, and more important, *macros should be used only when you need your own language constructs*; it follows that they shouldn't be used where a function can be as effective. Macros are our only solution if we need:

- Special evaluation semantics
- Customized syntax for frequent patterns or domain-specific notation
- To gain ground by precomputing intermediate data at compile time

On the other hand, we should also always ask ourselves whether there's a function-based (that is, not requiring special evaluation rules and therefore macros) way to achieve the same goal.

Hygiene

Traditionally, one of the biggest potential problems in writing macros is generating code that interacts with other code improperly. Clojure has safeguards in place that other Lisps lack, but there is still potential for error.

Code generated by a macro will often be embedded in other code, and often will have user-defined code embedded within it. In either case, some set of symbols is likely already bound to values by the user of the macro. It's possible for a macro to set up its own bindings that collide with those of the outer or inner context of the macro-users code, which can create bugs that are very difficult to identify. Macros that avoid these sorts of issues are called *hygienic macros*.

Consider a macro with an implementation that requires a let-bound value. The name we choose is irrelevant to the user of our macro and should be invisible to him, but we do have to choose *some* name. Naively, we might try x:

```
(defmacro unhygienic
    [& body]
    `(let [x :oops]
        ~@body))
;= #'user/unhygenic
(unhygienic (println "x:" x))
```

```
;= #<CompilerException java.lang.RuntimeException:
;=   Can't let qualified name: user/x, compiling:(NO_SOURCE_PATH:1)>
```

Clojure is smart enough not to let this code compile. As we explored in "quote Versus syntax-quote" on page 240, all bare symbols are namespace-qualified within a syntax-quoted form. We can see the impact in this case if we check the expansion of our macro:

```
(macroexpand-1 `(unhygienic (println "x:" x)))
;= (clojure.core/let [user/x :oops]
;=   (clojure.core/println "x:" user/x))
```

References to x are expanded to user/x, but let requires that names for new bindings be unqualified symbols, so this macro will always yield code that emits a compilation error. We could improperly "avoid" this problem via some clever quoting and unquoting:

```
(defmacro still-unhygienic
  [& body]
  `(let [~'x :oops]            ❶
     ~@body))
;= #'user/still-unhygenic
(still-unhygienic (println "x:" x))
; x: :oops
;= nil
(macroexpand-1 '(still-unhygienic
                  (println "x:" x)))
;= (clojure.core/let [x :oops]
;=   (println "x:" x))
```

❶ ~'x is using unquote (~) to force the use of the specified explicitly namespace-unqualified symbol x as the name of the let-bound value.

This will at least run, but we've introduced a major bug into our code. The problem is that the name x, which our macro is defining within a local scope, may collide with local bindings either outside or inside of the code emitted by the macro. Consider a simple breaking usage of this macro:

```
(let [x :this-is-important]
  (still-unhygienic
    (println "x:" x)))
; x: :oops
```

Here we're already using the name x for another local value, but the let form emitted by the macro silently clobbers x with its own value within that scope. A user of this macro might never know this is happening without reading its source code.

Thankfully, Clojure provides a simple mechanism for avoiding naming collisions like this in code emitted by macros, and it involves less work than the improper "solution" previously.

Gensyms to the Rescue

When setting up a binding in a macro, we'd like to dynamically generate a name that will never collide with a name outside the macro's scope or inside of bodies of code provided as arguments to our macro. Fortunately, Clojure has a mechanism and a simple syntax for generating such names: *gensyms*. The gensym function returns a symbol that is guaranteed to be unique. Every time it's called, it returns a new symbol.

```
(gensym)
;= G__2386
(gensym)
;= G__2391
```

gensym also accepts an argument: a string used as a prefix of the generated symbol.

```
(gensym "sym")
;= sym2396
(gensym "sym")
;= sym2402
```

You can use gensym whenever you like if you need a unique symbol, but its primary role is in helping us write hygienic macros:

```
(defmacro hygienic
  [& body]
  (let [sym (gensym)]          ❶
    `(let [~sym :macro-value]  ❷
       ~@body)))
;= #'user/hygienic
(let [x :important-value]
  (hygienic (println "x:" x)))
; x: :important-value
;= nil
```

❶ Now instead of the macro specifying the name to use for the new local binding, it takes a guaranteed-unique symbol from gensym...

❷ ...and uses syntax-unquote to place it in the code form returned from the macro.

Now our code is safe. The choice of x for *our* local binding has no chance of colliding with the macro-generated local binding that is using the gensym-generated name.

Gensyms in macros are common enough that there is a shorthand way of using them. Any symbol ending in # inside a syntax-quote form will be expanded automatically into a gensym, and will expand to the same gensym every time it appears. This is called an *auto-gensym*, and the following code is equivalent to the previous definition of hygienic:

```
(defmacro hygienic
  [& body]
  `(let [x# :macro-value]
     ~@body))
```

x# in the syntax-quoted form will be transformed into something like x__3507__auto__ in the expanded macro.

Inside a single syntax-quoted form, all occurrences of a given gensym expand to the same actual symbol:

```
`(x# x#)
;= (x__1447__auto__ x__1447__auto__)
```

This allows the same syntax-quoted form to contain multiple usages of the same gensym, identified by an easily recognizable name within the macro's source code.

```
(defmacro auto-gensyms
  [& numbers]
  `(let [x# (rand-int 10)]                    ❶
     (+ x# ~@numbers)))                        ❷
;= #'user/auto-gensyms
(auto-gensyms 1 2 3 4 5)
;= 22
(macroexpand-1 '(auto-gensyms 1 2 3 4 5))     ❸
;= (clojure.core/let [x__570__auto__ (clojure.core/rand-int 10)]
;=   (clojure.core/+ x__570__auto__ 1 2 3 4 5))
```

❶ We use an auto-gensym x# to establish a local binding within the body of code provided by the macro.

❷ We refer to that gensymed local binding by the same x# name.

❸ Macroexpanding our usage of the macro shows that each usage of the auto-gensym has been replaced with a unique symbol, guaranteed to not clash with any of our other named bindings.

However, you need to keep in mind that auto-gensyms are only the same within the same syntax-quoted form:

```
[`x# `x#]
;= [x__1450__auto__ x__1451__auto__]
```

This means that code such as this reimplementation of doto, which tries to use the same auto-gensym in multiple syntax-quoted forms:

```
(defmacro our-doto [expr & forms]
  `(let [obj# ~expr]                           ❶
     ~@(map (fn [[f & args]]
              `(~f obj# ~@args)) forms)         ❷
     obj#))
```

❶ Usage #1 of obj#, in one syntax-quoted form.

❷ Usage #2 of obj#, in another syntax-quoted form, this one within the unquote-splicing form. These will yield two different gensyms, though we are intending to refer to the same let-bound value in each.

is going to fail:

```
(our-doto "It works"
  (println "I can't believe it"))
;= #<CompilerException java.lang.RuntimeException:
;=   Unable to resolve symbol: obj__1456__auto__ in this context,
;=   compiling:(NO_SOURCE_PATH:1)>
```

because the two obj# auto-gensyms are within the scope of two different syntax-quote forms. In a case like this, we'll need to resort to using gensym manually again:

```
(defmacro our-doto [expr & forms]
  (let [obj (gensym "obj")]
    `(let [~obj ~expr]
       ~@(map (fn [[f & args]]
                `(~f ~obj ~@args)) forms) ❶
       ~obj)))
```

❶ At this point this syntax quote is pretty useless and should be replaced by (list* f obj args).

And now it works:

```
(our-doto "It works"
  (println "I can't believe it")
  (println "I still can't believe it"))
; It works I can't believe it
; It works I still can't believe it
;= "It works"
```

Letting the User Pick Names

If your macro needs to set up a binding that *is* visible to the caller of the macro, we still need to pick a name for this binding, and we still need to worry about hygiene.

We could choose a name and document the macro as always using this name. This is rarely a good idea, but it does happen. If your macro expands to code that interacts with Java, for example, you could document the macro as always setting up a binding for the symbol this.[11] A macro that deliberately "leaks" a name in this way is said to be *anaphoric*,[12] a characteristic that is generally avoided, since users of such macros must consistently remember which symbols are implicitly used to name locals within their scope.

An easier and generally far saner thing to do is let the user select the symbol(s) to use for bindings. Because macros don't evaluate their arguments, it's easy for the user to pass a symbol to the macro, which can be used within the generated code:

```
(defmacro with
  [name & body]
```

---

11. This is the case for proxy, and it's a rare exception to the rule that in Clojure names are always picked by the user. Another exception is the defmacro macro itself! See the discussion of &env and &form later in this chapter.

12. See "Removing Boilerplate" on page 507 for some examples of anaphoric macros.

```
   `(let [~name 5]
      ~@body))
;= #'user/with
(with bar (+ 10 bar))
;= 15
(with foo (+ 40 foo))
;= 45
```

Double Evaluation

A common and insidious problem with macros is known as *double evaluation*. It is insidious because we likely won't spot the problem in many cases. Double evaluation arises when an argument to the macro appears twice (or more) in the expansion. Consider the spy macro:

```
(defmacro spy [x]
  `(do
     (println "spied" '~x ~x)
     ~x))
```

This macro prints the value of the provided expression and returns it. It will behave as we expect as long as x yields a constant value. But as soon as x becomes computationally expensive and/or relies on side effects, we'll get surprising results:

```
(spy 2)
; spied 2 2
;= 2
(spy (rand-int 10))
; spied (rand-int 10) 9
;= 7
```

In the first case everything works fine because 2 is a constant value. In the second case, (rand-int 10) is called twice within the code emitted by the macro, yielding different results each time. This behavior is obvious if you look at the macro expansion:

```
(macroexpand-1 '(spy (rand-int 10)))
;= (do (println (rand-int 10))
;=    (rand-int 10))
```

This would be a *serious* issue if we were using a launch-missiles function here instead of the more innocuous rand-int. To avoid this problem, the rule is to always introduce a local (generally an auto-gensym) when a macro argument appears more than once in the expansion:[13]

```
(defmacro spy [x]
  `(let [x# ~x]
     (println "spied" '~x x#)
     x#))

(macroexpand-1 '(spy (rand-int 10)))
;= (let [x__725__auto__ (rand-int 10)]
```

13. To be more precise, when a macro argument appears more than once in a code branch.

```
;=   (println x__725__auto__ '(rand-int 10))
;=   x__725__auto__)
```

This will ensure that the provided expression is never evaluated more than once:

```
(spy (rand-int 10))
; spied (rand-int 10) 9
;= 9
```

Double-evaluation, even when worked around, is a *code smell* that may hint to your macro expansion doing some work that could be extracted into a function.

```
(defn spy-helper [expr value]
  (println expr value)
  value)

(defmacro spy [x]
  `(spy-helper '~x ~x))
```

In this case, there's no need to introduce the auto-gensym local.

Common Macro Idioms and Patterns

Talking about *macro patterns* might seem oxymoronic, since macros themselves should eliminate the last remaining patterns.[14] Rather than proscribe boilerplate here, let's put the focus on some style points that will help your macros be more Clojure-idiomatic.

Require that new local bindings be specified in a vector.   When a macro is to introduce a new local scope with bound names, it should expect to receive those names along with their initializers in a vector, often as the first argument to the macro. This helps to match the idiom established by core forms and macros in Clojure, including let, if-let, for, with-open, and so on:

```
(let [a 42
      b "abc"]
  ...)

(if-let [x (test)]
  then
  else)

(with-open [in (input-stream ...)
            out (output-stream ...)]
  ...)

(for [x (range 10)
      y (range x)]
  [x y])
```

for is an interesting example because the initializing expressions are not the values that are going to be set in the local names: x is not going to hold the value of (range 10) but

_____

14. The others having been captured in functions.

_____

successively all the values of (range 10). Thus you should always remember that *the initializers are not required to be the values*.

Don't be clever when defining vars.   There are a number of macros in Clojure that define vars, all of which are based on def or some macro derivative. If you're going to write such a macro, keep a few things in mind so that your macro's var-defining semantics are aligned with user expectations for such things:

Macros that define a var should have a name that starts with def.
> This will align your macro with other var-defining macros like defn, defn-, defmacro, and so on. The def prefix is a cue to your user that the macro will intern a new var, and that it should be used as a top-level form.

Accept the name of the var as the first argument.
> Order of arguments aside, implicitly generated var names are clever, but they require users to understand the implementation of your macro—decidedly counter to their objective as instruments of abstraction.

Define one var per macro form.
> As a corollary to the generally bad practice of defining vars with generated or implied names, don't define more than one var per macro form. Just as you would find it confusing if def or defn were to define multiple vars, your users will find it confusing if your macro defines multiple vars. The one exception to this is if the code your macro generates needs something defined in a separate (private!) var that users will not have to access or generally know about.

No complex behavior should be locked inside macros.   Macros should ideally be a thin layer on top of existing functions (or other macros)—or should be easily replicable by these. This goes back to our prior discussion in "When to Use Macros" on page 243.

There are a variety of counterexamples, including the for macro, where macros have a very complex expansion. However, for doesn't do anything that cannot be replicated by a combination of map, filter, mapcat, fn, and let. The complexity in the for expansion is only accountable to optimization and syntactic objectives: it does not hide or lock away any piece of exclusive functionality.

Macros should delegate most of their work to functions and keep only for them what can't be more easily done in functions: controlling evaluation.

The Implicit Arguments: &env and &form

Earlier in "Letting the User Pick Names" on page 248, we mentioned that the defmacro macro itself is one of the rare anaphoric macros in Clojure. defmacro introduces two implicit local bindings: &env and &form.

&env

&env contains a map whose keys are the names[15] of all the current locals (the values of this map are unspecified). It may be useful for debugging purposes:

```
(defmacro spy-env []
  (let [ks (keys &env)]
    `(prn (zipmap '~ks [~@ks]))))

(let [x 1 y 2]
  (spy-env)
  (+ x y))
; {x 1, y 2}
;= 3
```

&env can also prove itself useful to safely optimize expressions at compile time. Here is a very crude version of such a macro that evaluates the provided expression at compile time if it does not use any locals defined within the context of the macro's usage:

```
(defmacro simplify
  [expr]
  (let [locals (set (keys &env))]
    (if (some locals (flatten expr))       ❶
      expr                                  ❷
      (do
        (println "Precomputing: " expr)
        (list `quote (eval expr))))))       ❸
```

❶ Here we do a *very* crude search for references to the locals within the body of code provided to our macro.

❷ If we suspect any such usage, then we return the code unaltered.

❸ Otherwise, we evaluate the expression provided to our macro *at compile time*, and return that value in place of our macro's expression (after helpfully printing an informational message so we can know what's going on).

This macro allows us to optimize expressions that we suspect can be eliminated from runtime code while retaining the unoptimized derivation of such expressions in our source code (often a far better practice than manually precomputing value and using the resulting "magic" constants):

```
(defn f
  [a b c]
  (+ a b c (simplify (apply + (range 5e7)))))
; Precomputing:  (apply + (range 5e7))
;= #'user/f
(f 1 2 3)                ;; returns instantly
;= 1249999975000006
(defn f'
  [a b c]
  (simplify (apply + a b c (range 5e7))))
```

---

15. Note that metadata on keys of &env can't be relied upon, in particular in the presence of local aliases.

```
;= #'user/f'
(f' 1 2 3)                ;; takes ~2.5s to calculate
;= 1249999975000006
```

Because the `apply` expression in our function _f_ contains no references to function locals, the `simplify` macro optimizes it away into a constant value. This optimization takes the form of `simplify` precomputing that value at compile time, so that runtime usages of _f_ do not need to pay the (~2.5s) cost of summing the numbers in that `range`. On the other hand, the expression within the `simplify` usage in the `f'` function _does_ depend upon local bindings as indicated by `&env`; therefore, `simplify` performs no optimizations, leaving our expression to be fully evaluated at runtime.

Testing and debugging &env usage.   It can be difficult to test macros that use `&env`. We have two options at our disposal: either write your macro and use logging or other methods of observation to determine its operation (as we did above with the `println` in `simplify`), or we can take advantage of some of the implementation details of macros to test them in isolation.

Macros are currently implemented as functions that take two extra arguments in front of their regular signatures, the values of `&form` and `&env` when they are invoked by the Clojure compiler. However, as we saw in "When to Use Macros" on page 243, Clojure prevents us from using macros as functions in order to avoid a large class of errors that would result.

We can get around this by reaching into our macro's var, grabbing its implementing function, and using it directly—much like the compiler does:

```
(@#'simplify nil {} '(inc 1))       ❶
; Precomputing:  (inc 1)
;= (quote 2)
(@#'simplify nil {'x nil} '(inc x))
;= (inc x)
```

❶ The line noise preceding `simplify` looks like cursing—it is the sugared syntax for dereferencing a named var, equivalent to (`deref` (`var simplify`)), and generally useful for obtaining the value of a private var—and should constitute a warning by itself. This particular abuse of macros is useful for testing in a pinch, but relies on particular current implementation details in Clojure.

Here we're invoking the macro's implementing function with two arguments prior to the expression we're testing with `simplify`: a `nil` argument for its `&form` (which we know we're not using) and an `&env` map either containing or not containing a key for a hypothetical local binding. This allows us to see what code `simplify` will produce for a couple of expressions. Note that we can't test `simplify` by using `macroexpand` in this case, because it provides no way for us to mock out the `&env` map, as we can when touching the macro's implementing function directly.[16]

---

16. See "Testing Contextual Macros" on page 258 for our stab at an alternative macroexpansion function that does support this without the var-dereferencing line noise.

&form

&form holds the whole form currently being macro-expanded, that is, a list containing the name of the macro as a symbol (as found in the user code: including alias or renames) and the arguments to the macro. It's really the form as read by the reader.[17] This means &form has all the metadata specified by the user, such as type hints and added by the reader, like the line number of the macro's usage.

Let's take a look at two powerful usages of &form: emitting useful compile-time error messages from macros and ensuring that user-provided type hints are preserved by your macros.

Producing useful macro error messages

One key usage of this information is to ensure that any errors thrown by your macros provide accurate and informative messages. For example, consider a macro that accepts a bunch of vector triples[18]—it might build the corresponding ontology, precalculating various relationships and properties of that ontology so that that work does not have to be done at runtime:

```
(defmacro ontology
  [& triples]
  (every? #(or (== 3 (count %))
               (throw (IllegalArgumentException.
                        "All triples provided as arguments must have 3 elements")))
          triples)
  ;; build and emit pre-processed ontology here...
  )
```

The exception will only be thrown when one of the vectors provided as an argument to ontology does not have three elements. However, the accompanying message will be less than ideal:

```
(ontology ["Boston" :capital-of])                              ❶
;= #<IllegalArgumentException java.lang.IllegalArgumentException:
;=   All triples provided as arguments must have 3 elements>
(pst)
;= IllegalArgumentException All triples provided as arguments must have 3 elements
;=   user/ontology (NO_SOURCE_FILE:3)                          ❷
```

❶ The incomplete triple does throw an exception, but...

❷ The line number shown in the exception's stack trace is incorrect from the user's perspective—3 here is relative to the *macro's* source, *not* the usage of it.

---

17. Or, returned by a previous expansion.

18. *Triples* are a term for subject-predicate-object expressions, as found in semantic web technologies like RDF. Specific representations and semantics of triples vary from implementation to implementation, but a simplified example of a vector triple might be `["Boston" :capital-of "Massachusetts"]`.

The line number isn't a big deal in this simple, short REPL interaction, but an inaccurate line number may lead to wasted minutes or hours debugging a faulty macro usage in a real project with potentially large source files. We can fix this by using &form and its metadata:

```
(defmacro ontology
  [& triples]
  (every? #(or (== 3 (count %))
               (throw (IllegalArgumentException.
                        (format "`%s` provided to `%s` on line %s has < 3 elements"
                                %                                         ❶
                                (first &form)                            ❷
                                (-> &form meta :line)))))                ❸
          triples)
  ;; ...
  )
```

❶ We include the offending vector argument in the error message; this doesn't require &form, but is a nice touch in any case.

❷ The first element in &form is always going to be the name of the macro as identified by the user. We'll see the utility of this in a bit.

❸ Here we pull out the line number from the reader-supplied metadata on &form. This line number accurately identifies where the *user's code* uses the macro.

With these changes, the experience of using our macro is improved significantly in the case of a compile-time error:

```
(ontology ["Boston" :capital-of])
;= #<IllegalArgumentException java.lang.IllegalArgumentException:
;=    `["Boston" :capital-of]` provided to `ontology` on line 1 has < 3 elements>
```

Nice, now our error message is much clearer with regard to the line number. But, why bother reprinting the name used to identify our macro? It is possible to rename the symbols used to identify vars "imported" from another namespace by using the refer function and its derivatives—a very useful feature in order to use functions and macros from other namespaces that have the same or similar names.[19] So, if we switch to another namespace, we have the option of using our ontology macro via another name:

```
(ns com.clojurebook.macros)
;= nil
(refer 'user :rename '{ontology triples})
;= nil
```

Now our ontology macro is available as triples in the com.clojurebook.macros namespace. Thankfully, our revised ontology macro will throw errors that accurately (and helpfully) indicate the name of the macro *as present in the actual usage*:

---

19. refer is described in "refer" (page 323), and is also reused by use, described later in that chapter.

```
(triples ["Boston" :capital-of])
;= #<IllegalArgumentException java.lang.IllegalArgumentException:
;=   `["Boston" :capital-of]` provided to `triples` on line 1 has < 3 elements>
```

Without the use of (first &form) in building that error message, some degree of confusion might ensue before our hapless macro user remembered that he had renamed
ontology to triples in the current namespace.

Preserving user-provided type hints

Most macros discard the metadata attached to the forms within their context, including
type hints.[20] For example, here the or macro form does not propagate the ^String type
hint to the code it produces, resulting in a reflection warning:

```
(set! *warn-on-reflection* true)
;= true
(defn first-char-of-either
  [a b]
  (.substring ^String (or a b) 0 1))
; Reflection warning, NO_SOURCE_PATH:2 - call to substring can't be resolved.
;= #'user/first-char-of-either
```

 Such cases are rarely found in the wild, because type hints are usually
put upstream of interop calls, resulting in the type of the macro form
being determined through type inference:

```
(defn first-char-of-either
  [^String a ^String b]
  (.substring (or a b) 0 1))
;= #'user/first-char-of-either
```

We can verify that the hint metadata on the or expression is lost; here, the expression,
with metadata:

```
(binding [*print-meta* true]
  (prn '^String (or a b)))
; ^{:tag String, :line 1} (or a b)
```

But if we macroexpand the same expression, that metadata is gone:

```
(binding [*print-meta* true]
  (prn (macroexpand '^String (or a b))))
; (let* [or__3548__auto__ a]
;   (if or__3548__auto__ or__3548__auto__ (clojure.core/or b)))
```

However, there's no reason why the type hint on the or expression can't be preserved;
doing so simply requires using &form effectively in its macro definition. First, let's see
what or looks like, as implemented in clojure.core:

```
(defmacro or
  ([] nil)
```

---

20. We describe type hints in "Type Hinting for Performance" on page 366.

```
([x] x)
([x & next]
  `(let [or# ~x]
     (if or# or# (or ~@next)))))
```

What we need to do is ensure that the metadata on &form—which contains the user-provided type hint, if any—is propagated onto the expression returned from or. In many cases, we could simply wrap the outer level of our macro's body with a with-meta call to add &form's metadata to the returned expression, but we can't do that here;[21] instead, we'll need to put type hints where they belong: on a symbol:

```
(defmacro OR
  ([] nil)
  ([x]
    (let [result (with-meta (gensym "res") (meta &form))]
      `(let [~result ~x]
         ~result)))
  ([x & next]
    (let [result (with-meta (gensym "res") (meta &form))]
      `(let [or# ~x
             ~result (if or# or# (OR ~@next))]
         ~result))))
```

We can verify that the hint we're providing is being preserved by looking at the output of macroexpand again (notice that we're using our or variant, OR):

```
(binding [*print-meta* true]
  (prn (macroexpand '^String (OR a b))))
; (let* [or__1176__auto__  a
;        ^{:tag String, :line 2}
;        res1186 (if or__1176__auto__ or__1176__auto__ (user/or b))]
;   ^{:tag String, :line 2} res1186)
```

User-supplied metadata is now no longer lost, in this case resulting in the elimination of the reflective call:

```
(defn first-char-of-any
  [a b]
  (.substring ^String (OR a b) 0 1))
;= #'user/first-char-of-any
```

The pattern exemplified in the definition of OR above can be broken out into a reusable function that can be easily used with any macro:

```
(defn preserve-metadata
  "Ensures that the body containing `expr` will carry the metadata
   from `&form`."
  [&form expr]
  (let [res (with-meta (gensym "res") (meta &form))]
    `(let [~res ~expr]
       ~res)))
```

21. This is due to an unfortunate implementation detail: special forms (like let, the outermost form in the expression returned by or) cannot be hinted. Thus, we must introduce a local to put the hint on it.

```
(defmacro OR
  "Same as `clojure.core/or`, but preserves user-supplied metadata
   (e.g. type hints)."
  ([] nil)
  ([x] (preserve-metadata &form x))
  ([x & next]
    (preserve-metadata &form `(let [or# ~x]
                                (if or# or# (or ~@next))))))
```

Writing a `defmacro` variant that always uses `preserve-metadata` to maintain user-supplied metadata for macro expressions is left as an exercise for the reader.

Testing Contextual Macros

As we've seen, macros using `&form` and `&env` can't be easily tested. However, based on our knowledge of these arguments and of how macros are implemented, we can whip up an implementation of `macroexpand-1` that allows us to effectively mock `&env` to aid in testing and debugging:

```
(defn macroexpand1-env [env form]
  (if-let [[x & xs] (and (seq? form) (seq form))]
    (if-let [v (and (symbol? x) (resolve x))]
      (if (-> v meta :macro)
        (apply @v form env xs)
        form)
      form)
    form))
```

We can use `macroexpand1-env` to test how our contextual `simplify` macro behaves when used within different "environments" of locals:

```
(macroexpand1-env '{} '(simplify (range 10)))
; Precomputing:  (range 10)
;= (quote (0 1 2 3 4 5 6 7 8 9))
(macroexpand1-env '{range nil} '(simplify (range 10)))
;= (range 10)
```

And we can test and verify macros' handling of `&form` metadata by specifying the metadata attached to the code provided to `macroexpand1-env`. For example, say we modified the `spy` macro we tinkered with before to echo the line number of the macro's usage, obtained from the metadata on `&form`:

```
(defmacro spy [expr]
  `(let [value# ~expr]
     (println (str "line #" ~(-> &form meta :line) ",")
              '~expr value#)
     value#))
;= #'user/spy
(let [a 1
      a (spy (inc a))
      a (spy (inc a))]
  a)
; line #2, (inc a) 2
```

```
; line #3, (inc a) 3
;= 3
```

If we wanted to verify that that echoing of the line number worked without running the code the macro emitted, we could use `macroexpand1-env`:

```
(macroexpand1-env {} (with-meta '(spy (+ 1 1)) {:line 42}))  ❶
;= (clojure.core/let [value__602__auto__ (+ 1 1)]
;=    (clojure.core/println
;=      (clojure.core/str "line #" 42 ",")           ❷
;=      (quote (+ 1 1)) value__602__auto__)
;=    value__602__auto__)
```

❶ We override the `:line` metadata on the form we provide to `macroexpand1-env` to some unusual value we'll recognize...

❷ ...and we can verify that, yes, our macro is picking up and using the line number metadata on &form properly.

The body of `macroexpand1-env` is actually a perfect candidate for a macro: those nested `if-let` expressions and the repeated `form` aren't especially elegant. It would be better if we could collapse all of those `if-let`s into a single form, perhaps like this:

```
(defn macroexpand1-env [env form]
  (if-all-let [[x & xs] (and (seq? form) (seq form))
               v (and (symbol? x) (resolve x))
               _ (-> v meta :macro)]
    (apply @v form env xs)
    form))
```

We would like `if-all-let` to evaluate the `then` form only if none of the bound expressions evaluated to `false` or `nil`. A macro can do this for us:

```
(defmacro if-all-let [bindings then else]
  (reduce (fn [subform binding]
            `(if-let [~@binding] ~subform ~else))
          then (reverse (partition 2 bindings)))))
```

This satisfies our second implementation of `macroexpand1-env`, and is generally quite useful where we might otherwise have had nested `if-let` forms.

In Detail: -> and ->>

To explore how macros work to solve real problems, let's work up an alternative implementation of a commonly used macro in Clojure: `->`, which is very similar to its cousin, `->>`. Often called *threading macros*, these are included in `clojure.core` (with a number of derivatives with similar semantics in various third-party libraries), and are remarkably useful in cleaning up chained function calls and chained Java-interop method calls.

What we'd like to do is be able rewrite somewhat awkward code like this:

```
(prn (conj (reverse [1 2 3]) 4))
```

...and instead write code like this:

```
(thread [1 2 3] reverse (conj 4) prn)
```

This way, rather than reading code inside-out (which can be difficult with deeply nested calls), we can read our code sequentially, left-to-right as a series of successive actions: "Start with [1 2 3], reverse it, `conj` 4 onto it, then `prn` it."

It's not hard to envision a macro to do this. Given a series of forms, we'll take the first form and insert it as the second item in the second form, then take the resulting form and insert it as the second item in the third form, and so on.

Additionally, if any form after the first is not already a list, let's consider it a list of one item. This lets us avoid parens on single-argument functions like this:

```
(-> foo (bar) (baz))
```

and instead write:

```
(-> foo bar baz)
```

First, let's write a simple utility function to ensure that a form is a seq.

```
(defn ensure-seq [x]
  (if (seq? x) x (list x)))

(ensure-seq 'x)
;= (x)
(ensure-seq '(x))
;= (x)
```

Now, given two forms x and ys, we want a function to insert x as the second item in ys, ensuring that ys is a seq.

```
(defn insert-second
  "Insert x as the second item in seq y."
  [x ys]
  (let [ys (ensure-seq ys)]
    (concat (list (first ys) x)
            (rest ys))))
```

Although this is a normal function, remember that it will be called from our macro. Thus the values of x and ys will be data structures representing unevaluated source code.

We can write this code more concisely with a bit of syntax-quoting and unquoting; remember, you can use these mechanisms outside of the body of a macro:

```
(defn insert-second
  "Insert x as the second item in seq y."
  [x ys]
  (let [ys (ensure-seq ys)]
    `(~(first ys) ~x ~@(rest ys))))
```

We can do it even more concisely using `list*`, a function that we looked at in "Creating seqs" on page 92 that is used frequently in the implementation of macros and their helpers:

```
(defn insert-second
  "Insert x as the second item in seq y."
  [x ys]
  (let [ys (ensure-seq ys)]
    (list* (first ys) x (rest ys))))
```

Now let's write our macro, which we'll call `thread`. (`thread x`) should just return `x`. (`thread x (a b)`) should return (`a x b`), using our utility functions. (`thread x (a b)` (`c d`)) can thread the first two items and then recursively call `thread` on the result.

```
(defmacro thread
  "Thread x through successive forms."
  ([x] x)
  ([x form] (insert-second x form))
  ([x form & more] `(thread (thread ~x ~form) ~@more)))
```

It looks like it works, just as the standard `->` macro does:[22]

```
(thread [1 2 3] (conj 4) reverse println)
;= (4 3 2 1)
(-> [1 2 3] (conj 4) reverse println)
;= (4 3 2 1)
```

One question we haven't asked ourselves is whether we could write this macro as a normal function, to avoid the use of macros at all. It turns out we can, with a slight modification:

```
(defn thread-fns
  ([x] x)
  ([x form] (form x))
  ([x form & more] (apply thread-fns (form x) more)))

(thread-fns [1 2 3] reverse #(conj % 4) prn)
;= (4 3 2 1)
```

In this case, having to wrap some of our function calls in #() makes our code more verbose and slightly harder to read, as well as adding overhead to our code via extraneous function calls. Additionally, the functional version will not work with bare Java method calls, whereas the macro version, being a simple manipulation of lists and symbols, does.

```
(thread [1 2 3] .toString (.split " ") seq)
;= ("[1" "2" "3]")

(thread-fns [1 2 3] .toString #(.split % " ") seq)
;= #<CompilerException java.lang.RuntimeException:
;=   Unable to resolve symbol: .toString in this context,
```

---

22. A reimplementation of `->>` would be just as straightforward, and is left as an exercise. Hint: you'll need an `insert-last` function instead of `insert-second`.

```
compiling:(NO_SOURCE_PATH:1)>

;; This is starting to look a bit hairy...
(thread-fns [1 2 3] #(.toString %) #(.split % " ") seq)
;= ("[1" "2" "3]")
```

It seems that the macro variant of our threading operator does offer some compelling syntactic advantages over the purely function-based approach. Indeed, the threading macros in Clojure are often used to great effect in clarifying the application of functional pipelines to yield transformations over a single value or a collection of values.

The real implementation of -> is actually not much more complex than our `thread`. `clojure.core` provides a few other threading macros, including:

..

> Works just like ->, but only works with Java interop calls (and calls of static Java methods, which -> does not support). .. was introduced before ->, and it's rarely used now, but you may still see it in the wild.

->>

> Threads forms together by inserting each form as the *last* item in successive forms, rather than as the second item. This is used most commonly when transforming sequences or other collections through a series of functions. For example:
>
> ```
> (->> (range 10) (map inc) (reduce +))
> ;= 55
> ```

Hopefully this serves as a compelling example of the power and utility of macros.

Final Thoughts

As with any other Lisp, macros are essential to Clojure's expressive power. A little macrology goes a long way in eliminating eyesores and abstracting away common patterns in your code. However, they are by no means the most basic construct or the one you should reach for first: you can go a very long way with Clojure without creating a single macro.

Functional programming and data modeling already yield tremendous expressive power and allow us to abstract away most repeating patterns in our code. Macros are the *final* step, simplifying patterns of control flow and adding syntactic sugar to minimize or eliminate code awkwardness.

## CHAPTER 6

Datatypes and Protocols

While programming in other languages, many of us have experienced this situation: you have crafted beautiful interfaces obeying all laws of good design, just to realize that you must deal with an object provided by another module over which you have absolutely no control. There's little hope that the maintainers of this module will ever add support for your interface—be it for technical, political, or legal reasons. In no time you are now juggling (drowning in?) adapters and proxies.

The luckiest among us work in languages dynamic enough to allow *monkey-patching*, where classes are open and methods can be jammed into those classes when necessary in order to bridge the distance between one interface and another. Thankfully, the term is disparaging enough to make you twitch and think twice before using it, since such surgery carries an armload of complexity, caveats, and pitfalls.

The fundamental problem behind these symptoms has previously been named the *expression problem*:

> The Expression Problem is a new name for an old problem. The goal is to define a datatype by cases, where one can add new cases to the datatype and new functions over the datatype, without recompiling existing code, and while retaining static type safety (e.g., no casts).
>
> —Philip Wadler, *http://www.daimi.au.dk/~madst/tool/papers/expression.txt*

Some argue whether the expression problem in dynamic languages is still the expression problem as originally coined by Philip Wadler. We are not going to determine how many angels can dance on the head of a pin in this book, so we'll be satisfied to keep to our own *dynamic expression problem*. Phrased using more object-oriented parlance:

> The *dynamic* Expression Problem is a new name for an old problem. The goal is to have interfaces and type where one can create new types implementing existing interfaces and provide implementation of a new interface for an existing type, without recompiling existing code.

The first half of this goal—having new types to implement old interfaces—is commonly met: every object-oriented language offers this capacity. The second half—providing implementations of new interfaces to old types—is the interesting part of the problem, and the one that few languages ever attempt to address. We are going to see how Clojure solves it.

Protocols

The Clojure corollary to interfaces are called `protocols`.[1] *Interface* is a term best kept reserved for Java interfaces.

A protocol consists of one or more methods, where each method can have multiple arities. All methods have at least one argument, corresponding to the privileged `this` in Java and `self` in Ruby and Python.

The first argument to each method in a protocol is said to be privileged because a particular protocol implementation will be chosen for each call based on it and, more specifically, on its type. Hence, protocols provide single type-based dispatch. This is a very limited form of polymorphic dispatch and it had been chosen for protocols for pragmatic reasons, namely:

- That's what most hosts (e.g., the JVM, the CLR, and JavaScript virtual machines) offer and, more important, optimize;
- Despite being limited, it covers a wide range of needs

If you truly need unrestricted or multiple dispatch, Clojure has an answer in multimethods, explored in Chapter 7.

A protocol definition looks like this:

```
(defprotocol ProtocolName
  "documentation"
  (a-method [this arg1 arg2] "method docstring")
  (another-method [x] [x arg] "docstring"))        ❶
```

❶ Because the privileged argument is explicit, you can give it any name you wish: `this`, `self`, `_`, etc.

Unlike most other names in Clojure, the names of protocols and types are usually written in `CamelCase` because they compile down to native JVM interfaces and classes. This allows you to easily distinguish protocols and types from other entities in Clojure, and it allows for idiomatic usage from other JVM languages.

From a user standpoint, *protocol methods are functions*: there is no special syntax involved in using them, you can look their documentation up with `doc`, you can pass them to higher-order functions, and so on. However, a protocol should not be designed with the user but with the protocol implementer in mind. A good protocol should consist of a small set of methods with no overlapping concerns; a good protocol is one that is *easy to implement*. There's nothing wrong with a protocol having a single method.

---

1. This will sound familiar to Smalltalk or Objective C hackers.

Although protocol methods are functions, you cannot use destructuring or rest arguments in the specification of those methods within the def protocol form. For example, based on what we learned in "Destructuring function arguments" on page 38, you might think that this defines a protocol with a single method that accepts two positional arguments and some number of additional arguments gathered into the more seq:

```
(defprotocol AProtocol
  (methodName [this x y & more]))
```

However, because protocols generate a JVM interface—which cannot support all the argument structure variations that Clojure functions provide—methodName is taken to be a method that accepts *four* arguments, and only four arguments.

Ancillary or convenience functions have no reason to be part of a protocol. They should instead be built on top of protocol methods.

When necessary, user-facing functions and protocol methods may even belong to different namespaces to make explicit which are part of the public API and which are part of the implementor's API.[2] An example of this separation can be found in Clojure itself: the namespace clojure.core.protocols introduces a protocol called InternalReduce:

```
(defprotocol InternalReduce
  "Protocol for concrete seq types that can reduce themselves
   faster than first/next recursion. Called by clojure.core/reduce."
  (internal-reduce [seq f start]))
```

As users of Clojure and its sequence operations, we would never need to use or even know about this protocol. However, if we were to implement our own data structure, and wanted to provide optimized reduce functionality based on implementation-specific factors, implementing that protocol would be of interest to us.

As we explore protocols and datatypes, we'll use this Matrix protocol, which defines operations to access and update bidimensional sequential data structures (such as arrays or vectors or nested versions of the same):

```
(defprotocol Matrix
  "Protocol for working with 2d datastructures."
  (lookup [matrix i j])
  (update [matrix i j value])
  (rows [matrix])
  (cols [matrix])
  (dims [matrix]))
```

---

2. This is exactly analogous to the API/SPI (*service provider interface*) distinction in many Java libraries.

Extending to Existing Types

Our first implementation of this protocol will be a very naive one for vectors of vectors. "Vector of vectors" is not a type in Clojure or even in the JVM,[3] so we are simply going to extend the protocol to Clojure vectors:

```
(extend-protocol Matrix
  clojure.lang.IPersistentVector
  (lookup [vov i j]
    (get-in vov [i j]))
  (update [vov i j value]
    (assoc-in vov [i j] value))
  (rows [vov]
    (seq vov))
  (cols [vov]
    (apply map vector vov))
  (dims [vov]
    [(count vov) (count (first vov))]))
```

Let's stop and detail `extend-protocol`. The first argument is the name of the protocol (`Matrix` here). Then we have an alternation of symbols (denoting type names like `IPersistentVector`, the foundational vector interface in Clojure) and lists (method implementations for the previously specified type and extended protocol).

Method implementations are no different from regular functions. Unlike in Ruby or Java, there is no implicit `self` or `this`: the privileged first argument that determines which implementation of a protocol to dispatch to is explicitly passed as the first argument to the method. In this regard, protocol implementation functions are similar to methods in Python.

A noteworthy aspect of protocols is that *you are not required to implement all methods*: Clojure will simply throw an exception if you try to call an unimplemented method.[4]

`extend-protocol` is not the only way to extend a protocol to a type; also available are:

- Inline implementation
- `extend`
- `extend-type`

We will talk about `extend` and inline implementation later in "Reusing Implementations" on page 285 and "Inline Implementation" on page 281, respectively.

`extend-type` is the dual to `extend-protocol`: where `extend-protocol` allows you to extend one protocol to several types, `extend-type` allows you to extend several protocols

---

3. Java generics don't exist at the bytecode level, they disappear during compilation—this is known as *type erasure* and as a side effect, makes life simpler for implementors of dynamic languages.

4. The actual exception type varies depending on the way the protocol was implemented, so don't rely on it.

to one type. They share the same layout, only the places where protocol names and types names occur are inverted.

Example 6-1. Comparison of use cases for extend-type versus extend-protocol

```
(extend-type AType
  AProtocol
  (method-from-AProtocol [this x]
    (;...implementation for AType
    ))
  AnotherProtocol
  (method1-from-AnotherProtocol [this x]
    (;...implementation for AType
    ))
  (method2-from-AnotherProtocol [this x y]
    (;...implementation for AType
    )))

(extend-protocol AProtocol
  AType
  (method1-from-AProtocol [this x]
    (;...implementation for AType
    ))
  AnotherType
  (method1-from-AProtocol [this x]
    (;...implementation for AnotherType
    ))
  (method2-from-AProtocol [this x y]
    (;...implementation for AnotherType
    )))
```

A protocol can also be extended to `nil`, so you can potentially say goodbye to many null pointer exceptions by providing a sane default behavior for it:

```
(extend-protocol Matrix
  nil
  (lookup [x i j])
  (update [x i j value])
  (rows [x] [])
  (cols [x] [])
  (dims [x] [0 0]))

(lookup nil 5 5)
;= nil
(dims nil)
;= [0 0]
```

To use our protocol and the implementation of it for vectors of vectors, it would help to have a *factory function*[5] that creates an empty vector of vectors with particular dimensions.

```
(defn vov
  "Create a vector of h w-item vectors."
  [h w]
  (vec (repeat h (vec (repeat w nil)))))
```

Now, let's play:

```
(def matrix (vov 3 4))
;= #'user/matrix
matrix
;= [[nil nil nil nil]
;=  [nil nil nil nil]
;=  [nil nil nil nil]]
(update matrix 1 2 :x)
;= [[nil nil nil nil]
;=  [nil nil :x nil]
;=  [nil nil nil nil]]
(lookup *1 1 2)
;= :x
(rows (update matrix 1 2 :x))
;= ([nil nil nil nil]
;=  [nil nil :x nil]
;=  [nil nil nil nil])
(cols (update matrix 1 2 :x))
;= ([nil nil nil]
;=  [nil nil nil]
;=  [nil :x nil]
;=  [nil nil nil])
```

Good, this works well. We have effectively *extended* (implemented) a protocol to an existing type, vectors. This has been done in a sane, namespaced way: because each protocol's methods correspond with a set of namespaced functions, one protocol extension isn't going to clash with any other, even if they share some identical method names.

To make the point clear that we can extend a protocol to any Java type, let's provide another implementation of our Matrix protocol, this time for bidimensional arrays of floating-point doubles—which, unlike IPersistentVector, cannot be suspected of providing special support for protocols.

Example 6-2. Extending a protocol to a Java array

```
(extend-protocol Matrix
  (Class/forName "[[D")              ❶
```

---

5. Factory functions in Clojure fill the role of constructors and static factory methods found elsewhere. Clojure provides a number of factory functions you've seen already, e.g., hash-map, sorted-set, etc., and as we describe in "Constructors and factory functions" on page 275, you'll find yourself wanting to define your own as well.

```
(lookup [matrix i j]
  (aget matrix i j))
(update [matrix i j value]          ❷
  (let [clone (aclone matrix)]
    (aset clone i
      (doto (aclone (aget clone i))
        (aset j value)))
    clone))
(rows [matrix]
  (map vec matrix))
(cols [matrix]
  (apply map vector matrix))
(dims [matrix]
  (let [rs (count matrix)]
    (if (zero? rs)
      [0 0]
      [rs (count (aget matrix 0))])))))
```

❶ This Class/forName call allows you to obtain a reference to the Class corresponding to two-dimensional arrays of doubles, referred to as double[][].class in Java; see "Array classes" (page 444) for more on this notation.

❷ Arrays are *not* immutable, but we provide some degree of immutable semantics through our Matrix implementation that uses arrays, so it is as consistent as possible with our previous vector-of-vectors implementation: every update clones the outer array of arrays, clones the affected row, and swaps the clone with the updated value into the top-level array, which is returned. Of course, unrestricted mutability might be desirable for performance-intensive matrices; having separate protocols for such opposing semantics would make sense.

This implementation will be chosen for us by the protocol machinery based on the type of the first argument provided to each of its functions; here we can see array matrices performing as expected:

```
(def matrix (make-array Double/TYPE 2 3))
;= #'user/matrix
(rows matrix)
;= ([0.0 0.0 0.0]
;=  [0.0 0.0 0.0])
(rows (update matrix 1 1 3.4))
;= ([0.0 0.0 0.0]
;=  [0.0 3.4 0.0])
(lookup (update matrix 1 1 3.4) 1 1)
;= 3.4
(cols (update matrix 1 1 3.4))
;= ([0.0 0.0]
;=  [0.0 3.4]
;=  [0.0 0.0])
(dims matrix)
;= [2 3]
```

Now it should be clear that, despite fulfilling much the same role as Java interfaces, Clojure protocols are more potent and do not suffer from the dynamic version of the *expression problem*: we can bring any preexisting type in to satisfy the contract of our protocols without modifying those types or having any other special access to them.

However, we have so far only extended protocols to types defined in Java. Thankfully, Clojure provides its own ways of defining new types.

Defining Your Own Types

A Clojure type *is* a Java class, although a Clojure type definition is as easy as

```
(defrecord Point [x y])
```

or

```
(deftype Point [x y])
```

We'll discuss the many commonalities that `deftype` and `defrecord` share before diving into what makes each unique.

Both of these forms define a new Java class `Point`, with two `public` and `final` fields named x and y. Just like protocols (and unlike other names in Clojure), type names are usually written in `CamelCase` and not in `lower-dashed-case` because they do compile down to Java classes. Creating a new `Point` instance is as simple as calling its constructor—`(Point. 3 4)`—one argument per field in the same order as given upon definition, whether it was defined as a *type* or a *record type*. Because they are regular fields on Java objects:

- Accessing and updating their values is *much* faster than the same operations involving, for example, regular Clojure maps.
- You can access fields of `deftype` or `defrecord` instances by using Clojure's standard field access interop syntax:[6]

```
(.x (Point. 3 4))
;= 3
```

As-is, each field is typed as a default `java.lang.Object`; this is often perfectly sufficient for many models, and a necessity if the types of some values in your model may vary. However, if you need to, you can declare fields to be primitive types by using the same sort of metadata that is used to declare the types accepted and returned by functions. You can also optionally hint nonprimitive fields as you would hint method calls, although hints do not change the concrete type of the field as seen by, for example, a Java user of the defined type.

So, this defines a record type that has primitive `long` fields x and y, and an `Object` name that is hinted as a `String` within any inline method implementations that you might add to the type:

---

6. Records provide a more flexible abstraction for field access, which we describe in "Records are associative collections" (page 273).

```
(defrecord NamedPoint [^String name ^long x ^long y])
```

We discuss hinting and type declarations at length in "Type Hinting for Performance" on page 366 and "Declare Functions to Take and Return Primitives" on page 438, respectively, though neither are critical to building a fundamental understanding of how deftype and defrecord work.

It is sometimes useful to know what fields a particular type requires and provides, especially in the case of records, which can support holding auxiliary fields beyond what are defined for its constructor. This enumeration of defined fields is called a *basis*, available via a static method on the class defined by deftype or defrecord:

```
(NamedPoint/getBasis)
;= [name x y]
```

Each symbol within the basis retains the metadata provided in the original vector of fields, including type information:

```
(map meta (NamedPoint/getBasis))
;= ({:tag String} {:tag long} {:tag long})
```

We'll focus on records first: they are designed to be used to model and represent application-level data,[7] whereas deftype types are intended to define low-level infrastructure types, such as when you are implementing a new data structure.

The differences between the two facilities lie entirely with the defaults that records provide in terms of interoperating with the rest of Clojure and certain Java facilities, and certain capabilities that deftype provides that make it possible to optimize the low-level operations that they're designed to address. In the end, you should find yourself using records far more than deftype types for most classes of programs and problems.

Types Are Not Defined in Namespaces

When you define a new type with defrecord or deftype, the resulting class is defined as being in the Java package corresponding to the current namespace, and it is implicitly imported into the defining namespace, so you can refer to it by its unqualified name. However, when you use this defining namespace from another, types are not imported because they are host classes, *not* vars. *You have to explicitly import defined types even if you use or require the defining namespace.*

```
(def x "hello")
;= #'user/hello
(defrecord Point [x y])
;= user.Point                    ❶
(Point. 5 5)
;= #user.Point{:x 5, :y 5}
(ns user2)
(refer 'user)                    ❷
x                                ❸
;= "hello"
```

7. You might say that records and maps are the "POJO"s of the Clojure world.

```
Point                            ❹
;= CompilerException java.lang.Exception:
;=    Unable to resolve symbol: Point
(import 'user.Point)             ❺
Point
;= user.Point
```

❶ Defining a type `Point` while in the `user` namespace defines a new Java class `user.Point`. That type's unqualified name can be used directly because it is implicitly imported into the current namespace.

❷ `refer` is similar to `use`, but without the loading semantics—it presupposes the namespace already exists.

❸ x is now *referred* in the current namespace (`user2`).

❹ `Point` is not available though.

❺ `Point`, being a class, needs to be *imported* in the current namespace in order to refer to it via its short name.

You can learn about the finer points of Clojure namespaces in "Defining and Using Namespaces" on page 322.

Records

Often called *record types*, types defined by `defrecord` are a specialization of those defined by `deftype`. Additional facilities provided by records include:

- Value semantics
- Full participation in the associative collection abstraction
- Metadata support
- Reader support, so instances of record types can be created by simply reading data
- An additional convenience constructor for creating records with metadata and auxiliary fields as desired

 Clojure retains a vestigial "struct" map implementation—via the `def struct`, `create-struct`, `struct-map`, and `struct` functions—that should be considered deprecated at this point, and avoided. If you want a flexible struct, maps will often do just fine, as we described in "Maps as ad-hoc structs" on page 118; alternatively, if you need them, records are superior to the older `struct-map` implementation in every way. We'll talk about how to choose among these options in "When to use maps or records" on page 277.

Value semantics.   *Value semantics* implies two things: records are immutable, and, given two records whose fields are equal, those two records are themselves equal:

```
(defrecord Point [x y])
;= user.Point
(= (Point. 3 4) (Point. 3 4))
;= true
(= 3 3N)
;= true
(= (Point. 3N 4N) (Point. 3 4))
;= true
```

You should be used to such semantics from working with Clojure's data structures, which make the same guarantees. Records achieve this by automatically providing correct and consistent implementations of Object.equals and Object.hashCode that are dependent upon the values of records' fields.

Records are associative collections. Records participate in the associative abstraction,[8] so you can use with records all of the facilities you're used to using with maps.

For example, while the fields of both types and records may be accessed using interop forms like (.x instance), record fields can be accessed by functions—specifically, keywords, which as we saw in "Concise Collection Access" on page 111, are functions that look themselves up in the associative collection that they are called with. Such calls work just the same with records as you would expect when working with maps:

```
(:x (Point. 3 4))               ❶
;= 3
(:z (Point. 3 4) 0)             ❷
;= 0
(map :x [(Point. 3 4)
         (Point. 5 6)
         (Point. 7 8)])
;= (3 5 7)
```

❶ Note that when the keyword is explicit and its literal placed in function position, the compiler is able to optimize the access down to levels close to the (.x instance) raw field dereference.

❷ Default values for keywords that have no corresponding value in a record work as well.

Further, updating a field value is as simple as calling assoc on it, and all the rest of the associative and collection functions are at your disposal including keys, get, seq, conj, into, and so on. And, just like maps, records implement Java's java.util.Map interface, so you can pass records to Java APIs that expect to read data out of a Map instance.

While records are defined with a fixed set of fields, you can still associate new slots into a record that are not part of that initial set:[9]

---

8. Defined by the clojure.lang.Associative interface and described in "Associative" on page 99.

9. This characteristic, where a type or object with a fixed set of predefined fields can be "expanded" to include other values, is sometimes referred to in other languages and frameworks as an *expando* property.

```
(assoc (Point. 3 4) :z 5)                              ❶
;= #user.Point{:x 3, :y 4, :z 5}
(let [p (assoc (Point. 3 4) :z 5)]                     ❷
  (dissoc p :x))
;= {:y 4, :z 5}
(let [p (assoc (Point. 3 4) :z 5)]                     ❸
  (dissoc p :z))
;= #user.Point{:x 3, :y 4}
```

❶ A record can be extended with additional slots.

❷ dissociating a declared field produces a return value that is a simple map, not a record.

❸ However, dissociating an auxiliary slot does not degenerate the return value into a simple map.

Note that these additional slots are kept "off to the side" from a record's predefined fields in a regular Clojure hash map of their own, and have corresponding lookup and update performance characteristics; that is, they do not somehow become new fields on the record's underlying Java class:

```
(:z (assoc (Point. 3 4) :z 5))
;= 5
(.z (assoc (Point. 3 4) :z 5))
;= #<java.lang.IllegalArgumentException:
;=    No matching field found: z for class user.Point>
```

Metadata support.   Just as with other Clojure collections, you can retrieve and set metadata on records using `meta` and `with-meta` (and `vary-meta` as a consequence) without impacting records' value semantics:

```
(-> (Point. 3 4)
  (with-meta {:foo :bar})
  meta)
;= {:foo :bar}
```

See "Metadata" on page 135 for an overview of metadata and its use cases.

Readable representation.   You may have noticed that the REPL prints record instances with a particular syntax, distinct from regular Clojure maps and different again from arbitrary Java objects:

```
#user.Point{:x 3, :y 4, :z 5}
```

This is a record literal, the equivalent of square brackets used to denote vectors, colon-prefixed symbols to denote keywords, and so on. This means that you can print and read record instances to and from their textual representation just like any other Clojure literal:

```
(pr-str (assoc (Point. 3 4) :z [:a :b]))
;= "#user.Point{:x 3, :y 4, :z [:a :b]}"
(= (read-string *1)
   (assoc (Point. 3 4) :z [:a :b]))
;= true
```

This makes it just as easy to use records to store and retrieve data (in a file or database or other) as it is with any other value supported by the Clojure reader.

Auxiliary constructor. In addition to a constructor that accepts the defined fields of the type, records also offer a constructor that reflects some of their additional capabilities; namely, field extensibility and metadata support. This second constructor expects two extra arguments: a map containing slots beyond the fields specified when the record type was defined, and a map of metadata to attach to the created record:

```
(Point. 3 4 {:foo :bar} {:z 5})
;= #user.Point{:x 3, :y 4, :z 5}
(meta *1)
;= {:foo :bar}
```

This is semantically equivalent (and more efficient) than modifying a base record instance one step at a time like so:

```
(-> (Point. 3 4)
  (with-meta {:foo :bar})
  (assoc :z 5))
```

Constructors and factory functions

Constructors should generally not be part of your public API. Instead, you should provide one or more factory functions so that:

1. You can match the expected usage of callers, which is not necessarily provided for by the oftentimes too low-level constructors generated by an underlying model's `deftype` and `defrecord` forms.
2. You can apply such factory functions in a higher-order fashion to easily produce type and record instances from gobs of "regular" Clojure data.
3. You can maximize API stability for callers even if the underlying model implementations change.

A factory will not be as brittle as constructors to code change: as soon as you change a record type's list of fields, you change its constructor's signature, whereas factories allow you to add logic such as validation of arguments or producing derived or default field values. Clojure types don't allow you to define custom constructors, so anything that you would put into the body of a constructor in other languages needs to be placed into factory functions in Clojure.

Both `deftype` and `defrecord` implicitly create one factory function of the form `->MyType` that accepts field values positionally:

```
(->Point 3 4)
;= #user.Point{:x 3, :y 4}
```

Records also emit a second factory function of the form `map->MyType`, which accepts a single map that is used for populating the new record instance:

```
(map->Point {:x 3, :y 4, :z 5})
;= #user.Point{:x 3, :y 4, :z 5}
```

These are both useful for creating type and record instances from Clojure data, especially in conjunction with higher-order functions:

```
(apply ->Point [5 6])
;= #user.Point{:x 5, :y 6}

(map (partial apply ->Point) [[5 6] [7 8] [9 10]])
;= (#user.Point{:x 5, :y 6}
;=  #user.Point{:x 7, :y 8}
;=  #user.Point{:x 9, :y 10})

(map map->Point [{:x 1 :y 2} {:x 5 :y 6 :z 44}])
;= (#user.Point{:x 1, :y 2}
;=  #user.Point{:x 5, :y 6, :z 44})
```

For records, the map-based factory is also accessible as the static method **create** on the type, which can be a great help for Java consumers of libraries and types you define in Clojure:

```
(Point/create {:x 3, :y 4, :z 5})
;= #user.Point{:x 3, :y 4, :z 5}
```

While these provided factories are helpful, you'll still need to roll your own as soon as you need to add logic, derived fields, or validations to a factory function:

```
(defn log-point
  [x]
  {:pre [(pos? x)]}
  (Point. x (Math/log x)))

(log-point -42)
;= #<AssertionError java.lang.AssertionError: Assert failed: (pos? x)>
(log-point Math/E)
;= #user.Point{:x 2.718281828459045, :y 1.0}
```

Oftentimes, factories occur spontaneously in the writing process as an intermediate step between maps and records where you first start refactoring your code by introducing factories, which produce simple maps to make your code clearer. Such as:

```
(defn point [x y]
  {:x x, :y y})
```

When you later want to switch to records for a given type, you only have to rewrite the factory function to use your new record type. This thankfully often allows client code referencing the factory function to continue unchanged and unaware of the shift.

When to use maps or records

While there are excellent use cases for records,[10] it is often preferable to approach problems using regular maps first, moving on to records later as circumstances warrant.

Maps are the simplest way to get started writing code and modeling data because maps do not force you to predefine any types or schema at all, thus giving you more conceptual latitude when prototyping a feature. However, as soon as you perceive the need for type-based polymorphism (available via protocols for records and types) or performance-sensitive field access, you can switch to records and be done: most of your code (if not all) will work as is because of the abstractions shared between maps and records.

One pitfall when switching from maps to records is that *records are not functions*. So, `((Point. 3 4) :x)` will not work, while `({:x 5 :y 6} :x)` will. However, if you follow the recommendations in "Concise Collection Access" on page 111 on when it is appropriate to use maps as functions, there should be no overlap between the kind of maps used as functions and the kind of maps replaced by records.

Another trap is that maps and records can never be equal, so you have to pay extra attention when mixing maps and records to represent the same data.

```
(defrecord Point [x y])
;= user.Point
(= (Point. 3 4) (Point. 3 4))
;= true
(= {:x 3 :y 4} (Point. 3 4))
;= false
(= (Point. 3 4) {:x 3 :y 4}) ❶
;= false
```

❶ Clojure is thankfully well-behaved, and doesn't break the symmetric property of equality.

Types

`deftype` is the lowest-level type definition form in Clojure—in fact, `defrecord` is really just a macro that builds on top of `deftype`. As you might expect, many of the "creature comforts" of records are unavailable in types defined with `deftype`. It is fundamentally intended to be used to define low-level infrastructure types, as might be needed for implementing a new data structure or reference type; in contrast, maps and records should be used to house your application-level data.

What this low-level type form does offer is one key facility that is *sometimes* unavoidable at the lowest levels of an application or library: mutable fields!

Before jumping to mutable fields, let's first clarify that normal (immutable) field access with `deftype` instances is *only* possible via interop forms:

---

10. See Chapter 18 for a diagram to help guide your thinking in this area.

```
(deftype Point [x y])
;= user.Point
(.x (Point. 3 4))
;= 3
(:x (Point. 3 4))
;= nil
```

deftype types are not associative,[11] and so the most common pattern of using keywords as accessor functions is unavailable. Thus, we must rely upon the fact that types compile down to Java classes, with each immutable field in that class being defined as publicly available and final.

Mutable fields come in two flavors: volatile or unsynchronized. To declare a field as mutable, you have to qualify it with the metadata ^:volatile-mutable or ^:unsynchron ized-mutable, e.g.:

```
(deftype MyType [^:volatile-mutable fld])
```

This *-mutable metadata will compose without a problem with any field type declarations you may need to use.

"Volatile" here has the same meaning as the volatile field modifier in Java: reads and writes are atomic[12] and must be executed in program order; i.e., they cannot be reordered by the JIT compiler or by the CPU. Volatiles are thus unsurprising and thread-safe—but uncoordinated and still entirely open to race conditions.

On the other hand, an unsynchronized field is a "regular" Java mutable field whose use will be thread-safe only under the guard of a lock[13]...or in the most expert of hands.

While immutable fields are public, *mutable fields are always private* and only accessible from within method bodies provided inline with the type definition. Inline implementations will be covered in detail in "Implementing Protocols" on page 280; for now it will suffice to provide a simple example of a type that contains a single mutable field and implements the sole method of the Clojure interface that defines the deref abstraction, IDeref:[14]

---

11. Unless you were to define a type that implements Clojure's clojure.lang.Associative interface; we'll tackle something very similar to this in "Participating in Clojure's Collection Abstractions" on page 292.

12. According to the *Java Memory Model*, writes to *nonvolatile* long or double fields are not guaranteed to be atomic. See JSR-133, section 11.

13. If you're brave enough—and need wildly mutable fields badly enough—you can use the locking macro, described in "Locking" on page 225.

14. Any type that implements IDeref may be dereferenced with deref and therefore with the @ reader syntax, described in the Note on page 160.

Schrödinger's cat.

```
(deftype SchrödingerCat [^:unsynchronized-mutable state]
  clojure.lang.IDeref
  (deref [sc]
    (locking sc
      (or state
        (set! state (if (zero? (rand-int 2))
                      :dead
                      :alive))))))

(defn schrödinger-cat
  "Creates a new Schrödinger's cat. Beware, the REPL may kill it!"
  []
  (SchrödingerCat. nil))

(def felix (schrödinger-cat))
;= #'user/felix                             ❶
@felix                                      ❷
;= :dead
(schrödinger-cat)
;= #<SchrödingerCat@3248bc64: :dead>
(schrödinger-cat)
;= #<SchrödingerCat@b28eed01: :alive>
```

❶ Felix is still both alive and dead…

❷ …until we—or the REPL—kill him (or ensure his survival) as a side effect of dereferencing.

Mutable fields or reference/dataflow types?

Because the state of our SchrödingerCat is not determined until we "look in the box," it is equivalent to

```
(delay (if (zero? (rand-int 2))
         :dead
         :alive))
```

Most of the time, an application's mutability needs can be satisfied by Clojure's reference types (agents, atoms, and refs), dataflow types (futures, promises, and delays), or judicious use of java.util.concurrent classes. Using such facilities—all described in Chapter 4—is a far more satisfying option than touching mutable fields: they eliminate large swaths of complexity, focus mutability among a limited set of loci, and generally cut away opportunities for you to cause problems for yourself. In short, don't rush for mutable fields when you have better tools at hand!

As we can see above, setting a mutable field can be done by simply `set!`-ing the field as named in the `deftype` field vector with a new value, that is, a `(set! field value)`.[15] A mutable field can be accessed within the body of an implementation simply by referring to it.[16]

Now that we understand the different sorts of types in Clojure, we can resume our tour of protocols.

Implementing Protocols

There are two ways to implement a protocol for any given type:

1. Provide implementations for protocol methods when a type is initially defined via `deftype` or `defrecord`; this is called *inline implementation*.
2. Use the `extend*` functions to register implementations for a type with the protocol.

Let's contrast the two approaches in Examples 6-3 and 6-4 through implementing the `Matrix` protocol for the `Point` record type, where we'll consider a point to be a 2×1 matrix:

Example 6-3. Implementing a protocol inline

```
(defrecord Point [x y]
  Matrix
  (lookup [pt i j]
    (when (zero? j)
      (case i
        0 x
        1 y)))
  (update [pt i j value]
    (if (zero? j)
      (condp = i
        0 (Point. value y)
        1 (Point. x value))
      pt))
  (rows [pt] [[x] [y]])
  (cols [pt] [[x y]])
  (dims [pt] [2 1]))
```

Example 6-4. Extending a protocol to an already-defined type

```
(defrecord Point [x y])

(extend-protocol Matrix
  Point
```

15. This is the equivalent of `this.field = value` in Java, `self.field = value` in Python, and `@field = value` in Ruby.
16. Mutable fields in method body implementations behave like local bindings; that is, you can refer to them directly instead of doing something like `(.x this)`, and you can shadow their names just as easily as "real" local bindings established by `let` or in the argument vector of a function.

```
(lookup [pt i j]
  (when (zero? j)
    (case i
      0 (:x pt)
      1 (:y pt))))
(update [pt i j value]
  (if (zero? j)
    (condp = i
      0 (Point. value (:y pt))
      1 (Point. (:x pt) value))
    pt))
(rows [pt]
  [[(:x pt)] [(:y pt)]])
(cols [pt]
  [[(:x pt) (:y pt)]])
(dims [pt] [2 1]))
```

A minor difference between the two approaches is how you access field values: when you extend a type externally you have to access the types' fields using keywords (or interop forms like (.x pt)), while when you provide inline implementations, you can directly refer to field values by their name since they are in the lexical scope.

Beyond that, the differences between inline implementation and using extend-* functions are legion.

Inline Implementation

Generally, inline implementations provide better performance for two reasons: they have direct access to the type's fields, and calling protocol methods will be as fast as calling an interface method in Java.

Because each protocol is backed by a Java interface, implementing a protocol's methods inline results in a class that implements the protocol's corresponding interface, where you define that class's method bodies in those inline implementations. Furthermore, each call site of a protocol function first performs a test against the backing interface, which triggers the fastest path when it's available: a regular method call, something the JVM can recognize and is built to optimize aggressively.

However, some of that underlying machinery can poke through when using inline implementations; namely, clashes can occur between protocol methods with the same name and signature. You can't provide inline implementations for two protocols whose method signatures conflict, nor even one protocol whose method signatures conflict with any java.lang.Object methods, or perhaps most confusingly, if you attempt to provide an inline implementation for any of the interfaces for which defrecord automatically provides implementations, including java.util.Map, java.io.Serializable, clojure.lang.IPersistentMap, and others. In such cases, an error will be thrown:

```
(defprotocol ClashWhenInlined
  (size [x]))
;= ClashWhenInlined
```

```
(defrecord R []
  ClashWhenInlined
  (size [x]))                        ❶
;= #<CompilerException java.lang.ClassFormatError:
;=   Duplicate method name&signature in class file user/R,
   compiling:(NO_SOURCE_PATH:1)>

(defrecord R [])
;= user.R
(extend-type R                       ❷
  ClashWhenInlined
  (size [x]))
;= nil
```

❶ This is going to clash with the size method that is defined in java.util.Map, which is automatically implemented by records.

❷ All is well when we use extend-type to register an implementation for our record type with the protocol, because that extension does not impact the construction of the R type—it isn't retroactively modified to implement the interface backing the protocol.

Because inline extensions are baked into the type produced by deftype or defrecord, you cannot change those implementations at runtime without redefining the whole type. Doing so further means that you must reevaluate all code that directly depends on the type in question.[17] However, the most pernicious problem with inline implementations is that, because deftype and defrecord each create and define a new type, existing objects that predate the updated type will *never* utilize any updated inline implementations.

Thus, inline implementations, while tempting because they appear so familiar (methods in classes!), are more static than other protocol extension mechanisms, and are best kept as an optimizing step.

The exception to this general rule is that inline implementation is the only way for a Clojure type to implement Java interfaces.

Inline implementations of Java interfaces

Since inline implementation of a protocol is simply implementing a protocol's corresponding Java interface, the exact same approach can be used to implement methods of *any* Java interface, and as a special case, methods of java.lang.Object.[18] Just as with protocols, you are not required to implement all methods of an interface; exception-throwing stubs are generated for any unsupported methods.

---

17. This amount of code is tremendously reduced when you follow our advice from "Constructors and factory functions" on page 275 to implement a factory function for your types.

18. Any other class, abstract or not, cannot be extended inline. You must resort to gen-class or proxy, described in "Defining Named Classes" on page 374 and "Instances of Anonymous Classes: proxy" on page 372 respectively, to subclass any concrete type.

```
(deftype MyType [a b c]
  java.lang.Runnable
  (run [this] ...)
  Object
  (equals [this that] ...)
  (hashCode [this] ...)
  Protocol1
  (method1 [this ...] ...)
  Protocol2
  (method2 [this ...] ...)
  (method3 [this ...] ...))
```

Being able to extend Object base methods allows you to give value semantics to Point even when it's defined through deftype:

```
(deftype Point [x y]
  Matrix
  (lookup [pt i j]
    (when (zero? j)
      (case i
        0 x
        1 y)))
  (update [pt i j value]
    (if (zero? j)
      (case i
        0 (Point. value y)
        1 (Point. x value))
      pt))
  (rows [pt]
    [[x] [y]])
  (cols [pt]
    [[x y]])
  (dims [pt]
    [2 1])
  Object
  (equals [this other]
    (and (instance? (class this) other)     ❶
      (= x (.x other)) (= y (.y other))))
  (hashCode [this]
    (-> x hash (hash-combine y))))
```

❶ Inline implementations cannot refer to the type being defined.

 Implementing equals and hashCode is as tedious and risky in Clojure as it is in Java—having them implemented for us by defrecord is one of that form's biggest draws, after all. However, implementing these methods correctly is even a bit trickier for deftype types because you cannot refer to the type being defined in an inline declaration: if you try to replace (class this) by Point in the previous code, it will compile but (instance? Point other) will always return false. This is a known limitation of the current compiler. Other possible workarounds include calling a function from within the inline implementation that *can* refer to the defined class, or to test against an interface (or a protocol) in lieu of a concrete class.

Defining anonymous types with reify

Besides `defrecord` and `deftype` there is one other construct that accepts inline implementations: `reify`.

Unlike `deftype` and `defrecord`, `reify` is not a top-level form; rather than defining a named type, it evaluates to an *instance* of an unnamed type. Essentially, it is a way to create objects that satisfy any protocol (or implement methods of any interface or `Object`). This makes it analogous to anonymous inner classes in Java.

The overall layout of `reify` is identical to `defrecord` or `deftype`, but without any declaration of fields:

```
(reify
  Protocol-or-Interface-or-Object
  (method1 [this x]
    (implementation))
  Another-Protocol-or-Interface
  (method2 [this x y]
    (implementation))
  (method3 [this x]
    (implementation)))
```

Just as with types and records, you don't have to provide implementations for all methods of a given protocol or interface.

Instances created by `reify` form closures, leaving method implementation bodies with direct access to any local in the lexical scope. This is very useful to create adapters (as in Example 6-5) or one-shot instances (as in Example 6-6).

Example 6-5. Adapting a function as an ActionListener

```
(defn listener
  "Creates an AWT/Swing `ActionListener` that delegates to the given function."
  [f]
  (reify
    java.awt.event.ActionListener
    (actionPerformed [this e]
      (f e))))
```

Example 6-6. Using a reified FileFilter implementation to obtain only directory files

```
(.listFiles (java.io.File. ".")
  (reify
    java.io.FileFilter
    (accept [this f]
      (.isDirectory f))))
```

Such use cases overlap with those of `proxy`,[19] but:

---

19. See "Instances of Anonymous Classes: proxy" on page 372.

- `reify` is simpler: its method implementations are "baked in" just like those provided to `deftype` and `defrecord` forms, so dynamic updates are not directly supported.

- `reify` is more limited: it can only satisfy protocols and implement methods of Java interfaces and `Object`. Concrete classes may not be subclassed, whether they are abstract or not.

- Because all of `reify`'s method implementations are inlined into the host class, calls to those methods have zero overhead.

Reusing Implementations

In the Clojure model of protocols and types, there is no concept of hierarchy. As we'll see, that is not a limitation, insofar as type-based inheritance is *itself* a complicating limitation and Clojure provides a more powerful and flexible alternative.

Types can only ever satisfy protocols or implement interfaces—there is no way to rely upon type inheritance as in most other languages where you can define a new type that subclasses another concrete type, thereby inheriting the latter's method implementations. Clojure's answer to the need to reuse concrete method implementations lays with the function that provides the foundation of the `extend-type` and `extend-protocol` macros: `extend`.

`extend` takes as its first argument the type to extend and then an alternation of protocols and *implementation maps*, which map method names (as keywords) to functions that implement those methods for the specified type.

Let's use `extend` to add `Matrix` implementations for the `Point` record type:

```
(defrecord Point [x y])

(extend Point
  Matrix
  {:lookup (fn [pt i j]
             (when (zero? j)
               (case i
                 0 (:x pt)
                 1 (:y pt))))
   :update (fn [pt i j value]
             (if (zero? j)
               (condp = i
                 0 (Point. value (:y pt))
                 1 (Point. (:x pt) value))
               pt))
   :rows (fn [pt]
           [[(:x pt)] [(:y pt)]])
   :cols (fn [pt]
           [[(:x pt) (:y pt)]])
   :dims (fn [pt] [2 1])})
```

Since extend is a function and not a macro like extend-type and extend-protocol, the implementation map is taken as a *value* that we can pass around, manipulate, and combine with other implementation maps. With this flexibility available, we can model any permutation of implementation reuse we desire, from simple stuff like "inheritance" to more subtle notions like traits and mixins.

A simple example is defining default implementations for rows and cols that depend only upon type-specific implementations of dims and lookup:

```
(def abstract-matrix-impl
  {:cols (fn [pt]
           (let [[h w] (dims pt)]
             (map
               (fn [x] (map #(lookup pt x y) (range 0 w)))
               (range 0 h))))
   :rows (fn [pt]
           (apply map vector (cols pt)))})
```

Now we can provide an extension of Matrix to Point, which builds upon the default implementation by simply associng in our type-specific method implementations:

```
(extend Point
  Matrix
  (assoc abstract-matrix-impl
    :lookup (fn [pt i j]
              (when (zero? j)
                (case i
                  0 (:x pt)
                  1 (:y pt))))
    :update (fn [pt i j value]
              (if (zero? j)
                (condp = i
                  0 (Point. value (:y pt))
                  1 (Point. (:x pt) value))
                pt))
    :dims (fn [pt] [2 1])))
```

While this example is quite simple and isn't especially innovative with regard to the state of mainstream object-oriented class design, it does illustrate how, thanks to the protocol methods allowing you to treat method implementations simply as named functions, you can model whatever inheritance relationships you like, entirely dissociated from concrete types that might otherwise get in your way.

More interesting would be to leverage implementations as values to provide *mixins*— that is, a way to combine several discrete implementations of a single protocol in a meaningful way.

For this example, let's define a new protocol, Measurable:[20]

---

20. This example is largely inspired by the one provided in the Wikipedia article on mixins: *https://en .wikipedia.org/wiki/Mixin*.

```
(defprotocol Measurable
  "A protocol for retrieving the dimensions of widgets."
  (width [measurable] "Returns the width in px.")
  (height [measurable] "Returns the height in px."))
```

Then we define a new Button record type to which we extend the Measurable protocol, along with a bordered implementation map:

```
(defrecord Button [text])

(extend-type Button
  Measurable
  (width [btn]
    (* 8 (-> btn :text count)))
  (height [btn] 8))

(def bordered
  {:width #(* 2 (:border-width %))
   :height #(* 2 (:border-height %))})
```

Now we'd like to define a BorderedButton that combines the implementations of both Button and bordered. But, there's a problem: we don't have an implementation map for Button. Protocols are helpfully not just static names that we can use with extend, et al.; they name vars that contain a variety of useful bits:

Example 6-7. Contents of a protocol var's map

```
Measurable
;= {:impls
;=   {user.Button
;=     {:height #<user$eval2056$fn__2057 user$eval2056$fn__2057@112f8578>,
;=      :width #<user$eval2056$fn__2059 user$eval2056$fn__2059@74b90ff7>}},
;=  :on-interface user.Measurable,
;=  :on user.Measurable,
;=  :doc "A protocol for retrieving the 2D dimensions of widgets.",
;=  :sigs
;=    {:height
;=      {:doc "Returns the height in px.",
;=       :arglists ([measurable]),
;=       :name height},
;=     :width
;=      {:doc "Returns the width in px.",
;=       :arglists ([measurable]),
;=       :name width}},
;=  :var #'user/Measurable,
;=  :method-map {:width :width, :height :height},
;=  :method-builders
;=    {#'user/height #<user$eval2012$fn__2013 user$eval2012$fn__2013@27aa7aac>,
;=     #'user/width #<user$eval2012$fn__2024 user$eval2012$fn__2024@4848268a>}}
```

There is plenty of interesting stuff in there even if most—if not all—are implementation details.[21] Relevant to our mixin example, we can spot that (get-in Measurable [:impls Button]) yields the implementation map for Button for the Measurable protocol:

```
(get-in Measurable [:impls Button])
;= {:height #<user$eval1251$fn__1252 user$eval1251$fn__1252@744589eb>,
;=  :width #<user$eval1251$fn__1254 user$eval1251$fn__1254@40735f45>}
```

The missing piece is a means to combine multiple implementations of a given method into a new implementation. Such a function should take the functions to combine and another function to compute the new result given the result of the two other implementations:

```
(defn combine
  "Takes two functions f and g and returns a fn that takes a variable number
   of args, applies them to f and g and then returns the result of
   (op rf rg) where rf and rg are the results of the calls to f and g."
  [op f g]
  (fn [& args]
    (op (apply f args) (apply g args))))
```

At last we can define our BorderedButton type and extend Measurable to it, using + to combine results from our bordered map of implementations and the implementations already registered with Measurable for Button:

```
(defrecord BorderedButton [text border-width border-height])

(extend BorderedButton
  Measurable
  (merge-with (partial combine +)
    (get-in Measurable [:impls Button])
    bordered))
```

It's time to verify that a BorderedButton instance correctly computes its dimensions compared to a Button instance with the same text:

```
(let [btn (Button. "Hello World")]
  [(width btn) (height btn)])
;= [88 8]

(let [bbtn (BorderedButton. "Hello World" 6 4)]
  [(width bbtn) (height bbtn)])
;= [100 16]
```

 Another argument in favor of *not* inlining implementations prematurely is that such powerful reuse patterns are not available for types that include inline extensions. In such cases you'll have to resort to delegation and/or macros.

---

21. See "Protocol Introspection" on page 289 for a brief tour of the functions that form the supported API available for protocol introspection.

Protocol Introspection

Now that we've seen the soft underbelly of protocols in Example 6-7, we should mention the convenience functions for introspecting protocols: extenders, extends?, and
satisfies?, which collectively provide a supported API for answering common questions about protocols and their relationships with types.

extenders

Returns the classes that have been extended to a given protocol. For example, after
going through the examples involving the Measurable protocol in the last section,
we can see which types participate in that protocol:

```
(extenders Measurable)
;= (user.BorderedButton user.Button)
```

This is the equivalent of asking, "Which classes implement some Java interface
x?" Note that, because types can be extended to satisfy protocols *at any point at
runtime*, these results are only true for the point in time when a protocol is queried
via extenders.

extends?

Returns true only if a type has been extended to a protocol:

```
(extends? Measurable Button)
;= true
```

satisfies?

Is the analog of instance?: it asks whether a particular instance participates in a
given protocol, either by dint of having been extended to it via extend and its
derivatives:

```
(satisfies? Measurable (Button. "hello"))
;= true
(satisfies? Measurable :other-value)
;= false
```

...or by its type having provided inline implementations of the protocol's methods:

```
(deftype Foo [x y]
  Measurable
  (width [_] x)
  (height [_] y))
;= user.Foo
(satisfies? Measurable (Foo. 5 5))
;= true
```

In this latter case, because types that provide inline implementations are really just
implementing methods on the host interface that the protocol generates, there can
be overlap between satisfies? and instance? for the same object:

```
(instance? user.Measurable (Foo. 5 5))    ❶
;= true
```

❶ `user.Measurable` is the interface generated by the `Measurable` protocol that we defined at `#'user/Measurable`.

Protocol Dispatch Edge Cases

Since protocol methods produce namespaced functions, there can never be a conflict between two protocols' functions. However, there are some edge cases that have no corollary in typical object-oriented languages where protocol dispatch can produce some surprising results.

Competing implementations. The fact that protocols can be extended at any time and at runtime is a huge boon to interactive development and for allowing protocol implementations to evolve to accommodate tricky modeling or optimization problems.[22] However, if two implementations of the same protocol for the same type exist, then the last implementation that was loaded will replace the first—potentially to surprising effect if the implementation you expect happens to be loaded first.

Alas, this is a problem of policy rather than technology! The rule of thumb to avoid such conflicts is: if you are neither the protocol or type owner, *be prepared to retract your implementation*. The potential conflict between the two owners is usually settled by chronology: when the protocol predates the type, it's the type owner's responsibility to extend the protocol and vice versa.

Class hierarchies break "ties" when possible. A related situation is where two implementations of a single protocol exist for two related types, and both are applicable for a particular protocol method call. For example, say we extend a protocol to two related interfaces—`java.util.List` and `java.util.Collection`, maybe—and then call one of the protocol methods with a type that matches both:

```
(defprotocol P
  (a [x]))
;= P
(extend-protocol P
  java.util.Collection
  (a [x] :collection!)
  java.util.List
  (a [x] :list!))
;= nil
(a [])
;= :list!
```

In such cases, the protocol dispatch machinery uses class hierarchy relationships to make a decision, and will always choose the protocol implementation for the most specific type—in this case, the one for `java.util.List` "wins" since it extends the base `Collection` interface.

---

22. An example of the latter is described at *http://dosync.posterous.com/51626638*.

Unresolvable "ties" choose an arbitrary implementation. But, what happens if the two types extended to a protocol have no class hierarchy relationship? In that case, the protocol dispatch mechanism will select and cache an *arbitrary* implementation. The most likely scenario where this can occur is when protocols are extended to multiple high-level Java interfaces.

Consider a protocol to which we extend two implementations, each for an interface type, neither of which have any relationship to the other with regard to class hierarchy; here, `java.util.Map` and `java.io.Serializable`:

```
(defprotocol P
  (a [x]))

(extend-protocol P
  java.util.Map
  (a [x] :map!)
  java.io.Serializable
  (a [x] :serializable!))
```

What will happen if we call `a` with a Clojure map, which implements both of these interfaces?

```
(a {})
;= :serializable!
```

Okay...that's *one* reasonable result—but why that one and not the `Map` implementation? The trap lies in the fact that this dispatch choice (which protocols cache for each concrete type that is dispatched upon) *can be different* the next time you restart your application or REPL and call the same protocol function. For the above example, this means that you cannot know ahead of time if (a {}) will return `:serializable!` or `:map!`

There are a couple of options for resolving this:

1. Extend the protocol to concrete types that you know you want to support. There is never any ambiguity of dispatch between concrete types.[23]

2. Wanting to extend multiple unrelated high-level interfaces to a protocol may be a sign of a design problem, where the contract of the protocol is too broad. Revisit that contract.

3. Use multimethods. In contrast to protocols, multimethods do fail with an error if a call results in an unresolvable tie between dispatch values. Further, multimethods provide a "preference" mechanism that can be used to specify how to resolve such ambiguity.[24]

---

23. ...and thus never any ambiguity of dispatch among protocol implementations for `deftype` or record types.

24. Multimethods are described in detail in Chapter 7, with their preference mechanism discussed in "Multiple Inheritance" on page 313.

Participating in Clojure's Collection Abstractions

In "Schrödinger's cat" (page 279), we had a glimpse of how to make a custom type participate in one of Clojure's abstractions by making a type dereferenceable. Let's raise the bar a bit and work through a complete data structure implementation that is fully integrated into Clojure's abstractions: namely, an array-backed set, specialized to be more efficient in both performance and memory than standard tree-based hashing sets for very small numbers of items.[25]

Participating in a Clojure abstraction currently means extending certain Java interfaces that Clojure defines for each abstraction. Thus, all of our implementation work must be performed inline.[26]

In general, the most difficult part of participating in Clojure's abstractions is identifying which interfaces and methods are to be implemented, as such things are largely undocumented officially.[27] A helper function will get us most of the way there, though:

```
(defn scaffold
  "Given an interface, returns a 'hollow' body suitable for use with `deftype`."
  [interface]
  (doseq [[iface methods] (->> interface
                               .getMethods
                               (map #(vector (.getName (.getDeclaringClass %))
                                             (symbol (.getName %))
                                             (count (.getParameterTypes %))))
                               (group-by first))]
    (println (str "  " iface))
    (doseq [[_ name argcount] methods]
      (println
        (str "    "
          (list name (into '[this] (take argcount (repeatedly gensym)))))))))
```

By looking at the output of (ancestors (class #{})), we can see that clojure.lang.IPer sistentSet is the primary interface implemented by a Clojure set; providing it to scaf fold yields a good starting point for our own set implementation:

---

25. The tree-based implementation strategy used by most of Clojure's collections, which we took a close look at in "Visualizing persistence: maps (and vectors and sets)" on page 125, is excellent for general-purpose usage, but specialized access and usage patterns can be fertile ground for specialized data structure implementations.

26. In the long term, interfaces for core abstractions are planned to be replaced by protocols; this is already the case in ClojureScript, mentioned in "ClojureScript" on page 584.

27. Clojure Atlas is one tool that can help identify the interfaces backing Clojure's abstractions: *http://www .clojureatlas.com*.

```
(scaffold clojure.lang.IPersistentSet)
;   clojure.lang.IPersistentSet
;     (get [this G__5617])
;     (contains [this G__5618])
;     (disjoin [this G__5619])
;   clojure.lang.IPersistentCollection
;     (count [this])
;     (cons [this G__5620])
;     (empty [this])
;     (equiv [this G__5621])
;   clojure.lang.Seqable                  ❶
;     (seq [this])
;   clojure.lang.Counted
;     (count [this])                      ❷
```

❶ If all you wanted was to ensure your data structure was seqable, you'd only need to implement the seq method of clojure.lang.Seqable.

❷ Note that there are two count methods with the same signature; one of them must be elided.

To implement a Clojure set, we need to implement those methods, in addition to Object's hashCode and equals so as to ensure proper value semantics. All of those methods' contracts should be obvious except perhaps cons and equiv. cons, despite its name, is the method that backs conj; equiv is similar to equals, but ensures sane equivalence semantics when applied to numerics (see "Equivalence can preserve your sanity" on page 435). We'll not need to worry much about the special requirements of the latter, as our set is not a numeric type.

Example 6-8. An array-backed set implementation using deftype

```
(declare empty-array-set)
(def ^:private ^:const max-size 4)                              ❶

(deftype ArraySet [^objects items
                   ^int size
                   ^:unsynchronized-mutable ^int hashcode]
  clojure.lang.IPersistentSet
  (get [this x]
    (loop [i 0]
      (when (< i size)
        (if (= x (aget items i))
          (aget items i)
          (recur (inc i))))))
  (contains [this x]
    (boolean
      (loop [i 0]
        (when (< i size)
          (or (= x (aget items i)) (recur (inc i)))))))
```

```
  (disjoin [this x]
    (loop [i 0]
      (if (== i size)
        this
        (if (not= x (aget items i))
          (recur (inc i))
          (ArraySet. (doto (aclone items)
                       (aset i (aget items (dec size)))
                       (aset (dec size) nil))
                     (dec size)
                     -1)))))
clojure.lang.IPersistentCollection
 (count [this] size)
 (cons [this x]
   (cond
     (.contains this x) this
     (== size max-size) (into #{x} this)                    ❷
     :else (ArraySet. (doto (aclone items)
                        (aset size x))
                      (inc size)
                      -1)))
 (empty [this] empty-array-set)
 (equiv [this that] (.equals this that))                    ❸
clojure.lang.Seqable
 (seq [this] (take size items))
Object
 (hashCode [this]
   (when (== -1 hashcode)
     (set! hashcode (int (areduce items idx ret 0           ❹
                           (unchecked-add-int ret (hash (aget items idx)))))))
   hashcode)
 (equals [this that]
   (or
     (identical? this that)
     (and (or (instance? java.util.Set that)
              (instance? clojure.lang.IPersistentSet that))
          (= (count this) (count that))
          (every? #(contains? this %) that)))))

(def ^:private empty-array-set (ArraySet. (object-array max-size) 0 -1))

(defn array-set                                             ❺
  "Creates an array-backed set containing the given values."
  [& vals]
  (into empty-array-set vals))
```

❶ A key characteristic of collection implementations specialized for a particular char-
❷ acter of dataset is that once the dataset shifts outside of an implementation's "sweet
spot," that implementation should "promote" the data into a different sort of collection that is more suitable without moving outside of the abstraction in question.
Here, for a set optimized to contain small numbers of values, we promote the set's
data to a regular Clojure hash set once more than four items are to be held. A different
threshold might be found to be more appropriate for very specific usage patterns,

❸ equiv delegates to equals to align the behavior of ArraySet with the implementation
of clojure.lang.APersistentSet.

❹ Since our set implementation is backed by an array, we've had to use various operations—areduce, aget, aset, and so on—that we've not talked about yet, although
they have little to do with our current focus. See "Use Primitive Arrays Judiciously" on page 442 to understand Clojure's operations over arrays.

❺ The constructor for ArraySet is in no way suitable for end users—its fields are entirely
related to its implementation. Because of this, and all of the other good reasons we
talked about in "Constructors and factory functions" on page 275, we provide a
user-friendly array-set factory function.

Does this implementation work?

```
(array-set)
;= #{}
(conj (array-set) 1)
;= #{1}
(apply array-set "hello")
;= #{\h \e \l \o}
(get (apply array-set "hello") \w)
;= nil
(get (apply array-set "hello") \h)
;= \h
(contains? (apply array-set "hello") \h)
;= true
(= (array-set) #{})
;= true
```

So far so good, but...

```
((apply array-set "hello") \h)
; #<ClassCastException java.lang.ClassCastException:
;    user.ArraySet cannot be cast to clojure.lang.IFn>
```

This exception isn't surprising: we haven't implemented anything to allow ArraySet to
be callable as a function. To do this, we must implement the suitable aritics of the
clojure.land.IFn interface, which is implemented by all Clojure functions. This is entirely optional—there's nothing to say that a perfectly useful collection *must* be
callable—but that feature is very convenient, so we'll take a stab at adding it.[28]

More serious is this:

```
(= #{} (array-set))
;= false
```

We are breaking the symmetric property of =, a key part of its general contract. This stems from the fact that Clojure sets are by definition also Java sets, as defined by java.util.Set.[29]

Let's use scaffold again to see what we need to implement java.util.Set:

```
(scaffold java.util.Set)
;  java.util.Set
;     (add [this G__6140])
;     (equals [this G__6141])
;     (hashCode [this])
;     (clear [this])
;     (isEmpty [this])
;     (contains [this G__6142])
;     (addAll [this G__6143])
;     (size [this])
;     (toArray [this G__6144])
;     (toArray [this])
;     (iterator [this])
;     (remove [this G__6145])
;     (removeAll [this G__6146])
;     (containsAll [this G__6147])
;     (retainAll [this G__6148])
```

Don't panic: only the read portion of that interface needs to be implemented, since ArraySet is immutable and persistent. equals, hashCode, and contains are already done, so we are left with:

```
java.util.Set
  (isEmpty [this])
  (size [this])
  (toArray [this G__6144])
  (toArray [this])
  (iterator [this])
  (containsAll [this G__6147])
```

None of these methods are difficult to write. The only pitfall would be to leak the items array when returning from toArray; this would leave our internal array open to being modified underneath us, ruining our immutability guarantee. The implementation of iterator could be tedious if done naively, but is actually very simple as long as you remember that sequences are Java collections as well, and so we can just reuse the Iterator they provide:

---

28. Similarly, ArraySet does not yet support metadata, functionality defined by clojure.lang.IObj. It only defines two methods that are very easy to implement; we leave this as an exercise for the reader.

29. The same holds true for Clojure map implementations, which should also implement Java's java.util.Map interface.

Example 6-9. An improved array-backed set implementation using deftype

```clojure
(deftype ArraySet [^objects items
                   ^int size
                   ^:unsynchronized-mutable ^int hashcode]
  clojure.lang.IPersistentSet
  (get [this x]
    (loop [i 0]
      (when (< i size)
        (if (= x (aget items i))
          (aget items i)
          (recur (inc i)))))))
  (contains [this x]
    (boolean
      (loop [i 0]
        (when (< i size)
          (or (= x (aget items i)) (recur (inc i)))))))
  (disjoin [this x]
    (loop [i 0]
      (if (== i size)
        this
        (if (not= x (aget items i))
          (recur (inc i))
          (ArraySet. (doto (aclone items)
                       (aset i (aget items (dec size)))
                       (aset (dec size) nil))
                     (dec size)
                     -1)))))
  clojure.lang.IPersistentCollection
  (count [this] size)
  (cons [this x]
    (cond
      (.contains this x) this
      (== size max-size) (into #{x} this)
      :else (ArraySet. (doto (aclone items)
                         (aset size x))
                       (inc size)
                       -1)))
  (empty [this] empty-array-set)
  (equiv [this that] (.equals this that))
  clojure.lang.Seqable
  (seq [this] (take size items))
  Object
  (hashCode [this]
    (when (== -1 hashcode)
      (set! hashcode (int (areduce items idx ret 0
                            (unchecked-add-int ret (hash (aget items idx)))))))
    hashcode)
  (equals [this that]
    (or
      (identical? this that)
      (and (instance? java.util.Set that)                  ❶
           (= (count this) (count that))
           (every? #(contains? this %) that))))
  clojure.lang.IFn
  (invoke [this key] (.get this key))                      ❷
```

```
(applyTo [this args]                                                    ❸
  (when (not= 1 (count args))
    (throw (clojure.lang.ArityException. (count args) "ArraySet"))))
  (this (first args)))
java.util.Set
(isEmpty [this] (zero? size))
(size [this] size)
(toArray [this array]
  (.toArray ^java.util.Collection (sequence items) array))            ❹
(toArray [this] (into-array (seq this)))
(iterator [this] (.iterator ^java.util.Collection (sequence this)))   ❺
(containsAll [this coll]
  (every? #(contains? this %) coll)))

(def ^:private empty-array-set (ArraySet. (object-array max-size) 0 -1))
```

❶ equals can be simplified to test only if that implements java.util.Set, since that interface is now implemented by ArraySet.

❷ For direct invocations, clojure.lang.IFn consists of 21 different arities of invoke. Sets can only take one argument (the key to look up, as if via get), so we only implement that arity; an error will be thrown if an ArraySet is called with no or more arguments.

❸ For invocations via apply, IFn defines applyTo, which takes the seq of arguments provided to apply.

❹ sequence is preferred over seq because it never returns nil: seq, by returning nil, would cause a NullPointerException for empty sets.

❺ Since sequences are Java collections, we can just return the Iterator provided by our own seq.

Now we have a fully functional set implementation that plays nicely with others, and is callable just like Clojure's regular sets:

```
(= #{3 1 2 0} (array-set 0 1 2 3))
;= true
((apply array-set "hello") \h)
;= \h
```

But, is ArraySet of any benefit to us? Let's see how it compares to Clojure's general-purpose hash-set, using a mix of lookups, disj, and conj operations:

```
(defn microbenchmark
  [f & {:keys [size trials] :or {size 4 trials 1e6}}]
  (let [items (repeatedly size gensym)]
    (time (loop [s (apply f items)
                 n trials]
            (when (pos? n)
              (doseq [x items] (contains? s x))
              (let [x (rand-nth items)]
                (recur (-> s (disj x) (conj x)) (dec n)))))))))

(doseq [n (range 1 5)
```

```
        f [#'array-set #'hash-set]]
  (print n (-> f meta :name) ": ")
  (microbenchmark @f :size n))
; size 1 array-set : "Elapsed time: 839.336 msecs"
; size 1 hash-set : "Elapsed time: 1105.059 msecs"
; size 2 array-set : "Elapsed time: 1201.81 msecs"
; size 2 hash-set : "Elapsed time: 1369.192 msecs"
; size 3 array-set : "Elapsed time: 1658.36 msecs"
; size 3 hash-set : "Elapsed time: 1740.955 msecs"
; size 4 array-set : "Elapsed time: 2197.424 msecs"
; size 4 hash-set : "Elapsed time: 2154.637 msecs"
```

It looks like `array-set` will yield the same or better performance for very small sets compared to `hash-set`, and since it's using a simple Java array for storage, it will certainly consume less memory than the corresponding tree-based implementation used by `hash-set`.

Final Thoughts

Types, records, and protocols together shape a potent framework that puts the focus on data and avoids extraneous ceremony and complexity. This data-centric approach to types and abstractions allows us to model domains and interactions more faithfully, apply the whole language to those models—such as how we can work with records and maps in a uniform way using the core collection and associative abstractions and functions—and helps us to avoid having to make false choices due to often unnecessary complexities like class hierarchies.

## CHAPTER 7

Multimethods

We have previously talked about protocols: they introduce a common but limited form of polymorphic dispatch—namely type-based single dispatch. In this chapter, we'll explore *multimethods*, which expand dispatch flexibility to not only offer multiple dispatch, but even dispatch based on things other than argument type. That is, for a given multimethod, the implementation used for any given invocation can be chosen as a function of any property of the arguments, without one of them being privileged. Additionally, multimethods support arbitrary hierarchies and means of disambiguating multiple inheritance.

 In Java, one method name can have several signatures of the same length differing only by the types of the arguments, a situation called *overloading*. However this does not constitute a kind of multiple dispatch: the right signature is selected during compilation based on the types of the method's arguments. The only *dynamic* dispatch occurs on the type of the privileged argument: `this`.

Multimethods Basics

A multimethod is created using a `defmulti` form, and implementations of a multimethod are provided by `defmethod` forms. The mnemonic is that they come in the same order as in the word *multimethod* itself: first you define the *multi*ple dispatch then the *methods* to which calls are dispatched.

Let's look at an example: a function that fills XML/HTML nodes and whose behavior depends on the tag name, using the representation of XML defined by the `clojure.xml` namespace. An element is a map of three keys: `:tag` for the name (as a keyword) of the element, `:attrs` for a map of attribute names (as keywords) to values (as strings), and `:content` for a collection of child nodes and content.

```
(defmulti fill
  "Fill a xml/html node (as per clojure.xml)
   with the provided value."
```

```
(fn [node value] (:tag node)))            ❶

(defmethod fill :div                        ❷
  [node value]
  (assoc node :content [(str value)]))

(defmethod fill :input
  [node value]
  (assoc-in node [:attrs :value] (str value)))
```

❶ This is the *dispatch function*; the arguments to the multimethod are passed to this function to yield a *dispatch value*, which is used to select which method to invoke for those arguments.

❷ The :div here is a dispatch value. When the return of the dispatch function matches this dispatch value, the provided method implementation (which is just another function) is selected and invoked.

A multimethod's operation is nothing complex:

1. Take arguments.
2. Compute the dispatch value by invoking the dispatch function with the given arguments.
3. Select the implementation method that was defined to support the dispatch value.
4. Call the implementation method with the original arguments.

That's all. You could easily reimplement such a system in a few lines of Clojure using atoms and macros,[1] or in some amount of code in Ruby or Python.[2]

Multimethods certainly *look* a little different than other function definitions, in a couple different ways:

- A multimethod—despite defining a function—does not explicitly specify its arities. Instead, it supports all arities supported by its dispatch function.
- The defmulti form is what actually defines a new var, fill in our example above. Each defmethod form simply registers a new implementation method on the "root" multimethod; counterintuitively, defmethod does not define or redefine any vars.

So far we haven't exercised our code yet, let's make sure everything is working as expected:

```
(fill {:tag :div} "hello")
;= {:content ["hello"], :tag :div}
(fill {:tag :input} "hello")
```

---

1. This is left as an exercise to the reader.

2. Multiple dispatch systems similar to Clojure's multimethods exist for other languages; Philip J. Eby's PEAK-Rules (*http://pypi.python.org/pypi/PEAK-Rules*) for Python is one particularly mature one. A narrative exploration of implementing Clojure-style multimethods in Python can be found at *http://codeblog.dhananjaynene.com/2010/08/clojure-style-multi-methods-in-python/*.

```
;= {:attrs {:value "hello"}, :tag :input}
(fill {:span :input} "hello")
;= #<IllegalArgumentException java.lang.IllegalArgumentException:
;=   No method in multimethod 'fill' for dispatch value: null>
```

Here is a shortcoming of our approach so far: since we don't have a base case, `fill` works only on elements it knows; that is, those for which we have provided an implementation via `defmethod`.

Helpfully, there's a special dispatch value: `:default`.

```
(defmethod fill :default
  [node value]
  (assoc node :content [(str value)]))

(fill {:span :input} "hello")
;= {:content ["hello"], :span :input}
(fill {:span :input} "hello")
;= {:content ["hello"], :span :input}
```

It works, and we can even get rid of the implementation for `:div` since it's covered by the base case!

However, our regular dispatch values are already keywords: this means we can run into trouble if we want to extend `fill` to cover the `<default>` tag[3] in a specialized way.

Gladfully `defmulti` takes options, and there's a way to specify what the default dispatch value should be:

```
(defmulti fill
  "Fill a xml/html node (as per clojure.xml)
   with the provided value."
  (fn [node value] (:tag node))
  :default nil)                              ❶

(defmethod fill nil                          ❷
  [node value]
  (assoc node :content [(str value)]))

(defmethod fill :input
  [node value]
  (assoc-in node [:attrs :value] (str value)))

(defmethod fill :default                     ❸
  [node value]
  (assoc-in node [:attrs :name] (str value)))
```

❶ `defmulti`'s options are simply keyword/value pairs, here used to set the default dispatch value to `nil`.

❷ Here is the corresponding default implementation.

❸ This is now not the default implementation but the one for `<default>` elements.

---

3. Let's assume we are dealing with some specific XML format or that someone sneaked it into HTML5.

Toward Hierarchies

Let's refine `fill` so that we apply different behaviors for different `<input>` tags. For example, we want to check radio buttons or checkboxes when their `value` attribute matches the value arguments passed to `fill`.

The current dispatch function does not provide information on attributes so, to dispatch on the `type` attribute, we need to modify the dispatch function:

```
(ns-unmap *ns* 'fill)

(defn- fill-dispatch [node value]
  (if (= :input (:tag node))
    [(:tag node) (-> node :attrs :type)]
    (:tag node)))

(defmulti fill
  "Fill a xml/html node (as per clojure.xml)
   with the provided value."
  #'fill-dispatch                              ❶
  :default nil)

(defmethod fill nil
  [node value]
  (assoc node :content [(str value)]))

(defmethod fill [:input nil]
  [node value]
  (assoc-in node [:attrs :value] (str value)))

(defmethod fill [:input "hidden"]
  [node value]
  (assoc-in node [:attrs :value] (str value)))

(defmethod fill [:input "text"]
  [node value]
  (assoc-in node [:attrs :value] (str value)))

(defmethod fill [:input "radio"]
  [node value]
  (if (= value (-> node :attrs :value))
    (assoc-in node [:attrs :checked] "checked")
    (update-in node [:attrs] dissoc :checked)))

(defmethod fill [:input "checkbox"]
  [node value]
  (if (= value (-> node :attrs :value))
    (assoc-in node [:attrs :checked] "checked")
    (update-in node [:attrs] dissoc :checked)))

(defmethod fill :default
  [node value]
  (assoc-in node [:attrs :name] (str value)))
```

❶ Using `#'fill-dispatch` instead of simply `fill-dispatch` adds a layer of indirection that allows us to modify the dispatch function without touching `ns-unmap` or losing any already-defined methods. Using `fill-dispatch` captures the value of the dispatch function at the time `defmulti` was evaluated, and the dispatch function would not be updated subsequently. This is very useful when evolving code at the REPL.

Redefining a multimethod does not update the multimethod's dispatch function

Notice that in our example above, we `ns-unmap` `fill` from our namespace so we can redefine it. This isn't typically necessary when redefining functions, but `defmulti` has `defonce` semantics, so dispatch functions cannot be changed without unmapping the root var of the multimethod first. This means you have to unmap it from the current namespace before redefining it, or your changes will be silently ignored!

An interesting point of this iteration is that dispatch values are now a mix of `nil`, keywords and pairs of keywords and strings. *Dispatch values are not constrained to keywords*. That said, we'll soon see that keywords still play a special role in regard to multimethods.

For now, we should test our new code:

```
(fill {:tag :input
       :attrs {:value "first choice"
               :type "checkbox"}}
      "first choice")                    ❶
;= {:tag :input,
;=  :attrs {:checked "checked",
;=          :type "checkbox",
;=          :value "first choice"}}
(fill *1 "off")                          ❷
;= {:tag :input
;=  :attrs {:type "checkbox",
;=          :value "first choice"}}
```

❶ Calling `fill` with a checkbox element's map and the `:value` of that checkbox is properly yielding a checked checkbox...

❷ ...and calling `fill` with that checked checkbox and any other value results in an unchecked checkbox.

These results seem good but there's a fair amount of repetition in the latest iteration: checkboxes and radio buttons should share the same implementation, as should explicit text fields and implicit ones (`nil`) too. Furthermore the `text` behavior should be the default case for unknown types.

In short, we would like to specify that checkboxes and radio buttons are *checkable inputs* and that unknown input types should be treated as text inputs. This can be done by defining a hierarchy, which allows us to express the relationships among dispatch values, which our multimethod will use to refine its selection of method implementations.

Hierarchies

Clojure's multimethods allow us to define hierarchies to support whatever relationships your domain requires, including multiple inheritance. These hierarchies are defined in terms of relations between *named objects*[4] (keywords or symbols[5]) and classes.

"Hierarchies" being plural is no accident: you can have more than one hierarchy. There's the global (and default) hierarchy and ones you can create as needed via `make-hierarchy`. In addition, hierarchies and multimethods are in no way restricted to a single namespace: you can extend a hierarchy (through `derive`) or a multimethod (via `defmethod`) from any namespace—not necessarily the one in which they were defined.

The global hierarchy being shared, access to it is more guarded. Namely, *non-namespaced keywords (or symbols) cannot be used in the global hierarchy*. This helps prevent two innocent libraries from stepping on each other's toes by independently choosing to use the same keyword to represent different semantics.

You define a hierarchical relation with `derive`:

```
(derive ::checkbox ::checkable)      ❶
;= nil
(derive ::radio ::checkable)
;= nil
(derive ::checkable ::input)
;= nil
(derive ::text ::input)
;= nil
```

❶ Recall that `::keyword` is a shorthand for `:current.namespace/keyword`; thus, `::checkbox` here is equivalent to `:user/checkbox`. Also remember that `::keyword` is to `:keyword` as `` `symbol `` is to `'symbol`. See "Keywords" on page 14 for more details.

We have just described in the relationships that hold between different "classes": checkboxes and radio buttons are "checkable," and all "checkable" and "text" elements are input elements. You can test these relationships within the hierarchy using `isa?`:

```
(isa? ::radio ::input)        ❶
;= true
(isa? ::radio ::text)
;= false
```

❶ Derivation is transitive: `::radio` is a `::checkable`, which is an `::input`.

---

4. Named objects are objects on which you can call `name` and `namespace`, they implement the `clojure.lang.Named` interface.

5. Keywords are generally preferred though.

---

isa? is rarely used outside of the REPL. If you find yourself using it a lot in code, it means there's a multimethod waiting to be extracted. In this regard, it's very similar to `instance?`: generally its presence hints at a dispatch facility (Java interface, protocol, or multimethod) to be factored out.

There are a handful of other introspective functions: `underive`, `ancestors`, `parents`, and `descendants`, which are useful either when working at the REPL or can be leveraged to perform some metaprogramming stunts.

Classes and interfaces can also participate in hierarchies but *only as children of a derivation*, never as parents,[6] Said another way, outside of the class hierarchy implicitly defined by your Clojure environment's classpath,[7] classes and interfaces can only ever be leaves in a hierarchy.

```
(isa? java.util.ArrayList Object)
;= true
(isa? java.util.ArrayList java.util.List)
;= true
(isa? java.util.ArrayList java.util.Map)        ❶
;= false
(derive java.util.Map ::collection)             ❷
;= nil
(derive java.util.Collection ::collection)
;= nil
(isa? java.util.ArrayList ::collection)         ❸
;= true
(isa? java.util.HashMap ::collection)
;= true
```

❶ In the Java Collections framework, `Maps` and `Collections` are entirely separate. No dispatch mechanism that relies solely on these static types can provide a way to handle a `Map` and a `Collection` with a single method (short of falling back to, for example, `Object`).

❷ We can declare that `Map` and `Collection` are derived from a new identifier in the global hierarchy, called `::collection`.

❸ We can now use `::collection` as a target dispatch value in `defmethod`, as it now matches any classes that implement `Map` or `Collection`.

This aspect of hierarchies isn't relevant to our running example, though. We'll return to the topic of using classes and interfaces in hierarchies in "Multiple Inheritance" on page 313.

---

6. The only way to derive from a class or interface is to create a type with interop or `deftype`, `defrecord`, or `reify`.

7. See "A classpath primer" on page 331 for information about the classpath.

The whole Java class hierarchy is always part of any hierarchy, even when freshly created by make-hierarchy.

```
(def h (make-hierarchy))
;= #'user/h
(isa? h java.util.ArrayList java.util.Collection)
;= true
```

Thus isa? supersets instance?, in that it can be used to test whether a class is derived from another class, or whether a class implements an interface.

Independent Hierarchies

Currently fill-dispatch returns nil, keywords, and vectors. Two of them can't participate in hierarchies (nil and vectors) and the third can't participate in the global hierarchy because those keywords are not namespaced.

So we are left with the choice between having fill-dispatch return namespaced keywords, or using a private hierarchy.

derive implicitly mutates the global hierarchy, but when you use a custom hierarchy, you have to manage the mutation yourself. It's as simple as putting the hierarchy into a reference type such as refs, atoms, or vars. Var is a safe choice:[8] that's what is used for the global hierarchy.

Example 7-1. Implementing fill with a custom hierarchy

```
(ns-unmap *ns* 'fill)

(def fill-hierarchy (-> (make-hierarchy)                          ❶
                        (derive :input.radio ::checkable)
                        (derive :input.checkbox ::checkable)
                        (derive ::checkable :input)
                        (derive :input.text :input)
                        (derive :input.hidden :input)))

(defn- fill-dispatch [node value]
  (if-let [type (and (= :input (:tag node))
                     (-> node :attrs :type))]
    (keyword (str "input." type))
    (:tag node)))

(defmulti fill
  "Fill a xml/html node (as per clojure.xml)
  with the provided value."
  #'fill-dispatch
  :default nil
```

---

8. It's the safe choice because hierarchies generally don't change often and you want changes to them to be visible from all threads. If you have other requirements (e.g., transactional changes or dynamic scope), pick the relevant reference type. See Chapter 4.

```
  :hierarchy #'fill-hierarchy)                                    ❷

(defmethod fill nil [node value]
  (assoc node :content [(str value)]))

(defmethod fill :input [node value]
  (assoc-in node [:attrs :value] (str value)))

(defmethod fill ::checkable [node value]
  (if (= value (-> node :attrs :value))
    (assoc-in node [:attrs :checked] "checked")
    (update-in node [:attrs] dissoc :checked)))
```

❶ Both `input.type` and `::checkable` are means of avoiding potential collisions with legitimate tag names. `.` in a keyword has no special meaning—it's simply part of its name.

❷ Multimethods expect a reference type of some kind as the value of the `:hierarchy` option, not a hierarchy value; this allows you to update the hierarchy if necessary at runtime. In this case, we provide the `fill-hierarchy` *var* (rather than its value at the time of evaluating the `defmulti` form); we could use `alter-var-root` to modify the hierarchy dynamically, without redefining the multimethod's root.

All hierarchy-related functions (such as `derive`, `isa?`, `parents`, and so on) require the hierarchy value as an additional first argument. Out of this list, `derive` is the most peculiar because without an explicit hierarchy, it's a side-effecting function—modifying the global hierarchy—and with an explicit hierarchy, it's a pure function!

Our latest iteration on the `fill` code doesn't repeat itself, so this goal has been attained. The second goal is not a success though: indeed unknown input types, like text inputs, are not handled.

```
(fill {:tag :input
       :attrs {:type "date"}}
      "20110820")
;= {:content ["20110820"], :attrs {:type "date"}, :tag :input}
```

Not exactly what we had in mind! We haven't expressed that unknown input types should be treated as text. The problem is that the set of inputs of unknown types is open, so we can't create all the necessary derivations by anticipation. And, since the set of dispatch values is bigger than only those for input tags, we can't use the default value for covering unexpected input types.

Or can we? If we think *dynamically* instead of assuming that we must statically define our hierarchy ahead of time, we realize that hierarchies are *not* static. This means our default case can act as a safety net and dynamically define the needed derivation so that for a given new input type, the default case will be hit only once.

Example 7-2. Dynamically updating the hierarchy used by fill

```
(defmethod fill nil [node value]
  (if (= :input (:tag node))
    (do
      (alter-var-root #'fill-hierarchy
        derive (fill-dispatch node value) :input)   ❶
      (fill node value))                              ❷
    (assoc node :content [(str value)]))))
```

❶ We alter the value of the var dynamically, specifying that the dispatch value for the unknown :input node should derive from :input in our hierarchy.

❷ After making that change, we recursively call fill, which will dispatch to the :input method implementation now that we've updated the hierarchy with a new derivation suited for this case.

This trick works well:

```
(fill {:tag :input
       :attrs {:type "date"}}
      "20110820")
;= {:attrs {:value "20110820", :type "date"}, :tag :input}
```

A less clever way of achieving this result would be to introduce a fill-input multimethod and calling it from the :input case of fill.

```
(ns-unmap *ns* 'fill)

(def input-hierarchy (-> (make-hierarchy)
                         (derive :input.radio ::checkable)
                         (derive :input.checkbox ::checkable)))   ❶

(defn- fill-dispatch [node value]
  (:tag node))

(defmulti fill
  "Fill a xml/html node (as per clojure.xml)
   with the provided value."
  #'fill-dispatch
  :default nil)                                      ❷

(defmulti fill-input
  "Fill an input field."
  (fn [node value] (-> node :attrs :type))
  :default nil
  :hierarchy #'input-hierarchy)

(defmethod fill nil [node value]
  (assoc node :content [(str value)]))

(defmethod fill :input [node value]
  (fill-input node value))

(defmethod fill-input nil [node value]
  (assoc-in node [:attrs :value] (str value)))
```

```
(defmethod fill-input ::checkable [node value]
  (if (= value (-> node :attrs :value))
    (assoc-in node [:attrs :checked] "checked")
    (update-in node [:attrs] dissoc :checked)))
```

❶ Explicitly deriving :text and :hidden from the default case is no longer necessary. Plus, it's downright impossible because our default dispatch value is nil, which cannot participate in hierarchies.

❷ fill no longer depends on a custom hierarchy—only fill-input.

Making It Really Multiple!

So far, our example has exerted non-type-based dispatch but not multiple dispatch: the second argument (value) was carefully ignored in all previous dispatch functions.

That's not much of a big deal because most multiple dispatch works in the same way: the dispatch function computes one value, which gets matched to an implementation according to the applicable hierarchy. The multimethod system is unaware that our dispatch functions were only vetting the first argument.

However, dispatch values that are vectors are special-cased by isa?, element by element:[9]

```
(isa? fill-hierarchy [:input.checkbox :text] [::checkable :input])
;= true
```

As we already pointed out, the Java class hierarchy is included in all hierarchies, this means we can throw some classes into the mix if we need to:

```
(isa? fill-hierarchy [:input.checkbox String] [::checkable CharSequence])
;= true
```

We are going to leverage this feature to make fill smarter and react accordingly to the type of its value argument.

The first step is to modify fill-dispatch to return a vector of one keyword and one class.[10]

```
(defn- fill-dispatch [node value]
  (if-let [type (and (= :input (:tag node))
                     (-> node :attrs :type))]
    [(keyword (str "input." type)) (class value)]
    [(:tag node) (class value)]))
```

---

9. It works recursively: you can use vectors of vectors as dispatch values!

10. This example is based on Example 7-1 along with the dynamic modification of hierarchies as demonstrated in Example 7-2.

Now we'd like to say that the base case is to convert the value to a `String`, whatever its type is. However, checkboxes accept sets as values: a checkbox will be checked if and only if its value is in the set.

```
(ns-unmap *ns* 'fill)

(def fill-hierarchy (-> (make-hierarchy)
                        (derive :input.radio ::checkable)
                        (derive :input.checkbox ::checkable)))

(defn- fill-dispatch [node value]
  (if-let [type (and (= :input (:tag node))
                     (-> node :attrs :type))]
    [(keyword (str "input." type)) (class value)]
    [(:tag node) (class value)]))

(defmulti fill
  "Fill a xml/html node (as per clojure.xml)
   with the provided value."
  #'fill-dispatch
  :default nil
  :hierarchy #'fill-hierarchy)

(defmethod fill nil
  [node value]
  (if (= :input (:tag node))
    (do
      (alter-var-root #'fill-hierarchy
        derive (first (fill-dispatch node value)) :input)    ❶
      (fill node value))
    (assoc node :content [(str value)])))

(defmethod fill
  [:input Object] [node value]
  (assoc-in node [:attrs :value] (str value)))

(defmethod fill [::checkable clojure.lang.IPersistentSet]
  [node value]
  (if (contains? value (-> node :attrs :value))
    (assoc-in node [:attrs :checked] "checked")
    (update-in node [:attrs] dissoc :checked)))
```

❶ This new `first` is here to take only the keyword part of the dispatch value. Remember: you can only use keywords, symbols, or classes in hierarchies.

Now we can check and uncheck checkboxes by using the more flexible set notation for checkable values:

```
(fill {:tag :input
       :attrs {:value "yes"
               :type "checkbox"}}
      #{"yes" "y"})
;= {:attrs {:checked "checked", :type "checkbox", :value "yes"}, :tag :input}
(fill *1 #{"no" "n"})
;= {:attrs {:type "checkbox", :value "yes"}, :tag :input}
```

While other input elements and noninput elements are filled as we'd expect:

```
(fill {:tag :input :attrs {:type "text"}} "some text")
;= {:attrs {:value "some text", :type "text"}, :tag :input}
(fill {:tag :h1} "Big Title!")
;= {:content ["Big Title!"], :tag :h1}
```

A Few More Things

Multiple Inheritance

Our running `fill` example doesn't have a hierarchy complex enough to introduce multiple "inheritance." Such relationships arise frequently when you have multimethods dealing with interfaces.

Let's say we want a `run` function that can execute anything vaguely runnable (like `java.lang.Runnable` and `java.util.concurrent.Callable`):

```
(defmulti run "Executes the computation." class)

(defmethod run Runnable
  [x]
  (.run x))

(defmethod run java.util.concurrent.Callable
  [x]
  (.call x))
```

Let's test it on a function:

```
(run #(println "hello!"))
;= #<IllegalArgumentException java.lang.IllegalArgumentException:
;=   Multiple methods in multimethod 'run' match dispatch value:
;=     class user$fn__1422 -> interface java.util.concurrent.Callable and
;=                             interface java.lang.Runnable, and neither is preferred>
```

The exception is pretty self-explanatory: since Clojure functions implement both `Runnable` and `Callable`, the multimethod doesn't know which implementation to pick and hints that one should be *preferred*.

Preferences are expressed through the `prefer-method` function. This function expects three arguments: the multimethod considered and *two* dispatch values, the first being the one that should be preferred over the second:

```
(prefer-method run java.util.concurrent.Callable Runnable)
;= #<MultiFn clojure.lang.MultiFn@6dc98c1b>
(run #(println "hello!"))
;= hello!
;= nil
```

Now the multimethod knows which implementation to pick, to *prefer*, and runs without problem.

This preferences mechanism allows us to declaratively resolve *diamond problems*,[11] that is, situations where one class derives from the same superclass via two or more other intermediary superclasses. Hence you don't have to defensively design your hierarchies in fear of multiple inheritance. *Preferences make multiple inheritance explicit, and therefore easy to reason about.*

Introspecting Multimethods

There are a handful of rarely used functions that allow you to go meta with multimethods: `remove-method`, `remove-all-methods`, `prefers`, `methods`, and `get-method`. These functions allow you to query and update multimethods.

You'll notice that there's no `add-method` though. It's good to know that the `defmethod` macro, despite being a `def`-something form, isn't required to be a top-level expression. However, you may prefer to register an existing function as a method implementation; we can find out how to do this by taking a peek under the covers:

```
(macroexpand-1 '(defmethod mmethod-name dispatch-value [args] body))
;= (. mmethod-name clojure.core/addMethod dispatch-value (clojure.core/fn [args]
    body)) ❶
```

❶ The `clojure.core/addMethod` instead of just `addMethod` is an artifact of `syntax-quote`. Preventing it is awkward but Clojure is smart enough to know to ignore namespaces on Java methods names.

This suggests a simple implementation of `add-method`:

```
(defn add-method [multifn dispatch-val f]
  (.addMethod multifn dispatch-val f))
```

As a side note, it happens that this function can be found as a private function of the `clojure.pprint` namespace, under the name `use-method`. However, whether you are using `use-method` or the above exposed `add-method` you are relying on an implementation detail, so be prepared to actively maintain it with next releases of Clojure.

type Versus class; or, the Revenge of the Map

`class` has a close cousin, `type`. `(type x)` generally returns the same result as `(class x)`, except when x has `:type` metadata:

```
(class {})
;= clojure.lang.PersistentArrayMap
(type {})
;= clojure.lang.PersistentArrayMap
(class ^{:type :a-tag} {})
;= clojure.lang.PersistentArrayMap
```

---

11. Not always a diamond as Clojure's hierarchies don't have a universal root. In Clojure, this problem would best be named the *V problem*.

```
(type ^{:type :a-tag} {})
;= :a-tag
```

:type metadata is a low ceremony way of categorizing data into types and having these types participate in multimethods. Note that it also works if you put the metadata on other kinds of objects: vectors, sets, functions, and so on.

For example, let's extend our example from "Multiple Inheritance" on page 313 to make it so that our run multimethod will interchangeably accept Runnables, Callable, regular Clojure functions, as well as maps "typed" as runnable that contain any of these things in a :run slot:

```
(ns-unmap *ns* 'run)

(defmulti run "Executes the computation." type)          ❶

(defmethod run Runnable
  [x]
  (.run x))

(defmethod run java.util.concurrent.Callable
  [x]
  (.call x))

(prefer-method run java.util.concurrent.Callable Runnable)

(defmethod run :runnable-map
  [m]
  (run (:run m)))

(run #(println "hello!"))
;= hello!
;= nil
(run (reify Runnable
       (run [this] (println "hello!"))))
;= hello!
;= nil
(run ^{:type :runnable-map}
      {:run #(println "hello!") :other :data})
;= hello!
;= nil
```

❶ We now have type acting as the dispatch function for run, so that it will return the :type metadata on any passed maps, falling back to returning the class of the argument if no such metadata is available.

Of course, you could modify the dispatch function to explicitly check for a :run slot in any provided map to achieve the same end. However, what would happen if you wanted to be able to run some function you knew was available as the last element of vectors produced elsewhere in your application? You would need to modify your dispatch function to allow for that, thereby subverting a big part of the motivation of multimethods (and really, many of Clojure's other facilities): to allow you to disentangle operations from the data that is being operated over.

The Range of Dispatch Functions Is Unlimited

Our final example will help to illustrate the flexibility that is available to you with multimethods. So far, we've been working with multimethods whose dispatch functions return values based solely on their arguments. However, there is no requirement at all that that be the case.

Consider a messaging system where the handling of each message is significantly different depending upon its priority:

```
(def priorities (atom {:911-call :high
                       :evacuation :high
                       :pothole-report :low
                       :tree-down :low}))

(defmulti route-message
  (fn [message] (@priorities (:type message))))

(defmethod route-message :low
  [{:keys [type]}]
  (println (format "Oh, there's another %s. Put it in the log." (name type))))

(defmethod route-message :high
  [{:keys [type]}]
  (println (format "Alert the authorities, there's a %s!" (name type))))
```

This seems pretty straightforward:[12]

```
(route-message {:type :911-call})
;= Alert the authorities, there's a 911-call!
;= nil
(route-message {:type :tree-down})
;= Oh, there's another tree-down. Put it in the log.
;= nil
```

However, what if the message priorities themselves can change dynamically? No problem: just adjust the data that is driving the dispatch function, and the behavior of route-message can change significantly *without any changes to code or data*:

```
(swap! priorities assoc :tree-down :high)
;= {:911-call :high, :pothole-report :low, :tree-down :high, :evacuation :high}
(route-message {:type :tree-down})
;= Alert the authorities, there's a tree-down!
;= nil
```

This gives you a lot of latitude and power, perhaps just enough to solve the problem you have. At the same time—apologies for the mixed metaphor—it might be just enough rope with which to hang yourself. A multimethod whose behavior is not strictly dependent upon the values provided as arguments is, by definition, not idempotent.[13] That doesn't make such functions unreliable or evil or useless, just more difficult

---

12. Presumably our route-message implementations would do more than print something to standard out.

13. See "Pure Functions" on page 76 for more about idempotence, pure functions, and their benefits.

---

to understand, test, and compose with other functions compared to their idempotent cousins.

Final Thoughts

Following along the `fill` example, we have covered all of the essential features of Clojure multimethods.[14]

It takes some time to get accustomed to their power, to think outside of single type-based dispatch. Each time you envision writing a bunch of nested conditionals or a big `cond` or defining a plethora of types just to link your data with particular functionality, you should ask yourself whether a multimethod wouldn't serve you better.

---

14. You can find some additional examples that use multimethods in Chapter 15.

## PART III

Tools, Platform, and Projects

## CHAPTER 8

Organizing and Building Clojure Projects

Ironically, one of the most challenging aspects of adopting a new, promising programming language often has little to do with the language itself: you need to organize and build the codebase you've written in that new language into artifacts that can be distributed and used, either by other programmers as libraries, by end users, or installed into, for example, server environments as is done for web applications. The specifics of this challenge can vary greatly depending upon whether you're using the new language as part of an existing project or in an entirely new effort, and what your specific deployment requirements are.

It's impossible for us to cover all the ways in which you can organize your projects and redistribute the fruits of your Clojure labors, and differences of opinion in some of these areas can often outstrip their importance,[1] but it is incumbent upon us to set you on a good path that is in accordance with the typical approaches in the Clojure community. In this chapter, we'll give you some general hints on how to think about structuring Clojure codebases, and present the best ways to solve the build problem for Clojure projects using the two most popular build tools in the Clojure community, Leiningen and Maven.

Project Geography

Before getting into the mechanics of builds, we first need to establish how to organize your Clojure projects with regard to the physical placement of files as well as the functional organization of your codebase. This means talking about *namespaces*.

---

1. The entire question of "build" is perhaps the grandest bikeshed ever built, lagging in controversy and bile perhaps only behind the *tabs versus spaces* and *emacs versus vi* "debates": *http://bikeshed.org*.

Defining and Using Namespaces

As we said in "Namespaces" on page 20,[2] Clojure's namespaces:

- Are dynamic mappings of symbols to Java class names and vars, the latter containing any value you specify (most often functions, constant data, and reference types)
- Are roughly analogous to packages in Java and modules in Python and Ruby

All Clojure code is defined within namespaces. If you neglect to define your own, any vars you define will be mapped into the default user namespace. While fine for a lot of REPL interactions, that's almost never a good idea once you want to build something to last and be used by others. We need to know how to define namespaces idiomatically, how they map onto individual source files, and how they are best used to provide high-level structure and organization for your Clojure codebase. Clojure provides discrete functions for manipulating the minutiae of namespaces (very useful at the REPL), as well as a unification of those functions into a single macro that we can use to declare in one place a namespace's name, top-level documentation, and dependencies on other namespaces and Java classes.

in-ns.   def and all of its variants (like defn) define vars within the *current name-space*, which is always bound in *ns*:

```
*ns*
;= #<Namespace user>
(defn a [] 42)
;= #'user/a
```

Using in-ns, we can switch to other namespaces (creating them if they don't already exist), thereby allowing us to define vars in those other namespaces:

```
(in-ns 'physics.constants)
;= #<Namespace physics.constants>
(def ^:const planck 6.62606957e-34)
;= #'physics.constants/planck
```

However, we'll quickly discover that something is awry in our new namespace:

```
(+ 1 1)
;= #<CompilerException java.lang.RuntimeException:
;=   Unable to resolve symbol: + in this context, compiling:(NO_SOURCE_PATH:1)>
```

The + function (and all other functions in the clojure.core namespace) aren't available as they are in the default user namespace we've worked within all along—though they are accessible using a namespace-qualified symbol:

```
(clojure.core/range -20 20 4)
;= (-20 -16 -12 -8 -4 0 4 8 12 16)
```

---

2. If you've not digested that section yet, do so now; that is where we introduce namespaces at the most basic level, talk about symbols, vars, and how the former resolve to the latter.

Remember that namespaces are mappings of symbols to vars; while in-ns switches us to the namespace we name, that's all it does. Special forms remain available (including def, var, ., and so on), but we need to load code from other namespaces and map vars named there into our new namespace in order to use that code reasonably succinctly.

refer.   Assuming a namespace is already loaded, we can use refer to add mappings to its vars for our namespace. We defined a dummy function a in the user namespace earlier. We can establish mappings in our empty namespace for all of the public vars in user, allowing us to access a more easily:

```
user/a
;= #<user$a user$a@6080669d>
(clojure.core/refer 'user)
;= nil
(a)
;= 42
```

a is now mapped within our current namespace to the var at user/a, and we can use it as if it were defined locally. That's certainly easier than having to use namespace-qualified symbols everywhere to access vars in other namespaces.

refer can be used to do more than a simple "import" though: you can specify that certain vars be excluded, included, or renamed when they are mapped into the current namespace by using optional keyword args of :exclude, :only, and :rename, respectively. For example, let's refer to clojure.core, but exclude some functions and map some of the arithmetic operators to different names locally:

```
(clojure.core/refer 'clojure.core
  :exclude '(range)
  :rename '{+ add
            - sub
            / div
            * mul})
;= nil
(-> 5 (add 18) (mul 2) (sub 6))
;= 40
(range -20 20 4)
;= #<CompilerException java.lang.RuntimeException:
;=    Unable to resolve symbol: range in this context, compiling:(NO_SOURCE_PATH:1)>
```

Now we can use all the public functions[3] from clojure.core (except for range, which we excluded), and we're using different names for some of the arithmetic functions.

While clojure.core is always preloaded (and refered to in the user namespace), we'll often need more than that, and we'll want to define multiple namespaces ourselves in order to organize our codebases sensibly. We need a facility for loading namespaces.

---

3. refer will not bring in any private vars from the source namespace. See "Vars" on page 198 for details on private vars.

refer is rarely used directly, but its effects and options are available through use, which *is* widely used.

require and use.   When some code needs to make use of functions or data defined in public vars in another namespace, require and use are used to:

1. Ensure that the namespaces in question are loaded.
2. Optionally establish aliases for those namespaces' names.
3. Trigger the implicit use of refer to allow code to refer to other namespaces' vars without qualification.

require provides (1) and (2); use is built on top of it and refer to provide (3) in a succinct way.

Let's start with a new REPL, where we'd like to use the union function in the clojure.set namespace:

```
(clojure.set/union #{1 2 3} #{4 5 6})
;= #<ClassNotFoundException java.lang.ClassNotFoundException: clojure.set>
```

Wait, that namespace isn't loaded yet—only clojure.core is preloaded. We can use require to load the clojure.set namespace from the classpath;[4] afterward, we can use any function within that namespace:

```
(require 'clojure.set)
;= nil
(clojure.set/union #{1 2 3} #{4 5 6})
;= #{1 2 3 4 5 6}
```

Having to use fully qualified symbols to name vars can be a pain though, especially if the libraries you are using provide namespaces that are long or have a number of segments. Thankfully, require provides a way to specify an alias for a namespace:

```
(require '[clojure.set :as set])   ❶
;= nil
(set/union #{1 2 3} #{4 5 6})
;= #{1 2 3 4 5 6}
```

❶ The vector arguments provided to require and use are sometimes called *libspecs*: they specify how a library is to be loaded and referred to within the current namespace.

When you need to require multiple namespaces that share a common prefix, you can provide to require a sequential collection where the first element is the namespace prefix and the remaining elements are the remaining segments specifying the

---

4. See "Namespaces and files" on page 328 for how Clojure namespaces correspond to files on disk, and "A classpath primer" on page 331 for what the classpath is and why you should care.

---

namespaces you'd like to load. So, if we wanted to `require` both `clojure.set` and `clojure.string`, we would not have to repeat the `clojure` prefix:

```
(require '(clojure string [set :as set]))
```

`use` provides all of the capabilities of `require`, except that by default, it `refers` the given namespace after it is loaded. So, `(use 'clojure.xml)` is the equivalent of:

```
(require 'clojure.xml)
(refer 'clojure.xml)
```

In addition, `use` passes along all of its arguments to `refer`, so you can leverage the latter's `:exclude`, `:only`, and `:rename` options to their fullest. To illustrate, let's consider a scenario where we need to use `clojure.string` and `clojure.set`:

1. We're happy to `refer` all of the vars in the latter into our current namespace, but...
2. We have a number of local functions whose names conflict with those in `clo jure.string`; a simple namespace alias (using `:as` with `require`) will work there, but...
3. We need to use `clojure.string/join` a lot, and it doesn't conflict with any functions in our current namespace, so we'd like to avoid the namespace alias in that case.
4. `clojure.string` and `clojure.set` both define a `join` function; attempting to refer both of them in will result in an error, so we want to prefer `clojure.string/join`.

`use` can accommodate these criteria readily:

```
(use '(clojure [string :only (join) :as str]
               [set :exclude (join)]))
;= nil
join
;= #<string$join clojure.string$join@2259a735>
intersection
;= #<set$intersection clojure.set$intersection@2f7fc44f>
str/trim
;= #<string$trim clojure.string$trim@283aa791>
```

We can now access `clojure.string`'s `join` function without any namespace qualification, but the rest of `clojure.set` has been `refered` into our namespace (including `inter section`), and the entire `clojure.string` namespace is available via the `str` alias.

Using require, refer, and use Effectively

These functions in concert provide many subtle options, especially compared to the blunt instruments that are `import` in Java and `require` in Ruby. Using them effectively and idiomatically can be a tripping point for some new to Clojure.

A good default is to always use `require`, generally with an alias for each namespace:

```
(require '(clojure [string :as str]
                   [set :as set]))
```

This is roughly equivalent to `import sys, os` in Python. Because namespaces generally have multiple segments (compared to the single-token module names common in

---

Python), Clojure does not provide a default alias for required namespaces, but it does allow you to control the alias that is used. Of course, if the namespace in question is short, or you only use vars from it a few times, then a bare require without any alias is entirely appropriate.

Another commonly recommended pattern is to prefer use in conjunction with a namespace alias and an explicit included list of vars to refer into the current namespace:

```
(use '[clojure.set :as set :only (intersection)])
```

Insofar as this form of use provides you with a superset of all of the functionality provided by require and refer, using it means you can consolidate all your namespace references into a single use form. Even where you might otherwise use aliasing require forms, the equivalent use form is hardly longer and allows you to add refered functions to the :only argument very easily.

In any case, it is generally good practice to avoid unconstrained usages of use, that is, those that do not include an :only option to explicitly name the functions that should be refered into the current namespace. Doing so makes it clear what parts of other namespaces your code makes use of, and avoids any name collision warnings that may crop up as upstream libraries change and add functions that you may have already declared locally.

import.   While Clojure namespaces primarily map symbols to vars, often canonically defined in multiple other namespaces, they also map symbols to Java classes and interfaces. You can use import to add such mappings to the current namespace.

import expects as arguments the full names of the classes to import, or a sequential collection describing the package and classes to import. Importing a class makes its "short name" available for use within the current namespace:

```
(Date.)                                                    ❶
;= #<CompilerException java.lang.IllegalArgumentException:
;=    Unable to resolve classname: Date, compiling:(NO_SOURCE_PATH:1)>
(java.util.Date.)                                          ❷
;= #<Date Mon Jul 18 12:31:38 EDT 2011>
(import 'java.util.Date 'java.text.SimpleDateFormat)       ❸
;= java.text.SimpleDateFormat
(.format (SimpleDateFormat. "MM/dd/yyyy") (Date.))         ❹
;= "07/18/2011"
```

❶ Date is in the java.util package, and so usages of its short name will cause an error before it is imported into the current namespace.

❷ We can use Java classes and interfaces without any explicit importing at all, but such usage requires fully qualified classnames, which can be unpleasantly verbose.

❸ You can import classes into the current namespace by providing import with symbols naming the classes.

❹ After being imported, the classes' short names can be used to refer to them.

All classes in the `java.lang` package are always imported into every namespace by default; for example, `java.lang.String` is available via the `String` symbol, and does not need to be `imported` separately.

When you want to import multiple classes from a single package, you can provide to `import` the same kind of package-prefixed collection that `require` accepts for namespaces with the same prefix:

```
(import '(java.util Arrays Collections))
;= java.util.Collections
(->> (iterate inc 0)
  (take 5)
  into-array
  Arrays/asList
  Collections/max)
;= 4
```

It's a rare case, but be aware that you cannot import two classes with the same short name into the same namespace:

```
(import 'java.awt.List 'java.util.List)
;= #<IllegalStateException java.lang.IllegalStateException:
;=   List already refers to: class java.awt.List in namespace: user>
```

The workaround here (as in Java) would be to import the one that you use most frequently within your namespace, and use the other's fully qualified classname.

While Clojure's `import` is conceptually similar to Java's `import` statements, there are a couple of important differences.

First, it provides no analogue to the wildcard import used frequently in Java, such as `import java.util.*;`. If you need to import multiple classes from a single package, you will need to enumerate each of them, surely as part of a package-prefixed list as shown above.

Second, if you need to refer to an *inner class* (e.g., `java.lang.Thread.State`, `java.util.Map.Entry`), you need to use the Java-internal notation for them (e.g., `java.lang.Thread$State`, `java.util.Map$Entry`). This applies to any reference to inner classes, not just those provided to `import`.

ns.   All of the namespace utility functions we've looked at so far in this section should generally be reserved for use in the REPL. Whenever you are working on code you would like to reuse outside of a REPL, you should use the `ns` macro to define your namespaces.[5]

---

5. It may be tempting to take a transcript of what you get working within a REPL, paste it all into a *.clj* file (complete with bare `in-ns`, `refer`, et al. forms), and call it a day. We urge you to fight any such temptation. As we'll discuss in the next section, there are some rules of good hygiene when it comes to organizing Clojure code, and neglecting to fully specify your namespaces by using `ns` would be running counter to those guidelines for no benefit.

ns allows you to declaratively specify a namespace's name along with its top-level documentation and what it needs to have required, refered, used, and imported to load successfully and work properly. It is a very thin wrapper around these functions; thus, this pile of utility function calls:

```
(in-ns 'examples.ns)
(clojure.core/refer 'clojure.core :exclude '[next replace remove])
(require '(clojure [string :as string]
                   [set :as set])
         '[clojure.java.shell :as sh])
(use '(clojure zip xml))
(import 'java.util.Date
        'java.text.SimpleDateFormat
        '(java.util.concurrent Executors
                               LinkedBlockingQueue))
```

is equivalent to this ns declaration:

```
(ns examples.ns
  (:refer-clojure :exclude [next replace remove])
  (:require (clojure [string :as string]
                     [set :as set])
            [clojure.java.shell :as sh])
  (:use (clojure zip xml))
  (:import java.util.Date
           java.text.SimpleDateFormat
           (java.util.concurrent Executors
                                 LinkedBlockingQueue)))
```

All the semantics for require, refer, and so on remain the same, but since ns is a macro, (notice that keywords are being used here, e.g., :use instead of use), the extensive quoting of names is unnecessary.

 In the previous examples, we are excluding vars from clojure.core because their names (next, replace, and remove) conflict with same-named vars defined in clojure.zip, which we use without exclusions a few lines down. Our use of clojure.zip *would* override the mappings to the vars referred from clojure.core (with a warning), but explicitly excluding them here makes it clear to later maintainers that we're aware of the conflict.

Once defined, namespaces may be inspected and modified at runtime, usually via a REPL. We talk about the different tools available for working with namespaces at runtime in "The Bare REPL" on page 399.

Namespaces and files

There are some hard-and-fast rules about how Clojure source files must be organized:[6]

---

6. Like all rules, most of these can be broken if you have a good reason to do so, but such reasons are rare.

Use one file per namespace.   Each namespace should be defined in a separate file, and this file's location within your project's Clojure source root must correspond with the namespace's segments. For example, the code for the `com.mycompany.foo` namespace should be in a file located at *com/mycompany/foo.clj*.[7] When that namespace is required or used, e.g., by (`require 'com.mycompany.foo`), the file at *com/mycompany/foo.clj* will be loaded, after which the namespace must be defined or an error will result.

Use underscores in filenames when namespaces contain dashes.   Very simply, if your namespace is to be `com.my-project.foo`, the source code for that namespace should be in a file located at *com/my_project/foo.clj*. Only the filename and directories corresponding to the namespace's segments are affected—you would continue to refer to the namespace in Clojure code using its declared name (e.g., (`require 'com.my-project.foo`), not (`require 'com.my_project.foo`)). This is necessary because the JVM does not allow for dashes in class or package names, but it is generally idiomatic to use dashes instead of underscores when naming Clojure entities, including namespaces, vars, locals, and so on.

Start every namespace with a comprehensive ns form.   The first Clojure form in every namespace's "root" (and usually only) file should be a well-tended `ns` form; bare usages of namespace-manipulating functions like `require` and `refer` are entirely unnecessary outside of a REPL environment. Aside from just being good form, using `ns`:

1. Encourages the consolidation of what might otherwise be disparate usages of `require`, et al.

2. Makes it easy for readers and later maintainers of your code to get an immediate impression of how a given namespace relates to its dependencies since it is always positioned at the top of each file.

3. Leaves the door open for refactoring and other code-manipulation tools that need to modify sets of required namespaces, functions, and imported classes, since `ns` is a macro that can accept only unevaluated names for these things.[8] The unrestricted evaluation possible in conjunction with lower-level namespace-modification forms makes such tools infeasible.

Avoid cyclic namespace dependencies.   The dependencies among Clojure namespaces within any application must form a directed acyclic graph; meaning, namespace X cannot require a namespace Y which itself requires namespace X (either directly or via one of its dependencies). Attempting to do this will result in an error like this:

```
#<Exception java.lang.Exception:
  Cyclic load dependency:
  [ /some/namespace/X ]->/some/namespace/Y->[ /some/namespace/X ]>
```

---

7. These paths are relative to whatever source root you're using. We get into the physical layout of Clojure projects on disk in "Location, Location, Location" on page 332.

8. For example, *slamhound*, which adjusts which namespaces are required and used and which classes are imported in an ns form based on the code in a given file: *https://github.com/technomancy/slamhound*.

Use declare to enable forward references.   Clojure loads each form in each namespace's files sequentially, resolving references to previously defined vars as it goes. This means that referring to an undefined var will cause an error:

```
(defn a [x] (+ constant (b x)))
;= #<CompilerException java.lang.RuntimeException:
;=   Unable to resolve symbol: constant in this context, compiling:(NO_SOURCE_PATH:1)>
```

Many languages define compilation units that allow them to find all of the "dangling" identifiers within a program before resolving references to them; Clojure does not do this. However, all is not lost if, for the sake of clarity or style, you want to define higher-level functions before the lower-level ones they reference: use declare to intern a var in the current namespace, define your higher-level function (referring freely to the declared vars), and then define the vars that you had previously only declared:

```
(declare constant b)
;= #'user/b
(defn a [x] (+ constant (b x)))
;= #'user/a
(def constant 42)
;= #'user/constant
(defn b [y] (max y constant))
;= #'user/b
(a 100)
;= 142
```

The one wrinkle to be aware of is that, if you neglect to actually define a previously declared var, that var will yield an unusable placeholder value when dereferenced at runtime that will almost surely result in an exception when your higher-level code attempts to do something with it.

Avoid single-segment namespaces.   Namespaces should have multiple segments; for example, the com.my-project.foo namespace has three segments. The reason for this is twofold:

1. If you AOT-compile a single-segment namespace, that process will yield at least one class file that is in the default package (i.e., is a "bare" class not in a Java package). This can prevent the namespace from being loaded in some environments, and will always prevent the namespace's corresponding class from being usable from Java, due to that language's restrictions on use of classes in the default package.

2. Even if you're absolutely, positively sure you're never going to want to redistribute AOT-compiled class files for your single-segment namespace, you still run a higher risk of namespace clashes than is prudent, no matter how clever you are at naming things.

Don't think that we're recommending that you reach for the heights of absurdity when it comes to namespace segment depth; no one likes names like com.foo.bar.baz.factory.factory.factories.Factory. However, there is some happy middle ground between that and a single segment, readily clashing namespace like app or util.

Regardless of how you organize your namespaces, they (and all other code and resources your library or application depends upon) will end up being loaded via the *classpath*.

A classpath primer

For programmers unfamiliar with Java, the *classpath* can often be a source of confusion. The classpath is the search path that the JVM will use when looking for user-defined libraries and resources. This path can include both directories and *.zip* archives, including *.jar* files. Clojure being hosted on the JVM, it inherits Java's classpath system.

The classpath has its own idiosyncrasies, but it is not unique, and has many similarities to other search path mechanisms you are surely familiar with. For example, shells in both Unix and Windows environments define a PATH environment variable, which stores a concatenated set of paths where executables may be found. Ruby and Python also have search paths: Ruby stores its in the runtime variable $LOAD_PATH,[9] while Python relies upon the PYTHONPATH environment variable. In all of these cases, the search path tends to be automatically handled by a combination of system-wide settings and dependency management tools (such as Ruby Gems or Python's easy_install and pip).

The same autoconfiguration of the classpath is available through Leiningen and Maven, the tools most often used for managing dependencies in Clojure projects, as well as most popular Java IDEs and Emacs. For example, once you have defined your dependencies in your *project.clj* or *pom.xml* file, starting a REPL through either of these tools will result in those dependencies being added to the REPL's classpath automatically. The same applies if you are using Leiningen or Maven plug-ins that bootstrap full applications, such as when running web applications locally via lein-ring or jetty:run.[10]

However, if you need to start a Java process directly within a shell, you need to construct the classpath manually. Even if you never use Clojure from the command line, knowing how the classpath is defined in the most fundamental way will help you understand what more advanced tools are doing for you.

Defining the classpath. By default, the classpath is empty. This is an inconvenient difference compared to the other search path mechanisms we mentioned, which all include the current working directory (.) by default, so that libraries rooted there will be found at runtime.

To set the classpath for a Java process, specify it on the command line with the -cp flag. For example, to include the current working directory, the *src* directory, the *clojure.jar* archive file, and all *.jar* files in the *lib* directory, on Unix-like systems we'd do this:

```
java -cp '.:src:clojure.jar:lib/*' clojure.main
```

---

9. Also known as $:.

10. See "Running Web Apps Locally" on page 565 for details.

As with all other search path mechanisms, the classpath is defined in a platform-dependent manner due to differences in filename conventions on different systems. On Unix-like systems, the classpath is a :-delimited list of /-defined paths; on Windows, it's a ;-delimited list of \-defined paths. So, our example classpath above for Unix-like systems would translate to this one on Windows:

```
'.;src;clojure.jar;lib\*'
```

Classpath and the REPL.   The classpath can be inspected from Clojure at runtime:

```
$ java -cp clojure.jar clojure.main
Clojure 1.3.0
(System/getProperty "java.class.path")
;= "clojure.jar"
```

The primary classpath (held by the `java.class.path` system property) is defined when the JVM process starts via command-line parameter or environment variable, but it unfortunately cannot be changed at runtime. This is at odds with Clojure's normal development cycle, which tends to involve opening a persistent REPL session and leaving it open. Changes to the classpath require a JVM restart, and therefore a REPL restart.[11]

Location, Location, Location

There are two predominant project layout conventions used in Clojure projects, the defaults for which are defined by the predominant build tools used by Clojure projects.[12]

First, there's the "Maven style," which puts all source files under a top-level *src* directory but separates source files into separate subdirectories based on language and role within a project. Primary source code that defines public APIs or shipped features goes in *src/main*; code that defines unit and functional tests that isn't generally distributed goes in *src/test*, and so on:

---

11. There *are* ways to get around this. Clojure itself provides an `add-classpath` function, though it is deprecated and generally not recommended. Another is pomegranate (*https://github.com/cemerick/pomegranate*), which provides a maintained replacement for `add-classpath` that provides a way to add *.jar* files and transitive Leiningen/Maven dependencies to a Clojure runtime. Finally, all sorts of JVM module systems, including OSGi, the NetBeans module system, and JVM application servers of all stripes provide easy ways to augment or redefine the classpath within applications or individual modules. All of these mechanisms use facilities built in to the JVM (such as managed `ClassLoader` hierarchies) in order to enable such capabilities.

12. All (decent) build tools (including Leiningen and Maven) allow you to put source files wherever you want. These layouts are just the defaults, although it's hard to imagine a case where it'd be worth the trouble to not use those defaults.

Example 8-1. The "Maven-style" project layout

```
<project dir>
 |
 |- src
    |- main
       |- clojure
       |- java
       |- resources
       |- ...
    |- test
       |- clojure
       |- java
       |- resources
       |- ...
```

When using this sort of project layout, Clojure source files are rooted at *src/main/clojure*, Java source files[13] are rooted at *src/main/java*, and so on. The fact that the roles and types of files are reflected in the directory structure can make some activities simpler. For example, rather than having to use filename filters to select a set of files of a particular type from a source root, you can "blindly" refer to sets of files by referring to the directory where each type of file is rooted. This can greatly simplify the packaging of resources: if you have a set of resources that need to be included in a web application (images, JavaScript files, and so on), they can be grouped under *src/main/webapp*, and you can safely put resources that shouldn't be redistributed in a different source root that you can be sure is never referenced by your build and packaging process.

The Maven-style layout is the most standardized option available—its encouragement of source file location conventions means that projects that use it rarely deviate. The primary disadvantage of the Maven-style project layout is that file paths are longer due to the prefixing of *src/main*, *src/test*, and so on.

The other predominant project layout style is one that is difficult to characterize, because it can vary substantially from project to project:

Example 8-2. The "freeform" project layout examples

```
<project dir>
 |
 |- src
 |- test

<project dir>
 |
 |- src
    |- java
    |- clojure
 |- test
```

---

13. Assuming you have them; take a look at "Building mixed-source projects" on page 351 for some tips if your project is a Java/Clojure hybrid.

```
|- resources
|- web
```

Compared to the Maven-style layout, freeform project layouts optimize for shorter file path length (in part to make it easier to refer to files on the command line), and generally have fewer conventions that are reused from project to project outside of the existence of *src* and *test*. Source files of different types are often mixed within the same source root (e.g., both Java and Clojure source files might be rooted at *src*), though sometimes not depending upon a specific project's build configuration. You'll find that projects use this layout in conjunction with build tools other than Maven, including Leiningen.

The Functional Organization of Clojure Codebases

So far, we've only talked about mechanical ground rules—where files go, naming rules, the correspondence between namespaces and files, and so on. More subtle are the questions about how to organize Clojure code from a functional perspective:

- How many functions should be used to implement a particular algorithm?
- How many functions should a namespace contain?
- How many namespaces should a project contain?

Corollary questions related to other programming languages are usually easier to answer, in part because there are often particular requirements that end up explicitly defining "good style." Many frequently used frameworks in various languages have specific expectations about how plug-ins/components/models/extensions are defined (e.g., "one class per database table" or "one module per user interface component"), so that the shape of a codebase is determined in large part by incidental or mechanical characteristics of the libraries it uses and the broader environment it will be deployed into.

In contrast, you are rarely forced to hew to a particular organization of a Clojure application as a side effect of using a particular library or framework.[14] In particular, broad application of functional programming techniques and occasional, judicious use of macros allows you to structure Clojure libraries and applications to mirror the contours of your domain far more than is possible in other languages. It's fair to say that Clojure encourages you to think more clearly about your domain than you likely have for years, with the end result that your data or model will often naturally dictate your program's structure more than you thought possible.

That is all to say, outside of some very general principles, there's probably no such thing as a "typical structure" of Clojure programs. This notion may either be disconcerting or very appealing, depending on your background and expectations. For our part, we've

---

14. Even if you are extending or integrating an existing Java library or framework using Clojure, it is rare to not be able to sequester the relevant interop that hooks the Clojure functions and data into the framework, leaving you free to structure your Clojure codebase as best suits the domain or your chosen architecture.

---

found it consistently refreshing to be able to focus on the essentials of a feature or algorithm or domain, without the distractions that can come with particular sorts of order imposed by decisions made long ago and far away from the problems we aim to solve in our code.

Basic project organization principles

It would be poor form for us to vaguely talk about general principles and not mention at least a few that we have in mind:

- Keep different things separate, maybe in different namespaces: code that works with customer records should probably all be in one namespace, away from the namespace that loads templates for your web content.
- Keep related things together, maybe grouped into natural categories that are manifested as namespaces. For example, use the hierarchy implied by namespaces' names to indicate relationships, such as that between a high level API (say, `foo.ui`) and a lower-level or provider APIs (e.g., `foo.ui.linux` and `foo.ui.windows`).
- Define vars that contain implementation-specific data or functions `^:private` (or, private using the `defn-` convenience form for defining private functions) as much as possible. This keeps clients from unwittingly depending upon things likely to change, while still providing them a back door to access "behind the curtain" functions and data if absolutely necessary via the `var` special form (or its reader sugar `#'`).
- Don't repeat yourself: define constants only once in a designated namespace, and break common functionality out into utility functions and utility namespaces as warranted.
- Use the common *abstractions* of reference types, collections, and sequences when you can, rather than marrying any particular concrete implementation of any of them.
- Unpure functions should be considered harmful, and implemented only when absolutely necessary.[15]

In the large, your Clojure projects will benefit from the same attention to modularity and separation of concerns that yields benefits in projects written in any other language. Beyond that, remember that namespaces are an organizational tool provided solely for your benefit: a large application written using 500 namespaces will function and perform just as well as the same application piled into one huge namespace. Therefore, you should feel free to structure your applications to match the structure of your domain and suit your team's way of working.

---

15. Pure functions are critical to the successful and effective application of functional programming, a cornerstone of designing idiomatic Clojure libraries and applications. Read about functional programming in Chapter 2, and pure functions specifically in "Pure Functions" on page 76.

Build

"Build" is an umbrella term that has come to encompass more and more of the things we do *after* we've written the code but before the code has been delivered (another loaded term, given the complications of software as a service, cloud computing, and so on).

For our purposes here, we'll consider *build* to mean:

- Compilation
- *Dependency management*, which allows you to systematically use external libraries
- Packaging the results of compilation and other project assets into *artifacts*
- Distribution of those artifacts within a dependency management context

That overly formal description sounds more complicated than the activities it describes. You're likely doing these things already:

Table 8-1. Contrasting "build" solutions for different programming languages

	Compilation	Dependency management	Packaging	Distribution
Ruby	`rake`	`gem`, `rvm`	Gems	*rubygems.org*
Python	`distutils`, SCons	`pip`, `virtualenv`	Eggs	PyPI[a]
Java	`javac`, Ant, Maven, Gradle, etc.	The Maven model, Ivy	Jar files and variants thereof	Maven artifact repositories

[a] *http://pypi.python.org/pypi*

Because Clojure is a JVM language, it naturally reuses large swaths of that ecosystem's build, packaging, and distribution infrastructure and mechanics:

- Leiningen reuses much of the Maven infrastructure while providing a far more pleasant "UI" and Clojure-native development experience.
- There are plug-ins for Maven, Gradle, and Ant that aid in driving Clojure builds from those tools.
- Clojure libraries are packaged as *.jar* files, Clojure web applications are (usually) packaged as *.war* files,[16] and so on.
- Clojure libraries are distributed via Maven repositories, which are accessible to every Java (and therefore Clojure) build tool.

This alignment between Clojure and Java's build tooling and practices allows Clojure applications and libraries to depend upon and use Java libraries, and allows you to distribute libraries written in Clojure that programmers using other JVM languages (such as Java, Groovy, Scala, JRuby, Jython, and so on) can depend upon and use.

---

16. Heroku is an outlier in this respect, see "Clojure on Heroku" on page 587.

If you are already using Java or some other JVM language, you'll find that adding some Clojure to your codebase will have a minimal impact your existing build process. On the other hand, if you're coming from Ruby, Python, or some other non-JVM language, you can take comfort in the fact that Clojure build processes and configurations are nearly always far simpler than their Java-tailored corollaries.

Ahead-of-Time Compilation

As we mentioned in "The Clojure REPL" on page 3, Clojure code is *always* compiled—there is no Clojure interpreter. Compilation, which involves generating bytecode for a given chunk of Clojure code and loading that bytecode into the host JVM, can happen in two different ways:

- At runtime; this is what happens when you use the REPL, or when you load a Clojure source file from disk. The contents of source files are compiled into bytecode, and loaded into the JVM. This bytecode and the classes it defines are not retained after the host JVM has been terminated.
- "Ahead-of-time" (AOT) compilation is the same as this runtime compilation, but the resulting bytecode is saved to disk as JVM class files.[17] Those class files can then be reused in later JVM instances in lieu of the originating Clojure source files.

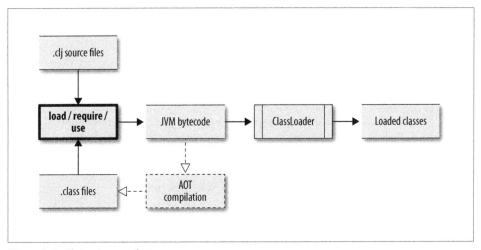

Figure 8-1. Clojure's compilation process

---

17. This is exactly analogous to `javac`, which saves generated class files to disk based on the contents of Java source files.

Clojure code can be loaded from source files or from AOT-compiled class files interchangeably, without any functional differences. Requiring a namespace—for example, (require 'clojure.set)—will search the classpath for the *clojure/set.clj* source file that defines that namespace, or from the corresponding AOT-compiled class files.[18]

Thus, outside of a few select circumstances, AOT compilation is entirely optional. Since Clojure libraries and applications generally have no technical reason to demand AOT compilation, it's reasonable to prefer to distribute Clojure sources when you can. In fact, AOT compilation can have some significant downsides:

1. JVM class files are by definition much larger on disk compared to the Clojure source files from which they are generated.

2. AOT compilation adds a discrete compile step back into the otherwise lightweight Clojure development cycle.

3. AOT compiling a project locks the Clojure library or application in question into the version of Clojure that was used to AOT-compile its sources. You cannot assume that code AOT-compiled with one version of Clojure can be deployed at runtime with another version of Clojure.

4. AOT compilation is *transitive*. If you AOT compile namespace foo that requires namespace bar, then bar will be AOT compiled as well, and so on. Depending upon the specific namespace dependencies within your library or application, this can result in a much larger scope of AOT compilation than you may expect given your build configuration.

 When all you need is to generate a single named class (or a handful) as an entry point for a Java framework, there is an easy way to break the transitivity: use gen-class (or the :gen-class option of ns) with a distinct implementation namespace specified by :impl-ns. Compilation doesn't follow such dependencies, so requiring the compilation of the gen-class namespace won't trigger a compilation of your entire codebase.

AOT compilation should be reserved for a few select use cases:

1. When you cannot or do not want to distribute source code.

2. When you want to use various class file engineering tools as part of your packaging process, such as obfuscators.

3. When startup time of your application is *absolutely critical*, such that you're willing to bear the costs of AOT-compilation. Loading AOT-compiled class files is far faster than getting to the same point from Clojure source files.

---

18. If both a source file and class files are available for a particular namespace, Clojure will give preference to the class files *unless* the source file has a newer modification date. This allows you to have both source roots and AOT compile target directories on the classpath in a REPL session and still be able to reload namespaces from updated source files as desired.

4. When you expect your Clojure code to be used from Java or another JVM language via named Java classes or interfaces generated by `gen-class`, `defrecord`, `deftype`, or `defprotocol`.[19]

We talk about some of the options for performing AOT compilation in Leiningen and Maven in "AOT compilation configuration" on page 349.

Dependency Management

Every software development team should use dependency management for their projects. Teams using Clojure are no different.

Not so long ago, there was a dark time when it was the norm to ship dependencies around the Internet in *.zip* and *.tar.gz* files, manually and carefully putting them in specific places in projects (often a *lib* directory), and adding the results to version control systems. Build processes would then refer to these dependencies using simple file paths, and they would either bundle the dependencies into distributed binaries or other artifacts or blithely assume that downstream users of the project would have the same versions of those dependencies already, or would know where to obtain them.

Modern demands have thankfully pushed out such practices in large part, given their reliance on manual tweaking and complete lack of repeatable process.

While Perl has CPAN (perhaps the granddaddy of all dependency management approaches), Python has `pip` and `virtualenv`, and Ruby has `gem` and `rvm`, dependency management on the JVM is dominated by Maven and the model it defined in the mid-2000s. Clojure fully embraces that model, regardless of which build tool you might use.

The Maven Dependency Management Model

Maven's dependency management model provides for:

- The identification and versioning of *artifacts* using *coordinates*
- The declaration of *dependencies* of artifacts and the projects that produce them
- The storage and retrieval of artifacts in *repositories* along with specifications of their dependencies
- The calculation of artifacts' *transitive dependencies*

Let's unpack these concepts and the broad strokes of the mechanics involved.

---

19. It is generally worth ensuring that you are AOT-compiling only those namespaces that include usages of these forms, if only to minimize the size of your packaged artifacts.

Artifacts and coordinates

An *artifact* is any file that is a product of a project's build process. Clojure libraries and applications are packaged just like those written using Java and other JVM languages. Concretely, this means you'll primarily be using and producing two types of artifacts:

- *.jar* files, which are *.zip* files that contain:[20]
  - — Clojure source files, JVM class files, and other assets (such as static configuration files, images, etc.) in a hierarchy mirroring their position in their source directory roots or compilation target directory
  - — Optional metadata in a `META-INF` directory entry
- *.war* files, which are also *.zip* files, are the JVM standard for packaging web applications. See "Web Application Packaging" on page 560 for more info about *.war* files and how they are used.

Rare Packaging Types

Regular, unadorned *.zip* or *.tar.gz* files are also found occasionally in Maven repositories, but these are more often used to transport noncode assets. For example, you might want to include a JVM installer with a client-side application installer that is constructed in an automated fashion at build time; zipping up the JVM installer and deploying it into your organization's Maven repository would ensure that your project could declare a dependency on it and script the inclusion of that installer.

In addition, application frameworks like the Eclipse and NetBeans rich client platforms have their own packaging types and requirements, although they are largely just variations on the *.jar* file theme and are rarely (if ever) used outside of the specific framework for which they are intended.

Artifacts of all types are identified using *coordinates*, a basket of attributes that together uniquely identify a particular version of an artifact:

- `groupId`, often an organizational or project identifier like `org.apache.lucene` or `com.google.collections`.
- `artifactId`, an identifier of the artifact within the organization or project, such as `lucene-core` or `lucene-queryparser`. Projects often produce multiple related artifacts under the same `groupId`, though it's common for smaller Clojure open source libraries to have the same `groupId` and `artifactId` when there is no distinction between the organization and project.
- `packaging`, an identifier of the type of artifact that is being referred to that corresponds to the file extension of the artifact itself. This defaults to `jar`, and is generally not specified in the default case.

---

20. You can read more about *.jar* files at *http://java.sun.com/developer/Books/javaprogramming/JAR/basics*.

- `version`, a version string that ideally follows the conventions of semantic versioning.[21]

In textual settings, Maven coordinates are often specified in a format like `groupId:arti factId:packaging:version`, so v1.3.0 of Clojure's jar is referred to as `org.clojure:clo jure:1.3.0` (remembering that the `jar` packaging is the default). Each project defines its own coordinates—sometimes in a Maven *pom.xml* file, sometimes in a *project.clj* file if you are using Leiningen. In any case, each time a project has been built and the author wishes to distribute the resulting artifacts, a corresponding *pom.xml* file is uploaded along with the artifacts to a Maven *repository*.

Repositories

When a set of artifacts is uploaded to a Maven *repository*, that repository generally indexes the versioning and dependency information in the *pom.xml* provided to it along with the artifacts; this is called *deployment*. From that point, the repository will be able to distribute the artifacts to any clients that wish to obtain them (almost always other developers whose projects depend upon the artifacts).

There are hundreds (maybe thousands) of public repositories in operation worldwide, but there are just few large ones that hold the majority of Maven artifacts:

- *Maven central*, the largest repository and default location where Maven-based build tools search for dependencies. All the official Clojure distributions and core libraries are released to Maven central.
- *Clojars.org*, an open Clojure community repository for which Leiningen provides simplified integration. Many very popular open source Clojure libraries are deployed to Clojars, including Ring, Clutch, and Enlive.
- Large open source organizations like Apache, JBoss, and RedHat maintain their own Maven repositories as well.

You will likely also work with two other types of Maven repositories at some point:

- Private/internal repositories are often maintained by companies and other organizations to house artifacts produced by their own projects, and sometimes to proxy public repositories such as Maven central or Clojars.
- The *local repository*, which is created by Maven and other Maven-based build tools at *~/.m2/repository*. This is where dependencies of your projects will be downloaded and cached for future use. You can also choose to *install* artifacts from projects you build into this local repository (which is conceptually the same process as deployment, but so named in order to distinguish the install action being targeted at the local repository).

---

21. Semantic versioning is a well-understood convention for specifying the magnitude of change between software versions. Read more about it at *http://semver.org*.

Dependencies

Just as every project defines its coordinates, every project defines its *dependencies*. Dependencies are expressed as references to other projects' artifacts, using those artifacts' coordinates. Using these specifications of dependencies, Maven and other Maven-based build tools can:

- Determine a project's set of *transitive dependencies*—that is, a project's dependencies' dependencies' dependencies, and so on. Put more formally, a project's dependencies form a directed acyclic graph, rooted at the project being built, run, examined, etc. It is a fatal error for a project's dependencies to form a referential cycle.

- Given a full set of a project's transitive dependencies, new REPLs and compilation and application processes can be started with the dependencies' artifacts added to the JVM's classpath; this allows code running in those processes to refer to classes, resources, and Clojure source files contained in those dependencies.

Resolving a project's dependencies is a straightforward graph traversal that you generally don't have to be aware of.[22] The only real caveat is the flexibility that exists in specifying dependency versions, which primarily comes in the form of *snapshots* and *version ranges*.

Clojure Is "Just" Another Dependency

Those with a background in Python, Ruby, and other languages that have their own dedicated runtime often have an expectation that you "install" Clojure, just as you might install some particular version of Ruby. This is not so.

Technically, Clojure is just another Java/JVM library, and therefore is just another dependency within your project; it is the JVM that you must install. Clojure then must be added to your application's classpath, usually with the help of Leiningen or Maven during development and testing.

The fact that Clojure is a JVM library can have some very tangible benefits in terms of deployment[23] and team and customer acceptance.[24]

Snapshot and release versions.   Within the Maven dependency model, versions are classified as either *snapshots* or *releases*. Most version strings—including examples like

---

22. Tools like Leiningen and Maven handle the sticky details for you. If you want to learn more about dependency resolution within the Maven model, *http://docs.codehaus.org/display/MAVEN/Dependency +Mediation+and+Conflict+Resolution* is a good reference.

23. When it comes time to deploy your application, there are various packaging options, including *.war* files for web apps, discussed in "Web Application Packaging" on page 560, *uberjars* for generalized application deployment, which are directly supported by Leiningen as mentioned in "Leiningen" on page 347, and other methods, all aiming to produce a single aggregated file containing all of your project's code and transitive dependencies, including Clojure.

24. See "Clojure is just another .jar file" on page 579.

`1.0.0`, `3.6`, `0.2.1-beta5`, and so on—are considered release versions, implying that such versions are fixed in time and will never change. This is enforced by all sane repositories, which will prevent a previously deployed artifact with a release version string from being updated. This supports the objective of repeatable builds: because released artifacts cannot change after they are deployed to a repository, once you've built and tested against a particular version of a dependency, you can forever rely upon those results.

Snapshot versions are entirely different. Denoted by version strings that end with a `-SNAPSHOT` suffix—such as `1.0.0-SNAPSHOT`, `3.6-SNAPSHOT`, or `0.2.1-beta5-SNAPSHOT`—snapshots are intended to identify artifacts produced from the bleeding edge of development. Thus, the same version number can refer to different concrete artifacts over time, as development releases are created and distributed to repositories.

For example, say you want to track ongoing development leading up to version `2.0.0` of a particular library because `2.0.0` will provide some key features your project needs. That library will likely distribute many builds with a version of `2.0.0-SNAPSHOT`, and as long as you specify that version string in your project's dependencies, you will always be working with and testing against the latest prerelease version.[25] You can then switch to using the `2.0.0` release version of the library once its authors finish their work and deploy the final release artifact to the project's repository.

Version ranges.   Say you have a dependency on version `1.6.0` of a library, but you might know that you could safely depend upon a library not breaking API compatibility until its next major release. Insofar as nearly all artifacts use semantic versioning, as in this case, it is often useful to define dependency versions in terms of *ranges of versions*. Maven supports a number of version range formats:

Table 8-2. Maven version range formats[a]

Range format	Semantics
`(,1.0]`	`x <= 1.0`
`1.0`	"Soft" requirement on `1.0`
`[1.0]`	Hard requirement on `1.0`
`[1.2,1.3]`	`1.2 <= x <= 1.3`
`[1.0,2.0)`	`1.0 <= x < 2.0`
`[1.5,)`	`x >= 1.5`

[a] Taken from *http://docs.codehaus.org/display/MAVEN/Dependency+Mediation+and+Conflict+Resolution*.

So, we can specify our dependency on the library as `[1.6.0,2.0.0)`, which will allow our project's artifacts to be resolved in conjunction with any version of the library between `1.6.0` (inclusive) and `2.0.0` (exclusive). Once `2.0.0` is released (perhaps breaking compatibility with the prior `1.x.x` releases given a bump in the major version

---

25. It is typical for Maven and tooling that depends upon it to check for new snapshots every 24 hours. If you're using Maven, passing a `-U` option will force that check to occur.

number), we'll need to test (and maybe tweak) our project to work with 2.0.0 and distribute a new release—perhaps specifying a version range dependency on the library of [2.0.0, 3.0.0).

Note that in the table above, a "bare" version number (e.g., 1.0) is noted as a "soft" version requirement. This means that if two different bare versions of a particular artifact are depended upon—for example, you depend on version 1.2 of a library, and one of your dependencies depends on version 1.6 of the same library—the later version will be selected and used in all builds, REPLs, and so on. This almost never causes any problems, but when it does, specifying a version range will eliminate the ambiguity. In this example, if you change your direct dependency on the library to [1.2,1.5], then version 1.5 will be selected.

This scenario and your usage of version ranges in general depends upon your assessment of the projects that produce the libraries you depend upon. If they use semantic versioning (of some sort) reliably, then version ranges can be a great way to ensure that the artifacts you produce will be used only with versions of their dependencies with which they are likely to be compatible. On the other hand, if your dependencies are versioned using some other scheme,[26] then version ranges may be less useful to you.

Build Tools and Configuration Patterns

Now that we've covered some key background on project organization and build concepts, let's look at some examples of working with the two most popular build tools in the Clojure community, Leiningen and Maven. This should only be considered a brisk overview though, so consider:

Each of these tools is deep in its own way, and this is not the place for a comprehensive treatise on the tools' capabilities and failings. Whichever build tool you choose, be sure to refer to its documentation and community resources to make the most of what it has to offer. Finally, we do provide some additional build examples specifically for web applications in Chapter 17.

Stick with what works.   As we said at the beginning of this chapter, it's impossible for us to provide any absolute truths–perhaps particularly when it comes to build tools. That said, there are some heuristics to help you in deciding which tool to use for your

---

26. An example of an unfortunate approach is to use date-of-release as the version number, such as 20110705. Even worse is the release of artifacts using things like Git or Mercurial commit SHAs like 8c7be13792, which are not only not amenable to version range specifications, they are not even monotonically increasing—thus, it's impossible to tell from such an artifact's coordinates which version is newer than another.

Clojure projects, which we discuss at length below in sections on Leiningen and Maven. There's one heuristic that should probably override others, however:

If your organization has standardized on a major JVM-based build toolchain, keep using it. There are Clojure plug-ins for Ant,[27] Maven, Gradle,[28] Buildr, and probably other systems we're not familiar with, so introducing Clojure into projects already using these tools is a straightforward matter and does not require disturbing a build and project management process that is already in place and working well.

Maven

Maven is probably the most commonly used build tool in the Java world. An open source Apache project,[29] its scope is far broader than most build tools: through an extensive third-party plug-in community, it aims to provide ways to manage the "full life cycle" of software projects, including things like integration and functional testing, code coverage, test reporting, and release management, in addition to the typical build processes of code compilation and packaging.

One of Maven's distinguishing characteristics is that you will find that other JVM-based tooling offers excellent integration with Maven, such as IDEs like Eclipse, NetBeans, and IntelliJ; team facilities like Hudson/Jenkins, Clover, and Cobertura; and auxiliary build tooling like NSIS, IzPack, javacc, ANTLR, and Selenium. If you'd like to have maximal integration between tools like this and your build tool, or those "full life cycle" activities are important to you or your organization, you should give Maven serious consideration for your Clojure projects.

Here is a basic *pom.xml* that will get you started with a simple Clojure project in Maven:[30]

Example 8-3. Basic pom.xml suitable for simple Clojure projects

```
<project xmlns="http://maven.apache.org/POM/4.0.0"
    xmlns:xsi="http://www.w3.org/2001/XMLSchema-instance"
    xsi:schemaLocation="http://maven.apache.org/POM/4.0.0
                    http://maven.apache.org/maven-v4_0_0.xsd">

    <modelVersion>4.0.0</modelVersion>
    <groupId>com.clojurebook</groupId>
    <artifactId>sample-maven-project</artifactId>
    <version>1.0.0</version>
    <packaging>clojure</packaging>
```

27. *https://github.com/jmcconnell/clojure-ant-tasks.*

28. *https://bitbucket.org/kotarak/clojuresque/wiki/Home.*

29. We recommend starting with the latest version of Maven 3, available from *http://maven.apache.org.*

30. There is an abundance of documentation available online related to Maven, including two free books that were written by its authors and are available at *http://www.sonatype.com/books.html*: *Maven by Example* is a tutorial-oriented introductory guide to Maven, while *Maven: the Complete Reference* is worth keeping handy for understanding the minutiae of the tool.

```
<dependencies>
    <dependency>
        <groupId>org.clojure</groupId>
        <artifactId>clojure</artifactId>
        <version>1.3.0</version>
    </dependency>
</dependencies>

<build>
    <resources>
        <resource>
            <directory>src/main/clojure</directory>
        </resource>
    </resources>
    <plugins>
        <plugin>
            <groupId>com.theoryinpractise</groupId>
            <artifactId>clojure-maven-plugin</artifactId>
            <version>1.3.8</version>
            <extensions>true</extensions>
            <configuration>
                <warnOnReflection>true</warnOnReflection>
                <temporaryOutputDirectory>true</temporaryOutputDirectory>
            </configuration>
        </plugin>
    </plugins>
</build>
</project>
```

This *pom.xml*:

- Defines Maven coordinates of `com.clojurebook:sample-maven-project:1.0.0`.
- Defines packaging of `clojure`, which prompts `clojure-maven-plugin` to add its AOT compilation and unit test goals to the corresponding Maven life cycle phases.
- Sets a single dependency of Clojure v1.3.0 (`org.clojure:clojure:1.3.0`).
- Adds the standard Clojure source directory as a Maven resource directory; this causes Clojure source files in that directory to be added to the *.jar* file produced by this project's build.
- Configures `clojure-maven-plugin` to run the AOT compiler in the "sanity check" mode described in "AOT compilation configuration" on page 349, warning when reflective interop calls are encountered and depositing the generated class files into a temporary directory (so they are not included in packaged artifacts).

Some typical workflows with a project using this *pom.xml* would be:

- `mvn clojure:repl` will start a new Clojure REPL with the classpath set to include all of the transitive dependencies of the project.
- `mvn package` will AOT-compile the Clojure source files as a sanity check and build the *.jar* file containing those files.

- `mvn test` will run all of the Java and Clojure tests present in your project (rooted at *test/src/java* and *test/src/clojure*, respectively)

- `mvn install`—in addition to what `mvn package` does—will *install* the *.jar* file in your local Maven repository.

- `mvn deploy`—in addition to what `mvn install` does—will *deploy* the *.jar* file to a remote repository that you would need to add into *pom.xml*.

All of the Clojure-specific functionality in Maven is provided by the `clojure-maven-plugin`,[31] which provides a plethora of options for controlling how and when it invokes Clojure's AOT compilation, runs specific Clojure scripts in your project, runs Clojure unit and functional tests, and so on. In addition, it provides a number of goals beyond `clojure:repl` that are useful in the course of development.

Aside from `clojure-maven-plugin`, there are hundreds of Maven plug-ins available to assist in automating various build, testing, and project management activities, as well as for enabling enhanced integration of Maven projects with external tools and environments. In general, simply search the Web for `foo maven plugin`, and you are likely to find a useful plug-in for the `foo` you are interested in.

Leiningen

Leiningen[32] is billed as "A build tool for Clojure designed to not set your hair on fire."[33] This mission was borne largely out of frustration with some of the complexity that Maven and Ant imply for the most common build requirements of Clojure projects. It aims to offer a simpler overall workflow for common tasks than Ant or Maven.

If you are coming from outside the JVM world—from Ruby, Python, or similar languages—you will likely find Leiningen more appealing than Maven. While it reuses parts of Maven under the covers, Leiningen provides a more Clojure-idiomatic treatment of the Maven dependency model, and a more lightweight development process. In particular, changing or extending Leiningen's build process can be done entirely within Clojure,[34] a refreshingly pleasant experience compared to what's required to build Maven plug-ins. The tradeoff is that Leiningen does not offer access to the array of third-party plug-ins and integration options in the Maven ecosystem, although the set of Leiningen plug-ins that are available continues to grow.[35]

---

31. *http://github.com/talios/clojure-maven-plugin*.

32. Leiningen, often referred to colloquially as "lein," is ostensibly pronounced as *LINE-ing-en*, although it's not rare to hear the alternative *LINE-in-gen*, either.

33. We recommend starting with the latest version of Leiningen, at least v1.7.0 or later: *http://leiningen.org*. All of the Leiningen examples in this book have been tested with v1.7.0, as well as the recently released preview of v2.0.

34. An example of a small local modification to a Leiningen build process is shown at "Building mixed-source projects" on page 351.

35. A partial list of Leiningen plug-ins can be found at *https://github.com/technomancy/leiningen/wiki/plugins*.

Here is a basic *project.clj* that will get you started with a simple Clojure project in Leiningen:

Example 8-4. Basic project.clj suitable for simple Clojure projects

```
(defproject com.clojurebook/sample-lein-project "1.0.0"
  :dependencies [[org.clojure/clojure "1.3.0"]])
```

`defproject` is a macro that defines a model of your project suitable for Leiningen. Aside from the key-value pairs that constitute the bulk of the project configuration, `defpro ject` requires the first two arguments to it to be the project's coordinates (specified using a Clojure symbol and a string, here `com.clojurebook/sample-lein-project "1.0.0"`, which corresponds to `com.clojurebook:sample-lein-project:1.0.0` in Maven notation).

`defproject` provides a shortcut where you can set the group and artifact ID to the same value with an unnamespaced symbol. This is most often done for open source projects where the project *is* the organization; for example, Ring (the Clojure web framework) has `ring "1.0.1"` as its first two arguments to `defproject`, resulting in Maven coordinates of `ring:ring:1.0.1`.

> Leiningen provides a command to create the scaffolding of a new project; invoking `lein new my-project` will create a new *my-project* directory containing a *project.clj* file (with coordinates of `my-project "1.0.0-SNAPSHOT"`), and placeholder source files and test source files.

This basic *project.clj* provides roughly the same configuration options as the sample Maven *pom.xml* discussed in "Maven" on page 345, with the difference that the root Clojure source directory is *src* rather than *src/main/clojure*, and the root Clojure test source directory is *test* rather than *src/test/clojure*. The real difference between the two approaches for such a simple project is that the behavior of the Leiningen build is dependent upon which `lein` commands are issued and in which order, whereas the Maven build enforces consistent ordering and semantics for each build phase.

Those differences aside, the basic Leiningen workflows are very similar to Maven's:

- `lein repl` will start a new Clojure REPL with the classpath set to include all of the transitive dependencies of the project.
- `lein test` will run all of the Clojure tests present in the project (usually housed in the *test* directory).
- `lein jar` performs the same packaging as `mvn package`, but does not automatically perform AOT compilation of the Clojure sources.
- `lein uberjar` will produce an *uberjar*, a *.jar* file just like that generated by `lein jar`, but with all of your project's transitive dependencies "unpacked" into it.

Uberjars are a commonly used for simple deployments, where an entire application can be delivered as a single file, executable with a single java invocation.[36]

- `lein compile` will AOT compile all of the project's Clojure sources based on the `:aot` configuration in *project.clj*. We talk about configuring Leiningen for AOT compilation next, in "AOT compilation configuration" on page 349.

- `lein pom` will generate a Maven-compatible *pom.xml* file that contains the project and dependency information in your project's *project.clj* file. It is this *pom.xml* file that would be used in deploying to a remote Maven repository or installed into your local Maven repository.

- `lein deps` ensures that all dependencies your project specifies are available, downloading them if necessary. This is generally done for you automatically (i.e., whenever the `:dependencies` vector is changed).

 As you can see, the notation used for describing dependencies in Leiningen and Maven is syntactically very different. However, the same information is being conveyed; this Leiningen dependency:

```
[org.clojure/clojure "1.3.0"]
```

is exactly equivalent to this one in Maven:

```
<dependency>
  <groupId>org.clojure</groupId>
  <artifactId>clojure</artifactId>
  <version>1.3.0</version>
</dependency>
```

Because it is more concise, and because it is much more widespread in the Clojure community (e.g., project *README* files are more likely to provide Leiningen-style dependency vectors than snippets of <depend ency> XML for use in Maven), from this point forward in the book, whenever we refer to a Clojure library used in an example, *we will provide the corresponding dependency using Leiningen's notation.*

AOT compilation configuration

Outside of defining dependencies and packaging artifacts, one of the most common things you need to do in a Clojure build process is AOT compile your Clojure sources. The motivations and tradeoffs associated with AOT compilation should be considered before proceeding, though. Please digest "Ahead-of-Time Compilation" on page 337 before deciding an AOT compilation is necessary or desirable for your project; oftentimes, it is not.

---

36. For example, `java -cp <path-to-uberjar> com.foo.MainClassName` or `java -cp <path-to-uberjar> clojure.main -m com.foo.namespace-with-main-fn`. The latter is most common with Clojure projects, and requires no AOT compilation; see the documentation for `clojure.main/main` for details.

In any case, both Leiningen and Maven provide straightforward ways of enabling, disabling, and configuring AOT compilation.

Leiningen.   By default, Leiningen will not perform AOT compilation on your project's Clojure sources. Configuring it to do so requires adding an `:aot` slot to the project configuration, where that slot's value may be:

- `:all`, which prompts Leiningen to AOT compile all namespaces found in your project
- A vector of namespaces specifying which namespaces within the project should be compiled.

Once you've added an `:aot` configuration, running `lein compile` will cause your project's Clojure namespaces to be AOT compiled.

Maven.   AOT compilation is enabled in `clojure-maven-plugin` by default, at least when using the `clojure` packaging as shown in Example 8-3. That packaging binds `clojure-maven-plugin`'s compilation goal to Maven's `compile` phase, so that AOT compilation is run after Maven's default Java compilation finishes.

If you're not using `clojure` packaging, you'll need to configure this phase binding explicitly:

```
<plugin>
    <groupId>com.theoryinpractise</groupId>
    <artifactId>clojure-maven-plugin</artifactId>
    <version>1.3.8</version>
    <configuration>
        <warnOnReflection>true</warnOnReflection>
        <temporaryOutputDirectory>false</temporaryOutputDirectory>
    </configuration>

    <executions>
        <execution>
            <id>compile-clojure</id>
            <phase>compile</phase>
            <goals>
                <goal>compile</goal>
            </goals>
        </execution>
    </executions>
</plugin>
```

Here we also see the two configuration parameters that are most relevant to AOT compilation: `warnOnReflection` and `temporaryOutputDirectory`. Respectively, these control whether `*warn-on-reflection` is enabled, and whether class files generated by AOT compilation are saved to the default *classes* output directory, or to a temporary directory.

AOT compilation as a sanity check.   Even if you don't want to distribute AOT-compiled class files, including AOT compilation in your build process (and ignoring the class file results) can be a useful sanity check on your Clojure project's code. Because

AOT compilation requires that the code in question be loaded, all referred libraries, namespaces, vars, and Java classes must be resolved and loaded; if there is a problem with any of those references, an AOT compilation step will uncover it.[37]

`clojure-maven-plugin` provides for this scenario; simply add `<temporaryOutputDirec tory>true</temporaryOutputDirectory>` to the plug-in's `<configuration>` element, and AOT compilation results will be directed toward a temporary directory (that is later deleted). This ensures that the AOT sanity check is performed, but its results won't leak into your packaged distribution.

Leiningen does not currently offer an easy way to perform AOT compilation but ignore the resulting class files when packaging a project's artifact(s). Currently, the best option is to invoke `lein compile` (to perform the AOT compilation), and be sure to invoke `lein clean` before using Leiningen to package your project for distribution.

Similarly, you can enable `*warn-on-reflection*` during the course of AOT compilation, which will cause Clojure to emit a warning for each instance of interop reflection or argument type mismatches it encounters in your code.[38] To enable these warnings, add a `<warnOnReflection>true</warnOnReflection>` element to your `clojure-maven-plu gin`'s configuration, or `:warn-on-reflection true` to your *project.clj* file for Leiningen.

Building mixed-source projects

If you want to add Clojure to an existing project, you may need to pay some attention to the order in which various parts of such hybrid projects are compiled.[39] Very simply, if your Java code needs to refer to named classes generated by Clojure's type definition forms in the same project, you'll need to AOT compile your Clojure sources before compiling your Java sources. Likewise, if your Clojure code needs to refer to classes defined in Java code, the Java sources would need to be compiled first.

 These build process concerns related to mixed-source projects may not be relevant at all if your Java code does not use your Clojure code within the same project, or if your Java code is interoperating with your Clojure code without referencing any Clojure-defined types.[40]

---

37. The same check can be done by loading code into a REPL, but it is generally good practice to ensure that such quality checks are regularly performed in a repeatable build, rather than in an interactive, rarely reproduced REPL session.

38. See "Type Hinting for Performance" on page 366 for details about interop type hinting, and "Type errors and warnings" on page 440 for more about the warnings that Clojure can emit for argument type mismatches.

39. For the sake of clarity, we'll assume here that your hybrid project includes Java as its only other non-Clojure language. Similar advice would hold if you were working on a Clojure/JRuby project or a Scala/Clojure project.

40. See "Using Clojure from Java" on page 385 for details of how to use functionality defined in Clojure from Java without defining new Java-referenceable types in Clojure.

In any case, you need to order the compilation steps in your build process to mirror the intra-project language dependencies. Both Leiningen and Maven provide for this straightforwardly.

Maven.   `clojure-maven-plugin` defaults to allowing Maven's Java compilation to proceed before AOT compiling your Clojure codebase. This can be changed by binding `clojure-maven-plugin`'s compilation goal's execution to a Maven phase that runs prior to `compile`, such as `process-resources`:

```
<plugin>
  <groupId>com.theoryinpractise</groupId>
  <artifactId>clojure-maven-plugin</artifactId>
  <version>1.3.8</version>
  <executions>
    <execution>
      <id>clojure-compile</id>
      <phase>process-resources</phase>
      <goals>
        <goal>compile</goal>
      </goals>
    </execution>
  </executions>
</plugin>
```

Leiningen.   Leiningen also defaults to using `javac` to compile Java code prior to any AOT compilation you have configured, as long as you have defined a location for where that Java code can be found using the `:java-source-path` `defproject` slot.

Leiningen allows you to reverse this order, but via programmatic means instead of making a change in configuration as in Maven. First, `:java-source-path` should remain undefined in our `defproject` configuration; otherwise, Leiningen's default compilation ordering will remain in effect. What we want to do is alter the behavior of its `compile` task so that `javac` runs after that task's default activity is complete. Leiningen bundles the robert-hooke library,[41] which provides a way to do this succinctly within our *project.clj* file:

```
(defproject com.clojurebook/lein-mixed-source "1.0.0"
  :dependencies [[org.clojure/clojure "1.3.0"]]
  :aot :all)

(require '(leiningen compile javac))                          ❶

(add-hook #'leiningen.compile/compile                         ❷
  (fn [compile project & args]                                ❸
    (apply compile project args)                              ❹
    (leiningen.javac/javac (assoc project :java-source-path "srcj"))))) ❺
```

❶ First we require the key Leiningen namespaces.

---

41. robert-hooke is a Clojure library that provides a superset of aspect-oriented programming (AOP) in Clojure; its application to problems usually solved by AOP frameworks in Java is described in "Aspect-Oriented Programming" on page 466.

❷ We want to add a hook to the driver function for Leiningen's `compile` task; to do this, `robert-hooke`'s `add-hook` function needs access to the driver function's var, `#'leiningen.compile/compile`.

❸ The hook function is provided with the original `compile` function occupying the `#'leiningen.compile/compile` var, the current `project` configuration, and all the other arguments that would have been passed to that original `compile` function. After `add-hook` returns, our hook function will be in complete control over the implementation of the `compile` task.

❹ First, we delegate to the original `compile` function, so that the usual Clojure AOT compilation can proceed.

❺ We need to `assoc` in a value for `:java-source-path` so that `javac` knows where to find our Java sources. This is usually included in the authoritative project model (defined by `defproject` at the top of the *project.clj* file); keeping it out of there ensures that `compile` won't attempt to run `javac` prior to compiling the project's Clojure sources.

With this in place, running `lein compile` will invoke our hook function, thus running the usual Clojure AOT compilation followed by using `javac` to compile the Java code we have rooted in the *srcj* directory.

 However you want to organize the code within a project, you should absolutely avoid *interleaving* source dependencies. An interleaving dependency would be where, for example, Java code uses a type defined in Clojure that implements an interface defined in Java, all within the same project. Such topologies *can* be resolved (perhaps more readily in Maven than elsewhere, given its ability to use any number of distinct source roots in conjunction with any number of compilation goal executions), but it's safe to assume that they are a symptom of a poor design.

Final Thoughts

Organizing codebases and software projects effectively is a domain unto itself. Hopefully we have provided you with enough of a jump start about how projects may be organized and built in the Clojure style to allow you to focus on learning Clojure itself and getting real work done using it.

## CHAPTER 9

Java and JVM Interoperability

Many languages provide their own purpose-built runtime; popular examples of this approach include Python (CPython), Ruby (MRI), and Java (the JVM).[1] In contrast, Clojure is fundamentally a *hosted* language, meaning that it targets an existing runtime, also the JVM.[2] This means that rather than reimplementing a variety of foundational facilities (e.g., garbage collection, just-in-time compilation, threading, graphics contexts, etc.) and libraries of all sorts (from basics like String handling to esoterica like cryptographic functions), Clojure simply reuses all of the work that's been done around the JVM.

Aside from simply being an implementation time saver, targeting a mature host is advantageous for the Clojure programmer as well:

- The JVM core facilities and ecosystem of libraries are backed by significant engineering organizations. This means that they are generally well-tested, widely used, and aggressively optimized, yielding performance characteristics typically required or desired by most practitioners.

- Being on the JVM means that there are standard routes of interoperability. Programs written in one language can call on functionality provided by libraries written in other languages, all in the same runtime, with the Java interfaces and the Java object model being the *lingua franca*.

- The Java and broader JVM communities are huge, guaranteeing the wide availability of libraries for every domain, an abundance of support materials, and a large pool of developers with deep platform expertise.

- Tools are available to support all phases of software development, including development environments, build tools, profilers, debuggers, and operations support.

---

1. Though starting with Java 7, changes to the JVM have been made exclusively with languages other than Java in mind—like Clojure—making it an explicitly polyglot runtime.

2. There are other implementations of Clojure that target other hosts; see "(dissoc Clojure 'JVM)" on page 583.

Making the most out of Clojure will likely require that you gain a thorough understanding of its relationship to its host, so you can leverage the best parts of the JVM, the libraries targeting it, and any prior investment you have in them.

The JVM Is Clojure's Foundation

You might think that Clojure being a hosted language implies that it is somehow divorced from the JVM in significant ways—similar to how some hosted scripting environments erect a sandbox out of which you cannot easily escape. Nothing could be further from the truth. There are many areas of Clojure that reuse foundational facilities in the JVM; to name a few of the most notable:

- Clojure strings are Java `String`s.
- Clojure `nil` is Java's `null`.
- Clojure numbers are Java numbers.[3]
- Clojure regular expressions are instances of `java.util.regex.Pattern`.
- Clojure data structures implement the read-only portions of the appropriate `java.util.*` collection interfaces; so, Clojure maps implement `java.util.Map`, vectors and sequences and lists implement `java.util.List`, and sets implement `java.util.Set`.
- Clojure functions implement `java.lang.Runnable` and `java.util.concurrent.Call able`, making them trivial to integrate into existing libraries and frameworks that expect these core Java interfaces.
- Behind its syntax and abstractions, Clojure function invocations *are* method invocations in Java; thus, Clojure functions and function calls carry no special runtime overhead.
- Clojure is never interpreted; rather, it is always compiled down to efficient JVM bytecode prior to being run, even in interactive settings like the REPL.
- Calling Java APIs from Clojure is semantically and mechanically the same operation as calling such APIs from Java.
  - Clojure functions compile down to classes.
  - Clojure's `defrecord` and `deftype` forms compile down to Java classes containing regular Java fields.
  - Protocols defined by `defprotocols` generate corresponding Java interfaces.

This deep level of integration means that using Java libraries from Clojure[4] (and vice versa) generally requires no special wrappers, conversions, or other subterfuge, and carries no performance penalty compared to equivalent Java code.

---

3. There are a couple subtle wrinkles to this; see Table 11-1 for details.

4. Which, remember, is a Java library itself; see "Clojure Is "Just" Another Dependency" on page 342.

Further, thanks to the depth of the Java standard library and the size of the community that has gathered around the JVM, it's rare for there not to be a JVM library (sometimes, many competing libraries) for every potential need you may have. This is usually a welcome change for those coming from environments where it is common to need to reimplement functionality in the preferred language.

Using Java Classes, Methods, and Fields

Clojure provides some simple forms for interoperating with its host's classes, methods, and fields; this makes working with Java libraries within Clojure very natural, and certainly more concise than the equivalent Java code.

Table 9-1. Clojure interop forms and their Java equivalents[a]

Operation	Clojure forms	Java equivalents
Create a new instance of a class ClassName	(ClassName.) (ClassName. arg1 arg2 …)	new ClassName() new Class Name(arg1, arg2, …)
Invoke an instance method on an object	(.methodName object) (.methodName object arg1 arg2 …)	object.methodName() object.methodName(arg1, arg2, …)
Invoke the a static method staticMethod in a class Class Name	(ClassName/staticMethod) (ClassName/staticMethod arg1 arg2 …)	ClassName.staticMethod() ClassName.staticMe thod(arg1, arg2, …)
Access the value of a static field FIELD in a class ClassName	ClassName/FIELD	ClassName.FIELD
Refer to a Class	ClassName	ClassName.class
Access the value of an instance field field in an object object	(.field object)	object.field
Set the value of an instance field field in an object object to 5	(set! (.fieldName object) 5)	object.fieldName = 5

[a] We're fibbing just a little here: There are actually only two fundamental host interop forms, . (a period) and new. The former provides method invocation and field access whereas the latter provides constructor invocation. Except for set!, all the forms above are expanded into various usages of . and new. This syntactic sugar is explained in "Java Interop: . and new" on page 44.

Examples 9-1 and 9-2 show a couple of quick REPL interactions where each of these interop forms are used to tap into some core classes in the Java standard library:

Example 9-1. Retrieving a web page using Java libraries

```
(import 'java.net.URL)              ❶
;= java.net.URL
(def cnn (URL. "http://cnn.com"))   ❷
;= #'user/cnn
(.getHost cnn)                      ❸
;= "cnn.com"
```

```
(slurp cnn)                                    ❹
;= "<html lang=\"en\"><head><title>CNN.com.........."
```

❶ The `import` macro imports the named class into the current namespace; in this case the platform-standard `URL` class.

❷ Here we create an instance of `URL` with a single string argument, and store the result in a var. The constructor usage here is equivalent to `new URL("http://cnn.com")` in Java.

❸ An invocation of the `getHost` method returns what we'd expect; this is equivalent to `url.getHost()` in Java.

❹ Clojure has a `slurp` function that will return the string content of a number of different types of objects, including `java.io.Files`, `java.net.Sockets`, byte arrays, and more.[5] Here we provide our `URL` instance to `slurp`, which returns to us the string content of the URL's page.

Using static methods and fields is just as easy:

Example 9-2. Java static method and field usage

```
Double/MAX_VALUE
;= 1.7976931348623157E308
(Double/parseDouble "3.141592653589793")
;= 3.141592653589793
```

A key consideration in the design of these interop forms was that they are entirely consistent with function position:[6] the "operation" being performed is always the first symbol in each form. Thus, in addition to being functionally analogous to "native" Java method and constructor calls, interop forms are entirely consistent with Clojure's syntax. This makes them as natural to read and write as non-interop code that uses regular Clojure functions, and enables the use of interop forms in conjunction with Clojure-native facilities like the `->` family of threading macros. For example, here is an idiomatic Clojure function that, given a decimal string, returns an uppercase hex String:

```
(defn decimal-to-hex
  [x]
  (-> x
    Integer/parseInt
    (Integer/toString 16)
    .toUpperCase))
;= #'user/decimal-to-hex
(decimal-to-hex "255")
;= "FF"
```

5. `slurp` actually relies on the `clojure.java.io/reader` function to return a `java.io.Reader` for all these different types of objects—in our example, using a variety of Java interop to open a `java.net.Socket` to the URL, obtain a `java.io.InputStream` from that socket, which is then wrapped with a `Reader`. `slurp` then takes over, trivially reading character data from the `Reader`.

6. Read more about *function position* in "Expressions, Operators, Syntax, and Precedence" on page 7.

The -> threading macro provides the result of each form as the first argument to the following form (converting bare symbols into single-element lists along the way), returning the result of the final form. So, the body of the decimal-to-hex function is equivalent to (.toUpperCase (Integer/toString (Integer/parseInt x) 16)); or, to this Java code:

```java
public String stringToHex (String x) {
    return Integer.toString(Integer.parseInt(x), 16).toUpperCase();
}
```

At least to our eyes, the usage of -> (and similar macros such as ->>[7]) leads to code that is far easier to read (you can look at it as a linear processing pipeline, which eliminates the need to "scrub" back and forth across an expression whose order of evaluation isn't simply left-to-right) yet entirely compatible with interop forms thanks to the consistent use of function position.

Accessing object fields.   Public fields are rare in Java APIs, and mutable public fields are particularly so. Nevertheless, Clojure provides easy access to them, and a way to set their value with its set! special form:[8]

Example 9-3. Accessing and setting the fields of a Java object

```clojure
(import 'java.awt.Point)
;= java.awt.Point
(def pt (Point. 5 10))
;= #'user/pt
(.x pt)
;= 5
(set! (.x pt) -42)
;= -42
(.x pt)
;= -42
```

Notice that set! uses the same syntax—(.x pt) here—for referring to the field to set as is used to retrieve the field's value.

---

7. See "In Detail: -> and ->>" on page 259 for a detailed explanation of -> and ->>.

8. set! is used in a few other situations where you are directly changing a mutable location; see "Specialized Mutation: set!" on page 45 for more.

The Java mutability (trap door | escape hatch)

While Clojure encourages the use of immutable values as a good default (as we discussed in Chapter 2), the same cannot be said of the majority language that shares Clojure's JVM host. Java's collections and its defaults in general encourage mutable object state. Since you can use Java libraries, classes, and objects from Clojure quite naturally, you can opt into mutable state without much ceremony at all. This can either serve as a useful escape hatch (especially when you need functionality that is only available as a Java library) or a nasty trap door (when you don't treat mutable Java objects with the caution they warrant). In any case, keep your wits about you when working with Java objects from Clojure, especially as you come to appreciate and rely upon Clojure's sane defaults.

Handy Interop Utilities

The vast majority of your usage of Java libraries will involve the core interop forms shown in Table 9-1. There are a couple of often-used utilities that you should be aware of, though:

class
> Returns the java.lang.Class of its argument; e.g., (class "foo") ⇒ java.lang.String

instance?
> A predicate function that returns true if its second argument is an instance of the Class named by the first argument, as in (instance? String "foo") ⇒ true

doto
> A macro that invokes a number of nested forms, providing the first argument to doto as the first argument to all later forms.

The purpose and usage of class and instance? should be fairly obvious, but doto warrants further explanation.

Many classes in the Java world are mutable, and frequently require initialization beyond what their constructors provide. A good example of this is java.util.ArrayList, which you often want to populate with some initial data:

```
ArrayList list = new ArrayList();
list.add(1);
list.add(2);
list.add(3);
```

Of course, Clojure provides literals for its own vectors,[9] but there are some unfortunate circumstances where an existing Java API may *require* an ArrayList (rather than

---

9. Note that Clojure's vector has nothing to do with java.util.Vector. See Chapter 3 for a full discussion of Clojure's data structures.

---

accepting any `java.util.List`, in which case a Clojure vector could be passed as an argument directly). In such cases, we could use `let` to create the `ArrayList`, populate it appropriately, and then return the `ArrayList` reference:

Example 9-4. Populating an ArrayList "manually"

```
(let [alist (ArrayList.)]
  (.add alist 1)
  (.add alist 2)
  (.add alist 3)
  alist)
```

That works, but is as verbose as Java. `doto` is a far better option here:[10]

Example 9-5. Using doto to populate an ArrayList more concisely

```
(doto (ArrayList.)
  (.add 1)
  (.add 2)
  (.add 3))
```

This does exactly the same thing as Example 9-4, but is obviously far more concise. The utility of `doto` is even clearer when more extensive operations need to be performed on or with a single object. For example:

Example 9-6. Using doto to manipulate java.awt.Graphics2D context

```
(doto graphics
  (.setBackground Color/white)
  (.setColor Color/black)
  (.scale 2 2)
  (.clearRect 0 0 500 500)
  (.drawRect 100 100 300 300))
```

This applies a series of operations to the `Graphics2D` object, resulting in a black square drawn within a white square in the graphics context, which the `doto` form itself returns.

Clojure's primary idiom is of working with values, rather than procedurally mutating fixed references. By providing you with a concise way to syntactically circumscribe any procedural initialization or other side-effecting operations, and implicitly returning the subject of those operations, which can be treated in later Clojure code as just another value, `doto` helps integrate interop with the host's mutable, stateful objects into this idiom.

---

10. `ArrayList` is familiar and a reasonable basis for a simple `doto` example, but of course, you can populate it with a Clojure collection straight away, as in `(ArrayList. [1 2 3])`.

Exceptions and Error Handling

Clojure reuses the JVM's exception machinery *in toto*,[11] with its familiar `try/catch/finally/throw` idiom. Thus, the pattern of error handling in Clojure will be familiar to anyone who has ever worked with languages that share that idiom, including Java, Ruby, Python, and many others.

Given that, blocks of code in Example 9-7 are equivalent with regard to their error handling:

Example 9-7. Parsing a string as an integer in Java, Ruby, and Clojure, with error handling

```java
// Java
public static Integer asInt (String s) {
    try {
        return Integer.parseInt(s);
    } catch (NumberFormatException e) {
        e.printStackTrace();
        return null;
    } finally {
        System.out.println("Attempted to parse as integer: " + s);
    }
}
```

```ruby
# Ruby
def as_int (s)
    begin
        return Integer(s)
    rescue Exception => e
        puts e.backtrace
    ensure
        puts "Attempted to parse as integer: " + s
    end
end
```

```clojure
; Clojure
(defn as-int
  [s]
  (try
    (Integer/parseInt s)
    (catch NumberFormatException e
      (.printStackTrace e))
    (finally
      (println "Attempted to parse as integer: " s))))
```

Parsing integers is a pretty mundane operation, but it makes it clear that the semantics and function of the `try`, `catch`, and `finally` forms in Clojure mirror those in Java and, for example, the corresponding ones in Ruby (`begin`, `rescue`, `ensure`):

---

11. There *are* a number of Clojure libraries that provide error-handling extensions that go far beyond what we describe here; in particular, Slingshot provides far more sophisticated modeling and handling of error states: *https://github.com/scgilardi/slingshot*.

try
:   Delimits the scope of an exception-handling form. It may contain any number of catch forms and an optional finally form, all prefixed by any number of expressions that represent the code's "happy path."[12] Assuming that happy path, the last expression in a try prior to any catch or finally forms determines the result of the try form.

catch
:   Specifies some code to jump to if an exception of the specified type (i.e., java.lang.Throwable, or any subclass thereof) is thrown in the course of the execution of the main body of the try form. The thrown exception is bound to the name provided after the exception type. The last expression in an activated catch form determines the result of the enclosing try form. Any number of catch forms may be specified.

finally
:   Specifies some code to execute just prior to the flow of control exiting the try form, regardless of the nature of that exit (that is, even if some code in the body of the try form threw an uncaught exception, the expressions in the finally form will be executed). The finally form does not influence the result of the try form at all; thus, it is only ever useful if some side-effecting action(s) need to be taken after the try is completed otherwise. The only wrinkle to this is that exceptions thrown from finally bodies will replace any exception thrown from the body of the corresponding try form (as is true in Java).

These are the foundations of the JVM's (and therefore Clojure's) general-purpose error-handling capabilities.

throwing exceptions. Clojure code can signal an exception using its throw form, which is exactly analogous to Java's throw and raise in Ruby and Python:

```
(throw (IllegalStateException. "I don't know what to do!"))
;= #<IllegalStateException java.lang.IllegalStateException: I don't know what to do!>
```

While you can syntactically raise any class or an instance of any class in Python, and you can even raise strings in Ruby, Clojure's throw must receive an instance of a class that extends java.lang.Throwable or some subclass of it:

```
(throw "foo")
;= #<ClassCastException java.lang.ClassCastException:
;=    java.lang.String cannot be cast to java.lang.Throwable>
```

Reusing existing exception types. One idiom that is often seen in Java codebases, but very, very rarely in Clojure code, is the definition of new exception types. Idiomatic Clojure code, when it does throw an exception, throws an exception of a standard type.

---

12. Worth pointing out is that Clojure's catch and finally forms must be included *within* a try; this makes explicit the semantic relationship between try (or, e.g., begin in Ruby) and catch and finally, the latter of which are syntactically treated as "top level" peers to try in nearly every other language.

There are over 350 exception types in the Java standard library; though it *can* happen, it is rare to come across a scenario where one of those exception types is not semantically sufficient to describe the error condition at hand. It's probably fair to say that 90 percent of all use cases are reasonably satisfied by one of the "core" exception types:

- `java.lang.IllegalArgumentException`
- `java.lang.UnsupportedOperationException`
- `java.lang.IllegalStateException`
- `java.io.IOException`

This is the general rule, but there are cases where a custom exception type is necessary. If you find yourself in such a situation, you may find the example custom exception type defined in "Defining a custom exception type" (page 378) to be helpful.

Escaping Checked Exceptions

While Clojure is hosted on the JVM, it does not inherit Java's *checked exceptions*. These are types of exceptions that may be declared to be thrown by Java methods; the Java compiler requires callers of such methods to either catch and handle thrown checked exceptions, or to declare that they throw those exceptions themselves. Checked exceptions have long been a controversial topic in the Java ecosystem,[13] with the rough consensus being that checked exceptions generally cause Java codebases to be more verbose and more difficult to maintain.

Clojure is thankfully not subject to the constraints of checked exceptions declared to be thrown by Java methods called from Clojure code, since checked exceptions are a fabrication of the Java compiler, and simply don't exist in the JVM at runtime.[14] So, we can (for example) create temporary files using a method that specifies that it can throw `java.io.IOException`, a checked exception:

```
(File/createTempFile "clojureTempFile" ".txt")
```

...outside the scope of any `try`/`catch` expression, and without any corollary to Java's `throws` declaration to indicate that that code may throw an `IOException`. This obviously allows Clojure to be more concise when calling methods with checked exception declarations compared to the equivalent Java code.

with-open, finally's Lament

The prototypical, most common usage of `finally` is in ensuring proper resource management. For example, here's a static utility method in Java for appending some text to a file:

---

13. *http://www.mindview.net/Etc/Discussions/CheckedExceptions* is a good exploration of the topic.

14. Incidentally, much like Java's generics thanks to erasure.

Example 9-8. Appending to a file in Java with manual resource management via finally

```java
public static void appendTo (File f, String text) throws IOException {
    Writer w = null;
    try {
        w = new OutputStreamWriter(new FileOutputStream(f, true), "UTF-8");
        w.write(text);
        w.flush();
    } finally {
        if (w != null) w.close();
    }
}
```

Notice the `finally` block where we conditionally close the `Writer` we open in the preceding `try` block. This pattern (or, the too-easy misapplication of it) is consistently the source of bugs in many programs that work with file, socket, database, and other resources that need explicit management. Because of this, Java 7 introduced a `try-with-resources` statement[15] that automatically closes, for example, file handles upon control exiting its scope, very similar to Python's `with`:

Example 9-9. Appending to a file in Java 7 using try-with-resources

```java
public static void appendTo (File f, String text) throws IOException {
  try (Writer w = new OutputStreamWriter(new FileOutputStream(f, true), "UTF-8")) {
      w.write(text);
      w.flush();
  }
}
```

Clojure provides an equivalent `with-open` form that ensures that resources are closed prior to control exiting its scope.[16] Here is an idiomatic translation of the `appendTo` method in Clojure, using the `with-open` form to ensure that the `Writer` is closed properly:

Example 9-10. Appending to a file in Clojure with automatic resource management via with-open

```clojure
(require '[clojure.java.io :as io])

(defn append-to
  [f text]
  (with-open [w (io/writer f :append true)] ❶
    (doto w (.write text) .flush)))
```

❶ We could have created an `OutputStreamWriter` and a `FileInputStream` manually ourselves, but the `writer` helper function is too convenient to bother.

---

15. See *http://download.oracle.com/javase/tutorial/essential/exceptions/tryResourceClose.html* for a primer if you're not yet familiar with it.

16. We can't pass up the opportunity to mention that `with-open` is implemented as a nine-line Clojure macro that you could easily write on your own—quite the contrast to the Godot-esque experience that is waiting for improvements delivered by maintainers of languages that lack macros. You can read about macros and what they enable in Chapter 5.

You can optionally bind multiple resources within a `with-open` form,[17] each of which will be closed before control exits `with-open`. Here's a naïve implementation of a copy function that demonstrates this:

Example 9-11. Appending to a file in Clojure with automatic resource management via with-open

```clojure
(defn copy-files
  [from to]
  (with-open [in (FileInputStream. from)
              out (FileOutputStream. to)]
    (loop [buf (make-array Byte/TYPE 1024)]
      (let [len (.read in buf)]
        (when (pos? len)
          (.write out buf 0 len)
          (recur buf))))))
```

This is a fine example of `with-open`, but a far better option would be to use the `copy` function (and the rest of the I/O utilities) in the `clojure.java.io` namespace[18] in preference to naïve implementations like this.

Type Hinting for Performance

You may have noticed some code examples that use syntax referring to Java class names, such as `^String` here:

```clojure
(defn length-of
  [^String text]
  (.length text))
```

The `^ClassName` syntax defines a *type hint*, an explicit indication to the Clojure compiler of the object type of an expression, var value, or a named binding.

The typical type hint syntax is expanded by the Clojure reader into metadata on the value following the hint. So, the `^String text` hinted binding form is expanded by the reader into the equivalent expression `^{:tag String} text`, which evaluates to the symbol `text` with the metadata `{:tag String}`. Clojure internally uses the term "tag" for type.

These hints are used by the compiler only to avoid emitting reflective interop calls; otherwise, they are unnecessary. So, if our code does not include an interop call, there is no need to include a type hint:

---

17. Any object whose class provides a nullary `close` method will work here. This matches the `close` method defined by the `java.lang.Closeable` interface, but because Clojure is a dynamic language, the resources you use in `with-open` do not need to actually implement that interface. This is called "duck typing" in many other dynamic languages.

18. *http://clojure.github.com/clojure/clojure.java.io-api.html*.

```
(defn silly-function
  [v]
  (nil? v))
```

Any hint you provide for v here would simply be left unused.

 Type hints on function arguments or returns are *not* signature declarations: they do not affect the types that a function can accept or return. Their only effect is to allow Clojure to call Java methods and access Java fields using compile-time generated code—rather than the much-slower option of using reflection at runtime to search for methods or fields matching the interop form in question. Thus, if a hint doesn't inform an interop operation, they are effectively no-ops. For example, this function hints its argument as being a `java.util.List`, but it can accept an argument of any type:

```
(defn accepts-anything
  [^java.util.List x]
  x)
;= #'user/accepts-anything
(accepts-anything (java.util.ArrayList.))
;= #<ArrayList []>
(accepts-anything 5)
;= 5
(accepts-anything false)
;= false
```

This is in contrast to signature *declarations*, which Clojure does provide, but *only* for primitive arguments and return types. We cover primitive type declarations in "Declare Functions to Take and Return Primitives" on page 438.

Avoiding reflective interop calls is key to ensuring maximal performance in code that is CPU-bound. In practice, little type-hinting is required in order to avoid reflection entirely, since the Clojure compiler provides for type inference based on the known types of literals, constructor calls, and method return types.

To illustrate this, let's add a type hint to some code in order to optimize it. Here's a function that returns a provided String, capitalized:

Example 9-12. An unhinted capitalization function

```
(defn capitalize
  [s]
  (-> s
    (.charAt 0)
    Character/toUpperCase
    (str (.substring s 1))))
```

This implementation works, but we'd probably like to speed it up a little bit:

Example 9-13. Timing the capitalization of "foo" 100,000 times

```
(time (doseq [s (repeat 100000 "foo")]
        (capitalize s)))
; "Elapsed time: 5040.218 msecs"
```

In this sort of case, where you suspect that type hinting may yield some benefits, turning on reflection warnings in the Clojure compiler is helpful; doing so indicates where reflective calls are being emitted:[19]

Example 9-14. Getting reflection warnings for the capitalize function from Example 9-12

```
(set! *warn-on-reflection* true)
;= true
(defn capitalize
  [s]
  (-> s
    (.charAt 0)
    Character/toUpperCase
    (str (.substring s 1))))
; Reflection warning, NO_SOURCE_PATH:27 - call to charAt can't be resolved.
; Reflection warning, NO_SOURCE_PATH:29 - call to toUpperCase can't be resolved.
; Reflection warning, NO_SOURCE_PATH:29 - call to substring can't be resolved.
;= #'user/capitalize
```

We see here that three interop calls are being emitted reflectively. We can address this by adding a single type hint (notice the ^String addition):

```
(defn fast-capitalize
  [^String s]
  (-> s
    (.charAt 0)
    Character/toUpperCase
    (str (.substring s 1))))
```

This will eliminate all three reflective calls. How can just one type hint impact all three reflective calls? This is where the Clojure compiler's type inference comes into play:

1. The let-bound name s is explicitly type-hinted to be a String. Therefore...

2. ...the .charAt call can be compiled down to a direct call to String.charAt. The compiler knows that this method returns a char, so...

3. ...it can properly select the char variant of Character.toUpperCase (rather than its int override).

4. Finally, the compiler again refers back to the explicit String type hint on s to inform its selection of String.substring when compiling the .substring interop method call.

---

19. The technique shown here is useful at the REPL, but you can get the same warnings from your build process if you want, with the benefit of actual line numbers. Refer to "AOT compilation as a sanity check" (page 350) for details.

How does this impact the performance of our revised `fast-capitalize` function? Let's see:

```
(time (doseq [s (repeat 100000 "foo")]
        (fast-capitalize s)))
; "Elapsed time: 154.889 msecs"
```

From 5 seconds down to .155 seconds. Not bad.

Type hints can be added to any expression. Consider this function, which has a reflective call to `String.split`:

```
(defn split-name
  [user]
  (zipmap [:first :last]
    (.split (:name user) " ")))
;= #'user/split-name
; Reflection warning, NO_SOURCE_PATH:3 - call to split can't be resolved.
(split-name {:name "Chas Emerick"})
;= {:last "Emerick", :first "Chas"}
```

If we could only hint let-bound names, we'd have to add a `let` form just to be able to hint a name we give the intermediate `(:name user)` value:

```
(defn split-name
  [user]
  (let [^String full-name (:name user)]
    (zipmap [:first :last]
      (.split full-name " "))))
;= #'user/split-name
```

No reflection, but that's a lot of work. Thankfully, we can hint the `(:name user)` expression:

```
(defn split-name
  [user]
  (zipmap [:first :last]
    (.split ^String (:name user) " ")))
;= #'user/split-name
```

No reflection, no added verbosity. Similarly, we can hint the return value of functions, so that all of their callers do not need to hint interop calls on their results:

```
(defn file-extension
  [^java.io.File f]
  (-> (re-seq #"\.(.+)" (.getName f))
    first
    second))

(.toUpperCase (file-extension (java.io.File. "image.png")))
; Reflection warning, NO_SOURCE_PATH:1 - reference to field toUpperCase can't be
  resolved.
;= "PNG"
```

Return value hints are added on functions' *argument vectors*:

```
(defn file-extension
  ^String [^java.io.File f]
```

```
(-> (re-seq #"\.(.+)" (.getName f))
    first
    second))

(.toUpperCase (file-extension (java.io.File. "image.png")))
;= "PNG"
```

Finally, we can provide type metadata on var names to indicate the type of value they contain:

```
(def a "image.png")
;= #'user/a
(java.io.File. a)
; Reflection warning, NO_SOURCE_PATH:1 - call to java.io.File ctor can't be resolved.
;= #<File image.png>
(def ^String a "image.png")
;= #'user/a
(java.io.File. a)
;= #<File image.png>
```

Arrays

Prior to the introduction of the `java.util` Collections API in Java 1.2, arrays[20] were one of the few ways you could hold large batches of objects. Now, arrays are rarely used to hold objects, but they remain an important tool when working with numeric and other primitive datasets. In any case, Clojure can handle Java arrays with aplomb, though you'll generally find that array-handling is one of the rare domains where Clojure is more verbose than Java out of the box given the latter's purpose-built syntax.

Table 9-2. Comparison of array operations

Operation	Clojure expression	Java equivalent
Create an array from a collection	`(into-array ["a" "b" "c"])`	`(String[])coll.toArray(new String[list.size()]);`
Create an empty array	`(make-array Integer 10 100)`	`new Integer[10][100]`
Create an empty array of primitive longs	`(long-array 10)` `(make-array Long/TYPE 10)`	`new long[10]`
Access an array value	`(aget some-array 4)`	`some_array[4]`
Set an array value[a]	`(aset some-array 4 "foo")` `(aset ^ints int-array 4 5)`	`some_array[4] = 5.6`

[a] Clojure's expression-hinting mechanism comes into play when setting values in arrays of primitives; see "Use Primitive Arrays Judiciously" on page 442 for details.

---

20. Don't confuse Clojure/Java arrays with Ruby's **Array**. Ruby's **Array** is similar to Java's **Vector**.

If your Clojure code is simply consuming arrays of objects, probably as returned by existing Java APIs, then there is no need to explicitly convert them to lists or other collections. Arrays are supported by Clojure's sequence abstraction,[21] so you can use them just like any other seqable collection:

```
(map #(Character/toUpperCase %) (.toCharArray "Clojure"))
;= (\C \L \O \J \U \R \E)
```

However, Clojure does provide some special support for primitive arrays. We cover that topic separately in "Use Primitive Arrays Judiciously" on page 442.

Defining Classes and Implementing Interfaces

Being able to call Java methods and instantiate classes is a good start, but you often need to define classes as well, implementing interfaces and sometimes extending an existing class. Clojure provides an array of class definition facilities, each of which offers a mix of different capabilities suited for different use cases.

Table 9-3. Comparison of key features of Clojure forms that define Java classes[a]

	proxy	gen-class	reify	deftype	defrecord
Returns an instance of an anonymous class?	√		√		
Defines a named class?		√		√	√
Can extend an existing base class?	√	√			
Can define new fields?				√	√
Provides default implementations of `Object.equals`, `Object.hashcode`, and various Clojure interfaces?					√

[a] If you know you need to define a new type in Clojure, but you're not sure which type-definition form to use, refer to the flowchart designed specifically for this purpose at Chapter 18.

21. Specifically, the seq function that underlies all of Clojure's various sequence operations will properly return a seq when provided an array.

All of these forms can be used to define classes and implement interfaces. Some of these forms—`deftype`, `defrecord`, and `reify`—also serve unique roles within Clojure that are unrelated to interoperability with Java classes and interfaces. Thus, we discuss them separately in Chapter 6.

On the other hand, the remaining two—`proxy` and `gen-class`—exist solely to support these usages in interop scenarios; we'll cover them here.

Instances of Anonymous Classes: proxy

`proxy` produces an instance of an anonymous class that implements any number of Java interfaces and/or a single concrete base class.[22] This anonymous class is generated only once, at compile time, based on the class and interface(s) specified. After that, the cost of each runtime `proxy` invocation is only that of a single call of the constructor of the generated class. This makes `proxy` the equivalent of defining and instantiating an anonymous inner class in Java.

To demonstrate the usage of `proxy`, let's see how we would use it to implement a basic least recently used (LRU) cache[23] with some building blocks available in the Java standard library.

The JDK provides a hash map implementation, `java.util.LinkedHashMap`, which provides the basic hooks for implementing a simple LRU cache: it can maintain entry iteration order based on last access, and it defines a method, `removeEldestEn try(Map.Entry<K,V>)`, which a subclass can override in order to inform the `LinkedHash Map` whether the oldest entry (based either on insertion or access order) should be removed.

Doing this with `proxy` allows us to exhibit all of its characteristics:

Example 9-15. Implementing a simple LRU cache using LinkedHashMap and proxy

```
(defn lru-cache                                    ❶
  [max-size]                                       ❷
  (proxy [java.util.LinkedHashMap] [16 0.75 true]  ❸
    (removeEldestEntry [entry]                     ❹
      (> (count this) max-size))))                 ❺
```

---

22. If you don't need to subclass an existing concrete class, you should prefer `reify` over `proxy`; the former is described in "Defining anonymous types with reify" on page 284.

23. See *http://en.wikipedia.org/wiki/Cache_algorithms#Least_Recently_Used* if you are not familiar with LRU caching.

---

❶ First, we set up a factory function so we can obtain instances of this cache as needed.

❷ proxy's method implementations form closures, so any values bound in the scope of a proxy usage are usable within those implementations. Here, we accept a max-size argument to the factory function, which our removeEldestEntry method implementation closes over. We'll compare that value to our map's size as our entry expiration criterion.

❸ proxy requires two vectors as its first two arguments:

1. The names of its superclass and/or implemented interfaces; note that the superclass must come first.

2. The arguments provided to its superclass's constructor. In this example, we're providing LinkedHashMap's default values for initial map size (16) and load factor (0.75), with a Boolean true that indicates that the underlying map should maintain access order rather than its default of insertion order. This is what turns the LinkedHashMap into a working LRU cache. Note that we could put any expressions into the vector of constructors, not just literals.

❹ proxy does not require you to provide a first this argument in its method implementations (unlike Clojure's other class-definition forms, reify, defrecord, and deftype). Rather, this is implicitly bound to the proxy instance...

❺ ...which we use to check the map's size. If it's grown larger than the closed-over max-size value, then we return true, indicating that the provided least recently used entry should be evicted from the cache. Of course, any criterion can be used to implement a cache eviction policy, but map size is a reasonable and common baseline.

Method implementations can be provided to proxy in any order.

Let's use our simple LRU cache at the REPL, and make sure it's working as we expect:

```
(def cache (doto (lru-cache 5)                          ❶
             (.put :a :b)))
;= #'user/cache
cache
;= #<LinkedHashMap$0 {:a=:b}>
(doseq [[k v] (partition 2 (range 500))]                ❷
  (get cache :a)                                        ❸
  (.put cache k v))                                     ❹
;= nil
cache
;= #<LinkedHashMap$0 {492=493, 494=495, 496=497, :a=:b, 498=499}> ❺
```

❶ First, we create a new cache using our lru-cache function defined in Example 9-15, adding one entry, a mapping between :a and :b.[24] We'll access this entry frequently, ensuring that it's never expired from the cache as the least recently used.

---

24. :a and :b are Clojure keyword literals. Clojure keywords are described in "Keywords" on page 14.

❷ We assemble a seq of 250 two-element lists using `partition`, each containing monotonically increasing integers as provided by `range`.[25] Each of these two-element lists is destructured[26] into "key" and "value" bindings with the [k v] destructuring form.

❸ Before adding each new entry to our cache, we access the entry corresponding to our :a key. This keeps this entry "hot," maintaining its position in the `LinkedHash Map` such that it is never offered to the `removeEldestEntry` method for potential eviction.

❹ We put each key-value pair from the seq of 250 pairs we built in ❷ into the cache. Once our `max-size` of 5 is exceeded, each `.put` should result in the least recently used entry being expired from the cache.

❺ After finishing our bulk `.puts`, we check the state of the cache...

...and, yes, the cache contains only five entries, and the [:a :b] entry that we kept hot remains; it was never offered to our `proxy`-implemented `removeEldestEntry` method, and was therefore never evicted. Only the [498 499] entry has been used more recently used than our [:a :b], as the last time we touched the map was to add the former.

Defining Named Classes

While `proxy` allows you to define anonymous classes at runtime within Clojure, there are often cases where you need to provide a static, standalone, named Java class for use by Java-centric consumers.[27] Clojure provides three forms that generate named classes, each of which embodies a different set of tradeoffs.

In conjunction with protocols, `deftype` and `defrecord` represent Clojure's principled approach to data and domain modeling. As a consequence, they eschew some of the more complicated aspects of the Java object model to make way for Clojure's idioms. Conversely, in order to be maximally efficient, `deftype` and `defrecord` are structurally the most similar to "regular" Java classes: they allow you to define new (optionally primitive) fields, and their method bodies are inlined into the class files they generate, making them as efficient as classes you might define in Java itself. We might say that `deftype` and `defrecord` reuse "the good parts" of the Java object model. While they can

---

25. An example involving a printable amount of data would be (`partition` 2 (`range` 10)) ⇒ ((0 1) (2 3) (4 5) (6 7) (8 9)).

26. You can read about Clojure's destructuring forms in "Destructuring (let, Part 2)" on page 28.

27. These consumers can be Java programmers if you are distributing Clojure code as a library, or existing JVM libraries, frameworks, and servers that require that certain implementation classes be statically named in configuration files and such. One common example of the latter are servlet containers; their *web.xml* file, described in Example 17-1, requires the specification of a named servlet class.

and are used for interop purposes when possible,[28] they have a much broader role within Clojure; thus, we discuss them separately and extensively in Chapter 6.

In contrast, `gen-class` provides more complete support for the Java object model—including defining static methods, subclassing concrete base classes, and defining multiple constructors and new instance methods—but is structurally very different from typical Java classes, with the generated class's methods delegating their implementation at runtime to regular Clojure functions.

gen-class

`gen-class` allows you to define Java classes whose method implementations are backed by regular Clojure functions. It is intended exclusively for interop contexts, and supports a broad subset of the Java object model that makes it possible to fulfill framework and library API requirements with few exceptions. It allows you to:

- Generate a Java class in any package and with any name
- Extend an existing base class, with access to the base class's protected fields
- Implement any number of Java interfaces
- Define any number of constructors
- Define static and additional instance methods, beyond those defined by the superclass and implemented interfaces
- Conveniently generate static factory functions
- Conveniently generate a static `main` method, for classes to operate at the command line

> `gen-class` is the only form in Clojure that must be *ahead-of-time (AOT) compiled*. Without it, `gen-class` forms are no-ops, as `gen-class` does not define a class at runtime like all of Clojure's other class-definition forms. With AOT compilation, `gen-class` forms emit Java class files that can be redistributed in *.jar* files and used by other Java libraries, referred to in Java programs, and so on.
>
> Learn more about AOT compilation in "Ahead-of-Time Compilation" on page 337. *All of the examples in this chapter that use gen-class assume that they've been AOT-compiled accordingly.*

Comprehensively describing all of `gen-class`'s options would likely require its own chapter. Rather, a couple of representative examples of `gen-class` usage will give you a good starting point for understanding how it works. Here's a Clojure namespace that implements very naive image resizing, which we can package into a self-contained, executable *.jar* file thanks to the `gen-class` definition:

---

28. As we'll see in some examples later in this chapter; see "Implementing JAX-RS web service endpoints" on page 383 and "Using deftype and defrecord Classes" on page 388.

Example 9-16. Providing static methods and a command-line utility via gen-class

```
(ns com.clojurebook.imaging
  (:use [clojure.java.io :only (file)])
  (:import (java.awt Image Graphics2D)
           javax.imageio.ImageIO
           java.awt.image.BufferedImage
           java.awt.geom.AffineTransform))

(defn load-image
  [file-or-path]
  (-> file-or-path file ImageIO/read))

(defn resize-image
  ^BufferedImage [^Image original factor]
  (let [scaled (BufferedImage. (* factor (.getWidth original))
                               (* factor (.getHeight original))
                               (.getType original))]
    (.drawImage ^Graphics2D (.getGraphics scaled)
                original
                (AffineTransform/getScaleInstance factor factor)
                nil)
    scaled))

(gen-class
  :name ResizeImage                                              ❶
  :main true                                                     ❷
  :methods [^:static [resizeFile [String String double] void]   ❸
            ^:static [resize [java.awt.Image double] java.awt.image.BufferedImage]])

(def ^:private -resize resize-image)                             ❹

(defn- -resizeFile
  [path outpath factor]
  (ImageIO/write (-> path load-image (resize-image factor))
                 "png"
                 (file outpath)))

(defn -main                                                      ❺
  [& [path outpath factor]]
  (when-not (and path outpath factor)
    (println "Usage: java -jar example-uberjar.jar ResizeImage [INFILE] [OUTFILE]
      [SCALE]")
    (System/exit 1))
  (-resizeFile path outpath (Double/parseDouble factor)))
```

❶ By default, gen-class generates classes with the same name as the namespace they're found in. In this case, the namespace (com.clojurebook.imaging) is Clojure-idiomatic, but does not fit with Java practice and is too long for a command-line tool anyway. Instead, we specify a class name to be generated in the default package, ResizeImage.

❷ We want to be able to use this class as a command-line tool, so we enable gen-class's main-method option. This will produce a public static void main String(args[]) method, which will delegate to the -main function in this namespace.

❸ Here we define two methods on the generated class, which are provided in the form [methodName [parameter types] returnType]. These methods are both static in this case, thanks to the ^:static metadata on each method's signature vector.

❹ By default, gen-class looks for method-implementing functions in the same namespace as the gen-class definition, and the same names as the defined methods but with a - prefix.[29] The static resize method we've defined conveniently has the same signature and semantics as our resize-image function. Thus, we simply alias the resize-image function into a new var with the name that the resize method will delegate to (-resize). We provide a dedicated implementation for the resizeFile method.

❺ Our main method provides some simple usage information, passing command-line arguments on to -resizeFile.

Once we AOT-compile this namespace, we'll have a ResizeImage class file that we can run from the command line or use from within a Java application via its static methods. For example, say we have an image in our current directory called *clojure.png*:

29. You can specify a different prefix by providing a string value to gen-class in a :prefix slot.

We can run our `ResizeImage` utility from the command line:

```
java -cp gen-class-1.0.0-standalone.jar ResizeImage clojure.png resized.png 0.5
```

Yielding our scaled image:

Those static methods on `ResizeImage` are of course accessible to any Java code as well:

```
ResizeImage.resizeFile("clojure.png", "resized.png", 0.5);
```

An important thing to note about `gen-class` is that it does not require you to change anything about your Clojure codebase. That `com.clojurebook.imaging` namespace would be a perfectly fine (albeit small) Clojure API, idiomatic in every sense; we're just using `gen-class` to provide a Java-friendly bridge to that namespace's functionality.

Defining a custom exception type.   As we said in "Reusing existing exception types" (page 363), it is generally the case that Clojure code reuses exception types that are already available in the Java standard library, or in other third-party libraries that a particular application might be using. However, there are some cases where a specialized exception type is called for, especially if you are collaborating extensively with Java-centric colleagues who expect to see a proliferation of exception types for each error condition.

Let's look at a custom exception type that allows us to provide a map of data alongside the usual `String` and root-cause `Throwable` that Java exceptions typically carry:

Example 9-17. Defining a custom exception type using gen-class

```
(ns com.clojurebook.CustomException
  (:gen-class :extends RuntimeException                                    ❶
              :implements [clojure.lang.IDeref]                            ❷
              :constructors {[java.util.Map String] [String]              ❸
                             [java.util.Map String Throwable] [String Throwable]}
              :init init
              :state info                                                 ❹
              :methods [[getInfo [] java.util.Map]                        ❺
                        [addInfo [Object Object] void]]))

(import 'com.clojurebook.CustomException)

(defn- -init                                                              ❻
  ([info message]
    [[message] (atom (into {} info))])                                    ❼
  ([info message ex]
    [[message ex] (atom (into {} info))]))
```

```
(defn- -deref                                                    ⑧
  [^CustomException this]
  @(.info this))

(defn- -getInfo
  [this]
  @this)

(defn- -addInfo
  [^CustomException this key value]
  (swap! (.info this) assoc key value))
```

❶ Our exception type subclasses `java.lang.Exception`...

❷ ...and implements one of Clojure's interface, `java.lang.IDeref`, allowing it to participate in the `deref` abstraction, which we described in the Note on page 160. Clojure clients will thus be able to use `deref` and `@` on this exception type in order to obtain its map payload, just like any other dereferenceable value.

❸ We define a couple of constructors. The map we're providing specifies (in part) that our `CustomException(java.util.Map, String)` constructor will call the `Exception(String)` constructor on our superclass. The values that are actually passed to the superclass's constructor are determined by the `:init` function we identify.

❹ Our exception type will have a single final field, which we'll call `info`. We'll see how that field is used in a bit.

❺ We define two methods, `getInfo` and `addInfo`. We'll see shortly how these make for a useful Java API for our custom exception.

❻ `gen-class` generates constructors based on the signatures we specify. Those constructors will call the `:init` function here with the same arguments they are provided, where we can do the same kind of initialization work that would be done in a regular Java constructor.

❼ The `:init` function must always return a vector of two elements: the first is a vector of arguments to be passed to the superclass' constructor; the second is the value that is set on the `:state` final field. We're storing an atom containing our info `Map` in our `:state` field; since we're using an atom to coordinate change to that info `Map`, we copy the provided (possibly mutable) `Map` into an immutable Clojure map.

❽ The `-deref` and `-addInfo` functions (implementing the `deref` and `addInfo` methods) show how we can interact with the atom we stored in the `CustomException`'s final `info` field.

In contrast to the `gen-class` usage we saw in Example 9-16, this `com.clojurebook.Cus tomException` namespace exists solely to define the `CustomException` class. For these sorts of scenarios, you can "inline" the `gen-class` configuration directly in the namespace declaration, leaving the generated class name to inherit the namespace's name.

Let's see how we might use this from Clojure, with the help of some dummy functions that could easily find corollaries in many large applications:

```
(import 'com.clojurebook.CustomException)
;= nil
(defn perform-operation
  [& [job priority :as args]]
  (throw (CustomException. {:arguments args} "Operation failed")))     ❶
;= #'user/perform-operation
(defn run-batch-job
  [customer-id]
  (doseq [[job priority] {:send-newsletter :low
                          :verify-billings :critical
                          :run-payroll :medium}]
    (try
      (perform-operation job priority)
      (catch CustomException e                                         ❷
        (swap! (.info e) merge {:customer-id customer-id
                                :timestamp (System/currentTimeMillis)})
        (throw e)))))
;= #'user/run-batch-job
(try
  (run-batch-job 89045)
  (catch CustomException e
    (println "Error!" (.getMessage e) @e)))                            ❸
; Error! Operation failed {:timestamp 1309935234556, :customer-id 89045,
;                          :arguments (:verify-billings :critical)}
;= nil
```

❶ perform-operation is throwing a new CustomException, providing an info map that contains the arguments that were passed to it as a seq.

❷ Any higher-level function (run-batch-job here) in the call chain can catch CustomExceptions and add new data into the exception's info map. Since we're in Clojure, we don't need to rely upon the addInfo method we created in our gen-class form—we just reach into the atom hanging off of the exception from its info field and merge in a map of content information: a customer ID and a timestamp of when the exception occurred.

❸ Our top-level function can also catch the CustomException; rather than adding more information to it, it:

- Dereferences (via the @ reader macro) the exception by using the deref method we defined, which returns the accumulated map of information it is carrying.

- Obtains the original message provided when the exception was created via the .getMessage method. Recall that we did not define this method; the classes generated by gen-class inherit methods implemented by their base class, just like regular Java classes.

Being able to pass arbitrary data along with exceptions like this can be very powerful. Depending on the domain, you could even include a function in the payload of an exception being thrown (or rethrown by a function or method in the middle of a call chain) that some higher level code could invoke to retry an operation, perhaps with different arguments.[30]

Using our new exception type from Java is straightforward as well:

```
import com.clojurebook.CustomException;
import clojure.lang.PersistentHashMap;

public class BatchJob {
    private static void performOperation (String jobId, String priority) {
        throw new CustomException(PersistentHashMap.create("jobId", jobId,
                "priority", priority), "Operation failed");
    }

    private static void runBatchJob (int customerId) {
        try {
            performOperation("verify-billings", "critical");
        } catch (CustomException e) {
            e.addInfo("customer-id", customerId);
            e.addInfo("timestamp", System.currentTimeMillis());
            throw e;
        }
    }

    public static void main (String[] args) {
        try {
            runBatchJob(89045);
        } catch (CustomException e) {
            System.out.println("Error! " + e.getMessage() + " " + e.getInfo());
        }
    }
}
```

The only differences here compared to our in-Clojure usage of `CustomException` is that the `.addInfo` method is preferable to attempting to perform the equivalent of `swap!` in Java on the atom we stored in the exception class's `info` field, and `.getInfo` is better that the `.deref` method, as the former is typed as returning a `java.util.Map`.

Annotations

Annotations in Java are a sort of statically defined metadata that can be attached to class, method, and field declarations. This metadata is available either at compile time for use by code-generation facilities and other compile-time processes or at runtime via Java's reflection mechanisms. Annotations were introduced in Java 5 as a way for users of libraries and frameworks to define behavior and semantics declaratively, but alongside the affected entities. This is in contrast to XML files and other configuration

---

30. Doing this would be a weaker instance of a one-off *restart* mechanism. Restarts are a key feature of *condition systems*, a generalization of exception-based error handling, found in Smalltalk and some other Lisps. Such systems allow any code that encounters an exceptional condition to provide one or more restarts that higher level code can opt into invoking. Again, we'd recommend looking at Slingshot if you'd like to experiment with more flexible error handling: *https://github.com/scgilardi/slingshot*

mechanisms that separate valuable metadata from what the metadata was intended to describe. Annotations are now in widespread use in many Java environments, so it's important for Clojure to be able to fit seamlessly into such contexts.

Annotations Are for Integration

Annotations are one area of Clojure's JVM host that regularly makes Clojure programmers cringe. Partly, this is because they can be a source of tragic complexity, even in Java. However, the real disconnect is that, compared to the combination of Clojure's metadata, macro system, and runtime compilation capabilities, Java annotations just don't do much given the amount of work and verbosity they typically involve.

So, while you'll find Clojure libraries and applications happily using nearly every other aspect of JVM interoperability that Clojure provides, few will willingly use Java annotations unless doing so is imperative from an integration standpoint.

Producing annotated JUnit tests

Clojure recognizes metadata attached to any of its class-generation forms as annotations of the resulting classes, methods, or fields. Let's take a look at an example, where we use the `org.junit.Test` method annotation from the popular JUnit test framework (*http://junit.org*) to specify which methods defined by a **gen-class** class are to be treated as tests.

Example 9-18. Using JUnit annotations to mark gen-class methods as tests

```
(ns com.clojurebook.annotations.junit
  (:import (org.junit Test Assert))
  (:gen-class
    :name com.clojurebook.annotations.JUnitTest
    :methods [[^{org.junit.Test true} simpleTest [] void]        ❶
              [^{org.junit.Test {:timeout 2000}} timeoutTest [] void]  ❷
              [^{org.junit.Test {:expected NullPointerException}}   ❸
                badException [] void]]]))

(defn -simpleTest
  [this]
  (Assert/assertEquals (class this) com.clojurebook.annotations.JUnitTest))

(defn -badException
  [this]
  (Integer/parseInt (System/getProperty "nonexistent")))        ❹

(defn -timeoutTest
  [this]
  (Thread/sleep 10000))                                          ❺
```

❶ An annotation on the `simpleTest` method of the generated `gen-class` class. `^{org.junit.Test true}` is equivalent to a bare `@org.junit.Test` annotation on a Java method.

❷ Here, we're specifying a value of `2000` milliseconds for the `timeout` field of the `org.junit.Test` annotation for the `timeoutTest` method. This is equivalent to a `@org.junit.Test(timeout=2000)` annotation in Java.

❸ Similarly, we're specifying that `badException` should throw a `NullPointerException` when called by providing that class as a value for the `expected` field of the `org.junit.Test` annotation. This is equivalent to `@org.junit.Test(expected=Null PointerException)` in Java.

❹ Our implementation for the `badException` method is attempting to parse what will be a nonexistent system property as an integer; this will throw a `NumberFormatExcep tion`, not the `NullPointerException` we are indicating in our annotation's `expected` value.

❺ Our implementation for the `timeoutTest` method will sleep for 10 seconds, longer than the 2 seconds defined as acceptable in our annotation's `timeout` value.

AOT compiling this namespace will produce a `com.clojurebook.annotations.JUnit Test` class that you can add to JUnit's runner. One test will pass (the `simpleTest` assertion will always be true), but the other two will fail due to the configuration we provided in our annotation metadata. The JUnit runner's output will include:

```
There were 2 failures:
1) timeoutTest(com.clojurebook.annotations.JUnitTest)
java.lang.Exception: test timed out after 2000 milliseconds
2) throwsWrongException(com.clojurebook.annotations.JUnitTest)
java.lang.Exception: Unexpected exception,
expected<java.lang.NullPointerException> but was<java.lang.NumberFormatException>
```

The annotations we provided in our `gen-class` `:methods` declaration completely determined the test criteria applied to the resulting class, and could be dropped into an annotation-driven JUnit test environment as-is.

Implementing JAX-RS web service endpoints

JAX-RS is one of the more popular web service standards in the Java world. It defines a set of annotation-based APIs useful for creating REST-style services using standard Java classes. Containers that implement the standard use the annotations to discover classes mapped to requested URLs, determine appropriate class methods to invoke based on requests' HTTP methods, and set things like response `Content-Type`.

Let's define a JAX-RS *resource* class in Clojure; we could do this using `gen-class` again, but let's use `deftype` this time to illustrate some of the variety you can apply in using Clojure's annotation support:[31]

---

31. For all the details on `deftype`, please refer to "Defining Your Own Types" on page 270.

Example 9-19. A web service implemented using JAX-RS annotations

```clojure
(ns com.clojurebook.annotations.jaxrs
  (:import (javax.ws.rs Path PathParam Produces GET)))

(definterface Greeting                                    ❶
  (greet [^String visitor-name]))

(deftype ^{Path "/greet/{visitorname}"} GreetingResource []  ❷
  Greeting
  (^{GET true                                             ❸
     Produces ["text/plain"]}
    greet
    [this ^{PathParam "visitorname"} visitor-name]        ❹
    (format "Hello %s!" visitor-name)))
```

❶ We use the `definterface` form to define a single-method interface called `Greeting` for our `deftype` class to implement. It accepts a single String argument.

❷ A `deftype` class is defined, with a `Path` class annotation that has a value of "/greet/{visitorname}"; this means that any request to the JAX-RS container that matches this URL pattern will be routed to our `GreetingResource` class.

❸ Our greet method implementation has two annotations on it: `GET`, which makes this method eligible for `GET` requests, and `Produces`, which defines the `Content-Type` that our JAX-RS container will specify when sending our response. In this case, we're just returning a string from our greet method, so "text/plain" is appropriate.

❹ The URL pattern we defined in our `Path` class annotation provides for a single parameter, `visitorname`. We specify that that URL parameter should be aligned with our `visitor-name` method argument by adding a `PathParam` annotation with the same name we used in the URL pattern.

Once AOT-compiled, our `GreetingResource` can be deployed into any JAX-RS container. We can get one running within the REPL, using the Grizzly embedded web server:

```clojure
(com.sun.jersey.api.container.grizzly.GrizzlyWebContainerFactory/create
  "http://localhost:8080/"
  {"com.sun.jersey.config.property.packages" "com.clojurebook.annotations.jaxrs"})
```

This causes a Grizzly instance to start serving on `localhost:8080`, searching the `com.clojurebook.annotations.jaxrs` package for resource handlers; our `GreetingResource` class will be found and be used as a candidate request handler. Accessing *http://localhost: 8080/application.wadl* will return the JAX-RS container's WADL descriptor, where we can see our resource URL, `visitorname` parameter, and `text/plain` media type:

```
% curl http://localhost:8080/application.wadl
<?xml version="1.0" encoding="UTF-8" standalone="yes"?>
<application xmlns="http://research.sun.com/wadl/2006/10">
    <doc xmlns:jersey="http://jersey.java.net/"
        jersey:generatedBy="Jersey: 1.8 06/24/2011 12:17 PM"/>
    <resources base="http://localhost:8080/">
```

```
<resource path="/greet/{visitorname}">
    <param xmlns:xs="http://www.w3.org/2001/XMLSchema"
        type="xs:string" style="template" name="visitorname"/>
    <method name="GET" id="greet">
        <response>
            <representation mediaType="text/plain"/>
        </response>
    </method>
</resource>
    </resources>
</application>
```

GET-ing any URL of the form *http://localhost:8080/greet/<some-name>* will produce the result we generate from our annotated JAX-RS resource class:

```
% curl http://localhost:8080/greet/Jose
Hello Jose!
```

Using Clojure from Java

For the moment, let's assume that you would like to call into a Clojure library from Java, and that library does not define any types or classes.[32] To use that codebase, you'll need to tap into the Clojure "native" functions and constant values it defines in namespaces. Thankfully, doing so from Java is straightforward:

1. Load the Clojure code you want to use. This means reusing the standard `require`, `use`, or `load` functions provided in Clojure's `clojure.core` namespace.

2. Obtain references to the vars corresponding with each function or value defined in the namespaces you care about.

3. Call the functions and use the values however your application requires.

All we need to demonstrate Java→Clojure interop are two vars, one providing a function, the other some value. The value will come from a simple Clojure namespace:

Example 9-20. Simple Clojure namespace

```
(ns com.clojurebook.histogram)

(def keywords (map keyword '(a c a d b c a d c d k d a b b b c d e e e f a a a)))
```

The function we'll use is `frequencies` from the `clojure.core` namespace; it accepts any seqable value, and returns a map of the seq's elements and counts of their frequency of occurrence in the seq.[33]

Here is a Java class that uses `frequencies` with the `keywords` value as well as many others.

---

32. The techniques shown here apply to any JVM language; simply transliterate the Java code shown in Example 9-21 into your preferred language.

33. The result is technically a histogram; see *http://en.wikipedia.org/wiki/Histogram* for an overview of what histograms are.

Example 9-21. Using Clojure code in Example 9-20 from Java

```java
package com.clojurebook;

import java.util.ArrayList;
import java.util.Map;

import clojure.lang.IFn;
import clojure.lang.Keyword;
import clojure.lang.RT;
import clojure.lang.Symbol;
import clojure.lang.Var;

public class JavaClojureInterop {
    private static IFn requireFn = RT.var("clojure.core", "require").fn();        ❶
    private static IFn randIntFn = RT.var("clojure.core", "rand-int").fn();
    static {
        requireFn.invoke(Symbol.intern("com.clojurebook.histogram"));            ❷
    }

    private static IFn frequencies = RT.var("clojure.core", "frequencies").fn(); ❸
    private static Object keywords = RT.var("com.clojurebook.histogram",         ❹
            "keywords").deref();

    @SuppressWarnings({ "unchecked", "rawtypes" })
    public static void main(String[] args) {
        Map<Keyword, Integer> sampleHistogram =
            (Map<Keyword, Integer>)frequencies.invoke(keywords);                 ❺
        System.out.println("Number of :a keywords in sample histogram: " +
                sampleHistogram.get(Keyword.intern("a")));                       ❻
        System.out.println("Complete sample histogram: " + sampleHistogram);
        System.out.println();

        System.out.println("Histogram of chars in 'I left my heart in san fransisco': " +
                frequencies.invoke("I left my heart in San Fransisco".toLowerCase())); ❼
        System.out.println();

        ArrayList randomInts = new ArrayList();
        for (int i = 0; i < 500; i++) randomInts.add(randIntFn.invoke(10));
        System.out.println("Histogram of 500 random ints [0,10): " +
                frequencies.invoke(randomInts));                                 ❽
    }
}
```

❶ First, we grab a couple of standard library functions we'll use later, `require` and `rand-int`. Notice that we're using the `fn()` method; this returns a Clojure function (all of which implement the `IFn` interface). The only difference between `fn()` and `deref()` is that the former performs the cast to `IFn` for you.

❷ Before we attempt to access our non-core Clojure namespace, we need to load it; we use `require` via our `requireFn` `IFn` reference for that here. This is exactly equivalent to evaluating (`require 'com.clojurebook.histogram`) in Clojure.

❸ Here, we get a reference to the `clojure.core/frequencies` var; this is equivalent to `#'clojure.core/frequencies` in Clojure.

❹ Here, we `deref` the value of the `keywords` var, which is that seq of keywords shown in Example 9-20.

❺ We call the `frequencies` function with our sample data using one of `IFn`'s `invoke()` methods. Note that these methods (just like `Var.deref()`) return an `Object`; Clojure is a dynamic language, so the type of the value in a var can be *anything*. This comes quite naturally within Clojure, but it does require some thought in a statically typed environment like Java: here we know that the `fre quencies` function returns a `Map`, and we know that the data we provided to it are `Keywords`, so we can safely cast `frequencies`'s result to `Map<Keyword, Number>`.

❻ Values returned by Clojure are regular Java objects, and we can use them as such. That `Map` of `Keywords` and `Numbers` can be accessed just as if a Java method produced it. Here, we obtain the interned `:a` keyword to see how many times it appears in the seq of sample data.

❼❽ Thanks to the generic treatment of various concrete types in Clojure, we can call `frequencies` with Java-originated `Lists` of random integers and `Strings`, and expect useful results.

After compiling this Java class, running it results in this output:

```
% java -cp target/java-clojure-interop-1.0.0-jar-with-dependencies.jar
        com.clojurebook.JavaClojureInterop
Number of :a keywords in sample histogram: 8
Complete sample histogram: {:a 8, :c 4, :d 5, :b 4, :k 1, :e 3, :f 1}

Frequences of chars in 'I left my heart in san fransisco':
{\space 6, \a 3, \c 1, \e 2, \f 2, \h 1, \i 3, \l 1, \m 1,
 \n 3, \o 1, \r 2, \s 3, \t 2, \y 1}

Frequences of 500 random ints [0,10):
{0 60, 1 61, 2 55, 3 46, 4 37, 5 45, 6 47, 7 52, 8 49, 9 48}
```

Two potential tripping points are worth mentioning here:

- Loading Clojure code (as we do with require in Example 9-21) requires that either the source file(s) or the AOT compiled class files for the namespaces in question are on your classpath.
- In general, you should obtain references to the vars you need to access *once* (usually holding them in a static reference). Further, if you don't expect the values they hold to change,[34] then it's wise to obtain their values once (via either fn() or deref()). This avoids the (small, but not insignificant) overhead of runtime var lookup.

After understanding the above, you'll be able to do nearly anything you want with Clojure functions and data from within Java. The remainder of the Java→Clojure interop story consists of being able to utilize types and protocols defined in Clojure from Java as well.

Using deftype and defrecord Classes

Each of these forms[35] generates a Java-accessible class. Because of that, you can create and use instances of these classes in Java as if they were written in Java from the start.

Consider the following namespace:

Example 9-22. Defining some classes using deftype and defrecord

```
(ns com.clojurebook.classes)

(deftype Range                                                    ❶
  [start end]
  Iterable
  (iterator [this]
    (.iterator (range start end))))

(defn string-range                                                ❷
  "Returns a Range instance based on start and end values provided as Strings
   in a list / vector / array."
  [[start end]]
  (Range. (Long/parseLong start) (Long/parseLong end)))

(defrecord OrderSummary                                           ❸
  [order-number total])
```

---

34. See "Dynamic Scope" on page 201 for details about when and how vars can change value over time.

35. We detailed gen-class in "Defining Named Classes" on page 374; deftype and defrecord are covered in Chapter 6.

When it is loaded, Clojure generates two classes, `com.clojurebook.classes.Range` and `com.clojurebook.classes.OrderSummary`. We can use them from Java just as if they were written in Java; you will even see proper code completion in your IDE for every field and method implemented by the Clojure-generated classes.

Example 9-23. Using deftype and defrecord classes defined in Example 9-22 from Java

```java
package com.clojurebook;

import clojure.lang.IFn;
import clojure.lang.RT;
import clojure.lang.Symbol;
import com.clojurebook.classes.OrderSummary;
import com.clojurebook.classes.Range;

public class ClojureClassesInJava {
    private static IFn requireFn = RT.var("clojure.core", "require").fn();
    static {
        requireFn.invoke(Symbol.intern("com.clojurebook.classes"));
    }

    private static IFn stringRangeFn = RT.var("com.clojurebook.classes",
            "string-range").fn();

    public static void main(String[] args) {
        Range range = new Range(0, 5);                              ❶
        System.out.print(range.start + "-" + range.end + ": ");     ❷
        for (Object i : range) System.out.print(i + " ");           ❸
        System.out.println();

        for (Object i : (Range)stringRangeFn.invoke(args))          ❹
            System.out.print(i + " ");
        System.out.println();

        OrderSummary summary = new OrderSummary(12345, "$19.45");   ❺
        System.out.println(String.format("order number: %s; order total: %s",
                summary.order_number, summary.total));
        System.out.println(summary.keySet());
        System.out.println(summary.values());
    }
}
```

❶ Here, we create an instance of the `Range` deftype class, providing two arguments as it requires.

❷ As is detailed in "Types" on page 277, `deftype` classes do not automatically implement any interfaces; however, we can access its two `final` fields by using the names specified in the `deftype` definition, and...

❸ ...since `Range` was defined to implement `Iterable`, we can obtain an `Iterator` from it and use it in a `for` loop just like any other `Iterable` instance.

❹ `deftype` and `defrecord` classes can often require a number of parameters of particular types depending on how those classes are used; thus, it is often wise to provide a factory function that simplifies their instantiation. Here, we're using the `string-range` factory function that accepts any destructurable collection containing two strings, returning a `Range` instance based on the parsed integer values of those strings. This helps us avoid having to pick apart and parse the numeric input from the command line.

❺ `defrecord` classes are just like `deftype` classes, except they provide default implementations of certain interfaces; here, we create a `defrecord` instance, and demonstrate `final` field access as well as its default implementations of a couple of methods from the `java.util.Map` interface.

Once we compile our Java class, we can run it and see some results:

```
% java -cp target/java-clojure-interop-1.0.0-jar-with-dependencies.jar
    com.clojurebook.ClojureClassesInJava 5 10
0-5: 0 1 2 3 4
5 6 7 8 9
order number: 12345; order total: $19.45
#{:order-number :total}
(12345 "$19.45")
```

When do you need ahead of time (AOT) compilation?

If you are using the results of any class-generating Clojure form from Java (including `deftype`, `defrecord`, `defprotocol`, or `gen-class`), you *must* AOT compile the namespaces containing those forms. Java's compiler needs to have those class files available on disk in order to compile Java code that uses Clojure-generated classes. This is in contrast to use of `defrecord`, et al., in a Clojure-only scenario; in that case, Clojure simply generates and loads the necessary classes at runtime and loads them into the JVM without ever producing a file on disk.

We discuss AOT compilation in "Ahead-of-Time Compilation" on page 337 and the compilation issues related to mixed-source projects in "Building mixed-source projects" on page 351.

Implementing Protocol Interfaces

Protocols enable the succinct creation of very flexible domain models within Clojure.[36] While you can extend protocols within Clojure to service existing Java classes and interfaces, you may come to need to have a Java class participate in an existing protocol without modifying your Clojure codebase. For this purpose, protocols generate an interface, which you can have your Java class implement. For example, here's a Clojure namespace that contains a single protocol and two implementations of it, one for strings, the other a default implementation that will be dispatched to for all `Objects`:

```
(ns com.clojurebook.protocol)
```

---

36. See Chapter 6 to read all about protocols.

```
(defprotocol Talkable
  (speak [this]))

(extend-protocol Talkable
  String
  (speak [s] s)
  Object
  (speak [this]
    (str (-> this class .getName) "s can't talk!"))))
```

The Talkable protocol defines one function, speak, and generates a com.clojure book.protocol.Talkable interface that has a single speak method. We can implement that interface easily in Java:

Example 9-24. Implementing a Clojure protocol in Java via its generated interface

```java
package com.clojurebook;

import clojure.lang.IFn;
import clojure.lang.RT;
import clojure.lang.Symbol;
import com.clojurebook.protocol.Talkable;

public class BitterTalkingDog implements Talkable {

    public Object speak() {                                                    ❶
        return "You probably expect me to say 'woof!', don't you? Typical.";
    }

    Talkable mellow () {
        return new Talkable () {                                               ❷
            public Object speak() {
                return "It's a wonderful day, don't you think?";
            }
        };
    }

    public static void main(String[] args) {
        RT.var("clojure.core", "require").invoke(                              ❸
            Symbol.intern("com.clojurebook.protocol"));
        IFn speakFn = RT.var("com.clojurebook.protocol", "speak").fn();

        BitterTalkingDog dog = new BitterTalkingDog();

        System.out.println(speakFn.invoke(5));
        System.out.println(speakFn.invoke(
            "A man may die, nations may rise and fall, but an idea lives on."));
        System.out.println(dog.speak());
        System.out.println(speakFn.invoke(dog.mellow()));
    }
}
```

❶ Our class's implementation of `Talkable`'s `speak` method.

❷ The protocol's generated interface is just like any other Java interface; here, we define and return an instance of an anonymous inner class that implements the protocol's interface.

❸ We need to load the `com.clojurebook.protocol` namespace in order for those `String` and `Object` extensions of the protocol to be available, and look up a reference to the `speak` var that the protocol defined.

As we can see, Clojure provides for bidirectional interoperability. While we've demonstrated that Clojure can use and participate in Java's abstractions, the same applies to Java participating in Clojure's key abstractions.

The output of this class' `main` method when run from the command line:

```
% java com.clojurebook.BitterTalkingDog
java.lang.Integers can't talk!
A man may die, nations may rise and fall, but an idea lives on.
You probably expect me to say 'woof!', don't you? Typical.
It's a wonderful day, don't you think?
```

Collaborating Partners

While Clojure provides a swarm of compelling features of its own, it is unabashedly a JVM language that takes full advantage of that platform's assets, including its maturity, efficiency, and reliable operational characteristics. This gives you the opportunity to take advantage of the vast ecosystem of Java libraries, frameworks, and community, as well as contribute back to that ecosystem in equal measure.

## CHAPTER 10

REPL-Oriented Programming

The quality of your tools is incredibly important, and can make or break the experience with a language, not to mention your degree of success more broadly. Clojure's REPL, which we picked apart in Chapter 1, is its most foundational tool—and, as we'll see, perhaps its most powerful as well.

As we've stressed from the beginning, Clojure is always compiled and has no interpreter. Further, as we learned in Chapter 5, Clojure's compiler is fully available at runtime, making the entirety of the language available at runtime—and therefore available in the Clojure REPL. This means that:

- Code you load and run in the REPL (say, in your development environment) will work and perform exactly the same as code loaded from files on disk (as they might be in a production environment).
- You can use a REPL to define and redefine any Clojure construct at any time.

The ramifications of these characteristics make the REPL an absolutely indispensable part of every Clojure programmer's toolchain in ways that are generally not true for REPLs and interpreters offered by other languages. Here, we'll explore some of the workflows enabled by the REPL that might just change how you approach developing software.

Interactive Development

Interactive development is a loaded term that has been taken to mean all manner of things, as most modern languages offer some degree of interactivity. Even Java developers can interactively evaluate expressions, for example, when an application is paused on a breakpoint in a debugger. And, of course, Ruby, Python, and others provide REPLs with varying levels of sophistication, although they are generally not integrated with other tools (like your editor), are limited to running in a command line, and their host languages often place significant restrictions on how and what code can be modified or redefined at runtime.

In contrast, interactive development in Clojure as enabled by its REPL relaxes each of these constraints. As you use Clojure, you'll find that building applications interactively with the aid of a persistent REPL session is the most productive approach you can choose, with little to nothing between your fingertips and what's going on inside of the Clojure runtime and the JVM.

Example 10-1. A tiny Swing "application"

```
(ns com.clojurebook.fn-browser
  (:import (javax.swing JList JFrame JScrollPane JButton)
           java.util.Vector))

(defonce fn-names (->> (ns-publics 'clojure.core)              ❶
                       (map key)
                       sort
                       Vector.
                       JList.))

(defn show-info [] )                                           ❷

(defonce window (doto (JFrame. "\"Interactive Development!\"")
                  (.setSize (java.awt.Dimension. 400 300))
                  (.add (JScrollPane. fn-names))               ❸
                  (.add java.awt.BorderLayout/SOUTH
                    (doto (JButton. "Show Info")               ❹
                      (.addActionListener (reify java.awt.event.ActionListener
                                            (actionPerformed [_ e] (show-info))))))
                  (.setVisible true)))
```

❶ fn-names is a JList; the model will contain symbols naming each public var in the clojure.core namespace, sorted lexicographically.

❷ The show-info function will remain a no-op for now. We'll fix that later.

❸ That list component will be held within a scrollable container that is added to a window that is sized sanely.

❹ Also added to the window is a button with a click listener that will call the temporarily no-op show-info function.

You can load this code into a Clojure REPL, or save it into a *com/clojurebook/ fn_browser.clj* file on your classpath[1] and load it via (**require** 'com.clojurebook.fn-browser). In either case, assuming you aren't using Clojure in a headless environment like a server, you'll see a Swing window like this one in a pop up:

---

1. The organization of Clojure codebases and the classpath concept are both described in Chapter 8.

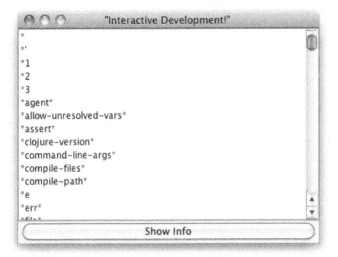

Unless you're still using a language that demands a discrete *write→compile→debug* cycle, being able to conjure up a UI from a REPL is not a huge revelation. What is a little more interesting is that we can seamlessly make changes to our running environment by just loading more code in any way that is convenient for us.

To demonstrate, let's make that Show Info button do something, as it is entirely inert so far. To do this, we simply need to redefine the show-info function that our click listener is delegating to do something interesting...such as pop up the documentation for the clojure.core function that is selected in the list:

```clojure
(in-ns 'com.clojurebook.fn-browser)

(import '(javax.swing JOptionPane JTextArea))

(defn show-info
  []
  (when-let [selected-fn (.getSelectedValue fn-names)]
    (JOptionPane/showMessageDialog
      window
      (-> (ns-resolve 'clojure.core selected-fn)    ❶
        meta                                        ❷
        :doc                                        ❸
        (JTextArea. 10 40)                          ❹
        JScrollPane.)
      (str "Doc string for clojure.core/" selected-fn)
      JOptionPane/INFORMATION_MESSAGE)))
```

❶ If a function name has been selected in the list component, we resolve it within the clojure.core namespace, using ns-resolve. This returns a var...

❷ ...which we obtain the metadata of...

❸ ...and get out of that metadata its :doc value, which is where Clojure stores documentation strings provided when vars are defined. See "Docstrings" on page 199 for more about documentation strings.

❹ The documentation for the function then forms the initial content of a JTextArea component, which is used as the "message" in the JOptionPane pop-up box.

You can load this code into the REPL or you can edit the *fn_browser.clj* file you created and reload it via (require 'com.clojurebook.fn-browser :reload).[2] In either case, once you redefine show-info, the button's click listener will call the newly defined function *without recreating, modifying, or otherwise touching that button.*

Selecting a function in clojure.core that has some documentation and clicking the Get Info button will pop up that documentation:

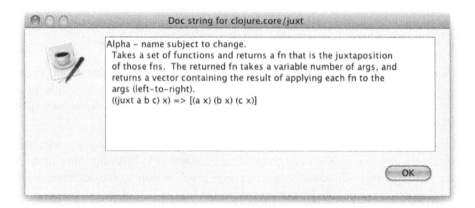

Using defonce to Avoid Var Clobbering

Once you have some code in a file that you are loading and reloading into a Clojure process—whether via the REPL or using the :reload and :reload-all options to use and require—you may have some var definitions that you *do not* want to reevaluate. For example, we would not want to be redefining the window and fn-names in Example 10-1; doing so would result in the creation of a new window and a new list component every time we reloaded the file.

The solution to this is defonce. Just like def and its brethren, defonce defines the value of a var in the current namespace, but it will not redefine any var that already has a value. Using defonce therefore allows us to mix the definition of vars that should remain fixed throughout the lifetime of our application (like window in our example, or perhaps

---

2. In the latter case, you would simply add the JOptionPane and JTextArea imports to the :import declaration in the file's ns form; loading the file will cause these additional class dependencies to be imported into the namespace. If you provide the :reload-all flag to require here, it would further cause all :required or :used namespaces to be transitively reloaded as well.

a database connection pool in a web application) and other vars that we may want to readily redefine through the course of development and perhaps into production settings.

This has been a particularly basic example, but hopefully illustrates some of the flexibility that Clojure's REPL interaction provides. As convenient as it might be to interactively tweak the behavior of user interfaces without restarting the application or rebuilding the window, the same kind of flexibility and immediate feedback applied to the development of data-intensive algorithms or complicated domain models yield immeasurable benefits.

The Persistent, Evolving Environment

To some, what we've demonstrated so far may appear to be only an incremental improvement over existing workflows, especially in languages like Ruby, Python, and PHP. After all, these and other languages can interactively load code, and can, in general, redefine various constructs when they are deployed in a long-running environment. The parallels only go so deep, though:

Clojure does not require a file-based workflow.   Python, Ruby, and PHP require that code be available on disk in order for it to be loaded.[3] While that's a perfectly reasonable option when using Clojure—as we alluded to in our previous example, you can use the `:reload` option when requiring a previously loaded namespace—it is by no means required. You can load code into a Clojure process without ever touching disk, either via direct REPL interaction (a.k.a. typing), or by using the REPL-oriented commands provided by your Clojure development environment to load files, namespaces, or entire projects at will.

Clojure's dynamicism is explicitly provided for by the language and runtime.   Many of the foundational aspects of Clojure's design explicitly encourage (or, *do not discourage*) dynamic redefinition of its constructs at runtime. The reification of namespaces and vars, the primacy of *loading code* versus requiring that code be available on disk or in an editor buffer, the widespread use of runtime bytecode generation and class loading, the narrowing of the space between compile time and runtime—these and many other metafeatures of Clojure conspire to make it usable as a persistent canvas upon which you may sketch your vision.

This may simply sound like hype...unless you have experienced a Clojure development environment equipped with nominal REPL facilities. Such environments allow you to readily pair your text editor to one or more persistent running REPLs. This pairing allows you to effortlessly move between writing code in an editor (or two, or nine)— where you can send single expressions or entire files' worth of code from that editor to

---

3. This isn't technically true in Ruby's case, but many tools and the cultural norms surrounding Ruby do push it in this direction.

your persistent REPL with a single keystroke—and interacting with the state of the Clojure runtime associated with that REPL in order to check intermediate results, experiment with half-formed ideas without sullying our projects' "real" source code, and in general interrogate the Clojure runtime to verify your work and guide your next steps. It is not uncommon for Clojure programmers to use the same JVM/Clojure process for days, incrementally modifying the runtime and their application's loaded code until its behavior meets their expectations and the tests they've defined.

At its best, this experience has sometimes been referred to as *flow*, a state wherein one's focus, clarity of vision, and ready access to critical information enables a heightened degree of ability, sense of control, and breadth of perspective. Clojure certainly doesn't have the market on flow cornered; programmers have described enjoying this state when using all sorts of languages. However, it's not unreasonable to speculate that Clojure enables it more than most, thanks in no small part to its rich REPL capabilities and experience, and thus its tighter feedback loop between program and programmer. This was discussed at length in a talk at the 2010 Clojure Conj:[4]

> Programming with a REPL is more like mentoring a partner in some ways. We can investigate its current state, what is happening with the machine, what our algorithms are doing underneath—all in a very rich way with the REPL.
>
> —Tom Faulhaber, *Lisp, Functional Programming, and the State of Flow*

Once you have an understanding of how the REPL works, and a sense of how it might be utilized in your programming practice, the best way to encourage this sort of experience is to make sure your toolchain is in order.

Tooling

Because of the complexity and verbosity of Java, "Java tooling" has always implied the use of truly Integrated Development Environments (IDEs) like Eclipse and IntelliJ IDEA: extensive code completion, refactoring, class hierarchy visualization, and other features aren't just niceties, they are hard requirements for most Java programmers. In contrast, dynamic programming languages (including Python and Ruby) generally demand only a capable text editor and a command prompt. Most Clojure programmers hew closer to the latter model,[5] with one key difference: while a capable text editor is a must, having access to a Clojure REPL—preferably well-integrated into one's editor and other facilities—is at least as important, if not more so.

Thankfully, accomplishing this is a straightforward task, and so reasonable Clojure support is available for a variety of popular editors (like Emacs, vim, TextMate, jEdit,

---

4. Video and slides available at *http://blip.tv/clojure/tom-faulhaber-lisp-functional-programming-and-the -state-of-flow-4539472*.

5. Many Clojure programming environments provide things like code completion and such as well, but we're talking about minimum expectations here, not the open set of what exists and what is desirable.

and so on) as well as IDEs (like Eclipse, Intellij IDEA, and NetBeans). Getting started with any of these options is fairly easy;[6] all other things being equal, we recommend using the tools you're already most comfortable with and that fit best into your existing style and workflow.[7] To give you some starting point for comparison, we'll briefly give an overview of the Clojure support provided by the two most popular tools used in the community that each represent orthogonal approaches to Clojure tooling (and tooling in general, perhaps): Eclipse and Emacs.

First, let's take a look at some of the basic practical tools that all Clojure REPLs provide that you'll want to be familiar with to enhance your programming experience.

The Bare REPL

You'll be using the Clojure REPL on a daily basis, and that means using its basic utilities. Regardless of whether you're using the most basic text editor with a REPL in a separate command line or the largest IDE with integrated REPL sessions, these utilities will be available and indispensable.[8]

REPL-bound vars. There are a number of vars that are typically only bound within a REPL session that provide conveniences necessary in an interactive environment.

- *1, *2, and *3 hold the values of the most recently evaluated expressions. For example, *1 corresponds to _ in Ruby and Python.
- *e provides the last uncaught exception that occurred in the REPL session. This is similar to the tuple of sys.last_type, sys.last_value, and sys.last_traceback in Python.

These vars and the automatic management of them can be very handy while interactively exploring APIs and your data:

```
(split-with keyword? [:a :b :c 1 2 3])
;= [(:a :b :c) (1 2 3)]
(zipmap (first *1) (second *1))
;= {:c 3, :b 2, :a 1}
(apply zipmap (split-with keyword? [:a :b :c 1 2 3]))
;= {:c 3, :b 2, :a 1}
```

---

6. See *http://dev.clojure.org/display/doc/Clojure+Tools* for pointers.

7. To stress the point: even if you're most comfortable with *notepad.exe*, you should use it as long as you have a REPL at the ready in a nearby terminal window. We think there are better options, and you may think so as well after a time, but there are few things more frustrating than trying to learn both a new programming language and a new set of tools all at the same time.

8. If you happen to be starting your REPL on the command line (i.e., via a direct java invocation) instead of using the REPL provided by Leiningen, Counterclockwise, Emacs, or really any other Clojure tool beyond the console, then you will almost certainly want one of JLine (*http://jline.sourceforge.net*) or rlwrap (*http://utopia.knoware.nl/~hlub/rlwrap/*). Clojure's built-in REPL does not provide things like command recall (i.e., hitting cursor-up to bring up the prior line sent to the REPL) or inline editing of the text not yet sent to the REPL; both JLine or rlwrap will add such capabilities to that built-in REPL.

`clojure.repl/pst` will print the stack trace of any exception provided, but will use the one bound to *e by default:

```
(throw (Exception. "foo"))
;= Exception foo  user/eval1 (NO_SOURCE_FILE:1)
(pst)
; Exception foo
;    user/eval1 (NO_SOURCE_FILE:1)
;    clojure.lang.Compiler.eval (Compiler.java:6465)
; ...
```

clojure.repl. Speaking of `clojure.repl`, it provides a bunch of utilities that are very handy at the REPL. You saw `pst` above; there's also `apropos`, which shows you which functions in loaded namespaces match a given regular expression or string:

```
(apropos #"^ref")
;= (ref-max-history refer-clojure ref-set
;=  ref-history-count ref ref-min-history refer)
```

`find-doc` does much the same, except it searches within documentation and prints all of the information associated with matching vars.

There's also `source`, which prints the source code of any function that was loaded from source:

```
(source merge)
; (defn merge
;   "Returns a map that consists of the rest of the maps conj-ed onto
;   the first.  If a key occurs in more than one map, the mapping from
;   the latter (left-to-right) will be the mapping in the result."
;   {:added "1.0"
;    :static true}
;   [& maps]
;   (when (some identity maps)
;     (reduce1 #(conj (or %1 {}) %2) maps)))
```

Finally, there's `doc`, which prints only the documentation for a given var; and `dir`, which prints a list of the public vars declared in the given namespace:

```
(require 'clojure.string)
;= nil
(dir clojure.string)
; blank?
; capitalize
; escape
; join
; lower-case
; replace
; replace-first
; reverse
; split
; split-lines
; trim
; trim-newline
; triml
```

```
; trimr
; upper-case
```

It is a rare Clojure REPL that doesn't start with `clojure.repl` loaded with its useful functions always available.

Introspecting namespaces

Namespaces are entities of their own, just as concrete and malleable as any data structure. There are a number of functions you can use to introspect and modify namespaces in the REPL; let's look at some of them.[9]

Note that, most of the time, you'll not have to touch these functions at all. However, if you have mistakenly defined some functions or data in a namespace, you can use these functions to find and potentially remove the offending definitions. This can help you to get out of some situations that would otherwise require restarting your application or REPL session, such as needing to define a `deftype` type with the same name as an existing Java class that you've already imported into a namespace.

ns-map, ns-imports, ns-refers, ns-publics, ns-aliases, ns-interns.   These functions all return a map of symbols that have been mapped within the given namespace to either a var or imported class. That is, where `refer` and `import` and `def` register symbols within a namespace, these functions report on those different kinds of mappings.

```
(ns clean-namespace)
;= nil
(ns-aliases *ns*)
;= {}
(require '[clojure.set :as set])
;= nil
(ns-aliases *ns*)
;= {set #<Namespace clojure.set>}
(ns-publics *ns*)
;= {}
(def x 0)
;= #'clean-namespace/x
(ns-publics *ns*)
;= {x #'clean-namespace/x}
```

ns-unmap, ns-unalias.   The former can be used to remove mappings of symbols to vars or imported classes, while the latter will remove a namespace alias.

```
(ns-unalias *ns* 'set)
;= nil
(ns-aliases *ns*)
;= {}
(ns-unmap *ns* 'x)
;= nil
```

---

9. `(apropos #"(ns-|-ns)")` will provide you with a more complete list you can explore on your own.

```
(ns-publics *ns*)
;= {}
```

remove-ns.   This is the "nuclear option" of namespace management. Where ns[10] will create a namespace, `remove-ns` will drop one from Clojure's authoritative name-space map.

```
(in-ns 'user)
;= #<Namespace user>
(filter #(= 'clean-namespace (ns-name %)) (all-ns))
;= (#<Namespace clean-namespace>)
(remove-ns 'clean-namespace)
;= #<Namespace clean-namespace>
(filter #(= 'clean-namespace (ns-name %)) (all-ns))
;= ()
```

This means that all code and data defined in vars interned in the dropped namespace become inaccessible, and *eligible* for garbage collection. Of course, if some reference to a function, protocol, or data defined in the dropped namespace is being held else-where, it will not be garbage-collected.

Structural editing of Clojure source code

While we are decidedly egalitarian when it comes to others' choice of text editors, there is one particular facility that is so compelling when editing Clojure source code that we must mention it: *paredit*, an editing mode that originated in the Emacs community that simplifies the editing of s-expressions, and is something that many Clojure programmers consider a must-have.

Most high-quality Java editors provide various structural selection fa-cilities, such as automatically inserting pairs of braces or expanding your selection to include the enclosing element, expression, or scope. paredit provides Clojure equivalents, and most implementations go far beyond the concepts supported in Java editors to include things like moving your cursor or selection one s-expression at a time, moving whole ex-pressions around, and automatically wrapping selected expressions with braces, brackets, or parentheses as needed to ensure that your source code is structurally sound.

In short, if you ever find it difficult to edit Clojure code—for example, easily selecting individual s-expressions or maintaining matching paren-theses, braces, or brackets—you would almost certainly benefit from using your editor's paredit-style features, or switching to an editor that provides them (most do).

---

10. Or, far less commonly, `create-ns`.

Eclipse

Eclipse—paired with Counterclockwise,[11] a plug-in that provides Clojure support within Eclipse—provides a comprehensive set of features for Clojure development: editing, code completion, REPL integration, introspection, debugging, and profiling. Eclipse certainly can't be considered lightweight, but in exchange, it does provide a compelling mix of tooling that is perhaps more approachable and accommodating for many programmers that appreciate familiar and discoverable user interfaces. In addition, if you need to work with Java as well as Clojure, possibly in the same project, then it is hard to beat (or, relinquish) the Java facilities that only IDEs like Eclipse offer.

Clojure editing. While Counterclockwise's Clojure editing support is not quite as sophisticated as that provided by Emacs, it is nonetheless very capable and among the best available. It provides a partial implementation of paredit,[12] excellent syntax highlighting, and a boatload of useful text-editing facilities it inherits from Eclipse. Each Clojure editor also feeds into Eclipse's standard "outline" view, which maintains a listing of all of the top-level expressions (usually function definitions) contained in the current file:

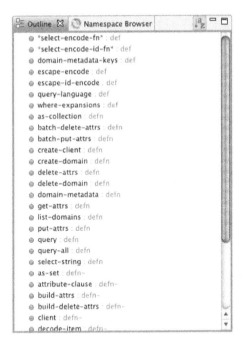

11. Go to *http://dev.clojure.org/display/doc/Getting+Started+with+Eclipse+and+Counterclockwise* to get started; the Counterclockwise project home is at *http://code.google.com/p/counterclockwise/*.

12. Described earlier in "Structural editing of Clojure source code" (page 402).

Eclipse and Counterclockwise provide a lot of hints within their respective interfaces to help you along in learning things like which commands are available and what the default keyboard shortcuts are in various contexts (some of which are different on different operating systems). For help at any time, refer to the "Clojure" menu (and contextual menu in editors) that Counterclockwise adds to Eclipse, as well as the Clojure editor reference page available by choosing "Dynamic Help" from the "Help" menu when any Clojure file is open.

REPL integration. Counterclockwise uses nREPL[13] (a Clojure REPL server and client library that is used by other Clojure tooling and is easily embeddable in Clojure applications) as the basis of its REPL integration. This allows you to connect and interact with any Clojure application running an nREPL server, which includes all the Clojure processes that you launch through Eclipse and Counterclockwise. Beyond being able to evaluate expressions, Counterclockwise's REPLs are integrated with the editor, allowing you to load code from open files and based on current selections, and include support for command history and code completion:

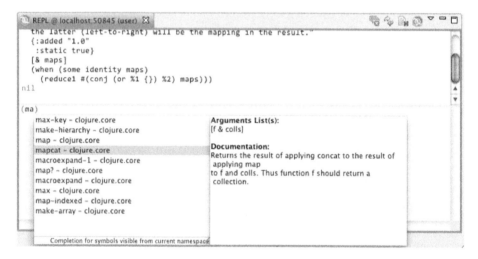

Once you have a running REPL, the same code completion as well as jump-to-definition actions become available in editors associated with the running REPL's project.

Namespace browsing. Counterclockwise also provides a graphical namespace browser. This view allows you to browse and search through all of the namespaces and vars loaded and defined in the Clojure environment to which the current REPL is connected:

---

13. *http://github.com/clojure/tools.nrepl.*

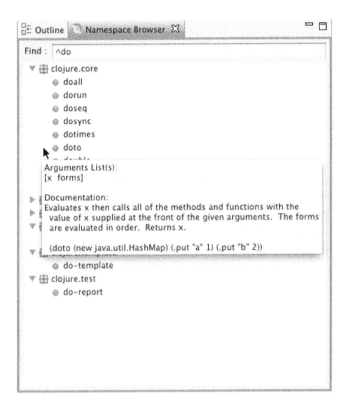

You can filter the list of vars (optionally using a regular expression as shown above). Hovering over a var name will display its documentation in a pop up; double-clicking will open the file the var is defined within and go to its definition.

Emacs

Emacs (*http://www.gnu.org/s/emacs/*) is a powerful and extensible text editor that has been a mainstay of Lisp programming for decades. Clojure support for Emacs is achieved by combining a number of modular tools and libraries.

There are two primary ways to work with Clojure in Emacs: `inferior-lisp` and SLIME. Both methods depend on having `clojure-mode` installed.

clojure-mode and paredit

Whether you use `inferior-lisp` or SLIME, `clojure-mode` and `paredit` are essential.

`clojure-mode` (*https://github.com/technomancy/clojure-mode*) provides Emacs with Clojure-specific editor functionality like syntax-highlighting, indentation, and code navigation. It also includes the helpful `clojure-test-mode`, which provides added shortcuts for automated testing using `clojure.test`. Instructions for setting up `clojure-mode` are found on its main project page.

In addition to `clojure-mode`, the aforementioned `paredit.el` (*http://www.emacswiki.org/emacs/ParEdit*) is a must-have minor mode for Emacs that provides support for automatic handling of parentheses; it is included in Emacs.

inferior-lisp

`inferior-lisp`[14] is the most basic way to use Clojure in Emacs. It is used to start a Clojure REPL in a subprocess, and displays this REPL in an Emacs buffer. You can use this REPL like any you might work with on a command line, but `inferior-lisp` also allows you to interactively send Clojure code from open source files in buffers to that REPL.

---

14. Named as such not to make a connotation regarding its quality, but to indicate that the Lisp being used is in a subprocess started by Emacs: *http://www.gnu.org/s/libtool/manual/emacs/External-Lisp.html*.

One advantage of `inferior-lisp` over SLIME is that `inferior-lisp` is built into Emacs, and setup involves setting a single variable in your Emacs configuration file (or via `M-:`) to tell Emacs how to invoke Clojure:

```
(setq inferior-lisp-program "lein repl")
```

The value of `inferior-lisp-program` can be a Leiningen invocation as above, an invocation of Java, or any other command that starts a Clojure REPL such as `mvn clojure:repl`, and so on. Once set, a Clojure REPL can then be started by executing the command `C-c C-z`. Note that the command in `inferior-lisp-program` is run in Emacs' current directory; depending on where you started Emacs, you may need to set its current directory (via `M-x cd`) before starting the `inferior-lisp` process. This is the fastest and easiest way to get Clojure up and running in Emacs:

```
(ns com.clojurebook.url-shortener
  (:use [compojure.core :only (GET PUT POST defroutes)])
  (:require (compojure handler route)
            [ring.util.response :as response]))
[]
(def ^:private counter (atom 0))

(def ^:private mappings (ref {}))

(defn url-for
  [id]
  (@mappings id))
-:--- url_shortener.clj  Top (5,0)     Git:master  (Clojure Fill)
REPL started; server listening on localhost port 55657
user=> #'com.clojurebook.url-shortener/app
user=> (in-ns 'com.clojurebook.url-shortener)
#<Namespace com.clojurebook.url-shortener>
com.clojurebook.url-shortener=> (dosync (alter mappings assoc :a 5))
{:a 5}
com.clojurebook.url-shortener=> █



U:**-  *inferior-lisp*  All L7   (Inferior Lisp:run)
```

Editing support is very basic compared to SLIME, but it may be all you need. The most common workflow when editing Clojure code in Emacs is to have one or more Emacs windows containing your source code, and an additional Emacs window containing a REPL buffer. Code can be edited in one window, and then sent to the REPL via one of many commands. Both `inferior-lisp` and SLIME offer this capability, though the commands differ (see Table 10-1).

Table 10-1. inferior-lisp

Keystroke	M-x command	Description
C-c C-z	run-lisp	Start the configured inferior-lisp process with the command set in inferior-lisp-program.
C-M-x	lisp-eval-defun	Evaluate the top-level form (such as a defn expression) under the cursor.
C-x C-e	lisp-eval-last-sexp	Evaluate the s-expression that precedes the cursor.
C-c C-l	clojure-load-file	Load the current file in its entirety.

SLIME

SLIME[15] is an Emacs library that provides advanced editing and REPL capabilities for many Lisps, including (but not limited to) Clojure. SLIME provides a more comprehensive development experience compared to inferior-lisp including a persistent command history, code completion, namespace introspection, a debugger, and so on.

Emacs' extensibility can be both a boon and a bane. Emacs can probably do anything you could possibly imagine a text editor doing, but setting it up to do so can be a daunting task.

In particular, setup instructions for SLIME and other Clojure-related tools for Emacs have changed repeatedly and rapidly as Clojure support for Emacs has evolved and matured. The Internet is currently littered with old blog posts and wiki entries giving outdated methods for setting up Clojure support in Emacs.

We suggest heading straight to *http://dev.clojure.org/display/doc/Getting +Started+with+Emacs* for installation and setup instructions, a wiki page that is consistently kept up to date by the maintainers of the various projects that provide Clojure support within Emacs.

In order to use SLIME, your Clojure project must be configured to provide a *swank* server; a corollary to nREPL, swank is SLIME's REPL interaction protocol. The easiest way to do this is to use lein to add swank-clojure (a Clojure implementation of swank) as a development-time dependency to your Leiningen project:

```
lein plugin install lein-swank 1.4.3
```

...or, you can add it to your *project.clj* file's vector of plug-ins permanently:

```
[lein-swank "1.4.3"]
```

SLIME can then be invoked from within Emacs via M-x clojure-jack-in once you have a file from the project for which you'd like to start the REPL open in the current buffer. If anything goes awry, be sure to check *http://dev.clojure.org/display/doc/Getting +Started+with+Emacs* for the latest instructions.

---

15. An acronym of *Superior Lisp Interaction Mode for Emacs*: *http://common-lisp.net/project/slime/*.

You can use all of the keybindings provided by `inferior-lisp` in SLIME, but the latter provides many more commands for sending code from a buffer to a running REPL and performing various operations and introspections within the context of the current file and within the Clojure/SLIME environment. Some examples are shown in Table 10-2.

Table 10-2. Common SLIME commands and their key bindings

Keystroke	M-x command	Description
C-c C-c	slime-compile-defun	Evaluate the top-level form under the cursor.
C-c C-k	slime-compile-and-load-file	Load the current file in its entirety.
M-.	slime-edit-definition	Jump to the definition of the symbol under the cursor.
C-c C-m	slime-macroexpand-1	macroexpand-1 the expression following the cursor.
C-c M-m	slime-macroexpand-all	macroexpand-all the expression following the cursor.
C-c I	slime-inspect	Display a navigable representation of the value of a given symbol or class.

The inspector.   Finding your way through the contours of a data structure or API can sometimes be daunting, especially when using some Java libraries. SLIME provides a way to visualize Clojure collections and Java objects and classes through its *inspector*. Just key `C-c I` and type in the symbol or expression for which you would like to inspect the value—or, put your cursor on a symbol of interest and type the keystroke:

```
      :dynamic true}
    *response-code* nil)

(defn- send-body
   [^URLConnection connection data]
   (with-open [output (.getOutputStream connection)]
    (io/copy data output)
    ; make sure streams are closed so we don't hold locks on files on Windows
    (when (instance? InputStream data) (.close ^InputStream data))))

(defn- get-response
-:---  http_client.clj   39% (52,5)   Git-master  (Clojure Hi Slime[clojure] Fill)
class java.net.URLConnection
--------------------------
Type: class java.lang.Class
---
Fields:
--▮
Methods:
   public java.lang.String java.net.URLConnection.toString()
   public java.net.URL java.net.URLConnection.getURL()
   public java.lang.Object java.net.URLConnection.getContent(java.lang.Class[]) thro →
   public java.lang.Object java.net.URLConnection.getContent() throws java.io.IOExce →
   public java.io.InputStream java.net.URLConnection.getInputStream() throws java.io →
   public java.security.Permission java.net.URLConnection.getPermission() throws jav →
U:%*-  *Slime Inspector*  Top L6     (Slime-Inspector)
```

You can do the same thing within values and classes included in the output of the inspector (or just hit return with your cursor over a symbol or value of interest), thus making it easy to visually dig through complicated APIs or large data structures.

Debugging.   When an exception is thrown at a SLIME REPL, you'll be dumped into the SLIME debugger. The debugger can also be invoked by manually setting breakpoints in your code:

```
(defn debug-me
  [x y]
  (let [z (merge x y)]
    (swank.core/break)))
```

Running (debug-me {:a 5} {"b" 5/6}) will give you something like Figure 10-1.

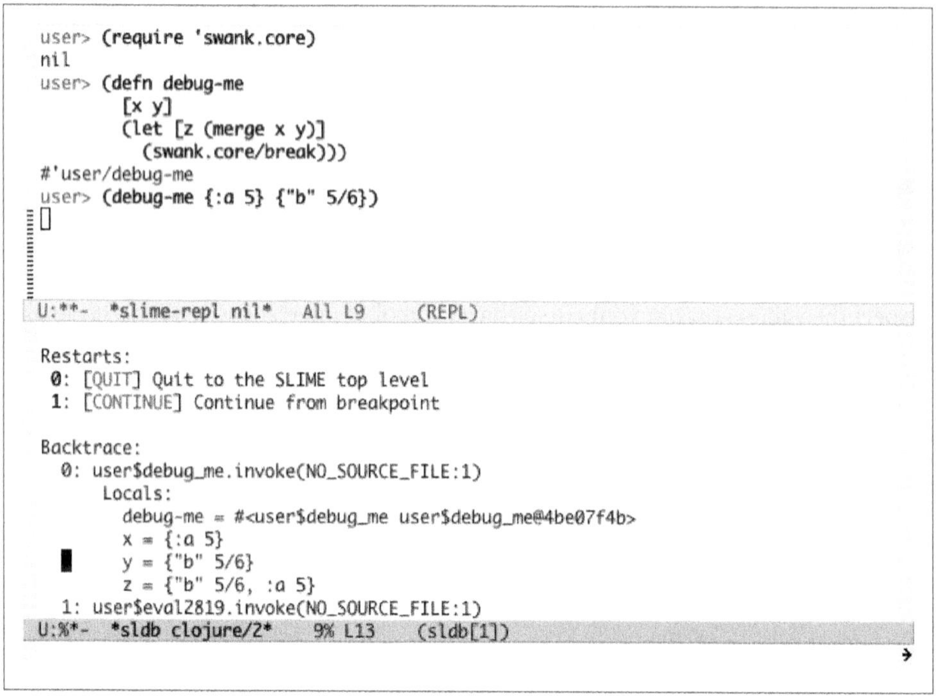

```
user> (require 'swank.core)
nil
user> (defn debug-me
        [x y]
        (let [z (merge x y)]
          (swank.core/break)))
#'user/debug-me
user> (debug-me {:a 5} {"b" 5/6})
[]
```
```
U:**-  *slime-repl nil*   All L9      (REPL)
```
```
Restarts:
  0: [QUIT] Quit to the SLIME top level
  1: [CONTINUE] Continue from breakpoint

Backtrace:
  0: user$debug_me.invoke(NO_SOURCE_FILE:1)
      Locals:
        debug-me = #<user$debug_me user$debug_me@4be07f4b>
        x = {:a 5}
        y = {"b" 5/6}
        z = {"b" 5/6, :a 5}
  1: user$eval2819.invoke(NO_SOURCE_FILE:1)
U:%*-  *sldb clojure/2*    9% L13     (sldb[1])
                                                       →
```

Figure 10-1. The SLIME debugger in action

Clicking parts of the backtrace causes locals and their values to be displayed as in the inspector, and you can dig into those values in the same ways as well.

Of course, when a debugger is active, Clojure is still live, and the REPL is still active, so arbitrary expressions can be evaluated: your program's current state can be inspected or tweaked, functions can be defined or redefined, and so on. In particular, the locals in scope from a swank.core/break call can be accessed and manipulated in the SLIME

REPL while the thread of execution that hit the breakpoint remains paused. This is a big advantage of programming in an interactive environment.

Debugging, Monitoring, and Patching Production in the REPL

In "The Persistent, Evolving Environment" on page 397, we talked about the "persistent, evolving environment" that the REPL provides in a development context. What was left unsaid there is that those environments to which the REPL connects us are not limited to development contexts. There is no technical reason why a REPL cannot be leveraged in "deployed" contexts—including production—to provide the same kind of dynamicism enjoyed in development.

Remember that the fundamental unit of interaction between you and a Clojure environment is *loading code*: very simply, evaluating expressions, from files on disk or provided as input to a REPL, which define functions and values and effect changes to the environment. No other special requirements apply. While some REPLs are tied to a local operating system process and console (including the default REPL provided by Clojure that we introduced in Example 1-1), that is by no means universal. In fact, many (if not most) Clojure development tools—including Counterclockwise for Eclipse and SLIME for Emacs—*only* use "remote" REPL processes.

When you start REPLs in these tools, a new JVM process is spawned as you would expect, but that process is initialized to start a REPL server, to which the tool connects: all of the code you load from such tools, and all of the interactions you have using their REPL user interfaces all occurs over a network pipe, albeit one connected to `local host`. Very simply, these REPL servers accept code sent to them as text, and apply the same *read*, *evaluate*, *print* process to that code as any other REPL, with the printed results sent back to your tool's REPL UI instead of to `*out*`.

 The Clojure REPL servers used by both Counterclockwise and SLIME— nREPL and swank-clojure, respectively—can be easily integrated into your application so you can open a REPL to deployed instances of your application, wherever they may be running. Both use Clojure libraries that are readily available as Maven dependencies. For details, check the projects' documentation for embedding at *http://github.com/clojure/tools.nrepl* and *https://github.com/technomancy/swank-clojure*.

In short, as long as you can get your deployed application to start a REPL server, and you can connect your Clojure tooling to it, you can interact with that remote Clojure environment using its REPL as if it were running under your desk. However, it's safe to say that, except perhaps in very special circumstances, you shouldn't be using a REPL connection to a deployed, nonlocal development runtime to do new development. Rather, a REPL connection to your production environment can be the most effective monitoring, debugging, and, occasionally, patching tool you could have.

Monitoring and runtime analysis. Because a REPL provides you with as high-fidelity a connection to a remote environment as you might have to a local Clojure environment, you have the opportunity to collect and monitor runtime data and events in ways that are impossible using other means. For example, capturing key event data in ways that you can access, manipulate, and analyze in the REPL can be very powerful. Here are a couple of trivial functions that enable this kind of usage:

```
(let [log-capacity 5000                              ❶
      events (agent [])]                             ❷
  (defn log-event [e]
    (send events #(if (== log-capacity (count %))
                    (-> % (conj e) (subvec 1))       ❸
                    (conj % e)))
    e)                                               ❹
  (defn events [] @events))                          ❺
```

❶ We define a capacity for our "log"—as a hardcoded size here, but this could just as easily be determined from a configuration setting.

❷ Our "log" is just an agent that holds an empty to vector to start. We're using an agent so we can update our log vector without potentially causing the thread calling log-event to block while updating, for example, an atom.

❸ When an event is logged, it's conjed onto the tail of our log vector. If the new event is going to overflow the defined capacity, then we trim the head of our log vector.

❹ We return the logged event so that log-event can be easily used within threading forms or composed with other functions.

❺ We define a simple accessor function so that the vector of events can be retrieved from the closure.

Let's see what we can do with our event-logging facility. Consider a web application where you'd like to track where your traffic is coming from, in particular to notice new "hot" referrers. To do this, you could capture a subset of each request's data via log-event; we'll dummy up some data here, simulating the logging of requests from a few referring domains:

```
(doseq [request (repeatedly 10000 (partial rand-nth [{:referrer "twitter.com"}
                                                     {:referrer "facebook.com"}
                                                     {:referrer "twitter.com"}
                                                     {:referrer "reddit.com"}]))]
  (log-event request))
;= nil
(count (events))
;= 5000
```

log-event is working properly in retaining a maximum of 5,000 events; the first 5,000 events rolled off the head of the vector. Now, when you connect to your remote web application via a REPL, you can do *anything you want* with this data; here, we can perform a simple summation, allowing us to see which referring domain sent us the most traffic over the last 5,000 requests:

```
(frequencies (events))
;= {{:referrer "twitter.com"} 2502,
    {:referrer "facebook.com"} 1280,
    {:referrer "reddit.com"} 1218}
```

Twitter was our site's top referrer over the last 5,000 requests (by dint of our gaming the dummy data by doubling the frequency of Twitter-referred "requests"). Of course, you could do a *lot* more than this; immediate improvements would be to capture more than just the referrer's domain, and perhaps truncate the events vector based on request timestamp so as to retain only the last 10 minutes of requests rather than a fixed number.

In any case, the upshot is that by being able to dig into your remote Clojure application using the REPL, you have all of the facilities of Clojure at your disposal to peek, poke, and analyze its state. Typical approaches to addressing these sorts of requirements— spooling data to disk or a database and analyzing it from there, or building dashboards and other status indicators into your application—are known quantities, but require resources and planning that may not be practical or possible. In any case, there is little that can beat the advantage of having a REPL handy to make *any* analysis instantly available.

Patching.   Once you've found the cause of a bug and determined the fix for it (presumably validating that fix in some kind of testing environment), getting that patch into a deployed application *without* prompting downtime can be a tall order depending on the specifics of your application and relevant local policies. However, with a remote REPL session, patching a deployed application is as simple as loading updated code.

Some care and preparation should go into this, though. In particular, there are some limitations to what can be updated when loading code in the REPL, as we discuss in "Limitations to Redefining Constructs" on page 415. In addition, there can be questions of logistics: if your patch requires changes to multiple files, you need to load them one at a time in the proper order. This is because the REPL you are connected to retains its remote classpath containing all the now-old code; require and use declarations will not magically find the updated code on your machine.

Beyond this concept of carefully patching a deployed application, there is the use case of rapidly iterating and updating a "live" environment. There are contexts where user requirements change so rapidly, and turnaround time of solutions is so critical, that it is advantageous to treat "production" as a development environment.[16] In such a situation, being able to jack your local tools into that deployed application with a REPL and push new code out at a breakneck pace is an edge that is hard to ignore.

---

16. Though this does exist in proper production environments, the most common example is a "user acceptance testing" context, where the faster you can deploy improvements, the happier your clients, customers, and partners will be.

Special Considerations for "Deployed" REPLs

If the concept of having an interactive connection to an application deployed to production is unsettling, we would remind you that JMX (Java Management Extensions) have for years provided a widely utilized though comparatively clumsy mechanism for dynamically making changes to a running Java application. That said, there are some things you should consider when using or making available a REPL from a production environment.

All changes are temporary. Just as in a development-context REPL, any changes you make within a deployed Clojure environment are strictly transient. Loading code or tweaking data structures via the REPL will impact the current JVM/Clojure process, but will be gone if you, for example, restart the deployed Clojure application. This is in contrast to certain workflows within the development context, where you have the option of making modifications to your project's source files, and loading that modified code—the next time you start a REPL for that project, that modified code will be what is loaded initially, making its effect persistent.

This is something to either simply be aware of when you are working in a REPL connected to a deployed application, or something to plan to work around. One work-around might be to ensure that any new code you load into a deployed application is mirrored by the deployment of a new artifact or executable to the remote environment, so that when the application is restarted, the changes you dynamically load via the REPL are always also present in the *.war* or *.jar* file(s), for example, corresponding to the modified code.

Network security and access control. No network implementation of a Clojure REPL provides anything in the way of security, including authentication and transport encryption. These issues are generally considered an orthogonal concern.

An easy way to resolve them in short order is to ensure that the REPL server running in your deployed application is bound to a network port that is safely behind the operating system's firewall.[17] You would then establish an SSH tunnel or use a VPN to gain access to the remote system, and connect to the running REPL server through that secure gateway.

Similarly, REPL servers do not enforce any sort of access control: once you have a REPL connection, you have unfettered access to the Clojure runtime and the environment it finds itself in. From a security standpoint, you should treat a REPL connection with the same care as you might treat an SSH session. There are ways to restrict the capabilities of a REPL, though, using an evaluation sandbox.[18]

---

17. This is likely to be the default, insofar as deployed environments typically expose ports used only for common network services, like HTTP, HTTPS, and SSH.

18. One such sandbox is *clojail*—*https://github.com/flatland/clojail*—which has been battle-tested through the evaluation of snippets of untrusted code in various Clojure IRC channels and on the puzzle site 4clojure.com.

Limitations to Redefining Constructs

The ability to interactively redefine parts of your Clojure application is nearly unlimited: everything from functions to top-level data structures to types specified via `deftype` and `defrecord` to protocols and multimethods can be redefined and modified at runtime (within the bounds of each construct's contract, of course), just by loading new or updated code. This capability is *nearly* unlimited though, with the "nearly" being mostly prompted by host limitations.

The fixed classpath.   The JVM's classpath cannot, in general, be modified or expanded at runtime. This means that you cannot load and use new dependencies that were not anticipated or available when the JVM/Clojure process was started. There are a number of workarounds for this limitation both in the JVM and Clojure communities.[19]

gen-class is never dynamic.   As described in "Defining Named Classes" on page 374, `gen-class` generates a static Java class strictly during ahead-of-time compilation, and at no other time. This class, by definition, cannot be updated at runtime. The JVM ecosystem has evolved approaches to reload and update static classes (like those generated by `gen-class`), but such methods are beyond our scope here.

Class instances retain inline implementations forever.   Inline interface and protocol implementations in classes defined by `deftype` and `defrecord` cannot be updated dynamically for existing instances of those classes. Workarounds here include delegating implementations to separate functions that you can readily redefine as necessary (which we did in the `reify`-based implementation of `ActionListener` in Example 10-1), and instead of providing functions named by vars when implementing protocols via `extend`, provide the vars themselves using the #' notation. Once you update the functions held by the latter, the new functions will be used to support the protocol implementations.

In addition to the these limitations implied by the JVM, you should keep in mind a couple of Clojure-specific issues:

Redefining macros does not reexpand usages of them.   If you define a macro, and use it in the definition of a function, redefining only the macro will not update the definition of the function. Remember that macros are used only at compile time: in order to have the new macro implementation "applied," all usages of that macro must be reloaded (and therefore recompiled) as well.

Redefining a multimethod does not update the multimethod's dispatch function.   As we pointed out in "Redefining a multimethod does not update the multimethod's dispatch function" (page 305), `defmulti` has `defonce` semantics, so dispatch functions aren't updated simply by loading a modified `defmulti` form. The workaround

---

19. One is pomegranate (see *https://github.com/cemerick/pomegranate* for details), which can add *.jar* files to your JVM's classpath, either directly from disk or by resolving them as Maven dependencies.

is to ns-unmap the multimethod's var—which unfortunately requires reloading each of the multimethod's method implementations as well.

Understand when you're capturing a value instead of dereferencing a var. Remember that def and friends intern a var in the current namespace, and vars contain the actual value you are defining. A var's symbol evaluates to the value the var holds at that point in time. That is exactly what you want if, for example, you are making a simple function call; however, if you name a var as an argument to another function, you are passing that var's value as the argument, not the var itself. Thus, if you attempt to redefine the var, the new value will not be taken into account:

```
(defn a [b] (+ 5 b))
;= #'user/a
(def b (partial a 5))        ❶
;= #'user/b
(b)
;= 10
(defn a [b] (+ 10 b))        ❷
;= #'user/a
(b)                          ❸
;= 10
```

❶ We define b to be a function, the function in the var a with a single argument partially applied.

❷ We redefine a...

❸ ...but because b has captured the original function a, our redefinition has no effect.

The workaround here is again to provide the var itself as the argument:

```
(def b (partial #'a 5))      ❶
;= #'user/b
(b)
;= 15
(defn a [b] (+ 5 b))         ❷
;= #'user/a
(b)                          ❸
;= 10
```

❶ We provide #'a to partial, instead of just a; this results in the function returned by partial capturing the *var* a, and not its value at that time.

❷ Now we can redefine a...

❸ ...and calling b now uses our redefined function now held by #'a.

In Summary

The Clojure REPL is a tool that can be used to smooth the passing of each hour of programming, speed the discovery of the cause of each new bug, and snatch victory from the gummy maw of failure in production environments. Using it effectively is necessary to gain the complete benefits of every quality Clojure toolchain, and understanding the full depth of its potential is part of the defining experience of programming in Clojure.

## PART IV

Practicums

## CHAPTER 11

Numerics and Mathematics

Many classes of applications remain safely ignorant of the details and subtleties of mathematics, regardless of the language or runtime being used. In such cases, it is often I/O overhead, database queries, and other factors that define an application's bottlenecks.

However, there are domains where numeric performance and/or correctness are critical, and the set of such cases seems to be growing: large-scale data processing, visualization, statistical analysis, and similar classes of applications all often require a degree of mathematical rigor not found elsewhere. Clojure gives you ways to choose how to optimize your application's usage of numerics to meet these demands along two different axes. Without sacrificing concision, expressiveness, or runtime dynamism, you can opt to:

1. Use primitive numerics to obtain maximum performance within the available range of those primitives.
2. Use boxed numerics to reliably perform arbitrary-precision operations.

In this chapter, we'll do a deep dive into how Clojure models numbers and implements operations over them.

Clojure Numerics

Our first step must be to understand the raw materials at hand, Clojure's numeric representations, shown in Table 11-1.[1] A good place to start would be to compare Clojure's numerics and those in Ruby and Python (those familiar with Java should be immediately comfortable, insofar as Clojure reuses Java's numeric representations).

---

1. See Table 1-2 for a refresher of the reader syntax that corresponds with each numeric type.

Table 11-1. Clojure's numeric types, with comparisons to representations in Python and Ruby

Numeric type	Clojure representation	Python equivalent	Ruby equivalent
Primitive 64-bit integers	`long`	None; Python and Ruby do not provide primitive numerics (all representations in both languages are boxed).	
Primitive 64-bit IEEE floating-point decimals	`double`		
Boxed integers	`java.lang.Long`	`int`[a]	`Fixnum`[b]
Boxed decimals	`java.lang.Double`	`float`	`Float`
"Big" ints (unbounded arbitrary-precision integers)	`java.math.BigInteger` and `clojure.lang.BigInt`	`long`	`Bignum`
"Big" decimals (unbounded arbitrary-precision decimals)	`java.math.BigDecimal`	`decimal.Decimal`	`BigDecimal`
Rationals (often also called *ratios*)	`clojure.lang.Ratio`	`fractions.Fraction`	`Rational`

[a] Python's `int` is 32 bits wide, and so the closer JVM equivalent is `java.lang.Integer`; however, as noted in the next section, Clojure widens all of its numerics to 64-bit representations, and so `long`s (or, in this case, Longs) are always preferred.

[b] The range of Ruby's `Fixnum` is implementation- and machine-dependent, usually 31 or 63 bits wide (the last bit is reserved to implement its fixnum semantics; see "Object Identity (identical?)" on page 433 for a brief discussion of fixnums).

Let's unpack some terminology and expand on some key facts from this table.

Clojure Prefers 64-bit (or Larger) Representations

While the JVM supports many smaller representations—such as 32-bit floating-point decimals and 32- and 16-bit integers (`floats`, `ints`, and `shorts`, respectively)—all of Clojure's reader forms and numeric operations produce 64-bit (or larger) numeric representations. All mathematics operations can work with these narrower types, but Clojure widens return values to their corresponding 64-bit representations. For example, incrementing a 32-bit integer produces a 64-bit long:

```
(class (inc (Integer. 5)))
;= java.lang.Long
```

This simplifies Clojure's numerics model compared to Java's, where there are three different integer representations and two different decimal representations.

Clojure Has a Mixed Numerics Model

Unlike most dynamic languages (including Ruby and Python), Clojure supports *primitive* numerics (e.g., `long` and `double`) alongside *boxed* numerics.

Primitives are not objects; they are value types that correspond directly to a machine-level type, to the point where certain numeric operations over primitives are implemented in hardware. Clojure reuses the JVM's `long` and `double` primitives, which correspond to the C/C++ types `long long` (also called `int64_t`) and `double`, respectively.

In contrast, boxed numbers *are* objects that are defined by classes; `java.lang.Long` is a box class whose sole purpose is to contain a primitive `long`, and `java.lang.Double` is the corollary that contains a primitive `double`.[2] Being objects, they incur a cost for each allocation, and so operations over them are necessarily slower: they must often be *unboxed* first (to obtain the primitive value within), and then the result of each operation may need to be boxed again (requiring an allocation of the box class appropriate for the primitive result value).

Why Do Long and Double Exist at All, Since They Don't Provide Any Semantic Advantages Over Their Primitive Counterparts?

Considered in isolation, it seems that the `Long` and `Double` box classes serve no purpose: using them in mathematical operations implies additional overhead, and they provide no advantages of range or precision like `BigInteger` and `BigDecimal`. The reason `Long` and `Double` (and the other Java box classes corresponding to the JVM's primitive types, such as `Boolean` and `Short`) exist is to allow JVM numbers to be used in all the scenarios where objects are useful.

For example, without these box classes, it would be impossible to store numbers in hash maps and other collections. The Java Collections API deals in objects exclusively.

We talk more about boxed numbers, specifically with how they impact Clojure, in "Optimizing Numeric Performance" on page 436.

Given the correspondence between primitives and machine types, and the allocation overhead associated with boxed numerics, working with primitives is always going to be faster—sometimes orders of magnitude faster, depending upon the specifics of an algorithm. On the other hand, the 64-bit numeric types natively provided by the JVM do have limits to their range and precision. To fill this gap, Clojure reuses `BigDecimal` and can work with `BigInteger`—Java's two unbounded numeric representations—and provides its own `BigInt`. These types are defined by classes, and therefore share the overhead associated with boxed numerics, but allow you to safely work with arbitrarily large or arbitrarily precise numbers.

So, we have two axes by which Clojure's numeric types may be understood: whether a particular representation is *primitive* or *boxed*, and whether its range or precision is limited or arbitrary. The different concrete representations of integers and decimals are shown in the matrix in Table 11-2 based on those axes.

---

2. Primitives are always denoted by lowercase names (like `double`), whereas boxed representations are always identified by their (capitalized) class name (like `Double`).

Table 11-2. Matrix comparison of numeric representations available in Clojure

	Limited range/precision	Arbitrary range/precision
Primitive types	`long, double`	*N/A*

Object types	`java.lang.Long,`
	`java.lang.Double`
		`clojure.lang.BigInt,`
		`java.math.BigDecimal,`
		`java.math.BigInteger`

While Clojure uses and provides many different numeric types, the semantics of its mathematical operations are consistent across types and when operations are performed with numbers of differing types. For example, `dec` always decrements its argument, regardless of the type of that argument, and always returns a number of the same concrete type:

```
(dec 1)
;= 0
(dec 1.0)
;= 0.0
(dec 1N)
;= 0N
(dec 1M)
;= 0M
(dec 5/4)
;= 1/4
```

Similarly, we can freely mix the types of numbers used in a single operation:[3]

```
(* 3 0.08 1/4 6N 1.2M)
;= 0.432
(< 1 1.6 7/3 9N 14e9000M)
;= true
```

When arguments to arithmetic operations are mixed, the type of the result is determined by Clojure's rules for widening of types. This is discussed in "The Rules of Numeric Contagion" on page 425.

Rationals

Rational numbers are the set of numbers that can be expressed as a fraction of two integers. For example, ⅓ and ⅗ are both rational numbers (equal to 0.333... and 0.6, respectively). Most languages—including Java, Ruby, and Python—support only integer and floating-point number representations and arithmetic. So, when a rational number is encountered, it is immediately "flattened" into the corresponding floating-point approximation:

---

3. A pleasant improvement over Java, especially since its mathematical operators cannot be used with numeric types providing arbitrary precision.

```
# Ruby
>> 1.0/3.0
0.333333333333333

# Python
>>> 1.0/3.0
0.333333333333333331
```

The perils of floating-point representations when used in various calculations are fairly well known (though rarely well understood). Here's a common example, back in Clojure:

```
(+ 0.1 0.1 0.1)
;= 0.30000000000000004
```

The error that slips into that result is simply the consequence of how floating-point numbers are represented.[4] Clojure avoids this by (a) allowing for rational number literals, and (b) not forcing rational numbers into an inexact floating-point approximation:

```
(+ 1/10 1/10 1/10)
;= 3/10
```

The flip side of this is that, when it *is* possible to flatten rational numbers into an integer without loss of precision, Clojure does so:

```
(+ 7/10 1/10 1/10 1/10)
;= 1
```

Ratios can be explicitly coerced to a floating-point representation:

```
(double 1/3)
;= 0.3333333333333333
```

and floating-point numbers can be converted to a ratio using the `rationalize` function:

```
(rationalize 0.45)
;= 9/20
```

The Rules of Numeric Contagion

When an arithmetic operation involves differing types of numbers, the type of the operation's return value is determined using a fixed hierarchy. Each numeric type has a different degree of *contagion*, where the argument to an operation with the highest degree of contagion determines the type of the return value (Figure 11-1).

---

4. Like many other runtimes, the JVM represents floating-point numbers according to the IEEE 754 specification. If you're interested in how a floating-point number boils down to bits in memory, the overview of the spec at *http://en.wikipedia.org/wiki/IEEE_754-2008* is a good jumping-off point.

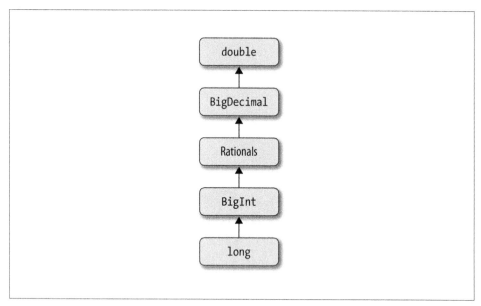

Figure 11-1. Clojure's numeric types, organized according to their relative degrees of contagion

Every mathematical operation must return a value of some concrete type, and there must be a defined way in which that type is chosen for operations involving heterogeneous arguments. The specific hierarchy that Clojure defines is ordered and implemented such that this coercion of the return value's type is never "lossy"; for example, every `long` can be coerced to a big int or rational or decimal without impacting the semantics of its value, while the reverse is not true.

This is trivially demonstrated:

```
(+ 1 1)    ❶
;= 2
(+ 1 1.5)  ❷
;= 2.5
(+ 1 1N)   ❸
;= 2N
(+ 1.1M 1N)  ❹
;= 2.1M
```

❶ Operations with homogeneously typed arguments return a result of that type.

❷ An operation involving a `long` and a `double` will always return a `double`.

❸ An operation involving a `long` and a `BigInteger` will always return a `BigInteger`.

❹ An operation involving a `BigDecimal` and a `BigInteger` will always return a `BigDecimal`.

The only wrinkle here is that any operation involving a double will return a double, even though doubles cannot properly represent the full range of the other numeric representations. This is because:

1. double (following the IEEE floating-point specification) defines some special values that cannot be represented by BigDecimals (specifically, the Infinity and NaN values).

2. double is the only representation that is inherently inexact—it would be questionable for an operation involving an inexact number to return a type of value that implied precision that does not exist.

The concept of contagion extends beyond the arithmetic operations provided by Clojure; they are just functions, and so the same rules apply for functions that you might write that accept numbers as arguments and are implemented using Clojure's operators. Consider a simple function that computes the sum of the squares:

```
(defn squares-sum
  [& vals]
  (reduce + (map * vals vals)))
;= #'user/squares-sum
(squares-sum 1 4 10)
;= 117
```

What happens when we add a double, a big int, a big decimal, or a rational to those being summed? We get a double, a big int, a big decimal, or a rational in return, respectively, regardless of the types of the other values being summed, consistent with the hierarchy of contagion we saw in Figure 11-1:

```
(squares-sum 1 4 10 20.5)
;= 537.25
(squares-sum 1 4 10 9N)
;= 198N
(squares-sum 1 4 10 9N 5.6M)
;= 229.36M
(squares-sum 1 4 10 25/2)
;= 1093/4
```

Clojure Mathematics

Knowing the types of available numbers and their representations is not sufficient to understand how mathematics is modeled in Clojure. Clojure's various arithmetic and equality operators provide additional semantic guarantees in order to support sensible results across all the numeric types in play and in the face of many common issues that arise in computational mathematics, such as the handling of overflow and underflow, controlling the promotion of arithmetic results, and collection equality.

Bounded Versus Arbitrary Precision

The 64-bit range of longs and doubles is quite expansive; integers $\pm 2^{63}$-1 can be represented and operated on, along with decimals $\pm 1.7976931348623157^{308}$. Most applications have no need for additional range or precision, so longs and doubles are often perfectly sufficient.

For those applications that do require additional range and/or precision, *arbitrary precision* numeric representations are available. These representations are *always* boxed; Clojure uses both `clojure.lang.BigInt` and `java.math.BigInteger` to represent arbitrary-range integers, and `java.math.BigDecimal` for arbitrary-precision decimals.

Why Does Clojure Have Its Own BigInt Class When Java Already Provides One in BigInteger?

This implementation detail has two origins.

First, `BigInteger` is somewhat broken, in that its `.hashCode` implementation is not consistent with that of `Long`:

```
(.hashCode (BigInteger. "6948736584"))
;= -1641197977
(.hashCode (Long. 6948736584))
;= -1641198007
```

This is really bad, causing situations where equivalent values can appear twice in a set (or be mapped to two different values in, for example, a hash map) simply because of the implementation detail of their concrete types.[5]

Second, while all operations involving `BigInteger`s must be performed using its (slower) software-based implementations, Clojure optimizes math involving `BigInt`s to use primitive (much faster) operations when possible, *as long as the values involved are within the range of primitive 64-bit longs*. This means that you often only pay the arbitrary-precision penalty for integer arithmetic when your data actually requires it.

In the end, you end up not generally having to care that there are two concrete arbitrary precision integer types in play; regardless of the types involved, the semantics of all of Clojure's numeric operations are unaffected by the particular types involved and their results are never a `BigInteger`.

To bring all this talk about precision and range down to earth, let's see what we can do with these arbitrarily large integers that we can't do with regular longs. Consider some value in a program that happens to be the maximum that can be represented in a long:

```
(def k Long/MAX_VALUE)
;= #'user/k
```

---

5. See "Equivalence can preserve your sanity" on page 435 for an example of this.

```
k
;= 9223372036854775807
```

That's a big number, but sometimes, it's not big enough:

```
(inc k)
;= ArithmeticException integer overflow
```

Clojure's primary math operators throw an exception on integer overflow instead of silently "wrapping around" the value, as discussed in "Unchecked Ops" on page 430. But, sometimes we really do need to work with values larger than the maximum value allowed by longs and doubles; in such cases, we have a couple of options:

Explicitly use arbitrary-precision numbers. Depending on the local requirements and context, this can be done either using the `bigint` and `bigdec` coercion functions:

```
(inc (bigint k))
;= 9223372036854775808N
(* 100 (bigdec Double/MAX_VALUE))
;= 1.797693134862315700E+310M
```

or by using appropriate literal notations. Remember from Table 1-2 that an N suffix produces a `BigInt`, and an M suffix produces a `BigDecimal`:

```
(dec 10223372636454715900N)
;= 10223372636454715899N
(* 0.5M 1e403M)
;= 5E+402M
```

Additionally, integer literals that exceed the limits of 64-bit `longs` are automatically promoted to be `BigInts`:

```
10223372636454715900
;= 10223372636454715900N
(* 2 10223372636454715900)
;= 20446745272909431800N
```

Utilize autopromoting operators for integer calculations. Using arbitrary precision explicitly is good if we control the inputs to a particular function; that allows us to use Clojure's primary arithmetic operators and rely on its (fast) numeric type contagion semantics to provoke the promotion of return values if necessary. If we know a particular calculation will require unbounded precision or range, we can supply arbitrary-precision inputs.

On the other hand, if we are implementing a calculation or algorithm that only *may* exceed the range of `long` integers, and contagion is not sufficient to ensure correct results, we can use the *prime*[6] autopromoting variants of Clojure's arithmetic operators to *auto*matically *promote* `long` results to `BigInts` that would otherwise overflow:

---

6. *Prime* here refers to the convention of using a prime mark (typically represented as an apostrophe, ') as a suffix of an operator's name to denote a variant of the baseline operator. See *http://en.wikipedia.org/wiki/Prime_(symbol)* for details of this notation outside of Clojure.

```
(inc' k)
;= 9223372036854775808N
```

These operators promote results *only as necessary* though; this ensures that results that are within the bounded range of 64-bit `long`s are not promoted:

```
(inc' 1)
;= 2
(inc' (dec' Long/MAX_VALUE))
;= 9223372036854775807
```

Prime variants are available for all of Clojure's mathematical operators that can cause an integer overflow or underflow: `inc'`, `dec'`, `+'`, `-'`, and `*'`.

There is a slight overhead associated with using the prime operators; each operation involving bounded representations must check the result and potentially redo the operation using `BigInt`s instead of `long`s. Such overhead is the price one must pay in order to obtain guaranteed correct results with a minimum of effort.

Unchecked Ops

Overflow and *underflow* are conditions where the result of an operation over integers exceeds what that integer's representation can support. The effects of underflow and overflow are likely familiar to anyone that has worked with numerical data in Java;[7] for example, this Java code:

```
System.out.println(Long.MAX_VALUE);
System.out.println(Long.MAX_VALUE + 1);
```

will yield this output:

```
9223372036854775807
-9223372036854775808
```

Ouch. Of course, none of us are ever intentionally incrementing maximum value constants, but the same thing happens if our calculations (unexpectedly) broach the defined limits of a given numeric representation.

Thankfully, all of Clojure's mathematical operators check for overflow and underflow and throw an exception if necessary:

```
Long/MIN_VALUE
;= -9223372036854775808
(dec Long/MIN_VALUE)
;= #<ArithmeticException java.lang.ArithmeticException: integer overflow>
```

This is decidedly better than having to track down bizarre behavior in your application because an operation overflowed *somewhere*, returning a semantically evil "wraparound" result.

---

7. Underflow and overflow are not an issue in languages like Python and Ruby, both of which apply autopromotion at all times to avoid these conditions for all of their mathematical operators.

However, there are some limited circumstances where you may want to retain the unchecked behavior of Java's operators:

1. You want to retain complete compatibility with Java's unfortunate semantics in this department—for example, if you're implementing a new version of some functionality in Clojure that was previously written in Java.
2. You want to avoid the (very small) cost associated with Clojure's overflow/underflow checks.

There are unchecked-* variants of all of Clojure's operators that do not perform underflow/overflow checks:

```
(unchecked-dec Long/MIN_VALUE)
;= 9223372036854775807
(unchecked-multiply 92233720368547758 1000)
;= -80
```

These variants are somewhat verbose (unchecked-multiply is pretty rough compared to *). An alternative is to set! *unchecked-math* to a true value prior to any top-level forms whose mathematical operations should all be unchecked:

```
(inc Long/MAX_VALUE)
;= #<ArithmeticException java.lang.ArithmeticException: integer overflow>
(set! *unchecked-math* true)
;= true
(inc Long/MAX_VALUE)
;= -9223372036854775808
(set! *unchecked-math* false)
;= false
```

 If you are going to use *unchecked-math*, it is most common to set! it at the top of a source file prior to the forms where unchecked ops should be used, optionally set!ing it back to false after those forms. *unchecked-math* *is reset for each source file that is loaded*, so you need to set it in each file that you use it; that is, you cannot set it once in a top-level namespace and expect that to take effect throughout subsequently loaded files. If this weren't the case, forgetting to reset *unchecked-math* back to false at the end of a file would "leak" the unfortunate semantics of unchecked ops throughout your (and others') code.

Note that you generally cannot use binding to set *unchecked-math*:

```
(binding [*unchecked-math* true]
  (inc Long/MAX_VALUE))
;= #<ArithmeticException java.lang.ArithmeticException: integer overflow>
```

This is because *unchecked-math* controls the operation of the compiler, but the bind ing form does not take effect until it is evaluated. This happens after (sometimes long after) the compiler has had its way with a given top-level form.[8]

Scale and Rounding Modes for Arbitrary-Precision Decimals Ops

One of the most frustrating things about using BigDecimal in Java is that many operations fail by default:

```
new BigDecimal(1).divide(new BigDecimal(3));

= java.lang.ArithmeticException:
=   Non-terminating decimal expansion; no exact representable decimal result.
```

While this code is already painfully verbose, making it work acceptably by specifying a rounding mode and maximum scale is even worse:

```
new BigDecimal(1).divide(new BigDecimal(3), new MathContext(10, RoundingMode.HALF_UP));

= 0.3333333333
```

Ruby's arbitrary-precision decimal implementation carries roughly the same cost, although the tradeoffs involved are different: instead of forcing you to thread a math context through each operation, math context parameters are set globally in the Decimal class.

Clojure provides a macro, with-precision, which simplifies this significantly. You provide your desired scale (and optionally, a rounding mode), and that information is threaded through all BigDecimal operations performed within the scope of with-precision *for you*:

```
(/ 22M 7)
;= #<ArithmeticException java.lang.ArithmeticException:
;=   Non-terminating decimal expansion; no exact representable decimal result.>
(with-precision 10 (/ 22M 7))
;= 3.142857143M
(with-precision 10 :rounding FLOOR
  (/ 22M 7))
;= 3.142857142M
```

And, if you really want to, you can set the scale and rounding mode without using with-precision by setting *math-context* to an appropriate instance of java.math.Math Context:[9]

---

8. An expression provided to eval within such a binding form *would* be compiled and evaluated using unchecked ops, since that compilation would be performed after the dynamic scope is established... although we cannot imagine why you would want to do this.

9. Since *math-context* is a dynamic var, you can change its value using either set! or alter-var-root. Which one you choose depends on whether you want your change to take effect on a thread-local basis or globally, respectively. You can read about dynamic scope in "Dynamic Scope" on page 201.

```
(set! *math-context* (java.math.MathContext. 10 java.math.RoundingMode/FLOOR))
;= #<MathContext precision=10 roundingMode=FLOOR>
(/ 22M 7)
;= 3.142857142M
```

Equality and Equivalence

Clojure provides three ways to determine the equality of values, which are embodied in three different predicate functions.

Object Identity (identical?)

Object identity, implemented by `identical?` in Clojure, is used to determine if two (or more) objects are exactly the same instance. This corresponds directly to `==` in Java (when used to compare object references), `is` in Python, and `equal?` in Ruby:

```
(identical? "foot" (str "fo" "ot"))
;= false
(let [a (range 10)]
  (identical? a a))
;= true
```

In general, numbers will never be `identical?`, even if provided as literals:

```
(identical? 5/4 (+ 3/4 1/2))
;= false
(identical? 5.4321 5.4321)
;= false
(identical? 2600 2600)
;= false
```

The exception is that the JVM (and therefore Clojure) provides for a limited range of *fixnums*. Fixnums are a pool of boxed integer values that are always used in preference to allocating a new integer. Ruby's fixnum semantics cover the entire range of its integers, while Python's fixnums are available only between –5 and 256.[10] The Oracle JVM's fixnum range is ±127[11] and so only results of operations that return integers within this range may be `identical?` to other integers of the same value:

```
(identical? 127 (dec 128))
;= true
(identical? 128 (dec 129))
;= false
```

In general, it's wise to not use `identical?` at all when comparing numbers.

---

10. This unusual range is an implementation detail of CPython.

11. The JVM's fixnum semantics are defined as part of its boxing conversions for primitive values (discussed in §5.1.7 of the Java Language Spec), and may differ in other versions and implementations.

Reference Equality (=)

This is what is most commonly referred to as "equality": a (potentially) type-sensitive, deep comparison of values to determine if they are structurally the same. Clojure's = predicate adopts the equality semantics of Java's reference equality, defined by `java.lang.Object.equals`.[12] `=` in Clojure is functionality equivalent to `==` in both Python and Ruby.

This yields generally intuitive and convenient results, especially when comparing collections of different concrete types:

```
(= {:a 1 :b ["hi"]}
   (into (sorted-map) [[:b ["hi"]] [:a 1]])
   (doto (java.util.HashMap.)
     (.put :a 1)
     (.put :b ["hi"])))
;= true
```

Note, however, that collections of different categories will never be = to each other. For example, while any sequential collection (e.g., a vector, list, or sequence) may be equal to another sequential collection of a different concrete type, a sequential collection will never be equal to a set, or a map.

The same dynamic applies to numeric equality. More precisely, = will only ever return true when comparing numbers of the same category, even if the numerical value being represented is equivalent. For example, all types of integers are usefully comparable using = (even integer types smaller than Clojure's preferred 64-bit longs), and the limited-precision decimals of different widths play nicely together as well:

```
(= 1 1N (Integer. 1) (Short. (short 1)) (Byte. (byte 1)))
;= true
(= 1.25 (Float. 1.25))
;= true
```

However, = will *never* return true for comparisons of equivalent numbers of different categories:

```
(= 1 1.0)
;= false
(= 1N 1M)
;= false
(= 1.25 5/4)
;= false
```

Clojure's = *could* obviate these type differences (as Ruby and Python do), but doing so would impose some runtime cost that would be unappreciated by those who need to maximize the performance of programs that work with homogeneous numeric data.

---

12. And, when comparing non-numbers, Clojure's = simply delegates to its arguments' implementation of `Object.equals`. The specifics of `Object.equals` are far more intricate than our summary here. It is absolutely worth your time to look at the javadocs for it and absorb them fully: *http://docs.oracle.com/javase/7/docs/api/java/lang/Object.html#equals%28java.lang.Object%29*.

Thus, Clojure opts to provide a third notion of equality, specifically to address the need for type-insensitive equivalence tests.

Numeric Equivalence (==)

Clojure's == predicate implements *numerical equivalence*, a measure of equality that is aligned with our intuitive understanding, unfettered by the artificial categories we use to delineate numeric representations. Where = returns false when comparing numbers of different implementation categories, == may return true if the values represented by the numbers provided are numerically equivalent:

```
(== 0.125 0.125M 1/8)
;= true
(== 4 4N 4.0 4.0M)
;= true
```

Note that even rationals are right at home being compared to their corresponding decimal representations when using ==.

== requires that all of its arguments be numbers; otherwise, it will throw an exception. This means that if you are not sure what the type of an argument might be, you need to either:

- Use =.
- If you need the equivalence semantics of ==, you need to guard its use with checks of its arguments (using number? will do here).

```
(defn equiv?
  "Same as `==`, but doesn't throw an exception if any arguments are not numbers."
  [& args]
  (and (every? number? args)
       (apply == args)))
;= #'user/equiv?
(equiv? "foo" 1)
;= false
(equiv? 4 4N 4.0 4.0M)
;= true
(equiv? 0.125 0.125M 1/8)
;= true
```

Equivalence can preserve your sanity

Java's notion of numeric equality can really hurt when heterogeneous types of numbers are used in collections. Because Java's collection implementations depend on each member's definition of equality (for things like determining membership in a set and locating a map entry given some key), and its numerics are defined to restrict equality based on implementation type, you can end up with degenerate situations like this:

```
java.util.Map m = new java.util.HashMap();
m.put(1, "integer");
m.put(1L, "long");
```

```
m.put(java.math.BigInteger.valueOf(1), "bigint");
System.out.println(m);
```

>> {1=bigint, 1=long, 1=integer}

Ouch: a map with three keys that we almost certainly would have preferred to have hashed out to the same entry—a recipe for producing incredibly subtle bugs. In contrast, Clojure's collections use its definition of equivalence for numeric keys and members:

```
(into #{} [1 1N (Integer. 1) (Short. (short 1))])
;= #{1}
(into {}
      [[1 :long]
       [1N :bigint]
       [(Integer. 1) :integer]])
;= {1 :integer}
```

Beware Mixed Floating-Point Equality Tests

As is always the case with floating-point decimals, care must be taken to account for the details of their representations. Just as simple operations can sometimes produce "incorrect" results:

```
(+ 0.1 0.2)
;= 0.30000000000000004
```

equality comparisons of different types of decimals can yield surprising behavior. Consider:

```
(== 1.1 (float 1.1))
;= false
```

Note that this is false even though we're using the type-insensitive == equivalency predicate. The issue is that the **float** (a 32-bit representation) needs to be widened into a **double** (a 64-bit representation), which cannot be done precisely for **1.1**:

```
(double (float 1.1))
;= 1.100000023841858
```

The same behavior occurs in Java, where this returns **false**:

```
1.1f == 1.1d
```

The causes of this are rooted in the IEEE floating-point specifications. Languages like Ruby and Python sidestep this issue by providing only one limited-precision decimal representation.

Optimizing Numeric Performance

Clojure provides all the raw materials needed to model and implement data- and mathematics-intensive algorithms clearly and concisely. However, while expressivity is important, performance is often an overriding concern in such cases—it's what drives

---

programmers everywhere who would otherwise prefer higher-level languages to implement performance-critical sections of their programs in languages like C and Fortran. That's a fine coping mechanism, and can always be a measure of last resort,[13] but is often a source of integration, build, and deployment complexity (not to mention a sap on developer productivity). Thus, the more we can do in our high-level language, the happier and more productive we'll be.

So, how can we maximize the performance of numerics-intensive code in Clojure?

Use primitives.   As we discussed in "Clojure Has a Mixed Numerics Model" on page 422, primitives are not burdened by the allocation and garbage-collection costs associated with boxed numbers, and most operations over them are implemented at very low levels (often the hardware itself). All other things being equal, the same algorithm[14] implemented to utilize primitives will often be an order of magnitude faster than if boxed numbers are used. Doing this within Clojure will allow you to implement algorithms that approach the runtime performance of the same functionality implemented in Java.

Avoid collections and seqs.   A corollary to the notion of using primitives whenever possible where performance is a concern is that you should avoid using collections and sequences in such circumstances. As we mentioned in "Why Do Long and Double Exist at All, Since They Don't Provide Any Semantic Advantages Over Their Primitive Counterparts?" on page 423, collections deal exclusively in objects, and cannot generally store primitive-typed values. When a primitive is added to a collection, it is automatically "promoted" to an instance of its corresponding boxed class—an approach to marrying primitive and object-based type systems called *autoboxing*, a dynamic that Clojure inherits from the JVM.

For example, adding a `double` to a list results in an instance of its box class (`java.lang.Double`) being allocated and initialized with the primitive `double` value. While allocation and the garbage collection that goes with it is remarkably fast on the JVM, the fastest possible allocation and garbage collection is that which doesn't happen. Thus, if you really want to push the performance of the hottest parts of your codebase as far as possible, avoiding such costs requires avoiding collections and sequences.

When you abstain from using collections and sequences, the natural fallback is to use arrays of primitives.

---

13. You can very readily call out to native libraries from within the JVM and Clojure. See *https://github.com/Chouser/clojure-jna* for a Clojure library that provides a concise way to use JNA (*https://github.com/twall/jna*).

14. An exponential-time algorithm will not outperform a polynomial-time algorithm, whether the former uses primitives or not. That's a long way to say: make sure you're using the right algorithm first, *then* worry about optimizing it if necessary.

Declare Functions to Take and Return Primitives

When Clojure compiles a function, it generates a corresponding class that implements clojure.lang.IFn, one of Clojure's Java interfaces. IFn defines a number of invoke methods; these are what are called under the covers when you invoke a Clojure function.[15]

All arguments and return values are Objects at (undecorated) function boundaries. These invoke methods all accept arguments and return values of the root type java.lang.Object. This enables Clojure's dynamic typing defaults (i.e., your functions' implementations determine the range of acceptable argument types, not static type declarations that are enforced by the language), but has the side effect of forcing the JVM to box any primitives passed as arguments to or returned as results from those functions. So, if we call a Clojure function with a primitive argument—a long, for example—that argument will be boxed into a Long object in order to conform to the type signature of the Clojure function's underlying invoke method. Similarly, if a function's result is a primitive value, the underlying Object return type ensures that such primitives are boxed before the caller receives the result.

While Clojure is unabashedly a dynamic programming language, it recognizes that optionally providing type information in order to optimize runtime performance is a winning tradeoff. Class-based type *hints*[16] enable the Clojure complier to avoid reflection when performing Java interop (such as invoking methods on Objects and so on), but hints do not change the signature of functions' implementing methods; those invoke methods continue to accept all Objects. In contrast, Clojure also provides for statically declaring the functions' arguments and return values to be primitives: specifically, of type double or long.

We can see this by examining the methods of the classes generated by functions. As a baseline, here's a function that takes a single argument that has no hints or type declarations:

```
(defn foo [a] 0)
;= #'user/foo
(seq (.getDeclaredMethods (class foo)))
;= (#<Method public java.lang.Object user$foo.invoke(java.lang.Object)>)
```

Notice that it declares a single arity of invoke; as expected, it accepts one argument of type Object, and returns a value of that type as well. We can also see that using a class-based hint does not impact the function's underlying invoke method signature:

```
(defn foo [^Double a] 0)
;= #'user/foo
```

---

15. And the methods you use if you happen to need to call Clojure functions *from* Java; see Chapter 9 to learn about some of the finer points of calling into Clojure from Java (or any other JVM-based language, for that matter).

16. We explore type hints extensively in "Type Hinting for Performance" on page 366.

```
(seq (.getDeclaredMethods (class foo)))
;= (#<Method public java.lang.Object user$foo.invoke(java.lang.Object)>)
```

Even though Double is semantically a number, it's still a class, and therefore results in an Object argument type.

Let's try again using the primitive type declarations that are available to us, ^long and ^double:

```
(defn round ^long [^double a] (Math/round a))
;= #'user/round
(seq (.getDeclaredMethods (class round)))
;= (#<Method public java.lang.Object user$round.invoke(java.lang.Object)>
;=  #<Method public final long user$round.invokePrim(double)>)
```

What changed is that Clojure is using the primitive type declarations to compile a primitives-safe fast path into the generated class, in the form of an invokePrim method, which accepts a primitive double and returns a primitive long. Calling this function now with a double will be as fast as if you had written the invokePrim method yourself in Java.

However, it will *not* accept a nonconforming argument:

```
(round "string")
;= #<ClassCastException java.lang.ClassCastException:
;=   java.lang.String cannot be cast to java.lang.Number>
```

Note that the exception complains about "string" not being a Number. We can indeed pass any boxed number...as long as it fits in the expected range:

```
(defn idem ^long [^long x] x)
;= #'user/idem
(idem 18/5)
;= 3
(idem 3.14M)
;= 3
(idem 1e15)
;= 1000000000000000
(idem 1e150)
;= #<IllegalArgumentException java.lang.IllegalArgumentException:
;=   Value out of range for long: 1.0E150>
```

On the other hand, you might notice that the usual invoke method with its Object argument and return types remains; this is to support the case when the function is being called with a boxed numeric argument. This means that you can continue to use functions with declared primitive argument types in conjunction with higher-order functions[17] like map and apply:

```
(map round [4.5 6.9 8.2])
;= (5 7 8)
(apply round [4.2])
;= 4
```

---

17. See "First-Class and Higher-Order Functions" on page 59 if you need a refresher on HOFs.

Both type hints and type declarations may be used in the specification of fields (and therefore, constructors) in `deftype` and `defrecord` types, which we discussed in detail in "Defining Your Own Types" on page 270.

Functions supporting primitive types are limited to four arguments

The preceding code looks like a free lunch: all of the expressive power of Clojure paired with the efficiency of the JVM's primitive numerics. Unfortunately, there is a downside: any Clojure function that is declared to accept or return a primitive type is limited to four arguments:

```
(defn foo ^long [a b c d e] 0)
;= #<CompilerException java.lang.IllegalArgumentException:
;=    fns taking primitives support only 4 or fewer args>
```

This is due to an implementation detail: in order to tap into the aforementioned efficiency without opting into a strictly static compilation process, each possible primitive-accepting function signature must be defined in a separate interface. With three possible argument and return types (`double`, `long`, and `Object`), even allowing for a maximum of four arguments produces a permutation of hundreds of distinct interfaces.

Type errors and warnings

The ability to declare primitive types for arguments and returns can lead to clearly inconsistent situations. Even though Clojure is a dynamic language, its compiler will throw compilation errors when it can detect a problem, either via direct analysis or type inference:

```
(defn foo ^long [^int a] 0)
;= #<CompilerException java.lang.IllegalArgumentException:
;=    Only long and double primitives are supported>
(defn foo ^long [^double a] a)
;= #<CompilerException java.lang.IllegalArgumentException:
;=    Mismatched primitive return, expected: long, had: double>
```

Similarly, if you have *warn-on-reflection* bound to `true`, the compiler will emit warnings when you are attempting to `recur` with values that will require boxing, because their type will not match the binding's declared (or inferred) type. Consider, a simple loop that counts down from 5 to 0:

```
(set! *warn-on-reflection* true)
;= true
(loop [x 5]
  (when-not (zero? x)
    (recur (dec x))))
;= nil
```

x here is inferred to be a `long` based on the literal that is provided, and the `recur` argument (the result of `(dec x)`) will also be a `long`, so there is no inconsistency. However, if we use the autopromoting `dec'` operator, it's possible that the `recur` argument will be a `BigInt`; Clojure catches this:

```
(loop [x 5]
  (when-not (zero? x)
    (recur (dec' x))))
; NO_SOURCE_FILE:2 recur arg for primitive local:
;                    x is not matching primitive, had: Object, needed: long
; Auto-boxing loop arg: x
;= nil
```

The same thing happens if we attempt to recur to a long binding with an incompatible primitive, such as a double:

```
(loop [x 5]
  (when-not (zero? x)
    (recur 0.0)))
; NO_SOURCE_FILE:2 recur arg for primitive local:
;                    x is not matching primitive, had: double, needed: long
; Auto-boxing loop arg: x
;= nil
```

These sorts of warnings are not limited to checks of primitive types within the local function body. Here, we have a function that returns double that instigates a warning when we attempt to recur with that return to a long binding:

```
(defn dfoo ^double [^double a] a)
;= #'user/dfoo
(loop [x 5]
  (when-not (zero? x)
    (recur (dfoo (dec x)))))
; NO_SOURCE_FILE:2 recur arg for primitive local:
;                    x is not matching primitive, had: double, needed: long
; Auto-boxing loop arg: x
;= nil
```

In such a situation, we can avoid the boxing and the warning by using long, one of the primitive coercion functions, to ensure that a primitive value of the right type is used:

```
(loop [x 5]
  (when-not (zero? x)
    (recur (long (dfoo (dec x))))))
;= nil
```

Clojure's coercion functions—short, int, long, double, float, and boolean—are only useful when you need to eliminate a compiler warning related to reflection or auto-boxing. For example, the usage of long above eliminated the prospect of autoboxing; here, we use double to eliminate a reflective call:

```
(defn round [v]
  (Math/round v))
; Reflection warning, NO_SOURCE_PATH:2 - call to round can't be resolved.
;= #'user/round
(defn round [v]
  (Math/round (double v)))
;= #'user/round
```

In particular, when used outside of such contexts, coercion functions *do not* return a value corresponding to the type they indicate:

```
(class (int 5))
;= java.lang.Long
```

In this way, they are most akin to type hints (discussed in "Type Hinting for Performance" on page 366), and should be used accordingly.

Use Primitive Arrays Judiciously

We already outlined how Java arrays may be used within Clojure in general in "Arrays" on page 370, but there are some special considerations that should be taken into account when working with arrays of primitive values.

Isolated mutation of local arrays is okay. Along the lines of, "If a tree falls in the forest and no one hears it, does it make a sound?," there are absolutely times where the use of mutable arrays is not only acceptable, but reasonable and entirely in line with Clojure idioms.

While Clojure strongly encourages the application of functional programming—including the use of immutable data structures, its sequence abstraction, maintaining a discrete split between state and identity, and all the rest described in Part I—it is fundamentally a practical language that won't get in the way if you really do need to bash around in a mutable array to get the performance characteristics you require.[18] Further, as long as your usage of mutable arrays is isolated (i.e., you don't let the mutable array escape from the hot code that needs it) and local (i.e., you're not mutating any arrays available globally or as an argument to one of your functions), you have a strong claim that your code is still functional in nature because it retains idempotent semantics.

A basic example where this approach is reasonable is in the construction of a histogram for a dataset. We used Clojure's `frequencies` function to obtain histograms for various datasets in Example 9-20, but let's look at what it would take to implement our own function to produce histograms. Assuming for now that we are working with bounded integer data, a vector might be the most appropriate representation:

```
(defn vector-histogram
  [data]
  (reduce (fn [hist v]
            (update-in hist [v] inc))
    (vec (repeat 10 0))
    data))
```

Let's get a sense of what its performance is like:

```
(def data (doall (repeatedly 1e6 #(rand-int 10))))          ❶
;= #'user/data
(time (vector-histogram data))
; "Elapsed time: 505.409 msecs"
;= [100383 100099 99120 100694 100003 99940 100247 99731 99681 100102]
```

18. The same philosophy is what produced transients, described in "Transients" on page 130, and the pinhole of mutability in `deftype`, covered in "Types" on page 277.

❶ Our dataset is just a sequence of random `Longs` (ensured to be fully realized by using the `doall` function).

`vector-histogram` is using Clojure's immutable vector data structure though—very efficient, but perhaps not efficient enough.[19] Let's try using a primitive array of longs to maintain the counts in our histogram:

Example 11-1. Building a histogram with a temporary array

```
(defn array-histogram
  [data]
  (vec
    (reduce (fn [^longs hist v]
              (aset hist v (inc (aget hist v)))
              hist)
            (long-array 10)
            data)))
```

This is *much* faster, by a factor of ~20×:

```
(time (array-histogram data))
; "Elapsed time: 25.925 msecs"
;= [100383 100099 99120 100694 100003 99940 100247 99731 99681 100102]
```

This is a perfect place to use a primitive array:

1. It matches the model and usage we need and puts no restrictions on the type of inputs it can work with (the `reduce` will work over any sequential collection, including other arrays).

2. The mutable array is only used locally, and never escapes the function. Thus, `array-histogram` is pure, and perfectly at home among other such functions in Clojure.

3. Using an array does not change the semantics a user would expect, including returning the same concrete data structure (a vector) as `vector-histogram`.

The mechanics of primitive arrays

If you want to create an array from an existing collection, you can use either `into-array` or `to-array`. The latter always returns an array of objects; the former will return an array of the type of the first value in the provided collection, or an array of a specified supertype:

```
(into-array ["a" "b" "c"])
;= #<String[] [Ljava.lang.String;@4413515e>
(into-array CharSequence ["a" "b" "c"])             ❶
;= #<CharSequence[] [Ljava.lang.CharSequence;@5acad437>
```

❶ Explicitly producing an array of a supertype of a collection's values can be particularly handy when interoperating with certain Java APIs that require such arrays.

---

19. Using a transient vector instead does provide significant performance gains, but only half that of the forthcoming array-based implementation.

You can also use `into-array` to produce arrays of primitives from collections of boxed values by providing the `Class` corresponding to the desired primitive type:

```
(into-array Long/TYPE (range 5))
;= #<long[] [J@21e3cc77>
```

Clojure provides some helper functions to create primitive or reference arrays: `boolean-array`, `byte-array`, `short-array`, `char-array`, `int-array`, `long-array`, `float-array`, `double-array`, and `object-array`. They take one argument, either the desired size or a collection:

```
(long-array 10)
;= #<long[] [J@12ee6d57>
(long-array (range 10))
;= #<long[] [J@676982f8>
```

Alternatively, except for `object-array`, you can provide both a size and a sequence, if the sequence is too short to initialize the whole array, it is padded with the default value for the corresponding type:

```
(seq (long-array 20 (range 10)))
;= (0 1 2 3 4 5 6 7 8 9 0 0 0 0 0 0 0 0 0 0)
```

`make-array` is used to create new empty arrays of any size or dimensionality, which are initialized to the default value for the type in question (`nil` for object types, `false` for Boolean arrays, and zero for primitive numeric arrays):

```
(def arr (make-array String 5 5))
;= #'user/arr
(aget arr 0 0)
;= nil
(def arr (make-array Boolean/TYPE 10))
;= #'user/arr
(aget arr 0)
;= false
```

Array classes.   While `make-array` allows you to create arrays of any dimensionality, there are cases where you need to obtain a `Class` corresponding to an array type; for example, to extend a protocol to an array of a particular type, as shown in Example 6-2. You can always get the `Class` of an array type using `class`:

```
(class (make-array Character/TYPE 0 0 0))
;= [[[C
```

But creating an array just to get a `Class` instance seems wrong somehow, akin to creating an array of some length in order to get a reference to that length's number.

Notice how the printed representation of the array `Class` above uses an unusual notation? This is how the JVM names classes corresponding to array types. While every box class provides a static `TYPE` field corresponding to its primitive's `Class`, there are no predefined `Classes` for nested arrays. Instead, you can use `Class/forName` to look up the `Class` for such types using the JVM's notation, for example:

```
(Class/forName "[[Z")
;= [[Z
(.getComponentType *1)
;= [Z
(.getComponentType *1)
;= boolean
```

The notation is a bit arcane, but it is regular. Each prefixed bracket indicates one level in the depth of the array type, so `"[Z"` corresponds to a one-dimensional `boolean` array, `"[[Z"` corresponds to a two-dimensional `boolean` array, and so on. There is a character reserved for each primitive type:

- Z—boolean
- B—byte
- C—char
- J—long
- I—int
- S—short
- D—double
- F—float

Array-specific type hints.   In general, unless Clojure knows what type of array you're working with, access and mutation operations will end up happening reflectively, thus working against arrays' usefulness as a local optimization. There is a set of type hints specifically intended for use with arrays:

```
^objects
^booleans
^bytes
^chars
^longs
^ints
^shorts
^doubles
^floats
```

You can see this at work in `array-histogram` in Example 11-1; if we hadn't hinted the `hist` argument to our reduce function, both the `aget` and `aset` operations turn into reflective calls, resulting in a running time *88x worse* than the our baseline histogram implementation that used immutable vectors!

Access and mutation.   `aget` and `aset` provide array access and mutation operations, respectively:

```
(let [arr (long-array 10)]
  (aset arr 0 50)
  (aget arr 0))
;= 50
```

Both operations require that the array's type be known in order to avoid reflection, usually provided by a suitable type hint. In this example, `arr` is known to be an array of longs since it's declared locally.

There are some special considerations when accessing and modifying values in multidimensional arrays, which we'll get to shortly.

map and reduce over arrays. map and reduce are pleasant to use, but they work with sequences that, as generic collections, can only hold objects. Thus, when applied to processing arrays, map and reduce prompt the liberal boxing of what had been primitive values.

Anything you can do with map and reduce can be unrolled into a loop expression, which does offer full primitive support. However, writing loop forms is error-prone insofar as you must track and manage indices into the array(s) being operated upon.

To spare us such things, Clojure provides `amap` and `areduce`, macros that are modeled after their functional counterparts but specialized to operate over arrays while avoiding autoboxing:

```
(let [a (int-array (range 10))]
  (amap a i res
    (inc (aget a i))))
;= #<int[] [I@eaf261a>
(seq *1)
;= (1 2 3 4 5 6 7 8 9 10)
```

amap expects four arguments: the "source" array to map an expression across, the name to give to the index (i here), the name to give to the result array that is initialized as a copy of the source array (res here), and then an expression whose result will be set at index i in the result array res.

areduce works in a similar way:

```
(let [a (int-array (range 10))]
  (areduce a i sum 0
    (+ sum (aget a i))))
;= 45
```

a and i play the same role as in amap. sum is the name of the accumulator (corresponding to the first argument of the function provided to reduce), followed by the accumulator's initial value, and then an expression whose value becomes the accumulator value for the next iteration—or, the result of the areduce form after the reduction is complete.

Multidimensional concerns. While aset and aget are easy to use with one-dimensional arrays, some additional care must be taken when working with multidimensional arrays. While the "terminal" values in multidimensional arrays are of the primitive type you specify, the intermediate levels are arrays of objects (other arrays). In addition, because it is impossible for aget and aset to provide arities for all possible array dimensionalities, they support multidimensional operations by recursively using apply to get or set each level of multidimensional arrays.

All of this adds up to potentially devastating performance for simple operations on multidimensional arrays:

```
(def arr (make-array Double/TYPE 1000 1000))
;= #'user/arr
(time (dotimes [i 1000]
        (dotimes [j 1000]
          (aset arr i j 1.0)
          (aget arr i j))))
; "Elapsed time: 50802.798 msecs"
```

Because **aset** does not provide a direct arity for N-dimensional arrays, **1.0** is getting boxed by **aset** when it uses **apply** to propagate its rest arguments. Further, there is no way for us to hint or declare that **arr** is an array of primitive arrays; thus, all the operations involved are happening reflectively. The only fast path for both **aget** and **aset** are when operating on a properly hinted one-dimensional array.

The "fix" is to unpack the multidimensional array manually, providing the necessary hinting:

```
(time (dotimes [i 1000]
        (dotimes [j 1000]
          (let [^doubles darr (aget ^objects arr i)]
            (aset darr j 1.0)
            (aget darr j)))))
; "Elapsed time: 21.543 msecs"
;= nil
```

Yes, that's a *2600×* performance differential compared to our prior naive usage of **aset** and **aget** with multidimensional arrays, and as fast as the equivalent Java code.[20]

Automating type hinting of multidimensional array operations

So, we know how to get optimal performance, but it involves some perhaps error-prone hinting and more code than we'd like: a separate **let**-binding is needed for each step down into the array. This calls for a couple of macros to automate the unpacking and proper hinting of operations on multidimensional arrays:[21]

Example 11-2. deep-aget

```
(defmacro deep-aget
  "Gets a value from a multidimensional array as if via `aget`,
  but with automatic application of appropriate type hints to
  each step in the array traversal as guided by the hint added
  to the source array.

  e.g. (deep-aget ^doubles arr i j)"
```

---

20. The equivalent Java code actually does essentially the same work, but Java's syntax is optimized to support concise array access and mutation, and its static compilation model can easily derive the interim types involved.

21. This approach was originally described in *http://clj-me.cgrand.net/2009/10/15/multidim-arrays*.

```
([array idx]
  `(aget ~array ~idx))                                                    ❶
([array idx & idxs]
  (let [a-sym (gensym "a")]
    `(let [~a-sym (aget ~(vary-meta array assoc :tag 'objects) ~idx]      ❷
       (deep-aget ~(with-meta a-sym {:tag (-> array meta :tag)}) ~@idxs)))))❸
```

❶ If we are accessing a one-dimensional array (indicated by the single index), then we use aget directly, and assume that the array symbol is properly hinted.

❷ If we're still "above" the terminal array, we obtain the next array down, making sure to hint the array argument to aget as ^objects.

❸ We make a recursive call to deep-aget with a-sym (that next array down), reapplying the terminal array type hint to it in case it is the terminal array; if it is, the single-index arity of deep-aget at <1> will receive the call, and perform the terminal aget.

deep-aset has to take a different approach than deep-aget, since it needs to use deep-aget to efficiently traverse the multidimensional array to get to where it can finally apply aset to the terminal array value:

Example 11-3. deep-aset

```
(defmacro deep-aset
  "Sets a value in a multidimensional array as if via `aset`,
  but with automatic application of appropriate type hints to
  each step in the array traversal as guided by the hint added
  to the target array.

  e.g. (deep-aset ^doubles arr i j 1.0)"
  [array & idxsv]
  (let [hints '{booleans boolean, bytes byte                             ❶
                chars char, longs long
                ints int, shorts short
                doubles double, floats float}
        hint (-> array meta :tag)
        [v idx & sxdi] (reverse idxsv)
        idxs (reverse sxdi)
        v (if-let [h (hints hint)] (list h v) v)
        nested-array (if (seq idxs)
                       `(deep-aget ~(vary-meta array assoc :tag 'objects) ~@idxs)
                       array)
        a-sym (gensym "a")]
    `(let [~a-sym ~nested-array]
       (aset ~(with-meta a-sym {:tag hint}) ~idx ~v))))
```

❶ A mapping is maintained between array hint symbols and primitive coercion function names; if array is hinted using one of the former, then the corresponding coercion expression will be used in conjunction with aset and the value given to deep-aset. This allows the user to, for example, set a value in a multidimensional array of doubles using a long, as the long will be coerced in the aset call via (double v).

Using `deep-aget` and `deep-aset`, we can get the same performance as we would if we were unpacking and hinting N-dimensional array manually:

```
(time (dotimes [i 1000]
        (dotimes [j 1000]
          (deep-aset ^doubles arr i j 1.0)
          (deep-aget ^doubles arr i j))))
; "Elapsed time: 25.033 msecs"
```

 When `*warn-on-reflection*` is set to `true`, calls to `aget` and `aset` on arrays whose type can't be inferred raise a warning...except for multi-dimensional arities!

Visualizing the Mandelbrot Set in Clojure

Let's take a look at a somewhat more interesting example than the overused Fibonacci and prime number generators that are often used for microbenchmarking numeric performance. Visualizing the Mandelbrot Set[22] (or really, any fractal shape visualization) has long been a common practicum, and it will serve well here as a demonstration of how to optimize numeric algorithms in Clojure.

The Mandelbrot Set is defined by a complex polynomial that is applied iteratively:

$$z_{k+1} = z_k^2 + c$$

where c (a complex number) is a member of the Mandelbrot Set if z_{k+1} is bounded as k increases when z_0 is initialized to 0. c's that produce unbounded results from this calculation are said to *escape* to infinity.

First, let's look at a naive implementation of the Mandelbrot Set in Clojure,[23] which includes a couple utility functions for rendering the results of that implementation:

Example 11-4. Mandelbrot Set in Clojure

```
(ns clojureprogramming.mandelbrot
  (:import java.awt.image.BufferedImage
           (java.awt Color RenderingHints)))

(defn- escape
  "Returns an integer indicating how many iterations were required
   before the value of z (using the components `a` and `b`) could
   be determined to have escaped the Mandelbrot set.  If z
```

22. See *http://en.wikipedia.org/wiki/Mandelbrot_set* for a gentle introduction to the Mandelbrot Set, the mathematics behind it, and how you can go about generating visualizations of it. We'd also be remiss if we didn't point you toward Jonathan Coulton's fantastic song and music video about the Mandelbrot Set and its creator/discoverer Benoît Mandelbrot: *http://www.youtube.com/watch?v=ES-yKOYaXq0*.

23. Simpler implementations are possible; for example, by using the `iterate` function to lazily calculate the result of the complex polynomial, and `take`-ing only as many results from the head of that lazy seq as dictated by our maximum iteration count. Such approaches are much more concise, but because they utilize lazy seqs and collections, the results of our calculations will be boxed—and thus, much slower.

```
  will not escape, -1 is returned."
  [a0 b0 depth]
  (loop [a a0
         b b0
         iteration 0]
    (cond
      (< 4 (+ (* a a) (* b b))) iteration
      (>= iteration depth) -1
      :else (recur (+ a0 (- (* a a) (* b b)))
                   (+ b0 (* 2 (* a b)))
                   (inc iteration)))))

(defn mandelbrot
  "Calculates membership within and number of iterations to escape
   from the Mandelbrot set for the region defined by `rmin`, `rmax`
   `imin` and `imax` (real and imaginary components of z, respectively).

   Optional kwargs include `:depth` (maximum number of iterations
   to calculate escape of a point from the set), `:height` ('pixel'
   height of the rendering), and `:width` ('pixel' width of the
   rendering).

   Returns a seq of row vectors containing iteration numbers for when
   the corresponding point escaped from the set. -1 indicates points
   that did not escape in fewer than `depth` iterations, i.e. they
   belong to the set.  These integers can be used to drive most common
   Mandelbrot set visualizations."
  [rmin rmax imin imax & {:keys [width height depth]
                          :or {width 80 height 40 depth 1000}}]
  (let [rmin (double rmin)
        imin (double imin)
        stride-w (/ (- rmax rmin) width)
        stride-h (/ (- imax imin) height)]
    (loop [x 0
           y (dec height)
           escapes []]
      (if (== x width)
        (if (zero? y)
          (partition width escapes)
          (recur 0 (dec y) escapes))
        (recur (inc x) y (conj escapes (escape (+ rmin (* x stride-w))
                                               (+ imin (* y stride-h))
                                               depth)))))))

(defn render-text
  "Prints a basic textual rendering of mandelbrot set membership,
   as returned by a call to `mandelbrot`."
  [mandelbrot-grid]
  (doseq [row mandelbrot-grid]
    (doseq [escape-iter row]
      (print (if (neg? escape-iter) \* \space)))
    (println)))

(defn render-image
  "Given a mandelbrot set membership grid as returned by a call to
```

```
`mandelbrot`, returns a BufferedImage with the same resolution as the
grid that uses a discrete grayscale color palette."
[mandelbrot-grid]
(let [palette (vec (for [c (range 500)]
                    (Color/getHSBColor 0.0 0.0 (/ (Math/log c) (Math/log 500)))))
      height (count mandelbrot-grid)
      width (count (first mandelbrot-grid))
      img (BufferedImage. width height BufferedImage/TYPE_INT_RGB)
      ^java.awt.Graphics2D g (.getGraphics img)]
  (doseq [[y row] (map-indexed vector mandelbrot-grid)
          [x escape-iter] (map-indexed vector row)]
    (.setColor g (if (neg? escape-iter)
                   (palette 0)
                   (palette (mod (dec (count palette)) (inc escape-iter)))))
    (.drawRect g x y 1 1))
  (.dispose g)
  img))
```

The mandelbrot function returns a grid, each member being the number of iterations
of the polynomial that was required before the corresponding point escaped to infinity;
points that never escaped to infinity and therefore are members of the set are represented by a −1 iteration count. The simplest (and admittedly crude) visualization of the
Mandelbrot Set can be obtained by printing asterisks and spaces to the console, which
is implemented in the render-text function:[24]

```
(render-text (mandelbrot -2.25 0.75 -1.5 1.5 :width 80 :height 40 :depth 100))
```

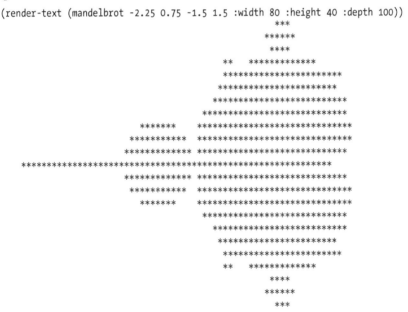

24. The nature of text—where characters are taller than they are wide—necessitates using a skewed aspect
    ratio (80 × 40 here) so the results look similar to image renderings that generally have 1:1 aspect ratios.

However, if we were to zoom in (i.e., change the domain of our visualization to focus in on smaller, interesting subfeatures of the set), we would need to perform many, many more iterations of the escape function than the 100 we're performing here. A quick timing of what that would require—for example, to generate a 1600×1200 image— shows that the implementation above is perhaps not as fast as we'd like:

```
(do (time (mandelbrot -2.25 0.75 -1.5 1.5
                :width 1600 :height 1200 :depth 1000))
    nil)
; "Elapsed time: 82714.764 msecs"
```

If you were to build an application to interactively explore the Mandelbrot Set (or perhaps perform some automated exploration of the same), this performance would be totally unacceptable.

The hottest part of this code is clearly the loop in the escape function. We can't do much about the complexity of the calculations it is performing—that is dictated by the Mandelbrot Set's definitional polynomial—but we can eliminate the numeric boxing that is going on.

As we discussed in "Declare Functions to Take and Return Primitives" on page 438, functions in Clojure are implemented by Java methods that accept java.lang.Objects as arguments, so the a0 and b0 double primitives that the mandelbrot function is calling escape with (the real and imaginary components of z in the Mandelbrot Set polynomial, respectively) end up getting boxed into Double objects. This cascades down to the types of the bindings in the loop form and kills the entire function's performance: initializing a and b with a0 and b0 implicitly types the former bindings as Double as well, so every single arithmetic operation in escape ends up having to unbox these values, with the results necessarily being boxed when they're rebound to a and b in the recur form.

The solution is to eliminate the untyped bindings in the first place; note the ^double type declarations for the a0 and b0 arguments in our revised implementation of escape, which is otherwise unchanged.

Example 11-5. Revised escape function declaring primitive numeric argument types

```
(defn- escape
  [^double a0 ^double b0 depth]
  (loop [a a0
         b b0
         iteration 0]
    (cond
      (< 4 (+ (* a a) (* b b))) iteration
      (>= iteration depth) -1
      :else (recur (+ a0 (- (* a a) (* b b)))
                   (+ b0 (* 2 (* a b)))
                   (inc iteration)))))
```

Now the escape function's generated class takes primitive doubles as its first two arguments. Clojure's type inference does the rest: the a and b bindings in loop are typed as double as well, permitting all of the arithmetic to work exclusively with primitive

---

arguments and avoiding the boxing of results when the arguments to recur are rebound to their corresponding names in the loop.

What's the concrete upshot? An order-of-magnitude improvement:

```
(do (time (mandelbrot -2.25 0.75 -1.5 1.5
                :width 1600 :height 1200 :depth 1000))
    nil)
; "Elapsed time: 8663.841 msecs"
```

With that improvement, we can reasonably go ahead and start exploring the set, using the render-image function to produce a rasterization of the Mandelbrot Set membership grid, shown in Figures 11-2 and 11-3.

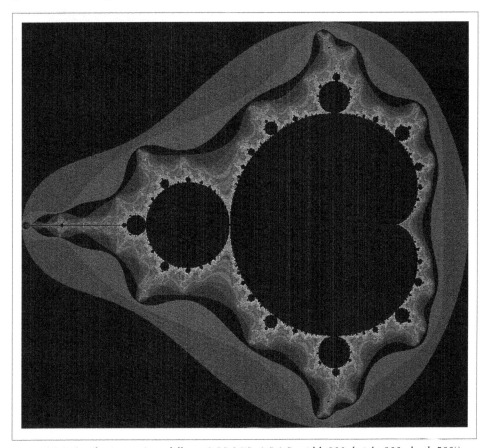

Figure 11-2. (render-image (mandelbrot -2.25 0.75 -1.5 1.5 :width 800 :height 800 :depth 500))

Figure 11-3. (render-image (mandelbrot -1.5 -1.3 -0.1 0.1 :width 800 :height 800 :depth 500))

`render-image` uses a fixed, discrete grayscale palette. Changing it so that it uses a colorful or continuous palette is left as an exercise.

If you're using a typical textual REPL,[25] then evaluating the above expressions will return a `BufferedImage` instance. You can save this image to disk using the JDK's `ImageIO` class and its `write` method:

```
(javax.imageio.ImageIO/write *1 "png" (java.io.File. "mandelbrot.png"))
```

which will save the image bound to `*1`[26] as a PNG to the file *mandelbrot.png* in your current directory. It would be easy enough to write a function to encapsulate this call.

There are all sorts of more advanced algorithmic techniques for speeding Mandelbrot Set calculations that would improve the running time of `mandelbrot` much further, but those are out of scope here. A few Clojure-specific optimizations might include:

- Instead of doing all of the computation within an imperative `loop`, recharacterizing it as a lazy sequence using, for example, `for` would allow you to trivially parallelize the computations using `pmap`.

- Returning a grid (seq of rows of point escape iteration numbers) from `mandelbrot` affords a great deal of flexibility. As we've seen, we can use the same resulting data structure to produce a text representation or a bitmap; similarly, a 3D renderer could be swapped in without changing `mandelbrot` or `escape`. Producing that grid does carry a cost though, so it might be worthwhile to thread a reference to a callback function through `mandelbrot` into `escape` so that each per-point action (whether that's printing a character to the console or painting a pixel on a bitmap) can be performed without any of the allocations associated with collections and sequences. Of course, that callback function should have its primitive arguments declared as we just did for `escape` to avoid boxing.

25. Clojure REPLs that support the display of mixed content are starting to appear; in such a REPL, evaluating `render-image` would immediately display the generated image without you having to save it to disk or otherwise get the image data out of the REPL. For an example of this, see *http://cemerick.com/2011/10/26/enabling-richer-interactions-in-the-clojure-repl*.

26. Remember that `*1` is always bound to the value of the last-evaluated expression in the REPL. See "REPL-bound vars" (page 399) for details and similar handy vars.

## CHAPTER 12

Design Patterns

Design patterns are generic, reusable solutions to recurring problems. A hallmark of object-oriented programming, they provide a common vocabulary that many in the Java and Ruby worlds are familiar with.

On the other hand, patterns can be a source of verbosity and boilerplate. To this point, Paul Graham observed that the existence and use of design patterns in a language are indicative of a weakness in the language itself, rather than a consequence of solving the problem at hand:

> When I see patterns in my programs, I consider it a sign of trouble. The shape of a program should reflect only the problem it needs to solve. Any other regularity in the code is a sign, to me at least, that I'm using abstractions that aren't powerful enough...

> —Paul Graham, *http://www.paulgraham.com/icad.html*

Graham was hardly the first to make this observation; Peter Norvig demonstrated some time ago (*http://www.norvig.com/design-patterns/*) that Lisps in particular either simplify or make invisible most design patterns. Clojure continues this tradition: thanks to powerful constructs like first-class functions, dynamic typing, and immutable values, many of the most common design patterns evaporate into thin air. And, with macros, Clojure gives you the tools you need to avoid creating boilerplate of your own.

Examples of Clojure code subsuming common design patterns are scattered throughout this book:

Listener, Observer.   A victim of first-class functions and dynamic typing, these are just functions that are called when a relevant event occurs; this can be seen with watches on references types in "Watches" on page 176. Outside of reference types, the preferred use of immutable values means that the scope of mutable things that you need to track is greatly minimized.

Abstract Factory, Strategy, Command.   If you have multiple implementations of any sort of functionality—whether it's to produce values of differing types or configurations, or to implement variations on an algorithm—there is no need to produce a

FactoryFactory[1] or a context to invoke your algorithm implementations. In both cases, just another function will do.

Iterator.   Iterators are completely supersetted by sequences, described in "Sequences" on page 89, and their use is effortless and declarative via functions like map.

Adapter, Wrapper, Delegate.   Made necessary by inflexible type hierarchies elsewhere, these are made unnecessary by protocols, which allow you orthogonally define new behavior for existing types without appeals to inheritance, adaptation, or wrapping. See Chapter 6.

Memento.   Layering a common API over top the mutation of an object solves the most mechanical of problems (API generality), but does nothing to address the glaring complexity of the mutable state itself. Immutable collections and records invert this strategy: mutable state is barred from values, retaining prior versions of those values is cheap and easy, and state transitions are left to reference types (each of which provides a different API to suit its respective concurrency and change semantics).

Template Method.   The limitations of class inheritance are well-known and felt daily by millions, yet it is used widely, often as the sole way to compose functionality within many languages. This dubious mingling of concerns is better recast as a higher-order function that can accept functions implementing the variable behavior while providing a canonical implementation of shared functionality. For example, if we needed to be able to call equivalent HTTP APIs offered by different providers based on some application-internal data structure, a HOF would allow us to define the provider-specific functionality as a separate function, while keeping the universal HTTP plumbing in one place:

```
(defn- update-status*
  [service-name service-endpoint-url request-data-fn]
  (fn [new-status]
    (log (format "Updating status @ %s to %s" service-name new-status))
    (let [http-request-data (request-data-fn new-status)
          connection (-> service-endpoint-url java.net.URL. .openConnection)]
      ;; ...set request method, parameters, body on `connection`
      ;; ...perform actual request
      ;; ...return result based on HTTP response status
      )))

(def update-facebook-status (update-status* "Facebook" "http://facebook.com/apis/..."
                              (fn [status]
                                {:params {:_a "update_status"
                                          :_t status}
                                 :method "GET"})))

(def update-twitter-status ...)
(def update-google-status ...)
```

---

1. Leave such things to the factory-building experts: *http://discuss.joelonsoftware.com/default.asp?joel.3.219431.12.*

Let's dig into some other common patterns in more detail, a couple of which are now so baked into common programming practice in other languages, it may take a little work to sift them out again.

Dependency Injection

In many object-oriented languages, *dependency injection* is a way to decouple a class from other objects upon which that class depends. Instead of an object initializing other objects internally, it accepts those objects as parameters that are often automagically supplied by the runtime or application container that is hosting your program.

In a static language like Java, this is accomplished by programming to interfaces rather than concrete classes. Consider this implementation of the ubiquitous pet store concept:

```java
interface IDog {
    public String bark();
}

class Chihuahua implements IDog {
    public String bark() {
        return "Yip!";
    }
}

class Mastiff implements IDog {
    public String bark() {
        return "Woof!";
    }
}

class PetStore {
    private IDog dog;
    public PetStore() {
        this.dog = new Mastiff();
    }

    public IDog getDog() {
        return dog;
    }
}

static class MyApp {
    public static void main(String[] args) {
        PetStore store = new PetStore();
        System.out.println(store.getDog().bark());
    }
}
```

Our pet store only works with mastiffs. If we want to change it to support different types of dogs, we have to alter and recompile the PetStore class. To make PetStore more reusable, we might rewrite PetStore like so:

```
class PetStore {
    private IDog dog;
    public PetStore(IDog dog) {
        this.dog = dog;
    }

    public IDog getDog() {
        return dog;
    }
}

class MyApp {
    public static void main(String[] args) {
        PetStore store = new PetStore(new Chihuahua());
        System.out.println(store.getDog().bark());
    }
}
```

Now the store's dog type has been parameterized. A particular type of dog is "injected" into our PetStore via its constructor; PetStore won't need to be recompiled each time we want to use a different dog. We can even use PetStore with classes that didn't exist when PetStore was written; we just have to implement the IDog interface and we're done. This allows us to easily create mock dog types for testing, for example.

The injection of dependencies is usually done by a "container" that uses runtime configuration to automatically initialize key objects with implementations of interfaces automatically discovered on the classpath or specified in its configuration. Depending upon the container implementation you're working with, this configuration usually takes the form of a separately managed set of configuration code or XML files.

Clojure turns this problem inside-out. Where bark is a method defined by our IDog classes in Java, Clojure code would define bark as a protocol method, detached from any concrete types.

```
(defprotocol Bark
  (bark [this]))

(defrecord Chihuahua []
  Bark
  (bark [this] "Yip!"))

(defrecord Mastiff []
  Bark
  (bark [this] "Woof!"))
```

Now, our pet store would look like this:

```
(defrecord PetStore [dog])

(defn main
  [dog]
  (let [store (PetStore. dog)]
    (println (bark (:dog store)))))
```

```
(main (Chihuahua.))
;= Yip!

(main (Mastiff.))
;= Woof!
```

Yes, that's it! Our PetStore is now one short line of code.

In Java, PetStore is limited to objects that implement the IDog interface. In Clojure, PetStore has no such limitation: it accepts any kind of parameter. As long as the Bark protocol is implemented for that type, things will work just fine. This allows us to do things that Java would never allow, such as extending Bark to classes we don't control. With this simple code:

```
(extend-protocol Bark
  java.util.Map
  (bark [this]
    (or (:bark this)
        (get this "bark"))))
```

...we can now use any Map as a dog, including a Clojure IPersistentMap or a Java HashMap, where the bark string can be mapped to either :bark or "bark":[2]

```
(main (doto (java.util.HashMap.)
        (.put "bark" "Ouah!")))
;= Ouah!

(main {:bark "Wan-wan!"})
;= Wan wan!
```

If you're using records, all of the fields are dynamic (unless declared to be primitive), so there are no types to drive automagical configuration as with dependency injection containers (either a good or bad thing depending upon your perspective). The upside is that, without a container,[3] the options available for configuration *expand*. For example, here's a suitable "configuration file" (really, just a file containing Clojure-readable data that we'll only read and not evaluate):

Example 12-1. petstore-config.clj

```
{:dog #user.Chihuahua{:weight 12, :price "$84.50"}}
```

Recall from "Readable representation" (page 274) that this #user.Chihuahua{...} notation is the readable representation of the named record type. We believe this compares *very* well to alternatives such configuring Spring beans using XML, @Bean annotations, or similar approaches offered by other dependency injection containers.

---

2. Other dog bark onomatopoeia courtesy of *https://en.wikipedia.org/wiki/Bark_%28utterance%29 #Representation*.

3. Note that you can absolutely opt to use "legacy" dependency injection containers (like Spring, Guice, et al.) with Clojure types and records.

An augmented `PetStore` factory function could read the configuration for our particular environment:

Example 12-2. configured-petstore

```
(defn configured-petstore
  []
  (-> "petstore-config.clj"
    slurp
    read-string
    map->PetStore))
```

Now we'll always get a properly "injected" `PetStore`:

```
(configured-petstore)
;= #user.PetStore{:dog #user.Chihuahua{:weight 12, :price "$84.50"}}
```

Strategy Pattern

Another common design pattern is the *strategy* pattern. This pattern allows the selection of a method or algorithm dynamically. Suppose we want to select a sorting algorithm at runtime:

```
interface ISorter {
    public sort (int[] numbers);
}

class QuickSort implements ISorter {
    public sort (int[] numbers) { ... }
}

class MergeSort implements ISorter {
    public sort (int[] numbers) { ... }
}

class Sorter {
    private ISorter sorter;
    public Sorter (ISorter sorter) {
        this.sorter = sorter;
    }

    public execute (int[] numbers) {
        sorter.sort(numbers);
    }
}

class App {
    public ISorter chooseSorter () {
        if (...) {
            return new QuickSort();
        } else {
            return new MergeSort();
        }
    }
```

```
    public static void main(String[] args) {
        int[] numbers = {5,1,4,2,3};

        Sorter s = new Sorter(chooseSorter());

        s.execute(numbers);

        //... now use sorted numbers
    }
}
```

Clojure has a very simple advantage over Java in this case. Whereas in Java, we need to put methods into classes, functions are first-class objects in Clojure. Translated literally, our Clojure code might look like this:

```
(defn quicksort [numbers] ...)

(defn mergesort [numbers] ...)

(defn choose-sorter
  []
  (if ...
    quicksort
    mergesort))

(defn main
  []
  (let [numbers [...]]
    ((choose-sorter) numbers)))
```

There are no classes in sight. Each function implementing the semantics of our algorithm can be called directly, without class definitions getting in the way of our specifying behavior.

You don't even have to give your sorting algorithm a name—an anonymous function works just as well. For example, the composition of Clojure's built-in **sort** function and then **reverse** to reverse the sort order is an anonymous function:

```
((comp reverse sort) [2 1 3])
;= (3 2 1)
```

Chain of Responsibility

While Clojure's facilities make many patterns unnecessary or invisible, a select few remain relevant and continue to impact our design and implementation of Clojure programs. One of these is a common form of flow control called *chain of responsibility*. In this pattern, an event is sent off to be processed by some set handlers. A handler can process the event or pass the event on to another processing handler. These handlers form a chain, and the event is passed down the chain until one of the handlers determines that the event should not be propagated further.

Chain of command is useful because it allows a process to be defined in multiple parts that can be composed and combined. No step needs to know anything about other steps in the process, other than how to pass control down the chain.

This concept shows up in many areas. Unix pipes are an example where textual data is passed from process to process. Filters on Java Servlets are another, where web requests are passed through a series of filters until or before a response is generated.

In Java, a chain of responsibility can be constructed by defining a series of "processor" objects and then initializing each with a pointer to the next processor.

```
abstract class Processor {
    protected Processor next;
    public addToChain(Processor p) {
        next = p;
    }
    public runChain(data) {
        Boolean continue = this.process(data);
        if(continue and next != null) {
            next.runChain(data);
        }
    }
    abstract public boolean process(String data);
}

class FooProcessor extends Processor {
    public boolean process(String data) {
        System.out.println("FOO says pass...");
        return true;
    }
}

class BarProcessor extends Processor {
    public boolean process(String data) {
        System.out.println("BAR " + data + " and let's stop here");
        return false;
    }
}

class BazProcessor extends Processor {
    public boolean process(String data) {
        System.out.println("BAZ?");
        return true;
    }
}

Processor chain = new FooProcessor().addToChain(
    new BarProcessor).addToChain(new BazProcessor);
chain.run("data123");
```

In this example, we use a simple protocol of returning Boolean true to indicate that set of data is unhandled, and false to continue passing data through the chain.

In Clojure, our basic unit of execution is the function rather than the class or method. This means we can implement something like a chain of responsibility by using simple function composition.

```clojure
(defn foo [data]
  (println "FOO passes")
  true)

(defn bar [data]
  (println "BAR" data "and let's stop here")
  false)

(defn baz [data]
  (println "BAZ?")
  true)

(defn wrap [f1 f2]
  (fn [data]
    (when (f1 data)
      (f2 data))))

(def chain (reduce wrap [foo bar baz]))
```

Here we define a function **wrap**, which takes two functions and composes them in a way similar to our Java example: f1 is run and if it returns true, f2 is run next. We can build a pipeline of functions in this way, which will run until a function terminates the chain or the chain runs out. We can then compose a series of functions by using a simple reduce.

Ring.   A more real-world example of a chain of command in Clojure is the Ring library, which we'll discuss in detail in Chapter 16. Ring is a library to process requests to a web server. A handler for a request is a function that accepts a request object in the form of a Clojure map, and returns a response object as another Clojure map.

Functions that modify and process these responses and requests are called *middleware*. Middleware can be composed in much the same way we did above in our example. Imagine we begin with a simple handler:

```clojure
(defn my-app
  [request]
  {:status 200
   :headers {"Content-type" "text/html"}
   :body (format "<html><body>You requested: %s</body></html>"
           (:uri request))})
```

We can then "wrap" this handler with middleware that performs a variety of other functions. One piece of middleware might parse web cookie data in the request and add a :cookie key to the request or response map. Another bit of middleware might do something similar for :session data. These kinds of middleware are already provided by Ring for your use, but it doesn't offer logging middleware that can log the request to a logfile; defining this middleware might look like so:

```
(defn wrap-logger
  [handler]
  (fn [request]
    (println (:uri request))
    (handler request)))
```

Depending upon the objectives of a piece of middleware, it can perform actions before or after passing the processing of the request to the next handler in the chain—or, if appropriate, not pass on the request at all. Our naive logging middleware simply dumps each request :uri to stdout before calling the next handler.

We can then use the cookies and session middleware provided by Ring along with the logging middleware we defined:

```
(require '[ring.middleware cookies session])
```

```
(def my-app (-> my-app
                ring.middleware.cookies/wrap-cookies
                ring.middleware.session/wrap-session
                wrap-logger))
```

This method of composition is very similar to comp, which we explored in "Composition of Function(ality)" on page 68, insofar as it yields a function that processes each bit of middleware in the reverse order of how they are included as arguments in the -> form. Because wrap-logger was the last middleware function to be invoked, the function it returns forms the outermost extent of the composed function, with my-app being the innermost piece.

Aspect-Oriented Programming

Aspect-oriented programming (AOP) is a methodology that allows separation of cross-cutting concerns. In object-oriented code, a behavior or process is often repeated in multiple classes, or spread across multiple methods. AOP is a way to abstract this behavior and apply it to classes and methods without using inheritance.

A common example is metrics. It's often desirable to produce and record timing metrics or other debugging information for running code. There is no easy way to compose this behavior into existing functionality in object-oriented codebases, so timing code ends up being added to particular methods of interest and then (hopefully!) commented out when it's no longer being used:

```
public class Foo
    public void expensiveComputation () {
        long start = System.currentTimeMillis();
        try {
            // do computation
        } catch (Exception e) {
            // log error
        } finally {
            long stop = System.currentTimeMillis();
            System.out.println("Run time: " + (stop - start) + "ms");
```

```
            }
        }
    }
```

Logging the runtime for a method requires altering the method, edits that we'd have to make repeatedly in order to instrument multiple methods. What we'd really like is a generally applicable way to "wrap" a method with some behavior. A function or method that does this is sometimes called *advice*.

If we have the capability to define advice separate from the methods that that advice will apply to, we gain a lot of flexibility:

- We can selectively apply[4] the advice on a per-method basis without modifying the methods themselves; debugging or other development-time advice (such as benchmarks or tracing) can be disabled entirely by changing a single configuration or choosing to simply not apply AOP transformations entirely.

- We can alter the behavior of the advice in one place rather than across multiple methods, so, for example, enhancements to code used to provide timings or other metrics need only be made once.

One implementation of AOP in Java is AspectJ (*http://www.eclipse.org/aspectj/*), an extension to Java that provides access to additional Java-like constructs for AOP. AspectJ provides its own compiler, which compiles AspectJ code into Java classes, which can then be weaved into your application's classes based on specifications of which methods and classes should be affected (called *pointcuts*). Let's look at an AspectJ example, starting with a class that contains a method for which we might want to obtain metrics:

```
public class AspectJExample {
    public void longRunningMethod () {
        System.out.println("Starting long-running method");
        try {
            Thread.sleep((long)(1000 + Math.random() * 2000));
        } catch (InterruptedException e) {
        }
    }
}
```

Next, we define a Timing aspect that will apply to all methods in this class:

```
public aspect Timing {
    pointcut profiledMethods(): call(* AspectJExample.* (..));      ❶

    long time;

    before(): profiledMethods() {                                  ❷
        time = System.currentTimeMillis();
    }

    after(): profiledMethods() {                                   ❸
        System.out.println("Call to " + thisJoinPoint.getSignature() +
```

---

4. The application of advice or other aspect transformations is often called *weaving*.

```
                    " took " + (System.currentTimeMillis() - time) + "ms");
        }
    }
```

❶ AspectJ has its own syntax for matching packages, classes, and method signatures; this pointcut matches all methods in the `AspectJExample` class, which we'll use to guide the application of the `before` and `after` advice.

❷ The aspect code that runs before affected methods obtains the current time so we can make a comparison to the time after the method returns.

❸ Code that is run after affected methods, wherein we naively dump the runtime of the method to stdout.

If we run a program that calls `AspectJExample.longRunningMethod`, then we'll see output similar to this:

```
Starting long-running method
Call to void com.clojurebook.AspectJExample.longRunningMethod() took 1599ms
```

Rather than potentially making modifications throughout our codebase in order to change or elide "profiling," changing the behavior of the AspectJ advice can be done in one place, or suspended entirely by just modifying the pointcut or not weaving the aspect into our methods or application to begin with.

Robert Hooke.   In Clojure, a superset of the functionality of aspect-oriented programming is easy to obtain thanks to vars and first-class functions. Functions can easily be passed as arguments to other functions, and Clojure allows vars to be redefined at runtime; these two features combine to allow easy "wrapping" of functions with other functions to modify behavior or results however you like.

The Robert Hooke library (*https://github.com/technomancy/robert-hooke*) provides a simple and powerful way to define advice (referred to as *hooks*) for functions. Back to our example above, setting up a hook to time a function is easy:

```
(defn time-it [f & args]
  (let [start (System/currentTimeMillis)]
    (try
      (apply f args)
      (finally
        (println "Run time: " (- (System/currentTimeMillis) start) "ms")))))
```

`time-it` is a regular Clojure function. It takes as its two arguments another function *f* and some set of arguments `args`, which will be the arguments the caller intended to pass to *f*. Our advice can do anything before or after calling *f* (if it decides to call *f* at all); in this case, we just record running time.

There's no contortion needed to allow `time-it` to invoke *f*; it simply calls it via `apply`, passing it the arguments in `args`. Note that thanks to variadic arguments, `time-it` works for any function regardless of how many arguments that function might require.

This advice can be applied to a function like so:

```
(require 'robert.hooke)

(defn foo [x y]
  (Thread/sleep (rand-int 1000))
  (+ x y))

(robert.hooke/add-hook #'foo time-it)  ❶
```

❶ The robert.hooke calls to add time-it hook to the var #'foo, which will affect all calls of its function.

And now when we invoke foo, we see the result of our time-it code running:

```
(foo 1 2)
; Run time:   772 ms
;= 3
```

Robert Hooke also provides the ability to temporarily or permanently disable or remove hooks:

```
(robert.hooke/with-hooks-disabled foo (foo 1 2))  ❶
;= 3

(robert.hooke/remove-hook #'foo time-it)          ❷
;= #<user$foo user$foo@4f13f501>
(foo 1 2)
;= 3
```

❶ with-hooks-disabled allows you to temporarily suspend the invocation of hooks on a particular named var.

❷ remove-hook will remove a particular hook from a var.

Note that this is all done at a REPL. Adding, removing, and temporarily suspending the invocation of hooks on a var can be determined entirely at runtime using whatever criteria are most suitable for your application.

Finally, because the addition and removal of hooks is done using regular functions (i.e., add-hook and remove-hook) on regular vars, there is no need for anything like the idiosyncratic AspectJ pointcut syntax we saw earlier. Excellent tools are available to introspect on the Clojure environment, so we can do things like add a hook to all vars in a namespace:

```
(require 'clojure.set)
;= nil
(doseq [var (->> (ns-publics 'clojure.set)
                 (map val))]
  (robert.hooke/add-hook var time-it))
;= nil
(clojure.set/intersection (set (range 100000))
                          (set (range -100000 10)))
; Run time:   97 ms
;= #{0 1 2 3 4 5 6 7 8 9}
```

All of this is done without any special language or compiler support, as is needed by AspectJ. In fact, the Robert Hooke library is a mere 100 lines of plain Clojure code; if it didn't exist already, you could write it yourself.

Final Thoughts

As we have seen, many common design patterns are trivial in Clojure, and in most cases, simply disappear into the language and its libraries entirely. Thanks to a focus on separating functions and data, along with first-class functions and the tools to combine and compose them, it's typical to complete designs and architectures in Clojure without appeal to design patterns that generally aim to manage and mitigate the relative complexity of object-oriented approaches like those embodied by Java and Ruby.

## CHAPTER 13

Testing

Conceptually, testing in Clojure is largely the same as it is in Java, Python, or Ruby. Regardless of the language you use, the objective is always to:

1. Construct a suitable environment.
2. Run some code.
3. Verify that the code behaved or returned as expected.

Of course, the details of each piece of this task can vary greatly between languages and testing frameworks. In this chapter, we'll survey ways to test in Clojure, focusing on `clojure.test`, the test framework that is included in the language's standard library.

Immutable Values and Pure Functions

In an object-oriented language like Java or Python or Ruby, testing can be a complicated matter. Objects tend to have numerous, subtle interactions with each other. Mutating one object may end up mutating any number of other objects, or the behavior of one object may implicitly rely upon the state of others. These interactions are often combinatorial in nature, making it difficult to reliably account for all the environmental characteristics that can change our programs' behavior, and therefore more difficult to test.

As we detailed in Chapter 2, Clojure encourages the use of immutable values and pure functions. Code written in line with such sensibilities is greatly simplified from a testing perspective: if your functions' results are determined only by their arguments, then simple unit tests are all that are required to ensure suitable test coverage. Of course, integration and functional testing will still be necessary for those parts of your applications that consist of more than pure functions.

Mocking

In object-oriented languages, a common test aid is to resort to *mock* objects, which simulate the behavior of real objects or services upon which some code depends. Given a suitably constructed mock, code under test can be more effectively isolated to prevent possible bugs or variable behavior in the dependency from unduly affecting test results.

Mock objects can be a lesson in incidental complexity, especially in statically typed languages. Interfaces may need to be created for the express purpose of being able to create mock objects, and mock-motivated data types are often necessary to present a uniform API for data obtained either from a live service or a mock of that service.

Mocks are often not necessary when testing in Clojure. Given immutable collections and records, there is simply never any reason to mock data per se; you can go so far as to capture data from production environments, persist it, and reuse it as test data, without any wrappers, conversions, or type gymnastics.[1] "Mock data" in Clojure is just...more data.

One relevant corollary to mocking in other languages is the need to mock Clojure *functions*. Consider a function that looks up the address for a given username:

```
(defn get-address
  [username]
  ;; access database
  )
```

This function will fail in any environment where the source database isn't available or hasn't been configured suitably, and tests involving this function will fail if a database *is* available, but contains different data than what the tests expect.

`with-redefs` is one solution to this problem. It temporarily replaces the root values of a set of named vars with some other values, executes its body, and then resets the original root values of those vars; effectively, the affected vars are mocked:

```
(with-redefs [address-lookup (constantly "123 Main St.")]
  (println (address-lookup)))
; 123 Main St.
```

You can use `binding`—described in "Dynamic Scope" on page 201—in much the same way, but `with-redefs` is more appropriate in many cases, especially when testing:

- `with-redefs` imposes no limitations on the vars that may be affected, in contrast to `binding`, which will only work on vars marked as `^:dynamic`.

---

1. Some testing situations have a special need for *generated* test data—a concept that has gained some exposure thanks to Haskell's QuickCheck—but such data remains immutable and amenable to all the generic data-manipulation facilities in Clojure. There are many Clojure libraries that provide various test data generation facilities, including `test.generative` (*https://github.com/clojure/test.generative/*), ClojureCheck (*https://bitbucket.org/kotarak/clojurecheck*), and `re-rand` (*https://github.com/weavejester/re -rand*).

- `with-redefs` has none of the thread-local semantics of dynamic bindings, that is, all threads, agents, futures, etc. see the temporary root value of the affected vars.
- Dynamic vars affected by `binding` can have their bound value `set!`ed. This doesn't prevent `alter-var-root` from being used on vars temporarily modified using `with-redefs`, but not having `set!` available when it's not necessary can be a reasonable precaution.

In short, the length of rope dynamic vars and `binding` provide is often longer than you need when testing, enabling cleverness that might not be desirable within that context.

In any case, both `with-redefs` and `binding` can be used in conjunction with the fixture facility provided by `clojure.test` to ensure that key vars are mocked as necessary for the scope of testing, either to have functions return known constant values, or to retarget operations, for example, to access a particular database based on local test configuration. We'll talk more about fixtures later in "Fixtures" on page 479.

clojure.test

`clojure.test` is the "official" Clojure test framework. It's a simple library, but one that is sufficient for many tasks.

 There are other popular test frameworks for Clojure that provide more sophisticated semantics and capabilities. The most popular of these is Midje, available at *https://github.com/marick/Midje*.

Assertions in `clojure.test` use the `is` macro. `is` evaluates a single expression, tests whether the result is logically true, and returns that value. `is` will report any failures, including the actual values that were obtained, along with the (optional) message provided with the assertion, if any:

```
(use 'clojure.test)

(is (= 5 (+ 4 2)) "I never was very good at math...")
; FAIL in clojure.lang.PersistentList$EmptyList@1 (NO_SOURCE_FILE:1)
; I was never very good at math...
; expected: (= 5 (+ 4 2))
;   actual: (not (= 5 6))
;= false

(is (re-find #"foo" "foobar"))
;= "foo"
```

is defines a number of special assertions that can be used within expressions.[2] For example, `thrown?` will test that a certain type of error is thrown in the course of the expression's evaluation:

```
(is (thrown? ArithmeticException (/ 1 0)))                                    ❶
;= #<ArithmeticException java.lang.ArithmeticException: Divide by zero>
(is (thrown? ArithmeticException (/ 1 1)))
; FAIL in clojure.lang.PersistentList$EmptyList@1 (NO_SOURCE_FILE:1)
; expected: (thrown? ArithmeticException (/ 1 1))
;    actual: nil
;= nil
```

❶ is returns the exception when a `thrown?` assertion passes.

`thrown-with-msg?` is similar, but also tests that some regular expression can be found within the error's message:

```
(is (thrown-with-msg? ArithmeticException #"zero" (/ 1 0)))
;= #<ArithmeticException java.lang.ArithmeticException: Divide by zero>
(is (thrown-with-msg? ArithmeticException #"zero" (inc Long/MAX_VALUE)))      ❶
; FAIL in clojure.lang.PersistentList$EmptyList@1 (NO_SOURCE_FILE:1)
; expected: (thrown-with-msg? ArithmeticException #"zero" (inc Long/MAX_VALUE))
;    actual: #<ArithmeticException java.lang.ArithmeticException: integer overflow>
;= #<ArithmeticException java.lang.ArithmeticException: integer overflow>
```

❶ Clojure throws an `ArithmeticException` when a nonpromoting operator will result in an overflow condition; this exception has a message that doesn't contain `#"zero"`, so the assertion fails.

You can document tests and augment failure reports by using the `testing` macro, which causes the description of a failing test's scope to be included in the error report:

```
(testing "Strings"
  (testing "regex"
    (is (re-find #"foo" "foobar"))
    (is (re-find #"foo" "bar")))
  (testing ".contains"
    (is (.contains "foobar" "foo"))))
; FAIL in clojure.lang.PersistentList$EmptyList@1 (NO_SOURCE_FILE:1)
; Strings regex
; expected: (re-find #"foo" "bar")
;    actual: (not (re-find #"foo" "bar"))
```

Defining Tests

There are two ways to define tests. First and probably most useful, tests can be defined as standalone functions via the `deftest` macro. This macro simply defines a zero-argument function for you (as per `defn`) with some metadata attached to its var that

---

2. You can add your own special assertions to is too, by defining a new method for the `clojure.test/assert-expr` multimethod. See the documentation for the `clojure.test` namespace for details: *http://clojure.github .com/clojure/clojure.test-api.html*.

marks it as a test. deftest tests are otherwise identical to normal functions, can be called from the REPL, and so on:

```
(deftest test-foo
  (is (= 1 1)))
;= #'user/test-foo
(test-foo)
;= nil
```

It's common to define tests in a set of namespaces separate from your library or application, often in a test subdirectory of your project. As we described in Chapter 8, Clojure's most commonly used build tools look in these directories for tests and can run them for you.

All clojure.test tests are actually defined as vars that have a function located in the :test slot of their metadata. We can see this in the test we defined above:

```
(:test (meta #'test-foo))
;= #<user$fn__366 user$fn__366@4e842e74>
```

The function you call via (test-foo) just delegates to this :test function. This may seem like a silly detail, but it makes it possible to do things like bundle tests with the functions they are testing, something the with-test macro helps you do.[3] It takes any form that defines a var as its first argument, and any number of other forms as additional arguments that will comprise the body of a test function that is stored in the metadata of that var:

```
(with-test
  (defn hello [name]
    (str "Hello, " name))
  (is (= (hello "Brian") "Hello, Brian"))
  (is (= (hello nil) "Hello, nil")))
;= #'user/hello
```

Defined this way, we can call and use hello in our application however we need to without running any tests:

```
(hello "Judy")
;= "Hello, Judy"
```

The body provided to with-test after the var-defining form is bundled up into a function that is stored in the :test slot of the var's metadata; this is the test function:

```
((:test (meta #'hello)))
; FAIL in clojure.lang.PersistentList$EmptyList@1 (NO_SOURCE_FILE:5)
; expected: (= (hello nil) "Hello, nil")
;   actual: (not (= "Hello, " "Hello, nil"))
;= false
```

---

3. You can think of this approach as a more structured version of Python's doctest module or the Ruby corollary, rubydoctest, with the commonality being the co-location of tests with the definition of the functions under test.

Helpfully, the `clojure.test/run-tests` function uses this metadata to dynamically find tests in one or more namespaces and run them all. Thus, it can find tests in a loaded source file as well as tests defined at the REPL:

```
(run-tests)      ❶
; Testing user
;
; FAIL in (hello) (NO_SOURCE_FILE:5)
; expected: (= (hello nil) "Hello, nil")
;   actual: (not (= "Hello, " "Hello, nil"))
;
; Ran 2 tests containing 3 assertions.
; 1 failures, 0 errors.
;= {:type :summary, :pass 2, :test 2, :error 0, :fail 1}
```

❶ If no namespaces are specified, `run-tests` searches for vars with `:test` functions in `*ns*`.

In contrast to the build-compile-test cycle in many languages, Clojure makes it easy to test functions as they're written via utilities like `run-tests`.

One caveat of this approach is that, once defined, tests stay defined as long as the JVM is alive. Loading a file from disk or requiring a namespace containing tests will not drop and redefine those tests, so unwanted tests will persist and `run-tests` will continue to find and run them until you restart the JVM—something we'd like to avoid if possible. Thankfully, you can undefine a var (and thus its test) using `ns-unmap`:[4]

```
(ns-unmap *ns* 'hello)
;= nil
(run-tests)
; Testing user
;
; Ran 1 tests containing 1 assertions.
; 0 failures, 0 errors.
;= {:type :summary, :pass 1, :test 1, :error 0, :fail 0}
```

Alternatively, we could have altered the metadata on `hello` to not contain the `:test` function; for vars, we define in conjunction with `with-test`, this will allow us to continue to use the underlying function:

```
(with-test
  (defn hello [name]
    (str "Hello, " name))
  (is (= (hello "Brian") "Hello, Brian"))
  (is (= (hello nil) "Hello, nil")))
;= #'user/hello
(alter-meta! #'hello dissoc :test)
;= {:ns #<Namespace user>, :name hello, :arglists ([name]),
;=  :line 2, :file "NO_SOURCE_PATH"}
(run-tests *ns*)
```

---

4. We talk more about `ns-unmap` and other namespace introspection and manipulation functions in "Defining and Using Namespaces" on page 322 and "Introspecting namespaces" on page 401.

```
; Testing user
;
; Ran 1 tests containing 1 assertions.
; 0 failures, 0 errors.
;= {:type :summary, :pass 1, :test 1, :error 0, :fail 0}
(hello "Rebecca")
;= "Hello, Rebecca"
```

Test "Suites"

You can call other test functions from within tests without a problem:

```
(deftest a
  (is (== 0 (- 3 2))))
;= #'user/a
(deftest b (a))
;= #'user/b
(deftest c (b))
;= #'user/c
(c)
; FAIL in (c b a) (NO_SOURCE_FILE:2)   ❶
; expected: (== 0 (- 3 2))
;    actual: (not (== 0 1))
```

❶ Failure reports helpfully include the "stack" of test functions that led to the failure; the stack here is the list (c b a).[5]

Defining "suites" of tests in this way is convenient, but clashes with the default behavior of run-tests (and therefore with the test-running functionality of Clojure build tools): because it invokes the :test function from the metadata of all vars, it will run subtests directly, even if they are being called as part of the "suite." At best, this will lead to longer test runtimes as tests are invoked redundantly; at worst, you'll get a proliferation of duplicated failure reports:

```
(run-tests)
; Testing user
;
; FAIL in (b a) (NO_SOURCE_FILE:2)
; expected: (== 0 (- 3 2))
;    actual: (not (== 0 1))
;
; FAIL in (c b a) (NO_SOURCE_FILE:2)
; expected: (== 0 (- 3 2))
;    actual: (not (== 0 1))
;
; FAIL in (a) (NO_SOURCE_FILE:2)
; expected: (== 0 (- 3 2))
;    actual: (not (== 0 1))
;
```

---

5. The unfortunate notation here indicates the call chain—c called b called a—*not* a single call, that is, evaluating (c b a) will fail, since functions defined via deftest take no arguments, including the one named c above.

```
; Ran 6 tests containing 3 assertions.
; 3 failures, 0 errors.
;= {:type :summary, :pass 0, :test 6, :error 0, :fail 3}
```

There are a couple of ways to avoid this. First, you can define a primary entry point for run-tests on a per-namespace basis; this entry point must be a function called test-ns-hook, and it must have a zero-argument arity. When test-ns-hook is present, it will be the only function in its namespace that run-tests will invoke. This gives you complete control over which tests are run and how they are composed:

```
(defn test-ns-hook [] (c))
;= #'user/test-ns-hook
(run-tests)
; Testing user
;
; FAIL in (c b a) (NO_SOURCE_FILE:2)
; expected: (== 0 (- 3 2))
;   actual: (not (== 0 1))
;
; Ran 3 tests containing 1 assertions.
; 1 failures, 0 errors.
;= {:type :summary, :pass 0, :test 3, :error 0, :fail 1}
```

Alternatively, you can just put subordinate assertions in regular functions. These won't have :test metadata, and therefore won't be found and invoked by run-tests:

```
(ns-unmap *ns* 'test-ns-hook)          ❶
;= nil
(defn a
  []
  (is (== 0 (- 3 2)))))
;= #'user/a
(defn b [] (a))
;= #'user/b
(deftest c (b))
;= #'user/c
(run-tests)
; Testing user
;
; FAIL in (c) (NO_SOURCE_FILE:3)          ❷
; expected: (== 0 (- 3 2))
;   actual: (not (== 0 1))
;
; Ran 1 tests containing 1 assertions.
; 1 failures, 0 errors.
;= {:type :summary, :pass 0, :test 1, :error 0, :fail 1}
```

❶ Let's first drop the test-ns-hook we defined earlier.

❷ Notice that the test "stack" for this failure is only (c) and not (c b a) as before. This is because run-tests only tracks test scope, not that of regular functions like a and b.

Fixtures

Fixtures provide a way to set up and then tear down services, database state, function mocks, and test data, thereby ensuring that all the tests within a namespace are invoked within a controlled context. They are similar to the setUp and tearDown methods (or @Before and @After annotations) found in xUnit unit testing libraries, but offer essentially unbounded control over the test environment.

A fixture is simply a higher-order function that accepts a single function argument that is the test or set of tests that should be invoked within the context established and torn down by the fixture. Fixtures can be defined anywhere, reused across test namespaces, and any number of them can be utilized for each namespace.

You can apply fixtures to a namespace in two ways:

- Fixtures can be invoked for *each* test found in a namespace. For a namespace that contains *n* tests, your fixture will be called *n* times, each time with a function corresponding to a single test.

- Alternatively, fixtures can be invoked *once* for an entire namespace, where the context it establishes will apply to all test functions in that namespace. For a namespace that contains *n* tests, your fixture will be called only once with a function that will invoke all of the namespace's test functions.

In either case, fixture implementations take this general form:

```
(defn some-fixture
  [f]
  (try
    ;; set up database connections, load test data,
    ;; mock out functions using `with-redefs` or `binding`, etc.
    (f)
    (finally
      ;; clean up database connections, files, etc.
      )))
```

Whether you choose the *each* or *once* option for a given fixture, the behavior of fixture implementations is highly dependent upon what you're testing and the details of your test environment(s).

The *each* or *once* options cover most requirements, but they do mean that fixtures in clojure.test offer a subset of the flexibility available when you define your own test-ns-hook. Whereas fixtures have two defined "life cycles," you have *complete* control over what runs, when it runs, and what is performed before and after each test within a test-ns-hook implementation. Fixtures happen to be more convenient most of the time; in particular, using them does not force you to explicitly manage the search for and invocation of test functions in a namespace, bookkeeping that you implicitly take on when using test-ns-hook.

Fixtures and `test-ns-hook` are mutually exclusive; if you define the latter, then the former will *not* be applied.

To get our hands dirty with fixtures, let's look back at `configured-petstore`, a function we defined in Example 12-2 and repeated below with some supporting records and a protocol:

```
(defprotocol Bark
  (bark [this]))

(defrecord Chihuahua [weight price]
  Bark
  (bark [this] "Yip!"))

(defrecord PetStore [dog])

(defn configured-petstore
  []
  (-> "petstore-config.clj"
    slurp
    read-string
    map->PetStore))
```

A test for `configured-petstore` is easy to write; we just need to compare the `PetStore` it produces to a known value:

```
(def ^:private dummy-petstore (PetStore. (Chihuahua. 12 "$84.50")))

(deftest test-configured-petstore
  (is (= (configured-petstore) dummy-petstore)))
```

`configured-petstore` loads a record from a particular file on disk, `"petstore-con fig.clj"` in the current directory. Therefore, this test will fail without if that file doesn't exist or isn't populated with data properly corresponding to our expected `dummy-pet store` value:

```
(run-tests)
; Testing user
;
; ERROR in (test-configured-petstore) (FileInputStream.java:-2)
; expected: (= (configured-petstore) dummy-petstore)
;   actual: java.io.FileNotFoundException: petstore-config.clj
    (No such file or directory)
;   at java.io.FileInputStream.open (FileInputStream.java:-2)
;     ...
;
; Ran 1 tests containing 1 assertions.
; 0 failures, 1 errors.
;= {:type :summary, :pass 0, :test 1, :error 1, :fail 0}
```

We need to ensure that a suitable file is present so that the result of calling `configured-petstore` can be verified. This calls for a fixture. We already have an expected Pet

Store instance (held in `dummy-petstore`); having our fixture dump the readable representation of that record and its fields to the file that `configured-petstore` requires is a simple matter:

```
(defn petstore-config-fixture
  [f]
  (let [file (java.io.File. "petstore-config.clj")]
    (try
      (spit file (with-out-str (pr dummy-petstore)))  ❶
      (f)                                              ❷
      (finally
        (.delete file)))))                             ❸
```

❶ Here's where we write the readable representation of `dummy-petstore` to "petstore-config.clj". Note that we're using `pr` here instead of `print` or `println`; the latter functions produce human-readable output, whereas `pr` and `prn` produce Clojure readable output.

❷ `f` here is either a test function, or a function that will call all test functions within the namespace. Which one it is depends on whether our fixture is registered to run `:once` for a namespace, or once for `:each` test function within a namespace.

❸ It's good form to clean up a fixture's effects as much as possible. If we didn't do this, then "`petstore-config.clj`" would persist across test runs, perhaps falsely enabling other tests to pass.

With our fixture defined,[6] all that remains is to register it. We'll use the `:once` life cycle:

```
(use-fixtures :once petstore-config-fixture)
```

With our fixture registered, we can be sure that `configured-petstore` will be invoked with known data in place, thus allowing the test to pass:

```
(run-tests)
; Testing user
;
; Ran 1 tests containing 1 assertions.
; 0 failures, 0 errors.
;= {:type :summary, :pass 1, :test 1, :error 0, :fail 0}
```

We could just as easily have registered `petstore-config-fixture` as an `:each` fixture, so that it would be applied once for each test function in the namespace.

Growing an HTML DSL

As a live example of testing during development, let's use tests to help us build a library to generate HTML. The result will be a simple-minded version of Hiccup (*https://github*

---

6. There is technically no need to define fixtures in top-level vars; you could just as easily pass fixtures as function literals to `use-fixtures`.

.com/weavejester/hiccup), a library that produces HTML that mirrors the structure of defined or generated Clojure collections.

Our goal is to be able to write HTML snippets like this:

```
[:html
 [:head [:title "Propaganda"]]
 [:body [:p "Visit us at "
         [:a {:href "http://clojureprogramming.com"}
          "our website"]
         "."]]]
```

And compile them into HTML like this:

```
<html>
  <head><title>Propaganda</title></head>
  <body>
    <p>Visit us at <a href="http://clojurebook.com">our website</a>.</p>
  </body>
</html>
```

Here, vectors (or really, any sequential collection) represent HTML elements where the first value is the element name, the second is an optional map of its attributes, and remaining values are the contents of the element, which can be either strings or additional vectors representing child elements.

Let's write some tests to get started. We know that our eventual HTML-generating function is going to be pure; it's going to accept some input, and produce some result without any external dependency or effect. We'd hate to have to write (is (= expected (f input))) over and over; so, most of our tests will likely use are:

```
(deftest test-addition
  (are [x y z] (= x (+ y z))
    10 7 3
    20 10 10
    100 89 11))
```

are is a helper macro in clojure.test that templatizes assertions. For example, the are form above macroexpands into this:

```
(do
  (clojure.test/is (= 10 (+ 7 3)))
  (clojure.test/is (= 20 (+ 10 10)))
  (clojure.test/is (= 100 (+ 89 11))))
```

are helps to minimize the repetition of each assertion, but we'll still need to repeat the transformation, for example (= expected (f input)). A short macro will help us avoid that as well:

```
(defmacro are* [f & body]
  `(are [x# y#] (~'= (~f x#) y#)
     ~@body))
```

Now we can write tests like this:

```clojure
(deftest test-tostring
  (are* str
    10 "10"
    :foo ":foo"
    "identity" "identity"))
```

Let's assume we'll have a function html that accepts a sequential collection and returns a string containing HTML. We'll further assume a helper function attrs that produces attribute strings for inclusion in HTML elements. We'll implement those functions incrementally to match the expectations we codify in our tests.

These tests should be a sensible starting point:

```clojure
(require 'clojure.string)

(declare html attrs)

(deftest test-html
  (are* html
    [:html]
    "<html></html>"

    [:a [:b]]
    "<a><b></b></a>"

    [:a {:href "/"} "Home"]
    "<a href=\"/\">Home</a>"

    [:div "foo" [:span "bar"] "baz"]
    "<div>foo<span>bar</span>baz</div>"))

(deftest test-attrs
  (are* (comp clojure.string/trim attrs)    ❶
    nil ""

    {:foo "bar"}
    "foo=\"bar\""

    (sorted-map :a "b" :c "d")
    "a=\"b\" c=\"d\""))
```

❶ We're cheating a bit here; trim will allow us to ignore leading or trailing whitespace emitted by attrs, which we know ends up being handy for certain edge cases.

Now for our code. A good first try:

```clojure
(defn attrs
  [attr-map]
  (->> attr-map
    (mapcat (fn [[k v]] [k " =\"" v "\""]))
    (apply str)))

(defn html
  [x]
```

```
    (if-not (sequential? x)
      (str x)
      (let [[tag & body] x
            [attr-map body] (if (map? (first body))
                                [(first body) (rest body)]
                                [nil body])]
        (str "<" (name tag) (attrs attr-map) ">"
             (apply str (map html body))
             "</" (name tag) ">")))))
```

Let's see how it does with our tests.

```
(run-tests)
; Testing user
;
; FAIL in (test-html) (NO_SOURCE_FILE:6)
; expected: (= (html [:a {:href "/"} "Home"]) "<a href=\"/\">Home</a>")
;   actual: (not (= "<a:href =\"/\">Home</a>" "<a href=\"/\">Home</a>"))
;
; FAIL in (test-attrs) (NO_SOURCE_FILE:20)
; expected: (= ((comp clojure.string/trim attrs) {:foo "bar"}) "foo=\"bar\"")
;   actual: (not (= ":foo =\"bar\"" "foo=\"bar\""))
;
; FAIL in (test-attrs) (NO_SOURCE_FILE:20)
; expected: (= ((comp clojure.string/trim attrs)
;                 (sorted-map :a "b" :c "d"))
;              "a=\"b\" c=\"d\"")
;   actual: (not (= ":a =\"b\":c =\"d\"" "a=\"b\" c=\"d\""))
;
; Ran 2 tests containing 7 assertions.
; 3 failures, 0 errors.
;= {:type :summary, :pass 4, :test 2, :error 0, :fail 3}
```

Oh no...what's wrong? It looks like attrs might be the source of all the trouble. We
have what look like Clojure keywords in our results, for example (attrs {:foo
"bar"}) is emitting ":foo =\":bar\"". We should be calling name on those keywords to
get a bare string for attribute names. Let's fix that, along with the spurious space between attribute names and the = character:

```
(defn attrs
  [attrs]
  (->> attrs
    (mapcat (fn [[k v]] [(name k) "=\"" v "\""]))
    (apply str)))
```

Now we can rerun just test-attrs to see how it works since we're focused on fixing
this attrs function:

```
(test-attrs)
; FAIL in (test-attrs) (NO_SOURCE_FILE:20)
; expected: (= ((comp clojure.string/trim attrs)
;                 (sorted-map :a "b" :c "d"))
;              "a=\"b\" c=\"d\"")
;   actual: (not (= ":a =\"b\":c =\"d\"" "a=\"b\" c=\"d\""))
```

Better, but it looks like we forgot the space before each attribute. A simple fix:

```
(defn attrs
  [attrs]
  (->> attrs
    (mapcat (fn [[k v]] [\space (name k) "=\"" v "\""]))
    (apply str)))
```

How are we doing now?

```
(test-attrs)
;= nil
(run-tests)
; Testing user
;
; Ran 2 tests containing 7 assertions.
; 0 failures, 0 errors.
;= {:type :summary, :pass 7, :test 2, :error 0, :fail 0}
```

Excellent, it looks like we've got some clean code. Let's see what it produces for our original example:[7]

```
(html [:html
        [:head [:title "Propaganda"]]
        [:body [:p "Visit us at "
                [:a {:href "http://clojurebook.com"}
                 "our website"]
                "."]]])
;= "<html>
;=   <head><title>Propaganda</title></head>
;=   <body>
;=     <p>Visit us at <a href=\"http://clojurebook.com\">our website</a>.</p>
;=   </body>
;= </html>"
```

The nice thing about a templating DSL like this is that, because HTML is represented by regular Clojure data structures end-to-end, we have all of the great facilities available for working with those data structures—and therefore HTML:

```
(html (list* :ul (for [author ["Chas Emerick" "Christophe Grand" "Brian Carper"]]
                   [:li author])))
;= "<ul><li>Chas Emerick</li><li>Christophe Grand</li><li>Brian Carper</li></ul>"
```

That's a whole lot more attractive than using what typically passes for an API to an HTML DOM, or committing atrocities like putting strings of HTML into your code and interpolating data into them. In the realm of options for producing HTML in Clojure, solutions like this (where Hiccup is the canonical implementation) represent one extreme, whereas other options like Enlive (which we use in examples in Chapter 16) represent a more traditional model where HTML content generally starts life as a template asset that is then programmatically populated.

---

7. No, html doesn't provide pretty-printing; we formatted out the string literal a bit so it would fit well on the page.

Relying upon Assertions

Our HTML generation functions are decent, but someone somewhere will inevitably attempt to abuse the API. For example, the Clojure-standard representation of XML (as produced by *clojure.xml*) looks like this:

```
{:tag :a, :attrs {:href "http://clojure.org"}, :content ["Clojure"]}
```

That's quite different than our vector-based HTML representation. Unsurprisingly, html will do odd things with this map, since it's not at all what it's expecting:

```
(html {:tag :a, :attrs {:href "http://clojure.org"}, :content ["Clojure"]})
;= "{:content [\"Clojure\"], :attrs {:href \"http://clojure.org\"}, :tag :a}"
```

Cripes, it returns a string! That's appropriate insofar as we somewhat lazily use html recursively to process the contents of element vectors, but this particular result is clearly not useful if we imagine a user that (perhaps reasonably) thinks she might be able to serialize a *clojure.xml* data structure to an HTML string using our html function. This is a situation where we'd like to fail as quickly as possible.

Enter assertions. Assertions test a condition and throw an error if the condition is not true:

```
(defn attrs
  [attr-map]
  (assert (or (map? attr-map)                                  ❶
              (nil? attr-map)) "attr-map must be nil, or a map")
  (->> attr-map
    (mapcat (fn [[k v]] [\space (name k) "=\"" v "\""]))
    (apply str)))

(attrs "hi")
;= #<AssertionError java.lang.AssertionError:
;=    Assert failed: attr-map must be nil, or a map
;=    (or (map? attr-map) (nil? attr-map))>
```

❶ We're using assert to verify the types of arguments, but it can be used anywhere in your code to enforce any invariant you can express.

Because assertions throw an error, they may not be the best tool to use in production code, where you might not want to pay the runtime costs associated with verifying assertions. Clojure allows us to enable and disable assertions by setting the *assert* var true or false, respectively.

Because assert is a macro, *assert* should be set before you *compile* code that uses it. When *assert* is false, calls to assert will be elided from the compiled function entirely, yielding no runtime cost.

```
(set! *assert* false)        ❶
;= false
(defn attrs
  [attr-map]
  (assert (or (map? attr-map)
```

```
                (nil? attr-map)) "attr-map must be nil, or a map")
  (->> attr-map
    (mapcat (fn [[k v]] [\space (name k) "=\"" v "\""]))
    (apply str)))
;= #'user/attrs
(attrs "hi")
;= #<UnsupportedOperationException java.lang.UnsupportedOperationException:
;=   nth not supported on this type: Character>
(set! *assert* true)        ❷
;= true
```

❶ The state of *assert* can be set at any time: on a per-namespace basis, for your entire application based on a system property or environment variable, or, as we do here, at the REPL.

❷ We set *assert* back to true to support later examples.

attrs above is compiled with assertions disabled, so we're now getting much less helpful nth not supported on this type errors, due to the function passed to mapcat attempting to sequentially destructure the string's characters. On the other hand, within an application that has been well-tested—perhaps using a mixture of assertions, unit tests, and functional testing—disabling assertions in production environments would eliminate the former's runtime cost.

Preconditions and Postconditions

The two most common use cases for assertions are testing inputs and outputs to functions. Because of Clojure's emphasis on the use of pure functions, many functions' inputs and outputs may be all there really is to test.

fn (and therefore derivatives like defn) has direct support for writing assertions to test inputs for *preconditions* and test output for *postconditions*. Preconditions are evaluated before the body of the function; postconditions are evaluated after the body of the function has been executed, but before the return value is delivered to the caller. If any condition evaluates logically false, then an error is thrown. This facility can be used to ensure that function arguments and return values meet defined criteria at runtime without cluttering the function body with checks and inconsistent throwing of exceptions while potentially reusing validation functionality across a codebase.

If the first value in the body of a Clojure function is a map with :pre or :post keys, this map is considered a map of pre- and/or postcondition expressions, and will be expanded to calls to assert when the function is compiled.[8]

The values for :pre and :post should be vectors, where each item in the vector is a separate assertion. Function parameters can be referred to in the preconditions. The value being returned from the function is bound to % in postconditions, similar to how

---

8. If a map is the only expression in a function body, it is treated as the function's return value, rather than a map of pre- and postconditions.

the first argument in a function literal is denoted. Let's recast our definition of attrs
and html using reasonable pre- and postconditions:

```
(defn attrs
  [attr-map]
  {:pre [(or (map? attr-map)                                          ❶
             (nil? attr-map))]}
  (->> attr-map
    (mapcat (fn [[k v]] [\space (name k) "=\"" v "\""]))
    (apply str)))

(defn html
  [x]
  {:pre [(if (sequential? x)                                          ❷
            (some #(-> x first %) [keyword? symbol? string?])
            (not (map? x)))]                                          ❸
   :post [(string? %)]}                                               ❹
  (if-not (sequential? x)
    (str x)
    (let [[tag & body] x
          [attr-map body] (if (map? (first body))
                            [(first body) (rest body)]
                            [nil body])]
      (str "<" (name tag) (attrs attr-map) ">"
           (apply str (map html body))
           "</" (name tag) ">"))))
```

❶ As before, we'll require that attrs will only accept nil or map arguments.

❷ The precondition for html is a little more complicated. If its argument is a sequential
collection, its first argument must be a string, keyword, or symbol. Otherwise...

❸ ...it can be anything other than a map.

❹ The postcondition for html only requires that its return value be a string. This could
get a lot fancier here and do things like verify that the generated HTML parses
cleanly, is compliant based on some DTD, and so on.

These conditions will help flag some common errors. Looking back at the case where
someone might use a *clojure.xml* element map to produce HTML using our function:

```
(html {:tag :a, :attrs {:href "http://clojure.org"}, :content ["Clojure"]})
;= #<AssertionError java.lang.AssertionError:
;=    Assert failed: (if (sequential? x)
;=                      (some (fn* [p1__843#] (-> x first p1__843#))
;=                            [keyword? symbol? string?])
;=                      (not (map? x)))>
```

Note that pre- and postconditions compile down into `assert`s within the body of their host function. This means that conditions are affected by the state of *assert* in the same way, and that it is impossible to add, remove, or change a function's conditions after it is compiled.[9]

9. One workaround for this is Trammel, a library focused on providing support for dynamic *contracts programming* in Clojure that uses conditions heavily along with record and type invariants to ensure program correctness: *https://github.com/fogus/trammel*.

## CHAPTER 14

Using Relational Databases

Relational databases are a mainstay of software development, and have been for decades now. It is a rare organization that does not use an RDBMS somewhere, and a rare programmer that does not find herself needing to get data in and out of one at least occasionally. Java has a rich history of quality support for relational databases via JDBC; thanks to its close relationship via the JVM, Clojure easily and fully takes advantage of that history.

We have many options for interacting with relational databases from Clojure. `clojure.java.jdbc` is a simple yet powerful library that acts as a thin layer between Clojure and JDBC. Korma is another Clojure library that provides a more Clojure-native interface. And finally, if Clojure's libraries do not suit your style or if you are looking to mix Clojure into an existing Java-based application, you can always fall back to one of the many mature and robust Java database libraries or frameworks. In this chapter, we'll explore setting up and using Hibernate from Clojure.

clojure.java.jdbc

Whether you use a native Java library or one of Clojure's many libraries, connecting to a database in Clojure will always utilize JDBC, the lowest-level API abstraction for interacting with relational databases in Java. The `clojure.java.jdbc` (*https://github .com/clojure/java.jdbc*) library wraps JDBC, so it is easier to use from Clojure:

```
[org.clojure/java.jdbc "0.1.1"]
```

In terms of dependencies, you need to pair JDBC and `clojure.java.jdbc` with a JDBC driver corresponding with the database you are using. There are hundreds of JDBC drivers for nearly every database in existence, so finding one for your needs should be easy enough. Here are some Leiningen coordinates for JDBC drivers for popular databases:

```
[org.xerial/sqlite-jdbc "3.7.2"]          ; SQLite
[mysql/mysql-connector-java "2.0.14"]     ; MySQL
[postgresql "9.0-801.jdbc4"]              ; PostgreSQL
```

All our examples will use the SQLite (*http://sqlite.org*) driver. Since SQLite is an "embedded" database—that is, the database engine runs in-process, with database files stored wherever you specify, rather than connecting to a potentially remote database server—all the code we show will work without having to set up and run a separate database. Thanks to the abstraction provided by JDBC, only minimal modifications would be required to use the same code with MySQL, PostgreSQL, Oracle, and others.

With `clojure.java.jdbc` and the `org.xerial/sqlite-jdbc` JDBC driver (*http://www.xerial.org/trac/Xerial/wiki/SQLiteJDBC*) library added to a project, we can dig into working with a database from the Clojure REPL.

All `clojure.java.jdbc` operations require a "spec" to operate:

```
(require '[clojure.java.jdbc :as jdbc])
;= nil
(def db-spec {:classname "org.sqlite.JDBC"
              :subprotocol "sqlite"
              :subname "test.db"})
;= #'user/db
```

Here, db-spec is a map of configuration data that `clojure.java.jdbc` will use to:

1. Locate our JDBC driver (via the `:classname` value).
2. Configure that driver and the connections it produces as we require.

Each JDBC driver will require a slightly different spec. For example, the spec for a MySQL session may look similar to this:

```
{:classname "com.mysql.jdbc.Driver"
 :subprotocol "mysql"
 :subname "//localhost:3306/databasename"
 :user "login"
 :password "password"}
```

Alternatively, `clojure.java.jdbc` specs may be created to specify a `javax.sql.Data Source` directly:

```
{:datasource datasource-instance
 :user "login"
 :password "password"}
```

...find one via JNDI:

```
{:name "java:/comp/env/jdbc/postgres"
 :environment {}} ; optional JNDI parameters for initializing
   javax.naming.InitialContext
```

...or, for many popular databases,[1] you can dispense with the map convention and provide a URI-style connection string like this:

```
"mysql://login:password@localhost:3306/databasename"
```

---

1. As of this writing, a connection string may be used with PostgreSQL, MySQL, SQLite, HSQLDB, and Derby.

If you are already familiar with JDBC, any of these methods should seem familiar; deriving an appropriate URI connection string or database spec from a JDBC-style connection string should be trivial.

Once you have your database spec settled, you can start using the `clojure.java.jdbc` API:

```
(jdbc/with-connection db-spec)
;= nil
```

`with-connection` is used to open a connection to our database. With no further body provided to `with-connection`, a connection will be opened and immediately closed; this is a useful sanity-check at the REPL, as an incorrect username, password, or database URL will result in an exception.

All expressions within the scope of `with-connection` are executed in the context of a live, open database connection. The connection is closed or freed automatically when control exits that scope.[2]

We can use `create-table` to create a table named "authors" and define a couple of columns. Keywords or strings can be used for table and column names; the latter are most appropriate for table/column names containing characters that cannot be represented as keyword literals:

```
(jdbc/with-connection db-spec
  (jdbc/create-table :authors
    [:id "integer primary key"]
    [:first_name "varchar"]
    [:last_name "varchar"]))
;= (0)
```

`insert-records` is a simple function that inserts data into the database, returning a seq of maps containing the keys generated for each inserted record. Keys in the maps correspond to columns in our table:

```
(jdbc/with-connection db-spec
  (jdbc/insert-records :authors
    {:first_name "Chas" :last_name "Emerick"}
    {:first_name "Christophe" :last_name "Grand"}
    {:first_name "Brian" :last_name "Carper"}))
;= ({:last_insert_rowid() 1}
;=  {:last_insert_rowid() 2}
;=  {:last_insert_rowid() 3})
```

`with-query-results` is used to fetch data from the database. The use of `doall` here is important; we'll explain it in detail shortly, in "Dealing with laziness" (page 495):

---

2. A common idiom in Clojure, this is just one example of automatic resource management. You will find many similar `with-*` functions for opening and closing file handles, network connections, and so on. See "with-open, finally's Lament" on page 364 for a discussion of `with-open`, the most commonly used `with-*` function in Clojure.

```
(jdbc/with-connection db-spec
  (jdbc/with-query-results res ["SELECT * FROM authors"]
    (doall res)))
;= ({:id 1, :first_name "Chas", :last_name "Emerick"}
;=  {:id 2, :first_name "Christophe", :last_name "Grand"}
;=  {:id 3, :first_name "Brian", :last_name "Carper"})
```

Note that throughout this example, we're dealing exclusively with native Clojure data types. Table and column names are keywords; database handles are maps; maps are used to insert data into the database, and querying the database returns a seq of maps. This fits with Clojure's design philosophy of having a few generic data types with many functions that operate on them.[3] Accessing fields in each row of the result set is a simple keyword lookup in a map. For example, we can produce the full name of each author in the table via a simple map.

Example 14-1. Transforming a result set using map

```
(jdbc/with-connection db-spec
  (jdbc/with-query-results res ["SELECT * FROM authors"]
    (doall (map #(str (:first_name %) " " (:last_name %)) res))))
;= ("Chas Emerick" "Christophe Grand" "Brian Carper")
```

You can apply any of the facilities available to you in Clojure to processing result sets.

with-query-results Explained

with-query-results is the primary way you'll get data out of your database. (with-query-results res query & body) will execute the query within the database, and then evaluate body where the query's result set is bound to a local called res. The result set itself is a lazy sequence of Clojure maps.

with-query-results supports *parameterized queries*, a common feature of SQL libraries where string query templates contain placeholders for query parameters that are provided separately and then interpolated by the database. Parameterized queries promote query reuse, which can increase the performance of queries that are run multiple times, and are also a boon to security compared to the dangerous equivalent: building queries via string concatenation, thereby opening the door to SQL injection attacks.

Queries should be a vector where the first item is a string of SQL, and subsequent values correspond to each parameter placeholder in the string query. For example:

```
(jdbc/with-connection db-spec
  (jdbc/with-query-results res ["SELECT * FROM authors WHERE id = ?" 2] ❶
    (doall res)))
;= ({:id 2, :first_name "Christophe", :last_name "Grand"})
```

❶ ? in the query represents a parameter, and 2 is the value we bind to this parameter.

---

3. Perlis is relevant here, see "Abstractions over Implementations" on page 84

Note that the types of the values you provide to be bound to parameters isn't of critical importance. Clojure being a dynamic language, the values you provide will be interpolated into the base SQL statement as appropriate. If you pass in a value of an unacceptable type (e.g., a type your JDBC driver is unable to coerce into the proper type), JDBC will throw an exception.

Dealing with laziness.   You may have noted the use of `doall` in conjunction with `with-query-results`. The result set returned by `with-query-results` is a lazy sequence,[4] each record within it is realized only as it is needed. This means that we can process positively huge datasets returned by queries without necessarily running into resource limitations, but we need to tread carefully, since the source of that data is a transient database connection. Consider this seemingly straightforward example:

```
(jdbc/with-connection db-spec
  (jdbc/with-query-results res ["SELECT * FROM authors"]
    res))
;= ({:id 1, :first_name "Chas", :last_name "Emerick"})
```

Whoa, that query only returned one row when we should expect three. The problem is that `with-query-results` returns `res`, our lazy result set, without evaluating it. The REPL eventually tries to print the lazy seq, which finally forces evaluation of its contents. But now it's too late: the database handle has been closed (because we have left the scope of `with-connection`) and we end up seeing incomplete (or no) results.[5]

The solution is to consume everything we need from the result set while the connection to the database is still alive. Certain operations, like `reduce`, will implicitly force the realization of the result set seq; transforming the result set seq using other operations that produce lazy seqs will themselves need to be wrapped in a call to `doall`, as we did in Example 14-1.

If all we want is to run a query and fetch the results in their entirety, we can easily set up a utility function to do this for us:

```
(defn fetch-results [db-spec query]
  (jdbc/with-connection db-spec
    (jdbc/with-query-results res query
      (doall res))))
;= #'user/fetch-results
(fetch-results db-spec ["SELECT * FROM authors"])
;= ({:id 1, :first_name "Chas", :last_name "Emerick"}
;=  {:id 2, :first_name "Christophe", :last_name "Grand"}
;=  {:id 3, :first_name "Brian", :last_name "Carper"})
```

---

4. See "Lazy seqs" on page 93.

5. Other JDBC drivers will throw an exception when you attempt to read data from a closed connection; the SQLite driver appears to prefetch the first row for us, thus the single-row result.

Transactions

Performing database operations as a single transaction is a simple matter of wrapping your code in a transaction form. transaction accepts any number of forms and executes each in turn as part of a single transaction. If an exception is thrown, or if the operation(s) performed will violate a constraint established in your database schema, the transaction will be rolled back. If the body of transaction finishes executing without error, the transaction is committed.

```
(jdbc/with-connection db-spec
  (jdbc/transaction
    (jdbc/delete-rows :authors ["id = ?" 1])
    (throw (Exception. "Abort transaction!"))))     ❶
;= ; Exception Abort transaction!
(fetch-results ["SELECT * FROM authors where id = ?" 1])
;= ({:id 1, :first_name "Chas", :last_name "Emerick"})     ❷
```

❶ Here we throw an exception to forcibly abort our transaction.

❷ Data in our database is untouched.

transaction is a macro that handles the minutiae of starting a transaction and ensuring the transaction is rolled back in the case of an exception. It also handles the drudgery of disabling autocommit on your JDBC connection object if necessary, restoring its original value when the transaction form's evaluation is complete.

Suppose we wanted to set the transaction isolation level of our connection to TRANSACTION_SERIALIZABLE. clojure.java.jdbc doesn't directly support this, but thanks to Clojure's dynamic nature, good Java interop support, and philosophy of avoiding data-hiding, we can still do it.

TRANSACTION_SERIALIZABLE itself is a static member in the java.sql.Connection class, so it can be referenced in Clojure as java.sql.Connection/TRANSACTION_SERIALIZABLE. We can access the dynamically bound current connection within the scope of with-connection via clojure.java.jdbc's connection function. Knowing this, we can set our transaction isolation level like so:

```
(jdbc/with-connection db-spec
  (.setTransactionIsolation (jdbc/connection)
    java.sql.Connection/TRANSACTION_SERIALIZABLE)
  (jdbc/transaction
    (jdbc/delete-rows :authors ["id = ?" 2])))
```

Connection Pooling

with-connection is easy to use, but by default it opens and closes a new database connection every time it's called. This is straightforward, but can be a big bottleneck.

Connection pooling is a means of creating a cache of database connections that can be reused over and over again. Many application servers provide DataSource-based connection pooling, often addressable via JNDI. If you aren't using an application server, you'll likely want to use c3p0 (*http://www.mchange.com/projects/c3p0*), one popular lightweight connection pooling library that can be deployed in any context:

```
[c3p0/c3p0 "0.9.1.2"]
```

With c3p0 added as a dependency in our project, we can easily set up a simple function to take a map-style database spec and return a `DataSource` that is backed by a c3p0 connection pool:

```
(import 'com.mchange.v2.c3p0.ComboPooledDataSource)
; Feb 05, 2011 2:26:40 AM com.mchange.v2.log.MLog <clinit>
; INFO: MLog clients using java 1.4+ standard logging.
;= com.mchange.v2.c3p0.ComboPooledDataSource

(defn pooled-spec
  [{:keys [classname subprotocol subname username password] :as other-spec}]
  (let [cpds (doto (ComboPooledDataSource.)                              ❶
               (.setDriverClass classname)
               (.setJdbcUrl (str "jdbc:" subprotocol ":" subname))
               (.setUser username)
               (.setPassword password))]
    {:datasource cpds}))
```

❶ c3p0's `ComboPooledDataSource` is a `DataSource` (Java's standard interface for any database connection source), so it can be used without modification with `with-connection`.

Connections will be initialized when first used, and then retained (based on the configuration of the pool) for use by subsequent calls to `with-connection`.

```
(def pooled-db (pooled-spec db-spec))
; Dec 27, 2011 8:49:28 AM com.mchange.v2.c3p0.C3P0Registry banner
; INFO: Initializing c3p0-0.9.1.2 [built 21-May-2007 15:04:56; debug? true; trace: 10]
;= #'user/pooled-db

(fetch-results pooled-db ["SELECT * FROM authors"])
; Dec 27, 2011 8:56:40 AM com.mchange.v2.c3p0.impl.AbstractPoolBackedDataSource
  getPoolManager
; INFO: Initializing c3p0 pool... com.mchange.v2.c3p0.ComboPooledDataSource
; [ acquireIncrement -> 3, acquireRetryAttempts -> 30, acquireRetryDelay -> 1000, ...
;= ({:id 1, :first_name "Chas", :last_name "Emerick"}
;=  {:id 2, :first_name "Christophe", :last_name "Grand"}
;=  {:id 3, :first_name "Brian", :last_name "Carper"})

(fetch-results pooled-db ["SELECT * FROM authors"])
;= ({:id 1, :first_name "Chas", :last_name "Emerick"}
;=  {:id 2, :first_name "Christophe", :last_name "Grand"}
;=  {:id 3, :first_name "Brian", :last_name "Carper"})
```

The second query will reuse the same connection as the first (as is hinted by the lack of initialization logging on the second `fetch-results` call). c3p0's default configuration is suitable for many applications, but we recommend taking advantage of the plethora of configuration options it offers in your local implementation of `pooled-spec` so as to maximize throughput.

Korma

Korma (*http://sqlkorma.com*) is an up-and-coming domain-specific language for working with relational databases in Clojure. It aims to provide a "batteries included" and Clojure-native database interaction experience; to that end, it takes care of generating SQL for many different popular databases, and handles administrative tasks like managing connection pooling via c3p0. For those familiar with Ruby's ActiveRecord or a similar object-relational mapper, Korma should seem familiar, although it is decidedly not an Object-Relational Mapping framework.

To use Korma, we need to first add a dependency for it to our project:

```
[korma "0.3.0"]
```

Prelude

Let's set up some tables and insert some data to work with, using `clojure.java.jdbc`.

```
(require '[clojure.java.jdbc :as jdbc])

(def db-spec {:classname "org.sqlite.JDBC"
              :subprotocol "sqlite"
              :subname "test.db"})

(defn setup
  []
  (jdbc/with-connection db-spec
    (jdbc/create-table :country
                       [:id "integer primary key"]
                       [:country "varchar"])
    (jdbc/create-table :author
                       [:id "integer primary key"]
                       [:country_id "integer constraint fk_country_id
                                     references country (id)"]
                       [:first_name "varchar"]
                       [:last_name "varchar"])
    (jdbc/insert-records :country
                       {:id 1 :country "USA"}
                       {:id 2 :country "Canada"}
                       {:id 3 :country "France"})
    (jdbc/insert-records :author
                       {:first_name "Chas" :last_name "Emerick" :country_id 1}
                       {:first_name "Christophe" :last_name "Grand" :country_id 3}
                       {:first_name "Brian" :last_name "Carper" :country_id 2}
                       {:first_name "Mark" :last_name "Twain" :country_id 1})))

(setup)
;= ({:id 1, :country_id 1, :first_name "Chas", :last_name "Emerick"}
;=  {:id 2, :country_id 3, :first_name "Christophe", :last_name "Grand"}
;=  {:id 3, :country_id 2, :first_name "Brian", :last_name "Carper"}
;=  {:id 4, :country_id 1, :first_name "Mark", :last_name "Twain"})
```

Our tables are defined as having a many-to-one relationship between authors and countries. Setting up Korma to use our database is easy:

```
(use '[korma db core])
(defdb korma-db db-spec)
```

defdb defines a connection that Korma can use; this command accepts the same arguments as the connection maps we pass to clojure.java.jdbc, so we reuse our db map here.

The defdb form evaluated most recently is set as the "default" connection, which will be used for all queries. This is handy if you have only one database to connect to, which covers the majority of use cases. defdb also helpfully sets up a connection pool for your database connection, letting you avoid the bookwork of doing it manually.[6]

The next step to set up Korma is to define *entities*, which are specifications to tell Korma the properties of your database tables. Entities are similar to "models" in Ruby's ActiveRecord. Our entities might look like this:

```
(declare author)

(defentity country
  (pk :id)
  (has-many author))

(defentity author
  (pk :id)
  (table :author)
  (belongs-to country))
```

defentity defines, among other things, the relationship between our tables in the database.

Queries

Having defined our table relationships, queries are straightforward:

```
(select author
  (with country)
  (where {:first_name "Chas"}))
;= [{:id 1, :country_id 1, :first_name "Chas",
     :last_name "Emerick", :id_2 1, :country "USA"}]
```

Korma's select macro is a DSL for doing SQL SELECT queries. select accepts a variety of functions that can be used to build queries. The with function we use here, for example, tells Korma to include a relation, which we previously defined with defentity. Note the country key/value pair included in our results.

---

6. You can use Korma's get-connection function to obtain a connection from the pool it set up, for example, (get-connection korma-db). This allows you to reuse Korma's connection pool if you happen to need to do something that requires using clojure.java.jdbc.

A more complex query:

```
(select author
  (with country)
  (where (like :first_name "Ch%"))
  (order :last_name :asc)
  (limit 1)
  (offset 1))
;= [{:id 2, :country_id 3, :first_name "Christophe",
     :last_name "Grand", :id_2 3, :country "France"}]
```

`order`, `limit`, and `offset` are straightforward representations of corresponded SQL clauses. More interesting is the `where` function, which is itself a miniature DSL for building SQL `WHERE` clauses. `where` can handle fairly complex conditions:

```
(select author
    (fields :first_name :last_name)
    (where (or (like :last_name "C%")
               (= :first_name "Mark"))))
;= [{:first_name "Brian", :last_name "Carper"}
;=  {:first_name "Mark", :last_name "Twain"}]
```

If we'd like to take a look under the hood to see the raw SQL produced by Korma, we can use the `sql-only` function:

```
(println (sql-only (select author
                    (with country)
                    (where (like :first_name "Ch%"))
                    (order :last_name :asc)
                    (limit 1)
                    (offset 1))))
;= ; SELECT "author".* FROM "author" LEFT JOIN "country"
;= ; ON "country"."id" = "author"."country_id"
;= ; WHERE "author"."first_name" LIKE ?
;= ; ORDER BY "author"."last_name" ASC LIMIT 1 OFFSET 1
```

Why Bother with a DSL?

Of course, you could run SQL queries from Clojure via strings of raw SQL statements. This is exactly what `clojure.java.jdbc` requires you to do, in fact. But there are advantages to Korma's approach.

A string of SQL is structureless, and manipulating such a string is difficult. Given `SELECT * FROM foo ORDER BY bar`, how would you alter this query to select something other than *? How would you add a `WHERE` clause? We would most likely need a full SQL parser.

Instead of structureless strings, Korma represents queries as simple Clojure maps. In fact, we can build these queries ourselves piece by piece, using `select*` instead of `select`:

```
(def query (-> (select* author)
               (fields :last_name :first_name)
               (limit 5)))
;= #'user/query
```

Let's see what that query map looks like:

```
{:group [],
 :from
 [{:table "author",
   :name "author",
   :pk :id,
   :db nil,
   :transforms (),
   :prepares (),
   :fields [],
   :rel
   {"country"
    #<Delay@54f690e4:
      {:table "country",
       :alias nil,
       :rel-type :belongs-to,
       :pk {:korma.sql.utils/generated "\"country\".\"id\""},
       :fk
       {:korma.sql.utils/generated "\"author\".\"country_id\""}}>}}],
 :joins [],
 :where [],
 :ent
 {:table "author",
  :name "author",
  :pk :id,
  :db nil,
  :transforms (),
  :prepares (),
  :fields [],
  :rel
  {"country"
   #<Delay@54f690e4:
     {:table "country",
      :alias nil,
      :rel-type :belongs-to,
      :pk {:korma.sql.utils/generated "\"country\".\"id\""},
      :fk {:korma.sql.utils/generated "\"author\".\"country_id\""}}>}},
 :limit 5,
 :type :select,
 :alias nil,
 :options nil,
 :fields (:last_name :first_name),
 :results :results,
 :table "author",
 :order [],
 :modifiers [],
 :db nil,
 :aliases #{}}
```

Altering a query is now as simple as manipulating the baseline Clojure map produced by select*, which is what Korma functions like order, limit, and offset do. Now, rather than constantly defining them in their entirety, we can build queries incrementally and execute them when we like by using the exec function; this lets us reuse parts of queries and encapsulate query transformations in reusable functions, all ways to cut down on code repetition.

The latest versions of Ruby on Rails' venerable ActiveRecord (version 3.0 as of this writing) has moved to a very similar method of forming SQL queries using method calls on query objects. In Ruby on Rails, you might write something like this:

```ruby
employees = Person.where(:type => "employee")
# ... later ...
managers = employees.where(:role => "manager").order(:last_name)
managers.all.each do |e|
  ...
end
```

Doing this with Korma is very similar:

```clojure
(def employees (where (select* employees) {:type "employee"}))

;; ... later ...
(let [managers (-> employees
                   (where {:role "manager"})
                   (order :last_name))]
  (doseq [e (exec managers)]
    ; ... process results ...
    ))
```

Pseudolaziness.   Queries built this way are "lazy," in that data isn't fetched from the database until the query is explicitly executed using Korma's **select** function. This is a different sort of laziness from Clojure's lazy data structures; it might more accurately be called "query-on-demand."

Suppose we have a table of all humans who ever lived. We could specify that we always want records from this table to be sorted by date of birth. Then before fetching the data, we can narrow it down with predicates and apply LIMIT and OFFSET to paginate the query.

```clojure
(def humans (-> (select* humans)
               (order :date_of_birth)))   ❶

(let [kings-of-germany (-> humans
                          (where {:country "Germany" :profession "King"}))]   ❷
  (doseq [start (range 0 100 10)
          k (select kings-of-germany                                          ❸
                   (offset start)
                   (limit 10))]
    ...)
```

❶ If we were to execute this query as-is, the result set would be billions-of-records large. However, humans captures the ordering we intend to enforce throughout our usage.

❷ Within a particular context, we can refine our query parameters as necessary...

❸ ...and use that refinement as the basis for even more fine-grained queries—like pagination—without having to restate all of the criteria that we'd previously accumulated in our query map.

Hibernate

If you are already using Java or another JVM language for RDBMS work, it's likely that you're using Hibernate (*http://www.hibernate.org*), easily the most popular Java object/relational mapping library. One of the advantages of Clojure is being able to use Java libraries and frameworks seamlessly, and Hibernate is no exception.

Hibernate has a very different philosophy from Clojure: it operates by creating objects, mutating them, and translating those mutations into database queries. However, Clojure is flexible enough to allow Hibernate to work with very little fuss.

Setup

Let's set up Hibernate to let us create, access, and update the `authors` table from earlier in the chapter. First, we'll need to add Hibernate as a project dependency:

```
[org.hibernate/hibernate-core "4.0.0.Final"]
```

Most usage of Hibernate from Clojure will likely involve using domain objects already built in Java.[7] Here's a vanilla Java class that represents author name data, using a mix of Hibernate and JPA annotations to indicate that it represents a database entity and specify the usual autoincrementing behavior of the `id` field:

```
package com.clojurebook.hibernate;

import javax.persistence.GeneratedValue;
import javax.persistence.Id;
import javax.persistence.Entity;
import org.hibernate.annotations.GenericGenerator;

@Entity
public class Author {
    private Long id;
    private String firstName;
    private String lastName;

    public Author () {}

    public Author (String firstName, String lastName) {
        this.firstName = firstName;
        this.lastName = lastName;
```

7. You *are* able to write Hibernate/JPA `Entity` classes using Clojure, quite easily. Refer to "Annotations" on page 381 for other examples of using Java framework annotations in conjunction with Clojure type definition facilities. In the case of Hibernate/JPA, you will need to use `gen-class`, since entities require a default/no-argument constructor to create entity instances when performing queries.

```
        }

        @Id
        @GeneratedValue(generator="increment")
        @GenericGenerator(name="increment", strategy = "increment")
        public Long getId () {
            return this.id;
        }
        public String getFirstName () {
            return this.firstName;
        }
        public String getLastName () {
            return this.lastName;
        }

        public void setId (Long id) {
            this.id = id;
        }
        public void setFirstName (String firstName) {
            this.firstName = firstName;
        }
        public void setLastName (String lastName) {
            this.lastName = lastName;
        }
    }
```

Rather than spec maps like those accepted by `clojure.java.jdbc` or Korma, Hibernate is generally configured using a *hibernate.cfg.xml* XML file. This one specifies that it should target an in-memory SQLite database.

Example 14-2. rsrc/hibernate.cfg.xml

```
<!DOCTYPE hibernate-configuration SYSTEM
"http://hibernate.sourceforge.net/hibernate-configuration-3.0.dtd">
<hibernate-configuration>
  <session-factory>
    <property name="hibernate.connection.driver_class">org.sqlite.JDBC</property>
    <property name="hibernate.connection.url">jdbc:sqlite::memory:</property>
    <property name="hibernate.dialect">org.hibernate.dialect.HSQLDialect</property>
    <!-- Drop and re-create the database schema on startup -->
    <property name="hbm2ddl.auto">create</property>
    <mapping class="com.clojurebook.hibernate.Author"/>
  </session-factory>
</hibernate-configuration>
```

Finally, if we're using Leiningen, we just need to add a couple of keys to our *project.clj*; one to indicate the source root for Java code we'd like it to compile (i.e., *Author.java*), and another to indicate the resources root, where we placed our *hibernate.cfg.xml* file:

```
    :java-source-path "java"
    :resources-path "rsrc"
```

This leaves our project structure looking like so:

```
|-- project.clj
|-- rsrc
|    `-- hibernate.cfg.xml
|-- java
|    `-- com
|         `-- clojurebook
|              `-- hibernate
|                   |-- Author.java
```

We can now compile our Java class and start a REPL to start seeing how we can use Hibernate from Clojure:

```
% lein javac
...
% lein repl
```

We first need to import the required Java classes from Hibernate, and our new Author class:

```
(import 'org.hibernate.SessionFactory
        'org.hibernate.cfg.Configuration
        'com.clojurebook.hibernate.Author)
```

Hibernate requires setting up a session factory object to allow us to open and close database sessions and run queries. It's important that the factory be instantiated only once. In Java, we might make a utility class with a `static final` member representing the session factory. The factory would be instantiated at the time the class was loaded. This kind of Java code is not uncommon, and is in fact straight from Hibernate's documentation (*http://docs.jboss.org/hibernate/core/3.3/reference/en/html/tutorial.html*):

```
public class HibernateUtil {
    private static final SessionFactory sessionFactory = buildSessionFactory();

    private static SessionFactory buildSessionFactory() {
        try {
            return new Configuration().configure().buildSessionFactory();
        }
        catch (Throwable ex) {
            System.err.println("Initial SessionFactory creation failed." + ex);
            throw new ExceptionInInitializerError(ex);
        }
    }

    public static SessionFactory getSessionFactory() {
        return sessionFactory;
    }
}
```

In Clojure, we can have a much simpler solution, using `defonce` and `delay`:

```
(defonce session-factory
  (delay (-> (Configuration.)
             .configure
             .buildSessionFactory)))
```

As the name implies, defonce behaves like def, defining a var to have some value, but leaving any existing definition intact, even if we reload the namespace that contains the session-factory definition. delay ensures that the -> expression that actually creates and configures the session factory isn't evaluated until it is dereferenced; this allows us to load or AOT-compile the source file without unintentionally attempting to connect to our configured database.

Persisting Data

Our *hibernate.cfg.xml* is set up to use an in-memory SQLite database, so it is bare when our REPL starts up. A typical approach to doing this in Java might go like this:

```java
public static void saveAuthors (Author... authors) {
  Session session = sessionFactory.openSession();
  session.beginTransaction();
  for (Author author : authors) {
    session.save(author);
  }
  session.getTransaction().commit();
  session.close();
}

saveAuthors(new Author("Christophe", "Grand"), new Author("Brian", "Carper"), ...);
```

A naive translation of this to Clojure would be something like add-authors here:

Example 14-3. add-authors

```clojure
(defn add-authors
  [& authors]
  (with-open [session (.openSession @session-factory)]
    (let [tx (.beginTransaction session)]
      (doseq [author authors]
        (.save session author))
      (.commit tx))))

(add-authors (Author. "Christophe" "Grand") (Author. "Brian" "Carper")
  (Author. "Chas" "Emerick"))
```

Running Queries

Now that we have persisted some data, let's try to fetch a list of rows in our authors table and print their names. In Java, we might do something like this:

```java
Session session = HibernateUtil.getSessionFactory().openSession();

try {
  return (List<Author>)newSession.createQuery("from Author").list();
} finally {
  session.close();
}
```

This code can be translated to Clojure in a very straightforward way:

Example 14-4. get-authors

```
(defn get-authors
  []
  (with-open [session (.openSession @session-factory)]
    (-> session
      (.createQuery "from Author")
      .list)))
```

Of course, since we're in Clojure, we have a fair bit more flexibility in terms of manipulating the data we obtain from our Hibernate query:

```
(for [{:keys [firstName lastName]} (map bean (get-authors))]  ❶
  (str lastName ", " firstName))
;= ("Carper, Brian" "Emerick, Chas" "Grand, Christophe")
```

❶ bean here converts any JavaBean-style Java object into a Clojure hash map, with each getter corresponding to a slot in that map with keyword keys of the same name as the getters in that JavaBean.

The `.list` method on the Hibernate query object returns a `java.util.ArrayList` of results. We are able loop over it using `doseq` because Clojure ensures that all `java.util.List`s are seqable.

Removing Boilerplate

Our Clojure code works, but it can be improved.

Note the repetition in our two functions. Opening and closing the session and beginning and committing transactions are two things we'll have to do over and over.

In Java, you might be stuck retyping this code over and over; not so in Clojure. A good first step was using the Clojure built-in `with-open` macro, which allows us to automatically open a connection or handle object, run some code, and then ensure that the handle or connection is closed once we're done using it. Because Hibernate sessions are closed with a standard `.close` method, `with-open` works on Hibernate sessions.

However, we can do better. `with-open` requires us to specify a name for the `session` local; with a macro on top of `with-open`, we can simply say that as a matter of convention, it will always be named `session` within the body of that macro:

```
(defmacro with-session
  [session-factory & body]  ❶
  `(with-open [~'session (.openSession ~(vary-meta session-factory assoc
                                          :tag 'SessionFactory))]  ❷
    ~@body))
```

❶ The first argument, `session-factory`, is a form that will be used to obtain an open session. All further arguments are forms executed in the context of that session being open.

❷ Without hinting `session-factory`, the compiler will not know that (`.openSession factory#`) will return a Hibernate `Session`, and so all calls involving `session` will be reflective. However, we can't just hint the unquoted `session-factory` symbol, as that would apply to the `~session-factory` form, and not to the user-provided symbol bound to `session-factory` within the macro. The fix is to modify the metadata of the symbol bound to `session-factory`, so that value will be hinted appropriately. Note that the value of `:tag` is itself a *symbol*, not a class.

Rather than use a gensym to establish a "safe" local binding that will not shadow existing bindings or "leak" into user code within the body of `with-session`, we *want* to have `session` bound within that scope to the Hibernate `Session`. To do this, we force the emission of an unqualified (un-namespaced) symbol using `~'session`.[8] A bare `session` symbol in the macro at this point would have caused a compilation error, as macroexpansion would have automatically qualified the symbol to the current namespace, e.g., `user/session`, which cannot be used as names for local bindings.

With this macro in place, we can rewrite Example 14-4 to be somewhat more concise:

```
(defn get-authors
  []
  (with-session @session-factory
    (-> session
        (.createQuery "from Author")
        .list)))
```

That's not a *huge* benefit on its own, but multiplied over dozens, hundreds, or thousands of Hibernate interactions involving an open session, it's some progress. More significant would be a corollary macro for executing operations within the context of a Hibernate transaction:

```
(defmacro with-transaction
  [& body]
  `(let [~'tx (.beginTransaction ~'session)]   ❶
     ~@body
     (.commit ~'tx)))
```

❶ Because Hibernate `Transaction` objects provide useful methods (just like `Session` objects), we implicitly bind the current `Transaction` to the `tx` local so user code can access it easily. This makes `with-transaction` an anaphoric macro as well.

Here, `session` is a name that we expect to be already bound to the value of a currently open session; thus, `with-transaction` will work seamlessly with the anaphoric `session` name bound in `with-session`. The generated code will begin a transaction, execute additional forms in `body`, and then commit the transaction. This allows us to produce a *much* simpler implementation of Example 14-3:

---

8. By establishing an implicit binding visible to user code, `with-session` is an *anaphoric* (sometimes referred to as *unhygienic*) macro. See "Hygiene" on page 244 and "Letting the User Pick Names" on page 248 for more about anaphoric macros.

```
(defn add-authors
  [& authors]
  (with-session @session-factory
    (with-transaction
      (doseq [author authors]
        (.save session author)))))
```

Pushing boilerplate and syntactic complexity like that involved in the bookkeeping of sessions and transactions out of the codebase we need to touch on a daily basis can make it easier to read, more enjoyable to work with, and perhaps most important, less prone to error.

Final Thoughts

Clojure has excellent support for working with relational databases. The JVM and JDBC provides a great foundation of comprehensive database support to build upon, pure Clojure options offer powerful and composable layers of additional functionality on top, and, if the need arises, it is easy and practical to fall back to mature Java frameworks like Hibernate.

## CHAPTER 15

Using Nonrelational Databases

After years of relational databases being the only functionally available choice for application developers needing to persist data, a number of new classes of databases have come to be regarded as legitimate alternatives to the ubiquitous RDBMS. These databases are each generally very different from each other. Despite their differences, key-value stores and column- and document-oriented databases share a common thread of presenting alternatives to the orthodoxy of the relational data model that has dominated for so long; thus, they are often collectively referred to as nonrelational databases.[1] These data stores' unique capabilities and increasing popularity make them common components in new Clojure applications, so it's worth seeing what such a combination looks like.

CouchDB is a document-oriented nonrelational database that defines a data model and architecture that fits well with Clojure's strengths and world view. The combination is particularly potent, allowing for the relatively simple implementation of many types of applications, from typical web frontends to pleasantly extensible messaging systems.

To start, it would be helpful to describe a couple of CouchDB features that are particularly relevant to Clojure:

- Its data model consists exclusively of JSON documents, which are trivially converted to and from Clojure's data structures.
- It uses an append-only btree-based storage system that defaults to ensuring data durability and operational atomicity.
- It uses *MVCC* for coping with concurrent modifications from multiple clients, the same optimistic, versioned change-management model that Clojure's software transaction memory uses.
- It allows for the definition of nontrivial queries in terms of data transformations called views, which may be implemented in nearly any language, including Clojure.

---

1. Or, more popularly (and unfortunately) as "NoSQL" databases.

Clojure's persistent data structures and focus on well-defined concurrency semantics make it a very natural pairing with CouchDB, which is similarly defined in terms of immutable documents that have clear semantics around the durability, atomicity, and conflict-management of changes.

Getting Set Up with CouchDB and Clutch

CouchDB is a very mature database (despite its 1.2.0 version label, which we'll be using in our examples), and extensive documentation may be found for it both online at its Apache project site[2] and in the O'Reilly book.[3] Those looking to completely understand it should refer to those resources.

To get started using CouchDB from Clojure, you'll first need to have CouchDB running locally.[4] In all of our examples, we'll be using the API provided by Clutch (*https://github .com/clojure-clutch/clutch*), a Clojure library that provides comprehensive support for CouchDB's facilities. To use Clutch, just add it as a dependency to your project:

```
[com.ashafa/clutch "0.3.0"]
```

Basic CRUD Operations

Let's explore CouchDB from the REPL, starting with the basics: creating, updating, and deleting documents.

Example 15-1. Simple CouchDB interaction in a REPL

```
(use '[com.ashafa.clutch :only (create-database with-db put-document
                                get-document delete-document)
                         :as clutch])

(def db (create-database "repl-crud"))                          ❶

(put-document db {:_id "foo" :some-data "bar"})                 ❷
;= {:_rev "1-2bd2719826", :some-data "bar", :_id "foo"}
(put-document db (assoc *1 :other-data "quux"))                 ❸
;= {:other-data "quux", :_rev "2-9f29b39770", :some-data "bar", :_id "foo"}
(get-document db "foo")                                         ❹
;= {:_id "foo", :_rev "2-9f29b39770", :other-data "quux", :some-data "bar"}
(delete-document db *1)                                         ❺
;= {:ok true, :id "foo", :rev "3-3e98dd1028"}
(get-document db "foo")                                         ❻
;= nil
```

2. *http://couchdb.apache.org*—(the wiki is a particularly rich trove of detailed information).

3. Written by members of the CouchDB development team and available free online and in print at *http:// guide.couchdb.org*.

4. Or, you can use a free hosted CouchDB instance from Cloudant for everything but the Clojure view server examples: *https://cloudant.com*.

❶ First, we create a scratch database for our REPL interaction.

❷ Here we create a document using a Clojure map. `put-document` returns the created document, which will be the same as the map provided, except for the addition of the `:_rev` slot. Note that we're defining `:_id` here, which serves as the "primary key" for the document; if we leave that undefined, CouchDB will assign our new document a UUID `:_id`.

❸ An update operation. Notice that the `:_rev` slot's value has been updated in the return value, because we've updated that document.[5]

❹ A simple get operation, which always returns the latest revision of the requested document; you can optionally request prior document revisions.

❺ A delete operation. Though we're providing the full document map in this case, note that we only really need to provide a map containing `:_id` and `:_rev` values that match the latest version of an existing document.

❻ A get operation returns `nil` if no document with the specified key exists.

The direct parallels between their respective data representations make interactions between Clojure and CouchDB very natural. CouchDB uses JSON throughout for data representation (key/value maps with string keys and scalar, array, or other key/value map as values), which maps onto Clojure's maps, vectors, and scalars perfectly. Fortunately, the JSON parser that Clutch uses (*https://github.com/clojure/data.json*) converts the string keys of JSON maps into Clojure keywords; this allows for easy lookup of key/value pairs and traversal of nested structures using functions like `get-in`, or Clojure's threading macros, `->`, `->>`, and so on.

The consequences of this can be illustrated by seeing how we can trivially drill into a document retrieved from CouchDB:

```
(clutch/create-document {:_id "foo"
                         :data ["bar" {:details ["bat" false 42]}]})
;= {:_id "foo", :data ["bar" {:details ["bat" false 42]}],
;=  :_rev "1-6d7460947434b90bf88f033785f81cdd"}
(->> (get-document db "foo")
  :data
  second
  :details
  (filter number?))
;= (42)
```

The upshot is that documents stored in and retrieved from CouchDB *are* "Clojure-native" data structures for all intents and purposes, and therefore amenable to all of Clojure's idiomatic facilities for querying and processing data. This simplifies applica-

---

5. Remember that `*1` is a REPL-bound var that holds the value of the last-evaluated expression, similar to `_` in Ruby's IRB and in the Python interpreter. See "REPL-bound vars" (page 399) for more about REPL-bound vars.

tion code significantly and brings relative clarity and ease to data modeling, often one of the most difficult aspects of database usage.

Views

CouchDB does not offer SQL or anything similar for performing ad-hoc queries. On their own, documents may only be indexed by a single "primary" string key.

The alternative provided by CouchDB is called *views*. Views are very similar in concept to the materialized views offered by some relational database systems. Views:

- Are stored and accessed separately from their "source" database
- Are defined programmatically (using almost any language, including Clojure as we'll see shortly) and ahead of time
- Reflect changes to the source database's documents upon access

The primary insight behind CouchDB's views is that nearly all of an application's data access can be enumerated, and so the flexibility (and attendant runtime cost) associated with SQL and other ad-hoc query mechanisms is generally unwarranted. In contrast, CouchDB views must always be defined in the database prior to accessing them,[6] with the benefit that accessing them will always be extremely fast, regardless of the amount of processing needed to produce the views' data.

To get started with views, let's load a dataset of hypothetical logging messages into a new database, named *logging*. We'll use Clutch's `bulk-update` function for this, which hooks into CouchDB's _bulk_docs API; this is the most efficient route for loading large amounts of data into CouchDB:

```
(clutch/bulk-update (create-database "logging")
  [{:evt-type "auth/new-user" :username "Chas"}
   {:evt-type "auth/new-user" :username "Dave"}
   {:evt-type "sales/purchase" :username "Chas" :products ["widget1"]}
   {:evt-type "sales/purchase" :username "Robin" :products ["widget14"]}
   {:evt-type "sales/RFQ" :username "Robin" :budget 20000}])
```

A Simple (JavaScript) View

By default, CouchDB views are defined using JavaScript; we'll start there to get familiarized with accessing views from Clojure, and then go on to implement a couple of views in Clojure itself.

Regardless of what language you use to implement views, they are defined by a map function, and an optional reduce function.

---

6. While you can create temporary views in an ad-hoc fashion, such views will always be *far* slower than "regular" views configured and stored ahead of time.

The *reduce* concept is defined somewhat differently in CouchDB than it is in Clojure and other functional programming languages, as well as in other data processing systems such as Hadoop and the MapReduce model popularized by Google. The semantics of reduce (and the CouchDB-specific notion of *rereduce*) is tied to CouchDB's B-Tree data indexing strategy. See *http://wiki.apache.org/couchdb/Introduction_to _CouchDB_views#Reduce_Functions* in the CouchDB documentation/ book for more information.

Our first view will cover an obvious usecase: report on how many log message of each type have been lodged. Implementing this requires defining a map and a reduce function:

```
function(doc) {
  emit(doc["evt-type"], null);
}

function (keys, vals, rereduce) {
  return rereduce ? sum(vals) : vals.length;
}
```

You can create this view using *Futon*, the administrative frontend provided with CouchDB,[7] or via Clutch like so:

```
(clutch/save-view "logging" "jsviews"          ❶
  (clutch/view-server-fns :javascript          ❷
    {:type-counts                              ❸
     {:map "function(doc) {
            emit(doc['evt-type'], null);
          }"
      :reduce "function (keys, vals, rereduce) {
               return rereduce ? sum(vals) : vals.length;
             }"}}))
```

❶ jsviews specifies the name of the *design document* where our view will be stored. Design documents are special documents within a CouchDB database that are dedicated to holding code to drive views, filters, and other in-database functionality.

❷ This view is implemented using JavaScript, which we must specify so that the design document may be configured properly.

❸ type-counts is the name of the view; you can provide many views at once to view-server-fns, just by adding another entry to the provided map.

---

7. If you're running CouchDB locally, you can access Futon at *http://localhost:5984/_utils*.

Now we're ready to query our view:

```
(clutch/get-view "logging" "jsviews" :type-counts {:group true})
;= ({:key "auth/new-user", :value 2}
;=  {:key "sales/purchase", :value 2}
;=  {:key "sales/RFQ", :value 1})
```

And there are our record counts, keyed on the log messages' :evt-type slot. get-view returns a lazy sequence of result documents from the named view; this means that view results of thousands or millions of documents may be consumed and processed from Clojure without difficulty. And again, these view result documents are just more Clojure maps and values, making it easy for us to produce a slightly more useful aggregated form with some Clojure seq processing:

```
(->> (clutch/get-view "logging" "jsviews" :type-counts {:group true})
  (map (juxt :key :value))
  (into {}))
;= {"auth/new-user" 2, "sales/purchase" 2, "sales/RFQ" 1}
```

As you might expect, these counts are updated as necessary as new log messages stream into the database.

The :group query option we're using above is a shortcut that reduces the view's values for each uniquely keyed record. Without it, we'd get a single result, with a value of 5. Views have all sorts of query options that we won't touch on here; please refer to the CouchDB documentation (*http://wiki.apache.org/couchdb/HTTP_view_API#Querying_Options*) for more information.

Views in Clojure

Writing CouchDB views in JavaScript is convenient, insofar as just about everyone knows JavaScript, and CouchDB comes with a JavaScript *view server* implementation out of the box.

CouchDB views are produced by feeding the source code defining a set of views along with JSON corresponding to "source" documents into a separate process called a *view server*. View servers simply read this data from stdin and emit what should be stored for the view results on stdout. The simplicity of implementation means that it is very straightforward to implement a view server in almost any programming language.

You'll almost certainly never need to consider writing a new view server: there are implementations for dozens of languages, including Clutch's implementation for writing views in Clojure.

However, there are very good reasons for using a non-JavaScript view server, all of which are certainly true when it comes to the Clojure view server provided by Clutch:

- You can take advantage of a richer, likely more familiar language.
- Your chosen view server's language almost surely has access to higher quality, more comprehensive libraries than are available in CouchDB's prepackaged JavaScript view server
- If your views involve any kind of intensive processing, your chosen view server's language likely provides a more efficient runtime than JavaScript's.

Configuring your local CouchDB instance to use Clutch's view server for Clojure views usually requires using the `configure-view-server` function in your Clutch-enabled REPL:[8]

```
(use '[com.ashafa.clutch.view-server :only (view-server-exec-string)])

(clutch/configure-view-server "http://localhost:5984" (view-server-exec-string))
```

The `configure-view-server` function creates a Clojure view server entry in your CouchDB instance, with a shell command that CouchDB will use to run the view server as necessary.[9]

First, let's take a look at a port of our simple JavaScript view to a Clojure view. Here, we're using Clutch to save the view to a different design document (`clj-views` instead of `jsviews`, which we used above for the JavaScript view):

```
(clutch/save-view "logging" "clj-views"
  (clutch/view-server-fns :clojure
    {:type-counts
     {:map (fn [doc]
             [[(:evt-type doc) nil]])
      :reduce (fn [keys vals rereduce]
                (if rereduce
                  (reduce + vals)
                  (count vals)))}}))
```

CouchDB's (and therefore Clutch's) view API is the same, regardless of which language your views are implemented in, so outside of specifying the different design document, our code for accessing the Clojure view is unchanged from before:

```
(->> (clutch/get-view "logging" "clj-views" :type-counts {:group true})
     (map (juxt :key :value))
     (into {}))
;= {"auth/new-user" 2, "sales/purchase" 2, "sales/RFQ" 1}
```

---

8. ClojureScript (see "ClojureScript" on page 584) can be used with Clutch to define Clojure views in CouchDB that do not require the configuration of a new view server—very convenient, especially if your CouchDB is hosted by Cloudant or elsewhere: *https://github.com/clojure-clutch/clutch-clojurescript*.

9. This setup invocation is a convenience for REPL use only; please refer to the Clutch README at *http://github.com/ashafa/clutch* for more information about setting up CouchDB to be Clojure view server ready in general terms.

Simply swapping braces for parens is not the objective here though; by writing views in Clojure, we can take advantage of all of its facilities when producing data for a view, including using any existing Clojure and Java libraries as necessary.

Consider the problem domain associated with our dataset, that of event logging from what we can suppose is a sort of e-commerce application. The concrete event types we see here appear to be related in some hierarchy (e.g., `sales/purchase` and `sales/RFQ` clearly being related). It would be trivial (regardless of the language you are writing views in) to split event types on the slash character and use CouchDB's view collation features (*http://wiki.apache.org/couchdb/View_collation*) to naturally group the emitted counts based on the implicit hierarchy. While that would be reasonably useful, it forces our event types into a strict hierarchy. Getting around this through creative event type naming or using some kind of manifold event typing (e.g., making `:evt-type` an array of types) is possible, but inelegant, less flexible, and more complex.

A better solution would be to define our event types in terms of Clojure's ad hoc hierarchies;[10] for example:

Example 15-2. Defining our event hierarchy

```
(ns eventing.types)

(derive 'sales/purchase 'sales/all)
(derive 'sales/purchase 'finance/accounts-receivable)
(derive 'finance/accounts-receivable 'finance/all)
(derive 'finance/all 'events/all)
(derive 'sales/all 'events/all)
(derive 'sales/RFQ 'sales/lead-generation)
(derive 'sales/lead-generation 'sales/all)
(derive 'auth/new-user 'sales/lead-generation)
(derive 'auth/new-user 'security/all)
(derive 'security/all 'events/all)
```

We can then use that representation in our view server to expand each concrete event type into all of its parent types, some of which may never actually appear as a log message's `:evt-type`, but that may represent something significant to the business in question. Taking this route allows us to succinctly provide for event types that impact multiple concerns. Here is a Clojure view implementing this strategy:

Example 15-3. A hierarchy-augmented Clojure view

```
(clutch/save-view "logging" "clj-views"
  (clutch/view-server-fns :clojure
    {:type-counts
     {:map (do
             (require 'eventing.types)              ❶
             (fn [doc
               (let [concrete-type (-> doc :evt-type symbol)]   ❷
                 (for [evtsym (cons concrete-type              ❸
```

10. Read more about hierarchies and multimethods in Clojure in Chapter 7.

```
                              (ancestors concrete-type))]
                  [(str evtsym) nil])])))
    :reduce (fn [keys vals rereduce]                              ❹
              (if rereduce
                (reduce + vals)
                (count vals)))}}})

(->> (clutch/with-db "logging"
       (clutch/get-view "clj-views" :type-counts {:group true}))
  (map (juxt :key :value))
  (into {}))
;= {"events/all" 5,
;=  "sales/all" 5,
;=  "finance/all" 2,
;=  "finance/accounts-receivable" 2,
;=  "sales/lead-generation" 3,
;=  "sales/purchase" 2,
;=  "sales/RFQ" 1,
;=  "security/all" 2,
;=  "auth/new-user" 2}
```

❶ First, we ensure that the namespace that defines the relationships between our known concrete event types and their "ancestral" types is loaded. This happens only once, when the view map is materialized in the view server and before any documents are processed. Note that the required namespace (eventing.types in this case) must be on the view server's classpath.

❷ We convert each :evt-type string into a symbol, so that...

❸ ...that symbol's ancestors in the defined hierarchy can be obtained. A single view result is emitted for each symbol, including one for the concrete :evt-type.

❹ The reduce function remains unchanged from our previous simple counting view.

The results of the view are now a lot more interesting. By defining our event type hierarchy in Clojure, not only have we been able to get "departmental" rollups of event counts, but the cross-functional events are treated far more usefully than a lexicographical naming scheme would allow for:

- auth/new-user events are properly related to lead generation in addition to their natural alignment under security.

- The scope of sales/purchase events have been broadened to include accounts receivable and finance.

Even better, our hierarchy of event types in Clojure can be added to or reorganized as needed, entirely independent of the different modules or applications that are producing the actual events. For example, when new auditing requirements dictate that user registrations are to be tracked and retained along with a broad spectrum of other business data, the security/all parent may be declared a child of a new audit/all event type, thereby including auth/new-users in the audit scope without the user authentication system changing anything about how it emits those auth/new-user events.

View functions must be pure

One thing to remember when writing views is that *you are not in control of when your view is invoked, or how many times it is invoked.* This CouchDB implementation detail is irrelevant when writing views using JavaScript, because it provides no facilities for doing I/O or other side-effecting operations. However, when writing views in Clojure (or really, any other non-JavaScript language), you need to ensure the functions you write are pure.[11] For example, sending a notification email every time your view processed an event of type `sales/purchase` would be a disaster: that email would be sent every time a purchase event document changed, or when the database is compacted, or (just to drive the point home) any time CouchDB decides it needs to invalidate the view results for that purchase document.

_changes: Abusing CouchDB as a Message Queue

CouchDB provides a change notification API (called _changes) that allows clients a great deal of flexibility in defining how to react in response to data flows.

Briefly, _changes works like so:

1. An HTTP connection is opened to the _changes URL for the CouchDB database of interest.

2. Wait. When any change occurs in the database in question (any document creation, deletion, or update), a JSON map is sent to the client describing the affected document ID and revision.

3. If you have elected to be notified of changes continuously, repeat from 2.

The simplest of all _changes usage via Clojure might be using Clutch's `watch-changes` function to echo all change notifications to *out*. Here, we'll create a new database for our _changes experimentation, set up a Clutch watch function for that database, and add a few documents to see what happens:

```
(clutch/create-database "changes")
(clutch/watch-changes "changes" :echo (partial println "changes:"))        ❶

(clutch/bulk-update "changes" [{:_id "doc1"} {:_id "doc2"}])                 ❷
;= [{:id "doc1", :rev "5-f36e792166"}
;=  {:id "doc2", :rev "3-5570e8bbb3"}]
; change: {:seq 7, :id doc1, :changes [{:rev 5-f36e792166}]}
; change: {:seq 8, :id doc2, :changes [{:rev 3-5570e8bbb3}]}
(clutch/delete-document "changes" (zipmap [:_id :_rev]
                                          ((juxt :id :rev) (first *1))))
;= {:ok true, :id "doc1", :rev "6-616e3df68"}
; change: {:seq 9, :id doc1, :changes [{:rev 6-616e3df68}], :deleted true}
```

---

11. See "Pure Functions" on page 76 for a discussion about referential transparency and pure functions.

```
(clutch/stop-changes "changes" :echo)                          ❸
;= nil
```

❶ Register a new watch function with the name :echo on the changes database; this one will just echo _changes notifications to *out*.

❷ We'll now be notified of all changes made in the database we're watching; these notifications correspond to calls to the echo function we registered.

❸ stop-changes will unsubscribe our watch function from the database's _changes feed.

This mechanism is exactly analogous to the watches[12] that are available for Clojure-native reference types such as atoms, vars, refs, and agents. Conceptually, each CouchDB database is contained within a separate atom; when a change is made to the database, that change is sent off to an agent associated with your watch-changes call.

In addition, CouchDB allows for the definition of "filter" functions that allows you to opt into a programmatic filtering of the documents that will be included in the feed of changes delivered by _changes. These filter functions can be defined using any language—just as with view functions—and their application can be parameterized when you start receiving notifications from _changes via Clutch's watch-changes, as we'll see shortly.

The possibilities for building very flexible event-driven applications using these facilities are quite boundless. From a systems perspective, the fact that CouchDB effectively serves as both a message queue (or perhaps more precisely, provides a superset of event queue functionality) and your likely primary data store (or "system of record" in data warehousing parlance), has a variety of attractive characteristics as well, including:

• The lack of any synchronization overhead or impedance mismatch between a primary database and a separate dedicated message queue (such as RabbitMQ, ActiveMQ, or one of the various JMS implementations).

• Simplified operational considerations: all things being equal, running one system is always easier than running two.

Just because you *can* use CouchDB as the basis for a bespoke message queue does not mean that you *should*; with great power comes great responsibility, and all that. Off-the-shelf message queues are extraordinarily good at what they do, and they address many common use cases very well. That said, it is our opinion that a savvy practitioner should always be on the watch for alternatives that might solve unique problems elegantly or typical problems more simply.

---

12. See "Watches" on page 176 for more details on watches.

À la Carte Message Queues

Let's combine all of what we've learned about how to effectively use CouchDB from Clojure to implement an asynchronous work queue based on the events being emitted into the *logging* database we considered earlier. First, a refresher on what that data looks like:

Example 15-4. Sample event data

```
{:evt-type "auth/new-user" :username "Chas"}
{:evt-type "auth/new-user" :username "Dave"}
{:evt-type "sales/purchase" :username "Chas" :products ["widget1"]}
{:evt-type "sales/purchase" :username "Robin" :products ["widget14"]}
{:evt-type "sales/RFQ" :username "Robin" :budget 20000}
```

Now, you could add a single watch for changes in the *logging* database, and instead of echoing those events to *out*, do something useful with them; that's a perfectly valid thing to do, especially if your requirements are relatively simple. However, most real-world systems need some additional levers to pull to control event processing loads and more ably support modular design requirements.

We can assume that our typical website or application will be generating all sorts of events; some will only need to be retained for some period of time, some will need to go into a long-term archive, and others will need to be acted upon as soon as possible. Earlier, we defined a hierarchy over the concrete event types in our sample dataset. Let's now build a parallel hierarchy that defines how different types of events should be consumed:

Example 15-5. Defining a partial event processing hierarchy

```
(ns eventing.processing)

(derive 'sales/lead-generation 'processing/realtime)
(derive 'sales/purchase 'processing/realtime)

(derive 'security/all 'processing/archive)
(derive 'finance/all 'processing/archive)
```

Take note that three of the four declarations here make no reference to concrete event types at all, but the hierarchies that are rooted at our processing "levels" fully apply to them nonetheless by dint of the relationships we defined earlier between the concrete event types and our broader event type categories (such as 'security/all'). In our example, this saves a fair bit of typing, but the real win comes when multiple teams are independently building separate modules or applications that are all emitting event data: each team can maintain its own event type hierarchies (representing functional, business, or organizational relationships as necessary) without necessarily coordinating with whomever is writing the module(s) or application(s) that will be coordinating the processing of those events.

We can now create a _changes filter that will allow us to select events whose type isa?[13] is another type that we've defined:

Example 15-6. Creating a message-type _changes filter

```
(clutch/save-filter "logging" "event-filters"
  (clutch/view-server-fns :clojure
    {:event-isa? (do
                  (require '[eventing types processing])
                  (fn [doc request]
                    (let [req-type (-> request :query :type)
                          evt-type (:evt-type doc)]
                      (and req-type evt-type
                        (isa? (symbol evt-type) (symbol req-type)))))))}))
```

This filter is parameterized (note the usage of the query param held by the **request** object), so we can pick and choose which events to be included in the stream delivered from _changes based on the hierarchies we've defined. Before we go any further, let's echo _changes again, but with some additions:

```
(clutch/watch-changes "logging" :echo-leads (partial println "change:")   ❶
  :filter "event-filters/event-isa?"                                       ❷
  :type "sales/lead-generation"                                            ❸
  :include_docs true)                                                      ❹

(clutch/put-document "logging"                                             ❺
  {:evt-type "sales/RFQ" :username "Lilly" :budget 20000})
;= {:_id "8f264da359f887ec3e86c8d34801704b",
;=  :_rev "1-eb10044985c9dccb731bd5f31d0188c6",
;=  :budget 20000, :evt-type "sales/RFQ", :username "Lilly"}
; change: {:seq 26, :id 8f264da359f887ec3e86c8d34801704b,                  ❻
;          :changes [{:rev 1-eb10044985c9dccb731bd5f31d0188c6}],
;          :doc {:_id 8f264da359f887ec3e86c8d34801704b,
;                :_rev 1-eb10044985c9dccb731bd5f31d0188c6,
;                :budget 20000,
;                :evt-type sales/RFQ,
```

13. See Chapter 7 for details of isa? semantics.

```
;                    :username Lilly}}
(clutch/stop-changes "logging" :echo-leads)
;= nil
```

❶ Similar to before, we'll watch for changes on the *logging* database...

❷ ...specifying our hierarchy-aware filter...

❸ ...parameterizing that filter so that only changes to lead-generation events are emitted...

❹ ...and requesting that the full contents of documents are included in the change notification objects, rather than the default of only their :_id and :_rev slots.

❺ When we create a new document, with an :evt-type that is a descendant of our specified lead-generation type...

❻ ...our watch receives the notification as we'd expect, along with the full content of the associated event.

This is all driven by the fact that, thanks to the hierarchies we've defined, (isa? 'sales/RFQ 'sales/lead-generation) returns true in our filter.

We can set up as many database watches as we need to correspond with various service or event priority levels, or simply to meet processing demands (especially if the processing involved is idempotent). Each watch serves as a discrete queue, at least from our application's perspective. And, again enabled by the hierarchies, processing implementations can be contributed by any number of potentially domain-specific modules.

Let's implement such a system. First, we define a multimethod[14] in some central location:

```
(ns eventing.processing)

(defmulti process-event :evt-type)
```

Then, we add process-event implementations as necessary, aligned with the hierarchies we've defined. At this point, all of the facilities of multimethods are available to us. Our process-event implementations simply echo some descriptive text to *out*; of course, real implementations of such methods would do something far more substantial: for our scenario, they'd send an invoice, cause product to be drop-shipped, add a lead to a CRM system, and so on.

Example 15-7. Implementing processing of sales-related "realtime" events

```
(ns salesorg.event-handling
  (use [eventing.processing :only (process-event)]))

(defmethod process-event 'sales/purchase
  [evt]
```

14. See Chapter 7.

```
    (println (format "We made a sale of %s to %s!" (:products evt) (:username evt))))

(defmethod process-event 'sales/lead-generation
  [evt]
  (println "Add prospect to CRM system: " evt))
```

Finally, we can set up our watch, which will drive the processing of each event, after pulling out the actual document that triggered the event in the first place, removing the CouchDB-specific :_id and :_rev slots, and converting the concrete :evt-type string into a symbol so its dispatch within the process-event multimethod is driven by the hierarchy we've built up and not the strings returned to us by CouchDB. We'll do that at the REPL here, and then again recreate the five events we've been looking at:

```
(require 'eventing.processing 'salesorg.event-handling)

(clutch/watch-changes "logging" :process-events
  #(-> %
     :doc
     (dissoc :_id :_rev)
     (update-in [:evt-type] symbol)
     eventing.processing/process-event)
  :filter "event-filters/event-isa?"
  :type "processing/realtime"
  :include_docs true)

(clutch/bulk-update "logging"
  [{:evt-type "auth/new-user" :username "Chas"}
   {:evt-type "auth/new-user" :username "Dave"}
   {:evt-type "sales/purchase" :username "Chas" :products ["widget1"]}
   {:evt-type "sales/purchase" :username "Robin" :products ["widget14"]}
   {:evt-type "sales/RFQ" :username "Robin" :budget 20000}])
; Add prospect to CRM system:  {:evt-type auth/new-user, :username Chas}
; Add prospect to CRM system:  {:evt-type auth/new-user, :username Dave}
; We made a sale of ["widget1"] to Chas!
; We made a sale of ["widget14"] to Robin!
; Add prospect to CRM system:  {:budget 20000, :evt-type sales/RFQ, :username Robin}
```

Final Thoughts

Clojure and CouchDB are both well-suited to dealing with heterogeneous, loosely structured datasets—a defining characteristic of dynamic, prototype-driven, ready-fire-aim development processes as well as an often much-needed salve for applications needing to integrate well with unchangeable legacy systems. Together, they are a potent combination, with Clojure bringing a great deal to the table in terms of maximizing the utility of CouchDB's views and filters and providing a number of facilities that enable you to make the most of CouchDB's features, model, and extensibility.

## CHAPTER 16

Clojure and the Web

Web development can easily be considered the ubiquitous domain: with rare exception, if you are a programmer today, not only do you know how to build web applications, you probably build or work on them regularly. This being the case, any ostensibly general-purpose language had better offer a compelling workflow and set of tools for building web apps. Clojure clears that bar handily.

Being hosted on the JVM and sporting excellent interop features, Clojure didn't have to start from scratch with bare sockets or an Apache module: all the good parts of the battle-tested array of Java web infrastructure was waiting to be leveraged. At the same time, the Clojure ecosystem has evolved its own set of idioms and principles of good web app architecture that contrasts significantly with typical Java practice.

The "Clojure Stack"

We've consistently repeated the mantra of good Clojure design: emphasizing common abstractions over concrete types and implementation details, pure functions with immutable data over side-effecting methods with mutable state, and the flexible assembly of these fundamentals into composites that are themselves reliable building blocks. It should then come as no surprise that there is no definitive "Clojure stack," at least compared to the monolithic framework bonanza that often constitutes web "stacks" in other languages. Instead, the Clojure community has grown a number of modular libraries over the years that collectively satisfy all of the requirements of the web developer, but that leverage Clojure's fundamental abstractions and emphasis on functional programming. You and your team can use those parts to build a stack that works for you and your applications, domain, and personal style and skills.[1]

This philosophy may seem counterintuitive to many experienced Rails, Django, or Lift developers. The features that are in such "complete stacks" are there for a reason:

---

1. Alternatively, you can start with one of the newer "batteries-included" web frameworks that have emerged of late; we mention these at the end of the chapter.

people tend to re-implement them if they're not there. However, given the context these frameworks operate within—full of object-oriented models with explicit controllers and views—there are few common abstractions, so effectively and efficiently composing small focused modules is often nigh on impossible. Given how easy this is in Clojure, such towering frameworks just don't save as much work as they do elsewhere. In short, if you're used to a fuller stack, try to keep an open mind until you've worked through a few apps; we suspect you'll not find a lot to want for.

We'll talk about web applications in three parts,[2] where each piece can be addressed by a different library (often chosen from a number of options):

- Request and response plumbing are those bits that either run an HTTP server or hook your application up to one, build request objects corresponding to incoming requests, and then produce an HTTP response as required.
- Routing is how requests get to the handler code you designate.
- Templating is how the response your handler produces is serialized to HTML (or whichever output media type you require).

What we'd like to show you is one particularly popular combination of libraries:

- Ring for the foundational request and response plumbing
- Compojure for routing
- Enlive for templating

Others quite happily mix and match other options to suit particular requirements or personal taste. Moustache[3] is another good option for routing. For templating, Hiccup[4] is a popular choice, clostache[5] borrows the Mustache[6] templating style available in many other languages' frameworks, and it's even straightforward to use things like JSPs, Velocity, stringtemplate, or other libraries from the pure Java web space.

If after trying the constellation we demonstrate here you'd like to explore some of these other options, a good starting point for comparing them is *http://brehaut.net/blog/2011/ring_introduction*.

---

2. There can certainly be more or less depending on your requirements, to address authentication, form validation, content negotiation, and on and on. There are quality Clojure libraries for all of these requirements, but covering all of the nooks and crannies of web development would require a separate book. For now, we'd just like to get you started down a good path.

3. *https://github.com/cgrand/moustache*.

4. Available at *https://github.com/weavejester/hiccup*. To get an immediate flavor for Hiccup, look at "Growing an HTML DSL" on page 481 again, where we reimplemented a naive subset of it as an exercise in testing.

5. *https://github.com/fhd/clostache*.

6. *http://mustache.github.com/*.

The Foundation: Ring

As you've seen throughout this book, Clojure excels at data transformation. However, we are actually most fortunate when there is no need for a transformation to occur: that is, when a suitable format exists for your domain, don't go out of your way to invent a new one. In that spirit, and with some inspiration from Python's WSGI and Ruby's Rack, Ring's[7] SPEC defines a standard data schema to represent web requests and responses using Clojure data structures, and a couple of key architectural concepts based on function composition: *adapters*, *handlers*, and *middleware*.

Understanding the Ring SPEC[8] is crucial to being able to effectively build web applications in Clojure. We'll explore each of its aspects here, including some parts of the SPEC verbatim as appropriate.[9] We encourage you to read the Ring SPEC in its entirety at least once, and keep it close at hand as you learn to work with the data and abstractions it defines.

Requests and Responses

Whereas many other frameworks define fixed APIs for accessing web request data—like the requested URI, request headers, query and post parameters, body content, and so on—and still other APIs for sending web responses, Ring represents both requests and responses as regular Clojure maps. In both cases, these maps must contain certain slots, may contain others, and can be used to hold any other data you require in the course of processing them.

Ring request maps (Table 16-1) contain these keys (optional slots *italicized*).

Table 16-1. Ring request maps

Key	Description of value
`:server-port`	The port on which the request is being handled.
`:server-name`	The resolved server name, or the server IP address as a string.
`:remote-addr`	The IP address of the client or the last proxy that sent the request.
`:uri`	The request URI, as a string. Must start with "/".
`:scheme`	The transport protocol, must be one of `:http` or `:https`.
`:request-method`	The HTTP request method, must be one of `:get`, `:head`, `:options`, `:put`, `:post`, or `:delete`.
`:headers`	A Clojure map of downcased header name Strings to corresponding header value Strings.
`:content-type`	The MIME type of the request body as a string, if known.

---

7. *https://github.com/mmcgrana/ring*.

8. Published at *https://github.com/mmcgrana/ring/blob/master/SPEC*.

9. Ring and its SPEC are MIT-licensed, Copyright © 2009–2010 Mark McGranaghan.

Key	Description of value
`:content-length`	The number of bytes in the request body, if known.
`:character-encoding`	The name of the character encoding used in the request body as a string, if known.
`:query-string`	The query string, if present.
`:body`	A `java.io.InputStream` for the request body, if present.

This schema encapsulates the fundamental data associated with a single HTTP request. For example, say you tried to access the URL *https://company.com:8080/accounts? q=Acme*; the corresponding Ring request map would look something like this:

```
{:remote-addr "127.0.0.1",
 :scheme :http,
 :request-method :get,
 :query-string "q=Acme",
 :content-type nil,
 :uri "/accounts",
 :server-name "company.com",
 :content-length nil,
 :server-port 8080,
 :body #<ByteArrayInputStream java.io.ByteArrayInputStream@604fd0e9>,   ❶
 :headers
{"user-agent" "Mozilla/5.0 (Macintosh; Intel Mac OS X 10.6) Firefox/8.0.1",
 "accept-charset" "ISO-8859-1,utf-8;q=0.7,*;q=0.7",
 "accept" "text/html,application/xhtml+xml,application/xml;q=0.9,*/*;q=0.8",
 "accept-encoding" "gzip, deflate",
 "accept-language" "en-us,en;q=0.5",
 "connection" "keep-alive"}}
```

❶ Because this is a simple GET request, the `:body InputStream` will be empty; thus, both `:content-type` and `:content-length` are `nil`.

This is a regular Clojure map, and can be processed and augmented just like every other map you've seen.

Likewise, Ring responses are also maps (Table 16-2); they require only two slots, and an optional `:body`.

Table 16-2. Ring response maps

Key	Description of value
`:status`	The HTTP status code, must be greater than or equal to 100.
`:headers`	A Clojure map of HTTP header names to header values. These values may be either Strings, in which case one name/value header will be sent in the HTTP response, or a seq of Strings, in which case a name/value header will be sent for each such String value.
`:body`	Optionally a String, a Clojure sequence of strings, a `java.io.File`, or a `java.io.InputStream`.

Perhaps now you can start to see the outlines of how web requests are handled with Ring: your code will take whatever actions are appropriate for a given request map and return a suitable response map. For example, the preceding GET request we considered might reasonably evoke a page of HTML from a web application; this response would look something like this:

```
{:status 200
 :headers {"Content-Type" "text/html"}
 :body "<html>...</html>"}
```

Alternatively, we can provide other types of response :body; if a response should correspond to a static file we have on disk, we can provide that directly:

```
{:status 200
 :headers {"Content-Type" "image/png"}
 :body (java.io.File. "/path/to/file.png")}
```

Finally, as we'll see in detail later, Ring is entirely capable of servicing HTTP API calls that don't necessarily require a body. If an HTTP PUT request was received to upload a file, an appropriate response might be to indicate that it was accepted and the corresponding server-side resource was created by simply returning a 201 HTTP status code:

```
{:status 201 :headers {}}
```

At this point, you might reasonably wonder how we get ahold of these maps that represent requests, and how we get our web servers to turn Ring response maps into proper HTTP responses. That particular piece of glue is provided by an *adapter*.

Adapters

A Ring adapter provides a bridge between a Ring application and the local implementation details of the HTTP protocol and/or server. In short, when an HTTP request is received, an adapter deconstructs it into a request map and passes it to the Ring application to be processed. That invocation must return a response map, which the adapter uses to send an HTTP response back to the client.

You'll likely never need to write your own adapter, but it's important to know how they fit into the overall Ring architecture. Many adapter implementations exist, allowing Ring applications to sit behind various different HTTP servers and HTTP APIs:

Servlets. Ring itself includes an adapter that allows Ring applications to surface as Java servlets, suitable for deployment into any Java web application server. This is discussed in more detail in "Web Application Packaging" on page 560.

ring-jetty-adapter. Also included with Ring is the ring-jetty-adapter, an adapter that uses an embedded Jetty (*http://jetty.codehaus.org/jetty/*) HTTP server to service requests. This is the most common way to run Ring applications, and we'll see it in action shortly.

ring-httpcore-adapter. This adapter (*https://github.com/mmcgrana/ring-httpcore -adapter*) is very similar to ring-jetty-adapter, but uses an embedded Apache HTTPCore server instead of Jetty.

Aleph. If you get the impression that Ring is *really* lightweight, you'd be right. In fact, the core contribution of Ring is not any of its particular implementations of anything (which are, indeed, slight); rather, it is the well-considered definition of the request/response data schema and key concepts of *adapters*, *middleware*, and *handlers* that makes it important. Indeed, thanks to these abstractions, Ring—the canonical implementation of which is fundamentally synchronous in nature to suit the synchronous nature of most web applications—can itself be swapped out for other Ring-compatible implementations. A notable example is Aleph,[10] which offers a Ring-compatible adapter that uses Netty[11] to serve responses to clients *asynchronously*, without requiring any changes to your Ring application.

Other adapters have also been written to bridge Ring applications to, for example, Mongrel and FastCGI-capable servers.

Now we are ready to look at the part that does the "real" work in a Ring application, *handlers*, and how we can bring them together with our preferred adapter to start building web apps.

Handlers

A Ring handler is just a function that accepts a request map and returns a response map. All Ring applications consist of a bunch of handler functions, chained and composed and delegated to as necessary to support the desired behavior and functionality.

Let's start with a simple echo server. First, add a dependency for Ring to a project:[12]

```
[ring "1.0.0"]
```

Now we can fire up a REPL and write a web app:

Example 16-1. Starting a Ring application from the REPL

```
(use '[ring.adapter.jetty :only (run-jetty)])
;= nil
(defn app                                            ❶
  [{:keys [uri]}]
  {:body (format "You requested %s" uri)})
;= #'user/app
(def server (run-jetty #'app {:port 8080 :join? false}))  ❷
;= #'user/server                                     ❸
```

---

10. *https://github.com/ztellman/aleph.*

11. *http://www.jboss.org/netty.*

12. Please don't be spooked by the prevalence of `"1.0.0"` version numbers here. All of the projects mentioned have been in heavy use for many years; the `"1.0.0"` designation was recently bestowed on many of them all at once, in part to recognize their stability.

---

❶ Our handler function. All handlers take a single Ring request map argument, and must return a Ring response map. To start, we're simply echoing back the URI of the request as plain text.

❷ We're using the Jetty adapter. All adapters are implemented as a function that takes two arguments: the Ring handler function to use to service requests, and a map of options for the adapter. Here we're requesting that Jetty run on port 8080, and that we should not "join" on the thread that Jetty will use; not specifying this would cause our REPL to block waiting for the Jetty server to shut down.

❸ We opted to retain a reference to the Jetty server in the server var. This gives us the option (if we so choose) to stop the Jetty server by calling (.stop server).

We can now visit our running Ring web app:

That's nice, but notice that the URI does not include our query parameters, ?at=world. Because we started the Jetty adapter with our handler's var (i.e., #'app) rather than passing our handler function itself, we can readily redefine the handler without restarting Jetty:

```
(defn app
  [{:keys [uri query-string]}]
  {:body (format "You requested %s with query %s" uri query-string)})
;= #'user/app
```

The results are immediately available:

Surely we can do better than that, though. It would be quite horrible to have to pick apart query parameters ourselves from a string. However, the Ring SPEC for request maps doesn't say anything about query and form parameters being available in any other form.

Thankfully, we're far from being stuck. A particular bit of Ring *middleware* addresses this common requirement.

Middleware

Middleware is any enhancement or modification of the effect of handlers. Remember that, because Ring requests and responses are Clojure maps, they can be transformed readily, and since handlers are just functions, it is trivial to produce composites of different functions to yield aggregate behavior. This typically manifests in middleware as a higher-order function that accepts one or more handlers (maybe with some configuration), which returns a new handler with whatever composite functionality is desired.

Let's make that really concrete. As we just saw, Ring requests do not by default contain any kind of structured representation of query parameters. We can change this by adding a bit of middleware to our application; it is the middleware that will decorate the original request map it receives from the Jetty adapter with our query parameters usefully broken down into a map:

```
(use '[ring.middleware.params :only (wrap-params)])
;= nil
(defn app*                                                        ❶
  [{:keys [uri params]}]                                          ❷
  {:body (format "You requested %s with query %s" uri params)})
;= #'user/app*
(def app (wrap-params app*))                                      ❸
;= #'user/app
```

❶ We're now defining our handler as **app***, so the middleware-enhanced handler can be placed in the **app** var, the one the Jetty adapter has retained.

❷ Instead of looking for **:query-string** in the request map, our handler now expects a value in **:params**.

❸ The composition of our handler and the middleware happens via a simple HOF call. A new handler is returned by **wrap-params**, which now forms the outermost layer of our application—after doing its work to parse out all of the parameters in the request's query string and POST body (if any), it will call the handler function we provide with the request map, newly decorated with all of the parameters in the **:params** slot.

Let's take a look:

```
You requested /hello with query {"at" "world"}
```

Fabulous, we now have parameters upon which we can base application behavior.

Ring includes a bunch of different bits of middleware that you can mix into your web application as desired, from parsing cookies and session data out of request headers to short-circuiting requests for static files to supporting multipart form submissions and file uploads.[13] While Ring doesn't apply any middleware to handlers by default, some other Ring-based web frameworks do.

Finally, since middleware is really just a form of function composition, creating new middleware is extraordinarily easy. An example of some trivial middleware is included in Ring on page 465. Due to its ease of implementation and degree of flexibility, you'll find that many extensions to Ring are implemented in terms of middleware.

Conceptually, Ring middleware is similar to Java servlet filters: both approaches allow for the post-hoc modification of web requests and responses. On the other hand, the implementation and use of middleware is staggeringly easy—just the definition and then invocation of a higher-order function—compared to the relatively maze-like adventure that is implementing the various interfaces associated with servlet filters and configuring them as necessary upon deployment. More significantly though, servlet filters often cannot be effectively composed because of conflicting custom `ServletRequest` and `ServletResponse` types, and if a servlet happens to imperatively send content out the door on the wire of a `ServletResponse`, a filter is helpless to stop it. This is where middleware shines: benefiting from the Ring model where requests and responses are immutable collections that always hew to a single common abstraction, middleware can *always* be composed effectively...after all, they're just functions!

Routing Requests with Compojure

So far, we've defined a single function that handled all requests; aside from the simplest of applications, this will never do.[14] We want to be able to structure our applications naturally, separating logically distinct functionality into different Ring handlers in potentially different namespaces, pulling them all together in just the right arrangement. We could try to pick apart request URI strings to delegate request handling to other functions; however, just as we composed our Ring handler with some middleware to augment our application, there are better ways to achieve our ends.

Very simply, *routing* is the selection of a handler that should be used to respond to a web request, and *routes* are patterns of incoming request attributes that are used to drive that selection process. Abstractly, you can easily imagine defining web applications in terms of a table of routes that correspond to particular handlers defined in various namespaces (Figure 16-1).

---

13. Look on Ring's main GitHub page for a full list of included middleware: *https://github.com/mmcgrana/ring*.

14. Of course, if you are writing a very small, contained HTTP service, a single Ring handler running in Jetty may be perfect without any further adornment.

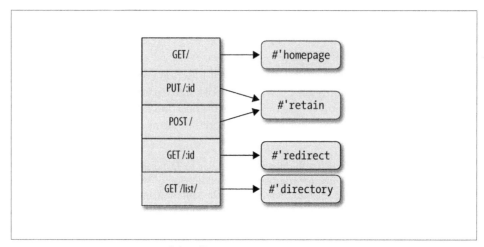

Figure 16-1. Pairing routes up with handlers

When a GET request is received for the root of the application (/), that request will be routed to the homepage handler. When a PUT request is received for any URI with a single segment (represented by :id in the diagram), that request will be routed to the retain handler; the same goes for any POST request to the root of the application, and so on.

Let's build a complete web application that has routes matching the diagram in Figure 16-1. The result will be a simple URL-shortening HTTP service,[15] similar to bit.ly, tinyurl.com, and so on; such services allow users to specify and use shorter URLs that redirect to their canonical counterparts. To do this, we'll use Compojure (*https://github .com/weavejester/compojure*), the most popular library for defining *routes* for Ring applications, and one that has taken cues from the URL routing features in many frameworks you may be familiar with already, including Ruby on Rails and Django.

Let's start a new REPL session with Compojure included in our project's dependencies, which should now include both Compojure and Ring:

```
[compojure "1.0.1"]
[ring "1.0.1"]
```

We should first consider what kind of model we should have for storing URLs and their shorter identifiers. We want to focus on building the web side of things, so let's just keep this state in a map in memory using a reference type.[16]

---

15. You might call it a *REST* service, but the semantics of REST are tricky to get right, as Roy Fielding (the originator of the REST term) points out in, for example, *http://roy.gbiv.com/untangled/2008/rest-apis-must -be-hypertext-driven*. We're happy enough to say that ours will be a well-behaved HTTP service.

16. If we were going to properly build this service out for real usage, we could quite easily use one of the databases discussed in Chapters 14 or 15 in place of in-memory state.

Which reference types should we use? We'll allow users to request the assignment of short URL identifiers, so we need to protect against conflicts where an identifier is already taken, and we need to coordinate changes to our map so that concurrent requests can't add identically keyed entries. This calls for holding our primary mapping in a ref: each modification to the map will be performed transactionally, so we'll be able to safely avoid clobbering already-registered identifiers, and concurrent conflicting requests (e.g., if two clients both want to register a URL for the same shorter identifier) will never produce inconsistencies in our model.

On the other hand, we don't need such stringent guarantees for the automatically generated identifiers we use for when users *don't* provide an identifier of their own. We could go with some form of hashing or random identifiers, but the easiest approach is to use an incrementing counter. An atom is the perfect candidate for maintaining that counter.[17]

So, we have our in-memory model, a counter in an atom, and a map in a ref:

```
(def ^:private counter (atom 0))

(def ^:private mappings (ref {}))
```

We should have a couple of dedicated functions for working with this state. Not only will they make it trivial to test our core functionality outside of a web context, if we were going to transition to building a database backend, our only work would consist of reimplementing these two functions:

```
(defn url-for
  [id]
  (@mappings id))

(defn shorten!
  "Stores the given URL under a new unique identifier, or the given identifier
   if provided.  Returns the identifier as a string.
   Modifies the global mapping accordingly."
  ([url]
   (let [id (swap! counter inc)          ❶
         id (Long/toString id 36)]       ❷
     (or (shorten! url id)               ❸
         (recur url))))
  ([url id]
   (dosync
     (when-not (@mappings id)            ❹
       (alter mappings assoc id url)
       id))))
```

❶ swap! will return the new value in the counter atom, which is guaranteed to be unique for this invocation of shorten!.

---

17. Because modifications to the state of the ref's mapping may end up retrying due to request contention, some automatically generated identifiers pulled from the counter will be dropped on the floor. This seems reasonable, but worth being aware of.

❷ This Long/toString call converts the numeric ID to a base-36 string, which is much more compact for larger values than a simple base-10 str of the ID.

❸ We reuse the other arity of shorten! to attempt to store the automatically generated ID ⇒ URL mapping. If it fails (because the ID already exists in mappings), then we simply recur to retry.

❹ When the ID we are aiming to add doesn't exist yet, we assoc it with the canonical URL in the map and return the short identifier, or nil otherwise.

Let's see how well our model works:

```
(shorten! "http://clojurebook.com")
;= "1"
(shorten! "http://clojure.org" "clj")
;= "clj"
(shorten! "http://id-already-exists.com" "clj")
;= nil
@mappings
;= {"clj" "http://clojure.org", "1" "http://clojurebook.com"}
```

Looking good so far. Now let's build out a couple of functions to handle the sorts of HTTP requests we can expect. retain will be the web "frontend" to shorten!; it delegates the actual interaction with our mappings to shorten!, and returns appropriate response maps based on whether a URL (and optional provided ID) could be stored:

```
(defn retain
  [& [url id :as args]]
  (if-let [id (apply shorten! args)]
    {:status 201                                              ❶
     :headers {"Location" id}
     :body (list "URL " url " assigned the short identifier " id)}  ❷
    {:status 409 :body (format "Short URL %s is already taken" id)}))  ❸
```

❶ If we successfully store a URL with a particular ID, then retain will return a Ring response with a :status of 201 (an HTTP response code indicating that a resource was successfully created), along with a Location header containing the stored ID (which nonbrowser HTTP clients may find useful), and a textual :body that is suitable for human consumption.

❷ Remember from Table 16-2 that Ring response bodies can be a number of different types, including a seq of strings.

❸ The only reason why we wouldn't be able to store a URL with a short identifier is if the user requested an ID that was already taken. In this case, we return a response with a 409 :status (an HTTP response code indicating a "conflict" preventing the requested action from taking place).

redirect will be the function that looks up a requested ID, responding with a browser redirect if the ID is known and corresponds to a URL:

```
(require 'ring.util.response)
```

```
(defn redirect
  [id]
  (if-let [url (url-for id)]
    (ring.util.response/redirect url)
    {:status 404 :body (str "No such short URL: " id)}))
```

If the given id is found in our mappings, then redirect uses a utility function in Ring's ring.util.response namespace[18] to send an appropriate redirect response (corresponding to an HTTP :status of 302).

Now, retain and redirect are technically *not* Ring handlers: while they return Ring responses and are therefore useful helpers, they do not accept request maps. This isn't required, but we've constrained the scope of these functions to make them simpler, more concise, and easier to test.

Finally, we can define our Compojure routes, in the same order as they are depicted in Figure 16-1:[19]

Example 16-2. Compojure routes for a URL shortener service

```
(use '[compojure.core :only (GET PUT POST defroutes)])
(require 'compojure.route)

(defroutes app*
  (GET "/" request "Welcome!")
  (PUT "/:id" [id url] (retain url id))
  (POST "/" [url] (retain url))
  (GET "/:id" [id] (redirect id))
  (GET "/list/" [] (interpose "\n" (keys @mappings)))
  (compojure.route/not-found "Sorry, there's nothing here."))
```

defroutes defines a var (app* in this case) containing a single Ring handler that attempts to dispatch incoming requests to each of the Ring handlers provided in its body in order. The first handler that returns a non-nil value short circuits the dispatch process, and that returned value is used as the return value of the "top level" Ring handler defined by defroutes.

Routes in Compojure define both a Ring handler and the patterns used to match requests to that handler. Each route consists of:

- The HTTP method for which the handler should be invoked. These methods are macros provided by Compojure that correspond to common HTTP verbs like GET and POST.[20]

---

18. ring.util.response contains a number of very useful utilities for creating and modifying response maps.

19. As much of a non sequitur as it is, we would be remiss if we did not suggest that you internalize Tim Berners-Lee's rant, "Cool URIs don't change": *http://www.w3.org/Provider/Style/URI.html*.

20. Other request method macros Compojure provides out of the box include PUT, DELETE, HEAD, and a special macro ANY, which acts as a wildcard. If necessary, route macros can be defined as needed for "nonstandard" HTTP verbs like COPY.

- A URI pattern that describes the `:uri`s for which the handler should be invoked.
- A binding form for the request and/or parameters and matched portions of the URI; names in this form will become locals for the body of the handler.
- The body of the handler, which can contain any Clojure code, and which should either return `nil` (indicating that the request was not handled and should continue to be dispatched to later routes), or some other value that can be used as the basis for a Ring response map.

Let's look at one of our routes:

```
(PUT "/:id" [id url] (retain url id))
```

This route will only match requests with a `:request-method` of `:put` (which corresponds to PUT in the HTTP protocol), and requests for URIs with a single segment; for example, `"/some-id"` will match, but `"/path/to/some-id"` will not. The `:id` portion of the URI pattern string causes that part of the URI to be bound to the `id` local established by the `[id url]` binding vector. The `url` local isn't mentioned in the pattern string; it is bound to the `:url` parameter (or `nil` if no such parameter is provided in the request). The behavior and return value is defined by the remaining Clojure code following the binding form.

Because Compojure routes evaluate to Ring handler functions, we can very easily get a feel for how they work at the REPL, and experiment with all of the options that Compojure routes offer.[21] For example, this is the same route we use in our URL shortener (although a different handler body is used here); we can see very clearly that parameters and named URI path segments are bound to symbols of the same name in the binding vector:

```
((PUT "/:id"
     [id url]
     (list "You requested that " url " be assigned id " id))
  {:uri "/some-id" :params {:url "http://clojurebook.com"} :request-method :put})
;= {:status 200, :headers {"Content-Type" "text/html"},
;=  :body ("You requested that " "http://clojurebook.com" " be assigned id "
  "some-id")}
```

 Note that the handlers produced by Compojure routes helpfully provide typical defaults for the `:status` and `:headers` slots of the response map. This allows you to simply return the body of the response if you know you're producing an error-free HTML page.

Path segments identified by a `:keyword` will match any character except for /, ., ,, ;, and ?; an asterisk path segment will match everything up to the next forward slash.

---

21. Ring requests are generally quite easy to construct, and we do so directly here. If you find yourself "mocking" Ring requests regularly (for testing, experimentation, or other purposes), you may find ring-mock useful: *https://github.com/weavejester/ring-mock*.

You can provide as many path segments as you like in your URI pattern, and bind any set of them as locals for the body of your handler.[22] If you have multiple path segments with the same name, a vector of each of the matching segments will be bound to the named locals:

```
((PUT ["/*/*/:id/:id"]
      [* id]
      (str * id))
 {:uri "/abc/xyz/foo/bar" :request-method :put})
;= {:status 200, :headers {"Content-Type" "text/html"},
;=  :body "[\"abc\" \"xyz\"][\"foo\" \"bar\"]"}
```

One really useful feature is that regular expressions can be provided to define the nature and scope of path segments. This is very similar to the regular expression-based :con straints in Rails, and is done by wrapping the URI pattern in a vector, and providing key/value pairs of path segment names and regular expressions. For example, we can specify that the :id path segment only contain digits by using the #"\d+" regular expression:

```
((PUT ["/:id" :id #"\d+"]
      [id url]
      (str "You requested that " url " be assigned id " id))
 {:uri "/some-id" :params {:url "http://clojurebook.com"} :request-method :put})  ❶
;= nil
((PUT ["/:id" :id #"\d+"]
      [id url]
      (str "You requested that " url " be assigned id " id))
 {:uri "/590" :params {:url "http://clojurebook.com"} :request-method :put})       ❷
;= {:status 200, :headers {"Content-Type" "text/html"},
;=  :body "You requested that http://clojurebook.com be assigned id 590"}
```

❶ The request doesn't match the defined route because the :uri path segment some-id isn't numeric, and so the route returns nil (thus signaling that request dispatching should continue on to the next route and handler).

❷ A request with a numeric first :uri path segment does match, and so the handler body is invoked, producing a non-nil response.

Finally, you can always provide a symbol or a map destructuring form as the binding form in a route; that will bind the entire request map for the handler's body:

```
((PUT "/:id" req (str "You requested: " (:uri req)))
 {:uri "/foo" :request-method :put})
;= {:status 200, :headers {"Content-Type" "text/html"}, :body "You requested: /foo"}
((PUT "/:id" {:keys [uri]} (str "You requested: " uri))
 {:uri "/foo" :request-method :put})
;= {:status 200, :headers {"Content-Type" "text/html"}, :body "You requested: /foo"}
```

The final route in Example 16-2 is a catch-all that allows us to control what should happen if none of the routes we define in the defroutes form match the request and

---

22. Alternatively, you can access path segments in a :route-params map that Compojure adds to the request.

return a non-nil response. This will return an HTTP status of 404, with the body defined by the handler body we provide to the `compojure.route/not-found` helper; in our case, a simple string will do.

Our application is complete, except it's not running yet! That's just a matter of simple bookkeeping though. First, since we are depending on request parameters being parsed out and added to Ring requests, we need to add in some middleware. Compojure conveniently provides two helper functions for doing this in its `compojure.handler` namespace: `api` wraps a Ring handler with a couple of pieces of Ring-provided middleware that takes care of all of the parameter handling we might need, and is most suited for use with HTTP services; `site` provides the same, but adds other middleware to support functionality you'd expect in a user/browser-facing website, like handling for cookies, sessions, multipart form posts and uploads, and so on. We'll opt for the former:

```
(require 'compojure.handler)

(def app (compojure.handler/api app*))
```

Now we just need to start up our application using the Jetty adapter:

```
(use '[ring.adapter.jetty :only (run-jetty)])
;= nil
(def server (run-jetty #'app {:port 8080 :join? false}))
;= #'user/server
```

All of this will be easily accessible from any web browser, but be well-formed enough that we can use the service programmatically with any HTTP library. In order to properly test our URL shortener service, we'll need to send PUT or POST requests to the service with form parameters properly set. This can be a little tricky to do, since browsers need a form in order to send either type of request. However, `curl` is a commonly used and widely available command-line tool that makes it relatively easy to test our service end-to-end. `curl` allows you to set the HTTP method with the -X argument, and will print out the full response from the server when executed with the -i argument.

Let's establish a couple of short URL IDs using PUT:

```
% curl -X PUT 'http://localhost:8080/sicp?url=http://mitpress.mit.edu/sicp/'
URL http://mitpress.mit.edu/sicp/ assigned the short identifier sicp

% curl -X PUT 'http://localhost:8080/clj?url=http://clojure.org'
URL http://clojure.org assigned the short identifier clj
```

curl will output the headers it receives from our service if we include the -i option; if we do this while POSTing to the service to get an autogenerated ID, we can see the service properly returning the 201 Created HTTP status code as well as the Location header:

```
% curl -i -X POST 'http://localhost:8080/?url=http://clojurebook.com'
HTTP/1.1 201 Created
Date: Sun, 18 Dec 2011 20:58:09 GMT
Location: 1
Content-Length: 58
Server: Jetty(6.1.25)
```

```
URL http://clojurebook.com assigned the short identifier 1
```

Now, if we try to register a short URL ID that is already taken, the service will properly reply with a failure, the 409 Conflict HTTP status that a programmatic agent could use to provide a helpful message to a user:

```
% curl -i -X PUT 'http://localhost:8080/1?url=http://apple.com'
HTTP/1.1 409 Conflict
Date: Sun, 18 Dec 2011 20:58:40 GMT
Content-Length: 28
Server: Jetty(6.1.25)

Short URL 1 is already taken
```

With some URLs now registered, we can use the /list/ route to get a listing of the known short identifiers:

```
% curl http://localhost:8080/list/
1
clj
sicp
```

Requesting any URI that has no corresponding route (or one that has a single segment but that does not correspond to any known short URL ID) properly yields a 404 Not Found response and message:

```
% curl -i http://localhost:8080/foo
HTTP/1.1 404 Not Found
Date: Sun, 18 Dec 2011 21:21:39 GMT
Content-Length: 22
Server: Jetty(6.1.25)

No such short URL: foo
```

And requests for all other nonshort URL ID paths return the generalized 404 response:

```
% curl -i http://localhost:8080/some/other/url
HTTP/1.1 404 Not Found
Date: Sun, 18 Dec 2011 21:21:53 GMT
Content-Length: 28
Server: Jetty(6.1.25)

Sorry, there's nothing here.
```

Finally, we can see that the redirection works properly by requesting a URI that *does* correspond to a short URL ID:

```
% curl -i http://localhost:8080/sicp
HTTP/1.1 302 Found
Date: Sun, 18 Dec 2011 20:59:12 GMT
Location: http://mitpress.mit.edu/sicp/
Content-Length: 0
Server: Jetty(6.1.25)

% curl -L http://localhost:8080/sicp                          ❶
```

```
<HTML><HEAD><TITLE>Welcome to the SICP Web Site</TITLE></HEAD>
....
```

❶ The -L option to curl instructs it to follow the HTTP redirect indicated by the 302 Found status code and the Location header.

The final code for our URL shortening service is reproduced here as it would appear in a source file.

Example 16-3. A functional URL shortener

```
(ns com.clojurebook.url-shortener
  (:use [compojure.core :only (GET PUT POST defroutes)])
  (:require (compojure handler route)
            [ring.util.response :as response]))

(def ^:private counter (atom 0))

(def ^:private mappings (ref {}))

(defn url-for
  [id]
  (@mappings id))

(defn shorten!
  "Stores the given URL under a new unique identifier, or the given identifier
  if provided.  Returns the identifier as a string.
  Modifies the global mapping accordingly."
  ([url]
   (let [id (swap! counter inc)
         id (Long/toString id 36)]
     (or (shorten! url id)
         (recur url))))
  ([url id]
   (dosync
     (when-not (@mappings id)
       (alter mappings assoc id url)
       id))))

(defn retain
  [& [url id :as args]]
  (if-let [id (apply shorten! args)]
    {:status 201
     :headers {"Location" id}
     :body (list "URL " url " assigned the short identifier " id)}
    {:status 409 :body (format "Short URL %s is already taken" id)}))

(defn redirect
  [id]
  (if-let [url (url-for id)]
    (response/redirect url)
    {:status 404 :body (str "No such short URL: " id)}))

(defroutes app*
  (GET "/" request "Welcome!")
```

```
  (PUT "/:id" [id url] (retain url id))
  (POST "/" [url] (if (empty? url)
                      {:status 400 :body "No `url` parameter provided"}
                      (retain url)))
  (GET "/:id" [id] (redirect id))
  (GET "/list/" [] (interpose "\n" (keys @mappings)))
  (compojure.route/not-found "Sorry, there's nothing here."))

(def app (compojure.handler/api app*))

;; ; To run locally:
;; (use '[ring.adapter.jetty :only (run-jetty)])
;; (def server (run-jetty #'app {:port 8080 :join? false}))
```

Composing routes.   Because `defroutes` dispatches to any Ring handler function, and `defroutes` itself creates a handler function, you can compose hierarchies of routes with zero effort. If we wanted to add an admin console to our URL shortening service, we could mix in the existing `app*` routes trivially:

```
(defroutes app+admin
  (GET "/admin/" request ...)
  (POST "/admin/some-admin-action" request ...)
  app*)
```

The only thing to keep in mind is that you'll want to keep "catch-all" routes (e.g., like those produced by `compojure.route/not-found`) out of groups of routes that you would like to compose into higher-level groups; otherwise, routes appearing after `app*` above would never be dispatched to or their handlers invoked.

Templating

Thus far, we have done just about everything a web framework can be expected to do, with the notable exception of actually producing complex HTML. While HTTP services and file servers are useful, most people think "HTML" when they hear "web application." Most web frameworks use template systems where HTML is intermingled with executable code or unevaluated "directives" that refer to bound variables defined for the scope of page generation, resulting in a populated page of HTML.

A sample of this approach is Ruby's ERB templating language:

Example 16-4. Example of an ERB HTML template

```
<h1>Hello, <%= @user.name %></h1>

<p>These are your friends:</p>
<ul>
<% @user.friends.each do |friend| %>
  <li><%= friend.name %></li>
<% end %>
</ul>
```

Those unfamiliar with ERB syntax may be puzzled, but this is not so dissimilar to Django templates or JSPs or any of a hundred other templating systems you might be familiar with. All of these systems work primarily by string substitution; in ERB's case, executing Ruby code found within <% and %> delimiters, and evaluating expressions within <%= and %> delimiters to obtain strings that should be included in the output. ERB templates run inside a context, so expressions like @user.name refer to a local inside the context, obtaining its name attribute.

This approach has been used by numerous languages and millions of programmers for years; this is even the primary mode of operation in the case of PHP. However, not all is well. The first obvious problem is that the HTML in these templates is tricky to debug and fine-tune; until we have a working web stack, we cannot make sure the template HTML works or make adjustments to its stylesheets. A similar problem exists with the code, in that it's difficult to test in isolation without mocking out a nontrivial environment with appropriate domain objects and such. In more precise terms, the coupling between our model and our view is stronger than we'd like. Finally, the ideal developer of such templates is both an expert at HTML and an expert at Ruby (or Python, or PHP) and the software stack driving the templates.

Despite the templating approach's popularity, people who are both expert web designers and expert software engineers are extremely rare. A designer is often commissioned to create HTML mockups and then developers modify the templates by hand, adding markup for their preferred templating languages. If there are design changes, they often come as updates to the original HTML documents, which the developers must revisit and carefully merge with their templated version. Obviously, this is not an optimal scenario. Can we do better?

Enlive: Selector-Based HTML Transformation

Enlive (*http://github.com/cgrand/enlive*) proposes a radical way to decouple code from templates: rather than defining a special local syntax for interpolating values into templates, Enlive templates are plain HTML files with no special tags, no special attributes, no special classes, and no special syntax. Instead, content is injected into templates by Clojure code that uses *selectors* (heavily inspired by CSS selectors) to specify what to modify, and Clojure functions that define what transformations to apply.[23]

This strict separation of concerns—design kept entirely isolated from code that transforms it—makes roundtrip collaboration between programmers and designers particularly easy. And, because the selectors that you might use to identify parts of a template to modify are likely the same as some of the CSS selectors used to style the produced

---

23. Templating is just a special case of transforming HTML or XML data: Enlive can also be used to scrape and extract content from HTML and XML documents using the same selectors it uses for templating. However, we'll only discuss the use of Enlive for templating here.

content, changes in the template that might impact the code that transforms that design are easy for designers (or, programmers engaged in design!) to identify ahead of time.

Testing the waters

The first step in using Enlive is usually to write the HTML file—what is referred to as the template *source*—but let's first get a sense of how Enlive works through some REPL tinkering. Add a dependency for it to your project:

```
[enlive/enlive "1.0.0"]
```

...and start a REPL.

```
(require '[net.cgrand.enlive-html :as h])
;= nil
(h/sniptest "<h1>Lorem Ipsum</h1>")
;= "<h1>Lorem Ipsum</h1>"
```

sniptest is a utility provided by Enlive that simplifies experimenting with and transforming snippets of HTML in the REPL. We're not specifying a transformation here, so our input is being returned unchanged.

```
(h/sniptest "<h1>Lorem Ipsum</h1>"
  [:h1] (h/content "Hello Reader!"))
;= "<h1>Hello Reader!</h1>"
```

[:h1] is a selector—corresponding to the CSS selector h1—that matches all h1 elements in the HTML being transformed. content is a HOF that returns a function that will set the body of matched elements to the value(s) provided to content. Enlive provides a large number of ready-made transformer HOFs that satisfy all of the common templating needs you might have in a typical web application, and its selectors provide a superset of CSS selectors for specifying where those transformations should be applied.

Let's pull the covers back a bit so we can understand how more sophisticated transformations are possible. Enlive has a html-snippet function that is used to parse any HTML content, returning a sequence of maps, each one representing an element with attributes and child content:

```
(h/html-snippet "<p>x, <a id=\"home\" href=\"/\">y</a>, <a href=\"..\">z</a></p>")
;= ({:tag :p,
;=   :attrs nil,
;=   :content
;=   ("x, "
;=    {:tag :a, :attrs {:href "/", :id "home"}, :content ("y")}
;=    ", "
;=    {:tag :a, :attrs {:href ".."}, :content ("z")})})
```

This representation of HTML/XML matches that produced and consumed by the functions in the clojure.xml namespace—another example where the selection of a common abstraction allows for simpler interchange of data and composition of functionality.

Knowing this, it's not hard to imagine how Enlive implements transformations:

1. Selectors traverse the tree that represents the HTML in question to find matching elements.

2. Those elements are passed to the transformation function paired with the each selector applied. The functions' results replace the selected elements.

Because these operations are carried out over Clojure's persistent data structures using pure functions, they can be chained, composed, and reused however your needs dictate:

Example 16-5. A less trivial HTML transformation

```
(h/sniptest "<p>x, <a id=\"home\" href=\"/\">y</a>, <a href=\"..\">z</a></p>"
  [:a#home] (h/set-attr :href "http://clojurebook.com")
  [[:a (h/attr= :href "..")]] (h/content "go up"))
;= "<p>x, <a href=\"http://clojurebook.com\" id=\"home\">y</a>, <a href=\"..\">go up</a>
   </p>"
```

Making the most of Enlive requires understanding how to construct appropriate selectors and transformer functions.

Selectors

Enlive selector syntax may seem daunting at first, but is in fact very easy to pick up if you know CSS much at all. Most of the time, adding colons in front of each step and wrapping everything into a vector suffices. For example, the CSS selector `div span.phone` becomes `[:div :span.phone]`, `#summary .kw` becomes `[:#summary :.kw]`, and so on.

Newcomers to Enlive often struggle with the meaning of nested vectors in selectors. The rule is easy, if not simple: *the outermost vector denotes chaining, all other vectors denote conjunction.* So, `[:div [:span :.phone]]` is equivalent to the above `[:div :span.phone]`. Conjunctive vectors can be nested *ad lib*: `[:div [:span [:.phone :.mobile]]]` is the same as `[:div :span.phone.mobile]`.

Note that the outermost vector is not optional, even if the selector has only one step: `:h1` is not a valid selector, `[:h1]` is.

Enlive also supports disjunctions. The equivalent of the CSS selector `div#info span.phone, div#info span.email` is the following: `#{[:div#info :span.phone] [:div#info :span.email]}`. However, unlike in CSS, disjunctions are not limited to the top level: `[:div#info #{:span.phone :span.email}]` or even `[:div#info [:span #{:.phone :.email}]]` are all different notations of the same selector.

 To summarize: sets denote disjunction, inner vectors denote conjunction, outermost vectors denote hierarchical chaining.

All other tests are performed with predicates, and as such can be extended at will. This is the case of attr?: the CSS selector a[class] becomes [[:a (attr? :class)]]. Take note of the nested vectors: a single vector selector—that is, [:a (attr? :class)]—is equivalent to a *[class] in CSS. The difference is marked:

```
(h/sniptest "<p class=\"\"><a href=\"\" class=\"\"></a></p>"
  [[:p (h/attr? :class)]] (h/content "XXX"))
;= "<p class=\"\">XXX</p>"

(h/sniptest "<p class=\"\"><a href=\"\" class=\"\"></a></p>"
  [:p (h/attr? :class)] (h/content "XXX"))
;= "<p class=\"\"><a class=\"\" href=\"\">XXX</a></p>"
```

Corollaries to most CSS selectors are provided in Enlive (including all the :nth-* pseudoclasses). Beyond that initial set, you can define your own selectors, which are themselves just functions. This can be accomplished using the pred or zip-pred HOFs that Enlive provides, which respectively take predicates on elements and predicates on zippers[24] and yield a function that Enlive can use as a *selector step*.

In attr=, Enlive already provides a selector for matching elements that have a particular attribute whose value matches a given value.[25] Let's define a new selector step function that matches elements that have *any* attribute whose value matches a given value:

```
(defn some-attr=
  "Selector step, matches elements where at least one attribute
   has the specified value."
  [value]
  (h/pred (fn [node]
            (some #{value} (vals (:attrs node))))))
```

Let's see how it works:

```
(h/sniptest "<ul><li id=\"foo\">A<li>B<li name=\"foo\">C</li></ul>"
  [(some-attr= "foo")] (h/set-attr :found "yes"))
;= "<ul>
;=   <li found=\"yes\" id=\"foo\">A</li>
;=   <li>B</li>
;=   <li found=\"yes\" name=\"foo\">C</li>
;= </ul>"
```

Enlive already gives us a lot of flexibility in controlling the effects of our transformations. As you can see, when that flexibility isn't enough for what you want to do, you can define your own selectors, using whatever criteria you desire.

Iterating and branching

So far we have seen how to identify nodes and how to transform them (as with, e.g., content or set-attr) but we have not covered the two pillars of templating: condition and iteration.

---

24. Recall that we discussed zippers in "Navigation, Update, and Zippers" on page 151.

25. attr= is used in Example 16-5.

The key to iterating and branching in Enlive is to understand that a transformation can be one of:

- A function of one element returning one element
- A function of one element returning a collection of elements
- nil, equivalent to (fn [_] nil)

It follows that, for example, displaying an optional message is as simple as using when, which evaluates to nil when its condition is logically false:

```
(defn display
  [msg]
  (h/sniptest "<div><span class=\"msg\"></span></div>"
    [:.msg] (when msg (h/content msg))))
;= #'user/display
(display "Welcome back!")
;= "<div><span class=\"msg\">Welcome back!</span></div>"
(display nil)
;= "<div></div>"
```

When a message is present, the when form evaluates to the (h/content msg) transformation function, which sets the content of the matched span element to the provided message. On the other hand, when there's no message to display, the when form evaluates to nil, and the message placeholder is removed.

Alternatively, you may need to retain the empty span because it is needed by client-side code; in that case, just use an if (or a cond or whatever other conditional you prefer) instead of the when form:

```
(defn display
  [msg]
  (h/sniptest "<div><span class=\"msg\"></span></div>"
    [:.msg] (if msg
              (h/content msg)
              (h/add-class "hidden"))))
;= #'user/display
(display nil)
;= "<div><span class=\"msg hidden\"></span></div>"
```

Iterating in Enlive is done with clone-for which looks and behaves a lot like for:

```
(defn countdown
  [n]
  (h/sniptest "<ul><li></li></ul>"
    [:li] (h/clone-for [i (range n 0 -1)]
            (h/content (str i)))))
;= #'user/countdown
(countdown 0)
;= "<ul></ul>"
(countdown 3)
;= "<ul><li>3</li><li>2</li><li>1</li></ul>"
```

Under the covers, a for comprehension yields a sequence of transformation functions (in the example above, n instances of (h/content (str i))), each of which is used to produce element(s) based on the single node selected by the selector. The resulting elements replace the original node.

A common need when it comes to iteration is to remove some attributes that were used to select the node in the first place—for example, an ID. This is done with the `do->` function, which composes transformations by applying them in sequence:

```
(defn countdown
  [n]
  (h/sniptest "<ul><li id=\"foo\"></li></ul>"
    [:#foo] (h/do->
              (h/remove-attr :id)
              (h/clone-for [i (range n 0 -1)]
                (h/content (str i))))))
;= #'user/countdown
(countdown 3)
;= "<ul><li>3</li><li>2</li><li>1</li></ul>"
```

Of course, `do->` can be used anywhere a transformation is expected since it evaluates to one itself, so there is no limit to how you can compose transformation functions.

Putting everything together

`sniptest` is a great exploratory aid that has allowed us to demonstrate all the basics of Enlive, but it's of little use in a real application. We need to load HTML from disk—or, more specifically, from our application's classpath. This is the job of `deftemplate` and `defsnippet`.

`defsnippet` defines a function that loads HTML from the file on our classpath that we can transform however we like as with `sniptest`. These functions are intended to be called from within other snippet or `deftemplate` functions as an easy way to compose discrete units of content. For example, assuming we have a file *footer.html* at the root of our classpath:

Example 16-6. footer.html

```
<div class="footer"/>
```

we can define a reusable `footer` snippet:

```
(h/defsnippet footer "footer.html" [:.footer]    ❶
  [message]                                       ❷
  [:.footer] (h/content message))                 ❸
```

❶ `footer` is the name of the var and function we're defining. `"footer.html"` is the path to the HTML file we're loading content from, and can be a string or an instance of `java.io.File`, `java.net.URL`, or `java.net.URI`. The third argument to `defsnippet` is a selector that indicates the root element within the loaded HTML file to which transformations should be applied. `[:.footer]` here ensures that we discard the `<html>` and `<body>` elements that Enlive adds implicitly when loading snippets and templates. A single HTML file can contain several snippets, each `defsnippet` selecting only the relevant nodes—it's handy to have many reusable components in the same file and to be able to preview them using just a web browser.

❷ An argument vector; this snippet function takes a single argument, message.

❸ The rest of the defsnippet form consists of pairs of selectors and transformers, as we've seen already.

 If you are using Leiningen, the best place to put HTML templates is inside the *resources* directory (the default for the :resources-path option in *project.clj*). With Maven, HTML templates are typically rooted within *src/main/resources*.

Unlike sniptest, calling a defsnippet function yields a sequence of maps representing HTML elements:

```
(footer "hello")
;= ({:tag :div, :attrs {:class "footer"}, :content ("hello")})
```

deftemplate works in much the same way, but you cannot define a root for the transformations to apply to, and instead of a sequence of maps representing HTML, deftemplate functions return a lazy sequence of strings containing HTML fragments that can conveniently be used as the :body of a Ring response map.

Knowing all this, we can easily reproduce the results of the ERB template we initially considered in Example 16-4. First, we define our template file:

Example 16-7. friends.html

```
<h1>Hello, <span class="username"/></h1>
<p>These are your friends:</p>
<ul class="friends"><li/></ul>
```

And then, either in our application or here in a REPL, we can define an Enlive template function and produce some complete HTML documents:

```
(h/deftemplate friends-list "friends.html"
  [username friends]
  [:.username] (h/content username)
  [:ul.friends :li] (h/clone-for [f friends]
                      (h/content f)))

(friends-list "Chas" ["Christophe" "Brian"])            ❶
;= ("<html>" "<body>" "<h1>" "Hello, " "<span class=\"username\">"
;= "Chas" "</span>" "</h1>" "\n" "<p>These are your friends:</p>"
;= "\n" "<ul class=\"friends\">" "<li>" "Christophe" "</li>" "<li>"
;= "Brian" "</li>" "</ul>" "\n" "</body>" "</html>")
```

❶ Remember that deftemplate returns a sequence of strings. Although it's unnecessary when returning content to a client via Ring, if you happen to need a concatenated string result of an Enlive operation, one is a quick (`apply str (friends-list ...)`) call away.

Now, we have reproduced the ERB template we initially considered, but it doesn't seem like we're very far ahead. The ERB template, while the source of a host of problems, has the apparent advantage of brevity. Even if we take into account that the ERB's code is embedded into its HTML content, it still seems like our Enlive corollary demands more code. That might be an acceptable tradeoff, given how much we've gained in other areas. After all, no approach is perfect.

The real benefits of Enlive come as our templates and functional requirements expand beyond the trivial. Since Enlive operations are all implemented as functions operating over a standard set of data structures, we can easily compose them. This is in sharp contrast to most templating systems, which operate at the level of strings and string concatenation.

To demonstrate, let's add a new class to each list item we produce in our example using do-> to compose two transformers:

```
(h/deftemplate friends-list "friends.html"
  [username friends friend-class]
  [:.username] (h/content username)
  [:ul.friends :li] (h/clone-for [f friends]
                      (h/do-> (h/content f)
                              (h/add-class friend-class))))

(friends-list "Chas" ["Christophe" "Brian"] "programmer")
;= ("<html>" "<body>" "<h1>" "Hello, " "<span class=\"username\">" "Chas"
;= "</span>" "</h1>" "\n" "<p>These are your friends:</p>" "\n"
;= "<ul class=\"friends\">" "<" "li" " " "class" "=\"" "programmer" "\""
;= ">" "Christophe" "</" "li" ">" "<" "li" " " "class" "=\"" "programmer"
;= "\"" ">" "Brian" "</" "li" ">" "</ul>" "\n" "</body>" "</html>")
```

We've hardly increased our code density at all, the change in question is distinct, and it is isolated within the code; meanwhile, our HTML template file hasn't been touched. For comparison, the traditional ERB method starts to devolve into line noise:

```
<h1>Hello, <%= @user.name %></h1>

<p>These are your friends:</p>
<ul>
<% @user.friends.each do |friend| %>
  <li class="<%= @friendclass %>"><%= friend.name %></li>
<% end %>
</ul>
```

Finally, let's add our footer into the page:

```
(h/deftemplate friends-list "friends.html"
  [username friends friend-class]
  [:.username] (h/content username)
  [:ul.friends :li] (h/clone-for [f friends]
                      (h/do-> (h/content f)
                              (h/add-class friend-class)))
```

```
    [:body] (h/append (footer (str "Goodbye, " username))))  ❶

  (friends-list "Chas" ["Christophe" "Brian"] "programmer")
  ;= ("<html>" "<body>" "<h1>" "Hello, " "<span class=\"username\">" "Chas"
  ;= "</span>" "</h1>" "\n" "<p>These are your friends:</p>" "\n"
  ;= "<ul class=\"friends\">" "<" "li" " " "class" "=\"" "programmer" "\""
  ;= ">" "Christophe" "</" "li" ">" "<" "li" " " "class" "=\"" "programmer"
  ;= "\"" ">" "Brian" "</" "li" ">" "</ul>" "\n" "<div class=\"footer\">"
  ;= "Goodbye, Chas" "</div>" "</body>" "</html>")
```

❶ Where content replaces the child content of a selected element, append appends to it. If we had used content here, the footer would be the only content in the <body> of the generated HTML.

You can call defsnippet functions directly from your template functions as we do above; or, you can pass snippet functions or the results of calls to them into template functions as arguments; or, you can even do things like look up and call snippet functions based on class names present in the HTML of your template files. Because all of the entities involved in building up Enlive templates are generic—functions that consume and produce collections adhering to common abstractions—it's entirely up to you as to how to combine templates and snippets to assemble complete pages.

Final Thoughts

Throughout this chapter, we've seen how a functional approach to software design yields small but very powerful abstractions that let us quickly produce server-side applications. We've made an HTTP service in 26 short lines. We've shown how we can take a radically different approach to web content generation with Enlive, cutting our templates away from our server code along a novel axis. We've seen everything you need to make a middling-sized web framework. With proper persistent storage, there are few if any web properties that you couldn't tackle with these components.

But even more interesting than what we've shown is what we haven't shown: a big stack with frameworks and generators. This might be considered a complaint leveled at the state of Clojure's web libraries. Those coming from Python or Ruby (or even Java) might be used to generators, fixtures, controllers, and views. Our examples have had none of these, and their absence may be jarring to an experienced web developer.

An experienced functional programmer might notice that this state of affairs is actually common for most functional languages. Because of the nature of functional programming, it's very easy to knit together complex systems from very simple, basic functions. For example, adding authorization to our bookmarking example could be achieved with the addition of one small piece of middleware. The lightweight nature of the libraries and abstractions involved makes this possible and easy, in sharp contrast to the extremely heavyweight authorization hooks in a full web stack like Django or Spring-augmented Java.

In fact, this lightweight functional approach has made such an impression that it has started to press influence back to the traditional web communities. Small "ultra-lightweight" web frameworks are springing up in every language, concerned with only basic routing, rendering, and simple modeling.

This is not to say that Ring and Compojure and Enlive are the final word on Clojure web development. A variety of "batteries-included" frameworks have begun to appear,[26] as well as various larger-stack frameworks and app servers.[27] However, it is telling that most of these new developments have been happy to build upon the foundational pieces we've explored here.

---

26. Such as Noir (*http://www.webnoir.org*) and Ringfinger (*https://github.com/myfreeweb/ringfinger*).

27. The most notable of which is Immutant, an application server for Clojure built on top of JBoss: *http://immutant.org*.

## CHAPTER 17

Deploying Clojure Web Applications

Once you're past a certain point of competence with Clojure and are on your way toward having a working application completed, you'll inevitably need to deliver its functionality to your users and customers. The modern era has tilted distribution norms toward server-side deployments (often "in the cloud") that clients interact with via web services and interfaces. In this chapter, we'll explore the various ways one can package and then deploy Clojure web applications, taking full advantage of the mature facilities that the JVM and Java ecosystem provide for doing so.[1]

Java and Clojure Web Architecture

Almost without exception, Clojure web applications are packaged and deployed as *servlets*, the same fundamental architecture used by web applications written in Java. Web servlets are simply Java classes that extend the `javax.servlet.http.HttpServlet` base class, which defines a programmatic interface for handling HTTP requests. There are methods for each HTTP request method (`GET`, `POST`, and so on), each of which accept request and response objects; each HTTP request method implementation examines the incoming request and coordinates the writing out of the response contents. Applications that follow the servlet specification (which boils down to implementing a single Java interface and following some packaging conventions) can be deployed as web applications to any of many dozens of app servers, many of which offer a variety of specialized capabilities on top of the baseline Java servlet support (like database connection pooling, message queue implementations, management and monitoring features, and so on).

---

1. There is no reason why the same practices and infrastructure that we describe here (tweaked in minor ways) cannot be effectively reused to deploy and manage server applications that do not expose web services. More broadly, client-side Clojure applications (for use in desktop or mobile environments) can follow the same general deployment path that Clojure web applications do: find how their Java cousins are deployed, and piggyback on the same infrastructure and processes.

With a few exceptions, app servers provide for *multitenancy*, so you can deploy multiple applications, each potentially containing multiple servlets, to the same app server (Figure 17-1). Nearly all app servers are also web servers (often with very mature, performant HTTP/HTTPS implementations), but you can also opt to deploy to an app server proxied by a dedicated web server (such as Apache httpd, lighttpd, or IIS).[2]

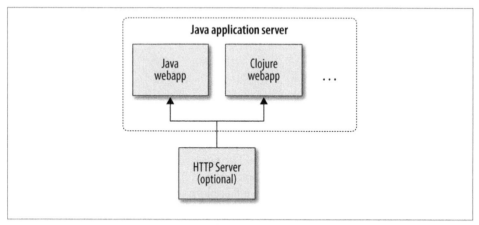

Figure 17-1. Java web architecture

By piggybacking on this architecture and ecosystem, Clojure web applications enjoy the same diversity of deployment targets and operational capabilities as their Java web application cousins.

> The Java server specification landscape is vast, of which servlets are one (admittedly foundational) part. Other specifications include standards for message queue support, directory access, and database persistence formalisms, defined by JMS, JNDI, and JPA, respectively. If your organization already has investments in these specifications, then you'll be pleased to know that Clojure can participate in and use those facilities just as readily as it can take advantage of the servlet spec. On the other hand, if you've never heard of these JEE (*Java Enterprise Edition*, née J2EE) standards, you'll be equally happy to know that you don't need to know anything about them in order to build and deploy fully featured Clojure web applications.

While you can implement servlets directly in Clojure (it's just a matter of subclassing the `HttpServlet` base class, after all), it is vastly preferable to use a Clojure web

---

2. Some app servers offer methods other than HTTP proxy for communication between an app server instance and a dedicated web server; for very high-load scenarios, these methods may be more efficient than HTTP proxying. For example, the Tomcat app server offers a set of Apache and ISAPI modules that implement a compact binary communications protocol: *http://tomcat.apache.org/connectors-doc/*.

framework (like Ring, examined in detail in Chapter 16) to abstract away from the programmatic (and decidedly imperative) nature of the servlet API. In Ring's case, each handler is a function that accepts a Clojure map argument that is an idiomatic translation of the data in the servlet's HTTP request object, returning a value that a Ring adapter writes out to the servlet's HTTP response object. These handlers are then combined with routes—pairings of HTTP request methods (again, such as GET) and URL matchers—to yield a single function that encapsulates the unified functionality of your application across all types of supported HTTP verbs and URLs. Ring provides a couple of adapters that delegate a concrete servlet's handler methods to that function.

If we "zoom" in on the Clojure web app in Figure 17-1, we can visualize the relationship between servlets and Ring:

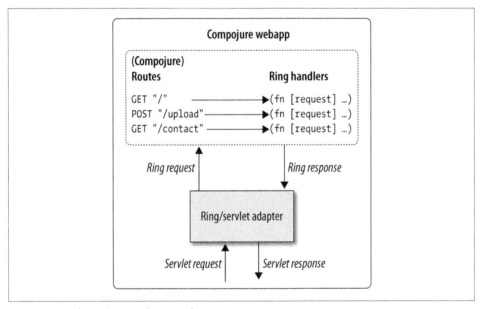

Figure 17-2. Clojure/Ring web app architecture

This bridging of the servlet architecture and Ring's model can be done a couple of different ways depending on what your deployment strategy is:

1. If you are going to use one of the embeddable app servers (Jetty and Glassfish being the most popular), you can produce a servlet wrapper at runtime and simply hand that to the app server running within the same JVM. With everything happening at runtime, and no special packaging or build process, this is perfect for development and local testing scenarios.

2. Deploying to a standalone app server[3] generally requires that you package your web app into a *.war* file. This packaging step is a trivial addition to whatever build process you have in place already and will allow you to deploy your Clojure web

application into any specification-compliant app server (including hosted platforms like Google App Engine[4] and Amazon's Elastic Beanstalk[5]).[6]

There are tradeoffs involved in both methods. Deploying to a standalone application server does involve some additional build and packaging configuration and process. On the other hand, going to production on top of an embedded app server (sometimes this is referred to as a *containerless* approach) forces you to create and maintain whatever bootstrap, deployment, and management processes you need, rather than simply reusing the (presumably better-tested) facilities provided by a standalone app server. We recommend that you do whatever you are most used to at first, and experiment with both options when possible so you can land on the best process for your project and team.

We already demonstrated how applications can be run from the REPL in the embedded Jetty runtime in Chapter 16; let's now tackle *.war* packaging, which will allow us to flexibly deploy to production-ready app servers and hosted platforms.

Web Application Packaging

A Java web application is packaged into a *.war* file, an extension of the *.jar* file packaging discussed in "Artifacts and coordinates" on page 340.[7] The typical *.war* file layout includes:

- Resources like HTML files and images that are statically served out of the "top level" of the *.war* file
- A variety of data rooted in a *WEB-INF* directory entry, under which you can find:
  - A *web.xml* file that describes how the *.war* file should be deployed into a web application server.
  - A *lib* directory entry, which can contain any number of nested *.jar* files. This is usually where all of the transitive dependencies of a web application are housed, and is what makes *.war* files self-contained deployable units (in contrast to other server application architectures that require extensive server

---

3. There are dozens of mature, well-supported app servers, each of which provides its own set of extra features on top of the foundational servlet and other JEE specifications.

4. *https://github.com/gcv/appengine-magic.*

5. *http://aws.amazon.com/elasticbeanstalk.*

6. Note that one of the most popular Clojure deployment targets of late, Heroku, has a significantly different take on application deployment; see "Clojure on Heroku" on page 587.

7. We are merely scratching the surface here of what you can control about how your web applications are managed and deployed, especially through setting various parameters in the *web.xml* file you include in your *.war*. You can read more about *.war* files and *web.xml* options at *http://java.sun.com/j2ee/tutorial/1_3-fcs/doc/WCC3.html.*

---

configuration to ensure that the dependencies of deployed applications are available).

—A *classes* directory entry, which contains Clojure source files, JVM class files (including class files resulting from AOT-compiling Clojure source), and other assets. This corresponds with the content of a typical *.jar* file, and is where the "top level" code for the web application is housed (in contrast to its dependencies).

The linchpin of the *.war* packaging convention is the *web.xml* file. It is how one defines how an application should be deployed; in part, it can:

- "Mount" individual servlets on particular paths, allowing a single *.war* file to contain multiple independent applications rooted at different paths
- Specify which classes of static resources (such as CSS, JavaScript, and image files) should be served by the app server directly without being handled by mounted servlets
- Configure behavior of user sessions, including session timeouts as well as which storage mechanisms should be used to retain session data
- Configure app-server-specific services and features

Here's a very simple example *web.xml* file, which defines a single servlet (`com.clojure book.hello_world`) that is mounted at the root (`/`) of the app server's context, and requests that the "default" servlet (every app server has one for serving static resources) should be responsible for serving a variety of static files defined by their file extensions:

Example 17-1. Simple web.xml file

```xml
<?xml version="1.0" encoding="UTF-8"?>
<web-app version="2.5" xmlns="http://java.sun.com/xml/ns/javaee"
         xmlns:xsi="http://www.w3.org/2001/XMLSchema-instance"
         xsi:schemaLocation="http://java.sun.com/xml/ns/javaee
                             http://java.sun.com/xml/ns/javaee/web-app_2_5.xsd">
    <servlet>
        <servlet-name>app</servlet-name>
        <servlet-class>com.clojurebook.hello_world</servlet-class>
    </servlet>
    <servlet-mapping>
        <servlet-name>app</servlet-name>
        <url-pattern>/</url-pattern>
    </servlet-mapping>
    <servlet-mapping>
        <servlet-name>default</servlet-name>
        <url-pattern>*.css</url-pattern>
        <url-pattern>*.js</url-pattern>
        <url-pattern>*.png</url-pattern>
        <url-pattern>*.jpg</url-pattern>
        <url-pattern>*.gif</url-pattern>
        <url-pattern>*.ico</url-pattern>
        <url-pattern>*.swf</url-pattern>
```

```
        </servlet-mapping>
</web-app>
```

This is the *web.xml* file that we'll use in our Maven-built Clojure web app; Leiningen takes a different approach where the *web.xml* file is generated from configuration housed in its *project.clj* file. As we'll see throughout the rest of this chapter, your choice of build tool does influence minor details related to the packaging and organization of our web application.

Building .war files with Maven

As we saw in "Maven" on page 345, Maven projects produce *.jar* files by default, at least when your *pom.xml* defines a `<packaging>` of `clojure` (or `jar`, the default). Changing `<packaging>` to `war` will result in your project being packaged up as a *.war* file any time `mvn package` is invoked (or any phase that depends upon `package`, such as `install` or `deploy`). Since we're not using the `clojure` packaging anymore, we also need to attach `clojure-maven-plugin`'s `compile` goal to Maven's `compile` phase:

Example 17-2. pom.xml suitable for simple Clojure webapp projects

```
<project xmlns="http://maven.apache.org/POM/4.0.0"
         xmlns:xsi="http://www.w3.org/2001/XMLSchema-instance"
    xsi:schemaLocation="http://maven.apache.org/POM/4.0.0
                        http://maven.apache.org/maven-v4_0_0.xsd">
    <modelVersion>4.0.0</modelVersion>

    <groupId>com.clojurebook</groupId>
    <artifactId>sample-maven-web-project</artifactId>
    <version>1.0.0</version>
    <packaging>war</packaging>

    <dependencies>
        <dependency>
            <groupId>org.clojure</groupId>
            <artifactId>clojure</artifactId>
            <version>1.3.0</version>
        </dependency>
        <dependency>
            <groupId>compojure</groupId>
            <artifactId>compojure</artifactId>
            <version>1.0.1</version>
        </dependency>
        <dependency>
            <groupId>ring</groupId>
            <artifactId>ring-servlet</artifactId>
            <version>1.0.1</version>
        </dependency>
    </dependencies>

    <build>
        <plugins>
            <plugin>
                <groupId>com.theoryinpractise</groupId>
```

```
            <artifactId>clojure-maven-plugin</artifactId>
            <version>1.3.8</version>
            <extensions>true</extensions>
            <configuration>
                <warnOnReflection>true</warnOnReflection>
                <temporaryOutputDirectory>false</temporaryOutputDirectory>
            </configuration>

            <executions>
                <execution>
                    <id>compile-clojure</id>
                    <phase>compile</phase>
                    <goals>
                        <goal>compile</goal>
                    </goals>
                </execution>
            </executions>
        </plugin>
        <plugin>
            <groupId>org.mortbay.jetty</groupId>
            <artifactId>maven-jetty-plugin</artifactId>
            <version>6.1.15</version>
            <configuration>
                <webAppConfig>
                    <extraClasspath>
                      src/main/webapp,src/main/resources,src/main/clojure
                    </extraClasspath>
                </webAppConfig>
                <reload>manual</reload>
            </configuration>
        </plugin>
    </plugins>
  </build>
</project>
```

This sample *pom.xml* also includes the baseline dependencies needed to use Compojure and Ring, and some configuration for the `maven-jetty-plugin`; the latter allows us to run our web application locally using the embedded Jetty app server, ideal for development and local testing.

Our simple webapp consists of a single handler; since we can include our own *web.xml* file when building it with Maven, we can rely on the app server to handle requests for static files, so no additional route is needed for images and such:

Example 17-3. com.clojurebook.hello-world

```
(ns com.clojurebook.hello-world
  (:use
    [ring.util.servlet :only (defservice)]
    [compojure.core :only (GET)])
  (:gen-class
    :extends javax.servlet.http.HttpServlet))

(defservice
```

```
(GET "*" {:keys [uri]}
    (format "<html>
            URL requested: %s
            <p>
              <a href=\"/wright_pond.jpg\">
                Image served by app server via web.xml <servlet-mapping>
              </a>
            </p>
            </html>"
            uri)))
```

Building .war files with Leiningen

lein-ring[8] is a Leiningen plug-in that provides a number of facilities useful for developing Ring web applications when using Leiningen. One of these is the production of *.war* files, with the *generation* of *web.xml* files based on configuration in your *project.clj* file. This approach is quite different (and *much* shorter and simpler!) than Maven's, where you must author the *web.xml* file yourself.

Example 17-4. project.clj suitable for simple Clojure webapp projects

```
(defproject com.clojurebook/sample-lein-web-project "1.0.0"
  :dependencies [[org.clojure/clojure "1.4.0"]
                 [compojure/compojure "1.0.1"]
                 [ring/ring-servlet "1.0.1"]]
  :plugins [[lein-ring "0.6.2"]]
  :ring {:handler com.clojurebook.hello-world/routes})
```

The only configuration that lein-ring requires is the :ring :handler slot, which is where you specify the namespace-qualified name of the var that holds your application's top-level request handler. From that name, lein-ring will generate a servlet class (in this case, called com.clojurebook.servlet), which will delegate requests to our handler, and a *web.xml* file that defines that servlet and mounts it at the root URL path (/). This is the equivalent of our specifying our own *web.xml* and using gen-class and defservice to generate the servlet class and request delegation in the Maven project.

With this *project.clj* in place, running lein ring uberwar will produce a *.war* file that we can use to deploy to any app server.

Since lein-ring is generating our *web.xml* file without specifying that the app server's default servlet should handle requests for static resources, we need to include a route in our main handler that will serve these assets from our classpath:

---

8. See *https://github.com/weavejester/lein-ring* for full documentation and details.

Example 17-5. com/clojurebook/hello_world.clj

```
(ns com.clojurebook.hello-world
  (:use
    [compojure.core :only (GET defroutes)]
    [compojure.route :only (resources)]))

(defroutes routes
  (resources "/")
  (GET "*" {:keys [uri]}
      (format "<html>
              URL requested: %s
              <p>
                <a href=\"/wright_pond.jpg\">
                  Image served by compojure.route/resources
                </a>
              </p>
              </html>"
              uri)))
```

lein-ring only allows you to define a subset of the configuration options available in *web.xml* files, and it does not currently allow you to provide your own *web.xml* file. Thus, if you wish to use certain servlet specification features (such as servlet filters, context parameters, and default servlet mappings—which we use in the Maven example to let our app server handle requests for static resources), you will need to:

- Use the leiningen-war plug-in[9] (which only builds *.war* files; it does not provide the local Jetty deployment features of lein-ring), or

- Add some additional scripting on top of your lein-ring usage to swap a customized *web.xml* file into the *.war* files it produces, or

- Use Maven.

Running Web Apps Locally

Whether you prefer Maven or Leiningen, Jetty is used to run web apps locally for development and testing. This allows you to rapidly prototype new features and bug fixes without going through a complete packaging and deployment cycle as required for "real" deployments to production or common remote testing environments.

Maven.   As noted in "Building .war files with Maven" on page 562, our sample we-bapp-ready *pom.xml* includes a configuration for maven-jetty-plugin. Invoke mvn jetty:run within a project with such a configuration, and Jetty will be started on localhost port 8080, running the project's web application. As you make changes to your Clojure code, static assets, or *web.xml* file, you will want those changes available to your application running in Jetty without stopping and restarting it fully. To do this, hit Return in the console where you started Maven; this will reload the Jetty webapp

---

9. *https://github.com/alienscience/leiningen-war.*

context that your application is running within, a far faster process than killing the Maven/Jetty process and starting it from scratch.

Leiningen.   Leiningen's support for running web apps locally is essentially the same as Maven's. `lein ring server` will start a Jetty server with all requests routed to the root handler provided in your *project.clj* file's `:ring :handler` slot. `lein-ring` takes a slightly different approach to loading changed files into your running webapp: rather than waiting until you request a reload of the application context, `lein-ring` reloads all of the Clojure source files in your project each time it receives a request using Clojure's `require` function.

Loading updated code via "remote" REPLs.   A more flexible code-loading solution than that offered by either `maven-jetty-plugin` or `lein-ring` is to bundle a REPL server with your web application, and configure it to start upon deployment. This will allow you to connect to the "remote" REPL server from your development environment (such as Eclipse + Counterclockwise or Emacs + SLIME), and load Clojure code when you want to, rather than having to rely upon a timeout, context-switch to the terminal from which Jetty was started, or potentially delay saving changes to disk until you're ready to have those changes loaded into your running app.

This is a general-purpose approach that is not limited to web applications, and not limited to local deployments; see Chapter 10 for details.

Web Application Deployment

Being able to package Clojure web applications into standard *.war* files gives us a lot of deployment flexibility: all of the deployment practices and facilities available for deploying Java web applications are therefore available for use with Clojure web apps. In general, the act of deployment requires the following:

1. Setting up and configuring an app server
2. Copying the *.war* file your build process is producing to your server
3. Restarting the app server if necessary
4. If necessary, reverting your application's *.war* file to a prior version (in case the last deployed version contained a regression, for example)

You can certainly do these things manually or in a custom way—programmers and system administrators have been doing "hands-on" application deployments for a *long* time. And, if your organization already deploys Java web applications, you can almost surely drop your shiny new Clojure web apps into that same process.

However, if you're game, there are some specific Clojure-friendly toolchains that can make application deployment a lot simpler, easier, and more automated than most other options. We'll take a look at one, Amazon's Elastic Beanstalk service, that is broadly applicable to Clojure web applications, automating the provisioning and configuration of servers and deployment of applications to those servers.

Deploying Clojure Apps to Amazon's Elastic Beanstalk

Amazon's Elastic Beanstalk (EB) is a *platform as a service* that provides a thin layer of automation and deployment management tools on top of Amazon Web Services's (AWS) lower-level EC2 compute and load balancer services. EB allows you to programmatically provision and control *environments* (collections of one or more application servers fronted by a load balancer), to which you can deploy different versions of your application.

The load balancers used by EB are integrated with this provisioning mechanism, so that when your application experiences higher load (based on metrics you define, such as number of requests or aggregate bandwidth utilized per minute), the corresponding EB environment is expanded to contain more app servers to service that load. Especially if your application uses AWS's database facilities[10] or some other hosted database that can be co-located in AWS,[11] EB can be a very compelling deployment option that addresses the entire development, deployment, and maintenance life cycle of your application.

AWS provides a comprehensive Java API to their services, including EB, so interacting with it from Clojure is straightforward. Conveniently, there is a Leiningen plug-in for interacting with EB, lein-beanstalk.[12]

Basic setup and deployment. A couple of changes need to be made to a Leiningen-ready web application project to make it ready for use with `lein-beanstalk`. First, add the `lein-beanstalk` plug-in to your *project.clj*'s `plugins` vector.

```
[lein-beanstalk "0.2.2"]
```

Second, we need to add a Compojure route to support Elastic Beanstalk's "heartbeat." At regular intervals, your deployed application will be polled with a `HEAD` request to its root (/) URI; if it doesn't respond successfully, then Elastic Beanstalk will assume the entire application is down and attempt to redeploy and restart it. For this example, let's reuse the URL shortener service we built in "Routing Requests with Compojure" on page 535; we'll set up the Beanstalk heartbeat route in its own namespace, and—as further confirmation of the composability of Compojure routes and Ring handlers in general—just roll in the top-level route from the actual URL shortener service:

---

10. AWS provides three "managed" database services that pair well with the minimal operational overhead that Elastic Beanstalk enables: DynamoDB and SimpleDB, both nonrelational in nature (the latter being the precursor to the former), and AmazonRDS, which offers relational Oracle and MySQL environments. One of us maintains a Clojure API for SimpleDB, available at *https://github.com/cemerick/rummage*.

11. Such as Cloudant for hosted CouchDB clusters: *https://cloudant.com*.

12. *https://github.com/weavejester/lein-beanstalk*.

Example 17-6. com.clojurebook.url-shortener.beanstalk

```clojure
(ns com.clojurebook.url-shortener.beanstalk
  (:use [compojure.core :only (HEAD defroutes)])
  (:require [com.clojurebook.url-shortener :as shortener]
            [compojure.core :as compojure]))

(compojure/defroutes app
  ; This HEAD route is here because Amazon's Elastic Beanstalk determines if
  ; your application is up by whether it responds successfully to a
  ; HEAD request at /
  (compojure/HEAD "/" [] "")
  shortener/app)
```

The last modification we'll need to make to the project is to add a suitable `:ring` `:handler` configuration, since `lein-beanstalk` reuses `lein-ring` to produce *.war* files for deployment. Here is what the URL shortener's *project.clj* file looks like with the `lein-beanstalk` plug-in in place along with a suitable `:ring` `:handler` configuration:

Example 17-7. project.clj

```clojure
(defproject com.clojurebook/url-shortener "1.0.0"
  :description "A toy URL shortener HTTP service written using Ring and Compojure."
  :dependencies [[org.clojure/clojure "1.3.0"]
                 [compojure "1.0.1"]
                 [ring "1.0.1"]]
  plugins [[lein-beanstalk "0.2.2"]]
  :ring {:handler com.clojurebook.url-shortener.beanstalk/app})
```

Finally, you need to put your AWS credentials into a definition in the file at *~/.lein/ init.clj*;[13] these will be used to authenticate all of your `lein-beanstalk` activity:

Example 17-8. ~/.lein/init.clj

```clojure
(def lein-beanstalk-credentials
  {:access-key "XXXXXXXXXXXXXX"
   :secret-key "YYYYYYYYYYYYYY"})
```

Once these changes are in place, we can deploy our application via Elastic Beanstalk. One command-line invocation will do it:

```
lein beanstalk deploy development
```

This command prompts `lein-beanstalk` to:

1. Produce a *.war* file for your web application using `lein-ring`.
2. Copy that file to Amazon's S3 service.

---

13. Security credentials like this should never be put in your *project.clj* file, or any other file in your project that might be checked into source control. The prospect of that can be bad enough in an internal setting, but outright disastrous if you happen to push such commits to a publicly accessible repository-hosting service like GitHub or BitBucket.

---

3. Create an Elastic Beanstalk application with the same name as your project's name, if one does not exist yet.[14]

4. Create an environment called `development` for the Elastic Beanstalk application.

5. Request that the *.war* file copied to S3 be deployed to the `development` environment.

When the `deploy` command is finished (which can take a couple of minutes, especially the first time you perform a deployment for a particular application or environment), `lein-beanstalk` will indicate that your application is live and ready to be accessed.[15]

Application versioning.   Elastic Beanstalk retains all prior versions of your application in S3, so you can roll back a deployment at any time through the AWS console. `lein-beanstalk` uses the version number declared in your *project.clj* file to create those EB version numbers, so it is easy to understand what you have deployed, and how that relates to prior versions of your application. You can see the most recent versions uploaded to Elastic Beanstalk by running the `lein beanstalk info` command:

```
% lein beanstalk info
Application Name: url-shortener
Last 5 Versions:  1.0.0-SNAPSHOT-20111219051007
                  1.0.0-SNAPSHOT-20111219045316
Created On:       Mon Dec 19 04:53:53 EST 2011
Updated On:       Mon Dec 19 04:53:53 EST 2011
Deployed Envs:    development (Ready)
```

When you are certain that what you have deployed is satisfactory, you can use `lein beanstalk clean` to remove any unused versions and their corresponding *.war* files from S3.

Environments.   You can have as many environments as you need within a given Elastic Beanstalk application, with whatever names you like. `lein-beanstalk` defines three by default: `development`, `staging`, and `production`, the first of which we used in our example above. You can change or add to these defaults in your *project.clj*; consult the documentation for `lein-beanstalk` for details.

You can get various operational details about a particular environment by running the `lein beanstalk info <environment-name>` command:

```
% lein beanstalk info development
Environment ID:    e-cnjm4hrqki
Application Name:  url-shortener
Environment Name:  development
Description:
```

14. For example, if you are using our sample `lein-beanstalk` project—which has coordinates of `com.clojurebook/url-shortener`, then the application name will be `url-shortener`. Elastic Beanstalk application names must be globally unique, so if you are using (anyone's) sample project, be sure you change the artifact ID to something you can be sure is unique.

15. ...at a URL of the form *http://your-project-name.elasticbeanstalk.com*. You can use a `CNAME` record in your domain's DNS configuration to point, e.g., *www.yourdomain.com* to this *elasticbeanstalk.com* domain, and transparently serve well-branded sites from Elastic Beanstalk.

```
URL:                  url-shortener-dev.elasticbeanstalk.com
Load Balancer URL: awseb-development-1574221210.us-east-1.elb.amazonaws.com
Status:               Ready
Health:               Green
Current Version:      1.0.0-SNAPSHOT-20111219051007
Solution Stack:       32bit Amazon Linux running Tomcat 6
Created On:           Mon Dec 19 05:10:44 EST 2011
Updated On:           Mon Dec 19 05:13:11 EST 2011
```

Going Beyond Simple Web Application Deployment

Of course, depending on your requirements and environment, there can be much, much more to application deployment than what we've covered here. Many projects (even very large, heavily trafficked sites) can happily spend their entire existence on a service like Elastic Beanstalk; however, others will have a need to automate processes beyond simply getting a *.war* file up into a running container. Fine-grained control over provisioning and configuration of web frontends and load balancers, complete control over your database facilities, custom network routing and monitoring, perhaps in a heterogeneous mix of cloud services and in-house infrastructure...any of these issues can encroach on what might have otherwise been a straightforward use of a single easy-to-use cloud service and demand some tooling beyond what can handle the common case. Pallet is a Clojure toolchain for addressing challenges like these; see "Pallet" on page 586.

Whatever tool you use or requirements you have, never forget that solutions that apply to Java applications uniformly apply to Clojure applications. Similarly, you can always use non-Clojure tools (whether Chef, Puppet, or other) to deploy and manage Clojure applications, simply by using the techniques and idioms those tools provide for Java and JVM applications generally.

## PART V

Miscellanea

## CHAPTER 18

Choosing Clojure Type Definition Forms Wisely

Clojure provides a number of different forms useful for defining types:

- `deftype`, `defrecord`, and `reify`, Clojure's primary datatype abstractions, explored in "Defining Your Own Types" on page 270
- Maps of all sorts, particularly useful for the most flexible *de facto* types, discussed in Chapter 3
- `proxy` and `gen-class`, which focus on providing comprehensive Java and JVM interoperability, covered in "Defining Classes and Implementing Interfaces" on page 371

Each of these forms represents a different set of tradeoffs. Especially when you are new to Clojure, it may be difficult to determine when one type-definition form should be used over another. When should you use `deftype` instead of `defrecord`, `gen-class` instead of `deftype`, or `proxy` instead of `reify`?

We have attempted to explore all of the nuances of these forms in the sections referenced above. However, it is sometimes helpful to have a visual reference for such things, even if it is summary in nature. With that in mind, we hope you will find the flowchart in Figure 18-1 useful. Starting with the premise that you would like to define a type in Clojure, it will guide you through the most significant points of distinction between the type definition forms in the language so that you can settle on the one that is right for your particular situation:[1]

---

1. The canonical and up-to-date version of this flowchart is maintained at *https://github.com/cemerick/clojure -type-selection-flowchart* along with a number of translations, including Dutch, German, Japanese, Portuguese, and Spanish so far.

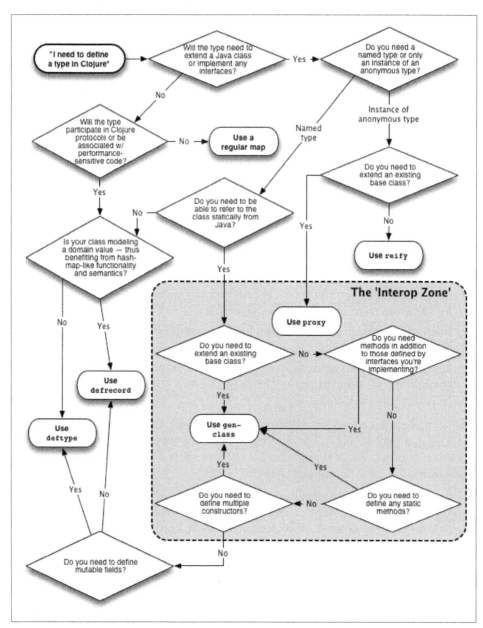

Figure 18-1. Choosing Clojure type definition forms wisely

"The *Interop Zone*" demarcates use cases (e.g., needing to define multiple constructors) and forms (proxy and gen-class) that are exclusively the domain of Clojure's JVM interoperability support. Using these forms is fine, but be aware that by doing so, you are stepping outside of Clojure's "native" abstractions. Unless you are defining a type for the express purpose of meeting interoperability requirements, one of Clojure's simpler type-definition forms may suit your needs better.

An example of "performance sensitive code" would be accessing slots in a hot loop. In such a situation:

- Regular maps will kill you.
- Using `:keyword` accessors with a record or `deftype` instance will deliver close-to-Java performance.
- Using direct field access (i.e., `(.field val)`) with a record or `deftype` instance will be as fast as Java by definition.

This doesn't mean that you should use field access all the time, or even most of the time. That's an optimization and should only be taken on when absolutely necessary, especially given the costs associated with it: efficient field access ties code that uses it to a particular type, which often complicates the implementation of generic functionality and limits composability.[2]

---

2. Recall that "premature optimization is the root of all evil." Thank you, Professor Knuth.

## CHAPTER 19

Introducing Clojure into Your Workplace

(or, Sneaking Clojure Past the Boss[1])

It is a sad fact that many programmers, if not the majority, use languages and tools every day that they begrudge. Either through historical accident, organizational inertia, or hard facts of the business, we often find ourselves stuck wishing we were using something, *anything* else to get our jobs done.

This *status quo* may be particularly frustrating if you've come far enough in your understanding and appreciation of Clojure that you'd like to be able to use it in your day job or on your next consulting engagement. What we'd like to do here is provide you with a brief guide, a cheat sheet, a set of talking points and strategies to help you successfully introduce Clojure into your workplace. In doing so, you'll hopefully end up having more productive days, less frustrating nights, and a more profitable business.

Just the Facts...

Clojure is new and innovative. In its relatively short history, Clojure has turned a lot of conventional programming language wisdom on its ear. It was unthinkable five years ago that a language would gain popularity that encourages functional programming, uses persistent immutable data structures by default, provides tractable concurrency and parallelism primitives, offers extensive metaprogramming facilities, and runs on the JVM with little to no performance differential compared to Java.

There's a lot more to that story, and there's no reason to believe that Clojure will not continue to push boundaries and cover new territory, even as what it offers already continues to mature and become more widely understood.

---

1. We're kidding, of course...mostly.

Clojure has tried, tested, reliable foundations. While Clojure itself is relatively new as programming languages go, it has deep roots. Rich Hickey (Clojure's creator) created no fewer than three projects prior to Clojure that focused on interoperability between a Lisp environment and the JVM and/or .NET.[2] These early experiments paved the way for the creation of Clojure, which has attained and validated its particular approach to balancing its Lisp language fundamentals and its host VM environment.

Of course, Clojure is heavily inspired in ways large and small by prior Lisp languages and environments, just as most modern languages (including Java, Python, Ruby, JavaScript, to name a few) have been. Especially attractive parts of that lineage are Clojure's wholehearted embrace of functional programming, and of macros, a meta-programming approach that, while validated by decades of use prior to Clojure's arrival, remains unparalleled outside of the Lisp family of languages.

In many ways, Clojure's targeting of the JVM closes the loop started when the original creators of Java and the JVM borrowed so much of what made early Lisp systems such pleasant, productive programming environments.[3]

Clojure lets you take advantage of all the benefits of the JVM. Many programmers, enticed by the expressiveness and relative flexibility of usually interpreted languages (such as Ruby and Python) have long pined for better runtimes. Especially for teams comfortable with the dynamic typing, Clojure provides the best of both worlds: top-notch expressivity stacked on top of the JVM, which in its nearly 20-year history has been crafted into an incredibly advanced, general-purpose computing platform.

Clojure being hosted on the JVM means that you benefit from all of the fruits of its widespread use: reliable operational and performance characteristics, a massive ecosystem of high-quality third-party libraries (both open source and commercial), mature server and tooling support, uncontroversial dependency management, and so on.

Clojure lets you reuse your investment in Java. If you use Java today, or otherwise have an existing investment in the JVM, Clojure helps you leverage that. Clojure web applications will run side by side with your other Java web applications without a hitch, you can call existing Java libraries from code you write in Clojure, and you can call Clojure functions and create instances of Clojure types from code you write in Java (or any other language that runs on the JVM, including JRuby, Jython, JavaScript [via Rhino], Scala, Groovy, and so on). Everything you've learned about builds, packaging, continuous integration, and JVM operations and tuning applies to the work you'll do with Clojure.

---

2. In chronological order: DotLisp, which worked with .NET (*http://dotlisp.sourceforge.net*); jFli (*http://jfli .sourceforge.net*), which targeted the JVM; and FOIL (*http://foil.sourceforge.net*), which could work with either VM.

3. Guy L. Steele, one of the creators of the original Scheme programming language and an author of both the *Java Language Specification* and *Common Lisp, the Language* (the basis of the ANSI Common Lisp standard) is widely quoted as having said, "We managed to drag a lot of [C++ programmers] about halfway to Lisp."

Clojure is an incremental addition to your existing JVM investment, not a radical departure.

"Clojure is just another .jar file".   A corollary of the fact that Clojure lets you reuse your investments in Java is that Clojure really is "just another *.jar* file." This means that you can package it as one dependency among others within a delivered application that includes Clojure source (or class files obtained from AOT-compiling such source), and your customers and clients will be none the wiser.

We're not suggesting that you subvert management or trick your customers. However, if you already legitimately have latitude and authority in choosing what you use to build software for clients and customers, then the use of Clojure as part of a complete solution is little different than choosing to build grammars using ANTLR, rightly abusing Lucene indexes as general-purpose datastores, or slipping into Visual Studio to build a sane launcher for your Java-based Windows desktop application.

Emphasize Productivity

Code less, do more.   Chances are very good that Clojure's solution to a given problem will be less verbose, less complex, and more comprehensible than a solution to the same problem in another language. There's *far* less mutable state to contend with. Concurrency and parallelism have consistent, simplified semantics, with locks and deadlocks eliminated. Classes and types are optional, and getters and setters are unnecessary. Syntactic patterns can be abstracted away with a judicious use of macros. The list goes on.

Taking advantage of Clojure will likely do for your personal level of productivity the same thing that Java did when you had been using C/C++, or the same thing Ruby or Python did when you had been using Java. Those benefits will scale up to your entire team as conceptual and design overhead imposed by the peculiarities of other languages is removed.

Programmers have been reaching for higher-level languages from the beginning; Clojure is just another step in that progression.

Clojure enables innovative solutions to complex problems.   A lot of what we've been talking about here has to do with Clojure's ability to fit in to existing investments, language preferences, and so on. But, some of the most tangible benefits of Clojure have to do with how it can help you stand out.

Most programming languages prescribe a particular architectural perspective, into which you must fit your domain. Clojure stands in stark contrast to this approach; it is structured to encourage the use of functional programming and modeling solutions in terms of purpose-built abstractions (enabled by things like protocols, records, and multimethods, for example). In doing so, Clojure forces you to "pay for" only those parts of the language that you use—where the currency involved isn't cash, but rather, modeling complexity and mental overhead.

This all means that when you design an API, a library, or a whole system with Clojure, that design is not encumbered by decisions that Clojure makes for you. This can make solutions to small problems extraordinarily simple, and can enable tractable implementations of very complex problems.

Clojure can give you an edge.   Would you use a tool that gave you or your organization an unfair advantage over your competition?[4]

Thinking back some years, what if you could use Ruby and Rails for web development in 1999? Or, what if you could build large-scale systems in 1990 using circa-2000 Java? We suspect you'd jump at such an opportunity.

Right now, if we squint, the world runs on Java, PHP, C/C++, and a smattering of "fringe" languages like Ruby and Python and Scala. We can safely assume that Clojure will not become as widespread as Java or PHP or C++, but we can definitively say that some of its key distinctions—for example, its software transactional memory architecture and its persistent functional data structure implementations—are being adopted, adapted, and sometimes used directly by other very capable programming languages. However, just as Java was not a Lisp just because the JVM's designers borrowed a raft of techniques and features from Lisp systems, languages that borrow capabilities and features from Clojure today are not equivalent to Clojure.

If you start using Clojure now, you may give yourself the opportunity to have an unfair advantage for years to come.

Emphasize Community

Clojure is open source and welcomes contributors.   Clojure is open source under a liberal-use license,[5] making it perfect for inclusion in commercial products and for use within commercial organizations (of course in addition to any noncommercial, charitable, or personal use).

While Clojure is itself the manifestation of one person's vision,[6] the project effort that surrounds Clojure is very inclusive: hundreds of individuals (many of them representing companies) are registered contributors[7] who have helped improve various aspects of

---

4. We would be remiss at this point if we did not reference Paul Graham's *Beating the Averages* essay, which is very relevant to this point: *http://www.paulgraham.com/avg.html*.

5. The Eclipse Public License, which allows for free commercial use and redistribution: *http://www.eclipse .org/legal/epl-v10.html*.

6. In Clojure's case, Rich Hickey, who has a role similar to Python's Guido Van Rossum, Ruby's Yukihiro Matsumoto, Perl's Larry Wall, and C++'s Bjarne Stroustrup.

7. All recognized contributors are listed at *http://clojure.org/contributing*.

the project. As of this writing, the Clojure language itself has a history of contributions from over 70 individuals.

The upshot is:

1. You'll never be restricted in your use of Clojure by legal externalities.
2. If you ever find a bug in Clojure's implementation, you can be confident that it will be fixed upstream—either by one of the existing contributors acting on a bug report, or by your own hand if you choose to become a contributor yourself.

Clojure has a large, growing, friendly community.   The Clojure community is large, and growing at a furious pace:

- The main mailing list (*http://groups.google.com/group/clojure*) has over 6,000 subscribers and is constantly active.
- The main IRC channel[8] regularly has over 400 people in it, and is constantly active.
- Major Clojure libraries and tools all have their own mailing lists (most of them hosted via Google Groups), monitored by the authors and lead developers.
- By the time you read this, at least six books on Clojure will have been published, all by major publishers.

Size isn't everything, though. While some programming languages and frameworks have somehow managed to gather hostile, toxic, ego-driven communities, Clojure's community is building a reputation as being notable in its friendliness and welcoming stance with regard to newcomers. In fact, when the 2011 State of Clojure survey[9] asked what factors were most frustrating in their use of Clojure, just 2 percent of respondents (the smallest subpopulation for that question) reported that "unpleasant community interactions" were an issue.

All of this means that when you want to talk with experienced, knowledgeable Clojure programmers—whether to offer or ask for help—you'll always have somewhere to go.

Clojure is widely used.   The core Clojure team maintains a wiki page where organizations using Clojure can make themselves known:

> *http://dev.clojure.org/display/community/Clojure+Success+Stories*

On that page, you'll find that: global, established corporations like Citicorp and Akamai use Clojure; startups like Backtype (now with Twitter), The Climate Corporation (née Weatherbill), and Woven use Clojure; consulting shops like Relevance use Clojure; and hardcore research shops like the Max Planck Institute for Molecular Biomedicine use Clojure.

---

8. *irc://irc.freenode.net/clojure* or in your browser at *http://webchat.freenode.net/?channels=#clojure*.

9. One of us has run a community-wide survey for the past two years to gauge the origins, mood, and priorities of the Clojure community; full results of the last editing of that survey are available at *http://cemerick.com/2011/07/11/results-of-the-2011-state-of-clojure-survey/*.

If your organization starts using Clojure, it will have good company.

Be Prudent

Don't try to put a square peg into a round hole. Like any tool, Clojure provides a number of affordances, and it shines the brightest when it is used in ways that allow those affordances to offer the most leverage. As much as you may like Clojure, and want to do work with it regularly, you should be sure that it is well-suited to your organization and its objectives before lobbying for its use.

Thus, if your company builds embedded systems using C++ (for example), it's probably not realistic to attempt to convince your teammates to replace that codebase with Clojure.[10]

Start small, start slow. Sometimes incremental measures are the best way to introduce something new into an existing system. With this in mind, perhaps it would be easy to start writing all of your projects' tests in Clojure, or perhaps use Clojure to build secondary or internal tools. Building up a track record of success for Clojure among your colleagues will often be far more convincing of its capabilities and benefits than any well-delivered pitch or presentation ever would be.

---

10. At least not overnight, and at least not now. But, some *are* working on compiling Clojure down to lower-level languages suitable for delivering "native" applications. For an example, see *http://nakkaya.com/2011/06/29/ferret-an-experimental-clojure-compiler/*.

## CHAPTER 20

What's Next?

If you've gotten all you can out of this book—or you want to look ahead to what's waiting for you once you have a firm grasp on Clojure's fundamentals—you might want to take a look at the projects and resources listed here. These are some of the coolest things we know of in the Clojure universe. Some of them will help you learn Clojure better, some of them might be useful to you in your "real" projects, and others are just too fun to not check out at least once.

Finally, because Clojure is a relatively new language with a community that is growing and building like mad, new awesome stuff pops up all the time. If you head over to *http://clojurebook.com*, we'll do our best to keep up with it all and point you at the best of the best.

(dissoc Clojure 'JVM)

There are two other well-supported implementations of Clojure that target other execution environments. If you like what you see here, but need to deploy outside of the JVM, then ClojureCLR or ClojureScript might be just what you need.

ClojureCLR

ClojureCLR[1] is a port of Clojure to the .NET CLR. It is not a naive cross-compilation; rather, it is maintained separately, and aims to provide the same degree of tight host interoperability for the CLR that Clojure does for the JVM. Given the differences between the JVM and the CLR, this means that ClojureCLR provides some facilities that Clojure does not.

While ClojureCLR has not seen as much use as Clojure proper, it is mature, well-tested, and represents a great option for anyone that needs to deploy applications on the CLR without leaving the comforts of Clojure.

---

1. *https://github.com/clojure/clojure-clr*; its maintainers blog at *http://clojureclr.blogspot.com*.

ClojureScript

ClojureScript (*https://github.com/clojure/clojurescript*) is a different animal entirely. It targets JavaScript (technically, ECMAScript 3), and therefore produces code that can be run in all modern browsers, as well as in other JavaScript execution environments such as Node.js, CouchDB,[2] and others, much in the same vein as CoffeeScript or Dart. This means that you can write ClojureScript—using macros, types, protocols, multimethods, and so on—and deploy it to any JavaScript host.

There are two caveats we should mention:

1. ClojureScript is very new. The project was first made public in 2011, and significant changes continue to be made as of this book's printing. That said, it is fundamentally quite stable; projects and sites using ClojureScript have been in production for many months.

2. There are nontrivial differences between Clojure and ClojureScript. This is due in part to the vast differences between JavaScript hosts and the JVM, but also because ClojureScript is a source-to-source compiler: rather than generating bytecode that is loaded into the host, the ClojureScript compiler necessarily generates JavaScript source code. An overview of the differences between Clojure and ClojureScript is available at *https://github.com/clojure/clojurescript/wiki/Differences-from-Clojure*.

ClojureScript was first introduced by Rich Hickey in summer of 2011 at a monthly meeting of ClojureNYC;[3] video of that introduction is at *http://blip.tv/clojure/rich-hickey-unveils-clojurescript-5399498*.

4Clojure

4Clojure (*http://4clojure.com*) offers small interactive Clojure programming challenges, ranging from the most basic parts of Clojure to mind twisters. Once you complete a problem, you can take a peek at other players' solutions. It has garnered quite a following, with thousands of people participating and hundreds of thousands of challenges solved.

While looking at others' solutions, do keep in mind that code golfing (*https://en.wiki pedia.org/wiki/Code_golf*) is a common practice on 4Clojure. Most of the tricks and ideas you'll see there are valuable; just don't take 4Clojure solutions as an authoritative style guide.

---

2. ClojureScript can be used with Clutch—used extensively in Chapter 15—to define views in CouchDB: *https://github.com/clojure-clutch/clutch-clojurescript*.

3. *http://www.meetup.com/Clojure-NYC/*.

Overtone

Overtone[4] is an open source audio environment written in Clojure that produces sounds and music via the SuperCollider[5] synthesis server. This allows you to write instruments and synthesizers in Clojure using very high-level abstractions, and mix them together (optionally with loaded samples from around the Internet) into full compositions however you like. Beyond programmatically making sounds and music, Overtone provides support for things like TouchOSC, the Monome, and other hardware inputs so that the noise you make with code can be further controlled by your gestures and touch, just like any other instrument.

Clojure Conj 2011 (*http://clojure-conj.org*) saw a presentation of Overtone by one of its project leads, which we highly recommend watching to get a feel for Overtone's history and general objectives: *http://blip.tv/clojure/sam-aaron-programming-music-with-over tone-5970273*.

core.logic

In "Putting Clojure's Collections to Work" on page 136 we talked about *relational-oriented* programming. The `core.logic` (*https://github.com/clojure/core.logic*) enables a form of logic programming known as *relational* programming, which, in terms of declarativeness, is the next step. Other examples of relational programming languages include SQL and Prolog. `core.logic` is oriented more toward the latter, in that it implements a form of miniKanren, a type of relational programming language that is well-suited for constraint logic programming.

With this extra declarativeness comes great features: a `core.logic` *goal* (the relational corollary of a function) makes no distinction between parameters and return value, therefore making it possible to run them "backward," so that you can obtain one (or several) possible arguments given a known "return" value.[6]

The simplest example of this power is `conso`, the relational counterpart of `cons`. Since goals ("relational functions") don't discriminate between arguments and return value, `conso` takes its "return value" as an extra third and last argument. Let's see it in action:

```
(use '[clojure.core.logic])

(run* [x] (conso 1 [2 3] x))     ❶
;= ((1 2 3))
(run* [x]
  (fresh [_]
```

---

4. *http://overtone.github.com*.

5. *http://supercollider.sourceforge.net*.

6. "Return" is so quoted to remind you that in relational programming, there's no such thing as a return value as you are used to in object-oriented or functional programming.

```
    (conso x _ [1 2 3]))) 				❷
;= (1)
(run* [x]
  (fresh [_]
    (conso _ x [1 2 3]))) 				❸
;= ((2 3))
(run* [q] 						❹
  (fresh [x y]
    (conso x y [1 2 3])
    (== q [x y])))
;= ((1 (2 3)))
```

❶ We first call it in the "obvious" way; the return value is a list of results, akin to a set of answers when solving an equation or the result set when executing a SQL query. The only solution to this program is (1 2 3).

❷ When called with the two first arguments unknown (x and _), and only asking for potential values for the first one, the only answer is 1. In this way, conso can be used like first.

❸ This time returning only the second argument, the only answer is (2 3); so, conso can also be used like rest.

❹ We can also return the first two arguments at once, a bit like destructuring the list, as in [x & [y z]].

When even a simple function like cons (or rather conso) becomes more expressive and powerful, it opens new ways to express elegantly solutions to difficult problems.

Pallet

We walked through a basic deployment process for Clojure web applications in Chapter 17, but your needs may go beyond what we presented there. Pallet (*https://github .com/pallet/pallet*) is a Clojure toolchain for addressing many of the complex challenges involved in the deployment of applications and management of computing infrastructure in an automated way. While tools like Chef and Puppet are finding increasingly common usage to automate system configuration, Pallet aims to offer a superset of their functionality—including automating provisioning of instances across multiple cloud providers.[7] Of course, being a Clojure tool, you configure, extend, and interact with Pallet (and therefore the hardware and servers and processes that make up your computing infrastructure), using Clojure code and through the REPL, so you can leverage all of the advantages of the language within the realms of provisioning, system administration, and configuration management.

---

7. Thanks in large part to the jclouds library, which provides a uniform abstraction over dozens of different cloud services: *http://code.google.com/p/jclouds*.

Avout

All of the discussion of concurrency in Chapter 4 was focused on in-process concurrency, coordinating interleaving and parallelized processes within a single Clojure runtime. Avout (*http://avout.io*) is a reimplementation of Clojure's atoms and refs (and therefore the latter's software transactional memory) for use in distributed, multiprocess applications. It is built on top of Apache Zookeeper (*http://zookeeper.apache.org*) but is designed for extensibility so new backends can be added. If Clojure's STM is attractive to you, but you need to have its transactional semantics apply across multiple applications (or instances of the same application running in different processes), Avout may be a natural fit.

Clojure on Heroku

While Chapter 17 presented a very typical web application deployment approach using a container (such as Tomcat on Amazon's Elastic Beanstalk), there are ways to run Clojure web apps *without* a container, and therefore without the packaging work that containers imply. While such *containerless* deployment options are a relatively new approach in the JVM space, they are becoming more and more common. One of the most popular to date is provided by Heroku (*http://heroku.com*)—a scalable application deployment platform that is itself hosted on Amazon Web Services—which now directly supports the deployment of Ring-based web applications using Leiningen[8] without requiring any separate compilation or packaging steps.

Heroku has the added benefit of offering application "add-ons"—managed database clusters, message queues, web services, and so on—that you can configure and use from within your Clojure project without having to set up and manage such things yourself. It is a proprietary platform, but it just might be paving the way for how all Clojure applications will be deployed in a containerless future.

---

8. See *http://devcenter.heroku.com/articles/clojure* for a full walk-through and documentation.

Index

Symbols

! (exclamation mark), 133
& (ampersand), 31
&env, 252–253
&form, 254–258
  arguments, 253
  macro error messages, 254
  user-provided type hints, 256–258
' (quote), 19, 24
* (asterisks), 202
math-context, 432
unchecked-math, 431
warn-on-reflection, 440, 449
+ function, 322
, (commas), 19
-> and ->> in macros, 71, 259–262
. special form, 44
.jar file, 340, 579
.tar.gz file, 340
.war files
  about, 560
  Leiningen, 564
  Maven, 562
.zip, 340
::collection, 307
:as, 34
:body, 530
:character-encoding, 530
:content-length, 530
:content-type, 529
:error-handler, 214
:headers, 529, 530
:or, 34
:query-string, 530

:reload, 397
:remote-addr, 529
:request-method, 529
:scheme, 529
:server-name, 529
:server-port, 529
:status, 530
:uri, 529
= (equality), 434
@ (at sign), 160
^:const, 200
_ (underscore), 28, 329
_changes, CouchDB, 520
{...} (braces), 6
~@, 242
404 Not Found, 543
409 Conflict, 543
4Clojure, 584

A

abstract syntax tree, 9
abstractions, 84–114
  associative, 99–103
  collection abstractions, 292
  collections, 87
  indexed, 103
  sequences, 89–99
    creating seqs, 92
    head retention, 98
    lazy seqs, 93–98
    versus iterators, 91
    versus lists, 92
  sequential and map collections, 29
  set abstractions, 105
  sorted, 106–111

We'd like to hear your suggestions for improving our indexes. Send email to *index@oreilly.com*.

stacks, 104
access, collections, 111–114
adapters, Ring, 531
add-watch, 177
advice, 467
agents, 209–224
    errors in agent actions, 212
    I/O, transactions and nested sends, 214–224
aget, 445, 446
Aleph, 532
algorithms, defined, 15
aliases, namespaces, 22
alter, 183, 184
alter-var-root, 207
amap, 446
Amazon, EB, 567–569
ampersand (&), 31
annotations, 381–385
    JAX-RS, 383
    JUnit tests, 382
anonymous classes, proxy, 372
anonymous functions versus function literals, 64
anonymous types, reify, 284
AOP (aspect-oriented programming), 466–470
AOT compilation
    about, 337
    configuration, 349
    need for, 390
APIs
    dynamic scope, 202
    manipulating code, 232
    size of, 85
appendTo, 365
applications, versioning, 569
arbitrary implementation, 291
arbitrary precision versus bounded, 428–430
arbitrary-precision decimals ops, scale and rounding modes, 432
arbitrary-precision numbers, 17
areduce, 446
argument vectors, 369
arguments
    &form and &env, 253
    destructuring function arguments, 38–40
    keywords, 39
    mutable arguments and functions, 56

performance, 438
primitive types, 440
rest arguments, 38
arithmetic functions, 78
arities
    functions, 37, 41
    Multimethods, 302
    performance, 67
ArrayList, 360
arrays
    classes, 444
    hints, 445
    Java, 370
    operations, 370
    primitive arrays, 442–449
        about, 443
        type hinting of multidimensional array operations, 447
ArraySet, 295
artifactId, 340
artifacts, Maven dependency management model, 340
aset, 445, 446
aspect-oriented programming (AOP), 466–470
AspectJ, 467
assertions, testing, 486
assoc, 100, 127
associative abstraction
    data structures, 99–103
    records, 273
asterisks (*), 202
at sign (@), 160
atoms
    concurrency and parallelism, 174
    operations on, 192
attrs, 483
auto-gensym, 246
autoboxing, 437, 441
autopromoting operators, 429
auxiliary constructor, 275
averaging numbers, 5
Avout, 587
await, 211
await-for, 212

B

back references, 138
bare version numbers, 344

barging, 194
BigDecimal, 423, 432
BigInt, 423, 428
BigInteger, 423, 428
binding
    local bindings: let, 27
    multiple resources, 366
    value to their keys' names, 34
    vectors, 250
    with-redefs, 472
binding conveyance, 206
blocks, Ruby, 40
boilerplate, Hibernate, 507
booleans, 13
bounded versus arbitrary precision, 428–430
boxed decimals, 422
boxed integers, 422
braces {...}, 6
branching, Enlive, 549
browsing namespaces, 404
build solutions, 336–353
    compilation, 337
    dependency management, 339–344
        artifacts and coordinates, 340
        dependencies, 342
        repositories, 341
    tools and configuration patterns, 344–353
        AOT compilation configuration, 349
        Leiningen, 347
        Maven, 345
        mixed source projects, 351
built-in operators, 233

C

catch, 363
chain of responsibility, 463–466
character literals, 13
checked exceptions, 364
chunking, 168
class, 360
classes, 371–385
    annotations, 381–385
        JAX-RS, 383
        JUnit tests, 382
    arrays, 444
    deftype and dfrecord classes, 388–390
    hierarchies, 290
    inline and protocol implementations, 415
    Java, 357–360, 371

    multimethods, 314
    named classes, 374–381
    proxy, 372
classpath
    JVM, 4
    limitations, 415
    namespaces, 331
Clojars.org, 341
Clojure
    collections and data structures, 83–157
    concurrency and parallelism, 159–226
    datatypes and protocols, 263–299
    design patterns, 457–470
    FP, 51–82
    future, 583–587
    general information about, 1–48
    introducing to your workplace, 577–582
    Java, 355–392
    macros, 229–262
    multimethods, 301–317
    nonrelational databases, 511–525
    numerics and mathematics, 421–455
    projects, 321–353
    relational databases, 491–509
    REPL (Read, Evaluate, Print, Loop), 393–
        417
    testing, 471–489
    type definition forms, 573
    web applications, 557–570
    web development, 527–555
clojure-maven-plugin, 347, 352
clojure-mode, 406
clojure.core, 323
clojure.java.jdbc, 491–497
    connection pooling, 496
    transactions, 496
    with-query-results, 494
clojure.lang.IEditableCollection, 132
clojure.repl, 400
clojure.set, 325
clojure.string, 325
clojure.test, 473–481
    defining tests, 474–476
    fixtures, 479
    test suites, 477
ClojureCLR, 583
ClojureScript, 584
clone-for, 550
Clutch, 512

code blocks: do, 25
code generation versus macros, 232
code-as-data, 9
codebases, functional organization of, 334
coercion functions, 441
collection abstractions, 292
collection literals, 19
collection types, destructuring, 28
collections and data structures, 83–157
  abstractions, 84–114
    associative, 99–103
    collections, 87
    indexed, 103
    sequences, 89–99
    set abstractions, 105
    sorted, 106–111
    stacks, 104
  collection access, 111–114
    idiomatic usage, 112
    keys and higher-order functions, 113
  Conway's Game of Life, 139–145
  data structure types, 114–122
    lists, 114
    maps, 117
    sets, 117
    vectors, 115
  identifiers and cycles, 137
  immutability and persistence, 122–134
    structural sharing, 123–130
    transients, 130–134
  macros, 235
  maze generation, 145–151
  metadata, 135
  navigation, update and zippers, 151–156
  performance, 437
command-line utility, 376
commas (,), 19
comments, 18
community, 580
commute, 185–189, 193
comp, 69
comparators, ordering, 107–111
compare, 107
compare-and-set, 174
compilation
  AOT, 337, 349
  macros, 230
  REPL, 4
Compojure

about, 536
routes, 539
compositionality, 68–76
  building a primitive logging system, 72–76
  higher-order functions, 71
concat, 242
concurrency and parallelism, 159–226
  about, 2
  agents, 209–224
    errors in agent actions, 212
    I/O, transactions and nested sends, 214–224
  agents and workloads, 217
  atoms, 174
  compared, 166
  coordination, 172
  delays, 160
  futures, 162
  Java's concurrency primitives, 224
  notifications and constraints, 176–179
    validators, 178
    watches, 176–178
  parallelism on the cheap, 166
  promises, 163
  reference types, 129, 170
  refs, 180–198
    mechanics of ref change, 181–191
    STM, 180
    transactional memory, 191–198
  state and identity, 168
  synchronization, 172
  vars, 198–208
    defining, 198–201
    dynamic scope, 201–206
    forward declarations, 208
    versus variables, 206
concurrency forms, dynamic scope, 206
concurrency primitives, Java, 224
concurrency-ref-mechanics, 215
cond, 42
conditionals: if, 42
configuration patterns, 344–353
configuration, AOT compilation configuration, 349
configure-view-server, 517
conj, 84, 87, 104, 114, 124
connection pooling, 496
cons, 93
constants, 200

constraints (see notifications and constraints)
constructors, factory functions, 275
constructs, redefining, 415
containerless approach, 560
contains?, 101
continue, 213
Conway's Game of Life, 139–145
coordinates, Maven dependency management model, 340
coordination, concurrency and parallelism, 172
core.logic, 585
core.memoize, 80
CouchDB, 511–525
    about, 512
    CRUD, 512
    message queues, 522–525
    views, 514–520
        Clojure, 516–520
        JavaScript, 514–516
    _changes, 520
count, 88, 92
Counterclockwise, 403
CRUD, nonrelational databases, 512
CSS selectors, 549
curl, 542
cycles
    about, 138
    collections and data structures, 137
cyclic dependencies, 165

D

data
    Clojure programs represented as, 11
    functions as, 59
    persisting data in Hibernate, 506
data structures (see collections and data structures)
databases (see nonrelational databases; relational databases)
dataflow variables, 164
DataSource-based connection pooling, 496
datatypes and protocols, 263–299
    about protocols, 264
    classes, 415
    collection abstractions, 292
    defining your own types, 270–280
        deftype, 277–280
        records, 272–277

extending existing types, 266–270
    implementing protocols, 280–288
        inline, 281–285
        reusing implementations, 285–288
    protocol dispatch edge cases, 290
    protocol inspection, 289
    using Clojure from Java, 390
debugging
    macros, 237
    REPL, 411–414
    SLIME, 410
dec, 424
declarations
    about, 367
    forward declarations, 208
declarative concurrency, 164
declare functions, 438–442
declare macro, 208
def, 26, 416
defdb, 499
defining vars: def, 26
defmethod, 301
defmulti, 302, 415
defn-, 199
defonce, 396, 415, 506
defproject, 348
defrecord, 270, 272, 282, 374, 415
defroutes, 545
defsnippet, 551, 554
deftemplate, 552
deftype, 270, 277, 282, 283, 371, 374, 415
deftype class, 388–390
delays, 160
dependencies
    clojure.java.jdbc, 491
    cyclic dependencies, 165
    cyclic namespaces, 329
    interleaving source dependencies, 353
dependency injection, 459–462
dependency management, 339–344
    artifacts and coordinates, 340
    dependencies, 342
    repositories, 341
deployment, 341
deref, 160, 162, 171, 194
derive, 308
deserialization, 12
design patterns, 457–470
    AOP, 466–470

chain of responsibility, 463–466
dependency injection, 459–462
strategy pattern, 462
destructuring, 28–36
collection types, 28
function arguments, 38–40
map destructuring, 32–36
sequential, 30–32
dfrecord classes, 388–390
Digital Subscriber Line (DSL) versus Korma,
500
disjunctions, 548
dispatch function
about, 302
multimethods, 305, 316
multiple, 311
dissoc, 100, 274
do expressions, implicit, 26
do forms, implicit, 40
do->, 551
do: code blocks, 25
doall, 97, 168, 495
doc, 400
docstrings, 199
dorun, 97, 167
doseq, 91
dosync, 182, 192
doto, 360, 361
double, 427
Double box class, 423
double evaluation, macros, 249
downloading Clojure, 3
DSL (Digital Subscriber Line) versus Korma,
500
dynamic expression problem, 263
dynamic redefinition, 397
dynamic scope, 201–206
concurrency forms, 206
visualizing, 203

E

each, 479
earmuffs, 202
EB (Elastic Beanstalk), 567–569
Eclipse, 403–405
editing
Clojure editing support, 403
source code, 402
efficiency (see performance)

Emacs, 405–411
clojure-mode and paredit, 406
inferior-lisp, 406
SLIME, 408
empty, 87
Enlive, 546–554
about, 547
iterating and branching, 549
selectors, 548
using, 551
ensure, 198
environments, 569
equality and equivalence, 433–436
numeric equivalence, 435
object identity, 433
reference equality, 434
equals, 283
ERB templates
templating language, 545
using, 552
error handling
agents, 212, 213
Java, 362–366
macros, 234, 254
escape hatch, 360
escaping checked exceptions, 364
eval
about, 46
Ruby eval versus Clojure macros, 234
Evaluate, 20
evaluating
suppressing: quote, 24
symbols, 23
event types, hierarchies, 518
exceptions
agents, 212
Java, 362–366
throwing, 363
try and throw, 45
types
custom, 378
reusing, 363
exclamation mark (!), 133
expanding macros, 237
expression problem, 263
expressions
about, 7
code blocks, 25
regular expressions, 17

values, 54
extend, 285
extend-protocol, 266
extend-type, 266, 282
extenders, 289
extends?, 289
extensibility, Emacs, 408
extra-positional sequential values, 31

F

factory functions
    constructors, 275
    protocols and vectors, 268
failed agents, 212
fallbacks, 194
false, 114
false values, 103
false?, 42
fields
    immutable fields, 278
    Java, 357–360
    mutable fields, 278
    object fields, 359
files, namespaces, 328–331
fill-dispatch, 308
filter, 113
filter functions, 521
finally, 363, 364
find, 102
find-doc, 400
fire-and-forget persistence mechanism, 217
first-class functions, 59–68
fixnums, 433
fixtures, 479
flow, 398
fn, 36–41, 487
for, 88
form-level comments, 18
forms, 23
    (see also special forms)
    comment forms, 18
    concurrency forms, 206
    expanding nested forms, 239
    println forms, 18
    type definition forms, 573
forward declarations, 208
FP (functional programming), 51–82
    about, 52
    compositionality, 68–76

building a primitive logging system, 72–76
    higher-order functions, 71
    first-class and higher-order functions, 59–68
    pure functions, 76
    values, 52–59
        about, 53
        comparing to mutable objects, 54–58
        unfettered object state, 58
frequencies, 442
function application, 65–68
function composition, 69
function literals
    versus anonymous functions, 64
    versus partial literals, 67
functions, 51
    (see also FP)
    anonymous functions versus function literals, 64
    arithmetic functions, 78
    arity, 41
    coercion functions, 441
    collections and, 111
    collections keys, 112
    constructors and factory functions, 275
    creating functions: fn, 36–41
    declare functions, 438–442
    dynamic scope, 204
    factory functions, 268
    filter functions, 521
    first class and higher order functions, 59–68
    first class values, 61
    indexed-step functions, 139
    keys and collections, 113
    multiple arguments, 36
    multiple arities, 37
    mutable arguments, 56
    mutually recursive, 37
    nesting literals, 41
    primitive types, 440
    protocols, 264
    pure functions, 78
    rest arguments, 31
    sequential collections, 29
    side-effecting functions, 80
    single-arity functions, 38
    symbols, 23

testing, 471
variadic functions, 38, 90
versus macros, 232
versus records, 277
Futon, 515
future, 583–587
4Clojure, 584
about, 162
Avout, 587
ClojureCLR, 583
ClojureScript, 584
core.logic, 585
Heroku, 587
Overtone, 585
Pallet, 586

G

Game of Life, 143
games
concurrency-ref-mechanics, 215
ref change, 181
gen-class, 371, 375–381, 415
gensyms, macros, 246
get, 101, 102, 103
GET, 536
group-by, 119
groupId, 340

H

handlers, Ring, 532
handling exceptions: try and throw, 45
hash-map, 118
hash-set, 117
hashmaps, 14
head retention, 98
Heroku, 587
heterogeneous arguments, 426
hexadecimal notation, 16
Hibernate, 503–509
boilerplate, 507
persisting data, 506
queries, 506
setup, 503–506
Hiccup, 481
hierarchies, 304–311
classes, 290
event types, 518
higher-order functions, 59–68

hints
arrays, 445
type hints
macros and &form, 256–258
multidimensional array operations, 447
history, 195
homogeneously typed arguments, 426
homoiconicity, 7, 9–12, 230
HTML DSL, 481–485
HTML templates, Leiningen, 552
html-snippet, 547
hygienic macros, 244

I

I/O, agents, 214–224
identifiers, collections and data structures, 137
identities
about, 138
concurrency and parallelism, 168
object identity, 433
identity, 2
IDEs (Integrated Development Environments), 398
if, 42
if-let, 42
IFn, 438
immutability, 122–134
immutable fields, 278
immutable functions, testing, 471
immutable objects, 52
immutable values, 52
import, 326
in-ns, 322
indexed abstractions, 103
indexed-step functions, 139
indices
destructuring, 33
issues with, 138
vectors, 29
inferior-lisp, 406
infix operators, 9
inheritance
limitations, 458
multimethods, 313
inline implementation of protocols, 281–285
example, 280
Java interfaces, 282
reify, 284

inline interfaces, classes, 415
inner classes, 327
inner map destructuring, 33
insert-records, 493
inspecting protocols, 289
inspector, 409
instance field access, 45
instance method
    calls, 9
    invocation, 45
instance?, 360
integers, 54
Integrated Development Environments (IDEs), 398
interaction styles, REPL, 6
interactive development, 393–398
interfaces
    inline implementation of Java interfaces, 282
    Java classes, 371–385
    using Clojure from Java, 390
    versus protocols, 264
interleaving source dependencies, 353
interop forms, 357
interop utilities
    Java, 360
Interop Zone, 574
interoperability
    Java, 44
    Java and JVM, 355
    numeric primitives, 16
into, 131
into-array, 444
introducing Clojure to your workplace, 577–582
    community, 580
    facts, 577
    productivity, 579
    prudence, 582
introspecting
    multimethods, 314
    namespaces, 401
invariants, 59
invoke, 438
invokePrim, 439
is, 473
isa?, 307
isolated mutation of local arrays, 442
isolation, 181

iterating, Enlive, 549
iterators
    about, 458
    versus sequences, 91

J

Java, 355–392, 557–565
    abstraction, 85
    arrays, 370
    classes and interfaces, 371–385
        annotations, 381–385
        named classes, 374–381
        proxy, 372
    classes, methods and fields, 357–360
    Clojure's foundation, 356
    concurrency primitives, 224
    dependency injection, 459
    exceptions and error handling, 362–366
        escaping checked exceptions, 364
        with-open and finally, 364
    inline implementation of protocols with Java interfaces, 282
    interfaces, 282
    interop forms equivalents, 357
    interop utilities, 360
    interoperability, 44
    maps, 85
    mutability, 360
    servlet filters, 535
    type hinting, 366–370
    using Clojure from Java, 385–392
        deftype and defrecord classes, 388–390
        protocol interfaces, 390
    web application packaging, 560–565
        .war files with Leiningen, 564
        .war files with Maven, 562
    web architecture, 558
    wildcard import, 327
java.io.Serializable, 291
java.lang, 327
java.lang.Integer, 55
java.lang.Runnable, 225
java.util.ArrayList, 115
java.util.Collection, 290
java.util.concurrent, 224, 225
java.util.concurrent.Callable, 225
java.util.List, 29, 290
java.util.Map, 291
JavaScript, views, 514–516

JAX-RS annotations, 384
JAX-RS web service endpoints, 383
JMX (Java Management Extensions), 414
JSON, 513
JUnit tests, 382
JVM (Java Virtual Machine)
    Clojure hosted on, 2
    reusing investment in, 578

K

keys, 118
    binding values, 34
    collections, 112
    destructuring, 33
keywords, 14
    arguments, 39
    associative collections, 273
    as functions, 112
    hierarchy, 306
Korma, 498–503
    queries, 499
    using, 498
    versus DSL, 500

L

lambdas, Python, 40
lazy seqs, 93–98
lazy-seq, 90, 93
lein compile, 353
lein-ring, 564
Leiningen, 347
    AOT compilation, 350
    compilation, 352
    HTML templates, 552
    .war files, 564
    web apps, 566
let, 27
letfn, 37
lexical scope, 201
libraries, dynamic scope, 202
Library Coding Standards style guide, 120
libspecs, 324
LIFO (last-in, first-out), stacks, 104
LinkedHashMap, 372
Lisp
    and Clojure, 2
    special forms, 24
list function, 239, 241

list*, 93
lists
    about, 8
    data structure type, 114
    quote ('), 19
    quoting, 25
    structural sharing, 124
    versus sequences, 92
literals (see collection literals; scalar literals)
live lock, 194
local arrays, isolated mutation of, 442
local bindings
    destructured value, 32
    let, 27
local consistency, validators, 189
locals, destructuring, 30
locking
    concurrency primitives, 225
    primitives: monitor-enter and monitor-exit,
        45
logging
    building a primitive logging system, 72–76
    databases, 522
    states, 216
    write-behind log, 215–217
Long box class, 423
loop special form, 28
loops
    loop and recur, 43
    replacing, 140
LRU cache, 372
lucene-core, 340
lucene-queryparser, 340

M

macroexpand-1, 237
macroexpand-all, 239
macroexpansion, 231
macros, 229–262
    -> and ->>, 259–262
    about, 229–235
        versus functions, 232
        versus Ruby eval, 234
        what macros are not, 231
    comment macros, 18
    debugging, 237
    getting started, 235
    hygiene, 244–250
        double evaluation, 249

gensyms, 246
names, 248
idiom and patterns, 250
implicit arguments, 251–259
&env, 252–253
&form, 254–258
testing contextual macros, 258
redefining, 415
syntax, 239–242
quote versus syntax-quote, 240
unquote and unquote-splicing, 241
when to use, 243
make-array, 444
make-hierarchy, 308
Mandelbrot Set, 449–455
many-to-one relationships, 499
map function, 62, 446
maps
collections, 28
data structure type, 117
destructuring, 32–36
Java, 85
metadata maps and vars, 199
nested maps, 121
structural sharing, 125
transient variants, 132
when to use, 277
math-context, 432
mathematics (see numerics and mathematics)
matrices, map destructuring, 33
Maven
AOT compilation, 350
clojure-maven-plugin, 347, 352
layout conventions, 332
repositories, 341
version range formats, 343
.war files, 562
web apps, 565
Maven dependency management model, 339–344
about, 345
artifacts and coordinates, 340
dependencies, 342
repositories, 341
maze generation, 145–151
memoization, 79
memory (see STM: transactional memory)
message queues, 522–525
metadata

&form, 254
about, 20
agents, 222
annotations, 381
associative collections, 274
collections and data structures, 135
constants, 200
docstrings, 200
macros, 256
maps, 199
multimethods, 315
realized?, 161
types, 278
var names, 370
metaprogramming, 577
methodName, 265
methods
functions, 264
Java, 357–360
protocols, 266
middleware
Ring, 534
using, 465
Midje, 473
mixins, 286
mocking objects, 472
modes
agent error handlers, 213
scale and rounding modes for arbitrary-
precision decimals ops, 432
monitor-enter, 45
monitor-exit, 45
monitoring REPL, 411–414
monkey-patching, 263
multidimensional arrays
performance, 446
type hinting, 447
multimethods, 291, 301–317
about, 301–303
hierarchies, 304–311
inheritance, 313
introspecting, 314
multiple dispatch, 311
range of dispatch functions, 316
redefining, 415
type versus class, 314
multiplayer games, 181
multiple arities, 37
multitenancy, 558

mutable fields, 278
mutable objects
    comparing to values, 54–58
    unfettered object state, 58
mutable state, 52
mutations
    primitive arrays, 445
    reference types, 28
mutually recursive functions, 37

N

named classes, 374–381
names, macros, 248
namespace-global identity, 198
namespaced keywords, 14
namespaced symbols, 15
namespaces, 322–332
    about, 20
    browsing, 404
    codebases, 334
    files, 328–331
    hierarchies and multimethods, 306
    introspecting, 401
    macros, 255
    projects, 322–328
    protocols, 265, 268
    types, 271
    vars, 198
natural keys versus synthetic keys, 137
nested collections, accessing values in, 29
nested forms, expanding, 239
nested maps, reduce-by, 121
nested send, 215
nested vectors, destructuring, 31
nesting, function literals, 41
networks, security, 414
new special form, 44
next, 90
nil, 13, 102, 114
nonrelational databases, 511–525
    CouchDB and Clutch, 512
    CRUD, 512
    message queues, 522–525
    views, 514–520
        Clojure, 516–520
        JavaScript, 514–516
        _changes, 520
notifications and constraints, 176–179
    validators, 178

watches, 176–178
nREPL, 404
ns, 327
ns-aliases, 401
ns-imports, 401
ns-interns, 401
ns-map, 401
ns-publics, 401
ns-refers, 401
ns-unalias, 401
ns-unmap, 401, 476
nth, 104, 115
number literals, 15
numbering states, 137
numeric literals, 16
numeric primitives, interoperability, 16
numerics and mathematics, 421–455
    equality and equivalence, 433–436
        numeric equivalence, 435
        object identity, 433
        reference equality, 434
    Mandelbrot Set, 449–455
    mathematics, 427–432
        bounded versus arbitrary precision, 428–430
        scale and rounding modes, 432
        unchecked ops, 430
    numerics, 421–427
        mixed numerics model, 422
        numeric contagion, 425
        rationals, 424
        representations, 422
    optimizing numeric performance, 436–449
        declare functions, 438–442
        primitive arrays, 442–449

O

objects
    fields, 359
    identity, 433
    instantiation, 45
    mocking, 472
    mutable objects
        comparing to values, 54–58
        unfettered object state, 58
    types, 424
    unfettered object state, 58
octal notation, 16
once, 479

operations, arrays, 370
operators, 7
opt-in computation, 161
or, 256
ordering, comparators and predicates, 107–111
outer map destructuring, 33
OutputStream, 214
overloading, 301
overriding local binding, 28
Overtone, 585

P

packaging, 340
Pallet, 570, 586
parallelism (see concurrency and parallelism)
parameterized queries, 494
paredit, 402, 403, 406
parentheses, 6
partial literals versus function literals, 67
partition, 141
patching, 413
path segments, 540
peek, 104
performance, 436–449
    declare functions, 438–442
    higher order functions and arities, 67
    immutable data structures, 123
    persistent data structures, 130
    pmap, 167
    primitive arrays, 442–449
        about, 443
        type hinting of multidimensional array operations, 447
    type hinting, 366–370
persistence, 122–134
    data in Hibernate, 506
    reference states, 215–217
    structural sharing, 123–130
        benefits, 129
        lists, 124
        maps, vectors and sets, 125
    transients, 130–134
plug-ins
    about, 3
    Leiningen, 347
    Maven, 347
pmap, 167, 206
pointcuts, 467

polymorphism, 84, 277
pop, 104, 114
POST, 542
postconditions, assertions, 487
postwalk, 236
pre- and postconditions, 40
precedence, 7
preconditions, assertions, 487
predicates
    ordering, 107–111
    testing, 549
    turning into comparators, 107
prefer-method, 313
preferences, multiple inheritance, 313
prime operators, 430
primitives
    64-bit integers, 422
    arrays, 442–449
        about, 443
        type hinting of multidimensional array operations, 447
    concurrency primitives, 224
    declare functions, 438–442
    locking: monitor-enter and monitor-exit, 45
    numeric primitives interoperability, 16
    numerics, 422
    performance, 437
    types, 424
println forms, 18
private vars, 198
productivity, 579
program state, 52
project.clj, 348
projects, 321–353
    build solutions, 336–353
        compilation, 337
        dependency management, 339–344
        tools and configuration patterns, 344–353
    codebases, 334
    layout conventions, 332
    namespaces, 322–332
        classpath, 331
        files, 328–331
promises, 163
protocols (see datatypes and protocols)
proxy, 371
pure functions, 76

PUT, 536, 542
Python
    destructuring and unpacking, 30
    lambdas, 40
    numeric types, 422
PYTHONPATH, 331

Q

queries
    Hibernate, 506
    Korma, 499
queues, message queues, 522–525
quote ('), 19, 24
quote versus syntax-quote, 240

R

random numbers, 77
ranges of versions, 343
rasterization, 453
rational numbers, 17
rationals, 422, 424
Read, 20
reader, 12–20
    collection literals, 19
    comments, 18
    scalar literals
        booleans, 13
        characters, 13
        keywords, 14
        nil, 13
        numbers, 15
        regular expressions, 17
        strings, 13
        symbols, 15
    syntax, 20
    transactional memory, 194
    whitespace and commas, 19
realized?, 161
records, 272–277–280
    constructors and factory functions, 275
    when to use, 277
recur special form, 28, 43
recursive functions, letfn, 37
redefining
    constructs, 415
    macros, 415
    multimethods, 415
redirect, 539

reduce
    about, 63
    Conway's Game of Life, 140
    CouchDB, 515
    over arrays, 446
reduce-by, 121
ref-history-count, 195
ref-max-history, 195
ref-min-history, 195
ref-set, 189
refactoring, 276, 329
refer, 323
reference equality, 434
reference states, 215–217
reference types
    about, 2, 170
    coordinated and asynchronous semantics, 173
    mutation semantics, 28
    using, 537
referential transparency, 79
refs, 180–198
    mechanics of ref change, 181–191
        alter, 183
        commute, 185–189
        ref-set, 189
        validators, 189
    STM, 180
    transactional memory, 191–198
        readers may retry, 194
        side-effecting functions, 192
        transaction scope, 193
        write skew, 196
regular expressions, 17
reify
    anonymous types, 284
    Java classes, 371
relational databases, 491–509
    clojure.java.jdbc, 491–497
        connection pooling, 496
        transactions, 496
        with-query-results, 494
    Hibernate, 503–509
        boilerplate, 507
        persisting data, 506
        queries, 506
        setup, 503–506
    Korma, 498–503
        queries, 499

using, 498

versus DSL, 500

releases, 342

remove, 114

remove-ns, 402

render-image, 453

render-text, 451

REPL (Read, Evaluate, Print, Loop), 3–6, 393–417

agents, 211

classpath, 332

debugging, monitoring, and patching production, 411–414

interactive development, 393–398

monitoring, 412

multimethods, 307

namespaces, 322

redefining constructs, 415

tooling, 398–411

bare REPL, 399–402

Eclipse, 403–405

Emacs, 405–411

transactions, 194

uploading via remote REPLs, 566

web applications, 532

REPL-bound vars, 399

repositories, Maven dependency management model, 341

representations, numerics, 422

require, 324

requirements, 3

responsibility, chain of responsibility, 463–466

rest, 31, 35, 38, 90, 114, 125

restarting agents, 213

result set, 495

retain, 539

return values, performance, 438

reusing exception types, 363

Ring, 529–535

adapters, 531

handlers, 532

middleware, 534

requests and responses, 529

web app architecture, 559

ring-httpcore-adapter, 531

ring-jetty-adapter, 531

Robert Hooke library, 468

root bindings, 201, 207

rounding modes, arbitrary-precision decimals ops, 432

routing requests, 535–545

rseq, 106

rsubseq, 106, 110

Ruby

blocks, 40

ERB templating language, 545

eval versus Clojure macros, 234

lists and hashes, 85

numeric types, 422

strings, 56

runtime

analysis, 412

compilation, 337

dynamic redefinition, 397

S

satisfies?, 289

scalar literals, 13–17

booleans, 13

characters, 13

keywords, 14

nil, 13

numbers, 15

regular expressions, 17

strings, 13

symbols, 15

scale, arbitrary-precision decimals ops, 432

scope

dynamic scope, 201–206

concurrency forms, 206

visualizing, 203

transactions, 193

security, networks, 414

select, 499

selectors, Enlive, 548

semantics

reference types, 173

reference types and mutation semantics, 28

value semantics, 272

send, 209

send-off, 209

sends, agents and nested sends, 214–224

sequences, 89–99

creating seqs, 92

head retention, 98

lazy seqs, 93–98

lists, 115

performance, 437
seq, 84
transients, 133
versus iterators, 91
versus lists, 92
sequential collections, 28
sequential destructuring, 30–32, 97
serializable snapshot isolation, 185
serialization, 13
servlets
    about, 557
    filters, 535
    Ring, 531
session factories, 505
set abstractions, 105
set function, 117
set!, 45, 206, 359
sets
    data structure type, 117
    structural sharing, 125
sharing (see structural sharing)
shorten!, 538
side effects
    defined, 76
    lazy sequences, 98
side-effecting functions, 80, 192
single-arity functions, 38
single-segment namespaces, 330
SLIME, 407, 410
slots, 118
snapshots, 342
sniptest, 547, 551
software transactional memory (see STM)
sorted abstractions, 106–111
sorted-map, 108
sorted-map-by, 108
sorted-set, 108
sorted-set-by, 108
source code
    printing, 400
    structural editing, 402
SPEC, 529
special forms, 23–45
    code blocks: do, 25
    conditionals: if, 42
    creating functions: fn, 36–41
        destructuring function arguments, 38–
            40
    defining vars: def, 26

destructuring, 28–36
    map destructuring, 32–36
    sequential, 30–32
exception handling: try and throw, 45
Java interoperability: . and new special
        forms, 44
local bindings: let, 27
looping: loop and recur, 43
primitive locking: monitor-enter and
        monitor-exit, 45
referring to vars: var, 44
suppressing evaluation: quote, 24
versus macros, 233
splicing, unquote and unquote-splicing, 241
split-with, 99
SQLite, 492
stacks
    abstractions, 104
    Clojure stack, 527
    space, 43
states
    concurrency and parallelism, 2, 168
    logging, 216
    numbering, 137
    reference states, 215–217
    vars, 198
static field access, 45
static methods
    calls, 9
    gen-class, 376
    invocation, 45
stepper, 145
STM (software transactional memory)
    about, 180
    agents, 214
strategy pattern, 462
strings
    about, 13
    Ruby, 56
struct map, 272
structs, maps as ad-hoc structs, 118
structural editing, source code, 402
structural sharing, 123–130
    benefits, 129
    lists, 124
    maps, vectors and sets, 125
subseq, 106, 110
suppressing, evaluations: quote, 24
swap!, 174

symbols
  about, 15
  evaluation of, 8, 23
  functions, 23, 112
  hierarchy, 306
  macros, 248
synchronization
  agents, 214
  concurrency and parallelism, 172
syntax
  about, 7
  for destructuring, 29
  macros, 239–242
  reader, 20
syntax-quote versus quote, 240
syntax-quoted lists, 242
syntax-quoting, 240
synthetic keys versus natural keys, 137

T

templating, 545–554
  Enlive, 546–554
    about, 547
    iterating and branching, 549
    selectors, 548
    using, 551
temporaryOutputDirectory, 350
testing, 471–489
  &env, 253
  assertions, 486
  clojure.test, 473–481
    defining tests, 474–476
    fixtures, 479
    test suites, 477
  contextual macros, 258
  HTML DSL, 481–485
  immutable values and pure functions, 471
  JUnit tests, 382
  mixed floating point equality tests, 436
  pure functions, 79
thread pools
  agents, 210
  defined, 225
threading macros, 259
threads
  agents, 210
  dynamic scope, 206
throw, 45
throwing exceptions, 363

time-it, 468
transactional memory, 191–198
  readers may retry, 194
  side-effecting functions, 192
  transaction scope, 193
  write skew, 196
transactions
  agents, 214–224
  clojure.java.jdbc, 496
  commute, 185–189
  conflicts, 185
  modifications, 182
  scope, 193
TRANSACTION_SERIALIZABLE, 496
transients, immutability and persistence, 130–134
transitive dependencies, 342
trap door, 360
trees, data structures and persistent semantics, 128
true?, 42
try, 45, 363
try-with-resources, 365
tuples, as vectors, 116
type definition forms, 573
type hints
  macros and &form, 256–258
  multidimensional array operations, 447
  performance, 366–370
types, 263
  (see also datatypes and protocols; reference types)
  about, 2
  errors, 440
  multimethods, 314
  numerics, 422

U

unary operators, 9
unchecked ops, 430
unchecked-*, 431
unchecked-math, 431
uncoordinated operations, 172
underscore (_), 28, 329
unfettered object state, 58
Unix, classpath, 332
unpacking, 30
unquote and unquote-splicing, 241
unquote-splicing operator, 242

uploading via remote REPLs, 566
URL shortener, 544
use, 324

V

validators
    enforcing local consistency, 189
    notifications and constraints, 178
vals, 118
value semantics, 272
values, 52–59
    about, 53, 138
    comparing to mutable objects, 54–58
    program state, 52
    unfettered object state, 58
    versus vars, 416
variables
    dataflow variables, 164
    versus vars, 21, 206
variadic functions, 38, 90
vars, 198–208
    defined, 21
    defining, 26, 198–201, 251
        constants, 200
        docstrings, 199
        private vars, 198
    defonce, 396
    dynamic scope, 201–206
        concurrency forms, 206
        visualizing, 203
    forward declarations, 208
    REPL-bound vars, 399
    symbols, 20, 44
    versus values, 416
    versus variables, 206
vary-meta, 135
vector?, 116
vectors
    argument vectors, 369
    bindings, 250
    data structure type, 115
    defined, 115
    HTML example, 482
    indices, 29, 100
    nested, 31
    nth, 104
    structural sharing, 125
    transient variants, 132
versioning

about, 129
    applications, 569
    snapshots and release versions, 342
    version string, 341
views, 514–520
    Clojure, 516–520
    JavaScript, 514–516

W

warn-on-reflection, 440, 449
warnings, primitives, 440
warnOnReflection, 350
watches, notifications and constraints, 176–178
web, 527–555, 557–570
    beyond simple web application deployment, 570
    Clojure stack, 527
    Java, 557–565
        web application packaging, 560–565
    Ring, 529–535
        adapters, 531
        handlers, 532
        middleware, 534
        requests and responses, 529
    routing requests, 535–545
    templating, 545–554
        Enlive, 546–554
    web application deployment, 566–569
        EB, 567–569
    web apps, 565
web app, 559
web crawlers, 218
when-let, 42
where, 500
white space, 19
why Clojure, 1
wildcard import, 327
Wilson's algorithm, 149
with, 499
with-connection, 496
with-meta, 135
with-open, 364, 507
with-precision, 432
with-query-results, 493, 494
with-redefs, 208, 472
workflow, Emacs, 407
workloads, agents, 217–224
write skew, 196

write-behind log, 215–217

Z
zero-arg arity, 38
zippers, 151–156
    Ariadne's, 154
    custom, 153
    manipulating, 152

About the Authors

Chas Emerick has been a consistent presence in the Clojure community since early 2008. He has made contributions to the core language, been involved in dozens of Clojure open source projects, and frequently writes and speaks about Clojure and software development generally.

Chas maintains the Clojure Atlas (*http://clojureatlas.com*), an interactive visualization of and learning aid for the Clojure language and its standard libraries.

The founder of Snowtide (*http://snowtide.com*), a small software company in Western Massachusetts, Chas's primary domain is unstructured data extraction, with a particular specialty around PDF documents. He writes about Clojure, software development, entrepreneurship, and other passions at *http://cemerick.com*.

Brian Carper is a Ruby programmer turned Clojure devotee. He's been programming Clojure since 2008, using it at home and at work for everything from web development to data analysis to GUI apps.

Brian is the author of Gaka (*https://github.com/briancarper/gaka*), a Clojure-to-CSS compiler, and Oyako (*https://github.com/briancarper/oyako*), an Object-Relational Mapping library. He writes about Clojure and other topics at *http://briancarper.net*.

Christophe Grand was a long-time enthusiast of functional programming lost in Javaland when he encountered Clojure in early 2008, and it was love at first sight! He authored Enlive (*http://github.com/cgrand/enlive*), an HTML/XML transformation, extraction, and templating library; Parsley (*http://github.com/cgrand/parsley*), an incremental parser generator; and Moustache (*http://github.com/cgrand/moustache*), a routing and middleware application DSL for Ring.

As an independent consultant, he develops, coaches, and offers training in Clojure. He also writes about Clojure at *http://clj-me.cgrand.net*.

Colophon

The animal on the cover of *Clojure Programming* is a painted snipe. The painted snipes (family Rostratulidae) comprise three species: the Greater Painted Snipe, the Australian Painted Snipe, and the South American Painted Snipe.

These shorebirds are distinct from the true snipes, and, as their name implies, also much more colorful. They may be more closely related to jacanas or sandpipers. Painted snipe live in marshes, swamps, and other wetlands, and they eat a varied diet of seeds, rice, millet, insects, snails, and crustaceans. They are solitary and "skulking," except during breeding season, so they are difficult to spot.

The Greater Painted Snipe (*Rostratula benghalensis*) lives in Africa, India, and Southeast Asia. The Australian Painted Snipe (*R. australis*), long considered a subspecies, is found only in Australia and is classified as endangered. These two species of painted snipe exhibit an unusual sexual dimorphism, with the females larger and more brightly colored than the males. They are polyandrous, with the female courting several males, and the males take responsibility for incubating the eggs and raising the chicks.

The South American Painted Snipe (*Nycticryptes semicollaris*) is found in the southern parts of that continent. It can be distinguished from the other painted snipes by its webbed toes. The South American Painted Snipe mates monogamously and doesn't display the same degree of sexual dimorphism as the Greater and Australian species. It is hunted for food in Chile and Argentina.

The cover image is from *Riverside Natural History*. The cover font is Adobe ITC Garamond. The text font is Linotype Birka; the heading font is Adobe Myriad Condensed; and the code font is LucasFont's TheSansMonoCondensed.

Have it your way.

Lightning Source UK Ltd.
Milton Keynes UK
UKOW05f1038271115

263517UK00001B/5/P